INSIDERS' GUIDE® SERIES

INSIDERS' GUIDE® TO

SAVANNAH
AND HILTON HEAD

SEVENTH EDITION

RICH WITTISH AND BETTY DARBY

INSIDERS' GUIDE®

GUILFORD, CONNECTICUT
AN IMPRINT OF THE GLOBE PEQUOT PRESS

The prices and rates in this guidebook were confirmed at press time. We recommend, however, that you call establishments before traveling to obtain current information.

To buy books in quantity for corporate use or incentives, call **(800) 962–0973** or e-mail **premiums@GlobePequot.com.**

Text design: Nancy Freeborn
Maps created by XNR Productions, Inc. © Morris Book Publishing, LLC

ISSN 1539-7378
ISBN 978-0-7627-4797-9

Printed in the United States of America

10 9 8 7 6 5 4 3 2 1

CONTENTS

CONTENTS

Directory of Maps

Greater Savannah Area

Highway Access to Savannah

River St.

Bay St.

Franklin
Square

Ellis
Square

Bryan St.

Johnson
Square

Congress St.

Reynolds
Square

Liberty
Square

Broughton St.

Warren
Square

Telfair
Square

State St.

Washington
Square

Wright
Square

York St.

Oglethorpe
Square

Orleans
Square

Oglethorpe Ave.

Columbia
Square

Greene
Square

Chippewa
Square

Hull St.

Colonial
Park
Cemetery

Perry St.

Pulaski
Square

Liberty St.

Crawford
Square

Madison
Square

Harris St.

Lafayette
Square

Charlton St.

Chatham
Square

Jones St.

Troup
Square

Monterey
Square

Taylor St.

Gordon St.

Calhoun
Square

Gaston St.

Whitefield
Square

Huntingdon St.

Hall St.

Gwinnett St.

Forsyth
Park

Hall St.

Gwinnett St.

Martin Luther King Jr. Blvd.

Jefferson St.

Tattnall St.

Barnard St.

Whitaker St.

Drayton St.

Abercorn St.

Lincoln St.

Habersham St.

Price St.

Broad St.

Savannah River

17

16

N

0   0.1   0.2 km
0   0.1   0.2 mi.

Downtown Savannah

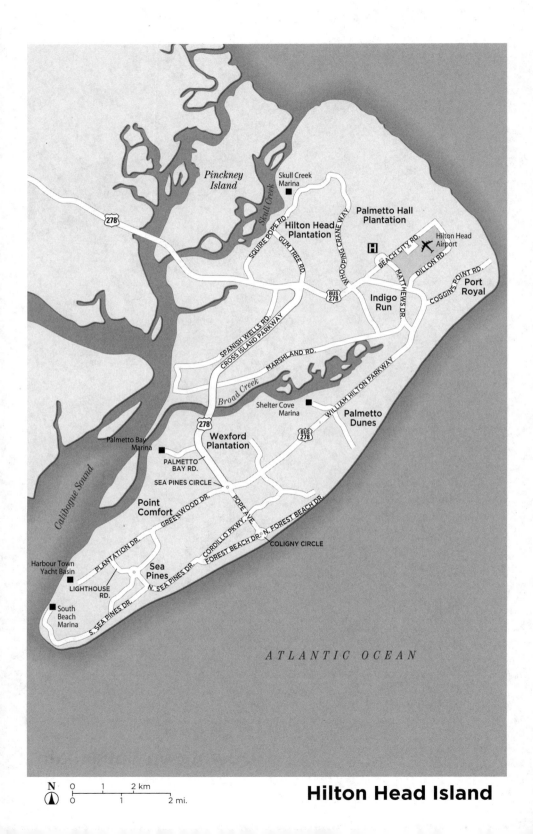

Hilton Head Island

PREFACE

We're having a wonderful time in Savannah, and we're glad that you are coming to join us. That's not just a postcard cliche. Savannah calls herself the Hostess City, and a traditionally welcoming attitude toward visitors is part of that legacy.

Long before tourism was considered an industry, hospitality was regarded around Savannah as something akin to religion. If you aren't gracious to guests, you "don't know how to act" and are "an embarrassment to your mother"—two of the deadliest faults possible in the South's social self-portrait. So relax: You are about to tour a city composed of people who, by and large, do know how to act and who have very proud mothers.

With the seventh edition of this book, we hope to give you the flavor of a city we have come to love, along with all the facts and figures you need to get yourself housed, entertained, fed, and properly toured. No, we're not native Savannahians—that's a multigenerational thing—but between the two of us, we've logged nearly 60 years in our adopted city. Job commitments brought us here with no real avowed intention of remaining, but over the years we forgot to leave.

Savannah is that kind of place. You could build a case that Savannah is a living laboratory for demonstrating the relativity of time. Time does seem to move at a different clip here. Change takes place slowly and is accepted even more slowly. Maybe languidly is a better term than slowly, because it emphasizes that there is something deliberate and intentional about this pacing. Pick the right hour at one of the downtown squares, when the traffic is still, look around at the massive oaks and stately townhomes, and you could easily erase 100, even 150 years off the calendar. Pick a marsh view at sunset, and you could erase a few thousand.

But don't get the impression we're a moldy, moss-draped museum, either. The corporate bigwigs and entertainment moguls of the day jet through the skies on corporate aircraft built here. The Port of Savannah is one of the nation's busiest, taking in goods from throughout the world. Baryshnikov danced here; John Travolta and Tom Hanks have filmed here; the PGA Championship Tour plays here. There's diversity in our universities and colleges. In short, Savannah has a place in the world's appointment books of today, not just in the history books.

Now, on to business. We've shared lots of things to do in these pages, based on years of entertaining visiting friends and relatives (and ourselves, too). We'll tell you how to chow down on some of the most delectable food imaginable and how to hole up in some of the most charming bed-and-breakfasts in the country. Parasailing, meeting alligators, retracing history, buying antiques, beach bumming, taking yourself out to the ole ball game—we tell you where and how (and how much it costs) to tap into these activities.

Additionally, if you're smitten with Savannah's celebrity cook, Paula Deen, we'll show you where to find that tasty home cooking she's always talking about. And if you've fallen in love with Savannah long-distance thanks to movies filmed here or the 1990s best seller *Midnight in the Garden of Good and Evil*, we've included some tips on connecting with those sights and scenes.

This is our seventh edition, newly updated and revised. The bulk of the changes are in predictable areas, as Savannah's restaurant, lodging, and nightlife scenes grow and change to accommodate her growing popularity. Revision and updating remains an ongoing process, to make sure that what you find within the pages of the guide you picked up last week accurately depicts the city you will find on your visit next week. You are invited to be part of this process. Comments, critiques, and suggestions are welcome, and they can be shared easily with us and our publishers, either online or on paper. (See How to Use This Book for details.)

Savannah gives herself lots of names, and others have added to the list: the Hostess City, the Coastal Empire, the Garden of Good and Evil, the Sovereign State of Chatham (Chatham County, that is), and so on. We firmly believe that, after your visit, you'll name her one of your favorite vacation destinations. We wager you'll be back. Like us, you may even forget to leave.

ACKNOWLEDGMENTS

Writing a book of this scope involves obtaining a lot of help from a lot of people. With that in mind, I offer special thanks to the following: John Burke and Michael Richter, who provided valuable information and insights for the fishing and boating sections of the Parks and Recreation chapter; Becky Bowden, who helped me get started in the right direction when I began writing the Hilton Head chapter; Ron Perry, a Hilton Head Realtor who aided me in gathering data on the island's planned communities; journalist Richard Fogaley, who gave us much-needed advice concerning Savannah's restaurants; Phyl Gatlin, who provided photographs for the Close-up in the Restaurants chapter; Preston Russell and Barbara Hines, authors of a splendid history of Savannah who graciously checked this book's History chapter for accuracy and content; Martha Giddens Nesbit, who allowed us to use a recipe from her *Savannah Collection* cookbook; and Cheryl Lauer, who lent her photographic skills to this endeavor along with encouraging words when they were needed.

Thanks also to many other folks who took time out of their busy schedules to talk with me or otherwise assist me. Among them are a horde of public relations and marketing specialists and other people who served as spokespersons for their respective businesses, agencies, and organizations. Those who were especially helpful were, from Savannah, John Howell of the Metropolitan Planning Commission, Lara Hoffman of the City of Savannah's Cultural Affairs Department, Ed Poenicke of the Chatham County Extension Service, Rick Lott of the Savannah Waterfront Association, Henry Lewandoski of Chatham County Mosquito Control, Scott Smith and Michael Jordan of the Coastal Heritage Society, Dr. Carol Brown of the Dr. Martin Luther

King Jr. Observance Day Association, Mike Beytagh of the St. Patrick's Day Parade Committee, Earl Etheridge of the City of Savannah's Department of Recreation Services, Vicki Blumberg and Lorenzo Bryant of Chatham County's Public Works and Park Services Department, Pat Metz of the U.S. Fish and Wildlife Service, Chica Arndt of Wormsloe Historic Site, and Duane Harris, Stuart Stevens, and Terry West of the Coastal Resources Division of the Georgia Department of Natural Resources.

Special thanks also to Hilton Head islander Charlie Clark of the Hilton Head Chamber of Commerce, and Ed Drane, Bud Culbertson, and Nan Johnson of the Town of Hilton Head Island. Many thanks to my editor, Meredith Phillips.

And thanks most of all to my wife, Linda, and daughter, Erica, for the love and support they gave me, particularly when the light at the end of the Insiders' Guide tunnel seemed somewhat dim.

—Rich Wittish

A massive project such as this can be daunting at best. Thanks to the help of dedicated professionals in the information field and ordinary Savannahians who were eager to share the good parts of our city, I was able to enjoy myself along the way.

Much of the information that goes into such a project comes by way of professional "question-answerers." Any well-run organization of any size has at least one individual or department, variously known as the public relations department, public affairs office, media contact, official spokesperson, and so on, whose job it is to field questions. Although it's their job to pass on information, they are to be commended for their cheerful attitude, enthusiasm about their mission, and attention to detail. One hesitates to start naming names in this category for fear of leaving someone out, so I'm intentionally keeping my list short here. The Savannah Police Department provided a solid briefing on alcohol regulations and their enforcement. Jay Self from the city's film office is always helpful. Everyone at Senior Citizens Inc. made a special effort to help me understand their many missions.

Writers take shameless advantage of their friends and family when working on such projects. My friends, acquaintances, and even coworkers no doubt tired of me constantly asking things like, "Yeah, but where else do you take visitors?" and "Where do you go at night when you don't go home?" I also leaned heavily on the expertise of friends. Cheryl Lauer took my photo and allowed herself to be recruited as photo liaison for the first edition. Suzanne Aikens was a big help on musical questions, for example, and Midge Schildkraut filled me in on Savannah's Jewish community. My mother, the late Rosalyn Darby, let me drag her along on tours to get an outsider's viewpoint (although that didn't work too well, since she was a regular visitor to the city for years). She even accompanied the small group I put together for my research mission to the drag show, and she said she had a nice time. Special thanks, too, to the hospitable folks at Wilmington Island's Sunrise Restaurant, who kept our coffee cups filled as my coauthor and I compared notes during planning sessions.

I shouldn't forget to give thanks to those who gave us something worth writing about. Savannah was planned, built, and preserved by visionaries, known and unknown, and populated in both the past and present by people interesting and hospitable enough to make it worth visiting (and living in). With that in mind, special thanks to anyone who preserved a building or defended a tree that a developer thought was inconveniently placed.

A closing word of thanks goes to Coleman Prophett, B. C. Akins, and Tommy Toles, the leaders of my first newsroom, who recognized the importance of teaching the trade to wet-behind-the-ears journalism students.

—Betty Darby

HOW TO USE THIS BOOK ?

We hope you'll treat this book as you would a valued traveling companion, taking it with you wherever you go during your time in Savannah, Tybee Island, and Hilton Head, and consulting it whenever you need help, advice, or answers to questions. Don't leave it home alone or in your hotel room; stick it in your travel bag, briefcase, or backpack so you'll have it handy when you need information on where to eat, shop, or spend the night.

We've organized this book so you can flip to whatever subjects interest you, while bypassing those that don't. Of course, it's our hope that eventually you'll take a look at every chapter because each contains valuable information and tips. Even if you're not a history buff, for instance, it's probably a good idea to read the History chapter early in the game so that you can have an understanding of Savannah's past—a past that plays a vital role in its present and comes alive when you walk along the city's streets and through its magnificent squares.

For the most part, we've arranged the content of chapters geographically, then alphabetically within geographic sections. This was done in an effort to make restaurants, accommodations, attractions, and other points of interest as easy as possible to find. (If all else fails, there's also an index.) We've divided the local area into four sections; you'll find an explanation of the territory the sections cover in the Area Overview chapter, and you can see where they are by referring to the maps at the front of the book. Another good way to find specific topics of interest is by looking in the extensive index in the back of the book. You'll note that the area code for almost every phone number listed is 912 (843 for places in South Carolina). Also

look for Insiders' Tips—marked with an **i**—that let you in on local secrets.

In addition to giving you a full rundown on the many topics you might expect to find in a guidebook, we've included a couple of chapters regarding subjects unique to Savannah. One chapter entitled "Savannah Celebrity" tells you how to get close to both the career and cooking of celebrity chef Paula Deen, as well as how to tour the places mentioned in the 1990s best seller *Midnight in the Garden of Good and Evil*. The other special chapter concerns Savannah's celebration of St. Patrick's Day, the city's favorite holiday.

We know that plenty of folks who make it to Savannah also have Hilton Head Island, South Carolina, on their travel itineraries. With this in mind, we have included a thorough chapter on Hilton Head, providing information on its history, accommodations, popular planned residential communities, restaurants and nightlife, and, of course, golf and tennis. In turn, we have also devoted an entire chapter to another nearby destination that you may not be so familiar with—fun and quirky little Tybee Island, which is part of Chatham County but very separate and distinct from Savannah.

We've done our darnedest to make this book as comprehensive and accurate as possible and to include the best that our area has to offer, and we've covered a lot of territory. Naturally, when you take on a project that's as massive and challenging as this one, you realize that omissions are inevitable and that most everyone has different tastes and opinions. If you discover a favorite restaurant, nightspot, shop, or other business that we've missed or something that's in error, please let us know so it can be added or corrected in future editions. We'll be updating, improving, and expanding our guide on a regular basis. You can contact us with comments or suggestions at editorial@GlobePequot.com, or by mail at:

RE: *Insiders' Guide to Savannah*
Reader Response/Editorial Department
The Globe Pequot Press
P.O. Box 480
Guilford, CT 06437

AREA OVERVIEW

Approach Savannah through South Carolina on U.S. Highway 17, and you find yourself on a two-lane road winding through marshland and passing by a few "gentlemen's clubs" that were video poker parlors and fireworks stands in their past lives. You're in the far reaches of the Lowcountry, and if you didn't know better, you'd swear you were in a desert . . . a desert where marsh grass stands in for sand. You're becoming convinced that you've driven all the way to Nowhere—that you've exiled yourself by automobile to the end of the world.

Then you round a bend of the highway, and suddenly you're staring at civilization in the form of the graceful towers of the Eugene Talmadge Memorial Bridge. Travel a bit farther, and you see the horizon to the left of the bridge filling with the low skyline of a city. In a few minutes, you leave South Carolina and the marsh behind and begin crossing the Savannah River into Georgia. On your left as you ascend the bridge is Hutchinson Island, where a recently built convention center and 16-story hotel herald the creation of a resort area. Cresting the crown of the bridge, you're 196 feet above the water and looking down and ahead toward your destination, the city of Savannah.

Glancing to your left, you see the golden dome of City Hall and a riverfront of brick cotton warehouses that have been converted into shops and restaurants. Beyond the waterfront, a canopy of trees stretches to the south, interrupted here and there by the spires of churches and the upper floors of a hotel, several office buildings, and an apartment complex or two. Off to your right, the river is bordered by manufacturing plants and the docks, warehouses, and towering cranes of the Georgia Ports Authority. Straight ahead

is a network of roadways, with some of the thoroughfares leading to the Southside and to west Chatham County, where many Savannahians live and many more do their shopping.

This seagull's-eye view of the area gives you a pretty good idea of the lay of the land, and your tires haven't even settled on Georgia ground yet. As you read deeper into this chapter, we'll give you a more complete picture of the region, including brief looks at some places you can't readily see from the bridge—Savannah's inshore islands.

As we mentioned in our How to Use This Book chapter, we've arranged many of the chapters in this guide by geographic sections. The boundaries and makeup of those sections are discussed here. Before we get into that, however, let us toss your way some nice-to-know, getting-grounded information about the Savannah area.

SAVANNAH STATISTICS

Savannah is the seat of government of Chatham County, one of the most populous counties in the largest state (in terms of area) east of the Mississippi River. Some 238,192 people live in Chatham, with 128,500 residing within Savannah's city limits. About a quarter of the county's 443 square miles are unincorporated, and there are also seven other municipalities within Chatham's borders: Bloomingdale, Garden City, Port Wentworth, Pooler, Thunderbolt, Vernonburg, and the city of Tybee Island.

The people who live here have a broad variety of backgrounds, jobs, and interests, which is what you might expect from a place that dates back to 1733 and serves as a port, a center of higher education, a tourist desti-

The wispy, gray vegetation hanging from the trees is Spanish moss, a plant that takes its moisture and nutrients from the air. This member of the pineapple family is not a parasite, but it can harm a tree if it covers too much foliage and blocks out the sunlight needed for photosynthesis. Don't lie in a bed of Spanish moss or drape it over your body; it is the home of mitelike creatures called red bugs that can cause skin irritation.

nation, a site for industrial plants, a home to the military, and a mecca for artists and historic preservationists. Because of its history, diversity, and charms, Savannah is a melting pot: Grab a morning cup of coffee at the Express Café & Bakery on Barnard Street, and you could be standing in line with a college student who just blew in from the North or a society matron whose ancestors walked up the Savannah River bluff with Georgia's founder, James Edward Oglethorpe.

Chatham County's population is about 55 percent white, 40.5 percent African American, 2 percent Asian, and 2 percent Hispanic. Inside Savannah's city limits, the African-American population is the majority. The growth rate from 1990 through 2000 was 7 percent, and projections indicate the county will continue to grow until the year 2015 at an annual rate of 0.7 percent to 1.5 percent, depending on which study you look at. Savannah's population is also getting older, with the percentage of people age 25 and younger declining and the percentage of folks age 65 and older increasing. The experts say this situation is the result of several factors, including a lower birth rate, the aging of the baby boomers, increased longevity due to medical advancements and healthier lifestyles, and the county's growing popularity as a retirement community.

A 2006 Savannah Area Chamber of Commerce report showed this partial accounting of the jobs in Savannah: manufacturing (9 per-

cent), retail trade (12.1 percent), professional and business services (11.6 percent), educational and health services (13.1 percent), leisure and hospitality (12.7 percent), and state and local government (12.2 percent). Among the county's major employers are Memorial Health University Medical Center, the Savannah College of Art and Design, St. Joseph's and Candler Hospitals, the Kroger supermarket chain, Gulfstream Aerospace Corporation, International Paper Company, Wal-Mart, Derst Baking Company, Great Dane Trailers, Tronox, Hunter Army Airfield, the Savannah-Chatham County Board of Education, and the governments of Georgia, Savannah, and the county.

According to the Georgia Department of Labor, a total of 161,200 people were employed in the Savannah metropolitan area in August 2007, with the region's unemployment rate at 4.5 percent that month. Per capita income in Chatham County in 2004 was $31,691.

The Savannah area is blessed with a climate classified as semitropical. Average seasonal temperatures are, in degrees Fahrenheit, 51 in winter, 66 in spring, 81 in summer, and 68 in autumn. From these figures, you can see that the best times to visit (as far as most folks are concerned) are the spring and fall. The days can get mighty hot and sticky during the summer—according to the Savannah Area Chamber of Commerce, the city on average experiences 67 days each year when the mercury climbs higher than 90.

Winters are fairly mild, with the temperature dipping below freezing an average of (ironically) 32 days a year. We seldom see snow, and the descent of even a few flakes is cause for excitement. The average annual rainfall is 49 inches, and Mother Nature delivers some frog-choking downpours now and then, particularly during summer afternoons. Because Savannah is in a low-lying area and much of the city's sewer system is antiquated, streets are prone to flooding when tides are high—be careful if you're driving around and get caught in a sudden storm.

This downtown fountain honors Savannah's German heritage. KYLE CASON

Being on the southeast coast, Savannah occasionally finds itself threatened by hurricanes. In recent years, the city has been spared the destruction caused by major storms. Savannah had close calls from Hurricane Hugo in 1989, Bertha in 1996, and Floyd in 1999, but the last hurricane to hit here was David in 1979, when winds as strong as 90 mph caused widespread power outages that lasted for several days.

That gives you the big picture. (For an at-a-glance version and a few extra facts, see the Vital Statistics page in this chapter.) Now let's look more closely at the four areas into which we've divided the county.

HERE'S LOOKING AT YOU, SAVANNAH

Historic Downtown

Our downtown area is bordered by the Savannah River on the north, East Broad Street on the east, Park Avenue on the south, and Martin Luther King Jr. Boulevard (once called West Broad Street) on the west. Downtown Savannah is the section most visitors come to see. It's the oldest part of the city—Oglethorpe landed here when he arrived to found Georgia more than 270 years ago. The city squares he laid out—those green jewels in Savannah's crown—are still here.

This is the site of the Historic District, 2.5 square miles of beautifully restored homes and historic churches. It's an area that's been designated by the U.S. Department of the Interior as a National Historic Landmark. It's a place of monuments, shady sidewalks, and a cemetery that's a park. It's where art students sit on curbs while sketching old buildings, where the Irish and others put themselves on parade on St. Patrick's Day, and where tourists look for places mentioned in the best seller *Midnight in the Garden of Good and Evil*. It's where fans of celebrity chef Paula Deen of Food Network fame, along with just plain hungry people, can dig into Paula's classic Southern cooking at her famous restaurant, The Lady and Sons.

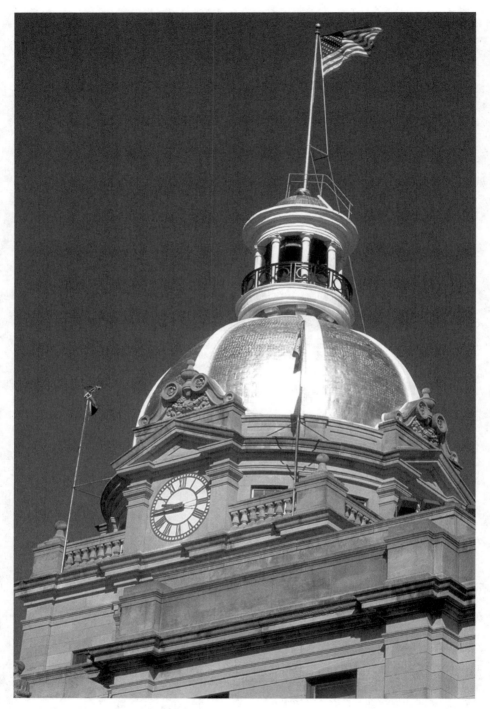

Savannah's City Hall sports a real gold dome. KYLE CASON

The downtown is also a place for fun, good eating, and shopping. River Street and City Market are here, with their stores and restaurants, and so is Broughton Street, which was once the city's main shopping district and has made a comeback after losing customers to the malls of the Southside (see our Shopping chapter). Downtown also hosts festivals, with many of Savannah's major annual events being held along the river, in City Market, and at Forsyth Park, a lush, green playground on Bull Street (see our Annual Events and Festivals chapter).

The downtown is the home of the city's financial district, Johnson Square, which is ringed by the main offices of several banks. There are also numerous museums and the Savannah College of Art and Design (SCAD). SCAD is the largest school of its kind in the nation, and its 7,000 students bring much vitality and creativity to the area (see our Education and Child Care and Arts and Culture chapters).

Interestingly enough, Savannah's downtown is not really "down," cartographically speaking. If you look at a map of the city, you'll see that the Historic District is in the northern part of town. That's because Savannah got its start on a bluff on the south bank of the river, causing the heart of the city to be north of everything else. When you're in downtown Savannah, you can't go much farther north and still be in Georgia. Savannah has not grown in that direction, across the north channel of the Savannah River (which is known as the Back River), because what's over there is mostly marshland, and it's also South Carolina.

Having said that, we must mention that when you're downtown on River Street gazing across the south channel of the Savannah River, you're looking at Hutchinson Island, a small part of Georgia that's being developed in a big way. The $98 million Savannah Harbor Resort complex has been created there, and the $83.5 million Savannah International Trade and Convention Center opened there in mid-2000.

i According to the Savannah Economic Development Authority, citing a Coldwell Banker report, a residence in Savannah that cost $217,351 would go for $266,000 in Atlanta, $270,000 in Charleston, $340,000 in Baltimore and Seattle, $715,000 in Chicago, and more than $1 million in Boston and San Francisco.

A significant part of the Hutchinson Island resort complex is a 403-room, 16-story Westin hotel that's emblematic of the growth in tourism being experienced by the city. Fueled by the popularity of *Midnight* and by the aggressive marketing efforts of the Savannah Area Chamber of Commerce and individual components of the city's hospitality industry, that growth—from 3.73 million visitors in 1995 to 6 million in 2003—has caused an upsurge in hotel building and expansion, a blossoming of new restaurants and specialty shops, and a proliferation of tour companies. According to the Chamber of Commerce, more than 6.5 million people visit Savannah annually, and tourism supports nearly 22,000 area jobs, according to a 2006 study.

Because Savannah hasn't been able to expand much to the north, most early development was southward, and much recent growth has been to the east and west.

Islands

The growth eastward has occurred principally on Chatham County's inshore islands, referred to as such because they're not on the Atlantic Ocean. They're separated from the mainland and neighboring islands by salt marsh, rivers, and tidal creeks. The islands in our Islands Area are those immediately east of Savannah—Oatland, Talahi, Whitemarsh, and Wilmington—and those southeast of the city—Dutch, Skidaway, and Isle of Hope. Because of its unique qualities and status as a destination for tourists, we have devoted a separate chapter to Tybee Island, which is also east of Savannah.

Savannah Vital Statistics

Nickname: Hostess City of the South

Mayor: Otis Johnson

Governor: Sonny Perdue

Outlying counties: Effingham, Bryan, Liberty

Population: Savannah, 128,500; Chatham County, 238,192; Georgia, 9.36 million

Area (sq. mi.): 65.1

Average temperatures: July, 82; January, 49

Average annual precipitation: Rainfall, 49 inches; snowfall, less than one-half inch

Major universities: Armstrong Atlantic State University, Savannah State University, Savannah College of Art and Design

Important dates:

Feb. 12, 1733: Founded as capital of Georgia, the thirteenth colony

1734: Becomes first city in North America planned on a system of squares; also becomes site of first agricultural experimental garden in North America.

1736: Becomes site of first Sunday school in America Oct. 9, 1779: Colonial army suffers crushing defeat in attempt to retake city from British during Siege of Savannah

1788: Becomes site of first African-American Baptist congregation in United States

1793: Eli Whitney perfects cotton gin on a plantation just west of Savannah

May 22, 1819: Serves as embarkation point for first steamship to cross Atlantic (SS *Savannah*)

April 19, 1862: Fort Pulaski, east of city, falls to first rifled cannon used in warfare

Dec. 21, 1864: Confederate Savannah surrenders to Union forces led by General William T. Sherman at the conclusion of his March to the Sea

1886: Opens first art museum (Telfair) in Southeast

1908, 1910, 1911: Hosts Grand Prix and Vanderbilt Cup auto racing

1911: Establishes first motorized fire department in United States

November 1955: Historic Savannah Foundation preservation group holds first general membership meeting

July 22–Aug. 2, 1996: Hosts yachting events of Summer Olympic Games

Major area employers: Gulfstream Aerospace Corp. (5,000), Memorial Health University Medical Center (5,351), International Paper Co. (970), St. Joseph's/Candler Health System (3,300), Kroger supermarkets (1,200)

Famous sons and daughters:
  Johnny Mercer, lyricist
  Conrad Aiken, poet
  Juliette Gordon Low, founder of the Girl Scouts
  Clarence Thomas, Supreme Court justice

Major airport: Savannah/Hilton Head International Airport

Major interstates: Interstate 95 (north-south), Interstate 16 (east-west)

Public transportation: Chatham Area Transit (CAT)

Military base: Hunter Army Airfield

Driving laws: Seat belts mandatory for occupants of the front seat of a vehicle and all occupants younger than 18; safety restraining systems required for children younger than 4 years old, but seat belts will suffice for those between age 3 and 4. Maximum speed limit under normal conditions 55 mph, 70 mph on rural interstates, and 65 mph on urban interstates. Speed limit decreases to 30 mph in business and residential districts. Headlights required between the half hour after sunset and the half hour before sunrise and when raining.

Alcohol laws: Drinking by persons younger than age 21 prohibited. Motorists 21 years and older considered under the influence of intoxicants when 0.08 gram or more by alcohol is present in the blood; for those younger than 21, the limit is 0.02 gram. Sunday sales of alcoholic beverages prohibited except in establishments that derive at least 50 percent of their food and beverage sales from the sale of prepared meals or foods. Sales of alcoholic beverages are prohibited between 2:55 a.m. on Sunday and 7:00 a.m. on Monday and between 3:00 and 7:00 a.m. other days.

Drinking on city streets prohibited except in the area bounded generally by the city limits on the north, West Boundary Street on the west, Jones Street on the south, and East Broad Street on the east. In this area, drinking from cans, bottles, or glasses is prohibited, and paper or plastic cups containing alcoholic beverages must not exceed 16 fluid ounces in size.

Daily newspaper: *Savannah Morning News*

Sales tax: 7 percent (4 percent state, 3 percent local option) on the purchase of all goods and some services

Room tax: 6 percent

Information for tourists:
  Savannah Area Chamber of Commerce
  Savannah Convention & Visitors Bureau
  101 East Bay Street, Savannah, GA 31401
  (912) 644-6400
  www.savannahvisit.com

The residential development of the eastside islands took off in the late 1980s, and Whitemarsh Island (pronounced "WHIT-marsh") was the fastest-growing part of the county in 1996, with Wilmington Island not far behind. Growth slowed on Whitemarsh in 1997, with most of the island being built out, but residential development continued on Wilmington, the fastest-growing part of Chatham during 1998. Most of the building on these islands has been residential, although a large shopping center and three schools have been constructed on Whitemarsh in recent years.

Despite the buildup, the eastside islands retain a natural beauty and laid-back quality. You can still take an evening stroll on an island street, look up at a sky brilliant with stars, and listen to the plaintive calls of mourning doves and the chuck-will's-widow. For the most part, the eastside islands remain quiet havens where folks sit on their docks and watch the marsh turn from gold to green as the seasons change; where oaks festooned with Spanish moss bend over roadways to create cool, verdant tunnels; where you can hop in your car, drive around the corner, and enjoy a meal of fresh seafood.

Farther to the south, you'll find the gated residential enclave of Dutch Island; Skidaway Island, site of The Landings, a private community of upscale homes, also gated; and Isle of Hope, with its dignified old houses adorning secluded narrow streets. The Landings covers much of Skidaway Island with 4,800 beautifully landscaped dwellings, 2 deep-water marinas, 6 private 18-hole golf courses, a fitness center, 4 clubhouses, 34 tennis courts, and more than 40 miles of biking and nature trails. Isle of Hope is entirely residential except for the marina on Bluff Drive (see our Relocation/Real Estate chapter). Bluff Drive is a lovely lane running alongside the Skidaway River, and it's our choice as the Savannah area's most picturesque street. The Isle is also the location of Wormsloe Historic Site, the place where one of Georgia's first settlers constructed a colonial estate (see our Attractions chapter).

Southside/Midtown

Southside/Midtown is the vast area south of Historic Downtown. Note that the locals refer to the northern portion of this area as Midtown. Midtown starts in the vicinity of the southern end of Forsyth Park and runs south to DeRenne Avenue, although some folks might tell you that it extends all the way to Oglethorpe Mall. (You can actually deduce how long someone has lived in Savannah by how far south they think the Southside begins.) Most of Savannah's Victorian District and all of the Thomas Square Streetcar Historic District are in Midtown. The districts are filled with Victorian-style frame houses and are on the National Register of Historic Places.

That distinction also applies to Ardsley Park and Chatham Crescent, two other areas in Midtown. Among the streets of Ardsley Park is one of Savannah's prettiest—oak- and azalea-lined Washington Avenue. At the eastern end of the avenue is Daffin Park, site of a lake and public tennis courts and athletic fields used by recreation league teams playing baseball, softball, football, and soccer. Daffin is also the stomping ground of professional athletes—the members of the city's minor-league baseball team, the Savannah Sand Gnats (see our Spectator Sports chapter). The Gnats play their home games at

i Snow seldom falls in Savannah (the last measurable accumulation was in December 1989), but one of the all-time favorite songs about wintry weather was written by a onetime resident, James L. Pierpont, who penned the words to "Jingle Bells" and worked as an organist at the Unitarian church in Savannah. Copyrighted in 1857, the song originally bore the title "One-Horse Open Sleigh." Whether Pierpont wrote the lyrics while living here has been a matter of good-natured dispute between Savannahians and residents of Pierpont's hometown of Medford, Massachusetts.

Grayson Stadium, which stands among the tall pines in the eastern portion of the park.

You'll find several shopping centers in Midtown, the main library (which has been renovated extensively), and much of Savannah's health-care community. Clustered just north of DeRenne Avenue, between Reynolds Street and the Truman Parkway, are numerous doctors' offices, pharmacies, medical laboratories, and two of the city's hospitals, Memorial Health University Medical Center and Candler Hospital (see our Health Care chapter).

Once south of DeRenne, you are in the part of town most locals call the Southside. It's an area of subdivisions, churches, recreational facilities, and commercial development. Savannah's main drag, Abercorn Street, turns into the area's primary retail strip here. We think of Abercorn south of DeRenne as the Land of a Thousand Curb Cuts. That's an exaggeration, but not much of one. The six-lane thoroughfare is nicked by the myriad entrances and exits to and from restaurants, motels, office complexes, convenience marts, both of Savannah's malls, auto dealerships, used-car lots, strip shopping centers, and megastores selling building materials, pet supplies, party goods, books, liquor, and office equipment. Interrupting this cascade of commercialism on Abercorn are St. Joseph's Hospital and the doctors' offices that have sprung up around it (see our Health Care chapter) and the campus of Armstrong Atlantic State University. The area we've designated as Southside/Midtown is also home to several other institutions of higher education, including Savannah State University, Savannah Technical College, and South University (see our Education chapter).

Outdoor activities abound in the Southside. Just east and southeast of Oglethorpe Mall is Bacon Park, a city- and county-owned recreational complex consisting of softball diamonds, soccer fields, tennis courts, a public golf course, a stadium where high-school football teams play, an aquatic center, and a lake surrounded by a walking/jogging track. Nearby is the site of the Chatham County track and field complex inside T. A. Wright Stadium at Savannah State University. Among the features of this world-class facility are an eight-lane track, a dual pole vault runway, a javelin runway, a steeplechase water jump, and shot put, discus, and hammer-throw circles.

The Southside past Oglethorpe Mall is where suburbia evolved in the 1960s and 1970s, mainly in the sprawling subdivision of Windsor Forest. Residential growth has continued in recent years farther out Abercorn Street at Georgetown, one of the fastest-growing areas in Chatham County in the 1990s (see our Relocation/Real Estate chapter), and in the Henderson Golf Club area.

To the west of the residential and commercial development of the Southside is Hunter Army Airfield, a 5,400-acre military post and site of the Army's longest runway. In 2006 a total of 7,100 soldiers and civilians were working at Hunter, the home of a Ranger battalion, units of the Third Infantry Division (Mechanized), and a Coast Guard air station. The bulk of the division is based an hour away at Fort Stewart, the largest Army installation east of the Mississippi River. With its 11,375-foot runway, Hunter serves as a location from which troops and equipment of the Third can be deployed throughout the world.

Two of Chatham's municipalities are in Southside/Midtown: Thunderbolt, a quaint fishing village of 2,278 people living alongside the Wilmington River, and Vernonburg, a settlement of 138 souls who reside on a handful of streets leading to the banks of the Vernon River. South of Vernonburg are the rustic residential communities of Beaulieu and Coffee Bluff.

West Chatham

West Chatham is where folks roll up their sleeves and get to work. It's where much of the area's industry flexes its muscles. This is the home of the county's largest manufacturer, Gulfstream Aerospace Corporation, which employs 5,000 people and produces corporate jet aircraft. West Chatham is the site of the headquarters of the Georgia Ports

A Gnasty Welcome to Savannah

"What just bit me?"

"What's that smell?"

Visitors to Savannah sometimes ask those questions even before inquiring about where to eat, what to visit, and how to find the Garden of Good and Evil.

The smell can hit you out on I-16, a few miles before you get to town, and the biting can begin as soon as you leave the safety of your car. You might think those unseen forces making lunch of your bare forearm are a figment of your imagination, but they're not. They're sand flies. Savannahians call them sand gnats and sometimes refer to them as "no-see-ums."

A sand gnat feeds on a human by slashing skin with its teeth and drinking the pool of blood that forms. Sounds gross, but you can't see this carnage taking place because your average sand gnat is about a millimeter long—so tiny it can fly through a standard window screen without grazing its wing tips. What you might see, particularly if you are prone to allergies, are small welts appearing where gnats have feasted. Try not to scratch; if you leave the bumps alone, they will disappear in about an hour.

Incidentally, the gnats biting you are females. They need the protein in blood for laying eggs. Sand gnats breed in the mud of salt marshes and are most prevalent in the spring and fall, but a few days of temperatures in the 60s can bring them out at other times. Although some folks recommend dousing yourself with a certain brand-name skin softener as a defense against sand gnats, entomologists say you can best fight these bugs by applying insect repellent containing the chemical compound DEET and by wearing long clothing and hats.

Savannahians have a love-hate relationship with sand gnats. They detest the gnat as an insect but adore it as the mascot of the city's minor-league baseball team. The management and fans of the Savannah ball club chose the Sand Gnat nickname when the team became an affiliate of the Los Angeles Dodgers organization in 1996. (As of 2007, they're now affiliated with the New York Mets.) Sand Gnat merchandise is so popular, it's a best seller among fans of minor-league teams.

Not nearly as lovable as the baseball team's bug-eyed mascot is the rotten-egg, cabbage-being-cooked smell that periodically wafts over Savannah. The odor emanates from the industries lining the banks of the Savannah River. The dominant component of the smell is sulfur dioxide, a pungent gas released during the manufacture of paper. Industry officials say they have spent big bucks attempting to eliminate the smell, and they assure us they have lessened it. The smell persists on occasion, however, especially during periods of extended wet weather. The sand gnats persist too. Savannahians have learned to live with both, and you can too.

Authority, which operates two deep-water terminals on the Savannah River. Most of the cargo handled on Savannah's docks is shipped in containers, and the city is one of the busiest container ports in the United States.

Many of the people who work at the port and the industries west of Savannah live in West Chatham's four municipalities. Of these, Garden City is the largest in terms of population—10,334 people call it home. Port Wentworth, the town closest to the river, has a population of 3,327, and Bloomingdale has 2,914 residents. Garden City and Bloomingdale grew considerably in 1998 when a majority of voters there opted for annexations that added about 7 square miles to Garden City and more than 1,000 acres to Bloomingdale. Pooler, a town of 9,114, is one of the fastest-developing parts of the region. West Chatham, long the setting for local industry, is rapidly taking on another persona—as the place where a dozen large, master-planned communities are taking shape. These communities, each covering at least 500 acres, will

> ℹ The city of Savannah and most of the area surrounding it receive water service from the city's Water Department. The water-delivery system utilizes 41 artesian wells.

combine residential and commercial development with green space. The construction of up to 40,000 new homes in these areas has been approved, and it's estimated that more than 100,000 people will eventually live in these communities—with names such as Godley Station, Rice Hope Plantation, and New Hampstead—when these projects are completed over the next 20 years.

West Chatham is also the location of Savannah/Hilton Head International Airport, where a $68.5 million terminal was opened in 1994 (see our Getting Here, Getting Around chapter). Close by the airport are CrossRoads Business Park, a state-of-the-art industrial park, and Crosswinds, a golf course that's lighted for nighttime play.

GETTING HERE, GETTING AROUND

Georgia's first city sits near the mouth of the Savannah River, which forms the boundary between Georgia and South Carolina. Take the Talmadge Bridge over the Savannah River and by the time you're back over dry land, you're in another state. Head south for about two and a half hours, and you've gone from Georgia's northernmost coastal point to the Florida border—a pretty short stretch between states, considering Georgia is the largest state east of the Mississippi.

The first Europeans to get to Savannah arrived in sailing vessels. Gen. James Edward Oglethorpe, Georgia's founder, came in 1733 to settle the colony and establish, among other things, a thriving port. Today, however, it's mainly cargo that arrives by ship. Although the rankings may vary from day to day, the Port of Savannah is the fourth-busiest container port in the United States, with several thousand ships making their way upriver every year to load or unload their goods. In 2001 the port crossed a significant milestone when it recorded its first year of handling more than a million TEUs, the volume measurement used to calculate containerized freight. And it has kept on growing—in the fiscal year ended in mid-2007, it handled more than 2.33 million TEUs. On a very rare occa-

> **i** Always lock your car downtown, just as you probably do in your own hometown. That turns vehicles into ovens in the summer. Locals often keep a towel or pillowcase in the front seat to drape across the steering wheel when they park to spare themselves scorched fingers later. During the summer, give serious consideration to choosing the city's parking garages, which offer shade, over metered spaces in the sun.

sion, you'll see a cruise ship that has docked in Savannah (an interest group is diligently advocating for expansion as a cruise destination), and the Intracoastal Waterway is traveled by private vessels, but most of our guests today come by plane, train, or—predominately—by car.

However guests arrive, Savannah is pretty easy to get to. Two interstate highways pass right through: Interstate 95, a continually busy superhighway that stretches from Florida to Maine, and Interstate 16, an interstate that connects Savannah to Macon (and Interstate 75) with some 165 miles of the wide-open interstate (translation: dull and often lightly traveled) you're likely to find in the East. And while we call it an interstate highway, it never leaves Georgia. Air travelers are going to find Savannah outfitted for them in a grand style, probably several cuts above what an experienced traveler would expect for a city this size. Savannah opened a new $68.5 million airport terminal in 1994. If you've ever navigated your way through big-city airports like those in Chicago or Atlanta, Savannah/Hilton Head International Airport will be a nice change. Like that of its namesake city, the pace is a little slower and friendlier at our airport, and there are no football-field-length corridors to run through in order to make your connections. On the other hand, it's attractive (well, as attractive as an airport can be), modern, and has all the relevant amenities.

Other transportation options include Amtrak and Greyhound, which make stops every day in Savannah.

Once you get here, there are several options to get you around, although the best way is still the oldest way—on foot, or as you might hear it called, "riding shank's mare." If you aren't interested in hoofing it, though, you'll find a well-developed system of taxis, a public bus system, a full array of rental car agencies, even "pedicabs," which are kind of a cross between a tricycle and a rickshaw, driven by strong-legged guides.

Overall, you should find Savannah to be a pretty friendly and easy place for traveling. You won't find elaborate freeway systems with HOV lanes or throngs of harried commuters rushing to catch their five o'clock train. Sorry, Savannah just isn't big enough for that stuff.

What we do have is a network of parkways that will take you around certain sections of the city. There are two-lane roads passing through beautiful marshes, and one-way streets designed to get you quickly from one place to another. And, of course, there are the squares—the very construction of which forces you to slow down . . . take your time . . . enjoy the scenery. This isn't to say we don't have congested streets and other roadways that seem more like speedways, especially in the commercial sections of the city. But big traffic jams are usually big news and might even make the morning paper the next day. Suburban sprawl has given us a fairly recent phenomenon—some commuter-hour congestion, especially on I-16 bound for the bedrooms of Effingham County, or on Abercorn Street's southern extremes approaching the Georgetown neighborhood and the entrance to I-95 en route to Richmond Hill's neighborhoods in adjacent Bryan County.

You may notice people also tend to move slower here, especially during the very hot and humid summer months. That doesn't always apply to driving, however, so don't dawdle if you've chosen the left lane of a busy street. And if you are lost, ask a local. More likely than not, he or she will be happy to get you headed in the right direction. Those of us who live or work in the Historic Downtown are particularly experienced at giving directions.

Having said all this, remember that Savannah is still a modern city, calling for the same commonsense security measures you need in any city. It may feel, particularly in the Historic Downtown, like a small town, but it isn't. Always use the same precautions you would in any city: Be aware of your surroundings, don't venture out alone at night, and keep your wallet or purse secure. There is street crime in Savannah and it has occasionally turned violent.

We have broken this chapter into two sections. Getting Here is just what you would expect: a look at the various modes of transportation to get you to Savannah. Getting Around helps you navigate once you've arrived. It includes a look at parking, public transportation, local roadways, and more.

GETTING HERE

By Air

Savannah/Hilton Head International Airport
400 Airways Avenue
(912) 964-0514
www.savannahairport.com
The Savannah/Hilton Head International Airport is about 10 miles north of Savannah. The exit number off I-95 is 104. Delta (800-221-1212) and USAirways (800-428-4322) are the largest carriers and also have been with the airport the longest. The other airlines are smaller, discount carriers including AirTran (800-247-8726), Continental Express (800-525-0280), United Express (800-241-6522), and Northwest (800-225-2525). Nonstop flights are available via various carriers to Atlanta, Charlotte, Newark, Cincinnati, Cleveland, Houston, Miami, New York (La Guardia), Washington, D.C., Dallas, Detroit, and Chicago. Additional nonstop destinations on weekends include Philadelphia and Pittsburgh.

The lineup at the airport is frequently fluid—new airlines, a few dropouts, shifting around of the offerings. Your travel agent or your favorite airline will know the latest picture. The Airport Commission is on a constant mission to beef up the offerings.

Oh, and if you are wondering about the name, Savannah/Hilton Head International Airport is correct, even though there are no international flights at the moment. (The name was amended to include Hilton Head since about half of the passenger traffic is bound there.) A small airline did offer flights to the Bahamas briefly, but the "international" portion of the title derives from the availability of customs facilities— meaning the airport is ready for international flights as soon as an airline jumps in there.

Although the airline getting you here may change, one constant will be where you will arrive. In May 1994, Savannah opened a $68.5 million terminal with eight gates, restaurants, gift shops, ATM machines, wireless Internet access, a postal center, and other traveler amenities. When passengers arrive or depart, they walk through Savannah Square, a relaxing seating area patterned after Savannah's famous downtown squares. A new parking deck added some 1,000 parking spaces to the existing stock early in 2000. Five more gates and 10,000 additional square feet of retail and concession space opened in 2007. A new "smart" parking garage, complete with technology to direct drivers to the nearest available vacant space, added 1,690 additional parking spaces later that same year.

Private Plane Service

Signature Flight Support
1001 Davidson Drive, Suite 150
Savannah/Hilton Head International Airport
(912) 964-1557
www.bba-aviation.com/flightsupport/
locations/sav
Signature Flight Support, part of the international BBA Aviation, is open daily from 6:00 a.m. to 10:00 p.m., with additional hours available on request. It offers tie-down service for single- and twin-engine planes, along with parking for jets. Fees depend on the aircraft. Repair service is available on call.

Savannah Aviation
34 Hangar Road
(912) 964-1022, (800) 544-8032
www.savannahaviation.com

Savannah Aviation offers maintenance for piston aircraft as well as pilot supplies. They'll teach you to fly, rent you a plane, or arrange a charter.

Rental Cars

Passengers have a choice of several rental-car agencies on the premises, although they tend to change and you should call ahead if it is particularly important to you to deal with a specific car rental agency. Serving Savannah/Hilton Head International are Alamo (800-327-9633; www.alamo.com), Avis (800-831-2847; www.avis.com), Budget (800-527-0700; www.budgetrentacar.com), Dollar Rent A Car (912-964-9001; www.dollar.com), Enterprise (800-736-8222; www.enterprise.com), Hertz (800-654-3131; www.hertz.com), National (800-227-7368; www.nationalcar.com), and Thrifty (800-367-2277; www.thrifty.com).

Taxi Service

The airport distributes a rate brochure (available either outside near all the cabs or inside near the baggage claim) that gives passengers an idea of what it will cost to take a taxi to local bed-and-breakfasts, hotels, motels, and inns. Maximum rates, set by the Savannah City Council, are $25 to the Historic District, $31 to Hutchinson Island, $50 to Tybee Island, $75 to Hilton Head Island, $50 to Bluffton, South Carolina, $60 to the Landings community; and between $33 and $38 to Savannah's Southside. Cabbies are allowed to charge an additional $5 per passenger in Georgia and $10 per passenger after the first two bound for South Carolina.

Taxi service at the airport can be arranged by calling the taxi stand at (912) 964-8016, or by simply showing up at the cab stand curbside, which is clearly marked and impossible to miss. We've never seen the cab stand unattended. Low Country Adventures (800-845-5582) provides airport shuttle service to and from Hilton Head (see our Hilton Head chapter).

There is no scheduled provider of limousine service to and from the airport. However, there are several private limousine services in the city, and these are listed later in this chapter. If you are interested in a ride from the airport, always inquire when calling as to whether the company has a permit to serve the airport.

By Train

Amtrak
2611 Seaboard Coastline Drive
(912) 234-2611, (800) 872-7245
(reservations)
The Silver Meteor and Silver Star take turns coming into Savannah as part of their treks along the eastern seaboard. Savannah is in the New York–Miami Amtrak corridor, and travelers have a choice of several departure times each day. Note that there is no train service currently to Atlanta, an omission advocacy groups periodically tackle.

The Amtrak station is about 4 miles from the Historic Downtown. Heading west on I-16, take the Chatham Parkway exit. At the stop sign turn left, then take your first right. The station is open every day from 4:30 a.m. to noon and from 4:30 p.m. to midnight. Taxicabs are at the station when each train pulls in. Rental cars are not available at the station.

By Bus

Greyhound Bus Lines
610 West Oglethorpe Avenue
(912) 232-2135
Savannah is on Greyhound Bus Lines' busiest eastern corridor—the stretch between New York City and Miami. Buses depart the city 23 times a day, 7 days a week, with the most frequent departures, as would be expected, headed north toward New York and south to Miami. There are also westbound options. If you are coming to Savannah on Greyhound, you will disembark at the terminal on the far western reaches of Oglethorpe Avenue, one of the Historic Downtown's main thoroughfares. Head out the front door of the station and walk to your left along Oglethorpe— within a few blocks you will be in the heart of the Historic Downtown. If you arrive at night,

use caution when walking, as you would in any city. The bus station's locale used to be on the fringes of the restored Historic District, but revitalization has moved into the area, and you'll find more foot traffic and less gritty surroundings. Taxi service is available at the bus terminal.

By Car

Savannah is reachable by car via two major interstates: I-95 from the north and south and I-16 running east and west. I-95 is the main artery along the eastern seaboard, stretching from Maine to the tip of Florida. It is especially busy in the Savannah area during spring, when snowbirds and spring-breakers are heading south for some winter relief. I-16 cuts an east-west path across middle Georgia before merging with I-75, which takes you into Atlanta. The following information is a helpful rundown on how to get to the main geographical sections of the city from either of these interstates.

To Historic Downtown

The best option to get to the Historic Downtown is to use I-16 heading east. There are a couple of clearly marked exits for downtown, but we suggest the one for Liberty Street. Want to swing by the Savannah Visitors Center for a pit stop and reassurance first? Take a left onto Liberty Street, then your next right onto Martin Luther King Jr. Boulevard (MLK), or take the Louisville Road exit, which is near

> **i** Bull Street is the dividing street for all Historic Downtown's east and west orientations. For example, you are on West Liberty Street if you are west of its intersection with Bull and on East Liberty Street if you are east of Bull. The street numbers start at the intersection with Bull and work their way up the farther east and west you go. For example, an address in the 200 block of West Liberty is 2 blocks from the intersection, as is an address in the 200 block of East Liberty—but they are 4 blocks apart.

the end of the interstate and has signs guiding you to the visitor center. You are now essentially a block from the traffic light where the interstate dumped you. The visitor center is on the western side of MLK, calling for a tricky left-hand turn into the parking lot. I-95 doesn't go directly into the city, so if you are traveling the north-south route, you'll need to take I-16 (the exit is clearly marked, although it features a wicked curve and tricky dual merge) for the final 10 miles or so.

To Islands

There are a couple of options to get you to Tybee or the eastern islands of Oatland, Talahi, Whitemarsh, and Wilmington. Take I-16 into the Historic Downtown area and get on any northbound street until you reach Bay Street. Continue east on Bay Street, which, in less than a mile, merges with President Street, then becomes President Street Extension. Follow the President Street Extension until it becomes Islands Expressway. In about 3 miles, it will merge with U.S. Highway 80, which is the main route to Tybee and the eastern islands.

A second option to get you to Tybee, along with the eastern and southeastern islands (Dutch and Isle of Hope), involves leaving I-16 at the 37th Street exit. Take 37th Street to Abercorn Street, take a right, then

> **i** It rarely snows in Savannah, but every few years we get a slight dusting or maybe some ice on the roads. Watch out! Even if you are an experienced driver from northern climes, be forewarned: The city has no snow removal equipment, most drivers don't have snow tires or tire chains, you can't get anywhere without crossing some form of bridge, and despite the fact that most Savannahians have no idea of how to drive in such conditions, a fair percentage will still pile into their cars to take in the novel sight of snow-draped palm trees.

proceed to Victory Drive, where you will turn left (east). To reach Skidaway Island, take a right off Victory onto Waters Avenue. To reach the southeastern islands, look for Skidaway Road off Victory Drive and take a right to get to Dutch Island and Isle of Hope. If you continue east on Victory, it will become US 80, which will take you to the eastern islands and Tybee.

To Southside/Midtown

If you are staying near the Southside, you might want to consider exiting I-95 at Highway 204 in the southern reaches of the county, about 20 miles south of the Historic Downtown. Highway 204 is also Abercorn Street, the main north-south thoroughfare running throughout the entire city. After exiting, head north. After about 3 miles you will enter the Southside—the city's main commercial district, with strip shopping centers, hotels, car dealerships, and Savannah's two malls.

Another option to get to the Southside or Midtown area from I-16: Take Lynes Parkway (Interstate 516). After about 4 miles, it turns into DeRenne Avenue, a main east-west thoroughfare. Take a right onto Abercorn Street off DeRenne, and you are at the edge of the Southside. If you go left onto Abercorn, you will be heading to Midtown and, beyond that, the Historic Downtown.

To West Chatham

The West Chatham communities of Pooler, Bloomingdale, and Garden City are all accessible from I-16 via various marked exits. From I-95 you can also take the Pooler Parkway, which will connect you to US 80 and take you through Bloomingdale, Pooler, and Garden City.

GETTING AROUND

Once you have made it to Savannah, there are several ways you can navigate within the city—from public transportation to a comfortable pair of shoes. Following are some ideas for getting around and a few things to watch out for while traversing the town.

Hitting the Road

Historic Downtown

If it wasn't for the squares, Savannah's Historic Downtown would follow a fairly simple grid pattern. There are 13 main north-south streets in the Historic Downtown, stretching from the northernmost point of the city—the Savannah River—south to Forsyth Park. These streets include (listed east to west) East Broad, Houston, Price, Habersham, Lincoln, Abercorn, Drayton, Bull, Whitaker, Barnard, Jefferson, Montgomery, and Martin Luther King Jr. Likewise, there are 23 main east-west streets, starting (for our purposes) at East Broad and ending at Martin Luther King Jr. (which was formerly known as West Broad). These main east-west roadways include River, Bay, Bryan, Congress, Broughton, State, York, Oglethorpe, Hull, Perry, Liberty, Harris, Charlton, Jones, Taylor, Gordon, Gaston, Huntingdon, Hall, Gwinnett, Bolton, Waldburg, and Park.

If our streets resemble a series of necklaces, then some of them are lucky enough to have pearls in the form of squares. In fact, six of the north-south streets—Montgomery, Barnard, Bull, Abercorn, Habersham, and Houston—have these jewels, making them the most beautiful streets in the Historic Downtown. Bull Street, however, is the most commanding strand. Located in the center of the Historic Downtown and easy to spot because it begins at golden-domed City Hall, Bull Street offers some of the most notable squares in the city, including the one where Forrest Gump waited for his bus and where the main plot unfolds in *Midnight in the Garden of Good and Evil*.

It is crucial that you understand how to navigate around the squares while traveling in the Historic Downtown. Imagine heading north or south on one of the six streets with squares. Every couple of blocks you are going to run into one. They're beautiful but they slow you down—not necessarily a bad

i Lost in Historic Downtown? Can't remember where you parked your car or how to get back to your hotel? Look for somebody doling out parking tickets. Under the "Ask Me" program, parking enforcement attendants—the ones buzzing around in those little blue-and-white carts writing parking tickets—are trained to assist tourists in need. They can give directions, help point out the nearest bathroom, even use their radios to track down misplaced cars.

thing—but local commuters opt for the plainer, straighter one-way Whitaker Street to get out of town and the equally straight, plain, and one-way Drayton Street to get in.

No, the squares aren't your standard traffic circles. There is only one lane, and traffic moves in a counterclockwise direction around a beautiful park filled with trees, benches, and in some instances, a monument or fountain. The traffic moves very slowly, so you have ample time to figure out where you would like to exit. When entering a square, always yield to any car making its way around the square—it has the right-of-way. Once the coast is clear, enter the square driving to your right. Because we have many visitors (and not a few locals) who don't understand that part about who has the right-of-way on the square, be cautious.

If you don't want to hit any squares, you can take a straight southbound route through the Historic Downtown on either Price Street or Whitaker Street. Both run one way. Drayton Street, a one-way northern thoroughfare, will get you all the way to the Savannah River without being interrupted by squares. These aren't, however, the prettiest routes. Note that you also will run into squares when traveling east to west in the Historic Downtown. The majority of the east-west routes pass by to the north or south of the squares, but a few intersect them. Again, when approaching a square from the east or west, you must yield to any traffic that is already making its way around the square. Once traffic has cleared, you enter the square by traveling to your right or going straight ahead. Liberty and Oglethorpe are the main east-west streets without squares, and they feature broad, tree-lined center medians. Other squareless east-west routes include Jones, Gaston, Broughton (the downtown business district's "main street"), and Bay. All of this sounds complicated. It isn't, as you will see. Yield when entering a square, travel to the right—as is quite obvious—and you'll do fine.

Islands

The eastern islands, including Whitemarsh, Talahi, Oatland, and Wilmington, are directly off US 80, which is also the only route to Tybee Island. It is a fairly wide, four-lane highway taking you through scenic marshlands before narrowing into a two-lane road as you near Tybee. Skidaway Road leads to Dutch Island and the Isle of Hope (but not, oddly enough, without some turns to Skidaway Island). Waters Avenue is the direct route to Skidaway Island. This well-marked, two-lane road is very busy and congested most times of the day. (Please see our Tybee Island chapter for more information on getting around there.) Pay particular attention to speed limits in school zones.

Southside/Midtown

Abercorn Street is the main artery running through Savannah's Southside. It begins at the Savannah River in the Historic Downtown, and in its early stretches is a charming, square-filled route through the Historic Downtown. It continues south some 20 miles to I-95, picking up additional lanes and additional traffic. All the motels, hotels, shopping centers, car dealerships, and other businesses in the Southside are either right on Abercorn or on a street just off this main drag. The six-lane street is heavily traveled and usually very busy. Try to avoid Abercorn during morning and afternoon rush hours—typically 7:30 to 9:00 a.m. and 4:00 to 6:00 p.m. If you are a road-warrior veteran of a gridlocked metropolis, however, you might find our version of rush hour amusing.

DeRenne Avenue, which becomes I-516 at its western end, is the main Southside east-west route. You will find two of the city's hospitals off DeRenne (one just off, and the other a few blocks north on Waters Avenue), along with gas stations, shopping centers, banks, and several medical offices. This road also is heavily traveled and should be avoided during morning and afternoon rush hours. Since this road serves hospital personnel, rush hour tends to start around 3:00 p.m. weekdays.

Victory Drive (US 80) is Midtown's main drag. It travels through residential neighborhoods and by shopping centers and Grayson Stadium, home of Savannah's minor-league baseball team, the Sand Gnats (see our Spectator Sports chapter). When traveling east, Victory Drive is the main route to Tybee and the eastern islands.

Eisenhower Drive is another major east-west road that accesses Hunter Army Airfield to the west and Skidaway Road to the east. It parallels DeRenne and Victory.

West Chatham

Bay Street, which runs right in front of City Hall in the Historic Downtown, continues to West Chatham, eventually taking you to Garden City and Port Wentworth. George Washington Highway, which turns into Augusta Road, is also another main thoroughfare for this part of town. US 80 runs through the area as well, taking motorists to Bloomingdale, Pooler, and Garden City.

Parking

When Oglethorpe designed the original city plan for Savannah, he didn't leave space for parking cars. That wasn't a problem at the time, but over the ensuing 270-plus years, it has caused some difficulties. You can find parking, generally, but it is not free, and it is often not as convenient as you would like in the Historic Downtown. We focus our parking information section on that part of town for a couple of reasons: It's the place most tourists want to roam, and it's the main area in the city where you have to pay to park. Venture outside the Historic Downtown to South-side/Midtown, Islands, or West Chatham, and you shouldn't have any trouble finding ample free parking. (An exception is Tybee Island, which is covered in a separate chapter.)

Despite the high volume of vehicles jostling for places in the Historic Downtown every day, a metered spot or one in a garage or parking lot usually is available. It's the daily downtown worker who finds parking an expensive nightmare, with meters vigilantly patrolled and waiting lists for monthly spaces in the city lots and prime private lots. As a visitor, you might not find a place right next to the square or shop you want to visit, but chances are good you will find one within comfortable walking distance. Be advised that it gets more crowded as you get closer to River Street—a main tourist hub overlooking the Savannah River. And remember that no matter how good the parking situation may be the rest of the year, it is going to be tough, if not altogether impossible, to get a spot near downtown on St. Patrick's Day. (See our St. Patrick's Day chapter for more information on the perils of parking during the city's big fest.)

Parking for the majority of the Historic Downtown area (and a little farther south) is metered, costing 30 cents to $1 an hour and more, depending on location. As we mention in other chapters, the downtown area is patrolled by vigilant parking enforcers who are out in force from 8:00 a.m. to 5:00 p.m., Monday through Friday. (Translation: It's free on weekends, provided you don't park any-where stupid like in front of a fire hydrant.) Leave your meter expired for even a minute or two, and chances are pretty good you are going to get a ticket. The majority of the tickets range between $8 and $15, and you have five days to pay up. After that, an additional $12 is tacked on. Wait 30 days to pay and your ticket suddenly costs you an additional $17. Parking meters are serious business in the city of Savannah, so take careful note of the time and carry change. Most merchants are friendly, but some are grouchy about mak-

i If you are going to depend on park-ing meters, keep plenty of change handy. Meters in prime locations or offer-ing the longest time span often take only quarters. None of them take pennies. By the way, the meter maids in Savannah haven't taken up working on weekends— at least not yet. Conversely, the ones at Tybee Island, our beach, are most vigilant on weekends.

ing meter change. Also, messages posted on some meters claim they are checked on Sat-urday—which is not true.

Parking Services is going high-tech down-town, with the installation of two new vari-eties of meter beyond the traditional put-in-a-coin-and-turn-the-handle versions. One requires parkers to walk to the middle of the block and buy a paper receipt from a machine, then return to the car and put it on the dashboard. Another version requires driv-ers to note the number of a parking space, walk to a midblock computer, and feed in coins. If all of this sounds likely to breed con-fusion, increase inconvenience, and enhance the chances you will get a parking ticket despite your efforts to comply—well, you are right. However, the newer meters take cur-rency and credit cards.

Metered parking is scarcer than ever since security concerns prompted the lifting of curbside parking near federal buildings, so read on to learn about your parking-garage options.

You won't find meters along Broughton Street, the main shopping district in the His-toric Downtown that is experiencing a resur-gence with new businesses, shops, and restaurants after years of decline. To help bring people into the area, the city allows free 2-hour parking along Broughton Street (with a few spaces that allow only 30 minutes of park-ing). While there are no meters, you can be ticketed for exceeding the time limit—it is monitored.

The State Street Parking Garage. BETTY DARBY

City Parking Garages

The city operates four modern parking garages, although they are of limited use during weekday business hours because most of the spaces are taken up by contract parkers. The Bryan Street Parking Garage at Bryan and Abercorn Streets is the nicest of the set, and it operates 24/7. The Robinson Garage at Montgomery and York Streets also is 24/7. The State Street Parking Garage at State and Abercorn Streets closes at 1:00 a.m. during the week—which will safely see you through dinner and most social events downtown except a steady club crawl. Hours are extended on weekends. The same hours apply at the Liberty Street Garage at Liberty and Montgomery Streets. Garage rates are $1 for the first hour and 75 cents for additional hours. Evening, weekend, and special event rates vary.

City Parking

The city operates a few public parking lots as well. Three are on River Street and cost $1 per hour. For easy access to the lots, from Bay Street take the Abercorn, Lincoln, or Barnard Street ramps to River Street. From the Lincoln ramp, turn left to reach the lots. From the Abercorn or Barnard ramps, turn either way on River Street to reach a city lot. Note that these are small lots; your best bet if visiting River Street is to park at the Bay Street level and walk down or ride the public elevator between City Hall and the Hyatt Regency Savannah.

There are a handful of private parking garages and lots in town. Many cater strictly to local businesses and have lengthy waiting lists to get in.

Visitor Parking Day Passes

Here's a real bargain. To take the hassle out of feeding meters, the city offers a Visitor Parking Day Pass. The pass, which costs $8, is valid for 48 hours and allows visitors to park at any meter in the Historic Downtown, at time-controlled lots and parking spaces, in the four city parking garages, or at the city parking lots. The pass, which must be displayed on the driver's-side dash, is not valid in all the areas you would expect—private parking lots, hotel parking garages, sweeping zones, freight zones, bagged meters (meters that are covered to tell you that parking is not allowed temporarily), etc.

You can purchase a day pass or find out more information on parking at the Savannah Visitors Center, 301 Martin Luther King Jr. Boulevard, or at the offices of City of Savannah Parking Services, 100 East Bryan Street (912-651-6470). The pass comes with a map showing parking locations. You can pick up a brochure outlining all the parking regulations at these locations, too.

Public Transportation

Chatham Area Transit
900 East Gwinnett Street
(912) 233-5767 (TDD)
www.catchacat.org
If you hear someone say they are going to "catch a CAT," they are referring to a ride on Chatham County's public bus system. Chatham Area Transit (CAT) has a fleet of buses (easy to spot with the outstretched cats drawn on their sides, although many of the buses are now defaced by advertising) traveling on 22 routes throughout the county.

CAT offers three free services, two of which are of particular interest to tourists. There's a free CAT shuttle making its way around the Historic District to some 30 stops, including hotels and prime shopping locations and historic squares. The shuttle bus looks like a well-groomed pseudo-trolley and is wheelchair accessible. Shuttle hours are from roughly 7:00 a.m. to 7:00 p.m. every day but Sunday, when they start just after 9:30 a.m. and run to about 5:00 p.m. CAT also operates a passenger ferry to Hutchinson Island, which is also free (more on that later). The third free service is a shuttle originating from the city's Liberty Street parking garage, designed to make that new facility on the edge of the business district more appealing to daily downtown workers—but anyone's welcome to ride it.

As far as the regular bus service goes, you can get just about anywhere you want by catching a CAT, including the city's two malls, the Historic Downtown area, and the Islands (except Tybee). CAT buses do not, however, go to much of West Chatham. All are wheelchair accessible. There are bicycle racks with a capacity of two bikes on the front of the buses. Fare is $1. Children shorter than 40 inches tall—the height of the fare box—get to ride free (limit two free children's fares per adult), and the fare for riders age 65 and older and persons with disabilities is half price. If you plan on doing a lot of traveling around Savannah on CAT, there is a weekly CAT Card—good for unlimited rides—available for $12. You can buy tickets at the Gwinnett Street office (although you'll never find it or get there without a car), a satellite office at 124 Bull Street, and in the Bull Street (main), Oglethorpe Mall, Carnegie, and Port City branches of the Live Oak Public Library.

Regular CAT buses run each day from 6:00 a.m. to midnight. Bus stops are marked with bright orange signs throughout the city. Some stops have a rain shelter, some have benches, and some are just standing points. There is no service on Thanksgiving, Christmas, or New Year's Day. CAT produces a comprehensive bus booklet, explaining everything from how to enter the bus to what routes will get you to different historic sites. The bus book, which also contains all the system's routes, can be found in area grocery stores, libraries, and malls, among other places. Its Web site, www.catchacat.org, is unusually well designed and informative for a government site.

CAT also operates a paratransit van system for Americans with Disabilities Act (ADA)–eligible riders. ADA-eligible visitors are welcome to use the TELERIDE service. In order to use the door-to-door service, visitors must present an ID card from their hometown transit system that proves their eligibility. TELERIDE costs $1.20 each way. For more information, call (912) 354-6900.

If you are in the Historic Downtown and want to purchase tokens, passes, or talk to someone about a route, stop in at CAT Central, 124 Bull Street, in the county's historic courthouse.

Taxis and Limousines

The best thing to do if you want taxi service in Savannah is to call the cab company directly. In theory, perhaps, you could hail a passing cab, but we've never seen it done—when we want a cab, we telephone and ask for one or go to the cab lineups outside major hotels and the airport. There are several companies in town, typically charging a maximum of $3.50 for the first mile and $1.80 per mile thereafter.

Limousine service also is available from a variety of local companies. Limos typically cost around $45 to $65 per hour, and some of the companies require a two-hour minimum. Advanced reservations are required to ensure prompt service.

Taxi services include Adam Cab Inc. (912-927-7466), Airport Taxi Service (912-269-5586), All American Cab (912-961-7433), Savannah Cab Company (912-236-2424), Toucan Taxi (912-233-3700), and Yellow Cab (912-236-1133).

For limousines, try A & E Luxury Limousine Service (912-354-2982), Low Country Adventures (912-629-0551, 800-845-5582), and First City Limousine (912-484-0455).

Bicycles

At present, Savannah is not exactly a bike-friendly city. In fact, because of its age, layout, and other considerations, there are only a few bike paths in town. However, relief may soon be in sight. In 1997 voters passed a measure that would allow several million dollars to be used to construct a series of bike paths throughout the county. That construction is still well in the future, however, so don't count on it to help you out much on your trip. Meanwhile, wear a helmet, follow traffic laws, and be aware that most motorists here don't have regular experience in sharing the roadway with bikes.

For the most part, bikes are not serious commuting or traveling modes in Savannah, although the growing student population at Savannah College of Art and Design is upping the bike census. This is not to say you can't get around on a bike in Historic Downtown or a few other places—more and more people do. It is just not the preferred (or the safest) mode of transportation. In fact, there is one Historic Downtown road, Bay Street, that we recommend completely avoiding on your bike. Bay Street is a very narrow, heavily traveled road where bikers will find themselves competing for space with 18-wheelers. In the summer of 1999, the city banned bike riding through the downtown squares in the name of pedestrian safety, although the ban does not apply to kids on bikes.

The designated bike paths in the city include the following (although bikes are legal on any surface street):

West to East Corridor: 52nd Street to Ward Street to LaRoche Avenue to the entrance of Savannah State University

North to South Corridor: Habersham Street to Stephenson Avenue to Hodgson Memorial Drive to Edgewater Drive to Hillyer Drive to Dyches Drive to Lorwood Drive to Tibet Avenue to Largo Drive to Windsor Road to Science Drive

McQueens Island Trail: 6 miles for hiking and biking between Bull River and Fort Pulaski along US 80

McCorkle Trail: Wilmington Island at Charlie C. Brooks Park, 7001 Johnny Mercer Boulevard

Walking

The best way to enjoy Savannah's Historic Downtown is with a comfortable pair of shoes. *Walking Magazine* dubbed Savannah one of the top 10 walking cities in the United States. To help find your way around on foot, we have included a walking tour in the Attractions chapter—that's a good place to start. Before you set out, however, here are a few tips, along with some rules of the walking road, to make your trip a little easier.

Enjoy the Squares, Carefully

Historic Downtown is only about 2.5 square miles, so it is fairly easy to see the entire area on foot. Savannah's famed squares make the trip even easier because they are perfect for strolling. Besides spacious walkways, there are also many benches in case you need to take a rest between jaunts.

A word of caution: Pedestrians don't get the same respect here they get elsewhere. Do not assume traffic will stop when you step into a crosswalk, no matter how clearly it is marked. In fact, if you do see someone yield to a pedestrian, check the car as it passes—it probably has out-of-state license plates. And when you are driving, don't be surprised that pedestrians casually jaywalk here. We don't recommend it—we just point out that it happens.

Crossing Bay Street

Although the Historic Downtown is generally very pedestrian friendly, one area that isn't is Bay Street. This is the main street running east to west in front of City Hall. Many tourists encounter Bay Street, as it must be crossed to reach River Street, the tourist haven running along the Savannah River. As mentioned in our Bicycles section, Bay Street is a very busy, narrow four-lane road that serves as the main throughway for 18-wheeler traffic trying to make it to other areas in the city. Many visitors think they can beat the traffic on Bay Street, get halfway across, and find themselves stuck in the middle, dangerously close to traffic and unable to safely pass to the other side. After experimenting with several options, the city went with increasing the number of traditional traffic lights to get pedestrians across. Most have a button-activated pedestrian signal: Push it, wait (and wait), then move quite briskly across. A few have audio features designed to serve the blind.

Getting to River Street

Savannah is built on a bluff overlooking the river, even though it probably looks flat to you. River Street runs along the Savannah

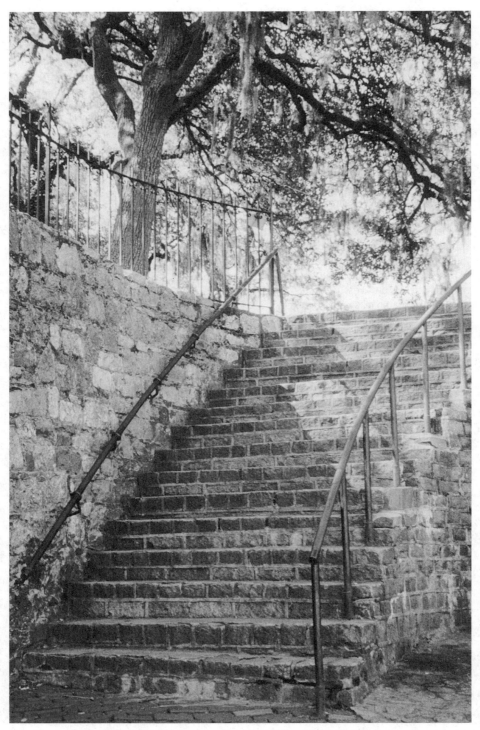

Steep stone stairs sweep down the bluff from Bay Street toward River Street. BETTY DARBY

River, which means it's lower than the rest of the city and can present a challenge to pedestrians. One of our favorite city projects was the 1998 installation of an elevator behind City Hall on Bay Street. The wheelchair-accessible elevator whisks riders down to River Street, avoiding the stairs and the cobblestone streets on its way. The elevator is between City Hall (can't miss that giant gold dome) and the Hyatt Regency Savannah (which, bless it, is a giant modern fortress that sticks out like a sore thumb and can't be missed either). Part of the elevator project included the installation of a public restroom facility on the River Street level. We've stopped in periodically and have been impressed with its upkeep. There's also a small information station with a friendly question-answerer, a brochure rack, and—most important in Savannah's climate—a water fountain. The more adventurous pedestrian might want to skip the elevator and hoof it to River Street. One option to get to River Street involves stairs. There is a hodgepodge of choices available—we prefer the wide, easily negotiated set that runs along the east (right-hand when you face the river) side of City Hall. All these stairs are old, and many aren't particularly easy to navigate, such as narrow slate steps curving along a stone wall with an aged metal railing. The steps tend to be beside the ramps that carry traffic to River Street. Be extremely careful, and if you want, walk down the ramps that cars use to get to the river.

Although you can avoid the tricky stairs this way, you won't avoid the cobblestone ramps, another potential pedestrian pitfall. The cobblestones are very beautiful and not as steep as the stairs, but beware walking on them with any type of heeled shoe. (Purists will point out that these are ballast stones, not proper cobblestones, but we figure a round, smooth rock is a round, smooth rock—whatever you call it.) These roads and ramps are uneven and difficult to walk on, even for people with the surest feet and flattest shoes. If you are not above sneaking, you

i There are some disadvantages to being close to sea level. Drenching thunderstorms are frequent in the summer, and if an incoming or high tide has filled up the drainage ditches (we call them canals), the water won't run off. Street flooding results, and in some areas—including well-developed residential areas—the water gets high enough to disable cars. Wait out really heavy storms—the flooding is usually short-lived. Better to spend some extra time indoors than to risk getting stuck in rising waters.

can duck into the elevator at the Savannah Hyatt Regency for a ride down to River Street—but you can't take a ride up without a room key.

Crossing the River

The development of the Savannah International Trade and Convention Center and the Westin Savannah Harbor Resort on Hutchinson Island—a midriver island between Georgia and South Carolina— added some transportation challenges. You can get to Hutchinson Island easily by road, via the Talmadge Bridge. But rather than drive for several miles, the resort and convention development is literally a stone's throw (well, more like a Tiger Woods' tee shot) from River Street. The obvious solution for auxiliary transportation between the two sites was a passenger ferry, and two ferries designed expressly for the route were delivered in 2004. They're known as the Savannah Belles Ferry System, operated by the Chatham Area Transit Authority, or CAT. The two vessels are named for historic women—the *Juliette Gordon Low*, named for the Savannah-born founder of the Girl Scouts, and the *Susie King Taylor*, named for a former slave who started one of the first schools for blacks in Savannah. The ferries are designed to look nostalgic and operate at about 20-minute intervals. After quibbling about fares for a couple years, the ferry trip is now free. Unless you are attending an event at the Savannah International Trade and Convention Center or staying at the Westin Savannah Harbor Golf Resort and Spa (or patronizing one of its amenities), you won't really need to use the ferry. We recommend it anyway, especially if you have children in your party. It's fun to see River Street from the vantage point of an arriving sailor.

Ferries operate seven days a week, weather and river conditions permitting, from 7:30 a.m. to 10:30 p.m. Ferry landings are at River Street behind City Hall, at the Savannah Marriott Riverfront, and on Hutchinson Island at the convention center.

Quick Trips

Here are a few suggested routes that may save you some time and frustration when getting from a few popular point As to point Bs. Note that all these jaunts are in the 15-to-20-minute range.

Historic Downtown to Oglethorpe Mall:

Option One: Take Whitaker Street south about 2 miles to Victory Drive. Turn left onto Victory Drive, then right at the second light onto Abercorn Street. The mall is about 4 miles down Abercorn Street. Turn left into Oglethorpe on Mall Boulevard.

Option Two: Take Bay Street east. In less than 1 mile it runs into President Street Extension. From President Street Extension, take Truman Parkway. After a couple of miles, exit to the right on Eisenhower Drive, then turn left onto Abercorn and look for Mall Boulevard after a couple of blocks.

Historic Downtown to Savannah Mall: Take I-16 4 miles west to the Lynes Memorial Parkway exit and go south. After 2.5 miles on the Lynes Parkway, exit at the Southwest Bypass (also known as the Veterans Parkway) and continue 7.5 miles until it ends at Highway 204. Turn left onto Highway 204, which becomes Abercorn Street, and the mall will be some 3 miles ahead on your left. Or just take one of the options to Oglethorpe Mall and opt to stay on Abercorn instead of turning onto Mall Boulevard; Savannah Mall is only a couple miles farther, on the right.

Historic Downtown to Savannah/Hilton Head International Airport: Take I-16 west to I-95 north. The airport is 14 miles away at exit 104 off I-95.

Historic Downtown to Amtrak station: Go west on Liberty Street, which turns into Louisville Road after less than a mile. Take a left onto Telfair Road, then a right onto Seaboard Coastline Drive.

HISTORY

Perhaps no other city owes as much to one man as Savannah owes to James Edward Oglethorpe, the English soldier and politician who founded Georgia. Oglethorpe was the mastermind and driving force behind the development of the colony of Georgia, whose first city was Savannah. He selected the site of the city and christened it, giving it the same name as the river that flows beside it. Oglethorpe supervised the first phase of the building of Savannah, and he nurtured the city during its infancy as a town. He defended it in its early years, militarily and financially.

More than that, Oglethorpe bestowed on Savannah a gift that has flourished throughout the decades and centuries since his passing. He designed and laid out the town and, in so doing, created the atmosphere that makes Savannah unique among cities. He left a legacy that has been admired and enjoyed by countless residents and visitors—a treasure that will be the pride of the city for as long as it stands.

OGLETHORPE AND HIS IDEA

Oglethorpe was born into a family that had a long history of service to England. After serving in the British army and fighting the Turks as the aide-de-camp of an Austrian prince, Oglethorpe was elected to the lower house of Parliament in 1722 at the age of 25. He developed an interest in the misfortunes of the poor, in particular the plight of debtors who had been thrown into prison by creditors hoping the debtors' friends would secure their release by paying the debts. He worked for prison reform and attempted to find solutions to England's unemployment problems.

Together with John Perceval, another member of Parliament, Oglethorpe hatched the idea of giving people who were out of work a fresh start by transporting them to a new colony in America that would be located between Spanish Florida and the English colony of South Carolina. Oglethorpe and Perceval petitioned King George II for a charter, which the king signed on April 21, 1732. The deal was not one-sided: The crown was motivated by the prospect of having colonists raise produce and procure raw materials to ship to England while serving as a market for English goods. The idea of having the new colony act as a buffer between the Spanish in Florida and thriving South Carolina was not lost on the royals either. To top it all off, the colony was to be named Georgia in honor of the king.

The colony would be managed by Oglethorpe, Perceval, and 19 other trustees, who would receive no pay and no land for their involvement. There were also rules for the colony: Slavery, lawyers, and "brandies and distilled liquors" (in particular rum) were prohibited, as were Catholics. In time, all would be allowed. Those who took advantage of the free passage to Georgia offered by the

i Among Savannah's tributes to founder James Edward Oglethorpe is a large bronze statue of the Englishman in Chippewa Square. The monument is the work of Daniel Chester French, sculptor of the Minuteman statue of Concord, Massachusetts. You'll notice that Oglethorpe faces toward Florida, still guarding his beloved Savannah against an invasion from the south.

trustees agreed to remain in the colony for three years, and each received a town lot for a house and 50 acres to farm. A colonist would not own the acreage and could occupy it only as long as he farmed it properly. Grants of 500 acres were available to people who paid their way to the colony.

The trustees adopted as their motto the Latin phrase *Non Sibi Sed Allis* (Not for themselves but others). It appears on Georgia's original seal, which also bears a rendering of a silkworm crawling across a mulberry leaf; it was hoped that the colony would produce silk in abundance.

BEFORE THE ENGLISH CAME

Although Oglethorpe brought a European-style civilization to this land known as Georgia, he and his little band of settlers were very much the new kids on the block. According to Max E. White, author of *Georgia's Indian Heritage,* human beings had existed in Georgia many centuries before. White states that "the earliest evidence of man's presence in Georgia and the Southeast is in the form of fluted projectile points identical to or very similar to those found west of the Mississippi and dated to about 12,000 years ago." In addition to discovering such rudimentary tools as projectile points, modern man has found other evidence of the native peoples of Georgia—shell middens and ceremonial mounds. The middens are piles of refuse "composed primarily of mussel shells discarded by prehistoric diners." "Many times," says White, "people were buried in these shell heaps and utilitarian objects, such as bone awls, projectile points, etc., were often placed with them." The remnants of shell middens can be seen in the Savannah area at Skidaway Island State Park (see our Parks and Recreation chapter).

Although Oglethorpe and his Englishmen were the first Europeans to make a go of settling in southeast Georgia, others had visited before them. Spanish explorer Hernando de Soto passed through in 1539–40 during his trek across what became the southeastern United States. After de Soto's countrymen established a settlement at St. Augustine, Florida, in 1565, they built Catholic missions and churches on Georgia's sea islands, the last of which was closed in 1702. French explorer Jean Ribault—who started short-lived settlements at what are now Jacksonville, Florida, and Beaufort, South Carolina—sailed along the Georgia coast in 1562.

"Almost all of Georgia was forest-covered when the Europeans first appeared on the scene," says White. The Native Americans living there were, for the most part, members of the Creek and Cherokee nations, "practicing an economy based on agriculture, hunting, fishing, and gathering." Most were Indians belonging to the Creek Confederacy, and one of them—Tomo-chi-chi—would have a significant impact on the survival of Oglethorpe's new colony.

A WHOLE NEW WORLD

Oglethorpe and his fellow trustees recruited 114 colonists comprising 35 families for the first voyage to Georgia and the task of starting a settlement there. Oglethorpe was the only trustee to make the trip. They left Gravesend, England, on November 17, 1732, aboard a 200-ton vessel named the *Anne* and arrived in what is now Charleston, South Carolina, on January 13, 1733. The settlers then made their way south down the South Carolina coast and, after transferring to smaller boats, landed in the new colony on February 1. That was the date of Georgia's founding according to the Julian calendar. When that calendar was abandoned in favor of the Gregorian calendar 19 years later, the date became February 12—the day now celebrated as Georgia Day (see GHS's Georgia Days in the Annual Events and Festivals chapter). Oglethorpe had gone ahead of the colonists several days before their landing and had chosen a site for the town of Savannah on a 40-foot-high bluff overlooking the Savannah River—Yamacraw Bluff. In a letter to the trustees explaining his choice of the site for a city, he stated that he "thought it healthy" and wrote, "The last and fullest consideration of the Healthfulness of the place was that an Indian nation, who knew the Nature of the Country, chose it for their Habitation."

The Indians were the 100-odd members of the Yamacraw tribe of the Lower Creek nation, led by an 80-year-old chief named Tomo-chi-chi (meaning to "fly up"). The Yamacraws would prove friendly and helpful to the colonists—providing them with food, interceding with other tribes on their behalf, and aiding them in their struggle against the Spanish. The Yamacraws had come to the coast some eight years before the English, led there by Tomo-chi-chi from what is now west Georgia. Other new neighbors were the Musgroves—Mary, an Indian woman, and her husband John, who was white. The Musgroves ran a nearby trading post called Musgrove Cowpen, and they would serve as interpreters for the Europeans and the Native Americans.

The colonists spent their first night in their new home camped out in an area that is now the site of a small park at Bay and Whitaker Streets. In the following days and weeks, Oglethorpe and Col. William Bull of South Carolina laid out the new city, and the settlers set about clearing the pine woods on the bluff with the help of black slaves from the neighboring colony. They also began cultivating a 10-acre plot that would be known as Trustees' Garden. On this parcel, at the current Bay and East Broad Streets, were planted fruit trees and the mulberry trees that were envisioned as the basis of Georgia's silk industry.

Things went well at the outset. By fall 1734, according to a letter from a South Carolina merchant who had visited the town, there were 80 houses and 40 more being built. During Georgia's first decade, the trustees sent more than 2,000 settlers. Other new arrivals brought diversity to the colony. Among them was a boatload of Jews from Portugal who established a Jewish congregation, Mickve Israel. It was the third founded in America and continues today as the South's oldest. Another was a group of Germans, the Salzburgers, who settled 21 miles upriver from Savannah in what is now Effingham County. Their community of New Ebenezer prospered, and the house of worship they built in 1769 is the oldest standing church in Georgia.

Also during the colony's infancy, Savannah became the site of the oldest orphanage in America with a continuous existence: Bethesda Home for Boys. The orphanage's founders, George Whitefield and James Habersham, came to Georgia in 1738 at the request of two Anglican ministers, the Wesley brothers, Charles and John, the latter of whom preached in Savannah during the mid-1730s and went on to found the Methodist church. Bethesda was situated southeast of the town on the banks of the Moon River, with the foundation of the first building being laid in March 1740. It is still in operation in a related capacity, and visitors are welcome to tour the site, a museum, and a chapel (see our Attractions chapter).

Oglethorpe remained involved with the colony during its first 10 years, and in July 1742, he led a contingent of soldiers and Indian allies in a battle that forever wrested control of the region from the Spanish in Florida. In the Battle of Bloody Marsh, his band of defenders surprised and defeated a numerically superior Spanish invasion force about 70 miles south of Savannah at St. Simons Island. The Spanish never attempted another invasion, and a peace treaty between Spain and England was signed in 1748.

i Famed storyteller Joel Chandler Harris in the spring of 2003 was recognized for his ties to Savannah with a historical marker placed on Bay Street. Harris, the author of the Uncle Remus tales, spent a significant part of his life in Savannah working for the daily newspaper. The location of the historical marker is at Bay and Whitaker Streets in a little park across from the former site of the *Savannah Morning News*.

Savannah's Priceless Jewels

The squares of Savannah lend the town a beauty and charm that's unique among American cities. But it's likely that James Edward Oglethorpe had defense as much as aesthetics in mind when he included the little parks in his plan for the city.

According to *Historic Savannah,* a survey of the city's buildings published by the Historic Savannah Foundation in 1979, "military considerations certainly played a major role" in the plan. The smallness of the squares and lots surrounding them "made the town more compact and easier to defend." The squares were also places where colonists living in nearby outposts could bring their families and livestock if attacked by Spaniards or Indians.

As conceived by Oglethorpe, the squares were at the center of the town's wards. Each ward had four "tythings," with each tything containing 10 lots for houses. In a ward, the tythings were on the northern and southern sides of the square, with the eastern and western sides of the square set aside as trust lots for public buildings. Oglethorpe laid out six wards and their squares. Four of these squares—now named Johnson, Wright, Ellis, and Telfair—were laid out in 1733, with Johnson being the first. Later, Oglethorpe laid out Reynolds and Oglethorpe Squares.

Eventually, a total of 24 squares were created. Two of them, Elbert and Liberty, have been "lost" to progress—bisected by Montgomery Street, they now exist as half-squares, with one half still parklike and the other half covered by public buildings. A third square, Ellis, was for 50 years covered by a parking garage, but it is now being restored.

No one knows for sure what inspired Oglethorpe to design Savannah as he did. "Perhaps his interest in town planning grew out of his friendship with an English architect, Robert Castell," surmises *Historic Savannah.* "Perhaps, because of his previous military service under Prince Eugene of Savoy, Oglethorpe followed the traditions of old Roman military camps. And perhaps he may have seen and utilized a plan of Peking, originally printed in 1688 and reproduced years later."

Castell, who died in debtors' prison, a circumstance that might have prompted Oglethorpe's interest in prison reform, had published a book called *The Villas of the Ancients,* and Oglethorpe owned two copies. According to historian William Harden, the book was "richly illustrated, and containing matter certainly of interest, and very probably of utility to one who might have in view the founding of a town or planning the laying out of pleasure grounds." Whatever Oglethorpe's inspiration, it lives happily on in the form of Savannah's priceless jewels, her squares.

The following is a list of Savannah's squares, with brief explanations of who or what they are named for:

Calhoun Square—for John C. Calhoun, a South Carolinian considered to be the Old South's greatest spokesman in the U.S. Senate

Chatham Square—for William Pitt, English prime minister and the Earl of Chatham during the period when Georgia was a royal colony

Chippewa Square—for the Battle of Chippewa, an American victory in Canada during the War of 1812

Columbia Square—for the female personification of the United States

Crawford Square—for William Crawford, a Georgia governor and U.S. secretary of the treasury

Elbert Square—for Samuel Elbert, a patriot of the American Revolution and a Georgia governor

Ellis Square—for Sir Henry Ellis, Georgia's second royal governor

Franklin Square—for statesman and inventor Benjamin Franklin, who at one time was an agent for Georgia in London

Greene Square—for Gen. Nathanael Greene of Rhode Island, Revolutionary War hero and short-lived owner of a plantation west of Savannah

Johnson Square—for Robert Johnson, the royal governor of South Carolina who aided Oglethorpe in establishing the colony of Georgia

Lafayette Square—for the Marquis de Lafayette, the Frenchman who was an important ally of the United States during the Revolutionary War

Liberty Square—in recognition of the nation's freedom and independence and for the Sons of Liberty, a group of young men who fanned the flames of revolution during the late 1700s

Madison Square—for James Madison, fourth president of the United States

Monterey Square—for the Mexican city captured by U.S. forces during the war with Mexico

Oglethorpe Square—for James Edward Oglethorpe, founder of Georgia

Orleans Square—for the Battle of New Orleans, an American victory in the War of 1812

Pulaski Square—for Polish Count Casimir Pulaski, who fought on the American side during the Revolutionary War and was killed during the Siege of Savannah

Reynolds Square—for John Reynolds, Georgia's first royal governor

Telfair Square—for the Telfair family, whose members made important contributions to Georgia in the areas of politics, business, the arts, and philanthropy

Troup Square—for Georgia governor George Michael Troup, who was also a U.S. senator

Warren Square—for Gen. Joseph Warren, a hero of the Revolutionary War

Washington Square—for George Washington, first president of the United States

Whitefield Square—for George Whitefield, one of the founders of the Bethesda orphanage

Wright Square—for Sir James Wright, Georgia's third royal governor

Colonial Cemetery is the final resting place of many early settlers. KYLE CASON

Oglethorpe left Georgia on July 22, 1743, never to return. Even before his departure, Savannah began to decline as the population dwindled due to the hardships of bringing civilization to a wilderness: insects, alligators, extremes in the weather, difficulties in growing crops. The colony remained a trusteeship until 1752, when the trustees, burdened by financial problems and turnover in their ranks, relinquished their charter to the crown a year before it was to expire. As Preston Russell and Barbara Hines wrote in their lyrical *Savannah: A History of Her People Since 1733*, "Non Sibi Sed Allis had fallen on its nose. The dream was long since dead, but Savannah was here to stay."

A ROYAL COMEBACK

Under control of the crown, Georgia's government changed from the benevolent dictatorship of the trustees to a more traditional setup headed by a governor and having an assembly of elected representatives. Under this arrangement, Georgia was upgraded from colony to province, with Savannah serving as the seat of government.

The first Royal Assembly met in Savannah in January 1755, and one of its first acts was to adopt a law allowing slavery. The first of Georgia's three royal governors, John Reynolds, began a two-and-a-half-year tenure in October 1754; he was succeeded by Henry Ellis, who gave way to James Wright in 1760. Wright, who ruled as governor until January 1776, was a godsend for Savannah's struggling economy. "In mere months, Wright led the youngest colony through stages of development that had required years in other colonies," states Edward Chan Sieg in his book *Eden on the Marsh: An Illustrated History of Savannah.* "Wright's administration was geared to accommodate the 'men of substance' who began to pour into Georgia from other colonies and from the plantations of the Indies. Aided by liberal credit policies and cheap labor, they transformed the coastal plains into the great plantations of legend. Wharf facilities and warehouses appeared on the bluff as shipping demands increased almost daily."

The major export was rice, the growing of which had been made possible by the repeal of the ban on slavery. The idea of making Savannah a silk-production center had flopped, apparently due to a combination of mismanagement and the silkworms' problems with the climate. By 1766, Wright was estimating that the province of Georgia was inhabited by as many as 10,000 whites and 7,800 black slaves—up from a total of 3,000 people nine years earlier—and that exports of rice had tripled over a six-year span.

i The Green-Meldrim House on Madison Square is the site of a meeting in January 1865 that inspired the famed "40 acres and a mule" declaration giving black freedmen land in Georgia, South Carolina, and Florida.

THE GREAT REBELLION

In the mid-1760s, many residents of England's American colonies reacted with outrage to what they deemed unfair taxation of imported items by the mother country. As the following decade unfolded, their dissatisfaction grew to the point that they sought independence from England.

The fervor for freedom took hold somewhat slowly in Savannah, but by mid-1774, it began to show itself in the actions of a group of dissidents called the Liberty Boys. Despite Governor Wright's efforts to stop them, they met several times to protest England's closing of the Boston Harbor as punishment for the Boston Tea Party. In January 1775, Noble Wimberly Jones, a Liberty Boy who had been speaker of the Royal Assembly, convened a meeting of Georgia's First Provincial Congress. Wright dissolved the body, but on July 4 a meeting of a second provincial congress was held, with the 102 delegates electing representatives to the colonies' Second Continental Congress.

In the interim, in May members of the Liberty Boys celebrated the opening shot of the American Revolution by breaking into the city's munitions room, stealing 600 pounds of powder, and shipping it to Boston to be used in the fight against the British. The powder really hit the fan on January 18, 1776, when three British warships showed up off the coast of Savannah. The newly established provincial government placed Wright under house arrest, putting an end to British rule in Savannah for the time being. The governor later slipped away and escaped on an English vessel.

On August 10, Savannahians aching for freedom celebrated the signing of the Declaration of Independence, a document endorsed by three Georgians, George Walton of Savannah and Lyman Hall and Button Gwinnett of nearby St. John's Parish. The new state of Georgia elected Archibald Bulloch as governor and completed a constitution in February 1777. Bulloch died during his first year in office and was replaced by Gwinnett.

Savannah, being in an exposed position on the far southeastern reaches of the new United States, paid for its location on December 29, 1778, when 3,000 British troops commanded by Col. Archibald Campbell routed the city's 700 defenders. The enemy had landed below Savannah two days before and slipped behind American Gen. Robert Howe and his forces. The British sacked the city, and James Wright returned to take control of Savannah. He and a small redcoat garrison found themselves under siege in September 1779 by a force of Frenchmen, Irishmen, and volunteers from Haiti. They were joined by a contingent of American troops from South Carolina, and on October 9, the overall commander of the allied forces, French Count Charles Henri d'Estaing, ordered an attack on a defensive position southwest of the city in an area near the existing Savannah Visitors Center. The assault on this position, the Spring Hill redoubt, was, in the words of authors Russell and Hines, "a disaster, the bloodiest single hour in the entire Revolution."

"Through three valiant advances and the staggering retreat," they wrote, "French and Americans were slaughtered by land and naval artillery from Spring Hill redoubt and from . . . ships in the river." The defenders lost 55 men; the attackers suffered more than

1,000 casualties, including the deaths of 2 men later immortalized in monuments in Savannah's squares—Casimir Pulaski, a Polish count who had brought a group of lancers to the fray, and Sgt. William Jasper, who fell while attempting to save the flag of his South Carolina regiment. Savannah remained in possession of the British until after the climactic Battle of Yorktown. Wright and his compatriots evacuated the city several months after that American victory in Virginia, and American forces took control of the city on July 11, 1782.

THE ANTEBELLUM ERA

The Revolutionary War left Savannah a shambles, but the city recovered and prospered in the years between the end of that fight for freedom and an even grimmer struggle in the 1860s. Much of Savannah's prosperity in the years after the Revolution and before the American Civil War was due to a machine invented in 1793 on a plantation west of the city. While serving as a tutor at Mulberry Grove—a plantation owned by the widow of Revolutionary War Gen. Nathanael Greene—a Connecticut schoolteacher named Eli Whitney perfected the cotton gin, a device for removing the seeds from cotton bolls. The machine helped revolutionize the cotton-producing industry and, in so doing, reinforced the value of slavery in the agrarian South—a circumstance that would bring disaster to the region and Savannah.

But in the early 1800s, cotton brought wealth to the city's port. On the subject of the city's transformation, Russell and Hines wrote, "In 1790 cotton exports were one thousand bales; by 1820 they were ninety thousand bales a year. In 1794 Savannah's population was 2,000 with export revenues under $500,000. By 1819 she was America's sixteenth largest city with exports exceeding $14,000,000." As Savannah prospered, its residents built elegant homes and other imposing structures. Probably the most famed of the designers of these buildings was architect

---

i During your stay in our town, you might hear someone referred to as being "Old Fort Irish." This means the person is of Irish descent and grew up in the area of northeast Savannah where Fort Wayne once stood. According to local historian James Mack Adams, the fort, which was also called the Fort of Savannah and Fort Provost, was built about 1760 and was abandoned in the mid-1800s. A gas works was built on the site, and Irish immigrants flocked to the area because of low rents. The fort site at Bay and East Broad Streets is now called Trustees' Garden and is the location of shops, apartments, offices, and The Pirates' House restaurant.

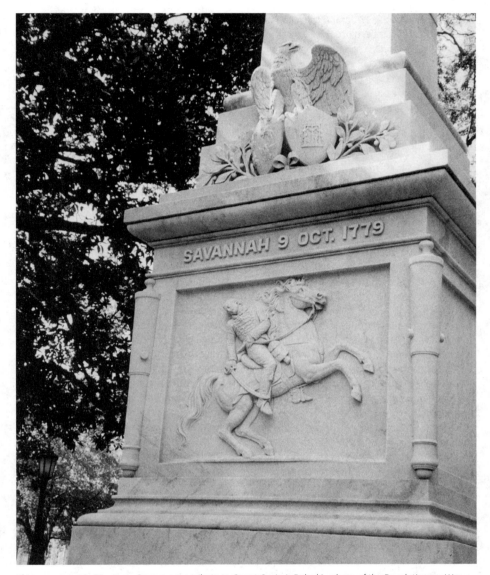

This monument in Monterey Square pays tribute to Count Casimir Pulaski, a hero of the Revolutionary War.
BETTY DARBY

William Jay, who came to the city from England in 1818, stayed for seven years, and is responsible for existing masterpieces such as the Owens-Thomas House, the Scarbrough House, and the Telfair Museum of Art (see our Attractions chapter).

Savannahians experienced some giddy high points during the years between the wars. Among the highest was the transatlantic voyage of the SS *Savannah*, a vessel that was bankrolled by local merchants and propelled by steam and sail. The ship left

Savannah on May 22, 1819, and arrived in Liverpool, England, a record-breaking 29 days and 11 hours later. On the return trip, the *Savannah* shattered that record by four days. A much more lasting achievement involving transportation occurred in 1847 when the Central of Georgia Railroad was completed, with Savannah as its eastern terminus. At that time, "Savannah reached its antebellum zenith," stated author Edward Chan Sieg.

"Now profits really soared and Savannah enjoyed a period of unprecedented growth. In addition to cotton, other sources of income were tobacco, rice, corn, lumber, and naval stores. . . . The population tripled, the city limits were extended, gas lighting made its appearance. Hospitals, churches, and orphanages grew in number for blacks and whites as excess wealth permitted the emergence of the charity traditions which were Savannah's birthright."

Other highly memorable moments occurred when two heroes of the revolution visited the city. In May 1791, while he was serving as the first president of the United States, George Washington came to town for four days and attended numerous get-togethers. One of these was a ball at which, according to William Harden's *A History of Savannah and South Georgia,* the Father of Our Country was "introduced to ninety-six elegantly dressed ladies." In appreciation of his stay, Washington presented the militiamen of the Chatham Artillery with two brass cannon used at Yorktown; they now occupy a spot on Bay Street just east of City Hall. The other visitor was Washington's French ally, the Marquis de Lafayette. He stopped over in March 1825 and was honored with a parade and many toasts.

Unfortunately, there were also some low points, including fires that destroyed large parts of the city in 1796 and 1820, deadly out-

ℹ️ Buildings stand on the site of Savannah's first "burying ground," situated on what is now York Street between Bull and Whitaker Streets. The first occupant: surgeon William Cox.

breaks of yellow fever in 1820 and 1854 (the epidemic of the former year killed 666), and a storm in 1804 that caused the drowning of more than 100 slaves, submerged Hutchinson Island, and greatly damaged many of the area's plantations. But as bad as those occurrences were, they were almost insignificant when compared to a disaster that was yet to come.

THE WORST KIND OF WAR

Disputes between Northern and Southern states over slavery and states' rights boiled over in the mid-1800s with cataclysmic results: the secession of Georgia and her Southern neighbors from the Union, the South's forming of a Confederacy, and the fighting of a war of the worst kind—a civil war. Although the war started in Charleston on April 16, 1861, when Confederate forces fired on and captured Fort Sumter, it was Savannah that, in the words of writers Russell and Hines, committed "the first belligerent act of the rebellious South."

Three months before Sumter, members of three militia outfits traveled by steamer from Savannah to Cockspur Island and seized Fort Pulaski, a large masonry edifice guarding the mouth of the Savannah River. Wrote Col. Charles H. Olmstead, who commanded the Confederates, "In due time Fort Pulaski was reached; its garrison, one elderly United States sergeant, made no defense, and the three companies of the First Volunteer Regiment marched in with drums beating and colors flying, and so for them a soldier's life began." Olmstead and others thought Fort Pulaski was impregnable. But 15 months after its bloodless seizure, shells from rifled cannon emplaced on Tybee Island by Federal troops left the thick walls of the fort looking like Swiss cheese (see our Tybee Island chapter). After 30 hours of bombardment, Olmstead realized that holding the fort was impossible and surrendered it and its 385 defenders.

Following Pulaski's fall, the new occupants of the fort and their comrades in the Union navy began a blockade of Savannah. The city's exports of cotton and other goods were thus bottled up, and the residents spent most of the war enduring the hardships of the siege by sea and mourning the loss of relatives and loved ones who fell on faraway fields of fire. Among those who died were brothers Joseph C. and William N. Habersham, killed in fighting near Atlanta on the same day in July 1864.

Later that year came Union Gen. William T. Sherman's devastating March to the Sea across Georgia. The prize at the end of the trek was Savannah. Sherman took it on December 21, but not before a battle at Fort McAllister south of Savannah near Richmond Hill (see our Day Trips chapter) and a skirmish at what would become the town of Pooler. The Union commander also allowed a force of 10,000 badly outnumbered Confederate defenders to slip out of the city and into South Carolina. In an oft-quoted telegram to President Abraham Lincoln that the commander in chief received on Christmas Eve, Sherman wrote, "I beg to present you as a Christmas Gift, the City of Savannah with 150 heavy guns and plenty of ammunition; and also about 25,000 bales of Cotton."

Savannah was out of the war, and its citizens settled in to cope with the city's occupation by Union troops. For the most part, it was a benign affair. "The occupation was a model of order, even occasional pleasantry, with both sides generally behaving like ladies and gentlemen," wrote Russell and Hines. Regardless of this, however, some of the women of the town refused to walk beneath the American flag.

BOUNCING BACK AGAIN

Unlike some Southern cities, Savannah survived the Civil War without being decimated by shell fire or burned to the ground, although a fire that broke out a month after the city's surrender destroyed 100 buildings. But the war took its toll, leaving the city bankrupt and its people in need of food. However, within a year of the end of hostilities, said Sieg in *Eden on the Marsh*, "Savannah was rolling again," a beneficiary of the rapid rebuilding of the

South's railroads and a resurgence in cotton production. In Savannah, "exports for 1867 exceeded fifty million dollars," wrote Sieg. "The predictors of doom following the loss of slave labor were proved wrong as a rising market pushed cotton production to levels never realized" under slavery.

After the war, Savannah and the rest of the South entered into an 11-year period of Reconstruction during which radical Northern politicians hoped to build a power base with the support of former slaves. Ultimately they failed, and slavery was replaced by a caste system and the creation of a so-called separate but equal society that was more separate than it was equal. In Savannah, "blacks entered a long period of assimilation," said Sieg. "As a result, they developed their own culture, built their own institutions, formed their own business associations, created their own art, music, and literature—and in the process, developed a black elite that led the march into the twentieth century." Among the institutions founded was the Georgia State Industrial College for Colored Youth, which is now Savannah State University (see our Education and Child Care chapter).

Economically, the last quarter of the 19th century saw the rice plantations around Savannah go out of business, turpentine and rosin from Georgia's pine forests rival cotton as the city's chief export, and the port enhanced by the dredging of the Savannah River shipping channel to a depth of 26 feet from 14 feet at the end of the war. There was also a spate of disasters during the last 25 years of the 1800s: Yellow fever killed more than 1,000 people in 1876, and the city was damaged by five significant fires, a tornado, two hurricanes, and an earthquake.

RACING INTO THE 20TH CENTURY

Savannah focused international attention on itself early in the 20th century by hosting Grand Prix and Vanderbilt Cup automobile racing in 1908, 1910, and 1911. During the first decade of the new century, the city expanded in other ways: A new City Hall was built, and much of the present-day skyline took shape. In the years that followed, Savannah began stretching southward from downtown with the creation of the city's first residential subdivision, Ardsley Park, after World War I (see our Relocation/Real Estate chapter). In the black community, residents formed the Negro Civic Improvement League to clean up overcrowded neighborhoods and started their own businesses, including the Wage Earners Savings Bank, which by 1915 covered a downtown block. (The bank building is now the site of the Ralph Mark Gilbert Civil Rights Museum, which you can learn about in our Attractions chapter.)

Not all was rosy, however. By the early 1920s cotton production in the South had fizzled out as laborers moved to the industrialized North and the boll weevil decimated Georgia's fields. Late in the decade came the Great Depression, and with it financial stagnation. During the 1930s, Savannah received an economic boost when the Union Bag and Paper Company set up shop just west of the city, bringing with it nearly 600 jobs and a payroll of $1 million. Union Bag, later known as Union Camp, was purchased by International Paper Company in the late 1990s and is still one of the city's largest employers. The company helped end Savannah's hard times, as did another, more far-reaching event—World War II.

ON THE HOME FRONT

Savannah contributed mightily to America's war effort. At the Southeastern Shipyard, some 15,000 workers built Liberty Ships. The city's little airport, Hunter Field, was appropriated by the military and turned into a huge air base. In 1943 it became a staging area for bomber aircraft and crews headed for duty in Europe; some 9,000 planes and 70,000 men were processed out of Hunter during the war.

With their airport gone, city officials began building another one in western Chatham County. It, too, was taken over by the government and became a training base for the crews of heavy bombers. Called Chatham Field, the base eventually became the site of Savannah/Hilton Head International Airport. Hunter continues to be used by the military and is now known as Hunter Army Airfield.

"The war turned Savannah from a sleepy, traditional, backward-looking town on a muddy river into a full-fledged, twentieth-century American city," wrote Edward Chan Sieg. "Savannahians gave what they had to the war effort, burying another generation of their youth and generously entertaining the youth of other cities." Savannah boomed, what with the influx of workers who came from the countryside to build ships and the city's popularity with military personnel from nearby bases, including the Marine Corps basic training complex at Parris Island, South Carolina.

The boom ended when the war did. The shipyard closed and most of the troops went home. "What remained was a partially deserted, once-fashionable Historic District," said Sieg. "Savannah had moved south to low-roofed suburbs, abandoning hundreds of high-ceilinged town houses to the dereliction of uncaring tenants, little or no maintenance, and, worst of all, unprofitable values. No wonder that the postwar business leaders reached the conclusion that if Savannah were to survive and flourish, the old city must make way for progress. But the preservationist attitude found its way into the lives of a handful of influential residents who became dedicated to the principle that demolition was not the only answer to decay."

PRESERVING THE PAST AND MAKING PROGRESS

Savannahians reacted with shame in 1946 when Great Britain's Lady Astor called the city "a beautiful lady with a dirty face." They were moved to action when the town's City Market on Ellis Square was demolished in 1954 and replaced with a parking garage. The following year, a group of seven women led by Anna C. Hunter chartered the Historic Savannah Foundation for the purpose of saving noteworthy structures from destruction. By the time of the foundation's first general membership meeting in November 1955, the organization had 700 members.

Its first project was saving the Isaiah Davenport House (see our Attractions chapter), and it was successfully followed by many others. Of the group's efforts, Russell and Hines wrote, "The foundation determined to reawaken interest in Savannah's heritage, to convince the public of the economic benefits of restoration, and to promote tourism. . . . During the next decade the foundation would deluge the city with a massive public relations campaign, arrange for a professional inventory of historic buildings, establish a revolving fund, and help establish a tourism and convention bureau within the Chamber of Commerce."

The group formulated a preservation plan that became a national model and the basis of the city's Historic Zoning Ordinance. By 1970 the foundation had saved more than 150 structures that were resold to individuals for restoration; the organization continues its efforts today from offices at 321 East York Street.

In recent years, the Savannah College of Art and Design (SCAD) (see our Education and Child Care chapter) has stepped forward as a leader in historic preservation. Among the many buildings the college has restored to house classrooms and offices are former public school buildings, the old Chatham County Jail, and portions of what was once the Central of Georgia Railroad complex. In the 1970s the city government beautified River Street by

i One branch of the most heavily traveled road in Colonial America—the Great Indian Warrior/Trading Path—reached to what would become Savannah, all the way from the Great Lakes. A historical marker on Liberty Street near its intersection with Martin Luther King Jr. Boulevard states that the path "passed through here."

creating Rousakis Plaza along the waterfront and started a revitalization of the Broughton Street shopping district that is a work in progress.

Since then, Savannahians have witnessed other progressive developments, including the construction of a new airport terminal, the replacement of the aging Talmadge Memorial Bridge across the Savannah River, improvements and growth at the city's port facilities, the revitalization of the Martin Luther King Jr. Boulevard corridor, and the construction of the Savannah International Trade and Convention Center on Hutchinson Island. In 1996 and 2004, Savannah found itself back on the international stage it had trod during the time of the great auto races: in 2004 as the news media and communications center for the G-8 summit meeting held on Sea Island, Georgia, and in 1996 as host of the yachting events of Atlanta's Summer Olympic Games. Fittingly, the opening and closing ceremonies of the games in Savannah were held at the eastern end of River Street, close to where James Edward Oglethorpe and his little band of colonists landed 263 years before.

BED-AND-BREAKFAST INNS

Scattered around the Historic Downtown are the city's "other" accommodations: bed-and-breakfasts, guesthouses, and inns. From a single suite in a privately owned 19th-century home to magnificently restored mansions, the city offers it all. Stay in one of these establishments for atmosphere carefully crafted for romance. In many cases, these accommodations are designed to create the impression you are staying in a luxurious private home.

There are more than 30 of these establishments to choose from, mostly in Historic Downtown, and the list continues to grow. According to local innkeepers, one of the latest trends in this niche of the hospitality industry is the upsurge of smaller establishments with fewer than five bedrooms. These take many forms, but generally it's a case of a homeowner deciding to convert a portion of a home into a bed-and-breakfast inn. There are more than 25 of these smaller establishments (more are coming), and they provide an interesting mix to the already established lot of bed-and-breakfast inns. In these home-based establishments, you may find yourself lodged in a restored carriage house or even occupy-

ing the full garden level of the owner's home. (A word of explanation is required: The lowest floor, or ground floor, is known as the garden level. In historic homes, the main entrance often is on the second floor, up a steep flight of steps, and that level is known as the parlor level.)

No matter which one you choose, there is one constant: Each establishment is as unique as its owner. There are lavish, sophisticated inns where sit-down breakfasts are served every morning promptly between 8:00 and 10:00 a.m. in a meticulously restored parlor, and there are relaxed and comfortable places where you may feel compelled to take off your shoes and prop your feet up on the slightly worn couch.

The decor can be just as diverse. Maybe you will find a beautiful courtyard with fountains and wrought-iron furniture just right for quiet conversations . . . perhaps there will be marble fireplaces, whirlpool tubs, and 18th-century antiques. Many bed-and-breakfast inns boast "Savannah Colors," a group of 56 historically accurate colors discovered by a local artist who went around scraping the newer paint off historic buildings and crawling through attics to uncover the hues Savannahians used to color their lives in earlier times. In these places, the restorations are so exacting you may feel transported back to another era. Some hosts won't be happy until you are dripping with Southern hospitality. One innkeeper told us she wanted her guests to feel like they had just visited one of their best Southern friends. But if privacy is what you are looking for, that can be found too. Check into a few bed-and-breakfasts in town, and you might not see the owners for the entire visit.

Another great reason to choose these accommodations is that no matter where you

i Don't forget about St. Patrick's Day. This is the busiest day of the entire year. If you are hoping to stay on or near the parade route, reservations should be made many months in advance. Some prime spots are booked a year ahead of time. And remember, if you like to party long and loud, you'll have plenty of company in Savannah for St. Paddy's—but you won't fit in with the B&B crowd. Do them—and yourself—a favor and check out more conventional accommodations. You'll find them listed in our Hotels and Motels chapter.

stay, one of the most beautifully preserved historic areas in the entire country awaits just outside your doorstep. Virtually all of Savannah's bed-and-breakfasts, guesthouses, and inns put you within comfortable walking distance of museum houses, squares, historic churches, monuments, art galleries, coffee shops, and restaurants. If you choose, you can park your car and not move it for your entire stay. (See our Tybee Island chapter for separate options there.)

Although owners may call their establishment a bed-and-breakfast, an inn, or a guesthouse, in many cases the terms are interchangeable. In fact, the most popular term to describe any of these types of establishments in Savannah seems to be *inn*. However, you may find everything from a 1-room inn to a 32-room inn.

Whatever the title, guests can expect to find the amenities expected in finer accommodations, including air-conditioning and private baths. Most accept major credit cards, and a few allow pets. Because of the age and historic value of the properties, many of these lodging options, especially guesthouses and smaller bed-and-breakfasts, no longer allow smoking inside. Even those that do allow smoking often restrict it to balconies or courtyards. Many have limited or no wheelchair access, since they are in old mansions. If stairs are a challenge for you, check out the situation by asking when you make reservations. Some inns don't allow young children, and although this may sound harsh to parents at first brush, we'll point out that the B&B experience isn't likely to appeal to kids anyway. Unless otherwise noted, assume that the listed establishments accept major credit cards and do not allow pets. Our listings will point out which accommodations do not allow children. Still, we suggest calling ahead to check on these details if they are a vital part of your travel plans. After all, you'll need to call ahead for reservations anyway—they're not just recommended, they're essential.

And one note on parking: Parking is at a premium in the Historic Downtown. Most of the area, including residential neighborhoods, has metered parking that is patrolled by very vigilant enforcers. Leave your meter expired for even a few minutes, and you are going to be ticketed. Do not make the mistake of thinking that because you have out-of-town license plates you will get a courtesy reminder—that doesn't happen here any longer. It is important to inquire about the parking situation when you call to find out about your accommodations.

Finally, because of the limited number of rooms available and the popularity of Savannah, innkeepers suggest making reservations at least one month in advance. At some places, you may find six weeks is needed. The spring months (anywhere from mid-February through April, depending on a year's given conditions) and fall are particularly busy ones for the B&B scene, so book as soon as possible. Choice weekends, including those featuring key Historic Downtown tours of homes or gardens, book up very quickly. To help with your reservations, there are several private reservation services in town, each having access to a portion of the market. Remember, each of these services and associations serves only a part of the market—none of them cover the full gamut, and many hotels are listed with several services. When making reservations, you may want to check with more than one service to get a good idea of what is available. Two associations have Web sites that will link you to reservation services at individual inns: www.historicinnsofsavannah.com, which includes seven mansions and four boutique hotels, and www.romanticinnsofsavannah .com, which represents 21 establishments and includes several Tybee facilities. Bed and Breakfast Reservations RSVP (912-354-4200; 800-729-7787) is a private reservation service representing about a dozen B&Bs and small inns and limited to those that are owner-operated. You can also make reservations at www.savannahres.com (800-310-1292) for about 20 participating inns, and the site includes links to those inns' Web sites. You can also find listings and links at the Savannah

Area Convention and Visitors Bureau's site, www.savannahvisit.com.

The following bed-and-breakfast listings are arranged in alphabetical order, and prices are indicated by the dollar-sign code explained in the Price Code featured below. You'll see a range of prices for some of these listings. Due to the wide variety of room options at some bed-and-breakfasts, it is not uncommon for one inn to offer both lower-priced accommodations and luxurious, upscale suites. Be specific when calling for details. The best deals are on weekday nights.

These entries are not meant to be an all-inclusive list of city inns. Instead, we hope to give a good sampling of the variety of special bed-and-breakfast inns doing business in Savannah. If you don't find something that sounds appealing in the following listings, refer again to the reservations services mentioned above. Chances are there are a few newcomers who cropped up between the researching of this book and your reading of it.

Price-Code Key

The dollar signs indicate the average cost for a one-night stay for two adults, not including taxes, gratuities, or add-on amenities. Many establishments have both high-season and off-season rates, and they define "season" differently, so check current prices, usually posted on the facilities' Web sites. Most establishments charge from $10 to $25 extra for additional guests. Please inquire about the additional fee when you call for reservations. Again, remember that reservations are essential. If you are on a really tight travel budget, chances are B&Bs aren't the accommodations for you—amenities and atmosphere come with a price tag.

$	**$99 and lower**
$$	**$100 to $150**
$$$	**$151 to $200**
$$$$	**$201 to $250**
$$$$$	**more than $250**

Azalea Inn and Gardens $$–$$$$$
217 East Huntingdon Street
(912) 236-2707, (800) 582-3823
www.azaleainn.com

Teresa and Micheal Jacobson are the new innkeepers at this veteran B&B near Forsyth Park. The home is a sprawling Victorian, circa 1889, and boasts seven rooms, two suites, and a carriage house. The dining room is decorated with murals depicting Savannah's history. Many of the rooms have fireplaces equipped with gas logs, and some have balconies and/or Jacuzzis. The inn is proud of its gardens. It also boasts a feature unusual for Savannah B&Bs—a swimming pool in the courtyard garden. Children over the age of 12 are welcome. The inn is nonsmoking throughout.

The Ballastone Inn $$$$$
14 East Oglethorpe Avenue
(912) 236-1484, (800) 822-4553
www.ballastone.com

The Ballastone is a magnificently restored, four-story 1838 mansion just off Bull Street, one of the historic area's main thoroughfares. Arriving guests will notice the beautiful Queen Anne staircase in the entryway and the warm, lavishly decorated parlor off to the right. Ceiling fans, rice poster and canopy beds, marble-topped tables, and fireplaces are some of the things you might find in one of the 18 individually decorated rooms. All are lavishly appointed and meticulously kept.

The Victoria Room, decorated in rich yellows, reds, and greens, has a massive king-size bed and whirlpool tub, while the Gazebo Room has deep greens and two queen-size beds. Besides the wonderful surroundings, guests enjoy afternoon Victorian tea along with evening hors d'oeuvres. There is a terry-cloth robe waiting in the bathroom and nightly turndown service with chocolates and cordials. On weekday mornings, you can choose to have continental breakfast in your room, the parlor, or outside in the courtyard. On Saturday and Sunday, guests are treated to a full breakfast at their choice of location.

The Ballastone Inn sitting room decorated for the holidays. COURTESY OF BALLASTONE INN

Children 16 years of age and older are welcome at The Ballastone. The inn has been recommended by *Brides, Glamour, Gourmet,* and *Condé Nast Traveler.* This is one of the inns that more closely resembles a small European hotel than a mom-and-pop bed-and-breakfast. Jennifer and Jim Salandi are the innkeeper-owners.

Bed and Breakfast Inn $$–$$$$
117 West Gordon Street
(912) 238-0518, (888) 238-0518
www.savannahbnb.com

This charming and well-established bed-and-breakfast was an early comer to the scene. The circa-1853 Federal row house on Gordon Row adjoins innkeeper Bob McAllister's home in one of the most attractive areas of the Historic Downtown. McAllister's a well-known host on the local scene, and his hospitality shows in the B&B's operation.

Rooms are furnished in a mixture of antiques and reproductions. (The innkeeper maintains antique chairs shouldn't be subjected to daily use, and guests shouldn't be subjected to antique chairs.) You'll love details such as pocket doors on the parlor level. Renovation has given the building a spacious deck overlooking a beautiful courtyard. The garden suites are prime rooms, complete with full kitchens and living and dining areas. You really won't need that kitchen, though. We can vouch for the freshly cooked breakfast, complete with a talented chef whose repertoire includes wonderful biscuits. If you can get a room over St. Patrick's Day—regular returnees fill most of them—you're in for a real treat, as the breakfast party here is a favorite stopping-off point as locals (including many parade participants) head in for the festivities. Children are welcome in some of the rooms.

i Because of regulations passed by local government, all new bed-and-breakfast inns opening in Savannah must provide off-street parking for their guests. That may be a headache for developers (not to mention a leg up to established inns that are "grandfathered"), but guests will ultimately benefit.

Broughton Street Bed & Breakfast $$$–$$$$$
511 East Broughton Street
(912) 232-6633, (877) 232-6633
www.broughtonst.com

Staying at the Broughton Street Bed & Breakfast is like having your own private town house in the heart of Savannah's Historic Downtown. The inn offers two rooms and a cottage at the quiet end of Broughton Street, essentially downtown Savannah's "Main Street," which is in the midst of a resurgence after years of decline. The master bedroom in the main building includes a four-poster bed, working fireplace, spacious bay window overlooking the street, and a small whirlpool bath and shower combination. The other bedroom has a queen-size bed with a view of the small rear courtyard. The cottage offers more privacy, but not necessarily more room. It has one bedroom and a sleeper sofa, and is decorated in a cozy, slightly more masculine style.

Except for the innkeepers' private quarters, guests get the run of the house, which includes a library with a huge, inviting leather couch and fireplace. There is a main parlor and dining room perfect for relaxing. All the rooms are nicely decorated with antiques. Wine and hors d'oeuvres are served in the evening. The inn is not wheelchair accessible. Children age 12 or older are welcome.

This inn, housed in a circa-1883 town house, was remodeled beginning in 1993. The owners subsequently operated it as a bed-and-breakfast until selling it in the spring of 2000. At the time of the sale, the furnishings were sold as well, but the new owners have outfitted it with a new supply of antiques and reproductions, and the resulting decor provides guests with the same kind of elegant ambience.

Columbia Square Inn $$$
125 Habersham Street
(912) 236-0444
www.columbiasquareinn.com

There are two things you notice when entering the Columbia Square Inn: the wonderful, wide heart-pine floorboards and the white walls. Although some innkeepers prefer lavish draperies and antiques to match, proprietor Barbara Wall's tastes are understated and elegant. There is no clutter here. The floors are nearly uncovered as are the windows, which reveal a view of the fountain in the center of Columbia Square and a magnificent magnolia tree reaching to the top of the home.

All rooms in the home, which the Walls restored several years ago (they occupy the ground floor), are spacious and decorated in the same manner. A leather settee or chair is neatly arranged in front of the fireplace along with a sofa to form a comfortable sitting area in each room. There are four-poster beds and armoires, and one of the rooms has an extra bedroom and a small veranda filled with gigantic ferns. Wall likes to give her guests their space, so everything they might need, from an ironing board to a cold drink, can be found in the rooms. There are small refrigerators, coffeemakers, and microwaves in each. She has found, however, that one of the most popular items she supplies are the Band Aids—to take care of the blisters that come from all that exploring. Continental breakfast is served in the rooms, but guests are welcome to spend their time in the other parts of the inn, including the parlor and dining room. Wall says that guests are delighted and surprised by the quiet conditions at her inn, which is, after all, situated in a prime location. There is no exterior signage. No children or pets allowed.

East Bay Inn $$$
225 East Bay Street
(912) 238-1225, (800) 500-1225
www.eastbayinn.com

If you are looking for the charm and ambience of a larger inn for a more moderate price, try the East Bay Inn. Located along bustling Bay Street, it features 28 rooms, each with 18th-century-style furnishings, hardwood floors, four-poster rice beds, high ceilings, and large beautiful windows. Some of the rooms have exposed brick walls that add to the charm. All are very nicely done and meticulously kept. You will feel comfortable whether here on business or for a romantic getaway.

Although one of the larger accommodations in this category, East Bay Inn still has an intimate feeling. Continental breakfast is served every morning in a small cafe that was formerly a bar. It features pretty tables for two covered in white linen. Evening cordials are presented in the lobby, which is decorated in deep greens and reds. The inn has one pet-friendly room, which requires advance reservations and a nonrefundable $35 pet fee. The inn is not wheelchair accessible.

Another nice addition to the inn's offerings is Skyler's restaurant. Located in the basement, with exposed brick walls and a huge, beautiful fireplace, Skyler's is a popular choice among locals, especially during the lunch hour. The menu is eclectic, offering items from fresh chow mein to chicken hoagies and crab cakes. You can't beat the teriyaki chicken Caesar salad! (Read more about it in our Restaurants chapter.)

Eliza Thompson House $$$$–$$$$$
5 West Jones Street
(912) 236-3620, (800) 348-9378
www.elizathompsonhouse.com

This gorgeous inn was an early arrival on the B&B scene, but it underwent a major redecoration and upgrading in 2000 and 2001. It fills two buildings. (There are 12 rooms in the main circa-1847 house and 13 in the courtyard addition or carriage house.) The Eliza Thompson House is run with the efficiency and style of a small European hotel, but it still ranks as a bed-and-breakfast because of its emphasis on personal amenities. It changed hands in 2001, becoming part of an eclectic Savannah-based chain.

Jones Street is a brick street in the residential portion of the Historic Downtown, almost completely canopied by the trees that line either side. Your views are either of this street or the meticulously maintained courtyard, which is equipped with a beautiful fountain complete with original iron sculpture. Guests can breakfast here or, on those rare occasions when the weather does not permit (we do have winter here, such as it is), in a glass-walled alcove overlooking it. Wine and cheese are served in the parlor in the late afternoons, and there's dessert and coffee in the evenings.

Rooms differ dramatically in style, although they are all traditionally furnished with antiques. You'll find a fabric-draped ceiling in one, a canopied bed in another. Look for the sumptuous imported bed linens throughout. Wheelchair-accessible (with a bit of effort) suites are available.

Foley House Inn $$$$–$$$$$
14 West Hull Street
(912) 232-6622, (800) 647-3708
www.foleyinn.com

When you first walk inside this 1896 brick home, you are struck by the rich burgundy and blue colors blanketing the walls and floors. The sumptuous design and detail extend throughout the parlor and all of the 19 individually styled rooms. Look out your window at Foley House Inn, and you will see beautiful Chippewa Square. Historic First Baptist Church is across the street, and a statue of Gen. James Edward Oglethorpe, the

i Reservations are a must, but while you are making them, be sure to check with the innkeepers on their cancellation policy. Some inns charge if you cancel, on the grounds that they turned away other reservations.

founder of Georgia, stands in the center of the square. (He's facing south, brandishing a sword to keep the Spanish colonists in Florida, which was part of the Georgia colony's early mission.)

In one suite decorated in deep pink, there is a canopied bed, two fireplaces, and a lovely bay window. In another, the walls are painted rich yellow, and red draperies hang in the sitting area situated by the bay window. They also frame the bed. A large, ornate armoire with his-and-her mirrored closets fills one wall.

All the rooms include fireplaces, and many have whirlpool baths. Tea and hors d'oeuvres are served each afternoon in the parlor, and guests can choose to have their continental breakfast there, in the small courtyard, or in their rooms. Evening cordials are also featured, as is concierge service for making all your dining and exploring reservations. Note that the inn is not conveniently wheelchair accessible. The food is considered particularly good at this inn.

The Gastonian $$$$–$$$$$
220 East Gaston Street
(912) 232-2869, (800) 322-6603

Everything about The Gastonian makes you want to come in and relax, from the magnificent verandas taking up one side of the house to the beautifully landscaped courtyard and warm rooms. Little details sometimes make the biggest impressions, and that is what you notice at The Gastonian. Come back from dinner, and you will find pralines on your pillow, the fireplace going (when the weather's right), and soft music playing on the radio. There is a concierge who is friendly and ready to make

> **i** Most bed-and-breakfasts provide DVD players or VCRs in at least some of their suites. If aching feet or stormy weather is keeping you inside, why not check out a video of a film made in Savannah? Check our Savannah Celebrity chapter for an inventory. Then settle back and see if you can spot your surroundings on the silver screen!

all your reservations, from dinner to horse-drawn carriage tours. The inn is actually two historic, wonderfully preserved mansions next to each other along Gaston Street. It is in a residential neighborhood, just a short walk from one of Savannah's most beautiful parks—Forsyth.

Georgian and Regency period antiques fill the main parlors, while all of the 18 rooms are styled individually. Each has a working fireplace, high ceilings, wooden floors, and Persian rugs, and is named for a noted Savannahian. In the Mary Hilyer Room, you will find a beautiful antique quilt with green and red flowers covering one wall. There is a whirlpool bath with a basket of Caswell Massey soaps and lotions nearby and a wonderful stained-glass window. French doors take you out to the veranda, where a wicker lounge chair awaits. Newlyweds often come to The Gastonian to have their pictures taken in the beautiful courtyard. There is also a sundeck with a hot tub—a perfect spot for enjoying continental breakfast. This inn has served as a temporary home for some of Savannah's visiting movie stars when the city was serving as a filming location.

Green Palm Inn $$–$$$$
548 East President Street
(912) 447-8901, (888) 606-9510
www.greenpalminn.com

This small bed-and-breakfast plays up its name: The handful of rooms are named for different species of palm tree, and the inn overlooks Greene Square. That puts this inn on the easternmost edge of the Historic District. It is one of the smallest and most affordable of the B&Bs. The house was built in 1987 and got the renovations that transformed it into a B&B in 1998. Look for atmospheric touches here like clawfoot bathtubs, a generous sprinkling of fireplaces (even in bathrooms), and British Colonial–style furniture. Guests can expect a hot breakfast as well as afternoon refreshments. Some of the rooms are equipped with Jacuzzis.

The Hamilton-Turner Inn $$$–$$$$$
330 Abercorn Street
(912) 233-1833, (888) 448-8849
www.hamilton-turnerinn.com

This glamorous Victorian boasts notable architecture, a prime location, and plenty of romance. The mansion—with an exterior as ornate as the Victorians could get it—was built in 1873, and among its claims to fame is the fact it was Savannah's first house with electric lighting. Like many of the grand homes in the Historic District, this four-story mansion fell on hard times in the middle of the last century. During the height of the popularity of the book *Midnight in the Garden of Good and Evil,* the house was used as a party venue and gift shop, capitalizing on the fact that the woman who was the "Mandy" character in the book lived there.

The hard times came to an end in 1998, when the Hamilton-Turner Inn opened as a 14-room bed-and-breakfast. It has since changed hands a few times and has moved steadily up the ranks of Historic District accommodations. Its location on Lafayette Square puts it square in the middle of the Historic District, with the Cathedral of St. John the Baptist as a neighbor and one of the city's most picturesque squares as its "front yard."

Guests climb steep entrance stairs to reach the parlor floor. But Hamilton-Turner is unusual in that it also has accommodations for disabled guests: a chair-lift, sort of an open-air elevator, goes from the ground level to one of the parlor-level suites. The public rooms include the front dining room, where breakfast is served, and a double parlor furnished with antiques.

There are bedrooms on every level of the house, differing mainly in how large and elaborately they are decorated. Most boast the high ceilings and sweeping windows of the building's construction period. Exceptions, however, are on the ground floor, a level that Savannah terms the garden level. The handful of rooms here feature brick walls and a cozier feel, and include some with private entrances.

i Did you enjoy your romantic bed-and-breakfast stay? Hang on to those business cards! Weekends at these plush homes-away-from-home are a popular and different gift for newlyweds and others who are celebrating. Of course, the price may make such a gift more feasible as a group offering from the office or a gang of friends.

Guests eat well here. They have their choice from a cooked-to-order menu that varies every day but always includes something sweet in keeping with the inn's "dessert begins at breakfast" philosophy. Wine and cheese are offered in the evenings.

The carriage house, across the courtyard from the main mansion, is a good choice for family groups. The inn welcomes children and small pets; check out the options when you book. And if you are lucky, you might catch a glimpse of a beaming bride and groom, since the Hamilton-Turner Inn hosts small destination weddings.

Joan's on Jones $$$
17 West Jones Street
(912) 234-3863, (888) 989-9806

Joan's on Jones is one of the most established of the smaller bed-and-breakfast inns in Savannah. Innkeepers Joan and Gary Levy have been welcoming guests to their Jones Street home since 1990. (That's a long time in the history of a relatively recent trend.) The experience has taught them many things, Joan says, including the ability to sense who wants attention and who wants to be left alone. Whichever you need, the Joneses are ready to satisfy.

The inn features two suites, both with private entrances and ample room. It is another establishment where you'll feel as if you have your own apartment in the heart of the city. These particular apartments are in a restored 1883 Victorian town house on one of the city's most scenic streets. The Jones Street

The Kehoe House is an elegant bed-and-breakfast. BETTY DARBY

Suite is painted a rich terra-cotta that Joan discovered in a local historic home and reproduced in her own. It is formally decorated and has pretty stained-glass windows and two fireplaces. Over one fireplace is a collection of old letters and other correspondence found behind the mantel during the restoration process. Reading lamps are over the bed for convenience, and there is a small kitchenette. The Garden Suite—just off a back courtyard that is perfect for relaxing with its lounge garden chairs—has a huge, brick cooking hearth, queen-size iron bed, and exposed brick walls. There is also a full kitchen. This suite is less formal but more intimate and romantic.

Children are welcome, and well-behaved dogs are allowed in the back suite for a nonrefundable fee. Continental breakfast is served each morning.

The Kehoe House $$$$–$$$$$
123 Habersham Street
(912) 232-1020, (800) 820-1020
www.kehoehouse.com

The Kehoe House stands catty-cornered to one of Savannah's preserved architectural treasures and house museums, the Davenport House, and has a commanding view of Columbia Square. The Kehoe House was built for an Irish immigrant who built a fortune in the iron foundry business. As his fortune and his family grew, he built this imposing brick Victorian. After its residential days, the building served other uses, including a stint as a funeral parlor. Former football star Joe Namath was one of a group of investors who held the property for a while.

The Kehoe has 13 rooms and is known for its European-style service. Guests are treated to a gourmet breakfast, afternoon tea, and evening wine with hors d'oeuvres. The fourth floor includes a party/banquet room, which is often the scene of bridesmaids' luncheons and business meetings.

This inn is unusual in that it is outfitted with an elevator—an amenity you are sure to appreciate after you spend the day following our advice that the best way to see Savannah is on foot. Also, this inn touts its rumors of hauntings.

912 Barnard	$–$$

912 Barnard Street
(912) 234-9121
www.912barnard.com
One of the few bed-and-breakfast establishments in Savannah's Victorian District, 912 Barnard is on the fringe of the Historic Downtown area. This section of the city is filled with large, elaborate, and beautiful (or formerly beautiful) Victorian homes and is one of Savannah's most active areas of restoration. On some blocks, you will find boarded-up homes in desperate need of rescuing, while others are well on their way to being revitalized.

This B&B bills itself as catering to the gay and lesbian community. There are only a handful of guest rooms at 912 Barnard, which is on a block where lots of restoration has taken place and is ongoing. This is one of the more affordable bed-and-breakfasts, but note that it does not accept credit cards. This nice Victorian row house is small, relaxed, and laid-back. There is a sit-down breakfast every morning in the dining room, where you will find the table decorated with a lace tablecloth and pretty antique china. The adjoining parlor, also decorated in antiques, is light, airy, and very relaxing with several beautiful windows to bring in the surrounding trees.

The Charleston Room, one of the guest accommodations, features a huge, wonderful bay window, a queen-size Charleston rice bed, sitting area, and fireplace. In the less-sedate Miami Room, you will find hubcaps from a 1972 Cadillac Seville lining one wall. The art deco–inspired room also has a private balcony, and if you look closely, you might find a pink flamingo or two. Personal checks, traveler's checks, and cash only.

Zeigler House
121 West Jones Street
(912) 233-5307, (866) 233-5307
If you are looking for elegance and the time-machine effect of period-perfect furnishings, check out Zeigler House. This circa-1856 home is freestanding and surrounded by lovely landscaping, which already sets it apart on Jones Street, where many homes stand shoulder-to-shoulder. The style is Italianate. The house is tall and relatively narrow, with an overall formal appearance.

That formality carries through to the inside, where the heart-pine flooring and other woodwork is displayed to good advantage. Elaborate ceiling medallions and chandeliers set the tone inside.

This is a small, owner-occupied inn, in business since 2003. Amenities include continental breakfast, and the rooms are also supplied with such equipment as microwave ovens and toasters. Some rooms have whirlpool tubs or private patios. Zeigler House is also blessed with that rarest of spe-

> **i** The bed-and-breakfast industry is a very fluid one. Even established, experienced, and successful innkeepers can simply tire of the business and decide to redesign that extra space as guest rooms for visiting grandchildren. Conversely, couples fixing up a roomy house may launch a bed-and-breakfast rather spontaneously to help pay off that renovation loan. Policies change too—one bad experience with a St. Bernard and an establishment that welcomed pets changes its mind. Our point here is that it's best to call ahead for reservations and confirmation of those essential travel details, like whether your cat is welcome.

cial touches in downtown Savannah: off-street parking. Of the five rooms, some can be combined into suites. The collection includes multi-room apartment suites geared toward longer stays. The bedroom decor draws heavily on luxury textiles and such architectural touches as exposed beams and painted brick walls.

HOTELS AND MOTELS

As you might have noticed while reading the Area Overview chapter, Savannah is a city of great diversity, and that characteristic holds true when it comes to the accommodations it offers its visitors. Savannah has several hotels that are large and contemporary, and others that are medium-size and quaint. It has motels that are moderately priced but comfortable, and others where, for a few dollars more, you'll be awash in amenities. Many of the hotels and motels offer suites in addition to rooms with the standard two double beds or one king-size bed, and a couple of establishments have nothing but suites.

For visitors seeking more of a personal touch, there are numerous bed-and-breakfast inns scattered throughout Historic Downtown; so many, in fact, we've devoted a separate chapter to them (see our Bed-and-Breakfast Inns chapter). Most of the hotels and motels described here are situated in one of two locations: on or very near Bay Street in Historic Downtown or on or just off Abercorn Street near Oglethorpe Mall in the Midtown area. There are many other motels in several nearby locales: on or near the beach at Tybee Island, which is about 25 minutes from downtown Savannah; in the Southside on Abercorn between Oglethorpe Mall and Savannah Mall; and out on Interstate 95, 10 or more miles from the heart of the city.

The motels at the beach are discussed in the Tybee Island chapter of this book. The accommodations between the malls and out on I-95 represent several major chains and should offer no surprises, but if your destination is Savannah and not the House of the Mouse or some other touristy spot in Florida, we recommend that you stay closer to our city and soak up some of the atmosphere of our historic old town.

You can be in the midst of that atmosphere by taking a room at a hotel or motel in the downtown area. In most cases, you'll pay accordingly for the location, but you can find some values if you're not too picky about the view from your room and the extras you receive.

Another cost-saving option is to stay at lodgings in the Midtown area. You'll be out of the mainstream of tourism but not by much—the motels and inns in Midtown are only 5 miles from Bay Street, which is about 12 to 15 minutes' traveling time if you avoid rush-hour traffic. Although most of these establishments are geared toward people on business trips, the innkeepers are more than happy to have tourists stay with them. Another reason to take a room in Midtown is that parking is free. That's not necessarily the case if you stay in Historic Downtown, and we've indicated in our listings if and what you'll have to pay to park at a hotel or motel there.

All of the hotels and motels described in this chapter accept major credit cards and have wheelchair-accessible rooms. Almost all have nonsmoking rooms, and many do not allow pets; if a hotel or motel does not have nonsmoking rooms or does accept pets, that information is included in our listing for the establishment.

You can expect that all accommodations will have color cable TV. If you're looking for

i When you visit Savannah, you're staying in "the most beautiful city in North America," according to *Le Monde*, one of the leading newspapers of Paris, France. *Conde Nast Traveler* magazine reader polls named Savannah one of the top 10 U.S. cities to visit multiple times.

premium channels, a phone call might be in order.

In season generally runs from mid-March through October. Some establishments decrease their rates during the hot summer months, and others jack them up on weekends, so you should call in advance to ascertain how much you'll have to spend. If you're planning to stay here on St. Patrick's Day weekend, expect to fork out considerably more than you would at any other time of year and make reservations months in advance. Some places set minimum stays of two or three days that weekend. (See our St. Patrick's Day chapter for more information.)

Price-Code Key

Each entry includes a symbol denoting a price range for the average one-night stay, in season, for two adults. Note that these prices do not include tax, gratuities, and add-on amenities such as premium movie channels or room service. Here's the code:

$	$110 or lower
$$	$111 to $150
$$$	$151 to $190
$$$$	$191 and higher

HISTORIC DOWNTOWN

The Promenade $$
412 West Bay Street
(912) 233-1011
www.promenadesavannah.com
This well-located hotel was previously a Best Western but is now called the Promenade. It is unusual in the downtown because it is more of a motel than a hotel and offers amenities at the lower end of the downtown rate schedule. The Promenade fronts on Bay Street, and the motel's rear building is on the western end of River Street, placing the three-story establishment about a block from the shops and restaurants along the river and in City Market (see our Shopping chapter). It's also within walking distance of much of the Historic District. If you want to do your sightseeing while

riding, hop on a tour bus or trolley at the motel's front door.

The Promenade—where a top-to-bottom renovation was completed in 2003 and another is in progress—offers guests deluxe, complimentary continental breakfasts from 6:30 until 9:30 a.m., and there's a fenced-in pool for swimming and sunning on the River Street side of the property. Eighty-seven of the rooms have two full-size beds, and the rest have king-size beds. Parking is free at this motel (a major break in the Historic District), which has been accommodating visitors to Savannah since the early 1970s.

Courtyard by Marriott $$$
Savannah Historic District
415 West Liberty Street
(912) 790-8287, (800) 932-2198
www.courtyard.com
The five-story Courtyard opened in late July 2001, adding 147 guest rooms and 9 suites to Savannah's inventory of overnight accommodations. The suites and 86 of the guest rooms offer king-size beds, with 9 of the rooms featuring spa-type bathrooms complete with whirlpool tubs. The other rooms have double queen-size beds.

The Courtyard, with a decor that's traditionally Southern in style, covers an entire block bounded by Martin Luther King Jr. Boulevard and Liberty, Montgomery, and Harris Streets. The main entrance is on Liberty, making the front door a short walk from the Savannah Visitors Center. The hotel's spacious courtyard—a lushly landscaped spot that creates an oasis in the heart of the downtown area—faces Harris Street and is also the site of a heated outdoor pool. Guests can relax here or at the hotel's spa, an exercise facility that includes a large whirlpool.

The Courtyard Cafe, which is in the northwest corner of the ground floor, is a roomy restaurant with plenty of windows to give diners a view of what's happening on Liberty Street and MLK. The cafe serves breakfast and dinner seven days a week, and the Camellia Room is the setting for cocktails and light appetizers from 5:00 to 10:00 p.m. Valet parking is available for $12 a day; no self-parking.

Doubletree Hotel Historic Savannah $$$
411 West Bay Street
(912) 790-7000, (800) 222-TREE
www.doubletree.hilton.com

One of the newest of the downtown hotels, the Doubletree Historic Savannah exudes the aura of the city's fine old homes. The public areas convey a bright, open, airy feeling that extends to the 150 spacious guest rooms with their 12- to 14-foot-high ceilings, European-style furnishings, and pastel decor. Seven of the rooms are suites complete with marble spa tubs and separate showers, 53 have king-size, four-poster mahogany beds, and the remainder offer double queen-size, two-poster beds. The designers of the hotel also took into account Savannah's Irish influence by incorporating Celtic touches into the surroundings—rugs feature a Celtic nautical knot motif, and shamrocks adorn room-number plates, the wallpaper border of the bathrooms, and the framework of mirrors.

The hotel emphasizes a bit of local history via the name of its full-service restaurant and bar, John Ryan's Bistro and Pub. Ryan was the owner of a nearby bottleworks that dates back to the mid-1800s, and photos of bottles that were unearthed during construction of the hotel decorate the walls of the library and pub.

Another tip of the hat to Savannah takes the form of the second-floor heated swimming pool, which fills an area reminiscent of one of the city's walled gardens. For the health conscious, there's a cardio fitness center on the second floor, which is also the site of meeting space covering 2,600 square feet and accommodating up to 200 people.

The hotel is on the southwest corner of Bay and Montgomery Streets, making it adjacent to City Market and just a short jaunt from River Street. Valet parking in a subterranean garage and side lot is available for $15 per day.

Hilton Garden Inn Historic District Savannah $$$
321 West Bay Street
(912) 721-5000, (877) 245-8854
www.hiltongardeninn.hilton.com

The Hilton Garden Inn Historic District Savannah, which opened as the Hilton Garden Inn in spring 2005, is the sister hotel to the nearby Doubletree, but the Garden has a more contemporary edge. This six-story establishment on Bay Street near City Market has 134 rooms, 34 of which are two-room suites. All of the guest quarters are equipped with refrigerators and microwave ovens, and the 12-foot-high ceilings lend a spacious feel. Small balconies grace 25 of the rooms. Pillow-top mattresses, cherry furnishings with stainless steel accents, and the green- and rust-hued decor add to the ambience. There's an all-you-can-eat Southern breakfast buffet available in an area off the lobby for $12.95, a small bar open from 4:00 to 11:00 p.m., and room service for lunch and dinner. An outdoor pool and spa area and a cardio-fitness center offer relaxation and recreation. Subterranean, valet parking is $15 per day; no self-parking.

Hampton Inn Savannah $$$
Historic District
201 East Bay Street
(912) 231-9700, (800) HAMPTON
www.hamptoninn.com

The Hampton Inn opened in January 1997, but the eight-story hotel fits right in with the city's Historic District. The stucco, brick, and ironwork of the exterior have the look of old

i As best we can determine, Savannah's first hotel was a place called the Mansion House on Bay Street. While poking around the Georgia Historical Society, we found an article from a *Savannah News-Press* magazine of 1969 stating the city's "earliest inns were the Mansion House, City Hotel, and the Screven (House), all of them operating about the middle of the last century."

Savannah. So does the lobby with its authentic gray bricks that were found on the site during construction, heart-pine floors from an old mill in central Georgia, antique and traditional furniture, Persian rugs, and a dark wood bar from England, purchased at a local antiques store. The regal way to stay at this Hampton is in a king special: a corner room with windows on two walls, a king-size bed, pullout love seat, wet bar, refrigerator, microwave, and videocassette recorder. The hotel has eight of these rooms, but you might need to make reservations early to get one.

The Hampton is at Bay and Abercorn Streets, 1 block south of River Street. Check out the glorious view of the Savannah River, the Eugene Talmadge Memorial Bridge, and Historic Downtown from the rooftop pool, but wear shades on a sunny day—it's bright up there. The hotel offers a complimentary, deluxe continental breakfast each day from 6:00 until 10:00 a.m. The hotel has 1,000 square feet of meeting space with limited food service, and catering is available. You can park in the hotel's underground garage for $10 a day, and if it's full, the fee will get you a spot at the city-owned garage across Abercorn.

Hilton Savannah DeSoto $$$$
15 East Liberty Street
(912) 232-9000, (800) HILTONS
www.desotohilton.com
The Hilton projects an aura that's both classical and rich: The lobby, hallways, and rooms are adorned with white and fuchsia columns, wood paneling, and burgundy and pale green furnishings. The 15-story hotel stands in the midst of the Historic District, and the views from upper-floor rooms are spectacular. The concierge floor—the 13th, numbered as such by hotel officials apparently unconcerned with superstition—offers what staff members call the "skyline view." You'll pay extra to stay there, but you'll get the view, a room featuring deluxe amenities such as the Hilton's trademark terry-cloth bathrobes and the use of a private lounge serving continental break-

fasts in the morning and drinks and hors d'oeuvres in the evening. Step out on the balcony of the lounge and enjoy a panoramic look at the graceful Eugene Talmadge Memorial Bridge and Savannah's riverfront. If you really want to stay in style, request a "corner king"—a room with a king-size bed, balcony, two large corner windows, and a bathroom equipped with a double vanity. You can dine on the premises at the first-floor Magnolia Restaurant, which serves breakfast, lunch, and dinner Southern style, and you can unwind at the Lion's Den lounge, where the bar brings back memories of TV's *Cheers* and the library is stocked with real books.

The hotel pool is on a second-floor deck that can accommodate outdoor gatherings of as many as 150 people. The Hilton has 20,000 square feet of space for meetings and other functions that can accommodate up to 850 people for a banquet; the Harborview Room, whose 15th-floor location makes it the highest meeting room in the city; and a 5,408-square-foot ballroom with 18-foot ceilings and elaborate crystal chandeliers. Also available for get-togethers is an atrium on the hotel's ground floor.

The Hilton was built in 1968 on the site of the DeSoto Hotel, which was constructed in 1890 and was a Savannah landmark for decades. A sitting room off the lobby of the Hilton affords guests a glimpse of the old hotel—the walls are covered with memorabilia, including framed banquet programs from visits by several U.S. presidents. Covered, secured parking is available for $10 a day, and valet service is $12.

Hyatt Regency Savannah $$$$
2 West Bay Street
(912) 238-1234, (800) 233-1234
www.savannah.hyatt.com
You can't sleep where James Edward Oglethorpe laid his head while founding Georgia in 1733, but you can get close by bedding down at the Hyatt Regency Savannah. The spot where Oglethorpe pitched his tent is in the small park on Bay Street in front of the

347-room hotel. But that's not the main attraction of the Hyatt Regency—the hotel's drawing card is its location overlooking River Street and the Savannah River. The hotel is built over the brick street.

This location places guests in the midst of Savannah's waterfront shops and festivals and affords terrific views of the river and the ships plying it. You'll pay extra for a room on the river, but where else can you get accommodations with a "Ships Passing Light" that activates when a huge oceangoing vessel glides by your window? On the fourth of the hotel's seven floors, you're at eye level with the decks of freighters and other ships as they make their way in or out of port. There are also great views of River Street and/or the river from the Hyatt's second-floor sundeck, various meeting rooms, a glassed-in restaurant aptly called the Windows Chop House, and an adjoining lounge named Vu. Speaking of glassed-in, that's a perfect description of the hotel's Harborside Ballroom, an 11,000-square-foot gathering place on River Street offering floor-to-ceiling views. The Hyatt has a total of 33,000 square feet of meeting space, including two ballrooms and a banquet room.

The hotel lobby is an atrium with the aura of a rain forest. Palm trees and bird-of-paradise plants adorn the floor of this open space, which stretches seven floors to the ceiling, and bright green philodendrons cascade from the balconies of interior rooms. The atrium is also the headquarters of guest services personnel, who can schedule tours of the city and help plan your stay, and you can board tour buses at the front door of the hotel. The Hyatt accommodates fitness buffs with an exercise room and a heated indoor pool. Valet parking is $17 per day; no self-parking.

Inn at Ellis Square $$$
201 West Bay Street
(912) 236-4440, (800) 542-7666
www.innatellissquare.com
The inn, a Days Hotel, was a Days Inn and Suites until a major renovation completed in mid-2005 that was a precursor to the revamping of Ellis Square itself. The 195-room inn, situated conveniently between River Street and City Market, features 57 suites decorated in a traditional style and featuring Southern accents. The inn is right on the Bay Street sidewalk and occupies the Guckheimer Building, which dates to 1851.

The hotel's elegantly roomy, ground-floor public areas are the sites of comfortable chairs, large fireplaces, Dominque's Lounge, and flexible meeting spaces that can accommodate anywhere from 20 to 200 people. Other features are an on-site concierge, an outdoor pool, and complimentary continental breakfasts available on a daily basis. Parking is in a garage at a fee of $9 per day.

The Mansion on Forsyth Park $$$$
700 Drayton Street
(912) 238-5158, (888) 711-5114
www.mansiononforsythpark.com
Native son Richard Kessler added The Mansion on Forsyth Park to his Kessler Collection of luxury hotels and resorts in 2005. Kessler, who was born in Savannah and grew up in nearby Effingham County, created The Mansion by purchasing the 18,000-square-foot Kayton-Granger-Huger House on the park, then buying adjacent property and building a four-story structure that houses the 126 rooms of his new boutique hotel. The original brick and terra-cotta mansion, which was constructed in 1888, is now the site of the hotel's fashionable 700 Drayton Restaurant, which serves nouvelle American cuisine "with a Savannah flair"; Casimir's Lounge; the Carriage Wine Cellar; and the 700 Kitchen cooking school.

The hotel is adorned with Brazilian mahogany, Italian onyx marble, and more than 400 pieces of original artwork. Other unusual accoutrements include Lalique crystal knobs adorning the front doors, three Bosendorfer pianos, and massive custom-made crystal chandeliers. Among amenities available to guests are the Marble Garden courtyard and waterfall, which are poolside; full butler service on the Bohemian Butler floor; and the Poseidon Spa, which offers massage therapy, rejuvenating body treatments, facials, specialty nail treatments, yoga and tai chi classes, a cardio-fitness facility, and men's and women's locker rooms with steam showers. Rooms have 9- to 12-foot-high ceilings, lime green or raspberry color schemes, pillow-top mattresses, and oversize soaking tubs or three-headed showers.

Unique features include a gallery that specializes in sales of art and jewelry, a London taxi that's a shuttle for guests, and a collection of women's hats dating from 1860 to 1960.

With its Viennese Ballroom, which covers 3,500 square feet and can seat 280, the hotel serves as a gathering spot for locals and guests alike. There's an additional 1,200 feet of meeting space in the form of private dining rooms on the second level of the restaurant. The aforementioned cooking school offers daily and weekly programs accommodating up to 16 participants.

The Marshall House $$$
123 East Broughton Street
(912) 644-7896, (800) 589-6304
www.marshallhouse.com
The Marshall House has the distinction of being one of Savannah's newest—and oldest—hotels. The 68-room luxury boutique hotel opened its doors August 1, 1999, after an extensive renovation. The hotel occupies the building that housed the original Marshall House, which was built in 1851 and closed in 1957 after a 147-year run, during which it was also a hospital for Union soldiers.

The new Marshall House combines its historic past with sophisticated features. Rooms offer pine floors, minibars, CD players, robes, and bathrooms with pedestal sinks. Also available are a 275-square-foot boardroom, a fully equipped business center, a 1,200-square-foot meeting room for corporate and social functions, and 45 Bistro, a restaurant offering fine dining.

Adding to the flavor of the hotel are historical memorabilia and locally produced art-work that tell the history of The Marshall House and of Savannah.

Guests are provided with workout privileges at the Downtown Athletic Club. Valet parking is $12 a day, with limited self-parking in a garage behind the hotel costing $8 a day.

The Mulberry Inn $$$
601 East Bay Street
(912) 238-1200, (877) 468-1200
www.savannahhotel.com
The Mulberry aims for a classic Savannah look and hits the mark. Traditional furnishings, oil paintings, polished hardwood floors, and chandeliers grace the lobby, and antique furniture is sprinkled throughout the hallways and sitting areas. Reproductions of antiques and burgundy and forest-green furnishings carry out the theme in the 145 rooms, 25 of which are suites. The two- and three-story establishment—an award-winning Holiday Inn and a member of Historic Hotels of America—surrounds a tree-shaded brick courtyard adorned with wrought-iron tables and chairs. Then there's the name of the inn, which refers to the mulberry trees planted by Georgia's colonists in an attempt to raise silkworms. The trees grew on a site that is now Trustee's Garden, across East Broad Street from the hotel.

Want more history? The Mulberry's got it. The two-story portion of the inn housing the lobby was built as a cotton warehouse and livery stable in the mid-1800s, then was converted to a Coca-Cola bottling plant in the early 1900s. The building was transformed into an inn and expanded in the 1980s. The front desk occupies the spot where the bottling machinery did its work, and there are photos on one of the walls of the lobby to prove it. The Mulberry's elegant Cafe Courtyard serves breakfast, lunch, and dinner, and the inn presents a complimentary tea each afternoon from 4:00 until 6:00 p.m. Hot and iced tea, coffee, and dessert treats are available for guests, and a singer and pianist provide delightful music. Other amenities include concierge and bellman services, a secured outdoor pool, a hot tub, an exercise center, and Sgt. Jasper's Tavern, a full-service lounge. The hotel has 3 meeting rooms, with the largest accommodating 125 people theater-style. The inn also offers full banquet and catering services. Parking at a garage across a side street is $12 per day.

Planters Inn $$$
29 Abercorn Street
(912) 232-5678, (800) 554-1187
www.plantersinnsavannah.com
Built in 1912 as the John Wesley Hotel, the Planters Inn has been thoroughly remodeled but retains the elegance and charm of the early days of the 20th century. The hotel's high ceilings, four-poster beds, lavish draperies, and antique furniture give you the feeling you've stepped back in time, but the friendly staff and the services they provide will make you aware you're very much in the present. Among the extras are nightly turn-down service, complimentary continental breakfasts served in the hospitality room from 6:30 to 10:30 a.m., and complimentary "after-noon wine" provided in the lobby from 5:30 to 7:30 p.m. every day but Sunday. Parking is available at a neighboring garage for $11.95 per night, and free valet service is offered.

The seven-floor hotel is on the site of a three-story residence built in 1812 as one of two twin houses. The other house still stands next door to the hotel. The exquisite lobby of the Planters Inn is part of the original house, which mirrored the one built beside it. If you decide to stay at this hotel, ask about a room with a fireplace (there are three on the seventh floor), a balcony (there are four), or a view of Reynolds Square, the little park in front of Planters Inn. The centerpiece of the square is a statue of John Wesley, the founder of Methodism, for whom the hotel was origi-nally named.

Quality Inn Heart of Savannah $$
300 West Bay Street
(912) 236-6321, (800) 221-2222
www.qualityinnhistoricsavannah.com

One of the operators of the Quality Inn Heart of Savannah likes to say that the tourist hot spots of River Street and City Market grew up around this motel on Bay Street. The Quality Inn opened in 1963, long before those two nearby areas became popular with visitors. The 2-story, 52-room motel continues to pro-vide guests with friendly service and well-maintained accommodations. Rooms with two double beds or queen-size beds are avail-able. There's no pool, but a complimentary continental breakfast is available in the lobby from 7:00 until 10:00 a.m. each day, and park-ing is free. Tour buses stop at the front door, and the folks at the front desk will help you make arrangements.

River Street Inn $$$$
124 East Bay Street
(912) 234-6400, (800) 253-4229
www.riverstreetinn.com
Guests of this inn experience a historic atmos-phere in the midst of the activity of River Street. The rooms of this hotel occupy the top three floors of a renovated five-story cotton warehouse on the Savannah River. The main entrance to the inn and its "parkside" rooms look out on Bay Street. Thirty-two of the inn's 86 rooms face the river, and several of these have small French balconies you can step out onto for a grand view of the street and the waterway.

Each of the inn's rooms is different; there are various decors featuring a mixture of authentic period antiques and reproductions, including four-poster and canopy beds. Hard-wood floors, area rugs, and polished brass bathroom fixtures complete the elegant look of old-time Savannah. The lower floors of the structure housing the River Street Inn were built in 1817 to store cotton for export, and the top three floors were added in 1853. The inn was opened in 1985.

Guests receive complimentary newspa-pers in the morning, use of the nearby Down-town Athletic Club, and homemade chocolates before retiring in the evening, and there's a wine reception in the afternoon. The inn can accommodate small meetings and conferences, with seating for 15 in its Board Room and for 40 in its Meeting Room. Parking is $10 per day.

Savannah Marriott Riverfront $$$$
100 General McIntosh Boulevard
(912) 233-7722, (800) 228-9290
www.marriott.com

When we think of the Savannah Marriott Riverfront, the word spacious leaps to mind. The atrium at the heart of the hotel has 7,000 square feet of carpeted space that can easily accommodate themed events and trade shows attended by as many as 500 people. As many as 108 rooms on the seven upper floors of the hotel open onto balconies with views of the atrium, the north side of which looks out on the Savannah River through expansive, floor-to-ceiling panes of glass. The hotel's 15,000-square-foot ballroom is the second largest in the city, and there are an additional 21,000 square feet of meeting space in the form of conference rooms and boardrooms.

Among the hotel's 46 suites are 4 deluxe models, each containing 1,430 square feet of space. You get the picture—everywhere you look, there are scads of space. The real lure of the Marriott, though, is its location on the Savannah River and the riverwalk at the eastern end of River Street. A total of 60 of the hotel's 379 rooms have balconies facing north to the water, and for $20 to $35 extra, you can be, as the Marriott folks say, "perched on the river" with a knockout view of passing ships. Special accommodations include rooms on the concierge floor and deluxe suites with walk-around wet bars, glass-topped dining tables, and large bathrooms featuring double vanities. Guests staying on the private, keyed concierge floor (the eighth) enjoy complimentary continental breakfasts, hors d'oeuvres in late afternoon, and a dessert buffet at night, Sunday night through Friday morning. Adding to the amenities available at the hotel is the Magnolia Spa, which opened in January 2005. This full-service spa is open daily and offers a full range of facials, massages, nail treatments, and body treatments.

There are two pools—one outside and the other in the atrium—and fitness and whirlpool rooms just off the atrium. You can get breakfast, lunch, and dinner and a great view of the river at the River's Edge restaurant, and lunch and dinner at the Atrium Bar. If you'd like a tour of the city, you can make arrangements at the trolley desk in the lobby. Guests who are delegates to meetings at the Savannah International Trade and Convention Center will find a shuttle service at the Waving Girl Landing boat dock adjacent to the hotel; the shuttle will take them across the Savannah River to the Trade Center and back.

Parking in one of the hotel's 620 spaces is $12 a day, with valet parking at $15 daily. The hotel, which opened in 1992 as a Radisson and was converted to a Marriott in 1994, hosted 750 athletes, trainers, and coaches while serving as the Olympic village for yachting events in 1996.

Thunderbird Inn $
611 West Oglethorpe Avenue
(912) 232-2661, (866) 324-2661
www.thethunderbirdinn.com

The owners of this restored vintage motel refer to it as "Savannah's hippest hotel." They took an establishment built in the mid-1960s and refurbished it—brightening up and modernizing the rooms, adding up-to-date features such as hair dryers and high-speed Internet access, and introducing amenities such as complimentary continental breakfasts and a concierge service. The two-story, 42-room Thunderbird retains the feel of its past but offers "the comforts of today." Rooms have king, queen, or double pillow-top beds. In keeping with its history, there's no pool or fitness room. Situated on the western edge of the Historic District, the motel stands in what was once a pretty rough part of town but is now an area that's being revitalized. It is relatively close to several Savannah College of Art and Design (SCAD) dorms.

The Westin Savannah Harbor
Golf Resort and Spa $$$$
1 Resort Drive
Hutchinson Island
(912) 201-2000
www.westinsavannah.com

The city's largest luxury hotel, the Westin rises majestically above the Hutchinson Island waterfront across the Savannah River from the Historic Downtown. The 16-story, 403-room hotel and its riverside neighbor, the Savannah International Trade and Convention Center, are the focal points of the island's Savannah Harbor development—the center-pieces of what is seen as the creation of a "second city" just north of Savannah's downtown area.

Built at a cost of $103 million and incorporating the features of local Regency-style landmarks in its architecture, the Westin opened in December 1999. The lobby and other public areas exude the atmosphere found in the city's fine old homes—high ceilings, hardwood floors, elaborate sconces, and walls painted in pastels. Adding to the ambience are many paintings and photographs by regional artists. The Savannah look is carried through the guest rooms, each of which features the Westin's "Heavenly Bed," an extremely comfortable seven-layer innovation consisting of a pillow-top mattress set covered with luxury thread count triple sheeting, a down blanket, and a duvet-covered comforter, with king-size goose down and feather pillows. The 55 rooms and suites on the hotel's club level—the top 2 floors— have balconies providing marvelous views, and guests staying at these lofty heights have access to a concierge lounge.

Speaking of lounges, the hotel has one that celebrates the work of one of Savannah's favorite sons, beloved lyricist Johnny Mercer. Named Midnight Sun after one of Mercer's songs, this elegantly clubby bar overlooks the river and specializes in drinks also named for Mercer tunes, such as "Blues in the Night." The Westin's restaurant, Aqua Star, can seat 145 and provides second-floor views of Savannah while serving a breakfast buffet each morning, a lunch buffet Monday through Saturday, brunch on Sunday, and dinner each evening. For special gatherings, there's a private dining room in the southeastern corner of the second floor, situated so it looks out on the river and the marina just east of the hotel. The Westin offers almost 20,000 square feet of meeting space that includes 11,500 square feet in the plush Grand Ballroom and 3,400 square feet in the first-floor Harbor Ballroom.

What really sets the Westin apart from other Savannah accommodations are the amenities available through the hotel's affiliation with the nearby Club at Savannah Harbor (see our Parks and Recreation chapter), which features an 18-hole, PGA-quality golf course designed by Robert Cupp and Sam Snead and a one-of-a-kind Greenbrier Spa. The par 72 course—managed by Troon Golf—plays more than 7,000 yards from its championship tees, and its clubhouse complex is the site of a pro shop, an exercise facility, a heated pool, four Har-Tru tennis courts, and the aforementioned spa. The spa is patterned after the spa at the famed Greenbrier resort in White Sulphur Springs, West Virginia, and is the first off-site facility to be licensed by the resort. The spa has 14 massage rooms, 2 steam rooms, 2 saunas, 2 Swiss shower rooms, 4 treatment rooms for sulfur and mud baths or body wraps, and a manicure and pedicure room.

Another unique feature of the hotel is the Westin's kids club, which provides daily activities for children such as scavenger hunts and arts and crafts. The club serves children ages 5 to 12 in the afternoons daily, at a cost of $25 per child, with a 10-child limit.

Valet parking at the hotel is $15 per night. If you stay at the Westin, you won't necessarily have to drive into town to see the sights. Although the Historic Downtown is across the river from the hotel, it's only a few minutes away by free ferry.

In a few rooms the hotel also accepts smaller dogs, with advance deposit and a non-refundable fee.

The luxurious Westin Savannah Harbor Golf Resort and Spa.

SOUTHSIDE/MIDTOWN

Clubhouse Inn of Savannah $
6800 Abercorn Street
(912) 356-1234, (800) CLUB INN
www.savannah.clubhouseinn.com

The folks at the Clubhouse Inn strive to create a "home away from home" atmosphere at their spacious motel on Abercorn Street. They serve a complimentary buffet each morning that gives guests the opportunity to enjoy a full breakfast in a glassed-in dining room looking out on the pool and patio. In the evenings from 5:00 until 7:00 p.m., the manager hosts a reception where each guest can have up to two complimentary mixed drinks. The two-story inn, part of a small chain of motels scattered throughout the United States, has 138 interior rooms that include 16 suites. Each suite has a bedroom with king-size, queen-size, or double beds and a sitting area/kitchen with a wet bar. Other rooms have either king-size beds or doubles. Pets are allowed for a fee of $25.

Country Inn & Suites by Carlson $–$$
7576 White Bluff Road
(912) 692-0404, (800) 456-4000
www.countryinns.com

This 62-room hotel brings a bit of the country to the hubbub of the Oglethorpe Mall area. You'll get a cozy feeling while lounging in the lobby, which has a fireplace, hardwood floor, Oriental carpet, and overstuffed chairs and couches, or while bedding down in the guest rooms and suites, featuring fluffy comforters, wreaths, and swags.

Guest rooms offer two queen-size beds or a king-size, and there are three types of suites: the country suite, which has a bedroom with two queen-size and a king-size bed and a living room with a sleeper sofa; the celebration suite, whose expanded living and bedroom area includes a king-size bed, whirlpool bath, and wet bar; and the home "suite" home, which has a kitchen, living room, and two bedrooms, one with a king-size bed and one with two queen-size beds. All suites come equipped with microwaves

and refrigerators. A particularly attractive feature of the Country Inn is its spacious indoor pool area, where you'll find a kidney-shaped pool, a whirlpool, and plenty of space for relaxing. The inn also offers a fitness room, a meeting room that accommodates 18 people, and a dining area where complimentary continental breakfasts are available from 7:00 to 9:30 a.m. There's also a social hour here from 5:00 to 7:00 p.m. Monday through Thursday at which complimentary beer, wine, and light snacks are served.

Holiday Inn Midtown $
7100 Abercorn Street
(912) 352-7100, (800) 255-8268
www.ichotelsgroup.com

As its name implies, this 171-room Holiday Inn stands smack-dab in the middle of town (not "downtown," "town," as in the larger city limits). The two two-story wings of the motel flank a courtyard that includes a spacious pool area set among palms and magnolias. Some rooms have king-size beds, others have two doubles, and all were completely renovated as part of a process that was finished in March 2000. The Marketplace restaurant serves breakfast and dinner, and Doubles, a 110-seat lounge, is geared for the after-work and after-date crowd. The Holiday Inn Midtown has a fitness room and offers same-day dry-cleaning service. The motel's several meeting rooms can accommodate up to 200 people.

Homewood Suites by Hilton $$
5820 White Bluff Road
(912) 353-8500, (800) CALL HOME
www.homewoodsuites.com/hws/savannah

The largest all-suite establishment in Savannah offers guests free local telephone calls and an Executive Center for business travelers. The Executive Center sports a typewriter, computer, and a DSL Interarrange to send and receive faxes at the front desk.

The 106 suites are configured as either one-bedroom "Homewood" suites, the hotel's most popular offerings; as master suites, which have fireplaces; or as two-bedroom, two-bath suites. Each suite features a fully equipped kitchen with two-burner stove, microwave, and full-size refrigerator; a sleeper sofa; and two telephones with dataports.

Leave a grocery list at the front desk, and your shopping will be done for you and charged to your room. In addition to the three-story building and two two-story buildings housing the suites, there is a spacious lodge that can accommodate 50 people for the hotel's complimentary, deluxe continental breakfasts and evening manager's receptions. The receptions, held from 5:00 until 7:00 p.m. Monday, offer guests beer, wine, soft drinks, and a light meal. A pool and whirlpool are situated just outside the lodge, and there is a court nearby where you can play basketball, tennis, or volleyball. If you need to burn off more energy, try the fitness room off the lobby in the lodge. The hotel also has two meeting rooms, one for up to 50 people and the other for 10, and an on-site laundry facility. Guests wishing to have a cookout will find two grills for their use under the huge oak tree that graces the property. Pets are allowed; check with the hotel for particulars.

Oglethorpe Inn and Suites $-$$$
7110 Hodgson Memorial Drive
(912) 354-8560, (800) 344-4378
www.oglethorpeinn.com
Although the Oglethorpe Inn and Suites (formerly the Masters Inn Suites) is near

i The Old Town Trolley swings by 12 motels on the Southside each morning around 9:00 a.m. to pick up people who want to take tours of Savannah's Historic District. The trolley makes a return trip at 3:00 p.m. If your motel isn't a regular stop, ask the desk clerk to call Old Town and have them come by and get you. Tour fees range from $18 to $22 for adults and are $9 for children ages 4 to 12 and free for kids younger than age 4.

Oglethorpe Mall and nestled amid the shopping centers and office parks of the Southside, this three-story hotel looks and feels as if it belongs in downtown Savannah. The hotel is built around an atrium decorated with palm trees, exotic plants, a gurgling fountain, and intricate black ironwork.

The Old South theme surfaces in the sitting rooms of the hotel's 51 suites. Each sitting room also contains a sofa, coffee table, easy chairs, and a small refrigerator, a microwave oven, and a coffeemaker. Six luxury suites have larger sitting rooms, king-size beds, and whirlpool bathtubs. All rooms are entered from the interior of the hotel. Guests can exercise in the outdoor pool at the rear of the hotel or in the fully equipped fitness room. Afterward, you can relax in the hotel's combination whirlpool bath-steam room. Many of the guests are businesspeople, and there is a conference room capable of seating 45.

Residence Inn by Marriott $$
5710 White Bluff Road
(912) 356-3266, (800) 331-3131
www.marriott.com
This Residence Inn has 66 one- and two-bedroom and studio suites under one roof. All suites have kitchens, and each of the two-bedroom accommodations has two full bathrooms, three televisions, and a wood-burning fireplace. Kitchens are equipped with refrigerators, microwaves, and coffeemakers, and the staff of the inn will do your grocery shopping for you. Just leave your shopping list at the front desk, and the groceries will be charged to your bill and deposited in your room by 6:00 p.m. Copies of USA Today and the Savannah Morning News are free, as is a hot breakfast buffet served in the Gatehouse sitting area. The Gatehouse is also the scene of social hours held from 5:00 to 7:00 p.m. Monday through Thursday— complimentary snacks, beer, wine, and other beverages are served. For those seeking recreation, you can enjoy an indoor pool and whirlpool, an exercise room, and an outdoor court for tennis,

basketball, or volleyball. Pets are welcome, but there is a $75 nonrefundable cleaning fee.

Savannah Midtown Courtyard by Marriott $$
6703 Abercorn Street
(912) 354-7878, (800) 321-2211
www.marriott.com/savch

Savannah's Courtyard by Marriott stands between two of the city's busiest thorough-fares, Abercorn Street and White Bluff Road, but the three-story hotel's beautifully land-scaped grounds will give you a feeling of being away from the madding crowd. The centerpiece of the hotel is the courtyard with its quaint gazebo and swimming pool. Just off the pool is an enclosed whirlpool surrounded by lots of space for lounging, and there's a fit-

According to the Savannah Area Chamber of Commerce, direct tourism spending in Chatham County totaled $1.4 billion in 2005, the most recent figure available at press time. The chamber also reported that 21 percent of that money was spent on rooms.

ness room near the lobby that sports state-of-the-art exercise equipment. The Courtyard's large dining area is open for breakfast daily (with a full meal priced at $8.95 and continental servings available). There are 144 interior rooms including 12 suites. Rooms on the upper floors open onto balconies. There are two meeting rooms, each of which can accommodate 24 people seated at tables.

RESTAURANTS

Your taste buds will be glad you came to Savannah—but your waistline might not be. The city offers a quantity and variety of restaurants completely out of proportion to its size. The recipe just adds up: Take plenty of fresh shrimp, crab, and fish from local waters, mix in the cultural contacts that go with more than 250 years as a seaport, consider the long growing season and the agricultural tradition of the South in general, then flavor with a generous helping of legendary Southern hospitality. The result is scores of restaurants serving just about every type of food imaginable.

The setting improves the flavor of food, as any good hostess will tell you. Savannah's restaurants serve their guests in unique settings that include the stonewalled halls of former cotton warehouses on the riverfront, balconies overlooking breathtaking marshes, historic mansions with antique furnishings, and unpretentious little places nestled under towering oaks.

Remember the scene in the movie *Forrest Gump* in which the character Bubba launched into an extensive list of ways to prepare shrimp? Well, in Savannah you'll find at least that many ways of serving this local favorite. If your day takes you out to Tybee Island, you're likely to spot shrimp boats, often working surprisingly close to the beach. And if your meal involves shrimp, you are about to discover what an amazing difference real freshness—as opposed to being iced down and flown inland—can make in its flavor.

With a little pushing and shoving, you can put Savannah's restaurants into four main categories: seafood, soul food or regional cooking, ethnic, and a sprinkling of haute cuisine. Some, of course, will defy labeling, and others will boast a menu that has a grip on more than one category.

We make no claims to offer a complete and comprehensive restaurant listing here. Instead, we've singled out places we like to go to, places our friends talk about, and places that have been fixtures for Savannah travelers for years. We've tried to make sure that we included something for every pocketbook, as well as something for every taste.

We've labeled our restaurants either Inexpensive, Moderate, or Expensive, because there are so many variables about tips, alcohol, dessert, and what have you. Of course, all things are relative—we think the price of a good Savannah meal is a bargain compared to larger cities. Also, you can run amok in the menu of an inexpensive place and wind up with an expensive meal, too—and vice versa. Still, this system will give you some idea of what to expect when the bill comes. You can count on inexpensive entrees to cost under $15, moderate entrees to cost up to $25, and expensive entrees to cost more than $25.

You'll also note that we haven't included chain restaurants, except in a very few exceptions where location or other circumstances make them especially significant. Savannah boasts a wide range of such chains, with many fine examples among them, but we feel our readers will already know what to expect from these restaurants. You'll find these listed in the Yellow Pages of your telephone directory.

Georgia law now prohibits smoking in restaurants, except on outdoor patios.

Parking in the Historic Downtown is always an adventure, so give yourself plenty of time to find a space, particularly if you have dinner reservations. Restaurants outside the downtown area generally have plenty of free nearby parking.

If your travels take you to nearby Tybee Island or Hilton Head, South Carolina, note that restaurants in those two locales (a smattering of eateries on Tybee, more than two dozen outstanding dining spots in Hilton Head) are discussed in the individual chapters that cover those two island destinations.

HISTORIC DOWNTOWN

Alligator Soul   Expensive
114 Barnard Street
(912) 232-7879, (912) 232-8038
www.alligatorsoul.com
Co-owner and executive chef Hilary Craig's love of Southern cuisine shines through in the dishes he serves at this cozy restaurant in below-street-level quarters on Barnard Street just north of Telfair Square. He's inspired to prepare Duck Three Ways—in separate courses as sautéed pate, as sausage wrapped in cabbage leaves, and as seared duck breast served with couscous and plum demiglace. His affection for pork manifests itself in another three-piece presentation that features roasted pork tenderloin, poached pork tenderloin with ginger snap pudding, and homemade smoked sausage with sauerkraut. Craig and his wife, Maureen, opened Alligator Soul in 2001 after coming to Savannah from Seattle, where they own and operate an award-winning restaurant of the same name. The atmosphere is akin to that of the cotton warehouses you'll find on River Street—lots of brick and exposed beams. Open nightly.

Belford's Savannah
Seafood & Steaks   Expensive
315 West St. Julian Street
(912) 233-2626
Belford's brings casual fine dining to the western end of City Market. Testifying to this approach are entrees such as shrimp, greens, and grits; the double-cut pork chop; and the stuffed filet—grilled filet mignon stuffed with shrimp and finished with béarnaise sauce. The atmosphere is light and airy, thanks to the tall, arched, unadorned windows lining the City Market and Congress Street sides of Belford's, which is housed in what was once a warehouse frequented by local grocers. The restaurant derives its name from the Belford's Wholesale Food Company, which was an integral part of City Market in the early 1900s, and a portrait of the Belford family is among the framed artwork decorating the eatery. Brick walls, highly polished wooden floors, captain's chairs, and tables covered with linen add to the classical feel of the place. Belford's serves lunch and dinner daily and breakfast Monday through Saturday, with brunch on Sunday.

The Cafe at City Market   Moderate
224 West St. Julian Street
(912) 236-7133
www.citymarket.com
Dine indoors at this restaurant in the eastern part of City Market, and you'll experience the atmosphere of a big-city bistro during the 1930s, '40s, and '50s, with recorded music to match (Sinatra is a favorite in the evenings). Dine outdoors, and you'll be sitting under an awning on an open-air deck "watching the world go by," as owner and chef Matt Maher puts it. At either location, you choose from a menu that's somewhat international in content and contains an item or two you've probably never encountered before, such as grilled cheese with artichoke hearts, mushrooms, and prosciutto ham, and black bean pizza. Also featured on the lunch menu is the Southern pecan chicken salad.

The dinner menu offers specialties such as stuffed chicken with asparagus, prosciutto ham, and provolone cheese, and Cuban tuna with black beans. There's room for 65 diners inside and 45 on the deck; you can smoke outside on the deck. Maher, who opened the cafe in 1991, recommends making reservations for dinner on weekends during the spring and summer.

Casbah Moroccan Restaurant   Moderate
118 East Broughton Street
(912) 234-6168
www.casbahrestaurant.com

Dinner at the Casbah turns into an evening-long event in which the food— which is very good—is only a part. Proprietor Sami Samir has re-created a bit of the atmosphere of Morocco in what started out as an abandoned storefront on the city's main shopping street.

The decor is now lush, dark, and romantic, with hassocks and other plush upholstered seating, floor-to-ceiling drapes, and a balcony from which a belly dancer descends. Guests are escorted to their seats, where a waiter opens and closes the meal by washing their hands from a decorative pitcher filled with rose water. The dancer comes on for short intervals throughout the evening, and the performances we've witnessed were interesting, entertaining, and quite decorous (although the dancers look more like college students than Middle Eastern belly dancers). The menu is heavily weighted with dishes like lamb cooked in honey and almonds, but even the less-adventurous palate will find an option here. Many dishes are variations on kebabs, in lamb, beef, or chicken (we opted for the dish featuring all three). For the appetizer course, we had a salad sampler, which features six different salads or relishes. The choices are not what we call light eating, but the meal is sedately paced, meaning you may still be able to manage, or at least share, a dessert. The staff is attentive, well versed on the dishes and customs, and experienced at putting guests at ease in unfamiliar surroundings. A wine list is available. Reservations are strongly recommended. Allow plenty of time—at least a couple of hours. Dress ranges from dressy casual to business attire, but women may feel more comfortable in pants, given the seating arrangements. There is a small gift shop selling Moroccan items, like tangines (cooking vessels). Open for dinner 5:30 to 10:30 p.m.

Clary's Cafe   Inexpensive
404 Abercorn Street
(912) 233-0402

4430 Habersham Street
(912) 351-0302

Visitors to Savannah know the original Clary's as the place where characters from *Midnight in the Garden of Good and Evil* congregated, but this cafe at Jones and Abercorn Streets was, as former owner Michael Faber once put it, "famous before The Book." Clary's opened in 1903 and, as a pharmacy and soda fountain, has been a hangout of Savannahians throughout its existence. Faber bought it in February 1994, during the week that *Midnight* hit the bookstores, and he renovated the building and converted the pharmacy into dining space. He made the most of the restaurant's connection to the book, with touches such as a stained-glass window depicting the Bird Girl and Midnight in the Garden T-shirts worn by employees.

As stated earlier, however, there's more to Clary's than its association with the best-selling book. The Midtown restaurant has extensive menus for breakfast, lunch, and dinner, and the downtown Clary's serves breakfast and lunch, each offering food made from scratch each day, including the four different soups. Among the breakfast specialties are the malted waffles and pancakes made with a special flour brought in from Michigan; for lunch, there are a variety of salads, burgers, sandwiches, and those aforementioned soups; and in the evening, featured items are the fillet of tilapia served on a seasoned oak plank, the old-fashioned pot roast, and the Triple Peaks salad, which has scoops of tuna, chicken, and shrimp salads on fresh greens and pasta salad. Faber, who was in the restaurant business in Chicago for 35 years before moving to Savannah in 1988, opened a second Clary's in Midtown in September 1998. The newer Clary's, at Habersham and 61st Streets, exudes the charm of the original, right down to the old-fashioned marble soda fountain and the leaded-glass windows. The menu at the Midtown location is the same as that of the downtown eatery, and there are 300 free parking spaces adjacent to the Habersham Street site.

Clary's was featured prominently in John Berendt's best seller about Savannah. BETTY DARBY

The Cotton Exchange Moderate
201 East River Street
(912) 232-7088

The oldest restaurant on River Street, The Cotton Exchange serves lunch and dinner in what was once a cotton warehouse built in 1799. The Exchange opened in 1971 and for a time offered mainly sandwiches, but the restaurant later expanded into the dinner market. Among the standouts on the dinner menu are the pasta dishes and the seafood platters. The folks at The Exchange haven't forgotten how to make outstanding sandwiches, in particular their Reubens and our favorite, a chargrilled hamburger they call the Congress. With your sandwich, you get a choice of a side dish, and we recommend the zesty German potato salad.

The Express Café and Bakery Inexpensive
39 Barnard Street
(912) 233-4683
www.expresscafeandbakery.com

This popular breakfast and lunch spot has a European air. We've never had anything here that wasn't good, and we've worked our way through the menu over the years: quiche, stuffed croissants, soup in bread bowls, sandwiches loaded with fresh vegetables, fresh baguettes, and so on. The desserts are special things as well. The Express opens at 7:00 a.m. weekdays and 8:00 a.m. weekends, closing at midafternoon.

i In a rush for lunch? Whip into Tanner's sandwich shop at 21 East Broughton Street and grab a couple of chili dogs and the orangiest orange drink you'll ever taste or see—a mixture of fresh and frozen orange juices, water, a little salt, and plenty of sugar. Tanner's, in business since 1942, is on the south side of Broughton near the corner of Drayton Street, and it's open in the morning and afternoon Monday through Saturday.

Garibaldi's Cafe Moderate–Expensive
315 West Congress Street
(912) 232-7118

A varied and sophisticated menu of continental dishes awaits at this small, attractive restaurant that is part of a small chain (there's another one in Charleston, South Carolina). Dinner is served nightly, and there's a full bar and extensive wine selections. Try the whole scored flounder in apricot sauce. Pasta dishes are staples, and there are always interesting seafood selections along with decadent desserts. Reservations are available, and dress is business attire on up. Dinner only.

Huey's Moderate
115 East River Street
(912) 234-7385

Huey's brings the Big Easy to Savannah with its New Orleans–style cuisine. With floor-to-ceiling windows right on the sidewalk, Huey's also offers a great view of the Savannah River, a circumstance that makes a breakfast of café au lait and beignets something special. For those unfamiliar with "N'awlins," beignets (pronounced "ben-yeas") are delectable French doughnuts.

Huey's also has some specialties for breakfast eaters with heartier appetites, including eggs Benedict and eggs sardou, the latter consisting of a bed of creamed spinach with artichoke hearts on a toasted English muffin with two poached eggs topped with hollandaise sauce.

For lunch and dinner, there are such dishes as red beans and rice served with andouille sausage, and muffuletta, a sandwich made with freshly baked bread, Genoa salami, cappicola ham, provolone cheese, and an olive dressing. The food is zesty but moderately spiced; if you want more zip, there's Tabasco sauce on your table.

Huey's has seating for 70 in its streetside dining room and for 20 in the adjacent patio bar. The restaurant has been in business on River Street since 1987.

Il Pasticcio Expensive
2 East Broughton Street
(912) 231-8888
www.ilpasticciosavannah.com

You'd never guess this large, upscale bastion of fine Italian cuisine once was a low-end department store. The dishes sport Italian names with English descriptions. Examples: Fettuccine ai Frutti di Mare, described as housemade fettuccine sautéed with shrimp, scallops, mussels, and clams in a spicy white wine sauce ($27) and Trota Farcita, which is baked trout stuffed with a fennel and caper relish, served with sautéed spinach and purple cabbage over a bed of saffron jasmine rice, topped with lemon juice and butter ($28). They're proud of their wines, and the dinner-only menu is creative and extensive, with ambience to spare. Consider this one on the dressy side, with reservations recommended. This restaurant is good for celebrity spotting during events like the Savannah Film Festival.

The Lady and Sons Moderate
102 West Congress Street
(912) 233-2600
www.theladyandsons.com

Paula Deen, host of the Food Network's *Paula Deen's Home Cooking,* is Savannah's newest celebrity. You can sample the food that made Paula famous here at her restaurant. And you can read more about Deen's kitchen-based empire in our Savannah Celebrity chapter later in this book.

There's a menu at this Southern comfort-food restaurant, but unless you are going to be in town long enough to return repeatedly, skip it and go directly to the buffet. This is the slow-cooked, perfectly seasoned stuff that Southerners consider real home cooking. Fried chicken, squash casserole, seasoned greens, fried green tomatoes, "hoecakes" (ask if you don't know), cheese biscuits—you get the picture. The buffet is $13 at lunch and $17 at dinner, and we predict that you can and will eat enough to stupefy yourself. If you opt for the menu, we recommend the crab cakes.

Lunch and dinner are served daily except for Sunday, when buffet-only service is from 11:00 a.m. to 5:00 p.m. A word of warning: If you eat the buffet for lunch, you won't be hungry for dinner—we speak from experience and we have hearty appetites.

The restaurant has new quarters in keeping with its new fame. A $4 million makeover turned an old hardware store into a three-story restaurant. Dining is on floors one and three, and the bar is on three as well. The second floor contains the kitchen and offices.

Locals have loved Deen's cooking for years, but with her show and her cookbooks, she has also built a national cult following. That means some growing pains for the restaurant. There's an efficient sign-in for those awaiting tables, and it can be quite a wait.

Mrs. Wilkes' Dining Room   Moderate
107 West Jones Street
(912) 232-5997
www.mrswilkes.com

Lunch at Mrs. Wilkes' is served beginning at 11:00 a.m., but the line of customers starts forming well before then on the shady sidewalk alongside Jones Street. The line usually moves at a fairly rapid clip, but the late owner, Sema Wilkes, would say that folks told her of waiting for two hours to get in the door of her establishment, which is on the garden floor of a three-story house. "They said it was worth the wait," said Mrs. Wilkes, who died in 2002 at the age of 95 and whose dining room is now operated by family members. It's worth the wait because dining at Mrs. Wilkes' is about more than eating lunch; it's about having a unique experience.

This is the same category of cooking—traditional Southern home-cooking—as Paula Deen's The Lady and Sons. Despite the celebrity, however, Mrs. Wilkes' is the one to choose if you can only visit one of these two restaurants during your visit.

At 11:00, after the first group of diners has filed in and taken their places around the seven 10-seat tables in the two low-ceilinged dining rooms, a member of the Wilkes family rings a little bell and says grace. Then the staff places heaping platters and bowls of Southern-style food on the tables, serving it country-style. Chatting with newly made acquaintances at your table, you dig in and pass around the platters and bowls (sometimes as many as 18 of them). After you've finished eating, you help clear your table, taking your dishes and silverware to the rear of the room. As you're leaving, a new group of 10 diners is admitted to take their seats at your table.

At our most recent visit to Mrs. Wilkes', the tables were loaded with fried chicken, barbecue chicken, beef stew, sausage, baked ham, collard greens, snap beans, black-eyed peas, squash, rice and gravy, okra and tomatoes, mashed potatoes, candied yams, pickled beets, apple salad, and macaroni salad.

The menu is changed on a daily basis, "because some people eat here every day," Mrs. Wilkes had said. However, you'll always be served beef stew, baked ham, and fried chicken, the last being a specialty of the house. When asked about her fried chicken by Bryant Gumbel during an interview on NBC's Today show, Mrs. Wilkes said, "If the Colonel's was as good, he'd be a general."

Mrs. Wilkes got started in the food service business in 1943 when her husband's job brought him to Savannah from the central Georgia town of Vidalia. L. H. Wilkes took a room at a boardinghouse in the building where Mrs. Wilkes' is now. Mrs. Wilkes would visit L. H. on weekends, got to know the owner of the boardinghouse, and eventually began helping her out by cooking for the boarders. The Wilkeses raised a family in Savannah and in 1965 bought the boardinghouse, which they restored and converted into apartments. Mrs. Wilkes also cooked and served meals, first for her neighbors, then for visitors; word of the quality of her food and her down-home hospitality spread, to the extent that Condé Nast Traveler magazine in 1990 named her place one of the 50 most distinguished restaurants in the United States.

Mrs. Wilkes' Dining Room serves delicious Southern home cooking. BETTY DARBY

Lunch at Mrs. Wilkes' is $13. The dining rooms are open Monday through Friday. Mrs. Wilkes' doesn't take credit cards, and smoking is prohibited. Dinner parties and catering can be arranged.

The Olde Pink House Restaurant & Planters Tavern   Expensive
23 Abercorn Street
(912) 232-4286

Experience Savannah as it was in post-Colonial days by dining at the Georgian-style mansion that is The Olde Pink House. This is the only restaurant in Savannah lodged in a historically significant house—a structure built in the late 1700s for wealthy merchant James Habersham Jr. and expanded in the early 1800s when it

was the Planters' Bank, the first such establishment in Georgia. Known also as the Habersham House, the building, on the northwest corner of Abercorn and Bryan Streets, has a pink exterior because it was constructed of bricks made from red clay and covered with white stucco; the red bled through the stucco, coloring it pink, and the structure has been painted that hue ever since. A tearoom was opened in the house in the 1930s, and it has been a restaurant for the past 50 years.

The Olde Pink House serves regional cuisine in seven elegant dining rooms occupying the upper two floors of the building, which has a basement housing the Planters Tavern. Examples of this type of cooking are the roast duck with wild berry sauce and hoppin' John, she-crab soup laced with sherry, Caesar salad with corn bread oysters, crispy scored flounder with apricot shallot sauce, and grilled pork tenderloin with collards and yams.

Before dining, you might want to walk downstairs to the tavern and relax with a drink while sitting in front of one of the large brick fireplaces on either end of the room, which was originally the house's kitchen. Take a good look around and you'll notice a metal door that once was part of a bank vault; it now leads to the restaurant's wine cellar. Other points of interest within the house are the oil painting of residents of old Savannah and notable Americans such as George Washington, a display featuring Habersham's somewhat gaudy shoe and knee buckles, and the staircase winding from the first floor to the second.

The Olde Pink House is open for candlelight dinners seven days a week, and jazz pianist Gail Thurmond performs in the tavern every evening but Monday. The bar is also the only place where smoking is allowed. Reservations are definitely recommended. If you're interested in dining in the restaurant's most romantic spot, ask for a table by a window in the second floor Office Room—it has a view of picturesque Reynolds Square.

Olympia Cafe   Moderate
5 East River Street
(912) 233-3131

This authentic Greek restaurant is a welcome respite from the glare and bustle of River Street. Brick walls and flooring, lots of plants, and soft lighting add to the atmosphere, but that's all incidental to the food. Favorites here include red snapper Aegean served with tomato sauce, spices, and feta cheese. Lamb chops marinated in olive oil and herbs before chargrilling are another favorite. Spanakopita is one of those dishes by which a Greek restaurant is measured, and you'll find this version of the flavored spinach pastry measures up well. On the lighter and less-expensive side of the menu, you can choose gyro sandwiches and chicken kebobs. On our last visit, we particularly enjoyed the Greek antipasto tray, even though we never quite figured out what some of the items on it were. Beverage selections include Greek coffee, and there is a full bar. Dress is generally nice and casual, but kick it up a notch for weekend dinners, when reservations are recommended. Don't be confused when you arrive—Olympia Cafe also operates a quick-and-casual take-out place on one side and a 35-flavor ice-cream parlor on the other.

The Pirates' House Restaurant   Moderate
20 East Broad Street
(912) 233-5757
www.thepirateshouse.com

This restaurant is a local institution. Locals have been coming here, and steering tourists here, for decades. It flirted with a stuffier atmosphere after a recent renovation, but its market reminded it that it did just fine in the old incarnation. The restaurant wanders from room to room, each of which is atmospheric (haunted, in fact, by some accounts). These quarters are Savannah's link to Robert Louis Stevenson's classic *Treasure Island*. When you have children in your party, it's hard to find a classy restaurant that accommodates younger patrons. The Pirates' House does this quite well, without damaging arrangements for adults out for a dress-up dinner. The menu is varied and includes lots of seafood. Locals head for the lunch buffet and always remember the fried chicken. The dessert menu is vast and intimidating: We suggest you consider dining here and skipping dessert, then making a return trip for dessert only before you leave Savannah. Nice casual will do for lunch, but brush up a little bit for dinner. There's full bar service. The restaurant also has a gift shop.

Ray's Famous Cafe   Inexpensive
146 Montgomery Street
(912) 232-4155

What makes Ray's Famous Cafe famous? Well, it's the clientele, much of which consists of members of the local courthouse crowd. You can see many of the town's attorneys, judges, and politicians here, either in the flesh or represented in the many caricatures that line the walls of the little cafe, which is on Montgomery Street just north of Oglethorpe Avenue and almost directly across from the Chatham County Courthouse. When former owner Ray Hord opened this restaurant in 1991, he called it the Uptown Country Cafe, but soon decided the name wasn't very catchy; so he changed it, and also altered the atmosphere of the place by asking *Savannah Morning News* political cartoonist Mark Streeter to drop by and make sketches of customers. And that's how Ray's Famous Cafe got to be famous. Although the caricatures have made Ray's an "in" place at which to eat lunch and breakfast, they're not the only things that bring people back. There are also the quality and variety of the home cooking and the promptness with which it's delivered. Ray's offers specials each day, with two meats and usually eight vegetables being featured. Ray's is open Monday through Friday and on Saturday morning.

The Riverhouse Restaurant   Expensive
125 West River Street
(912) 234-1900
www.riverhouseseafood.com

The Riverhouse and its bakery occupy four bays of an old cotton warehouse near the west end of River Street, and the bricks and thick wooden beams of the building lend charm to the upscale but casual atmosphere. Operated by the Harris family, which established it in 1982, The Riverhouse specializes in fresh seafood. Featured dishes include the grouper Florentine, which is served atop angel-hair pasta, and Atlantic salmon crowned

> **i** If you decide to get a take-out meal along River Street (or anywhere else near the water), resist the urge to share it with that single begging seagull that will invariably show up. Otherwise, hordes of its friends will arrive, and you will have no peace.

with whipped potatoes and baked. Among the appetizers are the seafood strudel—a light pastry filled with spinach, feta, shrimp, and crabmeat—and shrimp served on grits with a tasso gravy. The restaurant serves lunch and dinner, and "dessert only" customers are welcome any time in the bakery.

Saigon Restaurant   Moderate
4 West Broughton Street
(912) 232-5288

This is the latest addition to a trio of family-run Thai/Vietnamese restaurants (the others are Little Saigon and The King and I, described elsewhere in this chapter). This one has transformed a storefront on the city's former main retail street into a sleek-looking restaurant for lunch and dinner. Pick the subtler Vietnamese dishes, or follow the crowd to the trendier (and spicier) Thai menu. Our Thai favorites include bai ka pao, which is stir-fried meat (choose beef, chicken, or pork) with basil, garlic, onions, and mushrooms, and the green curry, which offers a choice of meat in curry, coconut milk, and vegetables. Ordinarily we don't bother recommending desserts—if a restaurant is really good, you won't have room for it anyway, we figure. But make an exception here. Basically, desserts are limited to ice cream—mango, coconut, and green tea flavors. The presentation is lovely, in an elaborate glass with sliced fruit and whipped cream with a filled cookie. Servings are large enough to serve two people amply. Our favorite—green tea ice cream.

The Shrimp Factory   Expensive
313 East River Street
(912) 236-4229
www.theshrimpfactory.com

This restaurant near the eastern end of River Street offers what owner Cheryl Harris Power likes to call "fine casual dining," meaning the atmosphere is relaxed but replete with special touches such as the salad being tossed tableside. The Shrimp Factory prides itself on its seafood, steaks, and chicken dishes, and as might be expected, you can find shrimp served "in so many ways" here—fried, with crab au gratin, with deviled crab, with sausage Creole, and with scallops. Pecan pie is a specialty of the house, as is the pine bark stew, which is best described as a "Southern bouillabaisse."

The restaurant occupies the bottom floor of a warehouse built in the 1820s for storing cotton, resin, and other products, and the building's heart-pine ceiling beams and rafters and brick walls give the Shrimp Factory a rustic feel. The restaurant has been in existence since 1977, and it's open seven days a week for lunch and dinner.

Six Pence Pub   Moderate
245 Bull Street
(912) 233-3156

A restaurant serving lunch and dinner daily, the Six Pence takes on the more convivial atmosphere of a pub as the evening unfolds. What you'll find here is what you might expect from a pub in Great Britain in terms of food and cozy atmosphere. Six Pence offers specials each day, with patrons having a particular liking for the shepherd's pie, the sausage (bangers, in England) and mashed potatoes, the French onion and potato soups, and a meat pie made with mushrooms, peas, onions, and carrots, and beef that's been marinated in beer.

Most of the memorabilia adorning the walls and bar is authentic—from the Toby mugs to the coronation collectibles dating from 1898 to the pub signs, some of which are more than 200 years old. Be sure to look for the ship's bell that's a replica of the one on the *Titanic* and was a souvenir gift from that ill-fated vessel's maiden voyage. Also search out the handwritten, hand-painted proclamations presented to King George VI in 1937.

The pub also has its own ghost, a fellow who reportedly hangs out in the basement and has a penchant for turning faucets and light fixtures on and off. Nicknamed "Larry" by former Six Pence owner Wendy Snowden, this apparition has the appearance of a young man from the late 1800s.

Skyler's   Moderate
225 East Bay Street
(912) 232-3955
www.skylersrestaurant.com

The co-owners of Skyler's—Nguyen Nguyet and Charles Coolidge—like to say their restaurant is "where East meets West." Nguyen, who's better known to patrons and friends as Ms. Moon, is a former resident of Vietnam, and Charles is a native of Atlanta; they worked together as chefs at the Hyatt hotel here and developed a cooking style that Coolidge deems a "fusion of Asian-Continental cuisine with coastal dishes." They took that style with them when they left the hotel and opened the original Skyler's on State Street in 1990. The restaurant quickly outgrew that location, and Ms. Moon and Coolidge moved it in 1993 to the cellar of the East Bay Inn, where there was more room and the ambience of a onetime cotton warehouse—brick floors and walls and a ceiling dominated by thick wooden beams. Skyler's specializes in crab cakes, roast pork, teriyaki chicken, and Caesar salad and seats its customers in Windsor chairs that make eating here an extremely comfortable experience. The main dining room accommodates 70 people, and there's a banquet room with seating for 60. Access to the restaurant is through the lobby of the East Bay Inn. Skyler's is open for lunch on weekdays and serves dinner Wednesday, Thursday, Friday, and Saturday.

Soho South Cafe   Moderate
12 West Liberty Street
(912) 233-1633
www.sohosouthcafe.com

What a place: a combination restaurant and art gallery in the minimally renovated lofty space once occupied by a garage. It's worth the trip just to look around, but the food could stand on its own anywhere. Soho South (which you will also hear called Soho Savannah, even though that isn't the official name) serves a sophisticated but affordable lunch. Your table might be from a patio suite or a circa-1950s dinette set. The quiche is the best

Close-up

Regional Cuisine Offers a Taste of Savannah

When you're in Savannah, you might run across some cuisine you're not likely to find in other parts of the country. Two examples, the Lowcountry shrimp boil and the oyster roast, combine food with other elements you might have noticed being mentioned throughout this book: Savannahians' love of getting together and their fondness for being outdoors.

You can order Lowcountry boil in a restaurant, and the same goes for oysters, but perhaps the best way to experience them is by attending an outdoor party at which they are the featured components. Lowcountry boil—also known as Frogmore stew because it supposedly originated in Frogmore, South Carolina, which is about 90 minutes northeast of Savannah—consists of smoked sausage, corn on the cob, and shrimp all boiled together in a large pot. Some cooks add other ingredients, with new potatoes seeming to be the most popular.

Oysters served at an oyster roast are roasted on a big piece of tin or steel that's supported by cinder blocks. A red-hot fire is built under the sheet of metal, and the oysters are placed on it and covered with wet cloth—burlap sacks do nicely. The oysters will steam open in about 20 minutes, and they're ready to eat. Special oyster knives are used to help dig the oysters out of their shells, and it's a good idea to wear gloves to prevent being cut by the oyster's tough exterior.

We think the best way to enjoy a Lowcountry boil or oyster roast is by standing around on a crisp day in autumn, chatting with friends, and diving into a pile of oysters or a big heap of sausage, shrimp, and corn that's been dumped on a table covered with newspaper. It doesn't hurt, by the way, if there's a keg of beer handy.

i If you're looking for a lunch or an afternoon snack that's healthy and fast, stop by the Brighter Day natural foods and organic produce store at the corner of Bull Street and Park Avenue. Brighter Day's juice bar deli caters to vegetarians by offering a variety of salads, soups, sandwiches, and smoothies—beverages made with fruit, fruit juices, and other stuff that's good for you and tastes good, too. You can carry out your food or eat inside or outside at small tables facing the south end of Forsyth Park. The deli is open daily from late morning until late afternoon.

available in Savannah and sells out early at lunch. Salads, soups, portobello mushroom burgers—we've never been disappointed here. Save room for the decadent desserts, which include a berry trifle-thing that's hard to resist. The clientele tends to be the local ladies-who-lunch crowd, with the occasional business lunch thrown in, and more and more tourists are getting steered here. The dinner menu is more complex and expensive (salmon Wellington, pepper-crusted filet mignon), but it retains a grilled salmon BLT and a char-grilled cheddar burger. Brunch is served on Sunday. Before you leave, swing by the restroom—even if you don't need the facilities, the decor is worth checking out. Also, we

Among other foods associated with this area are Savannah red rice, a dessert called trifle, and a cookie known as the benne wafer. The benne wafer has a taste all its own because it's made with benne seeds, which is what folks in the Lowcountry call sesame seeds. Trifle, a gift of the English colonists to Savannah, consists of pound cake that's been sprinkled with sherry, layered with custard, and topped with whipped cream. Savannah red rice goes great with fried chicken and seafood. The following is a recipe for this distinctly local dish provided by Martha Giddens Nesbit, who edited and wrote much of the food section of Savannah's daily newspaper for more than a decade and is the author of the *Savannah Collection* and *Savannah Entertains* cookbooks.

In her recipe, which serves four people, Martha uses four slices of bacon that have been fried crisp, crumbled, and reserved, one chopped onion, one chopped celery stalk, a cup of raw rice, one 16-ounce can of tomatoes, three-quarters of a cup of water, a teaspoon of salt, and a quarter-teaspoon of cayenne pepper.

Fry the chopped onion and celery in bacon fat, then remove some of the fat, if desired, and add the rice, tomatoes, water, salt, and pepper. Combine the ingredients and transfer them to a one and one-half-quart baking dish. Bake at 350 degrees for 20 minutes or until the rice is soft but not dry. Stir in the reserved bacon and serve hot or at room temperature.

Something else you're likely to encounter during mealtimes in Savannah is sweetened iced tea, which we call just plain ol' "sweet tea." Savannahians drink it year-round, and here's a good way to make a gallon-size pitcherful: Place three family-size tea bags in the basket of your automatic coffeemaker and brew up a full coffeepot of tea. Put about a cup of sugar in the pitcher and pour the hot tea on top. Stir it up and add a full coffeepot of water and stir again. When it cools, you've got sweet tea.

suggest you call ahead—this restaurant is one of our favorites, but it has a track record of changing its mind on what days it serves dinner (currently all week).

Spanky's Pizza Gallery & Saloon Inexpensive
317 East River Street
(912) 236-3009

308 Mall Way
(912) 355-3383

200 Governor Treutlen Road
Pooler
(912) 748-8188

1605 Strand
Tybee Island
(912) 786-5520
Ansley Williams, Alben Yarbrough, and Dusty Yarbrough opened the first Spanky's on River Street in 1976, intending to bring pizza to the area. They also served burgers and chicken sandwiches at the restaurant, which is housed in what had been a cotton warehouse. According to Williams, the chicken breasts used for the sandwiches were too large for the buns on which they were served, so the restaurateurs sliced off the excess chicken and, not wanting to be wasteful, battered and fried the strips of meat and sold them as "chicken fingers." Their concoction

was a hit with locals and has become a mainstay of eateries throughout southeast Georgia. The success of the River Street location led to the opening of Spanky's restaurants in other parts of the state and locally on the Southside near Oglethorpe Mall, in Pooler, and on Tybee Island (that one's called Spanky's Beachside). Williams and the Yarbroughs eventually went their separate ways, with Williams retaining ownership of the Spanky's on River Street and the Yarbroughs remaining involved with the others. Although the Spanky's restaurants have different owners, the menus are basically the same, with the chicken fingers, pizza, and burgers still featured. Another favorite of veteran customers are Spanky's Spuds, which are circular-sliced potatoes that are battered and fried. The restaurants are open daily for lunch and dinner.

Vinnie Van GoGo   Moderate
317 West Bryan Street
(912) 233-6394
www.vinnievangogo.com

Vinnie's serves pizza with real character—thin crust with fresh ingredients, including such options as spinach, artichoke, and broccoli, for dinner only. Experiment with pesto instead of regular sauce. A regular 14-inch pie is $9.00 to start, plus $1.50 for each ingredient. Dine in the cramped interior or at outside tables overlooking City Market (semi-enclosed when it's cold). Pizza is available by the slice, and one of those with the excellent spinach salad is an ample meal. Our personal favorite among the pizzas is feta, sun-dried tomato, and black olive. Beer is available. Get the wine list: Cork and screw-top are your options. Your most casual duds are probably too dressy for Vinnie's, but the food's tops. Cash only. Delivery via bicycle available downtown.

Walls' Barbecue   Inexpensive
515 East York Lane
(912) 232-9754

Ninety-five percent of the barbecue pork, fried chicken, deviled crabs, and other food sold at Walls' is taken out by customers. Walls' is essentially a building with a kitchen and counter on York Lane, which runs from Price to Houston Streets between York Street and Oglethorpe Avenue. If you want to eat in, there are three tables where you can sit. Walls' also offers fried fish, spare ribs, and vegetable plates, and all the dinners come with three sides from among red rice, potato salad, fries, cole slaw, and vegetables.

Margaret T. Weston, who runs Walls' along with her daughter, Teresa, says the business was started in the mid-1960s by her parents, Richard and Janie Walls, in a building in back of their cottage on York Street. "My daddy had a wood yard and he got tired of chopping wood, but he wanted security for my mother and me—he wanted us to be able to take care of ourselves." So the late Richard Walls started his barbecue business, choosing it, says Mrs. Weston with a smile, "because it was something he could get out of." Soon after the business opened, Walls began driving a taxicab, leaving Mrs. Walls and her daughter to do the cooking, and cook they have, much to the delight of Savannahians who love barbecue. Walls' is open for lunch and early dinner Thursday through Saturday.

ISLANDS

Basil's Pizza and Deli   Inexpensive
216 Johnny Mercer Boulevard
(912) 897-6400

This restaurant on Wilmington Island prides itself on being family operated (the name is derived from the Greek name of a son/grandson of the owners) and specializes in pizza and Mediterranean dishes. Among the combination pizzas are the Greek, eggplant Parmesan, and gyro varieties, and the menu includes Hellenic-inspired fare such as dolmades and spanakopita. Basil's also offers pasta, salads, and a broad array of sandwiches, and the pasta salad—made with bacon and broccoli—is as good as it gets. Basil's occupies a storefront in the Wilmington Island Shopping Center at the heart of the island.

Desposito's Seafood — Inexpensive
Macceo Drive
Thunderbolt
(912) 897-9963

On evenings when the weather's nice, Desposito's owner David Boone opens the windows of the enclosed porch of this little cinder-block and wood eatery at Thunderbolt. You can sit out there at tables covered with newspaper and eat boiled shrimp, crab legs, and steamed oysters as the breeze from the nearby Wilmington River wafts through the place.

Desposito's—which Walton Boone bought in late 1982 and son David took over in December 1996—also serves deviled crab; homemade chili, pecan pie, and potato salad; and the Lowcountry basket, which is filled with shrimp, corn on the cob, sausage, and the aforementioned potato salad. In addition to the porch, there's a dining room and a bar that serves beer and wine. Desposito's is open for dinner daily except Monday and for lunch on Friday, Saturday, and Sunday. MasterCard and Visa only are accepted. It's on the eastern side of the Wilmington River and north of U.S. Highway 80.

Driftaway Café — Moderate
7400 Skidaway Road
(912) 303-0999
www.driftawaycafe.com

We've been resisting the Driftaway Café for several years now, despite the recommendations of friends—the restaurant's popularity has outstripped its parking lot, and that intimidated us. We were finally lured inside by the promise that we could get really good fish tacos here. Now we can't stay away from the place, pea gravel parking lot or not. The Driftaway is a casual place, with covered and fan-equipped decks at front and back. The interior is cute without being cloying, with murals of local water scenes on the walls and a massive sculpture of a raging shark bursting through one wall. The best tables overlook the marsh at the rear, where you can see a real creek and a fake waterfall, with some kitschy statuary scattered around. On our first visit in really late summer, we enjoyed watching some really large snapping turtles in the creek and the butterflies feasting on the landscaping. But on to the food—the menu covers salads, sandwiches, and full entrees. It includes chicken and steak dishes, but we've found three favorites and an appetizer—all seafood—that meet our needs so well we haven't run rampant through the menu yet. The fish tacos ($10) are phenomenal: grouper strips flash fried in batter and served on flour tortillas with lettuce and some perfectly seasoned sauce. You can get the fish taco with grilled fish, too, but why mess with a good thing? Same goes for the "Full House Grouper Sandwich" ($11), a whopping plank of fish seasoned with remoulade sauce. The bread is completely superfluous, and the kitchen usually will hold it if you ask. For a more formal meal, we opt for the crispy scored flounder, which is flash fried and served with lots of a spicy apricot sauce. Our pet appetizer is crispy calamari ($8), and this is the only place we've ever found it that the texture wasn't rubbery enough to overwhelm the taste. Sides range from dressy (grilled asparagus) to down-home (homemade potato chips). There's a full bar and a large wine selection. Lunch and dinner seven days, 11:00 a.m. to 10:00 p.m. Monday through Thursday, and open to 11:00 p.m. on Friday and Saturday. Sunday brunch (heavy on egg dishes) starts at 10:00 a.m., and they close at 9:00 p.m. that day. Note that this place is in the Sandfly Community on the way to Skidaway Island.

Little Saigon — Moderate
4700-F US 80
(912) 897-1559

Savannah has a great many Asian restaurants, many of them quite acceptable but generally all tending to seem the same. Little Saigon is the happiest of exceptions. It evolved from an earlier Vietnamese/Chinese restaurant, and now serves Thai—the trendiest part of its menu—and Vietnamese, which to our way of thinking is a subtler and tastier side of the menu. This family-owned restaurant is one of those places you would never wind up at if a local didn't steer you that way. Little Saigon is in a nondescript strip shopping center, four lanes across from a Wal-Mart on the highway leading to the beach. Forget the unpromising-sounding location, because the offerings inside the sparkling clean restaurant are plenty promising. From the Thai options, diners can choose from a spiciness index of mild, medium, hot, and "Thai hot." (We love spicy food, but we've found that "medium" works just fine for us here—the staff gives solid guidance on the heat factor.) The menu has the classic Pahd Thai and a variety of curries. Our favorites, however, are among the simplest of the Vietnamese offerings: summer rolls, which are fresh chopped vegetables and shrimp (among other things) wrapped in rice paper, and the Vietnamese pork chop, which is grilled and seasoned and served sliced over jasmine rice. This restaurant has sisters: Saigon downtown and The King and I on the Southside.

Uncle Bubba's Oyster House   Moderate
104 Bryan Woods Road
(912) 897-6101
www.unclebubbasoysterhouse.com

Paula Deen, the star cook from the Food Network and The Lady and Sons Restaurant, is the figure behind this restaurant, which she opened with her brother, Bubba Hiers. Uncle Bubba's opened in 2004 in a renovated restaurant building on the marsh just off US 80, about halfway between town and the beach and visible from the highway. It features good marsh views and an extensive patio deck where food is served, weather permitting (and it usually does). The decor aims for a sort of retro-diner feel. It has also served as a filming site for Paula's party-themed series on the Food Network.

As you can probably tell from the name, they're big on seafood here. A signature dish is chargrilled oysters, which involve open flame, butter, and Parmesan cheese ($8 for a half dozen, $13 for a dozen). We can't vouch for those personally, however, because we haven't been able to resist the "Paula's Plate." These plates are filled with the homestyle cooking Deen serves up at her downtown restaurant, and are only available Sunday through Thursday—$9 for a classic meat-and-two-veg combo that varies day to day. Personally, we prefer Paula's cooking at Paula's other place, where you can go back for seconds, but it's a lot less hassle getting into Uncle Bubba's and the parking's free and available.

You'll recognize several of the Deen dishes on the menu, in fact. The restaurant serves both lunch and dinner daily, but we haven't noticed that much difference in the two menus. You'll find lots of crab, including a crab martini at dinner, which involves crab, asparagus, and tomato and whose only relation to the drink is the glass it comes in. Also count on fish, shrimp, and several non-seafood choices. You can drop $20 on an entree here if you like, but there are several viable selections at much more reasonable prices. Uncle Bubba's also serves fried dill pickles ($5), which are described as a Southern tradition. (If so, it's one we missed, but then again, we Southerners will fry anything.) They have a full bar (which we would have to utilize before eating fried dill pickles, but to each his own).

SOUTHSIDE/MIDTOWN

Barnes Restaurant   Moderate
5320 Waters Avenue
(912) 354-8745

4685 US 80 East
(912) 898-0220

The food here is predictable and it's family-friendly. The folks at the two Barnes restaurants pride themselves on the fact that everything from the barbecue sauce to the potato salad to the sweet iced tea is homemade. The sauce on Barnes's chopped pork and sliced beef barbecue is made according to a recipe developed by restaurant founder Nesbert Barnes and perfected over the years by his son, Hugh; it's spread on meat that's slow-cooked at low temperatures over oak and hickory wood. There's a step-by-step guide for making the tea, and an employee specifically designated to perform the task; if the tea maker is not present on a given day, the manager gets the job.

When Barnes opened in 1975, just south of where the existing building stands on Waters Avenue at 68th Street, it filled only take-out orders. A dining room was added three years later, and the existing restaurant opened in summer 1993. This Midtown eatery was renovated inside and out in 2004, with the interior given an "old Savannah" look and feel. The island restaurant went into operation two years later.

Today families, businesspeople, and retirees flock to Barnes for the barbecue and the tea. Chicken fingers, ribs, shrimp salad, and onion rings are other big sellers at both locations. Barnes serves lunch and dinner, and you're likely to encounter a line of customers waiting at the Waters Avenue restaurant if you get there around noon.

Bella's Italian Cafe   Moderate
4420 Habersham Street
(912) 354-4005
www.bellascafe.com

Located on Habersham Street between 60th and 61st Streets, Bella's is "where Savannah eats Italian," according to owner Joyce Shanks. She claims the manicotti at Bella's is the best south of Brooklyn, and she ought to know. She grew up in that New York borough, learning to cook manicotti and other Italian dishes in the kitchen of her grandmother, Bella. Joyce's manicotti is stuffed with a mixture of three cheeses, baked in marinara sauce, and topped with bubbling cheese. Her chicken Parmesan—a double chicken breast breaded, deep-fried, and baked with marinara and melted cheeses—is another popular entree, but we could make a meal of just Bella's breadsticks— yeast dough that's deep fried, tastes like doughnuts, and is served with marinara and herb butter.

Bella's, which has been at its existing site in Habersham Village shopping center since 1993 after a four-year stint at Savannah Mall, accommodates diners in cozy, family-oriented surroundings. The restaurant serves dinner seven days a week and lunch on weekdays. Beer and wine are available. Bella's doesn't take reservations, and it's a good idea to arrive early if you're dining on a weekend. There are only a few parking spaces in front of the restaurant but plenty of spots in the lot at the corner of Habersham and 61st. Bella's accepts major credit cards with the exception of Discover.

Carey Hilliard's Restaurant   Inexpensive
3316 Skidaway Road
(912) 354-7240

8410 Waters Avenue
(912) 355-2468

514 US 80
Garden City
(912) 964-5671

198 Pooler Parkway
Pooler
(912) 330-0700

5350 Highway 21
Garden City
(912) 963-0060

11111 Abercorn Street
(912) 925-3225

That there are six Carey Hilliard's in Savannah should tell you something about the popularity of these restaurants, which provide casual dining in an atmosphere geared toward families. Founder Carey Hilliard opened his first establishment in 1960 on Skidaway Road in what had been an A&W Root Beer stand. The drive-in, curb-service feature was retained, and all six restaurants offer it today. Order from your car, and you receive many of the amenities you would by dining inside, including china plates and silverware.

Barbecue has always been, and still is, a big seller at Carey Hilliard's, which serves lunch and dinner, but seafood dishes account for about half the orders these days. Among the favorites of customers are the fried shrimp, oysters, and deviled crabs. Seating at the restaurants averages 250. Beer and wine are available.

The Dawg House Grill   Inexpensive
6725 Waters Avenue
(912) 236-1557

If you've never experienced the off-the-wall enthusiasm that goes with college football, SEC style, you could get a taste of it here. The Dawg House Grill (and yes, Georgia bulldog fans do say it "Dawg") makes no secret of its allegiance to the University of Georgia Bulldogs—it's painted bright red and plays marching band renditions of football fight songs at the entrance. But you can't help but love a local restaurant that takes over what was a failed fast-food franchise and makes it work as a sit-down restaurant.

Argue about whether this is a sports bar or a restaurant. We call it a restaurant because we've eaten there, not drunk there. Suit yourself, however.

The menu here is classic bar food with mascot-themed names—dog bites are mini corn-dogs, and the "gator-hater" sandwich is really chicken and not gator. But the hamburgers are real hamburgers, and served in a variety of ways. We go the cheap route— rather than going for the fried green tomato appetizer and the hamburger as our entry, we order the fried green tomato burger and pick the tomatoes off for separate consumption. If it isn't fried here, it probably at least has melted cheese poured all over it—clearly the menu is geared toward young men capable of handling the calories. We asked about a dip listed on the menu once and the waiter started waxing poetic about a recipe that involved cheese, a gallon of sour cream, and a six-pack of Miller Lite. We skipped that.

In case you haven't figured this out, it is very casual. Open for lunch and dinner. Expect a bit of chaos if you show up during a game.

Elizabeth on Thirty-Seventh Street   Expensive
105 East 37th Street
(912) 236-5547
www.elizabethon37th.com

We knew this place attracted serious foodies, but did you know it also merited mention in the best seller *1,000 Places to See Before You Die*? It's also where locals celebrate and entertain to impress. This mansion-based restaurant produces a Southern regional menu that is hard to characterize, but sophisticated and appealing. (In other words, don't look for the overcooked or fried, flat qualities some folks consider regional cooking.) It makes the best of local offerings, but that does not mean you are faced with seafood selections only. Dress up and dig in for dinner daily from 6:00 to 10:00 p.m. Reservations are required.

Fiddlers Crab House and Oyster Barn   Moderate
7201 Hodgson Memorial Boulevard
(912) 351-2274
www.liveoakrestaurants.com

This big restaurant opened in 2007 as part of the local chain that includes several seafood restaurants on River Street and elsewhere. We were pleased to see it, since Savannah's Southside is oversupplied with chain eateries and a bit short on local ones. The rustic-looking building includes an off-the-roof water cascade that cools an outdoor patio, and a "moat" that should entertain the kiddies. Inside, the decor is rustic nautical, with walls made of old deck wood and tables with seashells buried in polyurethane. Check out the walls—they're a tribute to Savannah's family fishing and processing businesses, most of which are gone with the tide these days.

Look here for simple seafood dishes—not particularly fancy, creative, or gourmet stuff, but plain, affordable, and basically good. Prices and the interesting surroundings make this a good family location (although there is a full bar and a band on weekend nights). We usually opt for the grilled grouper Caesar salad (market price). There are some steak and seafood options for those averse to seafood.

Hirano's Restaurant
Inexpensive–Moderate
4426 Habersham Street
(912) 353-8337

13015 Abercorn Street
(912) 961-0770

Japanese cuisine became a major hit in Savannah with the opening of this small storefront restaurant on Habersham Street. Folks stand in line for a chance to order simple, fresh food from a limited menu. Large servings and reasonable prices are hallmarks here. The teriyaki chicken, served with rice and salad, runs less than $5, so if you pick your items carefully, this can be a budget meal as well as a real treat. Combination plates carry higher prices.

The food is prepared at open griddles behind the counter—this is not one of the showy knife-twirling restaurants. If you are eager to get started at the Habersham site, opt for a seat at the counter overlooking the cooking. Those seats come open more quickly than the small stock of tables. The Habersham location has a separate sushi bar, but call ahead if you are interested—it tends to keep shorter hours. Both the Hirano's serve a delicious California roll of avocado and cooked crab rolled in rice for those who are wary of traditional sushi.

Johnny Harris Restaurant
Moderate
1651 East Victory Drive
(912) 354-7810

Stepping into the main dining room at Johnny Harris is like fox-trotting back into the late 1930s and the 1940s, when this establishment was an elegant supper club on the outskirts of Savannah. The bandstand that occupied the middle of the floor is gone, but the room retains the charm of that bygone era. Remaining from those good old days are the dark wood paneling of the Old English decor and a 30-foot-high ceiling adorned for a starry, night-sky effect.

Perhaps the influx of thousands of college students has something to do with it, but area restaurants are now more likely to offer vegetarian, and even vegan, options on their menus. But if the menu doesn't actually use the word vegetarian, you might want to ask—Southern cooks traditionally use "side meat" such as salt pork or ham hocks as seasoning in vegetables.

You can also still slip into one of the booths lining the perimeter of the oval-shaped room and place an order by pushing a service button that illuminates a green light overhead.

The restaurant has been a favorite of Savannahians for decades, and many patrons bring their grandchildren and great-grandchildren so they can experience the atmosphere, service, and food—in particular the barbecue, fried chicken, prime rib, and crabmeat au gratin (meat of the crab's claw folded in a cream and cheese sauce). Johnny Harris is the oldest restaurant in Savannah and one of the oldest in Georgia, but you'll notice it's not in the Historic Downtown. It's in Midtown, on Victory Drive just east of Bee Road. That intersection is where the original restaurant was built in 1924 by a Southerner from out of town named Johnny Harris; the original wooden building was torn down, and the brick structure that houses the existing restaurant was built in 1936. Johnny Harris died in 1942, and the restaurant has been run by the Donaldson family of Savannah ever since.

Johnny Harris has seating under one roof for 275 people in the main room, the adjacent cafe area, a lounge with a full-service bar, and a banquet room that can accommodate up to 60. Smoking is allowed in the cafe area and lounge but prohibited in the main room. Johnny Harris serves lunch and dinner Monday though Saturday and takes but does not require reservations.

If you get the chance, stroll through the

restaurant's back hallways and take a gander at more than 60 framed menus hanging on the walls. They bear the autographs of well-known entertainers, politicians, and sports figures who have eaten at Johnny Harris. The first to scribble his signature was the late comedian Red Skelton; among the most recent was actor and filmmaker Clint Eastwood. You might also consider purchasing some of the restaurant's barbecue sauce to take home with you. It's bottled hot and sold at Johnny Harris and other outlets in Georgia, South Carolina, and Florida, and it is shipped worldwide via mail order.

The King and I   Moderate
798 Hodgson Memorial Boulevard
(912) 355-2100

This Thai restaurant is open for lunch and dinner. The owners have done a good job of transforming a strip mall's former coffee shop into an exotic but understated little haven for foodies in search of something different. A large marine aquarium well stocked with exotic fish sets the tone. The menu is pure Thai, with no other ethnic options and no weasel-out Americanized dishes either, so you might want to try somewhere else if you are dining with the timid. But on the other hand, you can order the degree of spiciness to your taste. The entrees divide into basically two groups—those served with Asian noodles and those served with basmati rice. We'd advise newcomers to focus on the dishes served with rice, as the noodles strike us as an acquired taste. And, if possible, save room for the fried bananas with ice cream and mango sauce (sharing recommended).

Larry's Restaurant   Inexpensive
3000 Skidaway Road
(912) 355-8272

Eat your vegetables at Larry's. You'll select three when you order an entree from the luncheon menu, which changes daily. (For information on what's cooking, call the menu line at 912-355-5821.) Among the favorite choices are the sweet potato soufflé, the squash casserole, and the turnip greens, and they go just fine with the fried chicken, beef stew, or chicken and dumplings. There's plenty more to choose from at this eatery, which has been serving breakfast and lunch on Skidaway Road a couple of blocks south of Victory Drive since 1981.

Larry's is a hangout of locals—one of those places where the parking lot is usually filled with vehicles (many of them pickup trucks), and the waitresses call customers by name. The food and atmosphere aren't fancy, but the home-style grub is good, plentiful, and inexpensive, and the air hums with the conversation of folks talking with longtime cronies or renewing old acquaintances. Larry's, which seats 150, is closed on weekends.

Rancho Alegre   Inexpensive
44 Posey Street
(912) 691-0110

Rancho Alegre is our nominee for Savannah's biggest culinary surprise. After all, who would expect to find a restaurant tucked away just off Abercorn Street near the eastern end of the Hunter Army Airfield runway, amid auto-repair shops and wholesale houses—one that serves Cuban cuisine, no less. But there it is, occupying what was once a residence before the commercialization spawned by nearby Oglethorpe Mall caught up with it. This rancho serves a variety of exotic-sounding dishes featuring chicken, beef, pork, and seafood, such as pollo a la Juliana (pepper chicken strips), ropa vieja (shredded beef slowly cooked in Creole sauce), masas de cerdo fritas (fried pork chunks), and camarones al ajilio (garlic shrimp). Most entries are accompanied by rice, beans, and sweet plantains. We're betting this is also one of few places in town where you can get Cuban coffee, flan, and fried yucca. The Rancho Alegre serves lunch and dinner Monday through Saturday. Posey Street, by the way, runs between Abercorn and White Bluff Road and is just south of Eisenhower Drive.

Sweet Potatoes   Inexpensive
6825 Waters Avenue
(912) 352-3434

This casual restaurant, which offers lunch and

dinner, is the downscale relative of the pricier and fancier Toucan Cafe (also described in this chapter)—but the food is still outstanding. The decor is simple and consists of bright paint and simple artwork. Basic meat and vegetables, cooked Southern style, are the mainstays here. There's a rotating list of daily specials, but you can count on some standard dishes as well. We recommend the vegetable plates, for which you select up to four dishes, simply because it is so hard to find restaurants that offer good selections of vegetables and cook them properly. Consider the dilled lima beans or the collards. (Always order collards in a restaurant: They take hours to fix properly and the smell lingers in the house.) True to its name, the restaurant offers some variant of a sweet potato dish every day— baked sweet potatoes, sweet potato soufflé, mashed sweet potatoes, even sweet potato salad. Beware, however, of the occasional offering of something called Wisconsin-style sweet potatoes—they are proof of the fact that while you can combine sweet potatoes and cheddar cheese, you really shouldn't.

Taste of India   Moderate
401 Mall Boulevard
(912) 356-1020
Savannah has a substantial Indian community, including college professors, physicians, hoteliers, and operators of retail shops. As a result, the city has a small handful of Indian restaurants. Our favorite is Taste of India. The restaurant's quarters formerly housed a barbecue restaurant, so there's something just a little incongruous about lush Indian decor against a knotty pine background. But instead of appearing overdone, the overall effect is one of exotic luxuriance.

We recommend a strategic approach. Plan plenty of time and gather up as large a group as you can. That way, each of you can order an appetizer and an entree, then taste them all. The menu is varied, with vegetarian dishes heavily represented. You can also choose from chicken, lamb, goat, and seafood entrees.

On the appetizer side, we recommend pau bhaji, a paste of mashed vegetables in garlic sauce that you eat on bread, or chicken samosa, a spiced meat pastry. For entrees, dishes we've personally experienced and can recommend include lamb sagwala, which resembles a lamb stew in a creamy spinach base. Less-adventurous souls can safely opt for the chicken curry. The staff offers options on how spicy you want your chosen dish to turn out. Some of the most intriguing-sounding items on the menu (which we have never mustered the nerve to try) are the yogurt-based drinks and what it describes as "Coca-Cola products imported from India," including Rim Zim and Thums Up.

Taste of India is open for lunch on weekdays, when it serves from a buffet, and for dinner seven days a week. It has a full bar.

Toucan Cafe   Moderate
531 Stephenson Avenue
(912) 352-2233
www.toucancafe.com
Nestled in the woods off Stephenson Avenue, the Toucan Cafe combines eclectic food, an interior that pulsates with the high-impact colors of the tropics, and an exterior that has a classic Mediterranean look. The cuisine reflects the influences of several exotic cultures—Jamaican jerk chicken and Jamaican jerk tilapia, both of which are served with black beans and mango salsa; chicken farfalle and shrimp farfalle, both served in a basil cream with bow-tie pasta; and Hellenic stuffed chicken, made with spinach and feta cheese, served over rice, and topped with marinated baby peas. Those are just a few of the dishes offered by owners Steve and Nancy Magulias who, in late 1998, moved the cafe to newly built quarters on Stephenson from a small storefront in nearby Eisenhower Plaza where the Toucan had been located since 1994.

The Toucan Cafe serves dinner and lunch Monday through Saturday; reservations aren't required but will be accepted for parties of five or more.

ℹ️ You can take care of some of your souvenir shopping while you dine out. Many restaurants sell sauces featured in their prize dishes or cookbooks drawing from their menu.

Tubby's Tank House   Moderate
2909 River Drive
Thunderbolt
(912) 354-9040

115 East River Street
(912) 233-0770
www.tubbystankhouse.com

Tubby's specializes in fresh seafood, much of it caught by part-owner Stan "Tubby" Strickland, a sport fisherman with a knack for hauling in mahimahi, grouper, tuna, and wahoo. In fact, says fellow owner Ansley Williams, Tubby's is a seafood restaurant because of Strickland's ability as an angler. Williams says that in 1994 when he, Strickland, and managing partner Ray Clark decided to start a new restaurant, they settled on opening a seafood place because Strickland "was catching so much fish we needed a place to distribute it." The result was Tubby's, a rustic-looking restaurant perched on the bluff at Thunderbolt.

In addition to the aforementioned sports fish, Tubby's serves shrimp, scallops, oysters, and Tubby's Tank Out, a seafood platter that, according to Williams, "is more than one human can eat." Burgers, chicken, and a variety of salads are available for those not inclined toward eating fish.

Tubby's serves lunch and dinner seven days a week, hosts oyster roasts on Thursday nights during the winter and Thursday sunset parties in the summer, and offers dancing in the back room on Thursday, Friday, and Saturday nights. A second Tubby's opened on River Street in February 1998. The menu at the downtown restaurant is similar to that of the original establishment, and the River Street location is also open for lunch and dinner each day of the week. Live entertainment is provided at night.

WEST CHATHAM

Love's Seafood Restaurant   Moderate
6817 Basin Road
(912) 925-3616

Love's is in southwest Chatham County 14 miles from the Historic Downtown, but city dwellers are more than happy to make the ride to this restaurant on the banks of the serene Ogeechee River. A major reason for the pilgrimages is Love's fried catfish, 90 percent of it caught in the river and all of it battered with a fine cracker meal that makes it so light it seems to float off the plate. Besides, says Fulton Love, who runs the restaurant with his wife, Donna, you can get there from downtown in 15 minutes if you take Interstate 16, Interstate 95, and Highway 204 to U.S. Highway 17 and the Chatham-Bryan County line.

The restaurant is where the US 17 bridge crosses the river, and has been there since 1949, when it was started as a fishing camp by Fulton's folks, O. F. and Thelma. If you've watched the movie *Forrest Gump*—and who hasn't?—you've seen the bridge and the restaurant in the scene where Forrest and his girlfriend part company. You can see the beautiful Ogeechee from about 250 of the 304 seats at Love's, but the best views are from the porch, which seats 50.

Love's serves steak and chicken fingers in an atmosphere that's rustic but upscale; however, the main draws here are the catfish and seafood, in particular the fried shrimp, shrimp and flounder stuffed with crabmeat, and the seafood fettuccine. Beer, wine, and mixed drinks are available.

Love's, which serves about 600 pounds of catfish a week and is probably the oldest catfish restaurant in Georgia, takes reservations for parties of 12 or more. It's open Tuesday through Saturday for dinner and Sunday for lunch and dinner; it's closed on Monday when the owners are, as they put it, "gone fishing."

Lovezzola's Pizza Restaurant   Inexpensive
320 US 80 East
Pooler
(912) 748-6414
www.lovezzolas.com

Pizza fans, rejoice! There is real pizza, as opposed to the franchise mass-production type, south of the Mason-Dixon Line. Paul Lovezzola has been hand throwing the dough for New York–style pizza at his restaurant for the past 19 years. This transplanted New Yorker hasn't lost his accent or his taste for slow-cooked sauces and individually prepared pizzas in those years.

Sit in his casual, family-style dining room at a table with red-and-white checked plastic tablecloths, and he'll point out his ancestral hometown on the map of Italy featured on the place mats. He serves up his pizza with the usual selection of toppings and offers pasta dishes, submarine sandwiches, and a salad bar as well.

His regulars include not only travelers along I-95 (he's just off exit 102) and expatriate Northerners but also a solid group of Southern converts who have been won over to the concept of pizza as a real food.

Pooler is one of Chatham County's municipalities on its western side, easy to find because it is close to the interstate and worth the drive for a taste of what pizza was before it became fast food. Takeouts are available, as is delivery in a limited area that includes the motels clustered around the Pooler exit off I-95.

NIGHTLIFE

After a day spent beaching, boating, shopping, eating, fishing, touring, visiting museums, checking out aged graveyards, and getting acclimated to the local heat and humidity, what do you do when the sun goes down? After an especially active tourist day, many folks would just opt to turn in early. Don't worry, though: You'll recover before your stay is over, and you'll want to sample Savannah's nightlife.

Savannah's traditional nightlife is an at-home thing. We have perfected the art of hospitality and party giving here, and the night's best food, drink, and entertainment is probably being served up in someone's backyard, on their dock, or in their living room. If you have friends, family, or savvy business acquaintances in town, chances are good you'll get a chance to see what we mean.

That doesn't mean you're out of luck if you don't have an invitation, however. Savannah has plenty of nightspots to entertain guests, and locals turn out too when they're tired of the homegrown party thing. The bar and entertainment scene falls into three general categories: River Street, a restored area along the Savannah River that was refurbished with just this sort of thing in mind; City Market, a restored quadrant of the Historic Downtown that's heavy on clubs and bars as well as shops; and a variety of watering holes and entertainment sites scattered along routes to the south of the city (the Southside, in local parlance).

If you don't have something very specific in mind (say, jazz or a sports bar), our advice is to follow your ear, literally. Visitors will fare better on River Street and in City Market, where there are lots of nightspots clustered together. You can follow the music you hear spilling out the doors and wander conve-niently from site to site. We're not scoffing at the Southside offerings: It's just that the nightspots there are more scattered, making it harder for someone unfamiliar with the terrain to get around.

Which brings us to the question of alcohol and the law. Savannah's folklore stresses the city's hard-drinking reputation, with tales that the town was never dry, even during Prohibition (which lingered long in Georgia, where some counties are still dry). You'll probably get tired of locals telling you the favorite question posed to a newcomer is, "What do you drink?"

Believe all this if you want to, but don't base your actions on it. Local law enforcement aggressively pursues alcohol offenses. Drivers can face charges with a blood-alcohol level of .08 percent, and unless you have a medical lab in your backseat, don't try to guess how many drinks it takes an individual to reach that level. Remember that the law prohibits open containers with alcohol in vehicles.

The law provides "zero tolerance" for alcohol levels in those younger than the legal drinking age of 21. In addition to drunken-driving laws that the Georgia General Assembly has tightened up in recent years, however, Savannah offers its own, city-specific reasons for designating a nondrinking driver, calling a cab, or drinking near where you are staying. Most of our tourist nightspots are in an area of narrow, often one-way, streets. Also, streets throughout the city tend to be lined with trees—either unyielding live oaks of massive girth or palm trees that are easily uprooted or snapped by collisions.

Don't be surprised (or flattered) to find yourself carded in many drinking establishments. Savannah has a large college and military population, and many soldiers and students are not of legal drinking age. With their licenses at stake, bars and restaurants tend to be thorough on the question of age. Although bars can stay open until 3:00 a.m., many of them pack it in early on slow nights, especially through the week.

Also note that city ordinances prohibit open bottles or cans on the street, but (as of this writing) if you want to wander out of a River Street watering hole or a City Market club, most places are glad to provide you with a plastic or foam cup. This practice, pretty unusual based on our experience with other cities, is under hostile scrutiny from Savannah City Council, however, so check with your bartender before you wander out with a cup of beer in case things have changed. (Remember, this go-cup leniency is in the city of Savannah, not the other municipalities.)

We've spent a lot of space covering alcohol, but we don't mean to give you the impression that all nightlife has to do with booze. We've included coffeehouses, which are growing in popularity, as well as movies and other activities. Also, Savannah is home to an active Alcoholics Anonymous family: If you want to catch a meeting and talk firsthand about alcohol-free nightlife in Savannah, call (912) 354-0993 for the extensive schedule.

The bars listed here are a sampling, but we think we've included at least something for everyone.

BARS

Churchill's Pub & Restaurant
13 West Bay Street
(912) 232-8501
www.thebritishpub.com
An after-hours kitchen fire drove this little bit of England out of its original home several years ago, but it's back in new (well, not new, but different) and expanded quarters. The massive carved mahogany bar will make you feel manor born! Downstairs, there are pool tables and dartboards. All in all, it's a nice, friendly place to have a drink, and the management is proud to point out that it's British owned.

i Dressed up for an evening on River Street? You won't want to risk cobblestones in dressy shoes, so if you park above the street—as you probably will have to—take the municipal elevator down to the river level. It is tucked between City Hall and the Hyatt Regency Savannah Hotel.

Churchill's is also a restaurant serving dinner, including such British fare as bangers and mash or roast beef with Yorkshire pudding. The menu also includes more conventional items such as fish dishes and sandwiches. We're not knocking the food, but we didn't have a problem determining to put this entry among the bars instead of among the restaurants. They claim to have 20 beers on tap (we didn't count, but there's obviously no shortage). Churchill's opens at 5:00 p.m. Sunday through Friday and at noon on Saturday.

Coach's Corner
3016 East Victory Drive
(912) 352-2933
The sports bar has become an American institution. Coach's Corner is a good example. More televised sports than you thought the airwaves could provide are on the multiple TV sets here. There's a full bar, but beer's the main drink of choice. A limited food menu is available, and we have friends who swear by the wings. Dress is casual, needless to say. Come by the Victory Drive site—it's in Thunderbolt, on the way to and from the beach—during October of a good season for the Atlanta Braves, and you can catch a giant motorized tomahawk chopping away, backed up by an occasional live chopper.

Crystal Beer Parlor
301 West Jones Street
(912) 443-9200
www.crystalbeerparlor.net
Of course there's a bar here, and of course it serves beer. But this is primarily a restaurant, a revival of an old Savannah favorite that

serves the best crab stew in town. Why are we putting it here in the listings of bars? Not just because of the name, but because of the entertainment. The Crystal Beer Parlor boasts live Dixieland jazz with the "Beer Parlor Ramblers" on Fridays, beginning around 7:30 p.m. This style of music is one of those you either love or hate, but if you fall in the "love" category, this band is a top performer. And if the music isn't to your taste, you can always sit in the back. There's no cover, and the restaurant (which serves both lunch and dinner) has its own parking lot.

Kevin Barry's Irish Pub
117 West River Street
(912) 233-9626
www.kevinbarrys.com

Savannah prides itself on its Irish heritage, not just during the elaborate St. Patrick's Day observance, but year-round. Just check out this pub. The stone-walled setting is dark and atmospheric, brightened considerably by a constantly changing program of authentic Irish performers every night (although we suggest calling ahead if this is essential to your evening; we've seen the schedule shift around a bit over the years). Count on acceptable food (including such Irish fare as potato soup and corned beef and cabbage), standard drinks, and an impressive collection of bottled and draft beers and ales. There's even a small gift shop for Irish goods. Brush up on your Irish history (and learn who the real Kevin Barry was) by reading the captions to the framed photos of figures who were either historic freedom fighters or long-dead terrorists, depending on your outlook.

Midnight Sun
Westin Savannah Harbor Resort
1 Resort Drive
Hutchinson Island
(912) 201-2000
www.westinsavannah.com

The Midnight Sun is the bar inside Savannah's Westin Savannah Harbor Resort, and it was designed with both local color and the view in mind. From within this clublike atmosphere, you can look out on both the hotel pool and the Savannah River, with River Street and Savannah's skyline beyond it. The name comes from a song by Savannah's favorite son, lyricist Johnny Mercer. So do the names of many of the drinks, and if the song title comes with a color, you'll find the drink color coordinated. (See what we mean by local color?) They even dub the martinis here "Mercertinis." The bar is open to the general public, not just hotel guests, and it adds another dimension to a River Street outing to take the ferry (hey, it's free!) across to enjoy the ambience and view Savannah from an angle few but sailors have enjoyed until recently.

Moon River Brew Pub
21 West Bay Street
(912) 447-0943
www.moonriverbrewing.com

This brewpub is Savannah's only on-premises microbrewery. We debated whether to list this one as a restaurant or a nightspot. On the one hand, they serve both lunch and dinner, and it's a lot more serious than typical bar munchies—oysters with pecan pesto and chicken walnut enchiladas, for example. Or there's the latest cross-cultural experiment—Bombay turkey mini burgers, which is a small patty of ground grilled turkey on a roll with bright yellow curry sauce. (We liked it but it was messy.) On the other hand, if made-on-the-premises beer is its reason for being, it's a nightspot, eh? Whichever side of the debate you agree with, know that you can get up to nine different (varying seasonally) fresh microbrews here in Imperial pints and half pints. Hours are 11:00 a.m. to 11:00 p.m. (except they don't close until 1:00 a.m. on weekend nights) and 10:00 p.m. on Sunday. The daily happy hour is 4:00 to 7:00 p.m.

Pinkie Master's Lounge
318 Drayton Street
(912) 238-0447

This modest neighborhood watering hole is legendary in Savannah as a political bar. Jour-

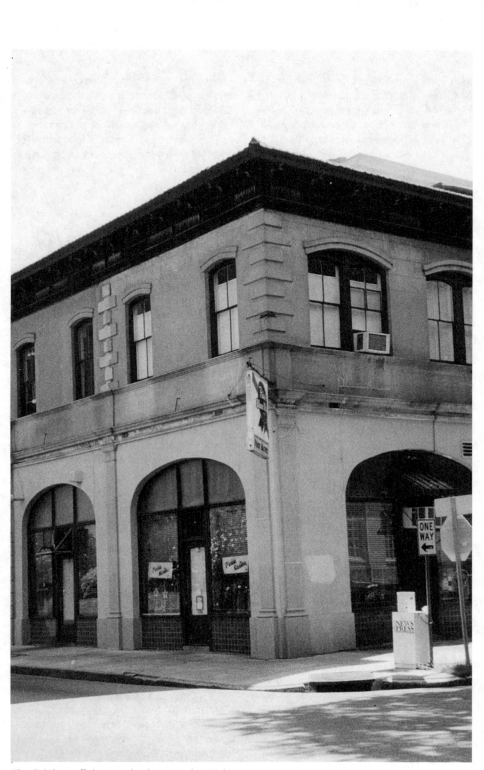

The slightly scruffy but popular downtown bar, Pinkie Master's. BETTY DARBY

i If you are invited for an evening at one of Savannah's several private clubs, be sure to ask your host or hostess about the dress code. Some have stringent prohibitions against women wearing pants, no matter how dressy.

nalists once plied local sources with alcohol here; Jimmy Carter (yes, that Jimmy Carter) once gave a speech standing on the bar. What you'll find today is a small bar where regulars talk back to the television set. There's an eclectic jukebox, darts, and a few game machines, along with the beer and the booze. We have friends who swear by this place, and you can't say it doesn't have plenty of atmosphere: Christmas decorations that never come down, a stuffed crow (at least we hope it's stuffed—maybe it's just dead), a rogue's gallery of politician's photos, and a soft-focus nude painting about which any of the regulars is willing to tell you lies. Drinks are cheap, the air is thick, and there's a sign above the bar reading TIPPING IS NOT A CITY IN CHINA. Looking back over this, we sound like we're running the place down, so we better 'fess up that we occasionally go here even when we aren't researching this book's various editions, and it's always interesting. There's a lot to be said for a place that refuses to gloss up for tourists.

Savannah Smiles
314 Williamson Street
(912) 527-6453

Savannah Smiles brought something different to the Savannah night scene. It features "Rock 'n' Roll dueling pianos" in an audience participation format that is a mix of rock 'n' roll standards and light comedy (with food 'n' drink in addition, of course). The show starts at 9:00 p.m., and the bar opens around 7:00 p.m. For ages 21 and up. Okay, so it's a bit hokey, but you're on vacation and you're never going to see these people again any-

way, so have fun. Finding it can be a bit of a challenge—Savannah Smiles is sandwiched between West Bay Street and River Street, sort of behind the Quality Inn, and chances are you won't be able to find a local who ever heard of Williamson Street. Closed Monday and Tuesday.

Vu Lounge
2 West Bay Street
(912) 238-1234

Before or after a nice dinner at one of the classier River Street restaurants, you may not be in the mood to nightcap it at one of the street's sing-along suds pubs. This is a nice alternative—a dressier place for a drink. The decor is upscale and subtle, the drinks are fine, and there's usually an inoffensive and unobtrusive musical lounge act. The whole thing would fall into the "very nice but forgettable" category if not for the view (hence the name). This bar is inside the Hyatt Regency Savannah (see our Hotels and Motels chapter) and has glass walls overlooking the Savannah River (literally—this portion of the hotel overhangs River Street). If you are lucky (or determined enough to stay put for a while), you'll get to see one of the giant container ships headed to or from the port upriver. Granted, you can see them from the street, too, but from the Vu's vantage point, you're more on eye level with the oceangoing giants. This lounge, formerly called M.D.'s, was remodeled extensively in 2005 and now includes an outdoor terrace.

Wet Willie's
101 East River Street
(912) 233-5650

This high-volume River Street bar caters to younger drinkers. The drinks are frozen concoctions with names like the infamous spring break potion, Sex on the Beach. Beware! Grain alcohol gives a single drink here the punch of at least two conventional alcoholic beverages. There's a light food menu, a small dance floor, and lots of loud recorded music.

Gallery Espresso is a popular coffee shop and art gallery. BETTY DARBY

BILLIARDS

B&B Billiards
411 West Congress Street
(912) 233-7116
On the fringe of City Market, this is a popular spot to shoot some pool and hang out with friends. Look for a mix of students, middle-aged locals, and the occasional tourist.

Capone's
1100 Eisenhower Drive
(912) 354-4848
This suburban pool parlor is also a bar and restaurant, and its location next to a shopping center multiplex makes it a good place to kill time before or after a movie. If you want to do any serious playing on weekends, arrive before 9:00 p.m.— that's when the wait for tables (there are 17 of them) starts to mount up. Open afternoons and evenings; hours vary.

COFFEEHOUSES

The coffeehouse boom has hit Savannah, and new venues seem to be springing up overnight. Here are two to get you going. Starbucks is located downtown at Broughton and Bull Streets (as well as in suburban shopping centers); we figure you know what to expect there.

Gallery Espresso
234 Bull Street
(912) 233-5348
www.galleryespresso.com
This is one of the city's first (and our personal favorite) on the coffeehouse scene. Coffee, both plain and in its multiple new forms, is augmented by a menu of baked goods and sandwiches, even wine. There's an occasional poetry reading or casual performance. The walls are home to displays by local artists,

Close-up

Club One and Lady Chablis: Anything but a Drag

In a city as inherently conservative as Savannah, you wouldn't expect tourism and the gay nightlife scene to intersect. You would be wrong.

Club One Jefferson has been the most prominent social setting, under various names, for Savannah's out-of-the-closet gay community since the 1980s. Its dance and performance scene had attracted occasional bolder and curious straights, but for the most part, Club One was a world unto itself. The Lady Chablis changed all that.

The flamboyant drag queen (is there any other kind?) caught the eye of author John Berendt when he was writing the book that would become the phenomenal best seller *Midnight in the Garden of Good and Evil*. The self-titled "Grand Empress of Savannah" is featured prominently therein. That alone was enough to make the performer famous, but then she went on to play herself in the movie version.

As the cult following for The Book grew, its readers flocked to Savannah. They wanted to gawk at The Book's houses, tour The Book's cemetery, and buy The Book trinkets. Most particularly, they wanted to get a look at The Lady Chablis.

And that presented the folks at Club One with a dilemma: How could they tap into that market without scaring the tourists back to Peoria, while at the same time keeping the flood of Book fanciers from displacing their regular clientele? Fortunately, they've come up with a smooth compromise. When Chablis is in town, they put on an earlier, somewhat tamer version of her show, reserving the stronger material for the later shows. It works well: Tourists get a sample of the strong stuff without a full dose, and the regular customers do not find their entertainment diluted, since the club's gay scene doesn't get moving until later anyway. Actually, the crowd has changed since this phenomenon began, and you're likely to find a mix of gays and straights at the bar and on the dance floor.

Don't misinterpret us here. Even though the early show (8:00 p.m. is early) is milder, it isn't mild. If you don't understand what a drag show is or are not at peace with the concept, don't go. Don't go if you can't take earthy language. Skip it if you feel too nervous, although we went to the early show with a group of friends (first-timers all) and didn't feel uncomfortable at all once we got there.

Chablis no longer lives in Savannah, but she was booked for 14 shows at Club One in 2007. The act is a big enough draw to rate its own page and multi-

and the exhibits have grown in quality and importance over the years. It's usually open until 1:00 a.m. Cozy and a good people-watching spot: The outdoor tables are particularly popular when the weather allows. Bring your laptop.

The Sentient Bean
13 East Park Avenue
(912) 232-4447
www.sentientbean.com
A friend once told us The Sentient Bean is a little piece of New York transplanted to Savan-

ple mentions on the club's website, www.clubone-online.com. The show bar is upstairs, and it's perfectly adequate but not particularly luxurious. It's also small. There are small tables on the front and along the sides and several rows of seats. Don't fret if you don't get a front seat—the place is small enough for you to see from all angles. In fact, if you're male, don't sit down front at all, unless you're willing to be flirted with by the performers. You'll have to fetch your own drinks from the bar on the upstairs level. Check the speaker location before you sit down: The room is small, but the speakers are big.

A drag show consists of female impersonators in drop-dead glamorous gowns and jewelry, dancing and lip-synching to recorded music. The show we caught featured one performer who was convincing as a beautiful woman, one performer who was convincing as an attractive woman who was trying very hard, one performer who was convincing as a homely but brave woman, and two others who were pretty unconvincing. The Lady Chablis emcees when she is there and performs several numbers. She also explains to the audience that they can come down front and tip performers if they wish. Bring folding money if you want to try that and don't worry: For the early show at least, it's a modest hand-to-hand exchange instead of the risque version you probably imagined (besides, the performers are wearing more clothes than the audience).

At the conclusion of the early show, Chablis comes back out to sign autographs, so bring your copy of The Book or Chablis' own book, *Hiding My Candy*.

Club One Jefferson has shows every weekend. Other performers vary, but drag shows are staples, along with the occasional beauty pageant or striptease act. In fall 2007, the weekend shows were the house troupe in "Queens of the Silver Screen." Normal cover is $6 to $10. Chablis tickets are now going for $25 a show, but be aware ticket prices will vary with the act.

Elsewhere in Club One Jefferson, you'll find multiple dance floors, full restaurant service, and a full bar. Dance music downstairs is Top 40, while the main level has techno and house music.

Pretty much anything goes by way of dress, but it's predominately casual. The club takes major credit cards and has an ATM on-site. Club One's at 1 Jefferson Street, just off Bay Street at the edge of City Market. It's rare in that it is open seven days a week. Hours are 5:00 p.m. to 3:00 a.m., closing an hour earlier on Sunday.

nah. We don't know about that, but we do know that if political advocacy has a center in Savannah, this must be it. Of course it serves coffee (fair trade and organic, to boot) and light food, but that's the least of it. It hosts live music, film screenings, poetry slams, speeches, classes, and what have you. The schedule stays pretty full, and attendance can be pretty good, too. You might want to drop by just to read the flyers on the walls to keep up with events geared toward the young, the liberal, and/or the involved. There is both

A walk on the beach can be a romantic conclusion to an evening out. Stroll out onto the Tybee Pier and Pavilion, lean against the rail, and watch the moon rise out of the Atlantic Ocean.

indoor and outdoor seating. The Sentient Bean is next door to Brighter Day, Savannah's oldest organic food store, and at the north end of Forsyth Park.

MOVIES

Savannah has typical movie offerings for a city its size, nothing more and nothing less. The blockbusters and major releases open here the same weekends they open everywhere else, but you may have to wait longer (or even until video) to catch, say, the Sundance winners or other non-mainstream fare. Our favorite is the Victory Stadium 9, the newest multiplex and currently the one doing the best job of cleanliness, upkeep, and enforcing civility.

Savannah has 48 movie screens scattered among 5 multiplexes and 1 small 2-screen independent. If that sounds like a lot of screens, don't get excited: Duplication eats up a lot of them. The daily newspaper has showtimes, but we've saved ourselves disappointment more than once by calling the recorded message to double-check. You'll find those numbers in the listings that follow. Diversions, the entertainment section that appears in Thursday's *Morning News*, contains a good little sketch map to help locate the theaters, all of which are outside the Historic Downtown. Ticket prices don't vary by more than a quarter or so—expect to pay in the range of $8.50 for a primetime adult ticket. Child, senior, and matinee tickets are available at discounts. Theaters offer same-day advance purchase options, and the newer ones even let you buy a day ahead and with credit cards. Most screens include stadium seating, meaning auditorium seating that is pitched so that you can see over the person

in front of you. They've also upscaled their amenities and gussied up the snack bars.

Carmike Cinema 10
(10 screens)
511 Stephenson Avenue
(912) 353-8683

Eisenhower Cinemas
(6 screens)
1100 Eisenhower Drive
(912) 352-3533

Regal Cinemas Savannah 10
(10 screens)
1132 Shawnee Avenue
(912) 927-7700

Victory Stadium 9
(9 screens)
1901 East Victory Drive
(912) 355-5000

Westside Cinemas
(2 screens)
403 U.S. Highway 80
Garden City
(912) 966-9101

Wynnsong 11
(11 screens)
1150 Shawnee Street
(912) 920-1227

There are a few other movie options, but they will require some checking on your part and some luck as far as scheduling. The Psychotronic Film Society shows "bizarre and otherwise unavailable" films at least once a month at The Sentient Bean, 13 East Park Avenue (see the schedule at www.sentient bean.com). The Lucas Theatre, a restored movie palace in the Historic District that primarily hosts touring shows and concerts, periodically runs movies, usually on a theme: holiday movies, for example, or movies made in Savannah. Savannah College of Art and Design, better known locally as SCAD, operates Trustees Theatre on Broughton Street i Planning on catching a popular movie on a weekend night? Swing by the theater during the day and get your same-day tickets in advance to ensure you won't be disappointed. All the local theaters have this service.

and occasionally shows movies that have become campus standards or are film show entries. SCAD also hosts an annual film festival in that theater, showcasing some genuinely avant-garde stuff.

GAMBLING

Diamond Casino
8010 US 80 East
(912) 897-3005, (877) 758-2597
www.diamondcasinosavannah.com
Okay, gambling is illegal in Georgia (except for the state-sponsored lottery). But coastal communities all over the country take advantage of the fact that, hey, it ain't that far to international waters, where anything goes. Gambling boat operations have been a bit of a gamble in Savannah, however; we've lost track of whether it's four or five such operations that have folded in the last 15 years or so. This one, though, might have staying power, since its launch has not been plagued with the problems of its predecessors. (Note to anyone doing business on the water: You cannot win an argument with the U.S. Coast Guard.) Also, the location (on the Wilmington River, well on the way to the beach) is considerably closer to the ocean, which means that non-gambling downtime that bores passengers and doesn't make money for owners is reduced.

The 164-foot *Midnight Gambler II* sails every day at 7:00 p.m., and at noon from Wednesday through Sunday. Trips are usually five hours, but figure six hours on Friday and Saturday nights. It would be a gamble to promise you what it costs—they keep changing it, from free to $10 to $5 to free. At the moment the boarding fee is $5, which is returned to you in gaming chips. Just remember, the ship doesn't make its money from admission, it makes it from what you gamble, so whatever the day's version of reality, you can expect the admission cost to be modest. Aboard are 220 slot machines, along with poker, roulette, craps, and blackjack. There's also food and drink.

ICE CREAM PARLORS

Leopold's Ice Cream
212 East Broughton Street
(912) 234-4442
www.leopoldsicecream.com
Okay, what's an ice cream parlor doing in a chapter on nightlife? After all, we could have put it in the Restaurants chapter, since Leopold's also serves soup and sandwiches. But the thing is, it is open at night near theaters and various places of activity, and it's nice to have somewhere to go after dark where the focus isn't on the bar. Leopold's is an institution in Savannah, dating back to 1919, but the operation hasn't been continuous. Stratton Leopold reopened it recently in new digs with the old fixtures, and it's a real trip back in time. They make their own ice cream, along with fountain delights like banana splits and hot fudge sundaes. There are tables outside as well as in the nostalgic interior. Check out the decor: Leopold is a major Hollywood producer when he isn't making ice cream (really!), and he's decorated the place with memorabilia from movies he's been involved with. Hours vary to as late as 10:00 or 11:00 p.m., and it's an easy walk from both the Lucas and Trustees theaters.

SHOPPING

Someday an enterprising psychology student is going to conduct ground-breaking research and discover what we already know: When you are traveling for pleasure, your hold on your purse strings is looser. Admit it! You'd never consider buying goofy-shaped mugs or snide T-shirts at home, at least not at full price. Ah, but when vacationing, that's a different story.

First of all, there are all those obligatory gifts—something for the neighbor who is feeding the dog, something for the grandkids or the grandparents, some kind of group offering for the office crowd. More important, however, are the travel gifts you buy yourself. These are things you would love under any circumstances: an attractive print, an antique armoire, the perfect addition to a prized collection. These things take on added significance when they remind us of a special trip, and we're more likely to treat ourselves to something we really want when we're shopping with the laid-back attitude of the vacationer.

So, if shopping is part of your vacation behavior, Savannah is your kind of vacation destination. Savannah is the regional shopping center for a large chunk of southeast Georgia; many people (outside of Brunswick, that is) consider it the only real metropolitan area until you get to Jacksonville, Florida (two and a half hours down Interstate 95), or in-state Macon (three hours west on Interstate 16).

With all this retail territory to cover, it stands to reason we had to be selective about what we included in this chapter. We'd like to share with you the rhyme and reason of what we left in and what we left out. First of all, we figured travelers don't need a comprehensive list of grocery stores and shoe shops. No,

we're not implying that you should travel hungry and barefoot, but because we know you are basically eating in restaurants and dragging your wardrobe around with you in a heavy suitcase, we left these and similar fundamental things out. We also skipped most of the chain stores: We don't mean to slight anybody, but our Wal-Marts probably look just like your Wal-Marts, and your hotel concierge or bed-and-breakfast host can point you in the right direction if you need one.

Instead, we've tried to concentrate on the needs of recreational shoppers while still steering the retail-impaired to the places where travelers are most likely to get the things they need. We concentrated on including shops that stock items of local or regional interest. Then we added places that struck us as unusual or interesting. Next, we included places where we like to browse and buy for ourselves.

ABOUT LOCATIONS

Before launching into our own category-by-category rundown of stores, we thought we would review the major shopping locations with you and provide a few pointers along the way.

River Street

River Street is literally along the Savannah River. It is reached by street ramps that lead down from the bluff-level Bay Street. In between these two levels is Factors' Walk. River Street is a major part of Savannah's tourist scene, and you'll find it is a prominent player for restaurants, nightlife, and annual events. But don't forget shopping! This restored waterfront strip features a steady progression of shops all along its length, beginning at the west end across from a small out-of-commission power plant (whose smokestacks make handy landmarks) and extending eastward many blocks until you reach the Waving Girl statue that is a local riverfront landmark. Factors' Walk, which parallels River Street halfway up the bluff, also features shops, although more widely scattered.

Parking is scarce. There are a few small private lots, where you pay as you enter. There's limited street-side parking on the various streets leading to River Street. Lots of motorists park illegally along River Street itself, but it's a bad idea—the city has cracked down on the long-winked-at practice. Use of the railroad track running down the middle of River Street was discontinued in early 1999, but even so, it seems unwise to park anywhere near a railroad track. (Talk of reviving a trolley to use those tracks surfaces periodically, but we'll believe it when we see it.)

We always opt to park at the Bay Street level and hike down, avoiding driving on tricky cobblestones. If you follow our example, however, watch your step and wear appropriate footwear: The stairs (located in each block) are steep and irregular, and once you get to the cobblestones, you'll find them as hard to walk on as they are to drive over. The going is much smoother once you get to the River Street level. The addition of a public elevator, tucked away between Savannah City Hall and the eastern side of the Hyatt Regency Savannah, has made life a lot simpler in this regard and, as a bonus, you'll find well-maintained public restrooms in the small building at the River Street foot of the elevator.

Don't expect much in the way of bargains on River Street: These shopkeepers saw you and your credit cards coming a mile away, and just as in any touristy area in any city, you'll find few discounts. Still, River Street offers a great variety, mingling local and regional goods, Savannah-themed merchandise imported from elsewhere, and generic trinkets and gifts. Even if you don't buy, you'll enjoy looking at goods that range from the genuinely artistic to the genuinely tacky (such as doormats bedecked with Confederate flags and the slogan "Yankee Go Home," which a shopkeeper assured us sell well to Northern visitors).

City Market

This restored area in the commercial section of the Historic Downtown runs from Barnard Street to Montgomery Street, north of Broughton Street. The complex is made up of nightclubs, restaurants, art galleries, and shops. The stores here tend to be more thematic—cat motif merchandise, New Age, outdoor furniture and gifts, and so on—than their cousins a few blocks away on River Street.

Broughton Street and Historic Downtown Areas

Broughton Street was where Savannah shopped before malls seized control of the retail world. It suffered the same fate as Main Streets all across America but has begun a comeback as a home to restaurants, college activities, and trendy shopping, including a slew of antiques dealers. In fact, some of the very best recreational shopping in the city can be done on Broughton Street. New upscale offerings stand side by side with the small low-end shops that kept the street going in its hard-luck days, things like wig shops and cut-price clothing shops. You'll also find two of Savannah's retail grand dames still in place. When other stores abandoned the main drag for suburban malls, Globe Shoe Company (17 East Broughton Street) and Levy Jewelers (101 East Broughton Street) dug in. These stores are where Old Savannah bought her shoes for debutante parties and her bridal silver, and while both stores now have other locations as well, they never closed their doors on Broughton.

You'll find plenty of intriguing stores scattered throughout the Historic Downtown. One eye-catching congregation clusters at the intersection of Bull and Liberty Streets near the Hilton Savannah DeSoto Hotel. The intersection of Jones and Whitaker Streets forms the nucleus for another appealing set of shops that mostly specializes in arts and home decor. They call themselves, collectively, the Downtown Design District, and capitalize on their proximity to both Mrs. Wilkes' eatery (see our Restaurants chapter) and Monterey Square (see our Savannah Celebrity chapter). You'll also find individual shops, especially antiques shops, sprinkled throughout the Historic Downtown.

Looking back over all these areas, here's how we'd put it in perspective: River Street is long on local color and has lots of shops cheek by jowl, where you can walk out one door and in the next. There's a variety of merchandise aimed at all age levels, and the compact location makes it easy to keep groups—be they children or merely hard-to-herd adults—together. Broughton Street's offerings aren't as likely to appeal much to children and are more widely spaced, but the merchandise is actually several cuts better, and oddly enough, the prices are more reasonable. City Market falls between these two descriptions, and you can stop by the other Historic District shops as you make your way around the city on tours, and so on.

MALLS AND SHOPPING CENTERS

Savannah has two malls, both south of downtown in a heavily trafficked area of suburban and chain-store development. There are various ways to get to them, but the most direct route and the one hardest to get lost on (although it's also the most crowded and traffic-light plagued) is straight out Abercorn Street from town. About 6 miles from the Historic Downtown, you'll spot Oglethorpe Mall on your left (you really can't miss it). Another couple of miles south, and you'll spot Savannah Mall on the right.

As for that ubiquitous American retail staple, the strip shopping center, Savannah has its share scattered mainly in the Southside/Midtown area. Because you know

> **i** Combine shopping with the national pastime. The Savannah Sand Gnats organization, the local minor-league baseball team currently associated with the New York Mets, sells a variety of caps, shirts, and so forth with the team's attractive (but pesky) logo.

what to expect in most of these—a grocery store, major discount retailer, chain or local drug store, etc.—we have left most of them out as a rule. However, there are a few exceptions, with interesting stores or interesting stories, which we have included here.

Oglethorpe Mall
7804 Abercorn Street
(912) 354-7038
www.oglethorpemall.com
Oglethorpe Mall is the city's original mall, with Sears, JCPenney, Belk, and Macy's as its anchors. There are more than specialty stores here, mostly on a single story, although some of the anchors have a second level. There's ample parking, but the multilevel parking deck comes in handy around the holidays and when it rains. You'll find a predictable array of stores inside (Gap, Victoria's Secret, CD stores, etc.), along with a few restaurants and a newly refurbished food court. Barnes and Noble opened here in 2000, and its daily 9:00 a.m. to 11:00 p.m. hours—complete with coffee shop—have made this an unlikely but popular late-night adult hangout.

If you are traveling with kids who are young (or look young), you need to be aware of mall policies requiring adult supervision of anyone age 16 or younger during most weekend business hours. From 4:00 to 9:00 p.m. on Friday, 1:00 to 9:00 p.m. on Saturday, and noon to 6:00 p.m. on Sunday, those younger than age 17 must be accompanied by a parent or guardian at least 21 years old. Anyone age 21 or younger will be asked for ID, with mall management considering driver's licenses, official state ID cards, college student ID cards, passports or visas, and mall employee IDs as acceptable identification.

Savannah Mall
14045 Abercorn Street
(912) 927-7467
www.savannahmall.com

Savannah still calls Savannah Mall, which opened in 1990, "the new mall," although by most cities' standards it isn't new anymore. Actually, this mall almost became known as "the mall that's in trouble," as its stock of anchor stores dwindled from four to one. But some savvy and recent lease coups, drawing on stores not usually thought of as mall staples, have given the new mall a new lease on life. First of all, the Bass Pro Shop took over what had been a two-story department store site. Now, it's a megastore for hunters, anglers, campers, and other outdoors types. There's both an outdoor and an indoor waterfall and massive aquariums featuring large examples of fish native to local waters (the long-nosed gar is one ugly fish, you'll discover). The space is so big they sell boats indoors. In 2004 the mall became home to Savannah's first Target store. Savannah Mall offers about 115 specialty stores, including a Waldenbooks, a Hallmark shop, and several restaurants. Behind the mall are neighboring rival multiplexes totaling more than 20 movie screens, so the mall is a convenient place to kill some time while waiting for Hollywood's latest.

Habersham Shopping Center
Habersham Street at 60th to 63rd Streets

This small strip shopping center runs along both sides of Habersham Street, from just after its intersection with 60th Street to 63rd Street. It appears modest at first glance—a small grocery store, a pharmacy, a dry cleaner, and other businesses clearly set up to serve the surrounding established neighborhood—but look closer and you'll find some interesting specialty shops. They include Punch and Judy, a children's store, and Merry Times, a card and gift shop. Other entries include a bakery and some nifty restaurants (which we cover in our Restaurants chapter).

Abercorn Common
8108 Abercorn Extension
www.abercorncommons.com

At first glance, this V-shaped strip shopping center won't strike you as anything special. It looks new and houses several nationally known names like Circuit City, Michael's, Home Goods, Books-a-Million, and Panera Bread (along with some still unleased space). What makes it interesting isn't immediately apparent: This is Savannah's first LEED-certified (Leadership in Energy and Environmental Design) retail development.

Developers took an aging and down-at-the-heels shopping center that wasn't living up to the potential of its location and, instead of just bulldozing it, tackled it as a "green" project. Demolition was held to a minimum, and conscious efforts were made to recycle or repurpose demolition debris to keep it out of landfills. New buildings were designed to be energy efficient, pavement was made permeable, and xeriscaping, or the use of landscaping plants that can survive in the climate without artificial irrigation, was called into play. The stores that are moving into this work-still-in-progress include a mix of local and national names, some of which we mention in more detail later (like Wild Birds Unlimited). But really, when was the last time you went to a shopping center where the parking lot design was actually interesting and significant?

Abercorn Walk
Abercorn Street and Janet Drive

This narrow, deep strip shopping center is on Abercorn, just slightly south of the major intersection of Abercorn and DeRenne, which marks the southward sprawl of retail in Savannah. The stores here are going to sound familiar to veteran shoppers: the Fresh Market, Ann Taylor LOFT, Chico's, Jos. A. Bank, Talbots. The significance is the upscale nature of the collected stores. It also rates mention because the Fresh Market is Savannah's first specialty grocery store (unless you count downtown's organic food shop, the venerable Brighter Day). You could hardly move in Fresh Market for the first month it was open, thanks to all the people who turned out for the novelty of unfamiliar produce, imported chocolates, and a deli case stocked with fancy takeout. We bought salmon there, and found it was wrapped and tied with the care and finesse rivaling anything we've managed to do with Christmas presents.

SHOPPING SAVANNAH

Anything south of, say, DeRenne Avenue is dubbed the Southside by Savannahians. This is where you'll find the strip malls, discount houses, shopping centers, megastores, etc. The Savannah Festival Factory Outlet Center, a typical example of this new kind of strip mall, is at the far southern edge of the city, where Abercorn is better known as Highway 204 and passes under I-95. This outlet center includes a Springmaid/Wamsutta factory store, Bugle Boy, and Bass Shoes, among many others.

East and west of Savannah, you'll find mainly grocery stores and other retail outlets in support of the suburban residential development there, with a few interesting shops thrown in and a large spate of beach-oriented shops at the end of the road on Tybee Island. (Check our Tybee Island chapter for more on shopping there.)

Now that we've roughly covered the general shopping areas, let's get more specific. We've divided our featured stores into categories. Join us on a quick shopping trip.

Antiques

In this section, we cover a sampling of both high-end and low-end antiques dealers. Serious collectors with serious budgets should seek out the upscale places; collectors and browsers will have better luck in the more mainstream, less expensive stores.

Abercorn Antique Village
201 East 37th Street
(912) 233-0064
www.abercornantiques.com
This rambling yellow Victorian home houses collections from more than 50 dealers. Look for French country furniture, statuary, oil paintings, crystal, jewelry, and so on. This is a good browsing location with a wide price range—stuff for the serious collector and less-pricey offerings as well. Lately, this veteran store has taken on a more design-oriented feel.

The Attic
224 West Bay Street
(912) 236-4879
Looking for antique fishing lures? Good examples can fetch $65 and up, and you'll find them among some of the other sports antiques here, along with fencing masks and old skis. It's an eclectic stock of mainly American antiques and collectibles—furniture, jewelry, glassware. It's not what you would call high end, but it's fun. The location itself is of interest to fans of *Midnight in the Garden of Good and Evil*, since it was the location of the financially ill-fated Emma's, a piano bar that is featured in that best seller.

Fran Campbell Antiques and Interiors Inc.
305 East 38th Street
(912) 238-5400
This shop specializes in upscale 18th- and 19th-century English and American furniture, Chinese export porcelain, antique accessories, and objets d'art. Design services are available. Hours aren't particularly regular, so call ahead.

Cobb's Galleries Inc.
122 East 37th Street
(912) 234-1582
This popular antiques shop keeps outgrowing its quarters. It is now located in a Victorian mansion at the corner of 37th and Abercorn Streets, the supposedly haunted Krouskoff House. That's appropriate, because owner Al

ℹ️ Sales taxes in Georgia vary by county, ranging from a minimum of 4 percent (the state's share) to as much as 7 percent, depending on local voter willingness to up the ante. In Chatham County (which includes Savannah and Tybee Island), it's 7 percent at the moment. Because the state exempts its share of the sales tax on groceries, expect to pay only the local sales tax on these. Also, state law exempts Bibles from sales tax, although you'll find many bookstore clerks are unaware of this.

Cobb wrote a book about a supposedly haunted bed that wreaked havoc in his household; you can buy a copy in the shop. Most of the stock is more conventional: an extensive collection of art pottery, about a thousand cookbooks, sports memorabilia, collectible liquor decanters, what have you. What's surprising about this shop is the sheer volume.

Habersham Antiques & Collectibles Market
2502 Habersham Street
(912) 238-5908
This used to be a nifty family-owned grocery store. Now, a collection of some 70 antiques dealers fills booth space where once Savannah's Ardsley Park matrons bought canned goods and prime cuts of meat. For the most part, these are not ultrafine antiques, although we're not talking junk, either. Our recent trip spotted some neat old books, lots of glassware, and some textiles. This is a good browsing site, a place to kill time while you look for that one missing prize piece for your collection of what-nots. Hours are 10:00 a.m. to 6:00 p.m. weekdays and 10:00 a.m. to 5:00 p.m. on Saturday. Once a year, the enterprise expands, spreading to the neighboring parking lot with a spring festival that brings other vendors in booths.

Savannah Galleries
30 East Bryan Street
(912) 232-1234
www.savannahgalleries.com

Here you'll find 10,000 square feet of high-end antique English, French, and American furniture, silver, porcelain, and Oriental rugs. Pieces range from elegant marquetry to rustic painted pine pieces.

Design services are available as are search services, and the staff will assist in building collections. Cleaning, repair, and appraisal of antique and modern Oriental rugs are also available. The owners, native Savannahians, have restored many fine old homes and are familiar with the furnishings such projects require. This establishment has been in operation since the 1960s and is experienced in shipping its merchandise.

Southern Antiques and Interiors Inc.
28 Abercorn Street
(912) 236-5080
www.southernantiques.net
This shop offers 12,000 square feet of high-end furniture, mostly English and Continental pieces from the 18th and 19th centuries. Reproductions are also available, usually made to order in the English workshops with which the firm has a relationship. Southern Antiques specializes in larger pieces and has both case goods and soft (upholstered) furniture. The store carries about $1 million in inventory and is experienced in shipping because the bulk of its business involves out-of-town customers. Custom constructions can be designed to fit specific spaces, and the time frame for custom work is less than that for placing special orders with commercial manufacturers.

Bookstores
The Book Lady
6 East Liberty Street
(912) 233-3628
Used and rare books are what you will find at The Book Lady, a quaint bookstore ideal for browsing. Besides art, architecture, religion, fiction, and the usual fare, you will also find sections called Pretty Books and Nice Old Books among the lot. There are also several local titles on Savannah and the area. For that

hard-to-find book, the store offers a search service.

Books-A-Million
8108 Abercorn Street
(912) 925-8112
This national retail chain offers thousands of titles, with deep discounts on best sellers. The selection of magazines is among the most extensive in the city. The local and regional section includes an extensive collection of Southern titles. The store also offers children's books, gifts, cards, and gift wrap. Grab one of the free book newsletters and settle in at the in-store coffee shop.

E. Shaver Bookseller
326 Bull Street
(912) 234-7257
Book lovers will delight in this independent bookstore, which occupies the ground floor of an Historic District home. The shop has become a fixture for both downtown residents and tourists. An impressive array of hardcover and paperback books is available, and the knowledgeable staff offers solid advice.

Local titles are well represented. The shop also offers an efficient book search service for older titles. A whole room is devoted to children's titles. Limited gift offerings include museum-style notecards, tote bags, and appointment calendars. This is what bookstores were before there were megachains.

Ex Libris
228 Martin Luther King Jr. Boulevard
(912) 238-2427
www.scad.edu
Ex Libris is part coffeehouse, part bookstore, and part gift shop, all put together by the Savannah College of Art and Design. The shop is on the western edge of the Historic Downtown and may be a little out of your way, but it's worth the trip. After browsing through art books, posters, framed art, and many other eclectic and fun items you most likely won't find anywhere else in Savannah, you can sit

and relax on the gigantic leather sofa and simply enjoy the beautifully restored building. A magnificent stairway takes up the center of the building and is the focal point of the room, along with "pillars" made out of hundreds of old books. The store is especially beautiful during the Christmas season, when the college opens its holiday shop and offers decorations and other festive items.

Candy

When we travel and need a gift for a hostess, or when we want to send a present with regional flavor (pun intended), we often opt for pralines. No one can claim these superrich candies (made of sugar, butter, cream, and pecans) are good for you, but at $14 and up per pound, your purse will probably stop you before you do yourself too much harm. You can find them made and sold in two shops on River Street. Although the shops would scream to hear it, we can't taste any difference. Pralines are available at shops in Savannah's malls, but the ones on River Street taste better.

River Street Sweets
13 East River Street
(912) 234-4608
Pralines are made right here, in full view, and there's usually someone near the door to offer you a sample. Display cases showcase other store specialties: confections of chocolate and nuts, spiced pecans, divinity, etc. There's a wide array of gift baskets and special packaging and an efficient shipping service.

Savannah Candy Kitchen
225 East River Street
(912) 233-8411
Kids of all ages will run rampant in this large candy store, which fills several rooms. In addition to pralines and other store-made specialties, you'll also find gourmet jelly beans and a staggering selection of other mass-produced candy—the kinds you remember from childhood and assumed no one sold anymore.

Choose from a wide selection of decorative tins to fill with goodies. This store also offers gift shipping.

Clothing

Cherub
51 Barnard Street
(912) 236-8722

Is little Missy a pouting toddler who was just born to walk the catwalk? Does your kindergartner long for haute couture? Got a fretful fashionista in your designer pram? This store can handle all of the above. Three Savannah women got together in 2005 to bring Savannah a high-end children's fashion store, also carrying gifts, accessories, bedding, and so on. Cherub's target demographic is from infant to, say, age six. But the kiddies had better have a pretty good allowance, since some of the pants are north of $50. We confess that such high-end kidswear names as Deux par Deux and Catamini don't mean much to us, but this is a fun and pleasant shop that should be a delight to the indulgent grandparent.

Gaucho
18 East Broughton Street
(912) 234-7414

250 Bull Street
(912) 232-7414

When browsing through either location of Gaucho, you might be reminded of those who believe you can never be too rich or too thin.

Gaucho had a wide selection of hats and accessories on our last visit, along with hand-painted blouses and, in the back, shoes. It's worth stopping by just to see the restoration at the Broughton Street site, especially the dressing-room area.

Jezebel
25 East River Street
(912) 236-4333

Twelve Oaks Shopping Center
5500 Abercorn Street
(912) 354-8889

This upscale ladies' clothing boutique fea-
tures casual and formal clothing for the Southern woman. Comfortable linen pants, dresses, and shirts perfect for weathering 90-degree temperatures are Jezebel hallmarks. Brands include Flax and Cut Loose, among others. Long flowing dresses, pants, and shirts with pretty prints are included in the mix, along with extravagant costume jewelry, shoes, hats, and more.

Dime Stores

Mack's 5 and 10 Cent Store
Medical Arts Shopping Center
4800 Waters Avenue
(912) 354-3025

You'll think this store is a time machine. This classic dime store opened in 1946 and moved to its current location in 1962, where not much has changed since. Although this is a fun store for browsing, it has a practical side too because, crammed into a tiny space, it somehow manages to have everything. When we needed pinwheels for a photo assignment, we knew, without question, we could find them here. People come here for stuff they still want but can't find elsewhere—things like hair nets, soft peppermint sticks, or flyswatters with wire mesh flaps. There are all sorts of housewares, along with plastic flowers, inexpensive toys, greeting cards, embroidered hankies, and cardboard cutouts for elementary-school bulletin boards.

Contemporary merchandise isn't ignored. You can find toys here for children in Memorial Health University Medical Center across the street. By the way, Mack's can still legitimately call itself a five-and-dime: Look hard enough, and you can still find items for these prices. We spotted tiny plastic animals for a dime and plastic rings and individual candies for a nickel.

Gifts and Fun Shops

Baskets, Bears & T's . . . Oh, My!
305 East River Street
(912) 232-4546

The title of this cozy shop pretty well describes the stock. The collection of stuffed animals includes both collectors' treasures and high-quality children's toys. Look for brands such as Ty, Russ, Boyd's Bears, Enesco, and other, smaller lines. Upstairs you'll find 2,500 square feet devoted to baskets of every imaginable shape, size, and material. T-shirts include both Savannah-themed versions and witty (but not vulgar) novelty shirts. Other stock includes dolls (such as the Susan Wakeen line), books of local interest, and plenty of furniture perfect for toys. Other gift and novelty items are scattered in among it all—things that owner/manager Carol Devine describes as "silly stuff . . . things that strike me at the moment."

Byrd Cookie Company and Gourmet Marketplace
6700 Waters Avenue
(912) 355-1716

You can buy these well-known local cookies all over town, but the advantage of choosing them from this shop is that you can sample the wide range of flavors here: Key Lime Coolers, Benne Bits, raspberry, butter cookies, and so on. They're sold in decorative tins ($10 each) that are excellent choices for those obligation gifts. One is sufficient for a solid token gift, or you can assemble a collection if you need something more impressive. A locally popular favorite is the benne wafer, a subtly sweet concoction made of unhulled sesame seeds. If you show up during a production run, you can even watch the manufacturing process through a glass window. In addition

i Shopping for Georgia lottery tickets? Your best bets are small convenience stores and gas stations. Most lottery vendors have prominently displayed signs. Time your lottery shopping spree so that you avoid 6:00 to just before 7:00 p.m.—that's when the daily drawing for the Cash 3 game is held, and there's a line of hopeful last-minute gamblers at many lottery outlets.

to Byrd Cookies and the Seckinger-Lee line of cookies and snacks that Byrd also produces, this shop features an array of clever gifts (most with a culinary theme), a selection of other gourmet food items, and fresh flowers. Note that it is closed on Saturday but open on Sunday. Shipping is available.

Charlotte's Corner
1 West Liberty Street
(912) 233-8061

This eclectic gift shop offers a little bit of everything, spread out over four rooms. There are lots of shirts—T-shirts, tank tops, sleep shirts, sweatshirts. Fancy children's clothing featuring appliques and smocking—the things that grandparents buy—are well represented in the stock. A line of fun clothes for adults is included, and there are plenty of toys. Woven afghans are offered in various motifs, including local ones. In addition to a line of *Midnight in the Garden of Good and Evil* merchandise, there are local souvenirs including other Savannah books, ornaments, and prints by local artists.

A Fine Choice
20 West State Street
(912) 650-1845

Owner Sherry Georges has packed a lot of varied gift merchandise into a small space, and she's hit upon a supply that isn't replicated all over town. It's also well organized for such a small shop with so much in it—pigs on these shelves, cats here, dragons there, paperweights here. We priced a set of three wise monkeys at $34 a set. The store also has a line of paperweights featuring Mount St. Helen's ashes. It also stocks unusual jewelry and a line of greeting cards.

Go Fish
106 West Broughton Street
(912) 231-0609

This store surprised us with a line of handicrafts that are very reasonably priced. It grew out of a missionary family's interest in helping the artisans they encountered in Third World countries and has expanded to a small chain (primarily in Georgia, Florida, and South Carolina) of stores selling Christian T-shirts and imported clothing, jewelry, and handicrafts.

We've been in several times and have not been accosted by any aggressive religious recruiting. The store's mission and focus are clearly explained in the literature scattered throughout the store, but aside from the religiously themed T-shirts, it could have been any store. The difference was the price on the home accessories—Indonesian woodcarvings at very low prices, like a line of elongated and brightly painted cat sculptures beginning at $25 and going up in height and price. The stock also included beaded jewelry and clothing made from batik fabrics. There are lots of affordable selections if you are chaperoning something like a Girl Scout troop, as so many Savannah visitors are. It's a friendly store and we drop in just to browse occasionally.

Half Moon Outfitters
15 East Broughton Street
(912) 201-9393
www.halfmoonoutfitters.com

This unique outdoor clothing and equipment company has transformed a rather pedestrian storefront on the city's former main shopping drag to a modern and appealing space. It fills two levels, and the renovation job is worth a trip inside even if you aren't interested in camping, kayaking, or backpacking. All the gear is here, from clothing to kayaks themselves, along with food supplies and a large collection of books. The shop was recently acquired by Half Moon Outfitters, a small chain of outdoor stores based in South Carolina. The staff is made up of friendly, knowledgeable young people who practice the lifestyle they sell, which makes them good sources of information if you are in need of advice on where best to camp, canoe, or what have you in this vicinity.

Midnight Star Pottery
1094 Eisenhower Drive
(912) 303-9599

This store is actually a pottery-painting studio where the customers pick out pieces of pottery, then go to work painting a one-of-a-kind creation. There are hundreds of pieces of pottery to choose from, including tiles, bowls, goblets, and vases. Many people make an outing to Midnight Star Pottery an event for family gatherings, wedding showers, or birthday parties. If you are a repeat visitor, note that this shop has moved from its original downtown site to the south.

The Paris Market
36 West Broughton Street
(912) 232-1500
www.theparismarket.com

The merchandise here is appealing, but The Paris Market is worth a visit just to see the primo restoration of the building that houses it. We remember when this store started as a small, crowded room-size shop in what is now called the Downtown Design District. Today, it occupies two spacious floors in a retail "palace" on a prominent corner of downtown's main drag. The ground floor has nostalgic wood flooring and is crowded with a dazzling collection of chandeliers (we couldn't muster up the nerve, or the visual acuity, to check the price tags). Downstairs, the floors are brick, and it is mirrors, ranks and ranks of them in all different (but massive) styles, that catch the eye. It is a great setting for merchandise, and the selection includes some surprisingly affordable things. We especially liked the filigree-scrolled initial ornaments outlined in pearls at $10 each (but alas, they were out of the B and the D). The stock is a mixture of new and vintage. There's also linen, dishes, soaps, decorating books, etc., much of it with a French or Parisian theme. In short, this is a nifty place to pick up a gift, or for the house-proud to groom their nests.

The Red Needle
1711 East Victory Drive
(912) 691-1071
www.redneedleyarns.com

Okay, knitting became a big thing while we

weren't looking. Suddenly, it's cool to whip out your knitting and stitch up a sweater (which it will probably be too warm to wear more than a few days per winter). If the process confuses you as much as it does us, you can check out The Red Needle. The store offers lessons, both in groups and individually, and provides a cozy space for needleworkers to gather and flash those needles. You'll find patterns and needles and other knitting accessories (with a few other needle arts also represented) in plenty. But the biggest draw is the yarn supply. Don't look for your basic synthetic Red Heart Super Saver hanks here: This is specialty yarn, often in natural fibers and unusual textures and treatments (and priced accordingly). The hours are primarily daytime, but there are periodic evening knitting sessions, which can be tracked on the Web site (where you can also order yarn). You might have to search around a bit to spot the store: Victory Drive is heavily trafficked (a main drag that is surprisingly beautiful when azaleas are in bloom or the ranks of palm trees down the center is freshly groomed). But dedicated needleworkers will find it worth the effort. After all, Victory is one of the routes to the beach!

Sails & Rails
125 East Broad Street
(912) 232-7201

It's hard to miss Sails & Rails in its new location on East Broad Street. It's the shop with the brightly displayed kites, flags, and windsocks blowing outside. This unique shop includes dozens of kites, along with flags from around the world and decorative ones for your front porch. Windsocks—ranging from those with pictures of snowmen on them to others shaped like whales—are also for sale, along with things for toy train enthusiasts. The new shop stands literally on the line between poverty and gentrification—with a nice bed-and-breakfast as a near neighbor, and a public housing project and low-income health clinic on the other side of the street.

Savannah Art Works
240 Bull Street
(912) 443-9331
www.savannahartworks.com

We struggled with whether to put Savannah Art Works in with the art galleries in our Arts and Culture chapter, or to put it here with gift shops. You could build a case either way, but since the affordable, artistic gifts and creations outnumbered the pricier wall pieces, we're calling it a gift shop. You may disagree, but either way you won't be disappointed with this entertaining and colorful shop. You'll find graphic cartoon dog prints and attractive and useful pottery, along with tiny 4-inch-square mini-paintings. Jane Wood, who owns the shop with Beth Martin, coils aluminum into an attractive and affordable (starting at $15) collection of vases, candelabra, and sconces. There's also plenty of stuff for deeper pockets. On our last visit, the back wall featured a display of dramatic black-and-white sketches ($125 and up), a trio of long and narrow paintings portraying either flying or falling vegetables (starting at $750), and fabric art done as pillows, purses, and wall hangings (up to $275). It's a friendly, well-positioned shop (you'll pass it if you do any serious walking in Savannah) and appears to be very supportive of local artists and craftspeople.

Savannah Scrapbooking
8805 White Bluff Road
(912) 920-4451
www.savannahscrapbooking.com

This specialty scrapbooking and paper crafts store stocks specialty Savannah-themed papers and die-cuts (primarily words, like "Savannah," "Tybee Island," "Forsyth Park," etc.) among its vast supply of acid-free papers and embellishments. When visiting scrapbookers hear that, they've been known to strike out for Savannah's Southside, where locals live and shop and tourists don't venture that often. This shop is now Savannah's only specialty scrapbook store, although you'll find some scrapbooking stuff in chain stores these days. At Savannah Scrapbooking, the racks

Savannah Art Works offers a mix of art and crafts. BETTY DARBY

store something like 2,000 different types of paper and all the latest innovations in accessories and design aids. The shop offers free table-time (if this is your hobby, you'll know what that means) and hosts crops into the night on occasion. Owner Jamie Danford says out-of-town visitors often attend and fit right in, and that during the day you might find a scrapbooking tourist at work while the spouse is on the golf course. Right now, the Web site is info-only, but she hopes to add ordering capability in the future.

True Grits
107 East River Street
(912) 234-8006
This gift shop specializes in nautical and Civil War items.

On the gifty side, choose from 250 different varieties of hot sauce, each label claiming to be deadlier than the other. You'll also see plenty of shirts, toys, mugs, and plates with Savannah scenes. Also, you'll find items with nautical themes: lighthouse figurines and lighthouse needlework kits; large, realistic wooden ship models; tables made from hatch covers or using four-bladed brass props as bases; and antique telescopes. Civil War merchandise includes replica swords and hats, many history books, and three different versions of Civil War–themed chess sets.

i If you've got military privileges, you'll find a PX and commissary at Hunter Army Airfield in Savannah.

Wild Birds Unlimited
8108 Abercorn Street, Suite 210
(912) 961-3455
http://savannah.wbu.com

Bird enthusiasts can stock up on birdseed, feeders, houses, binoculars, toys, gifts, and CDs here. This shop is geared to those who want to watch birds in the wild (including their own backyards), so it doesn't handle pet bird supplies. Some of the feeders and birdhouses double as lawn sculptures, including ornate, copper-roofed models. You'll also find a small stock of educational toys, and such unique items as hummingbird feeders and houses especially designed for butterflies and bats. The store relocated in late 2005 to Abercorn Commons, a redeveloped shopping center just past Oglethorpe Mall.

Home and Food

@ Home
320 West Broughton Street
(912) 201-0015

Some of the stock at this cute home accessory shop is kitschy almost-antiques or nostalgia items, while other stuff is just funky and fun. It all went over so well, they moved to larger quarters on Broughton Street. On a recent visit, we saw wooden Easter chicks, a diary/photo album, candles, and vintage linens. The stock also included several interesting books on theme decorating and lots of stationery and note cards.

Eclectibles!
10 West Broughton Street
(912) 443-9292

Look here for whimsical decor and light-hearted art. We found stock that ranged from

Roadside produce stands as well as regular grocery stores are good places to pick up Vidalia onions. These famous mild, sweet onions are grown only in and around nearby Vidalia and have acquired a dedicated national following of gourmets.

comical garden sculpture on stakes in the $32–$36 range to large serving trays with hand-painted olive motifs at $72, and some large cloisonné bells whose price we were afraid to check for fear we would end up buying them. Days and hours of operation are a bit erratic here.

One Fish, Two Fish
401 Whitaker Street
(912) 447-4600

This little shop expanded to a bigger one and then got bigger still, offering an array of trendy and unique gifts and other unusual merchandise. Our visit spotted gourmet goodies and gifts for pampered pets, and a few little jars of jellies and condiments for their human counterparts. The stock also includes trendy purses, ceramic flowers, and tons of other superfluous-but-so-desirable types of products. Look here for lavish linens and personal pampering items. One storefront down, but still within the same building, you'll find Circa Lighting, where you can buy lamps and lighting fixtures from a variety of periods and styles. It all adds up to a quaint and cozy little corner in which to browse. The restoration work, which stopped well short of the polished at a rustic and shabby-chic European look, merits a visit even if you are not in a buying frame of mind.

Peanut Shop of Savannah
407 East River Street
(912) 232-8612

Peanut brittle, roasted peanuts, and plain ol' peanuts, along with hard candy and Key lime jelly, are just some of the many things you will find inside the Peanut Shop. If you aren't sure what kind of peanuts you want, don't worry, there are usually several samples out so you can try before you buy.

24e
24 East Broughton Street
(912) 233-2274
www.twentyfoure.com

Broughton Street and the directions it has taken with revitalization never cease to amaze us. In the street's shabbier days—post-mall and pre-refurbishment—inexpensive furniture stores and very expensive rent-to-own furniture places were one of the standard fixtures of the place, along with vacant storefronts. Now, those are mostly gone, and scattered along Broughton are a handful of upscale, high-fashion furniture stores where style (and price) rival anything you might find in a major metropolitan area.

The finest of the new lot is 24e, which has put its address to modified use as its name. Over two floors in what was once two separate storefronts, you'll find displayed everything from knickknacks (ceramic penguins that shop co-owner Ruel Joyner Jr. calls a season signature item) to drop-dead furnishings. On the upstairs level, we found Italian leather sofas, overstuffed chintz armchairs, platform beds, and undulating chaise lounges. The accessory/gift-type stuff is on the lower level, including extremely expensive perfume lamps and reasonably priced glassware.

Despite the fact that the goods are mostly way outside our budget, we enjoyed browsing here. Even if you aren't in the market for furniture, don't miss that second level—it's worth the trip just to see the remnants of the old soft drink signs painted on what was once an exterior wall.

Thrifts and Flea Markets

This kind of shopping isn't for everyone, just the most dedicated bargain hunters. If you don't mind rolling up your sleeves, these places can be real treasure troves. Of course, you'll occasionally come away empty-handed, but if you are into the thrill of the chase, you won't mind a bit.

Goodwill Industries
310 Johnny Mercer Boulevard
(912) 897-3901

7220 Sallie Mood Drive
(912) 354-7423
Chances are your community has these stores, with donated goods, sorted and stocked by the disabled. But you should definitely check ours out: With our large military and college populations (which tend to be mobile), Savannah's Goodwills see lots of merchandise turnover. We have friends who have furnished entire beach houses with stuff from these stores. The Sallie Mood Drive location is the best place for furniture: It's in the back, behind swinging doors and easy to miss if you aren't specifically looking for it. We've bought three-drawer pine dressers rescued from dormitories for $35, current hardback best sellers for $2, glass ice buckets from the 1950s for $4, and so on. There are actually five locations, but these are the only two we've had much luck in. The Johnny Mercer location is the newest, and it has the best and brightest collection.

Keller's Flea Market
5901 Ogeechee Road
(912) 927-4848
www.ilovefleas.com
Ever wonder where people buy velvet wall-hangings depicting the Last Supper, wild stallions, and dogs playing poker? We've found them here ($10 each). In fact, if you go often enough and search diligently, we're convinced you can find just about anything in one of the 400-plus booths. Some are just tables under shed roofs; others are enclosed mini-stores. Don't expect anything fancy—this is the base of the food chain in retail shopping. Still, we've made some real finds here and had fun people watching.

Among the booths you'll find the equivalent of yard sales, estate sales, and salvage sales. Some have new merchandise, including designer label stuff that doesn't appear very convincing and pure junk that isn't masquerading as anything else. Handcrafters, small-scale importers, and collectors set up here. Go early on Saturday, and you'll see the antiques dealers scouting for stuff they'll clean up (and mark up) for their own shops. Our finds here have included an IBM Selectric typewriter for $35 (in need of some repair, but still worth it), used books, carved onyx

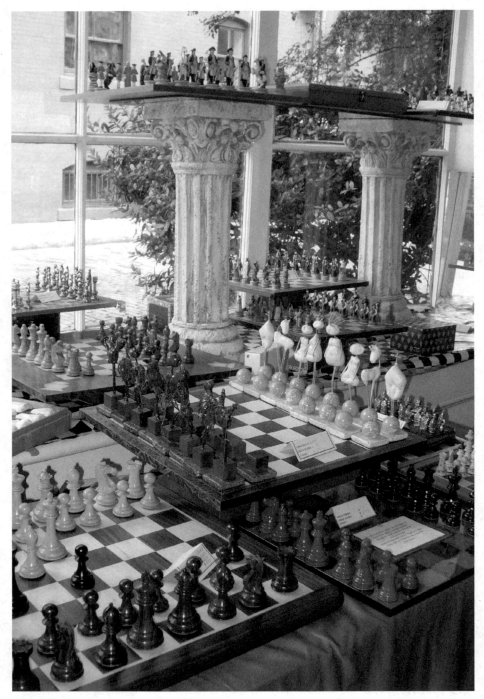

Decorative chess sets at Savannah Bulldog Cigar Company. BETTY DARBY parrots, and a possibly authentic (but probably not) poster from the 1955 World Series.

Other merchandise on a typical weekend includes fresh produce, houseplants and plants for landscaping, sports cards, T-shirts, and bumper stickers with politically incorrect slogans.

One section features exotic birds, reptiles, puppies, and chickens, but real animal lovers should give that section a wide berth. The market is open Saturday and Sunday. Ogeechee Road is also U.S. Highway 17, and the market is in the county's far southwestern section. About 2 miles past Savannah Mall, you'll spot the exit for US 17. Take the exit, turn left at the end of the ramp, and you'll soon see the market on your left. Dress casually or you'll look like an idiot.

Tobacco

Savannah Bulldog Cigar Company
244 Bull Street
(912) 232-2650

This smoking specialty shop stocks tobacco in all its forms, and chances are you don't realize how many forms that is. There are between 180 and 200 different types of cigars in stock at any given time, along with 30 blends of pipe tobacco (including their own custom blend, the Savannah Bulldog). Cigarettes include imported Dunhills, Export A (Canadian), and the American-made, additive-free Nat Sherman cigarettes in various sizes and shapes. The inventory even includes Indonesian clove cigarettes and Darsham Bidis, which is Indian tobacco wrapped in eucalyptus and flavored with strawberry or vanilla.

The Savannah Bulldog Cigar Company has accessories that include elegant lighters, cutters, punches, clippers, and humidors in fine

wood (the most expensive currently in stock is $1,250). They also stock books and magazines for cigar and pipe enthusiasts. It also stocks an array of chess sets and eclectic music CDs.

The most distinguishing feature at Savannah Bulldog Cigar Company, however, is the lounge, a small, comfortable room at the rear of the store with leather sofas and big-screen TV. Here customers from Savannah's business district (and tourists, of course) can relax with their smokes. Individual locker-size humidors with full temperature and humidity control are available for rental to house customers' personal tobacco collections. And, true to the name, you'll find one or more English bulldogs on the premises when you call.

Verdery's Lamps and Ye Ole Tobacco Shop
130 East Bay Street
(912) 236-1178

280 Eisenhower Drive
(912) 691-0807

Lamps and tobacco might sound like a strange combination, but the way the shopkeepers see it, it gives them something for both male and female shoppers. On the lighting side, they offer custom lamps and shades, along with repairs and restorative work. For tobacco enthusiasts, there's a walk-in humidor with more than 100 brands and 200 sizes of cigars, ranging in price from 65 cents to $29.95 each. The pipe tobacco selection includes Verdery's own custom blends. In addition to the usual line of American cigarette brands, they have imported Dunhills, Gauloises, and others, along with clove cigarettes and additive-free versions. The store also stocks pipes and leather goods for smokers.

ATTRACTIONS

Savannah is perfect for strolling, and we thought this chapter would be the perfect place to provide you with a little direction. With most of the city's best-known attractions in the Historic Downtown, a walking tour seemed in order to give your personal trek some guidance.

Here's the format: We provide detailed listings of many of the popular historic sites downtown, and in between we give explicit directions (in italics) on how to get from one location to the next. The tour takes in a little more than 2.5 miles; how long it takes depends on how fast you walk and whether you decide to take a detour or two and further explore some sites. We heartily encourage you to do so.

You will find many benches for leisurely breaks along the way. If you get hungry or have an urge to do some browsing, you will be passing by many restaurants and specialty shops. (If you stumble on a place that catches your fancy and is not listed in this chapter, chances are you can find out more about it in our Restaurants or Shopping chapters.) For another great dining option, pack a picnic before setting out. Each square you encounter—and we will cover nine—is perfect for relaxing near the magnolia trees while enjoying a good sandwich. If you've brought the dog along for a romp, be aware that the city has both leash and scoop laws. Do not bike through the squares.

We offer a basic map at the front of this book. If you need a further visual aid, several good maps of the Historic Downtown are available in shops around town and typically cost less than $5. The Savannah Visitors Center, located in the 300 block of Martin Luther King Jr. Boulevard near its intersection with Liberty Street, or the Savannah Area Chamber

of Commerce offices at Drayton and Bay Streets (912-644-6400) also provide a free visitors' guide that has a great map.

Following our Insiders' Historic Downtown tour, we provide information on other guided touring options in the city, plus a variety of other interesting attractions to explore both in Savannah's downtown and the outlying areas: the Islands, Southside, and West Chatham.

INSIDERS' HISTORIC DOWNTOWN WALKING TOUR

Whether you are coming to the Historic Downtown via the Talmadge Bridge or you're already there and wandering around on foot, you can't miss the gold dome on top of City Hall. Because of this, we decided to start our tour at this landmark on Bay Street and the northern tip of Bull Street. So look up (or down, depending on your vantage point), and when you spot the gold dome, head in that direction. Once you arrive, don't be shy—wander inside for a quick look around. You will be glad you did, and the office workers don't mind a bit. Also, don't be surprised if the gold dome is a bit cloaked. A major restoration project on City Hall moved to the dome and cupola in late 2007. It involves replacement of the unsound cupola with an exact replica and re-gilding of the gold dome. The project is slated to be finished by mid-2008.

City Hall
Bay and Bull Streets
(912) 651-6410, (912) 236-7284
Local architect Hyman Wallace Witcover designed and built City Hall in 1905 for an estimated $205,167. This price was to include

statues of chariots and horses on top of the structure, but budget constraints prevented them from being built. The exterior is composed of several materials, including rough-hewn granite blocks, colored limestone, and polished granite. The dome, rising 70 feet, was originally copper. However, in 1987 a local philanthropist donated $240,000 to the city, allowing the dome to be gilded with thin layers of 23-karat gold leaf. The gold was applied to the dome, cupola, and clock hands. Usually, most of the faces of the clock have the right time—but if your group is splitting up to tour, don't depend on it for your rendezvous time!

Inside the foyer you will find a lovely and intricate mosaic on the floor. Look up in the foyer, and you will see more detailed tiles. Go farther into the rotunda and look up for a pretty, circular view all the way up to the fourth floor and the stained glass in the dome. The original building directory is also in the rotunda on a giant tablet. Today, Savannah city offices are located throughout the community, but the second floor of City Hall is much like it was when the building was originally built. It still houses the mayor's office, clerk of council offices, and the council chambers. The stern and imposing council chambers have even stood in for courtrooms in a couple of Hollywood productions.

After leaving City Hall, head south on Bull Street. Look to your left while crossing Bay Street. The huge building on the corner opposite City Hall is the United States Custom House.

United States Custom House
1 East Bay Street
The magnificent columns in front of the Custom House each weigh 15 tons. Across the street are cannon presented to the Chatham Artillery in 1791 by George Washington.

In 1972 the structure was designated a historic custom house by the U.S. commissioner of customs. As you walk by, notice the wonderful ironwork fencing that not only decorates the building but also guards it. It is just

one of many fine examples of wrought iron you will notice throughout your walking tour. Although it is a landmark, it's also the working home of the Customs office, busy tracking the business of Savannah's port.

Continue south on Bull Street in the direction of Johnson Square.

Johnson Square
Bull Street, between Bryan and Congress Streets
This is Savannah's first square. It is named for Robert Johnson, the governor of South Carolina who helped the Georgia colony get established. During the early days of the colony, this was the center of activity for the city. In the center is a monument to Revolutionary War hero Gen. Nathanael Greene, who died in 1786; his grave is here as well. Today the square is the center of banking in Savannah. Stand in the middle and you will be surrounded by several banks. If you need to pick up some cash, this is a good spot to find an ATM. This is also a popular square for downtown workers to lunch in, and in spring and early summer there is often lunchtime musical entertainment.

On the eastern side of the square, look for pairs of gigantic green doors and majestic columns. They belong to Christ Church.

Christ Church
28 Bull Street
(912) 238-0434
Christ Church is known as Georgia's Mother Church. It was founded in 1733, on the exact spot where the first Christian religious service in Georgia was held. The current church replaced two churches that were destroyed. In 1735 John Wesley, the founder of Methodism, served as pastor here and founded what

---

i The Pirates' House at 20 East Broad Street, which is now home to a restaurant (see our Restaurants chapter) featuring a mysterious maze of rooms, is a former seaman's tavern built in 1794.

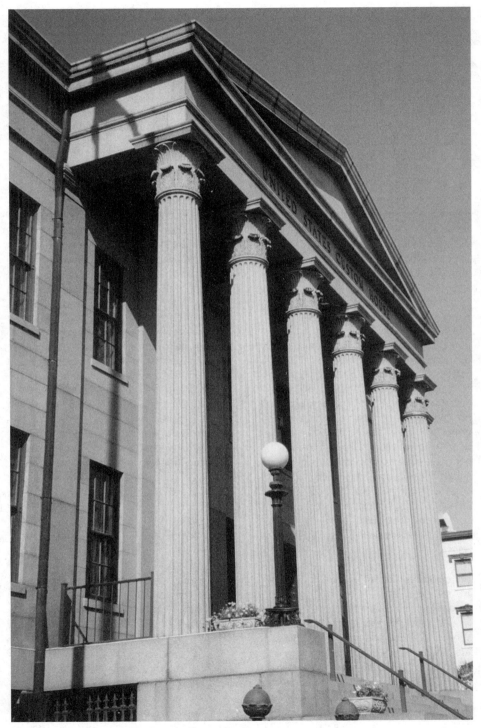

The U.S. Custom House turns an imposing face on Bay Street. BETTY DARBY is believed to be the world's first Protestant Sunday school.

Also interesting: Christ Church has one of the rarest church bells in the entire country. It is known as a Revere Bell and was created by Paul Revere and Sons, the company owned by the noted "British are coming" patriot. It is one of about 130 Revere bells, the majority of which are found in New England states; only a handful made it to the South. The bell in the tower is actually the third Revere Bell the church has owned. The first, purchased in 1816 for $716, cracked during shipment. The second cracked the second Sunday it rang. The third bell, as they say, was the charm. The church didn't have any significant problems with the third bell until 1995, when repairs needed to be made to the apparatus holding the bell. After a two-year repair job, the bell was rung again in early November 1997.

Continue heading south on Bull Street, crossing Congress Street and proceeding to Broughton Street. This is Savannah's original business district, and after decades of decline, it is becoming a shining example of what urban redevelopment can do. Look east and west to see many trendy shops and a restaurant selection that ranges from Thai to Moroccan to Italian (not to mention a good ol' hot dog place as well). Take a detour if you are hungry. If not, continue south on Bull Street to Wright Square, the second square on our trip.

Wright Square
Bull Street, between State and York Streets
Wright Square is named for Sir James Wright, the last royal governor of Georgia. The monument in the center is for William Washington Gordon, one of the founders of the Central of Georgia Railroad. (The railroad's offices used to be about a block away; you will pass the site on this walking tour.) The large boulder, taken from Stone Mountain near Atlanta, marks the grave of Tomo-chi-chi, the Yamacraw Indian chief who was instrumental in helping the founders get established in their new colony.

i John Houston, a former governor of Georgia, was named Savannah's first mayor in 1790.

Taking up the entire western side of the square is the federal courthouse. Made of Georgia marble, its architecture is a conglomeration of many styles: Spanish, French, Italian Renaissance, and Romanesque among them. On the eastern side of the square, you'll see the old Chatham County Courthouse, a light-colored brick building designed in 1889 by noted Boston architect William G. Preston. It now houses county offices. On the same side as the courthouse is Lutheran Church of the Ascension.

Lutheran Church of the Ascension
21 East State Street
(912) 232-4151
Massive red doors lead into Lutheran Church of the Ascension, formed in 1741 by German settlers. The current church was built between 1875 and 1879 and was designed by George B. Clarke, using Norman and Gothic styles. One of the church's most striking features is the Ascension Window, depicting the Ascension of the Lord.

Continue heading south on Bull Street. On the northeastern corner of Bull and Oglethorpe Streets is the Juliette Gordon Low Center.

Juliette Gordon Low Birthplace
142 Bull Street (corner of Bull Street and East Oglethorpe Avenue)
(912) 233-4501
www.girlscouts.org/birthplace
The Juliette Gordon Low Birthplace gives visitors an authentic glimpse of what life was like in the 1800s for one of Savannah's most prominent families—one that just happened to include Juliette Gordon Low, founder of the Girl Scouts.

But the Low Center isn't just about the Girl Scouts. This beautifully restored home, Savannah's first National Historic Landmark, is full of the Gordons' original belongings—from Georgian Revival chairs in the dining room to a painting of Niagara Falls by moonlight, a souvenir the Gordons bought some years after their honeymoon. When entering the main hallway, you will immediately notice the beautiful winding staircase with a rose-colored bull's-eye glass window in the background; it was installed in 1886 to give more light in the stairway. In the library is a brass chandelier original to the home. The south parlor, decorated in striking yellow, red, and green, has a pier mirror, installed in 1884.

Construction on the home began in 1818 in the newly fashionable English Regency style. William Washington Gordon and his wife, Sarah, were the first of four generations of the Gordon family to live in the home. William Gordon served as mayor of Savannah and is credited as a founder of the Central of Georgia Railroad. The house was eventually inherited by William Washington Gordon II and his wife, Eleanor Kinzie Gordon, the parents of Juliette Gordon. Juliette spent her childhood here.

i If you're venturing south of the Historic Downtown to do some sightseeing, be sure to take a drive down portions of two streets in Midtown—Victory Drive between Abercorn Street and Waters Avenue, and Washington Avenue between Bull Street and Waters. You'll see stately homes set amid huge, graceful oak trees and, if you hit it just right during the springtime, medians and yards bursting with the color of azaleas in bloom. Palm trees were first planted along Victory Drive in 1906 when it was called Estill Avenue, and this thoroughfare—which starts at Ogeechee Road, runs to the Wilmington River, and continues to Tybee Island as U.S. Highway 80— was once reputed to be the longest avenue of palms in the nation. When Estill Avenue was widened and extended in 1922, it was renamed Victory Drive in honor of the Americans who fought and died in World War I.

After passing through another generation of Gordons, the house was threatened with demolition in 1953. A concerned group of local Girl Scouts, including youngsters and adults, appealed to the national organization to save the birthplace of their founder, and the building was purchased by the Girl Scouts. It was restored and opened to the public three years later. Today, thousands of Girl Scouts from around the world make the pilgrimage to Savannah to visit the home of the group's cherished founder. The house is open from 10:00 a.m. to 4:00 p.m. Monday through Saturday (closed Wednesday from November to February) and from 11:00 a.m. to 4:00 p.m. on Sunday. Cost is $8 for adults and $7 for students ages 6 to 18. Recent renovations, which include a small elevator, have made the mansion relatively accessible to the handicapped, unusual among historic attractions.

Continuing south on Bull Street, you will pass the offices for the local school district on the left, housed in a rambling brick building that once housed a school and still sports nice frescoes above its entrances, and Independent Presbyterian Church on the right.

Independent Presbyterian Church
25 West Oglethorpe Avenue
(912) 236-3346
This church was founded in 1755 and is considered one of the most important Federal-style churches in the country. The original was designed by John Holden Greene of Rhode Island. It burned in 1889. The current building has an elevated mahogany pulpit, and the four Corinthian columns of the sanctuary were made from a single tree trunk that was carefully selected through exhaustive searches in the South. Woodrow Wilson married Ellen Axson, granddaughter of the church's pastor, here.

Continue south to Chippewa Square.

Chippewa Square
Bull Street, between Perry and Hull Streets
General James Oglethorpe is immortalized in bronze in the center of this square. First Bap-

A statue in Chippewa Square honors Gen. James Edward Oglethorpe, founder of the Georgia Colony.
BETTY DARBY

tist Church, organized in 1800, is on the northwestern corner of the square. Across the park on the northeastern corner is the Savannah Theater, home of a professional theatrical group that presents musical programs five days a week.

For movie buffs, this is the square where Forrest Gump sat waiting for the bus. The bench was placed on the far northern tip of the square. Next time you see the film, notice that traffic in the square is moving in the wrong direction! The beautiful building on the southwest corner is known as the Philbrick-Eastman House and is a fine example of Greek Revival architecture. It served as home for many prominent families; today, it houses a law firm. It was also a location for the movie *Now and Then,* which starred Demi Moore, Rita Wilson, and Melanie Griffith, among others.

While walking south through the square, look to your left along West Perry Street, and you will notice a row of magnificently restored private homes, among the many you will see on your trip today. You are getting into the more residential portion of the Historic District.

Continue south on Bull Street. After crossing Perry Street, notice a dolphin downspout on the home to your right. These interesting adornments to lovely houses are a common sight throughout Savannah. There are several boutiques, a coffee shop, and a few lunch spots in this area. Duck in to Gaucho to look for women's high fashion. (Check the Shopping and Restaurants chapters for more information.) Farther down Liberty Street is the Hilton Savannah DeSoto, built on the site of the DeSoto Hotel, which was razed in 1966. Next is Madison Square.

Madison Square
Bull Street, between Harris and Charlton Streets

Madison Square is named for James Madison, the fourth U.S. president. When entering Madison Square you will notice the Sorrel-Weed House on the northwest corner of the square. It was completed in 1841 and is an example of Greek Revival architecture. In

1997 the home was purchased and underwent an extensive $2 million renovation that restored it to its original condition. This renovation included painting the home its supposedly original bright orange color, which did not please neighbors and members of a local historic review committee. However, the homeowner won out, as you will see when walking by.

On the northeastern corner is E. Shaver Bookseller, a popular locally owned bookstore. If you need a break, this could be a good place to take it. On the southeastern edge of the square is a gigantic redbrick building that once was the Savannah Volunteer Guards Armory. This structure and the large building across the street on the southwest corner of the square—the old Scottish Rite Temple—are now owned by the Savannah College of Art and Design. The armory was the first building the art school founders purchased when they came to town in the late 1970s. At the time, there was an old greasy spoon inside, so complete renovation was needed. It was the first in a long list of buildings purchased and restored by the school; you'll find them throughout the Historic Downtown. Today the armory houses classrooms and Exhibit A, an art gallery that features artwork by students and professors and, at times, work by famous artists. It is open to the public free of charge. (For more information on the Savannah College of Art and Design, see our Education and Child Care chapter.)

Look to the northwest corner of the square. The Gothic brick mansion is the Green-Meldrim House.

Green-Meldrim House
1 West Macon Street
(912) 233-3845, (912) 232-1251

Built in 1853 by architect-builder John S. Norris for a wealthy cotton merchant, the Green-Meldrim House is best known as being headquarters for Gen. William T. Sherman, who gave the city of Savannah to President Lincoln as a Christmas present. The famous telegram to Lincoln, dated December 22, 1864, reads, "I beg to present to you as a Christmas Gift, the City of Savannah with 150 heavy guns and plenty of ammunition; and also about 25,000 bales of Cotton."

Today the home serves as a parish house and is owned by its neighbor, St. John's Church. When you walk by, notice the beautiful and elaborate ironwork and the oriel windows that give light from three sides. Inside are American black walnut wooden floors, elaborate moldings, marble mantels, and other original adornments. The home is open for tours from 10:00 a.m. to 4:00 p.m. on Tuesday, Thursday, and Friday, and 10:00 a.m. to 12:30 p.m. on Saturday. Admission is $7 for adults, $3 for students.

Continuing south on Bull Street, you will pass Jones Street, considered one of Savannah's most picturesque roadways. Notice the brick streets and wonderfully restored homes. It is well worth a short detour. It is also home to one of Savannah's most noted restaurants, Mrs. Wilkes', which is known for its Southern fare (see our Restaurants chapter). Next is Monterey Square.

Monterey Square
Bull Street, between Taylor and Gordon Streets

This is the final square on Bull Street. Its name commemorates the Battle of Monterey in the Mexican War. The square was laid out in 1847. In the center is a monument honoring Casimir Pulaski, a Polish nobleman who was killed during the American Revolution. He may or may not be buried under the monument that honors him; historians disagree. The monument was rededicated in 2001 after a restoration period of several years that saw its foundation standing empty.

During filming of the movie *Midnight in the Garden of Good and Evil,* set designers brought in their own monument. Now, when you see Monterey Square on the big screen, you'll know the monument is not the original. The square is surrounded by other significant sites used in the movie, including the home

where the book's main plot unfolds, the Mercer-Wilder House, commonly known as Mercer House, which is on the western edge of the square.

Mercer House
429 Bull Street
www.mercerhouse.com

Cited by Historic Savannah Foundation as nationally significant for its architectural style, this home was designed by John S. Norris and completed in 1871. The striking ironwork— including cast-iron window pediments, eight cast-iron balconies, and the sidewalk fence— is one of the house's signature features. The house was named for Confederate Gen. Hugh Mercer, songwriter Johnny Mercer's great-grandfather, but General Mercer sold the house. He never lived there nor did any member of the Mercer family.

In 1970, after the house was neglected and empty for many years, Jim Williams, the antiques dealer and central character in *Midnight in the Garden of Good and Evil,* finished a complete restoration of the home. Today the private home is owned by Dorothy Kingery, sister of the late Williams. She opened the home to limited public tours in 2004. Tickets are $12.50, and entrance is through the carriage house. For more details, see our Close-Up in this chapter.

Looking past Mercer House, on the southwest corner of the square, you will notice row houses along Gordon Street. One of these homes—7 West Gordon Street—has also had a brush with celebrity. If you are a fan of the PBS show This Old House, *you may be familiar with the renovation that took place here in 1996 at the home of Mills and Marianne Fleming. For several months, Norm Abram, Steve Thomas, and the rest of the crew from the popular series were in town helping restore the 1884 home, which made headlines when it was built for being one of the first homes in the city to have indoor plumbing. Across the square from Mercer House, on the eastern side of the square, is Temple Mickve Israel.*

Temple Mickve Israel
20 East Gordon Street
(912) 233-1547
www.mickveisrael.org
Temple Mickve Israel began with a group of Spanish-Portuguese Jews who came to Savannah in 1733, just five months after the founding of the colony. It is the site of the first Jewish congregation in the South and the third in the entire United States. It is also the only Gothic synagogue in the country. The temple was designed by Henry G. Harrison and houses the oldest Torah in America. There are also hundreds of documents, historical books, and letters from Presidents Washington, Jefferson, and Madison in the museum adjoining the temple. Tours of the sanctuary and museum take place Monday through Friday from 10:00 a.m. to 1:00 p.m. and 2:00 to 4:00 p.m. at a fee of $3 per person.

Continuing south on Bull Street, you will pass the George Armstrong House on the northwest corner of Bull and Gaston Streets. This massive building, constructed in 1920, was given to the city in 1935 and converted into Armstrong Junior College, predecessor of Armstrong Atlantic State University, which subsequently moved to Savannah's Southside. (For more on Armstrong Atlantic, see our Education and Child Care chapter.) Today it houses a law firm.

Across the street, on the northeast corner of Bull and Gaston Streets is the Oglethorpe Club, one of Savannah's most elite and private clubs. Straight ahead is Forsyth Park.

Forsyth Park
Bull Street, between Gaston Street and Park Avenue
This 30-acre park filled with azaleas, magnolia trees, walkways, park benches, and more is one of Savannah's most beautiful spots. If you are in need of a break during the walking tour, don't miss a stroll through Forsyth Park; in fact, we suggest a picnic. The park was laid out in 1851. One of its most recognizable and often photographed features is the white fountain near the center. Visit on the weekend, and you might see a bride and groom getting pictures taken beside the ornate swans and other creatures in the fountain.

The monument in the center of the park was erected by the United Daughters of the Confederacy and honors those killed during the Civil War. The park is also home to a Fragrant Garden for the Blind and is surrounded by beautiful and elaborately restored homes, many of which are Victorian in style. Across from the northwestern corner of the park is the Georgia Historical Society. (For much more on Forsyth Park, see our Parks and Recreation chapter.) The fenced-off area in the center is supposedly a work-in-progress on a casual refreshment stand/restaurant in cooperation with the city of Savannah, but work seems to be proceeding slowly.

Georgia Historical Society
501 Whitaker Street
(912) 651-2128
Dr. William Bacon Stevens, a physician who later became the Episcopal Bishop of Pennsylvania, and attorney I. K. Tefft are generally credited with organizing the Savannah-based Georgia Historical Society. The pair were soon joined by Dr. Richard D. Arnold, a founder of the American Medical Association. In 1839 the group incorporated one of the country's oldest (and the Southeast's first) historical societies.

Nearly 170 years later, the realization of their efforts can easily be seen in thousands of historic documents, artifacts, newspapers, and other source materials documenting Georgia's past. Visitors to the society will find everything in its massive archives, from copies of letters Gen. James Edward Oglethorpe wrote to the Trustees of the Colony to the grapeshot that killed Casimir Pulaski and was extracted from the Polish war hero's leg. There are minutes from the first Georgia Medical Society meeting, held in Savannah in 1804; photographs from the now-defunct YWCA; and family letters such as the one written by Garnett Andrews about the cotton gin Eli Whitney had invented.

The society also publishes, in cooperation with the University of Georgia, the highly acclaimed *Georgia Historical Quarterly,* a collection of scholarly articles. Entry to the Georgia Historical Society is free. The building is open to the public from 10:00 a.m. to 5:00 p.m. Tuesday through Friday and 9:00 a.m. to 3:00 p.m. on Saturday.

This is the midpoint of the walking tour. We will travel north for the next portion of the tour, heading back in the direction of City Hall, where we started. Continue 1 block east onto Gaston Street, crossing Drayton Street. Check out the many beautifully restored homes. Head north by turning left onto Abercorn and stay on this street until you reach Calhoun Square.

Calhoun Square
Abercorn Street, between Taylor and Gordon Streets

The first of the Abercorn Street squares on our tour was named for John Calhoun, a South Carolina statesman. It was laid out in 1851. When entering the square, you can't help but notice Wesley Monumental Methodist Church on the southwestern corner of the square. This Gothic Revival church was named for John and Charles Wesley, early figures in the history of Methodism. The sanctuary was built between 1876 and 1890. It features a Wesley Window opposite the pulpit, which contains the busts of the men for whom the church was named.

On the southeastern edge of the square is the Massie Heritage Interpretation Center.

Massie Heritage Interpretation Center
207 East Gordon Street
(912) 201-5070
www.massieschool.com

Honored as Georgia's oldest school in continuous operation, the Massie Heritage Interpretation Center is also the only remaining original building from Georgia's oldest chartered school system. The Greek Revival structure is listed on the National Register of Historic Places. It was completed in 1856 and is known for its gable roof, wood cupola, and cornice, among other features. Today, an enrichment program is offered to increase student understanding of Savannah's historic and architectural heritage. The center is open to the public from 9:00 a.m. to 4:00 p.m. Monday through Friday. Self-guided tours are $3; guided tours are $5.

Continue north on Abercorn Street. On your way, you will pass Clary's Cafe, a must for fans of The Book. It's the spot where Luther Driggers, the man rumored to have enough poison to kill the entire city, often hung out. Once a pharmacy with a lunch counter, it is now a restaurant. You will also pass Jones Street before entering Lafayette Square.

Lafayette Square
Abercorn Street, between Harris and Charlton Streets

This square, which was laid out in 1837, was named for Marquis de Lafayette, who visited Savannah in 1825. There are several significant buildings on this square, but when you enter it, you can't help but notice the Cathedral of St. John the Baptist, located near the northeast corner.

Cathedral of St. John the Baptist
223 East Harris Street
(912) 233-4709

This magnificent Gothic cathedral with its twin spires is one of Savannah's most noted landmarks. It is also the oldest Roman Catholic church in Georgia and the seat of the Diocese of Savannah. The parish organized in the late 1700s and erected its first church on Liberty Street. It wasn't until 1876 that the cathedral was built; tragically, it was destroyed by fire 20 years later.

When the cathedral was rebuilt, the original designs were used. One of the cathedral's most striking features is its stained glass. Most of it was executed by Innsbruck Glassmakers in Austrian Tyrol and installed around 1900. Other features include an Italian marble altar, the stations of the cross (which were

Close-up

Savannah's Most Famous (or Infamous) House Opens Its Doors to Public

During the height of the popularity of the book *Midnight in the Garden of Good and Evil*, Mercer House was under a sort of subdued siege. A thriving and opportunistic tourism subculture centered around the book was cashing in on the obsessive interest of fans. Nowhere could have been of more interest to those fans than Mercer House, the heart of John Berendt's loosely woven collection of Savannah stories centered around a fatal shooting there and the subsequent trials of the late Jim Williams.

The point is, though, that no one at Mercer House wanted this fame (although they did open the house up for filming of the movie version of the book). By the time the book was published, Williams was dead and the house was in the hands of his heirs as a private residence. Tour buses blared their version of the story outside the sedate mansion. Fans posed for pictures outside the house, or clambered up on the gate and low surrounding wall for better looks. Some went so far as to try to break in. Images of the house were reproduced on souvenirs of varying taste levels.

Dorothy Kingery, sister to Williams and the new owner of the house, fought back as best she could. She trademarked the facade of the house in an effort to deter its commercial exploitation. She even put the home on the market briefly, at a multimillion-dollar price that drew no takers.

The closest fans got for many years, at least legally, was through the carriage house. This two-story structure to the rear of the house was once the workshop where Williams worked on antiques. The family put the building to use as a small, upscale gift shop—one whose inventory did not include the kitschy *Midnight* stuff that was cropping up in shops all over town.

So things stood for the first decade after the publication of Berendt's book. An even larger percentage of the people featured in the book were dead by now. The fan fervor had died down some, although even today you can find tours and a gift shop dedicated to all things *Midnight*. Then, in 2004, quietly, with no fanfare and an extremely low-key approach, Kingery

imported from Munich), and the coat of arms of Pope John XXIII. The building just underwent a massive restoration, indoors and out, and is now fully open in its restored glory.

The Andrew Low House
329 Abercorn Street
(912) 233-6854
www.andrewlowhouse.com

On the northwest corner of Lafayette Square is the Andrew Low House, built in 1848 by Low, a wealthy cotton merchant. Low's son, William McKay Low, married Juliette Gordon, founder of the Girl Scouts. In fact, the carriage house in back of the home is the first official headquarters of the Girl Scouts of the U.S.A. Juliette Low left the building to the organization following her death.

opened the first floor of Mercer House (now increasingly known as the Mercer-Williams House) to paying guests.

The Mercer-Williams House is now the only private, occupied residence in Savannah that invites paying guests to tour it. Tours enter through the Carriage House, where a guide leads small groups through the courtyard and into the home's first floor. At the moment, that's all you get to see of the house. (Frankly, we still have trouble believing you can get inside the house at all: We would have bet money it would never have happened, and we wouldn't be surprised if the tours are discontinued one day with as little fanfare as they launched.)

At $12.50, the Mercer-Williams House is the priciest of the downtown house museums, although the price hasn't gone up in the three years it has been open. But it's also among the more interesting and beautiful. The downstairs rooms are fine display areas for the antiques Williams collected throughout his life. British Colonial pieces are among the most distinctive, Kingery herself says. The guides are knowledgeable about the home's interior features and the antiques displayed there.

This is a tour of Williams's house, and it focuses on his role in the preservation and restoration of Savannah's architectural treasures. It is not—repeat, not—a facet of the *Midnight in the Garden of Good and Evil* craze. You won't hear the book mentioned, and questions about things like where the shooting was will be deflected rather coolly. That shouldn't be surprising, though. Going into someone's house and asking awkward questions, even if you are a paying guest, is considered tacky, in local parlance.

The front of the house has no sign or other indication that it is open to tours, and we wonder how many tourists pose for snapshots there without ever realizing they could get in through the back door. The carriage house is directly behind the house, and a small, discreet sign gives tour details. The shop is worth a browse, too. It offers home decor and gift items of good quality, not extravagantly marked up. Although it isn't really a book store, the things we've bought on our few visits have all been books. And, as a sign of how much things have changed, that small stock of books on sale now includes *Midnight in the Garden of Good and Evil*.

The stunning home, with its elegant front gardens and beautiful ironwork, is built of stuccoed brick. It is now owned by the National Society of the Colonial Dames of America in the State of Georgia, whose members also donated its furnishings. Even the three-tiered fountain in the center of the square was donated by the organization. Some of the home's most noted guests have included Robert E. Lee and William Makepeace Thackeray. The home is open for tours from 10:00 a.m. to 4:30 p.m. Monday through Saturday (closed on Thursday) and from noon to 4:30 p.m. on Sunday. Cost to tour the house is $8.00 for adults and $4.50 for students, Girl Scouts, and Girl Scout leaders.

The Hamilton-Turner House
330 Abercorn Street

The Hamilton-Turner House is a Second Empire chateau built in the 1870s by a former mayor of Savannah. The Lafayette Square home was the first house in the city to get electricity and has many distinctive features, including a mansard roof and cast-iron balconies. In 1969 it was scheduled for demolition, but those plans were abandoned after the Historic Savannah Foundation stepped in. It has changed hands several times since then. (Read more about its current incarnation in our Bed-and-Breakfast Inns chapter.)

Flannery O'Connor House
207 East Charlton Street
(912) 233-6014

Noted Southern author Flannery O'Connor was born in this high-stoop, 19th-century home on the outskirts of Lafayette Square. She lived here as a child until 1938. The parlor floor has been restored to its original appearance and houses a small museum dedicated to the author. The home is open from 1:00 to 4:00 p.m. on Saturday and Sunday, and there is a $5 admission charge.

Continuing north on Abercorn Street, cross Liberty Street. On the east side of Abercorn Street is Colonial Park Cemetery.

Colonial Park Cemetery

Button Gwinnett, who signed the Declaration of Independence, and Edward Green Malbone, painter of miniatures, are two of the notable Georgians buried in this cemetery, the second public burial ground in Savannah. The cemetery, which takes up several blocks in the Historic Downtown, opened in 1750; it closed to burials 100 years later. Visitors are welcome to tour the cemetery and glimpse the old tombstones and inscriptions.

After exploring the cemetery, continue north on Abercorn Street, crossing Oglethorpe Avenue. As you cross Oglethorpe, you will pass the city's fire department headquarters. Next is Oglethorpe Square.

Oglethorpe Square
Abercorn Street, between State and York Streets

Oglethorpe Square was named for Georgia's founder, James Edward Oglethorpe. It was laid out in 1742. On the northeast corner of the square is one of Savannah's most famous museum houses, the Owens-Thomas House.

Owens-Thomas House
124 Abercorn Street
(912) 233-9743
www.telfair.org

Taking up an entire block on the eastern edge of the square is the Owens-Thomas House, considered to be one of the finest examples of English Regency architecture in the country. The home, with its columned entrance portico, brass inlaid staircase, and more, was designed by architect William Jay from 1816 to 1819 for cotton merchant Richard Richardson.

The home is made largely of tabby—an indigenous, concretelike material made of lime, oyster shells, and sand. The exterior is English stucco. The interior, which includes three rare built-in marble-top tables that belonged to the Richardsons, has many stunning features, including an entryway with a brass inlaid staircase and a drawing room with an unusual ceiling that makes the room appear to be round. The carriage house, also open for tours, is one of the earliest intact urban slave quarters in the South and opens into an English-inspired parterre garden.

In 1830, after the home had been used as a boardinghouse, George Welchman Owens, a congressman and former mayor of Savannah, purchased it for $10,000. The property remained in the Owens family until it was bequeathed to what is now the Telfair Museum of Art. The home is open from noon to 5:00 p.m. Monday, from 10:00 a.m. to 5:00 p.m. Tuesday through Saturday, and from 2:00 to 5:00 p.m. on Sunday. The cost to tour the house is $10 for adults, $4/$5 (depending on age) for children. Children younger than age five are free. Note that this house museum is part of the Telfair's three hold-

You can see the whole world in
Savannah, and it's sitting right near
one of the city's busiest intersections—
the meeting of Abercorn Street and
DeRenne Avenue. The world we're talking
about is what Savannahians refer to as
"The Globe," a steel sphere that's 60 feet
in diameter. The Savannah Gas Co.
erected it in the mid-1950s as an emergency holding station for natural gas and
soon painted it to depict Earth's oceans
and continents and with an arrow point-
ing to Savannah. The globe was featured
in the 1999 film *Forces of Nature*. It features a satellite-eye view of a hurricane
aimed right at Savannah. The latest
owner, a mortage company, has stuck its
name on the side.

ings—the other two are art museums, and
the best bargain is the $15 adult ticket that
gets you into all three attractions.

*One of Savannah's other noted museum
houses is just around the corner from the
Owens-Thomas House on East State Street. If
you would like to detour to this house, head
east on State Street and cross Lincoln. One
block on your left will be the Davenport
House.*

Isaiah Davenport House
324 East State Street
(912) 236-8097
www.davenporthousemuseum.org
As you walk around today in the Historic
Downtown enjoying the beautifully restored
homes and other sights, know that it was the
Davenport House that was largely responsible
for the preservation of the national treasure
that is the Historic District. In the 1950s, when
developers came up with a plan to demolish
the house, sell the brick, and put in a parking
lot, seven local women banded together to
stop it. That group, which later became the
Historic Savannah Foundation, raised $22,500
to purchase the home; such were the beginnings of restoration efforts in Savannah.

At the time of the rescue purchase, the
home was a tenement, divided into small
apartments and full of people. The Federal-
style home was originally built in 1820 by
master builder Isaiah Davenport, who used
the home as a kind of showcase for his work.
One of the incredible features of the house is
the delicate and ornate molding and plaster
work found throughout. The detail is so
incredible that in some cases it looks almost
like a wedding-cake border has been placed
around the edge of the ceilings. There is also
a lovely house garden and museum shop that
sells period items, note cards, Savannah specialty items, and more. The Davenport House
is open from 10:00 a.m. to 4:00 p.m. Monday
through Saturday, and 1:00 to 4:00 p.m. Sunday. Cost is $8 for adults, $5 for children.

*After viewing the Davenport House, head
west on State Street to Abercorn Street.
Again, travel north on Abercorn. As you cross
Broughton Street, you'll notice a large building on your right. Savannah College of Art
and Design has transformed this former
department store into a library. Continuing
along Abercorn Street, you will come to the
Lucas Theatre.*

Lucas Theatre
22 Abercorn Street
(912) 232-1696
www.lucastheatre.com
This Savannah landmark, built in 1921, served
not only as a theater but also as a general
center of entertainment for the city. It had
floors of imported marble, a dome ceiling surrounded by 600 incandescent lights, and 36
ornate boxes. However, it deteriorated with
the rest of downtown after World War II. A
group of citizens—Lucas Theatre for the Arts
Inc.—banded together to reopen the theater
and has been raising the millions of dollars
needed to complete the project. As part of
their fund-raising efforts, when the crew filming *Midnight in the Garden of Good and Evil*
was in town in 1997, it participated in a fund-
raiser for the theater. Among those in attendance were director Clint Eastwood and actor

Kevin Spacey. The theater is now in full operation (see our Arts and Culture chapter for more information) under the management of Savannah College of Art and Design.

After passing the Lucas Theatre, you will enter Reynolds Square, the last square on our walking tour.

Reynolds Square
Abercorn Street, between Bryan and Congress Streets

Reynolds Square was named for Capt. John Reynolds, who served as governor of Georgia in 1754. In the center is a statue of John Wesley, the founder of Methodism. On the northwestern corner of the square is The Olde Pink House, a popular eatery.

Continuing north on Abercorn Street, you will reach Bay Street. Look to the west and you will once again see the dome on City Hall, where the tour began. Directly across Bay Street is Factors' Walk and River Street.

Factors' Walk and River Street

Bay Street Factors' Walk is named for the cotton brokers (or "factors") who bought, sold, and shipped their wares along the banks of the Savannah River. This unique row of buildings, built on the bluff overlooking the water, rises two or three stories on the street side and three or more stories over the riverfront.

The focal point is the old Cotton Exchange, a redbrick building with the name COTTON EXCHANGE etched along the top of the facade. It was built in 1886 by William G. Preston and was one of the first buildings in the United States to be erected entirely over a public street. At one time this building was where the world price for cotton was set. While the brokers set the price of cotton, the lower floors served as cotton and naval warehouses with entrances at several levels, including on River Street.

Today both River Street and Factors' Walk are full of shops, restaurants, and galleries, all housed in the restored warehouses. It is a favorite spot for visitors. Take a stroll on the river for a fitting end to our tour.

GUIDED TOURS

Savannah abounds with guided-tour companies. Their offerings are varied—general history, ghosts and hauntings, African-American history, you name it. Modes as well as subjects vary: travel by air-conditioned minibus, open-sided pseudotrolley, horse-drawn carriage, riverboat, or plain old shank's mare (walking, in other words). The latest addition to the local tour scene is the Segway, those motorized "people movers" that look like a scale in a doctor's office, except they carry you around.

This is a very fluid industry. New tours are added constantly, schedules and itineraries change, etc. Although the following is not a comprehensive listing, it will get you started. We have avoided naming any one set of tours "the best." The quality of a given tour, we believe, really varies based on the guide more than the tour company. The city of Savannah requires guides to earn licenses by passing a test on local history and attractions every two years, so you can expect reasonable competence from any guide.

When you are making those required reservations, it's a good time to take advantage of the competitive nature of the industry. Ask specifically which sites are entered (most tours don't actually go inside buildings) and what perks are included. We've found that a constantly changing array of extras—discount coupons, refreshments, etc.—are put into play in an attempt to stand out in an industry where everyone is selling essentially the same thing. Remember, all prices are subject to change and are likely to increase slightly when the tourists return in large numbers each spring. The city also frequently revises the rules under which these tour companies operate, because the areas they tour through are also fully operational residential and business districts. They've also recently added a dollar-a-head fee as a tax. If you are just looking for a generic tour, you won't have any trouble getting a slot, even on a walk-up basis. If it's a specialty tour, however, plan ahead and make reservations by phone. These companies (some of them, anyway) have a tendency to come and go, so call ahead.

Boats

Savannah Riverboat Company
9 East River Street
(912) 232-6404, (800) 786-6404
www.savannahriverboat.com
This hour-long cruise takes you up and down the Savannah River on a replica riverboat, either the *Savannah River Queen* or the *Georgia Queen*. It's really the only good way for a tourist to get a firsthand look at the industrial and shipping side of the city—the bread and butter for many of us who live here. You can also get a waterfront perspective on historic structures. River Street from the water lends itself to good panoramic photos. Depending on river traffic, you may get to see some of the massive ships that make the port of Savannah among the busiest in the nation.

The daytime sightseeing cruise is narrated. Wear sunscreen! This company also offers a variety of other cruises, keyed around dinner and dancing, Sunday brunch, or even gospel music with a buffet dinner.

The sightseeing cruise is $17.95 for adults and $9.95 for those younger than age 12, plus tax. The meal cruises range from $32.95 to $44.95. A "murder afloat" mystery cruise with actors staging a "whodunit" is staged once a week (currently on Thursday nights) at a fare of $26.95 for adults and $18.95 for children. Prepaid reservations are required for most tours, except the daytime sightseeing. Note that schedules vary seasonally and can be affected by the weather.

Buses

In this category, we've grouped together big buses, minibuses, vans, and trolleylike vehicles—the whole motorized land travel thing. Reservations (again) are required and easily made by phone. Most tours make pickups at the visitor center at 301 Martin Luther King Jr. Boulevard, which has reasonably ample park-

Florence Martus is forever immortalized by the Waving Girl statue on River Street. For many years during the late 1800s and early 1900s, she greeted the ships that passed through the port of Savannah by waving a white cloth during the day and a lantern during the night, hoping to be the first to greet her returning husband (or, by some accounts, her returning fiancé). The Altrusa Club erected this statue in her honor.

ing if you are vacationing with a car. (The first half-hour of parking is free.) The tour companies use the large parking slots near the front entrance, and each space is marked with a posted sign identifying and advertising the company that leases that space. Convenient pickup is also available at most downtown hotels and bed-and-breakfasts. In fact, you can probably make arrangements for most tours to pick you up anywhere you like downtown—this is a competitive business. At least three companies—Old Savannah Tours, Old Town Trolley Tours, and Oglethorpe Tours—offer on-and-off-at-will trolley tours of the historic district; board and disembark at any of the tour company's designated stops outside historic district attractions. See details below.

Although most tours will take credit cards, some drivers do not have the means of processing them. If you plan on paying by plastic, mention that while making your reservations, because it may impact your selection of pickup locations. Also, prices don't include tips for the guide/driver, which most of the brochures and onboard signs shamelessly hustle for; they are strictly optional.

Old Town Trolley Tours of Savannah
234 Martin Luther King Jr. Boulevard
(912) 233-0083
www.historictours.com
This 90-minute tour offers reboarding options throughout the Historic Downtown on orange and green trolley-style vehicles. Tickets cost

This trolley-style bus is one of many vehicles used for guided tours. KYLE CASON

$20.70 for adults and $9.00 for children. The tour company also operates a gift shop downtown. It also offers a ghost tour on a trolley, "Ghosts and Gravestones," for $25 for adults and $10 for children.

Oglethorpe Trolley Tours
1115 Louisville Road
(912) 233-8380
www.oglethorpetours.com
This tour group absorbed the Gray Line of Savannah Tours in 2007. It offers a $10 on-off trolley tour, a complete history tour with admission to one attraction for $25 for adults and $10 for children, and riverboat and ghost packages. It also has a "Midnight in the Garden of Good and Evil" tour at $28 for adults and teens and $14 for children 5 to 11, including a drive out to Bonaventure Cemetery. The deluxe version goes outside the Historic District to include Isle of Hope, Wormsloe Historic Site, Bethesda Orphanage and Grayson Stadium, at a cost of $32 ($15 for those ages 5 to 11).

Victorian Lady Tours
(912) 236-1886
Ardis Wood dons Victorian costume to lead groups on customized tours. You can choose either walking tours or those conducted via various other transports, from your own car to a limo. The standard walking version lasts about two hours and costs $15 for adults and $7 for those younger than age 18. Rates for custom tours start at $45 per hour and go up. Options include downtown, the Colonial Coast, and the Lowcountry. The phone number reaches a recording; leave your number for a callback on specifics.

Horse-Drawn Carriages

Although children generally don't jump up and down at the prospect of a guided tour of historic sites, we've found horse-drawn carriages up the appeal significantly. Who knows? You may be lucky enough to see a chartered and decorated carriage ferrying a bride and groom from a wedding at one of the Historic Downtown churches. During rain or extreme heat, tours are not given.

Carriage Tours of Savannah
10 Warner Street
(912) 236-6756
www.carriagetoursofsavannah.com
Narrated tours are about an hour in length. Options include a daytime historic tour ($20 for adults, $10 for those ages 5 to 11), evening historic or ghost story tours ($19 for adults, $8 for children), and private carriage tours for couples, starting at $85. Tours depart from City Market.

Historic Savannah Carriage Tours
100 Aberdeen Street
(912) 443-9333
www.savannahcarriage.com
Pickup service can be arranged at hotels or at downtown locations. Fees are $20 for adults and $9 for children. Variations include a ghost tour and champagne tour. Departure is from the Hampton Inn at Bay and Abercorn Streets, or for private tours, by arrangement in the Historic District.

Magnolia Carriage Company
8 Warner Street
(912) 232-7727
Tours depart from City Market at $20 per person.

Walking

Walking tours have really taken off in recent years, and small wonder—all that's required is expertise and the ability to walk and talk at the same time. It seems to us there are new entries in this category constantly, so here's a sampling. Note, too, that many of the tour-bus companies offer a walking version as well. These tours generally depart from a specific downtown square, so check when you make your reservations. Remember, all such tours are offered weather permitting.

Ghost Talk, Ghost Walk
127 East Congress Street
(912) 233-3896, (800) 563-3896
The ghost tour is the mainstay (there are actually two different versions). They depart from Reynolds Square, beside the statue of John Wesley (one wonders what the famous preacher would have thought of it). Tours depart at dusk, varying according to the time of year, so call for information. Fees are $10 for adults and $5 for those younger than age 12. Other tours available include a Civil War version, a botanical tour, a historic architecture walk, and a literary walking tour. Rates vary; check when you make reservations.

The Savannah Walks
37 Abercorn Street
(912) 238-9255, (888) 728-9255
www.savannahwalks.com
This walking-tour firm offers a varied menu with different meeting points. Be sure to check on these things when you make your reservations. Fees are $15 for adults and $7 for children ages 6 to 16. Options include general tours, a "Midnight" tour, a ghost tour, a pub walk, a Civil War walk, and one featuring gardens. The historic homes walk is slightly higher ($22 adult, $14 children) because it includes admission to one of the city's house museums.

Sixth Sense Savannah
120 East Jones Street
(866) 666-3323
www.sixthsensesavannah.com
Lots of tour companies offer Savannah tours on a ghostly theme. This walking-tour company does it with a mixture of deadpan seriousness and arch humor (like the phone number, which spells out 666-DEAD). This company does not adopt the "all in fun" approach of many other ghost tours: These folks profess to believe, and even offer metaphysical readings on premises. The tour host is Shannon Scott, who has hosted some cable network TV programs on hauntings. Scott helped convince the American Institute of the

Paranormal to hold its annual convention in Savannah in 2002, and the group went on to bestow its "America's Most Haunted City" title on us. Tours start at 7:00 p.m.; there's a 9:30 p.m. version and a midnight one. Prices start at $18 for adults on the night tours and $20 for adults (16 and up) on the midnight tour.

Tootsy Tours
140 Johnny Mercer Boulevard, Suite 12
(912) 898-3111
www.tootsytours.com
These people offer specialty tours for Girl Scouts and for those with specific interests, specifically, black heritage, Jewish history, and natural history. They'll tailor a tour to fit your business meeting's downtime schedule, too. They also do regional tour work. Prices differ with the degree of customization.

Black History Tours

We thought these tours deserved to be singled out for separate mention as they cover a long-neglected aspect of American history. These are smaller operations than the heavy-duty commercial ventures discussed above. Our experience over the years has shown arrangements for these tours change frequently; confirm arrangements at the time of your trip.

Freedom Trail Tour
P.O. Box 1484
Savannah, 31402
(912) 398-2785
This tour is available seven days a week, with two tours daily in the winter and an extended schedule other months. Prices are $20 for adults and $12 for children, with discounts for seniors. The tour lasts about two hours and visits historic churches, the Ralph Mark Gilbert Civil Rights Museum, slave burial grounds, and sites of particular importance to African Americans. Departures are from the Visitors Center, 301 Martin Luther King Jr. Boulevard.

OTHER SAVANNAH ATTRACTIONS

What follows are listings of several other terrific Savannah attractions. Some are in the Historic Downtown but weren't covered by our walking tour; others are in the city's outlying areas.

Historic Downtown

Beach Institute
502 East Harris Street
(912) 234-8000
www.kingtisdell.org
The Beach Institute was established in 1865 by the American Missionary Association to educate newly freed slaves. Built in 1867, it was the first school in Savannah for African Americans and became a public school in 1919. The institute is an African-American cultural center and houses art, sculpture, and artifacts relating to the cultural contributions of black Americans. The star of its exhibits is the 238-piece collection of wood carvings by the late Ulysses Davis, Savannah folk artist. Lectures and other programs are frequently held. It is open from noon to 5:00 p.m. Tuesday through Saturday. Admission is $4 for adults, $2 for children.

First African Baptist Church
23 Montgomery Street
(912) 233-6597
Overlooking Franklin Square is First African Baptist Church. This church, which is still active, is descended from the oldest African-American congregation in the United States. George Leile, a slave, began making missionary visits to plantations up and down the Savannah River as early as 1774. A permanent congregation was formed at Brampton Plantation in 1788—the first black missionary Baptist church in Savannah.

Eventually, the congregation constructed the current building. It is the first brick building erected in Georgia by African Americans for African Americans; it was built by slaves who worked on it at night after being in the fields all day. The sanctuary has beautiful stained-glass windows framing the back of the altar, which displays pictures of the founding pastors. In the balcony are original pews with markings left by the slaves who built the church.

King-Tisdell Cottage
514 East Huntingdon Street
(912) 234-8000
www.kingtisdell.org

Built in 1869 by W. W. Aimar, this cottage, with its original gingerbread ornamentation, is in the Beach Institute neighborhood of the Historic Downtown and serves as a museum dedicated to preserving the African-American history of Savannah and the sea islands. Inside the small home you will find art objects, documents, and furniture of the 1890s. It is open from noon to 5:00 p.m. Tuesday through Saturday. Cost is $3.50.

Ralph Mark Gilbert Civil Rights Museum
460 Martin Luther King Jr. Boulevard
(912) 231-8900

More than 40,000 people toured Ralph Mark Gilbert Civil Rights Museum during its inaugural year of 1996. The museum chronicles the story of Savannah's civil rights struggles during the 1940s, 1950s, and 1960s. Along with traveling exhibits and special programming, it spotlights how Martin Luther King Jr. Boulevard, formerly known as West Broad Street, was once the center of the city's thriving black business community. Besides educating the community, the museum also serves as an educational resource for southeastern coastal Georgia.

Development of the museum took place over several years. More than $1.7 million went into the museum, which included the renovation of the Wage Earners Savings Bank building, where the museum is housed. The Wage Earners Bank is believed to be the second bank for African Americans in the nation. The museum is the brainchild of the late local historian and activist W. W. Law. It is named after the Rev. Ralph Mark Gilbert, a pastor at

i Want to see all of Savannah's museums for free? Plan your trip to Savannah around Super Museum Sunday. Every year the museums open up their doors free of charge to anyone who wants to stop by. You even get free transportation provided by the county's bus system. Not a bad deal. (See our Annual Events and Festivals chapter for more information.)

First African Baptist Church, who pioneered Savannah's modern civil rights movement. Admission is $4 for adults, $3 for seniors, and $2 for students. An expansion housing exhibit, meeting, and reception space is being built in a freestanding building behind the museum and is scheduled to open in 2008. (For information on the museum's annual anniversary celebration, look under May in our Annual Events and Festivals chapter.)

The Roundhouse Railroad Museum
601 West Harris Street
(912) 651-6823

The Roundhouse Railroad Museum includes the oldest and most complete antebellum railroad manufacturing and repair facilities still in existence in the United States. Thirteen of the original structures, which were built beginning in 1859, are still standing. Included are the roundhouse and turntable (where the engines were turned around) and the 125-foot brick smokestack. The site is a National Historic Landmark and is operated by the Coastal Heritage Society. It is open from 9:00 a.m. to 5:00 p.m. Monday through Saturday and from noon to 4:00 p.m. on Sunday. Cost is $4.25 for adults and $3.75 for students. Children younger than age 5 are free.

Savannah History Museum
Savannah Visitors Center
303 Martin Luther King Jr. Boulevard
(912) 651-6825

Delve into Savannah's colorful past at the Savannah History Museum, located in the old passenger station of the Central of Georgia Railroad that also houses the Savannah Visitors Center. The structure, a National Historic Landmark, features a variety of exhibits, including an 1890 steam locomotive that is still sitting on the original Central of Georgia tracks. A genuine antique cotton gin is on display, along with artifacts from the Civil War and other eras. A small theater shows a film that provides an overview of the city's history. The museum is open from 8:30 a.m. to 5:00 p.m. weekdays and 9:00 a.m. to 5:00 p.m. on weekends. It costs $4.25 for adults and teens, $3.75 for children ages 6 to 12. Kids younger than age 6 are free.

Ships of the Sea Museum
41 Martin Luther King Jr. Boulevard
(912) 232-1511
www.shipsofthesea.com
Scarbrough House and its related garden (a true undiscovered treasure) have added a lot of tone to this museum, previously housed on River Street. The exhibits are more formal now, showcasing paintings and intricate models. The collection also includes scrimshaw, ancient navigational tools, and a china cat figurine with its own risque story to tell. Learn about Savannah's maritime history while exploring this museum. The home, built in 1819 for the principal owner of the *Savannah,* the first steamship to cross the Atlantic Ocean, was designated a National Historic Landmark in 1974. Cost is $8 for adults, $6 for children age 7 and older (if you have a college ID you can get the discounted rate). Children younger than age 7 get in free. The museum is open from 10:00 a.m. to 5:00 p.m. Tuesday through Sunday. It is closed Monday.

Telfair Museum of Art
121 Barnard Street
(912) 232-1177
www.telfair.org
The Telfair is the oldest art museum in the South. Its permanent collection of paintings, prints, sculpture, and decorative arts is housed in a mansion designed by English architect William Jay for Alexander Telfair, son of Georgia governor Edward Telfair. The family lived here until 1875.

Among the museum's holdings are paintings by Childe Hassam, Frederick Frieseke, and Gari Melchers, along with Robert Henri, George Bellows, and George Luks. The museum also has a decorative arts collection that includes American and European objects from 1790 to 1840, including a rare Philadelphia suite of maple furniture, a secretary-bookcase commissioned from Duncan Phyfe of New York, and a dining table ordered from Thomas Cook of Philadelphia. The Jepson Center for the Arts, which opened in spring 2006, is a contemporary setting for more modern works, both from the Telfair's collection and in traveling exhibitions. It also houses educational facilities and is described in more detail in our Arts and Culture chapter.

The Telfair is open from 10:00 a.m. to 5:00 p.m. Monday, Wednesday, Friday, and Saturday (closed on Tuesday), 10:00 a.m. to 8:00 p.m. on Thursday, and noon to 5:00 p.m. on Sunday. Cost is $10 for adults, $8 for seniors, $5 for college students, and $4 for children ages 5 to 12. Children younger than age 5 are admitted free. Chatham County residents are admitted free on Sunday, but the regular rates apply to all others. Local governments or the museum periodically sponsor free admission on selected days.

Islands

Oatland Island Education Center
711 Sandtown Road
Oatland Island
(912) 898-3980
www.oatlandisland.org
A visit to Oatland gives you a good idea of what Georgia's first European settlers might have seen when they landed in 1733. Walk the 1.75-mile trail through the center's 75-acre forest of oaks, pines, and magnolias, and you'll encounter enclosures providing natural settings for animals native to the state: shorebirds, alligators, panthers, birds of prey, white-tailed deer, black bears, timber wolves,

and bison. The enclosures are large and wooded and the inhabitants are often hard to spot, but getting a look at them in their environment is worth the effort. The trail leads you to the Heritage Homesite area, where two log cabins (built in 1835, moved to Oatland and restored there) convey a feeling for life on the farm during pioneer days. Another Oatland feature is a barnyard where youngsters can see and feed farm animals.

Oatland, once cleared farmland where cotton was grown in the 18th and 19th centuries, was the site of a retirement home built in 1927 for railroad conductors. The home was in the center's main building, which later was used by the federal government as a test lab for the Centers for Disease Control until it was declared surplus in 1973. The Savannah-Chatham County School System (see our Education and Child Care chapter) took possession of the site for use as an environmental education center, and the main building now houses classrooms, offices, and a conference center. Although Oatland's main focus is on teaching students from local and out-of-county public and private schools, it is open to the public from 9:00 a.m. to 4:00 p.m. Monday through Friday and 10:00 a.m. to 4:00 p.m. on Saturday and Sunday.

Oatland hosts special events on selected Saturdays, such as its annual cane grinding festival, sheepshearing festival, the Medieval Festival, and the Halloween Hike (see our Annual Events and Festivals chapter). Admission to Oatland is $5 for adults and $3 for children. Sandtown Road runs south off Islands Expressway 4 miles east of Historic Downtown. The tour of the center's animal habitats is self-guided and takes about 90 minutes.

Old Fort Jackson
1 Fort Jackson Road
(912) 232-3945
www.chsgeorgia.org

Georgia's oldest standing brick fortification is an intriguing place. The fort perches right on the banks of the Savannah River—built there so its guns could fire on any vessel coming into Savannah—and chances are good you'll get an up-close view of an oceangoing ship during your visit.

Walk on the parapet of the fort and then investigate the structure's many nooks and crannies. Two powder magazines and most of the casemates are open to the public, and they contain displays of weaponry and tools used at the fort and artifacts from the CSS *Georgia*, a Confederate ironclad whose remains lay on the river bottom a few hundred feet away. Inspect 11 cannon. The 9-inch Dahlgren cannon is the largest functional piece of Civil War–era heavy artillery in the United States. Cannon-firing programs are presented daily from June 15 through August 15; call for more information.

Construction of Fort Jackson was begun in 1808 on the site of what had been an earthwork battery during the Revolutionary War. It was manned during the War of 1812 and expanded between 1845 and 1860. Confederate forces used it as headquarters of the Savannah River defenses during most of the Civil War, and it was garrisoned by Union troops after the city's surrender in December 1864. The only time it was fired upon was on October 1, 1862, when two Union steamers shelled it for about an hour during a reconnaissance mission. For a thorough rundown on the history of the fort, watch the 15-minute film that's shown in one of the powder magazines. The fort is not on an island, but we've placed it in this section because it's 3 miles from the Historic Downtown on the way to the eastside islands. To get there, take President Street Extension (also known as Islands Expressway) east to the red, white, and blue Fort Jackson sign; then turn left onto Woodcock Road and follow the brown signs to the fort. The nonprofit Coastal Heritage Society operates the fort under a lease with the state of Georgia. Admission is $4.25 for adults and $3.75 for students, senior citizens, and members of the military. There's no charge for children age 6 and younger.

The fort is open from 9:00 a.m. to 5:00 p.m. seven days a week, but it is closed on

Thanksgiving, Christmas, and New Year's Day. There are a variety of special programs available for groups, including Captain of the Guard and Mess and Muster dinners. The fort is also the site of the Coastal Heritage Society's Labor Day Lowcountry Boil and Auction (see our Annual Events and Festivals chapter).

Wormsloe Historic Site
7601 Skidaway Road
Isle of Hope
(912) 353-3023

You'll find the last architectural remnant of the Oglethorpe era in Savannah at Wormsloe Historic Site, which is at the end of Skidaway Road on the doorstep of the Isle of Hope, about 10 miles south of the Historic Downtown. After driving under a large masonry arch at the entrance to Wormsloe, you'll travel down an "avenue of oaks," a wide, crushed-stone road lined with majestic live-oak trees. After 1.25 miles, the road narrows to a walking trail. At this point, you'll find a parking lot and the Wormsloe museum.

Continue on foot down the trail about 0.25 mile, and you'll be looking at the remains of a fortified house where construction was started in 1739 during the 10-year span James Edward Oglethorpe spent founding and nurturing the colony of Georgia (see our History chapter). The builder and owner of the house—a physician, carpenter, and surveyor named Noble Jones—came to the new colony in 1733 with Oglethorpe and the first boatload of settlers. Three years later, Jones leased 500 acres from the Trustees of Georgia, land that would be part of a plantation he called Wormslow. The name was changed to Wormsloe in the mid-1800s by his great-grandson, and the plantation eventually grew to cover nearly 900 acres. Jones's descendants donated 822 of those acres to the Nature Conservancy in 1972, and the property was transferred to the state of Georgia, which manages the site via the Parks and Historic Sites Division of the Department of Natural Resources.

The house Jones completed in the mid-1740s was a five-room, one-and-one-half-story dwelling built into a fortlike, rectangular wall intended to protect its inhabitants from attack by the Spanish. The house and wall were made of tabby, a concoction of oyster shells, lime, and sand mixed with water. You can see parts of the foundation of the house and large portions of the wall. Other points of interest at Wormsloe are the museum and theater, where you can learn more about the site and the early days of the colony; a stone monument marking the first Jones family burial plot; nature trails; and the Colonial Life Area, which contains re-creations of outbuildings characteristic of Wormsloe's early period. This area is also the site of living-history demonstrations and programs presented during special events (see our Annual Events and Festivals chapter).

During your drive down the avenue of oaks, you may notice an elegant, two-story frame house on the eastern side of the road. This structure was built in 1828 and is home to the ninth generation of Jones's descendants; it is closed to the public. Wormsloe is open from 9:00 a.m. to 5:00 p.m. Tuesday through Saturday and from 2:00 to 5:30 p.m. on Sunday. It's closed on Mondays that are not legal holidays, Thanksgiving, Christmas, and New Year's Day. Admission is $4.00 for adults, $3.50 for senior citizens, and $2.50 for those 5 to 18 years old; children younger than age 5 are admitted free. This site is operated as part of Georgia's state parks system.

After you visit Wormsloe, take a few minutes to drive through nearby Isle of Hope, a community of narrow streets and beautifully preserved houses. Turn right after leaving Wormsloe, and you'll be on Parkersburg Road, which meanders through Isle of Hope until it reaches Bluff Drive, one of the prettiest streets in the Savannah area. A jaunt down Bluff Drive, which runs alongside the picturesque Skidaway River, is worth the time it will take to make this short detour. (For more on Isle of Hope, see our Relocation/Real Estate chapter.)

Southside/Midtown

Bethesda Home for Boys
9520 Ferguson Avenue
(912) 351-2040

Bethesda, America's oldest children's home, reposes on 600 oak-filled acres overlooking the Moon River (yes, that Moon River, the one made famous in the song by Henry Mancini and Savannahian Johnny Mercer). You can stroll or ride around the well-kept grounds of the main campus and visit the Bethesda museum and chapel, but the home's administrators ask that you report to the office after you arrive so that they know you're there. The museum—located in what was once the dining room of Burroughs Cottage, which was built in 1883 and is the oldest standing building at Bethesda—contains documents and artifacts pertaining to the history of the home and of coastal Georgia. Whitefield Chapel was completed in 1925 and is named for George Whitefield, one of the home's founders. It's a reproduction of Whitefield's church in England, and with its straight-back wooden pews, brick floor, and airy interior, the chapel is a spartan but beautiful place in which to spend a few moments in meditation. The chapel is open year-round; museum hours are from 9:00 a.m. to 5:00 p.m. Monday through Friday, and there's no admission, but donations are accepted.

Whitefield and his friend James Habersham started Bethesda in 1740 as a home for the orphaned boys of the fledgling colony of Georgia. The home has served more than 9,000 children and nowadays offers a residency program for 40 boys who are housed in 5 cottages staffed by cottage teachers. These days, few of the boys at Bethesda are orphans; most come from broken homes or from at-risk situations. They attend school at Bethesda through 12th grade. Through the years, according to Assistant Director Bill McIlrath, the mission of Bethesda has remained the same: "To teach the boys a good work ethic, to give them a good education, and to raise them in the nurture and admonition of the Lord."

Chatham County Garden Center and Botanical Gardens
1388 Eisenhower Drive
(912) 355-3883

See more than 900 varieties of trees, shrubs, and flowering plants when you visit this Savannah Area Council of Garden Clubs project on the Southside. The clubs maintain 10 acres of gardens featuring roses, perennials, herbs, and vegetables and separate gardens devoted to flowering plants that bloom during the different seasons of the year. There's also a garden for plants such as ferns that grow best in spots that don't get much sunshine. Some of the plants are labeled, so neophyte gardeners will be able to tell what they're looking at. A tabby walkway meanders through the gardens, and a small pond and a nature walk add to the ambience of this spot, which is nestled in a fairly well-developed part of town. The garden center is headquartered in an 1840s-era farmhouse that was moved to the Southside from a downtown location in 1991. The council presents lectures and courses on horticulture at the two-story house, which boasts features such as two fireplaces, heart-of-pine floors, and clam molding on the doors that's more than 150 years old. The center and gardens are on Eisenhower Drive at its intersection with Sallie Mood Drive; hours are from 10:00 a.m. to 2:00 p.m. daily, and admission is $2.

West Chatham

Bamboo Farm and Coastal Gardens
2 Canebrake Road
(912) 921-5460

If you like digging in the dirt and growing things, you should love this spot in southwest Chatham County that was once an experimental station where the federal government introduced plants from throughout the world.

Called the Bamboo Farm through the years by Savannahians because of the groves of the tropical plant grown there, the facility has a large collection of daylilies, a xeriscape garden, a cottage garden, and bamboo, of course—140 varieties of it. The bamboo collection is the largest in the United States open for viewing by the public, and there's also a grove of giant timber bamboo—the reason the farm was purchased for the U.S. Department of Agriculture in 1918. The bamboo grove, where stalks can reach a height of more than 70 feet and a diameter of 6 inches, originated with three seedlings planted on the site in 1890; 25 years later, it attracted the attention of plant explorer David Fairchild, who bought the 46-acre farm where the bamboo grew and donated it to the government.

The plant introduction station was closed in 1978, and the property was deeded four years later to the University of Georgia, whose Cooperative Extension Service operates it today, along with the government of Chatham County, as a center for coastal education. The farm offers a self-guided walking tour that will take you to (among other botanical treasures) the bamboo collection and grove, beds of ornamental and turf grasses, an experimental grove of different species of banana tree, a collection of crape myrtle trees that's probably the largest in coastal Georgia, and a variety of other interesting trees, including one whose fruit resembles popcorn.

The Bamboo Farm and Coastal Gardens holds a number of special events throughout the year, most of which require reservations, and makes available a 650-seat, open-air pavilion and a 100-seat conference hall. The farm is open from 8:00 a.m. to 5:00 p.m. Monday through Friday, from 10:00 a.m. to 5:00 p.m. on Saturday, and from noon until 5:00 p.m. on Sunday. Admission is free, and donations are accepted. The facility is on U.S. Highway 17, about 13 miles south of the Historic Downtown.

Mighty Eighth Air Force Heritage Museum
175 Bourne Avenue
Pooler
(912) 748-8888
www.mightyeighth.org

It's not unusual for veterans of World War II aerial combat to leave this museum's Mission Experience exhibit with tears in their eyes.

This re-creation of an Eighth Air Force bombing mission brings back vivid memories to those who flew over Europe—recollections of heavily defended targets, stricken aircraft, and fallen comrades. The panoramic, eight-screen theater and its B-17 flight are a featured part of the 90,000-square-foot museum in Pooler near the intersection of Interstate 95 and U.S. Highway 80 (exit 102 from I-95). In addition to the Mission Experience and other displays, the museum has a research library stocked with books pertaining to aviation and air warfare, an art gallery, Memorial Gardens, chapel, store, and restaurant.

The museum opened in May 1996. It honors the more than one million men and women who have served in the Eighth since its creation in Savannah on January 28, 1942, at the Chatham Artillery Armory on Bull Street at Park Avenue. A small command force worked there for a few months before moving to England, where the organization manned bases from August 1942 until May 1945 and grew to have more than 350,000 members during World War II. The Eighth flew more than 600,000 sorties against Nazi Germany and dropped more than 700,000 tons of bombs on enemy targets. Today, the building where the Eighth was born is the home of American Legion Post 135.

Besides the Mission Experience, the museum's exhibit area contains presentations featuring more than 15 units that were part of the Eighth; a mural and a scale model depicting a World War II bomber base in England; areas dealing with escape and evasion, prisoners of war, and the contributions of African-American airmen; a diorama portraying the raids on the Ploesti oil fields; a PT-17 Stearman trainer and a Messerschmitt Komet rocket plane on static display; and several other theaters. On display outdoors are an F-4 Phantom jet fighter, a MiG jet fighter, and a B-47 Stratojet bomber. The six-engine B-47 was a mainstay of the U.S. Air Force's Strategic Air Command during the early stages of the Cold War, and was a sight familiar to Savannahians in the 1950s, when Hunter Air Force Base (now Hunter Army Airfield) was the home of a B-47 wing. The museum is open from 9:00 a.m. until 5:00 p.m. daily except for New Year's Day, Easter, Thanksgiving, and Christmas. Admission to the exhibit area is $10 for adults and teens and $6 for children ages 6 to 12, with those younger than age 6 admitted free. There are discounts for members of the military, senior citizens, and groups of 20 or more. The library is open from 10:00 a.m. to noon and from 1:00 to 4:00 p.m. Monday through Friday.

Savannah-Ogeechee Canal Museum and Nature Center
681 Fort Argyle Road
(912) 748-8068
www.savannahogeecheecanal.com

The Savannah-Ogeechee Canal, which played a role in the commercial development of Savannah during the 1800s, lay virtually forgotten for a century until a group of Chatham Countians reclaimed a third of it from the tangle of foliage that had grown over it. These volunteers started their work in 1992 and now, organized as the Savannah-Ogeechee Canal Society, oversee the continued development of the waterway as a historic and recreational area.

The 16.5-mile canal, which once was 58 feet wide at water level, was completed in 1830 and links the Savannah and Ogeechee Rivers. It accommodated horse- and mule-drawn barges as much as 70 feet long, and also boats poled by their occupants. These barges and boats carried lumber, cotton, rice, naval stores, and other goods. Six 18-foot-wide locks, some originally made of wood and later replaced with brick, controlled the hydraulics of the canal, which faded from usage in the early 1890s because of the destructive effects of a hurricane, and because it could not compete with the region's railroads and road system.

You can get a splendid idea of what the southern portion of the canal was like by visiting the society's museum and 184-acre nature center, which is on Fort Argyle Road (better known as Highway 204), a little more than 2 miles west of exit 94 of I-95. The museum, a converted bungalow, has two exhibit rooms, one depicting the history of the canal and another displaying reptiles and amphibians that inhabit the area the waterway runs through.

Within view of the museum is Lock 5, which is on a trail you can follow for 0.4 mile along the canal south to Lock 6 and the Ogeechee River; this trail is the towpath that horses and mules trod while pulling barges more than 100 years ago. The Tow Path is one of several trails you can walk while at the nature center (see our Parks and Recreation chapter for more details). The museum and nature center are open from 9:00 a.m. to 5:00 p.m. each day of the year. Admission is $2 for adults and $1 for students and senior citizens; children age 5 and younger are admitted free.

SAVANNAH CELEBRITY

Published scandals and home cooking have both been very good to Savannah tourism. Fans of both have trekked to Savannah, and the tourism industry has responded with specialty tours, souvenirs, and classes.

The published scandal we refer to is John Berendt's nonfiction best seller *Midnight in the Garden of Good and Evil,* published in 1994. Set in Savannah, it tells a series of tales about local characters and eccentricities, but focuses mainly on a shooting death and subsequent series of murder trials.

The home cooking we refer to is that practiced by Paula Deen, who has built an empire out of fried chicken and cheese biscuits. In less than 20 years, Deen has gone from being a struggling, newly divorced housewife to the queen of a media and business empire that includes her two Food Network television programs, two restaurants, a growing library of cookbooks, her own magazine, a cooking school, and a line of products.

Both phenomena have drawn tourists to Savannah. Berendt's fans were trailing the blood-tinged scent of scandal, while Deen's followers are following their noses to tables laden with squash casserole and roasted oysters.

In the 1990s, Berendt's readers began to show up in the city, where *Midnight in the Garden of Good and Evil* became talked about so much that locals simply termed it "The Book." At its height, the resulting craze included multiple tours of Book-mentioned sites, a gift shop devoted to Book items, and even a newsletter. And even today, though the *Midnight* hour has passed to a large degree, you can still find plenty of specialty tours and souvenirs related to it. We cover those in more detail later in this chapter.

Just as the clock began to run out on *Midnight,* Savannah's next celebrity—and the woman around whom the next fan-driven phase of tourism would revolve—was beginning to come forward.

COOKING UP A FORTUNE

Paula Deen is building a national reputation and business empire on her home-style cooking skills. And she's taking Savannah along with her for the ride. Tourists make a beeline for her two Savannah restaurants, the tour that focuses on her career, and shops that sell her cookbooks, gift items, even her magazine. And, as the Next Big Thing after the *Midnight* phenomenon, it is appropriate that *Midnight* author John Berendt had a role in her discovery and subsequent success. He was fond of Deen's cooking, and he wrote the introduction for her first professionally published cookbook back in 1998, when his own book was still the center of attention in Savannah.

The Paula Deen story is a rags-to-riches tale that reads like the script for a sappy TV movie—except that it's true. The mother of two sons, she found herself divorced and unemployed in 1989. Lacking other job skills, she fell back on the Southern cooking techniques she had learned in her grandmother's kitchen.

i Savannah cannot lay claim to the origins of celebrity cook Paula Deen's thick Southern drawl, so prominently showcased on her Food Network program. She is originally from Albany, Georgia. In Savannah, we pronounce Albany much the same way a New Yorker would pronounce Albany. But a native of Albany, Georgia, will tell you he or she is from "AWL-benny."

She started small, as The Bag Lady. Helped by her sons, she packaged bag lunches for office workers in the downtown area. The next step was her own restaurant, run out of a nice but nondescript motel on Savannah's Southside, the section of town known for its strip shopping centers, suburbs, and adjacent military base. As she continued working her way up the ladder of the food business, her next stop was The Lady and Sons Restaurant in downtown Savannah, right in the midst of both the local business district and Savannah's tourist hub.

Even if things had stopped right there, the Deen story would have been an inspiring entrepreneurial tale. There were lines at the door to her restaurant every day, first with businessmen and later tourists jostling to get platefuls of fried chicken, collards, squash casserole, hoecakes, cheese biscuits, and other comfort food. She was making money and had built a sterling reputation for the quality of her food. She could have stayed a purely Savannah success story—but bigger things beckoned.

Deen had some successful appearances on a television shopping network, hawking her book and a line of seasonings. But her big break came with the advent of a regular show on the Food Network, a cable channel for foodies. Suddenly, Paula Deen went from being a good cook with a local following to a celebrity chef with a national following. And there was more to come on the heels of the program *Paula's Home Cooking*.

Success prompted Deen to move her restaurant a few blocks to a historic building she purchased and renovated, where she could serve bigger crowds and house more business enterprises. Her national fan following has followed her to Savannah, where it keeps her already crowded The Lady and Sons Restaurant packed. Now there's another TV program, *Paula's Party*, filmed at Uncle Bubba's Oyster House.

Those business enterprises keep coming. Deen understands marketing across various media—she's on TV, in cookbooks, in her own magazine, in personal appearances. You'll even find her in the movies, where she had a small part in *Elizabethtown*, starring Orlando Bloom.

Maybe you are visiting Savannah in search of all things Paula, in which case we can steer you to the things that will feed your fascination. Maybe you don't have cable television and don't follow the celebrity chef scene—we can still steer you to some of the best food you'll ever eat. Read on for details on the Deen scene. We'll start, appropriately enough, with the food.

The Lady and Sons
102 West Congress Street
(912) 233-2600
www.theladyandsons.com
www.pauladeen.com
This is Deen's flagship restaurant, and the one essential, cannot-miss stop for any serious Deen fan. You'll find it described in more detail in our Restaurants chapter. We will warn you that the place is very popular and requires some planning ahead. They start taking names for lunch seating at 9:30 a.m. and start serving at 11:00 a.m. Dinner is served beginning at 5:00 p.m. with table sign-up starting at 3:30 p.m. The cutoff times when they stop taking names strike us as pretty arbitrary. If, however, you get your name on the list, you do get seated. And as time has passed, the staff has learned better how to cope with the steady stream of fans. The lunch buffet is $12.99; the dinner version is $16.99; and you also have the options of ordering from the menu.

> ℹ️ It's a family thing: Paula Deen already has seven cookbooks in print, her sons have one, and now her brother, of Uncle Bubba's Oyster House fame (his real name is Earl Hiers), is getting in on the act. *Uncle Bubba's Savannah Seafood*, coauthored by Savannahian Polly Powers Stramm, was published in 2007.

And by the way, a word of warning: A public/private project near this restaurant involves tearing down a parking garage to restore a square, installing underground parking, building new buildings, and renovating existing ones. In other words, parking and congestion in the vicinity of the restaurant are likely to be amplified, at least into late 2008.

Uncle Bubba's Oyster House
104 Bryan Woods Road
(912) 897-6101

This is the second restaurant with which Deen is affiliated, named for her brother and launched after it became obvious The Lady's star was rising. The focus here is seafood, although a selection of Deen's country cooking is also available. Read more under Uncle Bubba's entry in our Restaurants chapter. This restaurant serves as the lunch location in the Paula Deen Tour (more on that later).

Success hasn't changed Paula Deen, except to make her a lot busier. But success has presented some challenges to her restaurants. The steady onslaught of hungry, impatient people seems to strain the attitudes of folks who take down names for those awaiting tables at both places. Don't be put off by the take-it-or-leave-it attitude of the list-keeper. Once you've cleared that hurdle, you'll find the staff inside friendly and welcoming.

The Paula Deen Tour
Old Savannah Tours
514 Berrien Street
(912) 234-8128
www.oldsavannahtours.com

This highly specialized tour will thrill Paula Deen fanatics, and it won't necessarily bore indulgent spouses and family members either. But if you haven't visited Savannah before and you aren't passionate about this celebrity cook, take another tour. For one thing, it is $54 for adults and $34 for ages 12 and under, a whopping price by local standards (but that's misleading, because it also includes a meal and souvenirs). For another thing, this tour can last as much as four hours, which (even if it does include lunch) takes a big bite out of a day.

The Deen tour cashes in on celebrity, just like similar theme tours cashed in on the popularity of *Midnight*. The difference is, anyone could launch a *Midnight* tour (and plenty did, and still do). But there is only one Deen tour, because the process virtually requires her blessing.

Only one tour is offered per day, beginning at 10:00 a.m. every day but Sunday. Advance reservations are strongly recommended—the tour company takes them even months in advance at its Web site. The tour passes through the Historic District and goes by places that were prominent in the development of Deen's career. Stops also include shops Deen recommends (usually food-related), lunch at Uncle Bubba's Oyster House, and a trip to the grounds of Bethesda Home for Boys, the historic orphanage whose grounds were the scene of Deen's televised wedding. Another local family-owned food business, Byrd Cookie Company (producers of Savannah's well-known benne wafers and other treats) is included on the tour except on Saturday, when it is closed in deference to the Seventh Day Adventist faith of the family behind it.

One of the prize benefits of the tour is a VIP seating pass to The Lady and Sons, Deen's flagship restaurant. The tour's pass lets participants bypass the usual wait, either for dinner that night or later in their visit.

There's no guarantee you'll meet Paula Deen on the tour (in fact, you probably won't, although it does happen), but it's not unusual to meet one of the two sons or her brother, Earl Hiers (Uncle Bubba).

The tour company really capitalizes on its Deen connections. It books a riverboat cruise heavily billed as being catered by The Lady and Sons. In 2007 it even scheduled two three-day tours that call on Albany, Deen's hometown, and Plains, hometown of former President Jimmy Carter, before returning to the regular Deen tour in Savannah on the third day. Now, we've been to Albany and it is a nice enough small town, but a tour like that should be reserved for only the most fanatical of fans.

Paula Deen's Cooking School
Various locations
www.theladyandsons.com/cooking.php

Paula used to teach a cooking school in Savannah, but at the moment it is on hiatus, probably because she's on a nationwide food tour on behalf of Smithfield Foods. We suspect the classes will eventually return—anything that sells out 11 months in advance at a price of $250 per person, as some of the classes did, is just too profitable to park forever. Registration is via the Web site at www.theladyandsons.com.

Cooking With Paula Deen Magazine
Hoffman Media
1900 International Park Drive, Suite #50
Birmingham, Alabama 35243
www.pauladeenmagazine.com

If Martha Stewart has her own cooking and lifestyle magazine, why not Paula Deen? This magazine is published six times a year, and the subscription price is $19.98. The publisher behind the glossy magazine is Hoffman Media, which also publishes two other food-oriented periodicals, *Taste of the South* and *Southern Lady*. The magazine has a central core of recipes, flanked at the beginning and end of the magazine by photo spreads and feature stories on Deen, Savannah, and other places in her life.

Meanwhile, if you want more Deen reading material, she has seven cookbooks in print already, along with what is described as a biography on her journey from troubled homemaker to successful entrepreneur, *It Ain't All About the Cookin'*. Also, there's a free newsletter you can sign up for at www.the ladyandsons.com.

Still haven't had your fill of this celebrity cook? She's marketing a line of sauces and mixes, aprons, magnets, even a line of coffee under her new husband's name, Captain

Michael's Coffee. You can buy at the store in her restaurants or via her Web site.

MIDNIGHT IN SAVANNAH

Although Savannah's *Midnight* phenomenon is not as all-consuming as it once was, it is still a viable tourism force. You would probably have to look long and hard to find a parallel for the financial windfall this book brought this city. Berendt's latest book is set in Venice—are gondola tours of scandal sites in that city's future? (It didn't really turn out that way, as lightning failed to strike twice.)

With *Midnight*'s curiously appealing set of character sketches loosely held together by a lurid murder case, the New York author created a phenomenon in the tourist world. His work gave rise to a plethora of themed guided tours and silly souvenirs, and at the height of its popularity, *Midnight in the Garden of Good and Evil* created enough of a furor to drive a statue out of a graveyard and make a drag queen into a local celeb.

The Book deals with homosexuality, murder, voodoo, weird social customs, and charismatic con men—not necessarily the most flattering portrayal imaginable. However, it was eagerly embraced by the local populace as well as the reading public.

Perhaps the locals just want their 15 minutes of fame, which *Midnight in the Garden of Good and Evil* certainly gives to Savannah and its residents. It seems that normally reticent people are willing to put up with the public airing of any amount of dirty laundry as long as it brings Clint Eastwood to town to film a movie about it.

The real answer, however, probably lies deep within a cash register. The city has discovered that the coattails of a best seller with a fan following are a comfortable and profitable place to ride.

There are still plenty of opportunities for Book fans to sample in person what they've experienced in print. One sure sign that the phenomenon is well past its peak, however, is this—the prices on the guided tours have not

The script for the movie of *Midnight in the Garden of Good and Evil* involved some significant revision from the book. Where the two conflict, believe The Book first.

gone up. The whole phenomenon might have had longer legs if the movie version had been more successful.

For the duration, we'll follow local practice and continue to call Berendt's best seller The Book—a shorthand we have all adopted in self-defense, since an eight-word title takes a while to say in a Southern drawl, and locals have trouble pronouncing Berendt's name.

A LITTLE BACKGROUND

Midnight in the Garden of Good and Evil was published in January 1994. Berendt, a columnist and former editor at *Esquire,* had spent several years living off and on in Savannah, collecting the stories that make up the book. The unifying thread of the book is the four murder trials that followed the fatal shooting of a young man by self-made millionaire antiques dealer Jim Williams. Mingled in are the stories of a flamboyant drag queen, a tax lawyer who excels as a bad-check artist and a piano player, white socialites who play cards and black debutantes who dance the minuet, an oddball genius with a penchant for poisons, and so on.

Random House quickly had a hit on its hands. The Book hit the *New York Times* bestseller list in March 1994 and pretty much stayed there for the ensuing four years.

Ah, but is The Book as true as it claims? That brings to mind what the character Huck Finn had to say about the Tom Sawyer story: that it was "mostly true but with some stretchers." The time lines, for example, are a little out of sync, and the slant of the stories can still spark debate among locals. Several of the names of central figures are pseudonyms, and that told-as-true tale about the dead cat, the dinner party, and the stomach pump is a classic urban legend—consider it modern folklore.

With book sales so brisk and a larger-than-life cast of characters on the page, it was inevitable that Hollywood would go Gardening. In May 1996, director Clint Eastwood began filming the screen version with Kevin Spacey in the Williams role, John Cusack as Berendt, and the Lady Chablis (the aforementioned drag queen) as the Lady Chablis. The story got a revision for the screen, and the city got an out-of-season face-lift, as the squares involved in the shooting were decked out in Christmas greenery in a month that qualifies as full summer in Savannah.

So now fans of The Book have had a refresher course, and those who haven't read it at least have an idea of what we are talking about. Let's move on to how visitors to Savannah can walk inside Berendt's pages.

TOURS

If you want to cover a lot of Book territory relatively quickly, the tour buses are your best bet. We're describing them in plural here because they offer essentially the same thing: a two- to two-and-one-half-hour tour that is mainly a drive-by of important sites from The Book, capped off with a cemetery visit. Be aware that tours have a tendency to run longer than advertised, so allow plenty of time. All tours require reservations, which can be made by phone. If this is an important event for you, call well in advance—while these tours aren't as popular as they once were, you can never tell. The various tour companies take the major credit cards, but

Early in The Book, lawyer and confidence man Joe Odom describes the Georgia-Florida football game as one of only two high holidays in Savannah, the other being St. Patrick's Day. For the record, Georgia broke a seven-game losing streak in that important series in 1997 and stunned the oddsmakers with a 37-to-17 victory—exactly three weeks before the scheduled debut of the *Midnight* movie.

Close-up

Savannah Filmography: 1975–2000

Note that accompanying dates are filming dates, not necessarily release dates.

2000: *The Gift*
1999: *The Legend of Bagger Vance*
1998: *Forces of Nature, The General's Daughter*
1997: *The Gingerbread Man, Midnight in the Garden of Good and Evil, Claudine's Return*
1996: *Wild America*
1995: *Something to Talk About*
1994: *Now and Then*
1993: *Forrest Gump, Camilla*
1990: *Goldenboy, Love Crimes*
1989: *The Rose and the Jackal, Flight of the Intruder, Glory*

1988: *The Return of Swamp Thing, The Judas Project*
1987: *My Father, My Son; 1969; War Stories*
1986: *Pals*
1983: *Solomon Northup's Odyssey*
1981: *All My Children, Tales of Ordinary Madness*
1980: *The Slayer, White Death, Scared to Death, When the Circus Came to Town, Fear, East of Eden, Mother Seton*
1979: *Gold Bug, The Ordeal of Dr. Mudd, Orphan Train, Hopscotch, Carny*
1978: *The Double McGuffin*
1977: *The Lincoln Conspiracy*
1976: *Roots*
1975: *Gator*

because tour drivers usually don't handle anything other than cash transactions, ask where you'll pay if you plan to use a credit card—it might affect which of the pickup locations you specify.

Tours pick up at the Savannah Visitors Center, 301 Martin Luther King Jr. Boulevard, which has reasonably ample parking. Stash your car and look for the large parking slots near the center's front door, marked with signs identifying the tour company that uses that spot—that's where you'll board. Major downtown hotels and some bed-and-breakfasts in the Historic Downtown also serve as pickup locations. Get details when you make your reservations.

Remember that Book-related tours are just part of a wider tour menu offered by each company. Others include ghost tours, walking tours, Civil War–themed tours, carriage tours, Savannah history tours, and the like. (See our

Attractions chapter for more on other types of guided tours.) The city of Savannah requires that tour guides pass a test and hold a license. On a typical tour, you'll drive by Mercer House, the mansion that was the site of The Book's fatal shooting; Club One, performance venue for the Lady Chablis (see our Nightlife chapter for details); various homes where lawyer and professional partier Joe Odom stayed, often without the owners' knowledge; the jail where Williams was incarcerated (now replaced by a structure outside town); the modern county courthouse where the first three trials were held; the ornate old federal courthouse that stands in for it in the movie version; and so on. The walking versions can't range far enough to include Bonaventure Cemetery, so choose another walking tour and opt for wheels if you are a Book fan—it just isn't the same without the graveyard.

Along the way, you'll get a chance to see the city's more conventional attractions as well, and chances are the tour guide will throw in a few comments about those. The highlight of all the tours is a visit to Bonaventure Cemetery, which you can read about elsewhere in this chapter. To connect with a Book tour, consult our tour listings in the Attractions chapter.

SEEING IT ON YOUR OWN

If you want to see some of The Book sites but don't fancy tours, you can get to many of them on your own. After all, the Historic Downtown itself is a character in the book. The following are some tips on what you can see solo. There's no shortage of maps in Savannah (hardly surprising in a city with a thriving tourism industry), and there's a good one in this very book. With a copy of The Book in hand and the map of the Historic Downtown you'll find at the front of our guide, you can find major Book sites such as Monterey Square.

Easily Accessed Sites

Now that you have a map, we'll list a few of the most easily found sites. We'll start with two general outdoor sites, where you can stand on the sidewalk and gaze, then move on to places you can actually get into.

Monterey Square
400 block of Bull Street, bounded by Taylor and Gordon Streets
This square is home to many of the central events in The Book, but it's worth a good look on its own merits. The massive central monument to Polish Count Casimir Pulaski, a hero of the American Revolution, has finally been

> **i** Savannah got its first look at the movie version of The Book on November 20, 1997, at a benefit for the Lucas Theatre restoration and the Frank Callen Boys and Girls Club.

returned to its pedestal, after a seemingly endless delay during its restoration. The absence was so long that when the movie of *Midnight* was filming on location, prop makers had to fake a version of the monument.

Mercer House
429 Bull Street
The famous house looks out on the square from Bull Street. This is where Williams lived and threw his famous parties, and where he shot his companion to death. It remains a private residence, although it opened to paying tours in 2004. See the Close-up in our Attractions chapter for details. Mercer House had claims to fame well before Williams's misfortunes. While lyricist Johnny Mercer ("Moon River," "That Old Black Magic," etc.) never lived there, he had close family ties to it.

Jackie Kennedy Onassis once showed up to tour it, and The Book claims she concluded that tour with a request for directions to the nearest Burger King. (It's a cute story, true or not, and if you believe it and want to follow in the footsteps of the rich and famous, the nearest Burger King is in the 600 block of Martin Luther King Jr. Boulevard.)

Next to Mercer House, across narrow Wayne Street, stands the home of the neighbors Williams feuded with. He gets in some sharp digs on them from beyond the grave, thanks to The Book. Again, this is a private house—no tours. Directly across the square from Mercer House stands the historic Temple Mickve Israel synagogue, whose congregation, along with many other Savannahians, was affronted when Williams hung a Nazi flag from his balcony to disrupt filming of a period movie.

Intersection of Bull and Gaston Streets
Remember, The Book maintains nothing counts unless it's North of Gaston Street (NOGS, for short). This is where Bull Street hits that great divide. The sweeping white brick building on the western side of Bull is Armstrong House, which crops up in the book several times, most prominently as the offices

of the lawyer who handled Williams's defense. On the eastern side you'll see the Oglethorpe Club, which also turns up in said Book. This is the city's most exclusive private club, with rigid membership requirements that include white skin, blue blood, and money that's yellowed with age.

Clary's Cafe
404 Abercorn Street
(912) 233-0402

Clary's was the setting where Berendt first encountered the Luther Driggers character, who tried to make goldfish glow and enjoyed toting about a bottle of poison. At the time, Clary's was a drugstore with a lunch counter. The drugstore is long gone, but the restaurant has grown. (Read more about it in our Restaurants chapter.) Clary's has opened a second location farther south in Midtown, but there's no Book connection.

Club One Jefferson
1 Jefferson Street
(912) 232-0200

The Lady Chablis performs in the drag show here periodically. For more details, check out the Close-up in our Nightlife chapter.

Telfair Museum of Art
121 Barnard Street
(912) 232-1177

This local art museum is the new home for the *Bird Girl* statue pictured on the cover of The Book. The figure once stood guard over the Trosdal family plot in Bonaventure Cemetery, and neither the statue nor the Trosdals are in the print version of the story. Family members had the statue removed when Book tourists overran the family plot to pose for photos beside it. (By the way, photography is not allowed inside the Telfair, a common enough prohibition by museums.) The Telfair is worth a visit in its own right (see our Arts and Culture chapter). Admission costs are $10 for adults, $8 for seniors, and $4 for children ages 5 to 12.

SOUVENIRS

The variety of Book souvenirs is impressive. Here's a very partial list: a woven afghan featuring book scenes, bookmarks picturing one of Joe Odom's rubber checks, paintings of Mercer House, a video "tour" with interviews of some of the real-life characters, coffee mugs and jewelry featuring the *Bird Girl* figure, a limited-edition candle shaped like the cover statue, postcards depicting the Lady Chablis, and miniature cookies in a tin patterned after the book cover. Several T-shirts are on the market.

The ultimate souvenir is, clearly, The Book itself. Of course, you'll find it in local bookstores, but you'll also spot it in local stores that have never sold any other book before. You'll find a huge supply of books that have been autographed by the author. Early in the phenomenon, there was a scandal about fake autographs at one supplier, and Berendt himself came forward to get that stopped. The book lists for $25, $10 in paperback. Some of the downtown souvenir places jack the price for an autographed copy. All the local independent booksellers and chains also carry the book, and we encourage you to keep your copy close at hand. The Lady Chablis holds an autograph session after her nightclub set. You'll never get a complete set of character autographs, however; many of the central characters have died.

An example of the hold The Book still has on local affections was clear when pianist and singer Emma Kelly died after a long illness. She was a well-known figure in Savannah and nearby Statesboro well before The Book came out, but The Book amplified that dramatically. Her funeral was front-page news in both cities. And when Jim Williams's Jaguar went on eBay in 2007, it got breathless newspaper coverage.

Random House has produced audio versions of The Book, both abridged and unabridged. If you haven't gotten around to reading it, these might be good options for car listening if you are driving into Savannah from some distance. Beware, however: The unabridged version runs more than 11 hours.

Bonaventure Cemetery: Good Fortune for Lovers of The Book

"Bonaventure" means "good fortune," which may strike you as a strange name for a graveyard. But once you visit this serenely beautiful place, chances are the name will seem more appropriate. Bonaventure Cemetery plays a prominent role in John Berendt's *Midnight in the Garden of Good and Evil*. It is here in this lush Victorian graveyard that the book's narrator drinks martinis and gets his introductory course on Savannah society. The massive cemetery stands under the moss-draped shade of towering live oaks, is peopled by row upon row of elegant statuary and headstones, and commands a waterfront view that would make a condo developer drool.

The graves made famous in the book include the Aiken family plot. Here, the parents of Pulitzer Prize–winning poet Conrad Aiken—killed in a murder-suicide—are buried. Conrad Aiken's own grave, marked by a bench engraved with poetry, stands alongside. Not too far away, you'll spot the graves of famed Savannah lyricist Johnny Mercer and his wife, Ginger.

This is the culminating point for the guided tours of Book sites. If you happen to be a nonfan of The Book, and you were swept along by a fervent spouse or group, hang in there. The 160-acre graveyard is well worth seeing in its own right.

Bonaventure was once an elegant plantation, but the grand home burned down more than once. Local folklore has it that the roof caught fire during a dinner party, and the guests finished the meal outdoors by the light of the burning house. If you are looking for ghost stories, there's a tale that you can still hear the revelry and breaking glass of that party at certain times. You'll find these tales repeated in The Book. The property became a cemetery in the 1800s and was put into city hands in 1907. It is still an active cemetery with an occasional burial, but the few remaining spaces are generally taken—don't get attached to the place.

Many important figures from the history of Georgia and the nation are buried here. There's Noble Jones, who arrived with James Oglethorpe at the beginning of the colony; several members of Georgia's Liberty Boys; and a number of prominent physicians, including Brodie Herndon, chief surgeon of hospitals for the Confederacy and the first doctor to perform a Caesarean operation in the United States. John Walz, sculptor of many of the impressive funerary statues in Bonaventure and other local cemeteries, is buried here. Ironically, there is no headstone at his grave.

If you want to visit Bonaventure Cemetery without a tour, here are some fairly detailed instructions. How you get there depends, of course, on where you start. Because we reasoned most visitors would be starting from the Historic Downtown, we launch our trek at the intersection of Bull and Liberty Streets, right beside the Hilton Savannah DeSoto Hotel. Set your trip odometer there; you have about 3.5 miles to go. Liberty Street is a major east-west thoroughfare downtown. Follow it east. You'll quickly leave the Historic District and pass through areas that include low-income housing and small industry. Don't be distracted by the large cemetery to your left shortly after you leave downtown—that's Hillcrest. The road forks just beyond that, so bear right. It will be fairly obvious in doing so that you are staying on the same road. The road assumes different names as you travel—from Liberty to Wheaton to Skidaway.

Immediately past a complex five-way intersection, you'll see the only real turn you'll make, a left onto 36th Street. It's identified by a street sign hanging between double traffic lights, and there's a turn arrow to help you make the turn in the increasingly heavy traffic you'll encounter. A McDonald's stands on the right just past this intersection; if you go past it, you've missed the turn. Just after you get on it, 36th Street merges into Bonaventure Road so seamlessly you probably won't even notice. Bonaventure Road is a narrow, two-lane road that winds through neat, modest housing and is lined by massive trees that are literally on the edge of the road. Pay attention!

Little Gracie marks the grave of a young girl in Bonaventure Cemetery. KYLE CASON

In just under a mile, where the road curves away to the right, you'll see the cemetery gates. Don't be distracted if a Forest Lawn Cemetery billboard is still in place in the vicinity. The sign on the gate identifies Bonaventure. There's a large, framed map just inside the entrance, but it gives locations by grave site number, not name. Instead, depend on the small wooden signposts stationed along the lanes between the plots. Book fans are looking for the sign marked Aiken and the nearby Mercer. The wooden marker signs are easy to follow.

Park with care, as there is a lot of tour-bus traffic. There's a small lot behind the office building just inside the gates if you are the hiking kind; there's also a grassy parking area for a few cars that's near the water and not far from the Aiken plot. Although we haven't heard of any trouble, it's an isolated spot between tours, so it's probably a good idea to lock your car and bring a friend.

Meanwhile, let's clear up some misconceptions in parting. Jim Williams, The Book's central figure, isn't buried at Bonaventure—or anywhere else in Savannah, for that matter. Instead, he was put to rest in his hometown of Gordon, Georgia. And Bonaventure is not the graveyard from which the Minerva character dug up the dirt for her voodoo spells, so leave the soil where you found it. It's history, not dirt.

Close-up

Great Savannah Books on the Other Side of Midnight

John Berendt's *Midnight in the Garden of Good and Evil* is not the first book to be set in Savannah, although you might get that impression the way some folks carry on. If you want to read more Savannah-as-a-setting books, we have some suggestions.

Here's a sample, starting with three books that have a *Midnight* connection, then moving on to more general topics.

More Than Mercer House: Savannah's Jim Williams and His Southern Houses, by Dr. Dorothy Kingery (Williams's sister, an academician), reviews Williams's role in the preservation of many significant buildings in Savannah and surrounding areas and tells tales of his outstanding antiques-finding adventures. For the most part, it is an attractive coffee-table book, featuring essays penned by Williams and family photos, as well as before-and-after restoration shots. It's a pretty book and a nice display copy, but only a genuine fan would find it absorbing. It does display that Southern touch of neatly omitting awkward topics: There's no reference to the series of shooting trials and jail time that marked the 1980s for Williams. You can buy the book in the author's store or order it by mail or phone (see store listings elsewhere in this chapter).

Hiding My Candy: The Autobiography of the Grand Empress of Savannah, by the Lady Chablis and Theodore Bouloukos, tells the story of the drag queen Berendt made famous. It includes pictures of the performer.

To Live and Die in Dixie, by Kathy Hogan Trocheck, is an installment in her mystery series about a housekeeper/sleuth. Trocheck was a newspaper reporter in Savannah before moving on to Atlanta, where most of her books are set. This 1993 mystery (published a year before The Book) features a rich antiques dealer implicated in the murder of an employee-house guest. He's known for disrupting movie filming with a Nazi flag and feuding with his Jewish neighbor over gentrification versus rehabilitating housing for the poor. The plot diverges from there, but Book fans will still catch the allu-

Basically, the same items are available at all stores that carry Book souvenirs. We've listed a store that devotes a large percentage of its stock to Book items, but you can find the same stuff in any number of general gift shops along River Street and even in scattered suburban and mall stores. We've also included Kingery's new store, a small but essential point for die-hard book fans. The only specific recommendation we make on these things concerns the cookies. If you want Byrd Cookie's Key Lime Coolers in the Byrd Girl commemorative tin, check out our Shopping chapter. Byrd Cookie operates a gift shop as part of its bakery, and it stands to reason this would be the cheapest place to get the cookies. We've seen them as expensive as $3 higher per box elsewhere. Besides, at sions. Trocheck has also written *Savannah Blues* under the pen name of Mary Kay Andrews.

Savannah Spectres and Other Strange Tales, by Margaret DeBolt, is a collection of local ghost stories that has become sort of the standard reference work on the topic hereabouts. Williams, of *Midnight* fame, crops up as the restorer of one of the more vigorously haunted structures in this collection.

Hooligans, by William Diehl, was published in 1984. It never attracted as much attention as Diehl's more successful works such as *Sharkey's Machine* and *Primal Fear*, which became movies. This tale of political corruption is set in a thinly veiled Savannah: "Oceanby" for Tybee, "Isle of Sighs" for Isle of Hope, and so on. Diehl was part of a productive writers' colony on St. Simons Island, about 90 miles south of Savannah as you near the Florida border.

Mercer House was the home of Jim Williams, a major player in The Book. KYLE CASON

Savannah, by Eugenia Price, is a historical romance distinguished by Price's research and a literary approach that stands far above the genre's norm. If you like what you read, you're in luck: This is the first of a four-volume saga set in Savannah. Price, who died in 1997, was another St. Simons Island author.

Byrd's you can sample the Key Lime Cooler and the other flavors available.

"The Book" Gift Shop
127 East Gordon Street
(912) 233-3867
www.midnightinsavannah.com
This shop occupies the garden floor (which is what we in Savannah call the ground floor of a building, topped by the parlor floor, followed by a second floor, which is really the third floor, and so on) of a building at Abercorn and Gordon Streets. Wander through several rooms to see a mix of Book souvenirs and general gifts. Stock includes shot glasses bearing the name of the Married Women's Card Club, which aptly illustrate the Southern idea of tackiness.

You'll find elements of a Book shrine along with the merchandise. The back room boasts some not-for-sale items such as a painting by Williams, a chair he once owned, a large collection of clippings about the phenomenon, and so on. Deborah Sullivan is the owner.

Mercer House Carriage Shop
430 Whitaker Street
(912) 236-6352

The carriage house behind Mercer House holds the tasteful gift shop that Williams's sister, Dorothy Kingery, has opened. You won't find any Book souvenirs, although copies of Berendt's book were in stock the last time we were there. You'll find a small selection of other books, including Kingery's own book about Williams's restoration and preservation successes in Savannah, and other gift items. This is also where you buy the tickets to the house tour. Note that while the house fronts on Bull Street, the carriage house fronts on Whitaker Street.

HOLLYWOOD IN SAVANNAH

Savannah has hosted at least 40 film or television projects since 1975, and it formalized the whole process by establishing a film liaison office at City Hall in 1995. True, there hasn't been a major production since *The Gift* wrapped in 2000, but we're poised and ready. Much seems to depend on incentives packages, which would have to be passed at the state legislative level.

Some of those productions have been

i If you are looking for arty souvenirs at low prices, the Telfair Museum of Art has a limited selection of posters, postcards, and the like for sale at token prices. For something even cheaper (i.e., free), look for the postcard reproductions that SCAD uses to announce gallery openings. We've found them stacked for giveaway in the college galleries and downtown coffee shops and eateries.

among the most critically acclaimed movies of our day. Some have starred the biggest names on the silver screen. Some have launched catchphrases into the lexicon of popular culture ("Life is like a box of chocolates . . ."). And some of them . . . well, some of them were *Return of Swamp Thing* and the like.

Examples of the outstanding include *Glory,* the historically based account of African-American soldiers in the Civil War that won three Oscars; *Forrest Gump,* which claimed six Oscars and solidified Tom Hanks's superstar status; and *Roots,* filmed here in part, which became the standard against which all miniseries are still measured. Going back even further, to 1962, when location shoots were rarer, the original *Cape Fear* was partially filmed here. City Hall and the downtown business district and Isle of Hope were on display. This original movie, since remade, featured Robert Mitchum at his creepiest.

If you want to experience some of Savannah's movie past in person, there's some interesting spots. Go to Chippewa Square, for example, where Bull Street flows around a statue of General Oglethorpe. Here is the filming site of the waiting-for-the-bus scene that was so crucial in *Forrest Gump.* Don't waste time looking for the bench—although Savannah's squares have plenty of real benches, that one was a movie prop. It was situated on the square's northern face, looking down Bull Street. Back in the movie's heyday, you could spot the occasional fan positioned there, hovering with his or her backside perched on empty air, "sitting" on the nonexistent bench for a Kodak moment.

The Legend of Bagger Vance had all the right ingredients for a megahit: star director (Robert Redford), star stars (Will Smith, Matt Damon, etc.), and lovely sets and costumes from its Depression-era setting. As is so often the way with Hollywood, the film was only a moderate success.

At the moment, Savannah's biggest brush with movie fame is a producer. Savannahians know Stratton Leopold best as the native son who came back home a few years ago and

Leopold's Ice Cream. BETTY DARBY

relaunched his family's ice cream parlor, not as a successful movie producer at home on such sets as *Mission Impossible 3* or the latest in the *Star Trek* franchise. That fact speaks well for both Savannah and Leopold.

Leopold's Ice Cream
212 East Broughton Street
(912) 234-4442
The Leopold brothers who launched this successful ice cream parlor back in the day merit a photo display at the front of the shop. Stratton Leopold's successful and high-powered movie career is memorialized toward the back. Here, you can see a movie camera, posters of the many films Leopold has been involved with, and a display case with trinkets and props from those films, including the famous "rabbit's foot" that Tom Cruise pur-

sued so desperately in the latest and best of the *Mission Impossible* movies (it looks suspiciously like the vacuum tubes we use at the drive-thru at the bank.)

The real star here is the food—homemade and hand-dipped ice cream like that the parents of aging Baby Boomers courted over. Tutti-frutti is the version of local fame. The

i The first decade of this century hasn't seen any major movies made in Savannah. When movie stars are in town these days, chances are they are watching movies, not making them—the Savannah Film Festival, a project of the Savannah College of Art and Design, always draws a celebrity audience. See details in our Arts and Culture chapter.

sandwiches are nothing to sneeze at, and you can get a real banana split or milk shake, too. The shop keeps late hours, so you can usually catch it open after a show at the nearby Lucas Theatre or other downtown outing.

This isn't the original location of the locally famous original, but walk through the door and you'd never know it. The latest Leopold saved the original fittings and has put them back into use.

ST. PATRICK'S DAY ☘

Kermit the Frog of Muppets fame occasionally has croaked out the melancholy little ditty "It's Not Easy Being Green." Obviously, Kermit has never hopped into the midst of St. Patrick's Day in Savannah, where it's not only easy being green, it's virtually mandatory.

On St. Patrick's Day in Savannah, people clothe themselves in outfits featuring every shade of green imaginable. They decorate themselves with green accessories, such as green beads, green-and-white-striped Cat in the Hat headgear, and green-and-white buttons conveying a variety of messages, the most prevalent being "Kiss Me, I'm Irish." The revelers color their hair, beards, and mustaches green and affix little green shamrock appliques to their faces. They even dye their dogs and the water of the city's fountains green.

On St. Patrick's Day in Savannah, people eat green grits and drink green beer, which tends to make some of them feel a wee bit green at the gills. On St. Patrick's Day in Savannah, people give themselves over to a wonderful green giddiness that permeates the atmosphere. Is this the work of the mischievous leprechauns—the little people of Irish lore? We're not sure, but we know it's there, wafting through the soft air of springtime, transforming human beings into creatures of whimsy.

WHY ST. PATRICK'S DAY?

You might be wondering why St. Patrick's Day has evolved as the most festive day of the year in Savannah, and why a city of fewer than 150,000 people has ended up playing host to some 500,000 revelers on that day.

These are good questions—ones on which we can only speculate. It's not enough to say that a large segment of Savannah's population is, or has been, Irish or of Irish descent. That's true of lots of cities that don't make anywhere near the fuss over St. Patrick's Day as does Savannah.

Part of the reason for the popularity of the day might stem from the fact that it's been celebrated here for a long time, longer than in most American cities. According to the late William L. Fogarty, who wrote a history of the local observance entitled *The Days We've Celebrated,* the first celebration here was in 1813 when the Hibernian Society, formed by Irish Protestants seeking to help their impoverished countrymen, held a private procession. The city's first public procession, which is recognized as Savannah's first St. Patrick's Day parade, was also held by the society and took place in 1824.

"Why and how this celebration could possibly have carried on these many years is perhaps one of the most fantastic mysteries of all," wrote Fogarty in 1980 as he attempted to answer questions regarding the parade's origin. "I don't know of anyone who could really give the actual reason. . . . Perhaps the answer would be the 'Pride of the Irish' has sustained it."

The observance was, for many years, mainly an Irish Catholic religious celebration aimed at honoring Patrick, the priest who brought Christianity to the Emerald Isle in the fifth century. Although the celebration remains religious in nature (many Savannahi-

> **i** In a quest to win strings of green beads from male onlookers, some females persist in baring portions of their anatomy on St. Patrick's Day, but this is behavior that will bring about their arrest if observed by the constabulary.

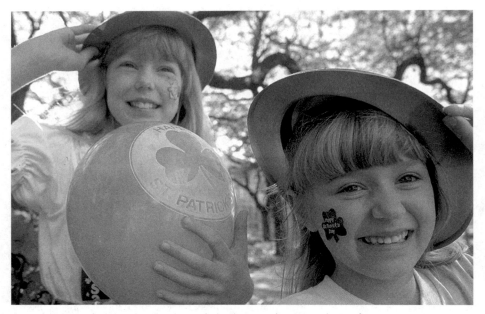

A tip of the hat and a big smile will make you feel welcome at the St. Patrick's Day festivities. PHYL M. GATLIN

ans begin the day by attending morning mass at the Cathedral of St. John the Baptist on Lafayette Square), the observance has become more secular over the years and has been adopted by other segments of the population, leading to the saying that "everyone's Irish on St. Patrick's Day."

Another reason for celebrating the day in a big way might have to do with its occurring at a time of year when Savannah is blessed with some of its best weather. The normal high temperature on St. Patrick's Day is 70, and the normal low is 49. There is a saying around here to the effect that "it never rains on St. Patrick's Day in Savannah." This is usually the case, although it doesn't always hold true: We recall one year when we stood and watched the parade with ice-cold rain running down our green-shirted necks, with only a jugful of mimosas (that's champagne mixed with orange juice) to keep us from deserting our posts.

On most St. Patrick's Days, however, the often dreary days of winter are over, and folks are just itching to get outside and cut loose. What better way to do so than with a citywide party?

IT'S MORE THAN JUST A DAY

The celebrating that is part of St. Patrick's Day festivities in Savannah occurs over a span of three or four days. St. Patrick's Day is observed on March 17, and the annual parade is held on that day except when it falls on Sunday—in that case, the parade is on Saturday, March 16. An especially rare exception will occur in 2008, when an extremely early Easter will put March 17 in Holy Week, leading to the observance being rescheduled for March 14. Some people celebrate by holding parties and get-togethers in their homes or by attending the invitation-only functions of Savannah's Irish societies. The latter range from the early-morning shenanigans of the Sinn Fein Society—which features green grits, Irish whiskey, and a master of ceremonies who continually announces "The bar is open"—to the comparatively staid, black-tie banquet held by the Hibernian Society.

The Hibernians pride themselves on their ability to attract banquet speakers of considerable note. In 1978 the Hibernian banquet speech was delivered by former Georgia governor Jimmy Carter, who at the time happened to be employed as president of the United States. Another, shorter speech Carter gave that day is the basis for one of Savannah's better St. Patrick's Day stories. In the mid-1960s, Carter developed a friendship with local character and bar owner Pinkie Masters. Pinkie—who reveled in telephoning local newspaper reporters and impersonating another character, onetime Georgia governor Lester Maddox—was fascinated with politics, and he became a fervent Carter booster. Carter didn't drink alcoholic beverages, but when he visited Savannah, he would invariably stop and see Pinkie at his lounge on Drayton Street near what was then known as the De Soto Hilton Hotel (see our Nightlife chapter for more about this well-known bar). Masters died in the latter part of 1977, and Carter was unable to attend the funeral, which drew a huge number of political dignitaries. When Carter came to Savannah on St. Patrick's Day 1978 for the 8:00 p.m. Hibernian banquet, he arrived in late afternoon at the Hilton, where a large crowd waited to greet him.

According to author William Fogarty, Carter's "first act" upon his arrival "was to sneak out through the [hotel's] underground parking garage, cross Drayton Street, and enter Pinkie Master's bar unannounced. Needless to say, Pinkie's family and friends who were operating the bar were flabbergasted, as were the customers in the bar." Carter "climbed upon the bar, where they have since added a plaque, and spoke to the crowd, then returned to the hotel. He had paid his respects to Pinkie."

The public partying on St. Patrick's Day occurs at Pinkie's and other watering holes throughout the city, but the bulk of the celebrating takes place on River Street, in City Market, and along Bay Street.

i The water of the Forsyth Park fountain is traditionally dyed green each year for St. Patrick's Day, but don't expect the Savannah River to be treated in similar fashion. The last and only attempt at turning the river green occurred in 1961 with less than desirable results. A thousand pounds of the chemical Uranine was used, and the outcome was a striped effect.

Most of the merrymaking happens on the day of the parade and the weekend closest to it. When the parade is on a Monday, Tuesday, or Wednesday, the partying will be on that day, the weekend before, and the day or days before. When the parade is on a Thursday or Friday, the celebrating will be on that day, the day before, and the weekend following. On parade day and weekends, River Street and City Market are packed with celebrators.

City Market (912-232-4903; www.savannah citymarket.com) hosts free live music and dancing in the courtyard. It's a very laid-back party that can last as long as five days, depending on when St. Patrick's Day falls. On St. Patrick's Day itself, the bands begin just as the parade passes nearby.

The Savannah Waterfront Association (912-234-0295; www.savwaterfront.com) hosts St. Patrick's Celebration on the River with 9 blocks of food booths, nationally known entertainment, and lots of people. Be prepared to literally rub elbows with fellow partyers as quite a crowd gathers here. Admission is free, and for legal drinkers a wristband can be purchased for $5 to drink beer outdoors. The wristband practice was begun in 1999 in an effort to curb underage drinking and, despite some initial outcry, the wristbands have become a fact of life. This festival goes on for several days from 10:00 a.m. to midnight, spanning the closest weekend to St. Patrick's Day and reaching its peak on the day itself.

The St. Patrick's Day holidays are also a time of traditional events such as the investiture of the parade grand marshal on the first Sunday in March, the gathering of Irish descendants at the Celtic Cross on the following Sunday, and the laying of a wreath at the Sgt. William Jasper Monument on the afternoon before the parade. There are also family-oriented events emphasizing Irish heritage and culture such as the Savannah Irish Festival at the Civic Center in mid-February and the Tara Feis festival in Emmet Park on Bay Street on the Saturday before the parade. For the athletically inclined, there's the St. Patrick's Day Rugby Tournament, held in Daffin Park on the weekend closest to the big day. (For more about all these events, see our Annual Events and Festivals chapter.) The focal point of the festivities, however, is the St. Patrick's Day parade.

THE PARADE

Savannah's St. Patrick's Day parade is the third oldest and one of the largest in the United States. It dates back to 1824, and only New York City's (1762) and Philadelphia's (1780) have been in existence longer. There are more entries—usually about 250—in Savannah's parade than those in Chicago (200), Philadelphia (101), Boston (100), or New York (75). With 10,000 marchers, Savannah has fewer than New York (150,000) and Chicago (20,000) but as many as Boston and more than Philly (9,700).

Savannah's parade covers a lot of pavement: specifically, 2 miles, making it almost as long in distance as the parades in Boston and Philadelphia (2.6 miles) and longer than New York's (1.5) and Chicago's (1). As you can imagine, given the number of people who march and how far they have to walk, the local parade takes quite awhile to unfold—almost three and a half hours. That being the case, it's a good idea to bring lawn chairs or stadium cushions so you can be as comfortable as possible while you watch, particularly if you arrive early and stake out a viewing spot closer to where the parade ends than

where it begins. The farther you are from the starting point, the longer you'll have to wait for the first marchers to reach you, maybe as long as an hour.

Speaking of beginnings and endings, the parade starts at 10:15 a.m. at Abercorn and Gwinnett Streets and ends at Bull and Harris Streets. The route of march is north on Abercorn to Broughton Street, east on Broughton to East Broad Street, north on East Broad to Bay Street, west on Bay to Bull, to the finish line. We think you'll find this event to be as enjoyable and festive as you can imagine, but don't go expecting to see something akin to the Tournament of Roses parade or Macy's Thanksgiving Day bash. There are floats in Savannah's parade, and they seem to be more numerous and elaborate each year, but you won't see anything that remotely resembles what you'd watch in Pasadena, California, on New Year's Day or on the streets of New York during the pre-Christmas holidays.

What you'll see in Savannah on St. Patrick's Day is more like a small-town parade that has grown to the point that it has burst clean out of its Kelly green britches. The down-home flavor of the parade is a big part of its appeal; one of the reasons we Savannahians keep going back year after year is to watch our relatives, neighbors, and coworkers as they march or ride by and wave and yell at each other. You'll see a lot of folks stepping out of or into the line of march as they shake hands and hug necks. And you're likely to see a woman or two dash from the sidelines to plant kisses on the cheeks of marchers, particularly those in uniform and especially members of the U.S. Army Rangers (home-based at Savannah's Hunter Army Air Field) and Benedictine Military School aggregations.

What you'll see are lots of high-school marching bands, numerous glad-handing politicians riding in convertibles, some beauty queens, several military color guards, the parade grand marshal, a gaggle of past grand marshals, and a multitude of men, women, and children of Irish descent, all dressed up in

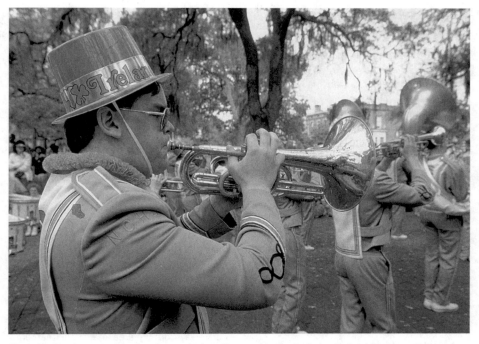

Music fills the air as marching bands parade down Savannah's streets during St. Patrick's Day activities.
PHYL M. GATLIN

their best greenery and marching in family groups or as members of Savannah's many Irish societies. Keep your eyes peeled for one of our favorite entries, the "Irishman at Large." You'll see college cheerleaders and dance teams, officials of the Catholic church, bagpipers, and detachments of soldiers, sailors, marines, and veterans' groups. People will be waving at you from more than 20 floats representing a variety of organizations and businesses.

Among our favorite parade units are those of the Shriners of Savannah's Alee Temple. The most outlandish of the Shriner groups is the Oriental band, which consists of a group of pillars of the community clad in colorful burnooses, jackets, and pantaloons and shod in brogans that have been spray-painted gold, turned up at the tips, and decorated with tiny bells. Other crowd pleasers from the

Shrine are its Dunecat Unit, whose members zip around in souped-up go-karts, and the Keystone Kops, who hand out citations to spectators amid much frenzied whistle blowing and scurrying around.

The parade occasionally has visiting celebrities, including, in recent years, units from the New York Police Department and the Budweiser Clydesdales.

In short, what you'll see at Savannah's St. Patrick's Day parade are lots of enthusiasm, a world of pride in being Irish, and the smiles of thousands of people having one heck of a good time.

The parade is put together by the St. Patrick's Day Parade Committee, and you can get a progress report on the upcoming edition of the parade at www.savannahsaint patricksday.com.

PRIME PARADE-WATCHING SPOTS

One of the best places from which to view the parade is Lafayette Square, which is on Abercorn Street between Charlton and Harris Streets. This is where the folks who judge the marching bands sit, so you'll see the bands performing at their best if you hang out here. Another good spot is the steps of the U.S. Custom House on Bay Street at Bull Street. The steps here are like bleachers, perfect for sitting and watching the festivities.

Here are some other good places for parade watching, as detailed by the *Savannah Morning News:*

The 600 block of Abercorn Street—where "the parade's performers aren't tired yet. The bands step higher; the people waving from their floats aren't yet suffering from arm fatigue."

East Broad Street between Broughton and Bay Streets—"a good place to see the picturesque variety of parade spectators. . . . SCAD (Savannah College of Art and Design) students tend to be in full bloom around here. Green dogs abound. So do green people."

Bay Street between East Broad and Bull Streets—"The closest convenient spot for those who've been cavorting down by the river."

We would also like to make this suggestion: To obtain a unique view of the parade, try getting a spot on the southern side of Calhoun Square (Abercorn and Gordon Streets), Lafayette Square (Abercorn and Charlton Streets), or Oglethorpe Square (Abercorn and

York Streets) or on the northern side of Wright Square (Bull and State Streets) or Chippewa Square (Bull and Hull Streets). You'll be watching the parade come straight at you rather than viewing it from the side, and it's a perspective that can be quite enjoyable.

PARKING ON ST. PATRICK'S DAY

If there is a downside to St. Patrick's Day, it might be locating a place to park. Metered spaces are free on this holiday, but vacant ones won't be easy to find unless you get to town real early. Another option is to park in one of the city's garages, which you can do all day for $10; here, too, an early arrival is mandatory. The garages are at State and Abercorn Streets, at Montgomery and York Streets, at Bryan and Abercorn Streets, and at Liberty and Montgomery Streets.

An alternative to parking downtown is to park away from the area and take a Chatham Area Transit bus into the city. There are regular bus routes to and from downtown (see our Getting Here, Getting Around chapter). A special shuttle runs nonstop continuously from the parking lot of Oglethorpe Mall to downtown on St. Patrick's Day for a nominal fee. The public transit organization here is the Chatham Area Transit Authority, known by the acronym CAT, and the slogan of the day is "I caught a CAT on St. Pat's."

Whatever you do, don't park on the parade route in a lot or space that's designated for use by a business or private individual. If there's a sign saying your car will be towed, that's probably what will happen, and you'll have to pay a minimum of $85 to get your vehicle back.

i You can drink alcoholic beverages in public in the parade festival area (bordered by River Street on the north, East Broad Street on the east, Jones Street on the south, and West Boundary Street on the west), but drinks must be in paper, Styrofoam, or plastic cups of no more than 16 ounces in volume.

ANNUAL EVENTS AND FESTIVALS

Savannahians love to party. They love their history. They also love getting outdoors and taking advantage of coastal Georgia's congenial climate. Is it any wonder, then, there's almost always something going on in Savannah? That something might be a festival attracting thousands of people or the commemoration of a historic event drawing a few hundred, but a week seldom passes in which there's nothing to do in Savannah.

We admit things slow down a tad during the summer months because of the heat, but that doesn't mean you can't get out and enjoy yourself. Grab your suntan lotion, cooler, and lounge chair and head for a day at the beach on nearby Tybee Island, just as Savannahians have been doing for more than a century.

Savannah's biggest party is its celebration of St. Patrick's Day, a green-hued blast bringing up to a half-million visitors to the city in mid-March. It's such a big deal we've devoted an entire chapter to it. But because we want to be sure you don't miss any of the fun, we've included in this chapter brief looks at significant happenings on that great day for the Irish and the days leading up to it.

As we indicated earlier, finding a parking space in Savannah can be a hassle, and the problem intensifies when a festival is held in the downtown area. It's a good idea—particularly if you're attending an event on River Street, where parking is extremely limited—to arrive early, find a spot on a street or in a lot a few blocks from the festival, then hoof it to your destination. Savannah is a city that's ideal for walking, and your stroll to and from the festival could be one of the most enjoyable parts of your day.

We need to mention one other thing before taking you through our month-by-month rundown of events and festivals:

Dates, times, and admission fees can change, so it's best to call ahead for the most current information. The telephone numbers included with the following write-ups are the numbers of the individuals, organizations, or agencies sponsoring or coordinating the events.

JANUARY
Historic Downtown

Emancipation Day Service
Location varies
(912) 234-6293, (912) 232-8507
By holding a special church service on New Year's Day, Savannah's Emancipation Association commemorates the signing of the proclamation that ordered the freeing of slaves in the Confederate states. During the 11:00 a.m. gathering, held at a different church each year, a participant reads the Emancipation Proclamation, a mass choir sings hymns, and speakers deliver addresses concerning the significance of that historic day in 1863.

Martin Luther King Jr.
Observance Day Activities
Various locations
(912) 234-5502
This monthlong tribute to civil rights leader Martin Luther King Jr. features a parade through downtown starting at 10:00 a.m. on the third Monday in January, the national day of observance for King Day. The observances wind up with the Freedom Ball at the Savannah Civic Center on the last Friday of January.

Heart and Stroke Gala
Hyatt Regency Savannah Hotel
2 West Bay Street
(912) 790-2900
The American Heart Association's premier

ℹ️ If you're looking to uplift your spirits during what can sometimes be a depressing time of year—late January—consider attending "Hymns for Hope," a musical program usually held on the Sunday before Super Bowl Sunday. Featuring local church choirs and gospel singing groups, this presentation takes place in the afternoon or early in the evening. Admission is $10 and benefits the Interfaith Hospitality Network of Coastal Georgia, a volunteer organization that aids homeless families. You can contact the network and get the specific details on "Hymns for Hope" by calling (912) 790-9446.

fund-raiser has a different theme every year and is held in late January or in early February, which is Heart Month. Tickets are $150 or $175 per person, and they entitle guests to a cocktail party with open bar at 6:30 p.m. and dinner with wine and beer at 8:00 p.m. A band plays popular dance music until midnight, and live and silent auctions add to the festivities.

FEBRUARY
Historic Downtown

GHS's Georgia Days
Various locations
(912) 651-2125
www.georgiahistory.com
This observance celebrating Georgia's founding and heritage unfolds during the first two weeks of February and usually focuses on the twelfth of the month—the day on which the first colonists landed in 1733. Georgia Week opens on the first day of February with a ceremony in a downtown square featuring a portrayal of a significant figure in the history of the state and wreath-layings at monuments throughout the city. Programs at historic sites and a lecture focusing on the aforementioned historic figure are part of the celebration,

which is presented by the Georgia Historical Society (GHS) in partnership with Chatham-Savannah public schools.

On the morning of Georgia Day, February 12, schoolchildren dressed as colonists and the Native Americans who welcomed them walk in a procession from Forsyth Park up Bull Street to City Hall on Bay Street. The Georgia Day Luncheon follows, with tickets priced at $25; the other events are free.

Black Heritage Festival
Various locations
(912) 691-6847
www.savannahga.gov/arts
www.savstate.edu
Various musical groups entertain with performances of gospel, reggae, blues, and jazz, and craftspeople at a marketplace at the Savannah Civic Center on Grand Festival Day (a Saturday) sell items related to African culture during this event, which is held during a week in early February. Funded by Savannah's Department of Cultural Affairs and presented by Savannah State University, this event highlights the multifaceted contributions of African Americans in the areas of music, the performing arts, and cuisine. Admission is free.

Super Museum Sunday
Various locations
(912) 651-2125
www.georgiahistory.com
More than 20 of the area's museums, educational institutions, and historic homes open their doors and invite the public in at no charge during this event, which serves as an activity of the Georgia Heritage Celebration and occurs on the Sunday before Georgia Day, February 12. Hours are from noon until 4:00 p.m. To determine if a specific museum participates in this program, contact the museum ahead of time. (You can find museums and their telephone numbers in the Attractions chapter.)

Islands

Colonial Faire & Muster at Wormsloe
Wormsloe Historic Site
7601 Skidaway Road
(912) 353-3023
Historical reenactors clad in the garb of Georgia's colonists make music and demonstrate craft skills, such as making candles and musket balls, at this program held in an open area near the marsh overlooking the Skidaway River. At the visitor center, you can view artifacts excavated from Wormsloe's tabby ruins and watch an audiovisual show about the founding of the 13th colony. The program takes place from 10:00 a.m. until 4:00 p.m. on the first Saturday and Sunday in February. Admission is free.

Southside/Midtown

Savannah Irish Festival
Savannah Civic Center
Liberty and Montgomery Streets
(912) 232-3448
www.savannahirish.org
This family-oriented event uses song, dance, and recitation to emphasize the heritage of the Irish and the contributions of Irish immigrants here and throughout the United States. In addition to the main stage, where much of this activity takes place, there are stages for children's entertainment and readings and discussions involving Irish culture and history. Vendors market Irish clothing, jewelry, and artifacts, and members of 12 local Irish organizations prepare and sell food, including shepherd's pie, Irish stew, and other ethnic dishes. The festival is on the second or third weekend in February from 11:30 a.m. to 7:00 p.m. on Saturday, and from 12:30 until 6:00 p.m. on Sunday. Admission to the festival is $11.50 per day or $20.00 for a two-day ticket. Children age 15 and younger are admitted free.

i Get a unique view of activities on River Street and stay out of the crowds by renting a hotel room facing the Savannah River, but be prepared for some late-night noise from musicians and merrymakers.

MARCH
Historic Downtown

First Saturday
Rousakis Plaza
River Street
(912) 234-0295
www.savwaterfront.com
Browse through the wares of artisans and craftspeople from throughout the Southeast and listen to various forms of music during First Saturday on the plaza on River Street. While enjoying the breeze blowing off the Savannah River, you might find yourself staring at a large cargo ship as it glides along the waterway, so close you'd swear you could reach out and touch it. The 40 to 60 open-air arts and crafts booths on the plaza offer a variety of treasures, everything from original oil paintings and watercolors to rocking horses fashioned from wood scraps. If you can't turn up something that catches your fancy among the artists' booths, visit the shops in the renovated cotton warehouses lining River Street.

Hungry? You have your choice of restaurants dishing up a variety of cuisine. The Savannah Waterfront Association presents First Saturday festivals from 9:00 a.m. to 6:00 p.m. on—what else?—the first Saturday of each month, with the exception of January and February. Some are part of expanded, more distinctive festivals: the Savannah Seafood Festival in November, Oktoberfest in October, the Fine Arts Festival in May, and Christmas on the River in December (see subsequent listings for more details on these festivals). Admission is free.

Grand Marshal Investiture Ceremony
Savannah Civic Center
15 East Liberty Street
(912) 233-4804

The St. Patrick's Day Parade Committee presents the parade grand marshal with his sash and recognizes civic dignitaries at this ceremony. The event takes place at 2:45 p.m. on the first Sunday in March, one week after the committee elects the leader of the parade. There is no charge for admission.

Celtic Cross Ceremony
Emmet Park
Bay and Price Streets
(912) 233-4804

Members of the city's Irish organizations gather at the Cathedral of St. John the Baptist for mass at 11:30 a.m. on the second Sunday of the month, then march in procession to Emmet Park, where they lay a wreath at the Celtic Cross and listen to a speech about their heritage. The cross, officially named the Irish Monument, was carved from a single piece of Irish limestone in County Roscommon, Ireland. The Savannah Irish Monument Committee erected the Celtic Cross in 1983, the 250th anniversary of the founding of Savannah and Georgia, to commemorate Georgians of Irish ancestry. The ceremony starts about 1:00 p.m., and it's open to the public.

Tara Feis
Emmet Park
Bay and Price Streets
(912) 651-6417
www.savannahga.gov/arts

The city of Savannah's Department of Cultural Affairs puts the emphasis on family-oriented activities at this Irish festival on the Saturday before St. Patrick's Day. Irish music and dancing, crafts demonstrations, storytelling, and poetry recitations fill the spotlight. Youngsters can participate in hands-on activities with a Celtic touch and enjoy carnival rides. Alcoholic beverages are prohibited in an effort to enhance the family-day atmosphere. The event, in sun-dappled

Emmet Park, runs from 11:00 a.m. until 5:00 p.m., and admission is as free as the Irish mist on a day in Killarney. In case you're wondering, feis is pronounced "fesh."

Sgt. William Jasper Memorial Ceremony
Madison Square
Bull Street, between Harris
and Charlton Streets
(912) 233-4804

On the eve of the St. Patrick's Day Parade, the parade grand marshal and his aides recognize the contributions of the military by walking from Johnson Square down Bull Street to Madison Square, where they lay a wreath at the monument honoring Revolutionary War hero William Jasper. A band or two that will be participating in the parade, often bagpipers, usually accompanies them. A 21-gun salute is fired during the ceremony, which occurs about 4:30 p.m.

St. Patrick's Day Parade
Various downtown streets
(912) 233-4804

Savannah's biggest annual event lasts upwards of four hours and involves thousands of participants. Some 250 units take to the streets for the parade, including marching bands, floats, and the city's numerous Irish organizations. The parade starts about 10:15 a.m. at Forsyth Park and winds its way around several of Savannah's squares and down its main thoroughfares. (For more information, see our St. Patrick's Day chapter.)

St. Patrick's at City Market
Jefferson and St. Julian Streets
(912) 232-4903
www.savannahcitymarket.com

City Market celebrates the big day with live music and dancing in the courtyard. This laid-back party occurs over a span of time that includes St. Patrick's Day and can last as long as five days, depending on when the holiday falls. On St. Patrick's Day, the bands crank up as soon as the parade passes nearby. It's free.

St. Patrick's Celebration on the River
Rousakis Plaza
River Street
(912) 234-0295
www.savwaterfront.com
The Savannah Waterfront Association sets up
food booths on the plaza and brings in nationally known entertainers to perform, but the
biggest attraction of St. Patrick's Day on the
River isn't eating or listening to music—it's
being part of the crowd that jams River
Street. This 9-block party is free for non-
drinkers, and it's the place to be during St.
Patrick's Day festivities if you like to rub
elbows with people—literally. Those wishing
to drink beer outdoors will have to purchase
$5 wristbands. The merrymaking is at its peak
on St. Patrick's Day and the weekend closest
to the holiday; the party cranks up about
10:00 a.m., and food sales and scheduled
entertainment end at midnight.

The Savannah Tour of Homes and Gardens
Parish House of Christ Church
18 Abercorn Street
(912) 234-8054
www.savannahtourofhomes.org
This granddaddy of Savannah's seasonal tours
brings you to a different neighborhood on
each day of its four-day run. Each three-hour,
self-guided walking tour takes you to approximately six private homes and/or gardens in
the Historic District. Hours are from 10:00
a.m. until 5:00 p.m. on Thursday, Friday, and
Saturday and from 11:00 a.m. to 4:00 p.m. on
Sunday, and participants are encouraged to
stroll from site to site at their own pace and in
any order they choose. Special events such as
luncheons, seminars, cemetery tours, and
teas are also presented, and they vary from
year to year. The event is held in late March.
Begun in 1935, the event is sponsored by the
Episcopal Church Women of Christ Church,
along with Historic Savannah Foundation, and
proceeds benefit outreach ministries of the
churchwomen and the foundation's preservation efforts. The fee for each walking tour is
$35, and it's essential to order tickets for the

tours and other activities ahead of time. The
tours always—yes, always—sell out. You pick
up your tickets at tour headquarters, the
Parish House of Christ Church.

Savannah Music Festival
Various locations
(912) 234-3378
www.savannahmusicfestival.org
The Savannah Music Festival—formerly
known as Savannah Onstage—enhances the
beauty of the city with two and a half weeks
of jazz, classical, blues, gospel, zydeco, and
other traditional American performances during late March and early April. The corner-
stone of this steadily growing festival is the
American Traditions Competition, which features solo vocalists presenting music that has
played a significant role in forming the cultural
heritage of the United States. Each year additional major events are incorporated into the
festival. Recent performers include Jazz at Lincoln Center Orchestra with Wynton Marsalis,
guitarist Buddy Guy, bluegrass singer and
mandolinist Ricky Skaggs, the Dave Grisman
Quintet, the Tallis Scholars, the Blind Boys of
Alabama, and the Derek Trucks Band, and
among recent productions were a new and
imaginative version of George Gershwin's
Porgy and Bess and *An Evening With
Beethoven,* featuring actress Mia Farrow and
the Beaux Arts Trio. The festival also reaches
students with free concerts and provides pre-
concert talks, films, and lectures about the
heritage of American music to children and
adults.

The American Traditions Competition in
2005 featured 30 contestants chosen from

> **i** You can find information on spe-
> cial, one-of-a-kind events in the
> pages of Diversions, a pullout section of
> the *Savannah Morning News* that appears
> in the daily newspaper every Thursday.
> This tabloid also contains feature stories
> about festivals being held locally and
> entertainers who are performing in
> Savannah.

among more than 100 entrants from throughout the United States. They participate in quarterfinal, semifinal, and final rounds over the course of a week, with the rounds held at the Lucas Theatre for the Arts. Tickets for individual events range from free to $65. The announced 2008 schedule includes the premiere of commissioned works by drummer Stewart Copeland, who recently completed a world tour with The Police, and jazz trombonist Wycliffe Gordon. A very partial list of performers ranged from the Blind Boys of Alabama performing soul gospel and the Atlanta Symphony Orchestra to Ricky Skaggs and Bruce Hornsby. Other performances ranged from Brazilian mandolin to a Persian lute master to Sacred Harp singing.

Islands

Sheep to Shawl Festival
Oatland Island Education Center
711 Sandtown Road
(912) 898-3980
www.oatlandisland.org
While musicians of the Savannah Folk Music Society fiddle and strum up a storm on the porch of a log cabin built in 1835, visitors watch an old-fashioned sheep shearing. This activity on a Saturday in March takes place at the education center's Heritage Homesite.

The main events occur about 11:30 a.m. and 2:00 p.m. when workers clip the sheep with hand-operated shears. Members of the Fiber Guild of the Savannahs card wool from the previous year's shearing, spin it into yarn, and, using a 150-year-old loom, weave yarn spun beforehand into a shawl. The shawl is raffled off, and the winner is announced near the end of the festival, which runs from 10:00 a.m. until 5:00 p.m. The center invites youngsters to try their hands at carding and spinning wool. Folks interested in viewing Oatland's wild and domesticated animals can walk the facility's 1.75-mile nature trail and visit the barnyard. Admission is $5 for adults and $3 for children, seniors and the military.

Southside/Midtown

St. Patrick's Day Rugby Tournament
Daffin Park
Victory Drive and Bee Road
(912) 234-5999
www.savannahrugby.com
Billed as one of the largest tournaments of its kind in the United States, this event is staged by the Savannah Shamrocks rugby club on the weekend closest to St. Patrick's Day. About 75 teams participate. There's no charge for roaming the sidelines and learning about this sport that's akin to American football and has been called "a ruffians' game played by gentlemen." The action starts about 9:00 a.m. on both days of the tourney, which was first held in 1979.

Spring Gardening Festival

Bamboo Farm and Coastal Gardens
2 Canebrake Road
(912) 921-5460
www/bamboo.caes.uga.edu
Swing into the planting season at the Bamboo Farm (see our Attractions chapter) by attending this program, which features garden exhibits and talks on horticulture. Also on the agenda are a container-gardening competition and a silent auction, and plant vendors will be on hand, perhaps offering that hard-to-find plant you've been looking for. Admission is $1 per carload for attending this festival, which is held from 9:00 a.m. to 3:00 p.m. on a Saturday in late March.

APRIL

Historic Downtown

Savannah Garden Exposition
Roundhouse Railroad Museum
601 West Harris Street
(912) 233-7787
www.savannahgardenexpo.com
During this festival in midspring, flowering plants and greenery adorn the bays where mechanics once repaired steam locomotives. Growers, antiques dealers, and other mer-

chants selling products to help your garden flourish set up shop in the bays. Exhibition gardens fill another portion of the Roundhouse, and window boxes created by local horticulturists brighten a long brick wall of the 19th-century railroad complex.

Lectures, seminars, gardening demonstrations, children's activities, and walking tours of Savannah add to the Expo, which is held from 10:00 a.m. to 6:00 p.m. on a Friday and Saturday in early April. Tickets go for $8 in advance and $10 at the gate, and proceeds benefit the Historic Savannah Foundation and the Isaiah Davenport House Museum.

NOGS Hidden Gardens of Savannah Tour
Garden Club of Savannah
(912) 961-4805
www.gcofsavannahnogstour.org

For more than 20 years, the members of the Garden Club of Savannah have, via this tour, enabled folks to glimpse a part of the city they would not otherwise see. As its name implies, this self-guided walking tour is your chance to get a look at some of the elegant gardens hidden behind the walls and gates of downtown homes. Chosen because of their beauty and unusual arrangement, eight gardens are opened to the public by their owners for only the two days of the tour.

You buy your tickets online, by mail from the Garden Club (P.O. Box 13892, Savannah, GA 31416), or at the Hilton Savannah DeSoto Hotel. A splendid way to end your walk is by finishing at the Harper-Fowlkes House on Orleans Square and attending the tea served there, a treat included in the $30 ticket price. A visit to the Massey Heritage Center and its garden is included on the tour, which is presented on a Friday and Saturday in late April, about the time Savannah is in full bloom. The gardens are open from 10:00 a.m. until 5:00 p.m., and light refreshments are served at the tea from 2:00 to 4:00 p.m. By the way, NOGS stands for North of Gaston Street, the locale of all the gardens on the tour.

Sidewalk Arts Festival
Forsyth Park
(912) 525-5100
www.scad.edu

The normally sedate slabs of the sidewalks leading through Forsyth Park pulsate with color in late April, when the Savannah College of Art and Design stages its Sidewalk Arts Festival. SCAD students, alumni, prospective students, children, and preteens cover the concrete with chalk drawings, creating an immense art exhibit on the ground. You'll see everything from reproductions of famous masterpieces to the flights of fancy of five-year-olds as you stroll through the park. Nearly 1,000 artists participate. Other attractions include the music of various bands and art projects for young children and preteens. The festival starts at 11:00 a.m. and ends at 5:00 p.m.

Confederate Memorial Day
Forsyth Park
(912) 232-3945

An observance that began in 1866 with women decorating the graves of husbands, sons, and brothers who fell while wearing the gray and butternut of the Confederacy continues in Savannah with a gathering at the Confederate Memorial monument in Forsyth Park on the Sunday closest to April 26, the day Gen. Joseph E. Johnston surrendered the last Confederate army at Greensboro, North Carolina. Civil War reenactors fire a 21-gun artillery salute, and there is a performance by a fife and drum corps. The solemn ceremony takes place in early afternoon.

Kids Day
Savannah Civic Center
Liberty and Montgomery Streets
(912) 355-8111
www.savj.org

One of the organizers of Kids Day is fond of saying this event gives children an opportunity to receive some education with a little e while having fun with a capital F. Kids Day shows children and their families the services available to them in the community and exposes youngsters to the arts and sciences via hands-on activities such as decorating pottery, delivering mock television weather reports, and listening to storytellers. Staffed by volunteers of the Jewish Educational Alliance and other members of the community, the event is free for adults and $1 for kids (or 50 cents with coupons distributed to schools and printed in the *Savannah Morning News*). Kids Day occurs on a Sunday in April from noon to 4:00 p.m.

West Chatham

Sunday Supper in the Strawberry Patch
Bamboo Farm and Coastal Gardens
2 Canebrake Road
(912) 921-5460
Held on a weekend in mid- or late April at the peak of strawberry-growing season, this Bamboo Farm fund-raiser gives folks a chance to get outdoors and enjoy a good ol' Southern supper—fried chicken, rice and gravy, fresh squash, field peas, Vidalia onions, sliced tomatoes, corn bread, iced tea, and strawberry shortcake, of course. The meal is served at the lakeside pavilion at the Bamboo Farm (see our Attractions chapter), but the berries are fresh from the farm's strawberry patch; the shortcake is provided by Mrs. Wilkes' (see our Restaurants chapter). It's a dessert combination that's tough to beat.

Those attending also enjoy self-guided tours of the gardens, and there's live entertainment and a silent auction. You need to make reservations for this get-together, which starts at 4:00 p.m.; cost of the meal is $15 per person.

Stand Up for America Day
Various locations
Port Wentworth
(912) 965-1999
www.portwentworthga.com
Residents of the west Chatham County town of Port Wentworth show their red, white, and blue colors from early morning until midnight on a Saturday in late April devoted to patriot-ism and fun. A parade featuring go-karts and bicycles decorated by youngsters starts at 10:00 a.m. near the city's elementary school, winds its way through town, and ends next to the fire station on Cantyre Street. That's also the site of a late-morning rally, craft sales, activities for children, and a nighttime street dance that goes on until midnight and includes a fireworks show about 9:00 p.m. Festivities start at 7:45 a.m. with a 5-kilometer run and a 1-mile fun walk.

MAY
Historic Downtown

Fine Arts Festival
River Street
(912) 234-0295
www.savwaterfront.com
Artists from throughout the nation display their paintings, photographs, and crafts during this festival on River Street's Rousakis Waterfront Plaza on the first weekend in May. Wine tasting, live music, and sales of food prepared by River Street restaurants add to the festivities. Admission is free to this event, a production of the Savannah Waterfront Association.

Kirkin' O' the Tartan
Independent Presbyterian Church
25 West Oglethorpe Avenue
(912) 236-3346
www.ipcsav.org
The Kirkin' O' the Tartan service begins with a procession of bagpipers and Scottish descendants bearing tartan banners representing their clans. After their entry into the church, the reading of scripture, the presentation of the banners, and a special sermon, there is more piping on the green outside the church. The service is at 11:00 a.m. on the second Sunday of May, and it's an occasion when many worshipers, Scottish and otherwise, rededicate themselves and their families to God.

Scottish Games and Highland Gathering
Bethesda Home for Boys
9520 Ferguson Avenue
(912) 233-6017
www.savannahscottishgames.com
Although tests of strength and dexterity are
the focal point of the Scottish Games, there's
more to the event than brawny laddies toss-
ing long poles ("cabers") and heaving sheaves
of hay into the air. Aye, there are winsome
lassies performing the dances of the Highlands and stouthearted bagpipers playing
their melancholy tunes. Also, members of
more than 50 Scottish clans bring a touch of
plaid to the green fields of the Bethesda
Home for Boys as they gather to parade,
socialize, and celebrate their heritage during
this festival on the first Saturday in May. The
event runs from 9:00 a.m. to 4:00 p.m. The
entry fee to the games is $10 for adults and
teens, $5 for children younger than age 12.

Ralph Mark Gilbert Civil Rights Museum
Anniversary Celebration
Ralph Mark Gilbert Civil Rights Museum
460 Martin Luther King Jr. Boulevard
(912) 231-8900
www.savannahcivilrights.com
Workshops and lectures inside the museum
and activities held at a local church in late
May emphasize the museum's founding in
1996. Workshops, lectures, and traveling
exhibits deal with aspects of African-American heritage, and so do the activities, which
include a food festival and entertainment by
dancers and musicians. Admission to the
museum is $4 for adults, $3 for senior citizens, and $2 for students.

Islands

War of Jenkins' Ear Observance
Wormsloe Historic Site
7601 Skidaway Road
Isle of Hope
(912) 353-3023
Wormsloe emphasizes the military aspect of
life in the Georgia of the 1740s with living-
history demonstrations on the last Saturday

i Wear comfortable shoes to outdoor
festivals, especially those on River
Street, where you'll be walking on cobblestones and uneven pavement. Be careful
if you use the steps leading from Bay
Street to River Street—they seem to have
been designed for people with long legs
and short feet.

in May. In a program running from 11:00 a.m.
to 4:00 p.m., members of the Wormsloe militia depict the lives of soldiers who fought in
the War of Jenkins' Ear—England's struggle
with the Spanish for possession of the southeastern portion of North America between
1739 and 1742. Admission is $4.00 for adults,
$3.50 for senior citizens, and $2.50 for children ages 6 to 18. Those age 6 and younger
are admitted free.

JUNE
Historic Downtown

First Saturday
Rousakis Plaza
River Street
(912) 234-0295
www.savwaterfront.com
See our March listing for more information on
this monthly event.

Savannah Asian Festival
Savannah Civic Center
Montgomery and Liberty Streets
(912) 651-6417
www.savannahga.gov/arts
A response to the contributions of Savannah's
growing Asian community, this one-day event
on a Saturday in June features displays and
entertainment reflecting the heritage of people of Chinese, Filipino, Indian, Japanese, Sri
Lankan, Nepalese, Korean, Thai, Pakistani, Tai-
wanese, and Vietnamese descent. A Vietnamese dragon dance ceremony, an Asian
fashion show, martial arts demonstrations,
and Vietnamese fan dancing are highlights.
Representatives of the Asian cultures, some

of them clad in native dress, display and sell arts and crafts at tables set up in the Civic Center arena and host workshops. You can purchase samples of Asian cuisine at food booths, and among the offerings are Chinese egg rolls, Indian curry, Thai beef, Filipino rice cakes, Vietnamese shish kebob, Japanese sushi, and Korean cucumber salad. The festival runs from 11:00 a.m. until 5:00 p.m. It's sponsored by Savannah's Department of Cultural Affairs, which means admission is free.

JULY

Historic Downtown

First Saturday
Rousakis Plaza
River Street
(912) 234-0295
www.savwaterfront.com
See our March listing for more information on this monthly event.

Fantastic Fourth Celebration
Rousakis Plaza
River Street
(912) 234-0295
www.savwaterfront.com
The sky above the Savannah River explodes in fireworks as folks gather on the plaza to celebrate the nation's birthday on July 4. Technicians shoot off shells 3 to 6 inches in diameter, including the largest projectile fired in Georgia, from nearby Hutchinson Island or

i If you happen to be near Johnson or Wright Squares around noontime on a Friday during the summer, amble on over and you'll likely be treated to some mighty fine sound provided by members of the local chapter of the American Federation of Musicians. From ragtime to jazz, their performances make lunchtime a special outdoor treat. They're on their outdoor "stages" from 11:30 a.m. to 1:30 p.m. during most of June, July, and August.

a barge in the river during a 22-minute, computer-synchronized "pyro-musical." Come early to stake out a good spot for viewing the show, and bring lawn chairs and a picnic supper to participate in what resembles a gigantic tailgate party. While you're waiting for the fireworks, you can listen to live music and people-watch. The free event opens about 5:00 p.m., and the rockets start bursting in air about 9:30 p.m.

AUGUST

Historic Downtown

First Saturday
Rousakis Plaza
River Street
(912) 234-0295
www.savwaterfront.com
See our March listing for more information on this monthly event.

Old Fort Jackson Labor Day Lowcountry Boil and Auction
Old Fort Jackson
1 Fort Jackson Road
(912) 651-3673
www.chsgeorgia.org
If you're going, you need to call ahead for reservations to this evening of fun, history, and food at the oldest standing brick fort in Georgia. The easygoing event on the Saturday of Labor Day weekend takes place within the brick walls of the structure, which was manned during the War of 1812 and used during the Civil War as a headquarters for the Confederacy's defense of the Savannah River (see our Attractions chapter). After visitors chow down on Lowcountry boil, barbecue, and all the trimmings, a live auction is held. The youngsters enjoy themselves scampering around in what amounts to a walled playground, and there's a cannon firing to further liven things up. Admission is $18 for adults and $12 for students. Children age six and younger are admitted free. Proceeds are used for the preservation of the fort.

Islands

Tools and Skills That Built the Colony
Wormsloe Historic Site
7601 Skidaway Road
(912) 353-3023
Wormsloe staff members in Colonial attire demonstrate carpentry, blacksmithing, and other skills essential to the development of Georgia. This living-history program is offered from 11:00 a.m. until 4:00 p.m. on the Saturday of Labor Day weekend. Admission is $4.00 for adults, $3.50 for senior citizens, and $2.50 for children ages 6 to 18. Those age 6 and younger are admitted free.

SEPTEMBER

Historic Downtown

First Saturday and Saltwater Shootout
Fishing Tournament
Rousakis Plaza
River Street
(912) 234-0295
www.savwaterfront.com
River Street serves as headquarters for the Saltwater Shootout Fishing Tournament during September's First Saturday event. In addition to enjoying the crafts, music, and food that are hallmarks of each First Saturday, festivalgoers can also watch anglers bring in their day's catch for weighing as the three-day tournament unfolds. Participants in the competition, an endeavor sponsored by the Greater Savannah Sports Council, compete during the first Friday, Saturday, and Sunday of September.

Savannah Jazz Festival
Forsyth Park
(912) 356-2399
www.coastaljazz.com
Forsyth Park and other venues heat up with the sounds of jazz for a week in late September when many of the finest musicians in the Savannah area and the South perform their special brand of American music. The park's the place to be for Blues Night on the Thurs-

day of the festival, for lively presentations on Friday night and Saturday afternoon and evening, and for a special Sunday afternoon session for children. The festival is funded by the city's Department of Cultural Affairs and organized by the Coastal Jazz Association, a nonprofit, community organization that depends on volunteers to run the event. Sessions are free.

Savannah Pride Festival
Rousakis Plaza
River Street
(912) 234-1134
www.savannahpride.org
This celebration of alternative lifestyles moves around a lot. After five years at a smaller venue, it built its way up to River Street and, later, to Johnson Square. The festival features dozens of entertainers and guest speakers addressing topics pertinent to the gay, lesbian, bisexual, and transgender community. More than 60 vendors are on hand, including folks representing community service agencies and those involved in sales of food, arts and crafts, and other merchandise. The event, held on a Saturday in mid-September, starts at 11:00 a.m. and progresses into the evening.

Islands

Medieval Festival
Oatland Island Education Center
711 Sandtown Road
Oatland Island
(912) 898-3980
www.oatlandisland.org
The clanging of sword fighting interrupts the normally serene environs of the Oatland Island Education Center on a Saturday in September when the Medieval Festival takes place. Costumed reenactors wield those weapons and also tell stories, roam through crowds of festivalgoers singing minstrel songs, and give demonstrations involving gypsy dancing and shooting a crossbow. Children's games and crafts and visits to a medieval village round out the activities, held

from 10:00 a.m. until 5:00 p.m. Admission is $5 for those four years old and older, with kids younger than four admitted free.

Southside/Midtown

Bethesda Labor Day Festival
Bethesda Home for Boys
9520 Ferguson Avenue
(912) 351-2040
www.bethesdahomeforboys.org

Held on Labor Day under the large, shady oaks at the Bethesda Home for Boys (see our Attractions chapter), this gathering for families offers live entertainment, kiddie rides, games, craft sales, and hot dogs and hamburgers, the last being made from Bethesda's homegrown beef. Special features have included antique automobile shows and live entertainment. Admission is free, but there is a $2 fee for parking. You buy tickets for games and food, and the prices won't set you back much. The festival runs from 10:00 a.m. until 4:00 p.m.

OCTOBER
Historic Downtown

Oktoberfest
Rousakis Plaza
River Street
(912) 234-0295
www.savwaterfront.com

If you happen to have a dachshund handy, you might want to enter it in the Wiener Dog Race, a comical competition that's become a featured part of the Savannah Waterfront Association's Oktoberfest event. Some 200 low-slung pooches "sprint" down the 50-foot racecourse as they seek to win prizes for their masters. The race—run in heats of four to six dogs until an overall winner prevails—benefits the local Friends of the Animals organization and costs $7 to enter. Watching is fun even if you don't have a dog running: Some pups never get out of the starting gate, and others wander around instead of heading for the finish line. The 2007 version featured a trio of

dogs put up by the crews of visiting U.S. naval vessels. The race is staged on the Saturday morning of the festival, which occurs during the first weekend of the month.

There will also be German food and music and plenty of beer. Booths manned by employees of River Street restaurants sell Wiener schnitzel, sauerbraten, bratwurst, and German chocolate cake, but there is also food for those whose tastes aren't Teutonic. Oompah band members decked out in lederhosen and Tyrolean hats provide much of the music, and festivalgoers are invited to join them in doing the arm-flapping, head-bobbing "Chicken Dance." Also, a headline entertainer usually performs at Oktoberfest. Admission is free, but the food is not. Hours of operation are 9:00 a.m. to midnight on Friday and Saturday and 9:00 a.m. until 6:00 p.m. on Sunday.

Picnic in the Park
Forsyth Park
(912) 651-6417
www.savannahga.gov/arts

Wine and dine under the stars and enjoy a pops classical concert by the Savannah Sinfonietta at this event on a weekend evening in early October. The more elaborate your picnic meal at tree-filled Forsyth Park, the better. Judges rate the best picnic, and festivalgoers seek to outdo one another with table settings and setups ranging from the elaborate to the unexpected. Candelabra, chandeliers, and chafing dishes make appearances, and some folks opt to embellish their picnics with formal rugs and dining room suites. Others get creative, building tropical huts for luaus or laying out an early Thanksgiving spread. If you prefer to simply sit on a blanket and nibble on a sandwich, that's okay, too. The concert and your seats on the grass are free of charge, courtesy of Savannah's Department of Cultural Affairs; you provide the food and drink.

Revolutionary War Memorial Celebration
Savannah History Museum
303 Martin Luther King Jr. Boulevard
(912) 651-6895
www.chsgeorgia.org

The Coastal Heritage Society uses this celebration to commemorate the climactic battle of the Siege of Savannah (see the History chapter), which was fought on the site of the Savannah History Museum and the nearby historic Roundhouse Railroad Museum. The ceremony is held about 7:00 a.m. on a Sunday in early October, with living history demonstrations offered throughout the weekend. Admission is free.

Historic Savannah Foundation Gala
Location varies
(912) 233-7787
www.historicsavannahfoundation.org
One of Historic Savannah Foundation's major fund-raisers starts with cocktails in private homes and moves to a site in one of the city's historic neighborhoods for a black-tie dinner party. The event is held in late October or early November, but the date and location vary. Tickets are $195.

Shalom Y'all Jewish Food Festival
Forsyth Park
(912) 233-1547
www.mickveisrael.org
Congregation Mickve Israel presents this opportunity to sample Jewish foods such as blintzes, potato latkes, matzo ball soup, knishes, kosher hot dogs, pastrami sandwiches, challah bread, and, of course, bagels with cream cheese and lox. These delectable items are sold from booths set up in Forsyth Park.

While you're strolling the park, be on the lookout for a booth manned by Arnold Belzer, the rabbi of the temple, who'll be dishing up portions of his own specialty, a type of stir-fry he calls "Ahmein Lo Mein." Live entertainment and activities for children add to the event, which runs from 11:00 a.m. until 4:00 p.m. on a Sunday in late October. Admission is free, and you purchase food and beverages by buying tickets at the park. Note that the best food sells out early.

Savannah Film Festival
Trustees Theater
216 East Broughton Street
(912) 525-5050
www.scad.edu
Hosted by the Savannah College of Art and Design, this presentation of film and video productions takes place during a week's time in late October and/or early November. The latest in feature-length films, shorts, animations, documentaries, and student work are screened at the Lucas Theatre and Trustees Theater in downtown Savannah, with workshops and gatherings at various other venues. Look for the trendy, the indie, the oldie, you name it. This week is always good for celebrity watching. Every year, the stars who attend to pick up awards become more A-list.

Islands

Halloween Hike
Oatland Island Education Center
711 Sandtown Road
Oatland Island
(912) 898-3980
www.oatlandisland.org
If you're seeking a "nonscary" Halloween experience for your child, take advantage of this walk along the trails and through the "Friendly Forest" at Oatland Island Education Center. As they frolic through the woods, young trick-or-treaters meet adults costumed as animal characters, who greet the children with hugs and goodies. Admission is $5 per child, and the center provides bags for collecting treats. You or another adult must accompany your child, and the little ones are encouraged to wear costumes and comfortable shoes. The center holds the hike on the Friday and Saturday before Halloween.

Southside/Midtown

Savannah Folk Music Festival
Various locations
(912) 786-6953
www.savannahfolk.org
The focal point of this completely free three-day musical jamboree is a concert at the

Roundhouse Railroad Museum in downtown Savannah. The concert consists of four to five acts featuring nationally recognized musicians. In recent years, folks such as singer-musicians Tom Rush, Mike Seeger, John Jackson, and Robin and Linda Williams have graced the stage. The concert, funded by Savannah's Department of Cultural Affairs, lasts from 1:00 to 7:00 p.m. on Sunday, the third day of the festival. Don't let the threat of rain scare you away; the museum affords plenty of shelter, so inclement weather won't stop the singing, picking, and grinning. The festival starts on a Friday evening in mid-October with performances of local musicians at City Market in downtown Savannah and continues Saturday night with an old-time country dance at the Notre Dame Academy gymnasium at Bull and 34th Streets. The whole shebang is presented by the Savannah Folk Music Society.

Savannah Greek Festival
Hellenic Center
14 West Anderson Street
(912) 236-8256
www.stpaul.ga.goarch.org

When we think of the Savannah Greek Festival, we can taste the baklava melting in our mouths. Those scrumptious pastries are just a sample of the tasty concoctions offered for sale at the Hellenic Center adjacent to St. Paul's Greek Orthodox Church in midtown Savannah during the third Thursday, Friday, and Saturday in October. Among other favorites of the patrons of the festival are the Greek salad, gyro sandwiches, and a spinach pie called spanakopita. While you're enjoying the food, sit back and watch the Hellenic Center's dance groups perform. You can also tour the church. Festival hours are 11:00 a.m. until 9:00 p.m. A $2 admission fee is charged on Saturday and after 4:00 p.m. on Thursday and Friday.

Coastal Empire Fair
520 West 63rd Street
(912) 354-3542
www.coastalempirefair.com

During 11 days in late October and early November when the weather turns chilly, the Coastal Empire Fair comes to town. The fairgrounds off Montgomery Street glow and throb with the lights and sounds of thrill rides, sideshows, and game booths. The 60-odd rides include about a dozen kiddie rides. This Exchange Club Fair Association extravaganza also features livestock shows, flower shows, and home demonstrations in skills such as canning and quilt making. The $20 admission fee allows you to hop on as many rides as you wish, and the price is reduced to $15 for special occasions such as days dedicated to students.

Bamboo Farm Annual Fall Festival
Bamboo Farm and Coastal Gardens
2 Canebrake Road
(912) 921-5460

Paint a pumpkin, buy some plants (perennials and fall annuals), or purchase sugar cane syrup at this celebration of autumn at the Bamboo Farm (see our Attractions chapter). For those seeking a bite to eat, there's a snack bar; the turnip green luncheon, featuring greens, roast pork, sweet potatoes, corn bread, and iced tea; and a hot-dog lunch. The kids will enjoy hayrides, pony rides, and a wildlife show presented by naturalist Okefenokee Joe. Adults might opt for the garden lecture and plant vendors. The last few years have featured workshops on the findings of an ongoing research program on growing bananas in Savannah—it can be done, with luck and skill.

This event takes place from 9:00 a.m. to 4:00 p.m. on a Saturday in late October. Admission is free, but there are charges for activities: $1 for a hayride, $2 for the wildlife show and pony rides, $3 for the hot-dog lunch, and $8 for the turnip green luncheon, for which reservations are required.

NOVEMBER

Historic Downtown

Savannah Seafood Festival
Rousakis Plaza
River Street
(912) 234-0295
www.savwaterfront.com
Fresh seafood prepared at booths on River Street's Rousakis Plaza is the main attraction of this event on the first weekend in November. Menus feature shrimp, crab, and crayfish—much of it caught in local waters. Festivalgoers munch away as they check out sales of arts and crafts, boogie to the beach and Cajun music provided by bands playing on the plaza's main stage, and enjoy the oyster-shucking contest. Hours are 9:00 a.m. to midnight on Friday and Saturday and 9:00 a.m. to 6:00 p.m. on Sunday. Admission is free.

Festival of Lights
Savannah Station
601 Cohen Street
(912) 236-7423
A fund-raiser for the programs of the nonprofit Parent and Child Development Services of Union Mission, this event on an evening in mid-November features a cocktail party and silent and live auctions. Held in the quaint brick surroundings of Savannah Station on the western fringes of the Historic District, this celebration for people of all faiths costs $100 per person to attend.

Telfair Art Fair
Telfair Square
121 Barnard Street
(912) 232-1177
www.telfair.org
The Telfair Museum's annual fair attracts about 65 artists from throughout the United States. They compete for cash awards and sell their creations to the public from displays under tents set up around Telfair Square. You can find paintings, sculpture, photographs, fabric, jewelry, and other fine arts at this exhibition, which takes place early in November. Hours are 10:00 a.m. until 5:00 p.m. on Saturday and 12:30 to 4:30 p.m. on Sunday. The fair is free.

Islands

Cane Grinding and Harvest Festival
Oatland Island Education Center
711 Sandtown Road
Oatland Island
(912) 898-3980
www.oatlandisland.org
Get a glimpse of the pioneer life of 1830s Georgia and do some early Christmas shopping by ambling through the Oatland forest and visiting the Heritage Homesite on a Saturday in November. At the end of your walk through a wood thick with oak, magnolia, pine, and vines of the muscadine grape, you'll find yourself in a small clearing where sugar cane is being processed. Farmers grind the cane into juice at a mill powered by a horse, then boil it into syrup. You can watch the entire operation, then buy a bottle of the sweet-smelling nectar to pour on your Sunday morning pancakes.

You might also want to poke your head into the cozy interiors of the two log cabins at the site and watch weavers at work and costumed women preparing corn bread, or you might hunker down on a bench and listen to members of the Savannah Folk Music Society as they perform songs from Georgia's past. Complete your day at Oatland by walking the nature trail to the wild-animal habitats and visiting the center's barnyard. If you need to get off your feet for a while, take a hayride through the forest. The festival opens at 10:00 a.m. and closes at 5:00 p.m. Admission is $5 for persons four and older; those younger than age four are admitted free.

DECEMBER

Historic Downtown

Holiday Open House
City Market
Jefferson and St. Julian Streets
(912) 232-4903
www.savannahcitymarket.com
On the first Friday evening of December, the courtyard at City Market glows with the soft light of luminarias as shop owners open their doors and offer complimentary refreshments to visitors. Strolling carolers sing Yuletide classics while Father Christmas—resplendent in his green velvet robe and red velvet cape and hat—talks with children about the spirit of the season and their plans for the holidays. This festive atmosphere takes place at City Market's Holiday Open House, which starts at sundown with the lighting of the luminarias and ends about 9:00 p.m.

Christmas for Kids
City Market
Jefferson and St. Julian Streets
(912) 232-4903
www.savannahcitymarket.com
It's been said that Christmas is for children, and City Market takes that to heart by offering a program for young people from 11:00 a.m. until 2:00 p.m. on the first Saturday of the month. This event gives youngsters the opportunity to decorate cookies, visit with Father Christmas, and make ornaments representative of Christmas, Hanukkah, and Kwanzaa. The entertainment varies from year to year, with puppet shows, a petting zoo, and performances by cloggers in the mix. It's all free.

Christmas on the River
River Street
(912) 234-0295
www.savwaterfront.com
Usher in the Christmas season on the first Saturday in December by shopping for gifts created by artists and craftspeople and watching a lighted parade starring Santa Claus. The arts and crafts vendors start selling at 9:00 a.m. on the riverfront plaza, and the parade begins at 6:00 p.m. on the western end of River Street. The parade lasts from an hour to 90 minutes and also includes high-school bands, color guards, floats, dance troupes, antique cars, and last, but most important, St. Nick riding in a carriage. After the parade, Santa poses for photos, and strolling musicians and local choirs perform throughout the day. Enjoy the parade but keep an eye out for flying candy flung from the floats to youngsters lining the route. Arts and crafts booths remain open until 6:00 p.m. In keeping with the spirit of the season, there is no charge for admission to this holiday festival.

Savannah River Bridge Run
Various downtown streets
(912) 355-3527
www.savannahbridgerun.com
Participating in either the 5- or 10-kilometer race will give you a unique view of Savannah—on foot from the Eugene Talmadge Memorial Bridge, a 1.4-mile span that rises 196 feet above the Savannah River. The longer race, held on the first Saturday in December, takes entrants from the starting line in the Historic District, over the bridge, and onto Hutchinson Island. The 10-K continues back over the bridge and into downtown. The 5-K begins on Hutchinson Island and comes across the bridge into Savannah. You can register ahead of time for $22 or enter on the day before the race for $30. Nearly 2,000 people compete in these two races. The race is particularly popular for a couple of reasons: 1) For obvious safety reasons, the towering Talmadge Bridge is closed to foot traffic at all other times, so this is the only way to see that stunning view at a human pace, and 2) Savannah's terrain is truly, utterly flat, so the steep slope of the bridge has novelty for local runners.

Downtown Neighborhood Association
Holiday Tour of Homes
Hilton Savannah DeSoto Hotel
15 East Liberty Street
(912) 236-8362
www.dnaholidaytour.net

Many of the homes on the tours offered during this mid-December event are decorated for Christmas in ways reflecting the lifestyles of their owners. The self-guided walking tours are on Saturday afternoon and evening and Sunday afternoon, with a different set of six to nine private homes featured on each day. The sponsoring Downtown Neighborhood Association selects homes in the Historic District that present a diversity of architectural design and decor. The Saturday-evening tour runs from 5:00 to 8:00 p.m., and candles light the interiors and exteriors of many of the residences visited. The Saturday afternoon and the Sunday tours run from noon to 4:00 p.m. Tickets are $30 per tour, and they can be picked up on the days of the event in the lobby of the Hilton Savannah DeSoto Hotel.

Tour organizers schedule special events for out-of-town tourgoers, including lectures pertaining to Savannah's architecture and history. Call ahead to find out more about what's available. The association, which has offered the tour for more than 20 years, returns revenues from the event to the community in the form of projects aimed at maintaining and improving the quality of life downtown.

New Year's Eve at City Market
City Market
Jefferson and St. Julian Streets
(912) 232-4903
www.savannahcitymarket.com

A live band creates a party atmosphere at City Market during the hours leading up to midnight on New Year's Eve. When the clock strikes midnight, hundreds of balloons strung across the courtyard are dropped amid the merrymakers. For Savannahians, this is as close as it gets to being in Times Square. The event is free, and the partying starts about 7:00 p.m. and lasts until 1:00 or 2:00 a.m.

Islands

Colonial Christmas at Wormsloe
Wormsloe Historic Site
7601 Skidaway Road
(912) 353-3023

While a Yule log is burned, carolers sing to the accompaniment of musicians playing a dulcimer and flutes at this Colonial Christmas celebration. Sip some apple cider and munch on cookies as you enjoy the festivities. This holiday program on the second Sunday in December runs from 2:00 to 5:00 p.m., and admission is $4.00 for adults, $3.50 for senior citizens, and $2.50 for those ages 6 to 18. Children younger than age 6 are admitted free.

Southside/Midtown

Christmas at Bethesda
Bethesda Home for Boys
9250 Ferguson Avenue
(912) 351-2040
www.bethesdahomeforboys.org

The boys of Bethesda (see our Attractions chapter) present a reenactment of the Magi's visit to the baby Jesus and sing Christmas carols during a program at their chapel. The boys and their guests then move to the gymnasium for an Old English Christmas celebration featuring the bringing in of a Yule log and visits from the Switch Man, who gives switches to kids who've been bad; the Cookie Lady, who gives cookies to kids who've been good; and Santa Claus, who has gifts for all the residents of the home. This observance occurs on an evening two weeks before Christmas and gets started about 6:00 p.m. The event is free and open to the public; donations are accepted.

KIDSTUFF

The time has come for a little brutal honesty. Savannah is a wonderful place. You can stay in romantic bed-and-breakfasts, stroll through history, shop for antiques, tour museums showcasing the treasures of gracious living in the past, dine in elegant restaurants on sophisticated dishes. In other words, Savannah's greatest attractions require a little, well, maturity, for full appreciation.

That's wonderful news for many travelers, but if your party includes kids, you're going to need a little help getting them to enjoy the wonders of this city. That's what this chapter is all about. The kids who have the privilege of growing up here have it made—a beach within easy striking distance, a water-oriented outdoor lifestyle that puts crab traps and fishing poles in the youngest of hands, a fanatically organized system of youth sports that covers all the major games (well, not ice hockey—this is the South, you know), a local theater scene that makes room for kids, you name it. Savannah also offers that increasingly rare opportunity of growing up in a place that has a sense of identity and uniqueness.

Chances are, though, that you are just passing through and hooking your kid or kids up to these homegrown attractions isn't really easy in the course of a few days.

With that in mind, we've compiled some suggestions for helping your kids enjoy their Savannah visit. We are not the home of any giant planned theme parks or prefab attractions, for which we should all be grateful. But we are the home of many wonderful things for kids to see and do with their parents while they enjoy themselves and learn something along the way. For organizational purposes, we grouped this chapter loosely along these lines. First of all, we wanted to cover the things that are unique to this city. With that in mind, we open with tips on how to help younger visitors enjoy the historic aspects of the city. Next, still focusing on Savannah flavors, we touch on ways to enjoy some of the unique wildlife of the region. Finally, we cover additional children's activities ranging from playgrounds to laser tag, stuff that is not unique to or even related to Savannah, but which could prove invaluable in keeping young vacationers busy.

Before we begin, though, let's touch on the issue of accommodations. If you are traveling with children, we recommend spending at least part of your stay at Tybee Island, the local beach. We've got a whole chapter on options there. Any child who tags along dutifully on historic site tours and antiques shopping rounds deserves a chance to dig in the sand and splash around in the ocean.

Some bed-and-breakfasts in Savannah welcome children, although many have age restrictions. Check beforehand. Personally, we recommend the selection of a hotel or motel with a swimming pool instead of a bed-and-breakfast with a Jacuzzi.

HISTORY FOR KIDS

Parents won't be able to resist the Historic District, no matter how much their children complain. Don't worry though: With a little preparation, you can make your trip through time more of an adventure and less like a field trip with a required school report afterward.

Most people choose at least one guided tour of the Historic District while they are in Savannah. It gets rid of a lot of orientation quickly, and you can go back later on foot to examine what really interested you. This option even works with kids, if you choose your tour carefully. You'll find the full menu of available tour options described in our Attractions chapter, so we won't review them here. Based on our experience with younger guests, however, take these things into consideration when choosing a tour: The purely historical versions won't really hold a child's interest, unless the entire tour group is made up of children on a planned trip and the guide can pitch his or her delivery solely to that age group. Also, find something else to do with the children if you are just dying to do one of the tours based on the best seller *Midnight in the Garden of Good and Evil*. The guide's patter isn't going to be too explicit, but there's no getting around the fact the book is about murder, homosexuality, transvestites, and larceny.

What does that leave in the tour category? Two really good options: carriage tours and ghost tours. Many city and suburban children have never had a close encounter with a horse, and the novelty of a carriage ride will appeal strongly (and make good family photos). If your children are old enough—say, at least second or third grade—you should check out the ghost tours, especially the walking or carriage versions. The stories are tame enough that they are unlikely to inspire screaming nightmares. (You know your own child best: Don't submit the timid to what the rest of us would consider a friendly chill.) The tours don't actually go inside any buildings, and the whole motif appeals to the adolescent sensibility. Actually, these popular tours have proliferated in recent years, and gotten hokier and sillier in the process. One you might consider for kids, especially if you have a camera along, is a ghost tour via a remodeled hearse (Hearse Ghost Ride, 912-695-1578, www.hearseghosttours.com). The price of this particular tour is $15 for adults, $10 for children 10 and under.

With younger children, you can add interest to historic sightseeing with the help of a locally produced little book. *Savannah Safari II* is the work of locals Polly Wylly Cooper and Emmeline King Cooper. It is a slim paperback volume, designed to serve as a coloring book if you so desire, that sends kids on a scav-

enger-style hunt for "animals" while touring the Historic District. The "animals" are the iron downspouts shaped like dolphins, the sculptured herons in the Forsyth Park fountains, and so on. Stretch the interest for older children by chipping in one of those disposable cameras so they can photograph their "animal" finds.

Savannah Safari II is $5 and available in local bookstores, which you'll find listed in our Shopping chapter.

Juliette Gordon Low Center
142 Bull Street
(912) 233-4501
www.girlscouts.org/birthplace

If your children are, have been, or aspire to be Girl Scouts, don't miss this wonderful house museum. In fact, it's your best bet among the museums for entertaining children. The birthplace and childhood home of Juliette "Daisy" Gordon Low is a virtual mecca for Girl Scouts from throughout the country, and you'll spot field trips full of them trooping around Savannah all the time. As a result, the staff at the center is experienced in the art of entertaining children without boring their adult escorts.

The elegant and beautifully preserved home of the wealthy Gordon family, which includes a masterpiece of a garden, works well for both age groups. Hours are 10:00 a.m. to 4:00 p.m. Monday through Saturday, and 11:00 a.m. to 4:00 p.m. Sunday. Closed the first two weeks of January, and Wednesday from November through February. Cost is $8 for adults and $7 for children. (Read more about it in our Attractions chapter.)

Ships of the Sea Museum
41 Martin Luther King Jr. Boulevard
(912) 232-1511
www.shipsofthesea.org

The kids can learn all about Savannah's maritime history at this museum, which has been relocated to one of Savannah's historic old residences. The more upscale setting probably lowered the kid appeal here, but it should ℹ️ Bicycling as a family can be a fun part of vacation. If you bring your own bike, bring your own helmet. If you rent a bike, insist on a helmet as part of the deal. Georgia law requires kids to wear a helmet when riding a bike, but it's a toothless law with no penalty and no enforcement, so the kids will have to depend on their parents to insist on this vital safety step.

still work for kids. Cost is $8 for adults, $6 for students and seniors. Family rate is $20. Children younger than age seven are free. The museum is open from 10:00 a.m. to 5:00 p.m. Tuesday through Sunday and is closed on Monday.

RIVER STREET

River Street, especially by day, can appeal mightily to the young tourist. All along the river are lots of shops, and while they are stocked with expensive gift items with the usual tourist-area markup, there are also plenty of wares geared toward kid tastes and kid pocketbooks. Follow them from shop to shop here and watch them buy candy and trinkets.

If luck is with you, your young entourage will get to spot one or more of the giant container ships, escorted by a team of tugboats, on its way upriver to the Georgia Ports Authority. These ships are such an imposing presence that even jaded teenagers will stop in their tracks to stare.

WILDLIFE

It's a shame for an inland kid to visit the coastal South and leave without seeing at least one alligator (from a safe distance, of course). Fortunately, that sighting can be arranged, along with such exotic fare as dolphins. Read on!

The Aquarium at Skidaway Island
30 Ocean Science Circle
(912) 598-3474, (912) 598-2496
Scout out Georgia's marine life at The Aquarium at Skidaway Island, where a major renovation was completed in September 2007. This small facility, operated by the University of Georgia Marine Extension Service, also includes a picnic area (which you may appreciate, because it is quite a drive out to Skidaway) and a walking trail. See 200 live animals—including fish of all shapes and sizes, turtles, and maybe even a small shark in the many wall tanks lining the exhibit hall. You owe this one to your kids if they have never seen a live flounder, our candidate for weirdest-looking fish in the world. Then go outside for a stroll along the Jay Wolfe Nature Trail, which passes by scenic marshes. The aquarium is open from 9:00 a.m. to 4:00 p.m. on weekdays and noon to 5:00 p.m. on Saturday. It is closed on Sunday and holidays. The cost is $4 for adults, $2 for children and seniors; children ages two and younger enter free.

Bull River Cruises
8005 Old Tybee Road
(U.S. Highway 80 East)
Tybee Island
(912) 898-1800
www.bullriver.com
This marina offers a variety of eco-cruises and charters, and bills itself as experienced in working with Girl Scout troops. Call for reservations. They're essential because these trips are keenly affected by the weather. No one can guarantee you a dolphin sighting, but it is highly likely. The real challenge is to make the trips long enough to justify the price and short enough to remain interesting if the local wildlife choose not to perform. Winter visitors are less likely to find these trips an option, although the marina will arrange custom trips, birthday parties, fishing charters, and other boating recreation excursions.

You wouldn't normally think of shopping for a child in a cigar store, but hear us out: The shops sell their empty cigar boxes, starting at $2. Even adamant nonsmokers will admit there's nothing better for storing those seashells than a cigar box. (Check out the listings for tobacco in our Shopping chapter.)

Lazaretto Creek Marina
US 80 East
(just across Lazaretto Creek Bridge)
Tybee Island
(912) 786-5848, (800) 242-0166
www.tybeedolphins.com
While enjoying the scenery of Fort Pulaski and the North Beach of Tybee Island, see friendly bottle-nosed dolphins playing in their natural habitat. The 90-minute tours cost $15 for adults and teens and $8 for children age 12 and younger. Diving and deep-sea/inshore fishing charters are available.

Oatland Island Education Center
711 Sandtown Road
(912) 898-3980
www.oatlandisland.org
You are virtually guaranteed to spot your alligator here at a natural-habitat facility operated by the local school system as an educational center. Other once-native animals—buffalo, wolves, birds of prey—and an authentic Colonial farm setting, complete with livestock, can also be seen. A self-guided outdoor hike takes you through marshes and around to the different animal and plant exhibits. Admission is $5, and free for those age three and younger. The center, which hosts many popular programs (see our Annual Events and Festivals chapter), is open from 9:00 a.m. to 4:00 p.m. Monday through Friday and 10:00 a.m. to 4:00 p.m. on Saturday (holidays impact Saturday hours). As teachers, the staff members are good with kids, so don't miss this attraction. Bring your own bug repellent, though—you'll need it. (For more on the center, see our Attractions chapter.)

Savannah National Wildlife Refuge
South Carolina Highway 170
(912) 652-4415
http://www.fws.gov/savannah/
Take a coastal safari through the 29,174-acre Savannah National Wildlife Refuge. It's full of freshwater marsh, tidal rivers, creeks, and bottomland hardwood swamps. While driving through the refuge, see if you can spot alligators, owls, hawks, turtles, snakes, or maybe even a bald eagle. The refuge is managed by the U.S. Fish and Wildlife Service. It is open seven days a week during daylight hours (except federal holidays), and visiting is free. The refuge is about 9 miles from downtown. (For more information and directions—which are a bit complex—see our Parks and Recreation chapter.)

Tybee Island Marine Science Center
14th Street parking lot
Tybee Island
(912) 786-5917
www.tybeemsc.org
Stroll the beach, toss a net into the ocean, then learn about what you find during a beach discovery walk held daily at the center. A tour guide leads the way and explains about Tybee's marine life. Don't forget to check out the stuff inside the center, too—you'll find a touch tank, aquariums, and shark displays. This isn't Sea World—expect a small, personalized experience. Open from 9:00 a.m. to 5:00 p.m. daily, closing at noon on Tuesday. Admission is $4 for adults and $3 for children, with those under three admitted free. (See our chapter on Tybee Island for more information.)

If you visit in the summer, the various branch libraries are in full swing with summer programs for kids. Call (912) 652-3600 to find the branch nearest you. Visitors are always welcome, and with a temporary card (cost $25), you can even check out books, videos, and tapes.

OUTDOOR ADVENTURE

Forsyth Park
Bull Street between Gaston Street and Park Avenue
Thirty acres perfect for letting off some steam are set aside in the Historic Downtown. There are swing sets, slides, and other contraptions for youngsters needing to get rid of some energy, along with plenty of open space to just plain run, beautiful magnolia trees, and scenery for Mom and Dad to enjoy, too. May we suggest a picnic?

Lake Mayer
Montgomery Crossroad and Sallie Mood Drive
(912) 652-6786
Bring your bike and take a spin around the 1.5-mile trail at Lake Mayer, located in the 75-acre community park of the same name. While there, you can also play tennis or basketball, play in the playground, or feed the ducks swimming in the lake.

Skidaway Island State Park
52 Diamond Causeway
Skidaway Island
(912) 598-2300
www.gastateparks.org
Camping sites, picnic areas, trails, playgrounds, and a swimming pool can be found at 533-acre Skidaway Island State Park, the only state park in Chatham County. Maps of the park and trails are available at the park office. If you don't want to tackle the trails alone, free guided hikes are available with

i Looking for kid-friendly restaurants that aren't fast-food franchises? Lots of restaurants cater to families, but if you're looking for a vacation dinner that will offer something for both adult and child appetites, try The Pirates' House downtown. The decor, along with tales of pirates and ghosts, will keep the kiddies entertained while you wait. (See our Restaurants chapter for more details.)

advance reservations. The pool is open Memorial Day to Labor Day and costs $3 per swimmer. Cost to enter the park is $3 per car, except on Wednesday when it is free. (For more information, see our Parks and Recreation chapter.)

THE OL' BALL GAME

Savannah Sand Gnats
Grayson Stadium
Daffin Park
1401 East Victory Drive
(912) 351-9150
www.sandgnats.com
If you happen to be in town during the Sand Gnats' season (early April through the end of August), round up the kids and take them to a ball game. Besides being entertained by the Gnats, the single-A affiliate for the New York Mets, kids and parents will have fun watching the dueling mascots and between-inning contests (including the classic one in which two people spin around dozens of times with their heads on the ends of bats, then try to make it to first base), munching on barbecue and boiled peanuts, and getting caught up in the atmosphere of this old-time ballpark. Games start at 7:15 p.m. on weekdays and Saturday and at 2:00 p.m. on Sunday until mid-June, when Sunday games begin at 4:00 p.m. General admission is only $7 for adults and $3 for students and children. Cheaper seats offer the best chance of catching foul balls. Parking is free around the stadium, which was extensively remodeled in 2005. (For much more on the Sand Gnats, see our Spectator Sports chapter.)

ENJOYING THE ARTS

Midnight Star Pottery
Eisenhower and Waters Avenues
(912) 236-3473
www.midnightstarpottery.com
Paint a bowl for your grandmother or a water dish for your favorite kitty at Midnight Star Pottery, a unique and enjoyable pottery-paint-

ing studio. Kids can spend hours choosing among the dozens of pottery pieces—included are plates, picture frames, pasta sets, tiles, napkin rings, even dog and cat dishes—and creating masterpieces. It's a lot of fun for Mom and Dad, too. Costs include the pottery items, which start at $2 for a tile and go up from there, and an hourly studio fee that starts at $6 per hour. The fee includes all creative materials (paints, brushes, glazes), firing, and instruction. The clock doesn't start ticking on the studio fee until you've picked out your piece of pottery, colors, and designs and have sat down to paint. In other words, if your child takes an hour trying to figure out just the right present to create for his or her teacher, it won't cost you anything extra.

THE LIGHT AT THE END OF THE TUNNEL

Tybee Island Lighthouse
30 Meddin Drive
(912) 786-5801
www.tybeelighthouse.org
Hike 154 feet to the top of Tybee Lighthouse for a great view of Tybee and Savannah. You'll also learn a few things about one of America's historic light stations. It opens at 9:00 a.m. and sells the last ticket at 4:30 p.m. (closes at 5:30). Closed on Tuesday. Cost, which includes admission to the Tybee Museum, is $6 for adults, $5 for seniors, military, and children age 6 to 14; children under 6 are free.

OPTIONS OF LAST RESORT

Did it rain after you rashly promised a day at the beach? Has too much walking left your feet too blistered to keep up with the kids? Then you might consider these options. They aren't unique to Savannah. In fact, they're the franchise-ish type thing that this book purposely doesn't include in most instances. But as any parent knows, when it comes to kids, it never hurts to have a fallback plan. All of these places cater to visiting birthday parties. All feature high noise and hyperactivity levels.

Adults who bring children here must summon up lots of fortitude. With that warning, here goes:

Chuck E. Cheese
6700 Abercorn Street
(912) 355-6420

The Flying Frogs
1100 Eisenhower Drive
(912) 356-0075
We lumped these two together because to us they are pretty much indistinguishable, despite the fact they are business rivals. Essentially, each is an indoor playground where kids are not only allowed to run wild but are encouraged to do so. Pizza is the menu mainstay. There are also games that pay off in points that kids can amass for prizes. At Chuck E. Cheese, there are giant animated figures that sing and perform skits. Chuck E. Cheese is open from 9:00 a.m. to 10:00 p.m. weekdays and Sunday and 9:00 a.m. to 11:00 p.m. Friday and Saturday. Flying Frogs features a kiddy train. Admission is free at Chuck E. Cheese, although you pay for the food and games. At Flying Frogs, admission is free, but there is a $1.50 charge for the maze and $1.00 for the toy train. The Flying Frog hours are 10:00 a.m. to 9:00 p.m. weekdays, 10:00 a.m. to 11:00 p.m. Friday and Saturday, and 11:00 a.m. to 8:00 p.m. Sunday.

Skukuzoo
Inside Savannah Mall
14045 Abercorn Street
(912) 921-7216
www.skukuzoo.com
A Savannah couple opened this indoor playground on Savannah Mall's second level early in 2003, and it quickly turned into a gathering place for moms and young kids. The playground, named after the Skukuza village in

i Let the kids try their luck at fishing. At Tybee's pier, you can rent gear and buy bait. We've seen some interesting catches there.

South Africa's Kruger National Park (where the owners honeymooned), features indoor play equipment designed around a jungle theme. There's a special play section for toddlers only, and the larger part is for kids ages 12 and younger. Come prepared for a high noise level! There's also an 18-hole indoor miniature golf course, equipped with golf clubs scaled to any size child. Video games and coin-operated rides round out the entertainment offerings. The concession stand sells pizza, sandwiches, and snacks, and there's a small stock of souvenirs. In the back, display cases feature some educational displays to make this destination eligible to handle elementary-school field trips. An adult must accompany the child, and the facility has an elaborate bracelet-matching system designed to make sure kids leave with the right adult. Admission is $5 for children (includes one round of golf), and free for adults and children 13 and up (golf, $3).

Star Castle
550 Mall Boulevard
(912) 354-5437

Star Castle was built as a giant for-pay playhouse for kids, and the architecture shows it—it's a pseudo-castle, complete with a "dragon" in the small pond by the door. But while the decor aims at a medieval theme, the entertainment is more up-to-date—laser tag, a skating rink, and an arcade full of electronic games and Skee Ball. There's a concession stand with the predictable kid-friendly pizza and sandwich menu.

There's no admission charge at the door, but you pay per activity. Laser tag is a simulated warfare game involving light-sensitive vests and laser "pistols." One game is $6.50 per player, with two games at $9.50 per player. Roller-skating session rates vary. Skate rental is $2.00. Arcade game charges vary.

Hours are 11:00 a.m. to 10:30 p.m. Monday through Thursday, 11:00 a.m. to midnight Friday and Saturday, and noon to 10:30 p.m. Sunday.

ARTS AND CULTURE

Savannah prides itself on its arts and culture scene, and justifiably so. The city is not only a consumer of the arts, but with the advent of a Savannah-based art college of growing repute, it is also a producer of the arts. Music, drama, and the visual arts are all well represented here, both in the form of outlets for local talent and in venues for touring artists of greater renown.

You can take your arts and culture on various levels in Savannah. You can don your designer duds and shop in ultrachic art galleries, picking up pieces by artists who never set foot on these shores; you can dress in jeans and pick up a sketch from a sidewalk artist on River Street; or you can rent a garret, buy a backpack, and enroll in art classes yourself. You can also work through the same type of strata musically as a concertgoer, a jazz follower in smoky nightclubs, or as a community band or civic orchestra performer bent on honing your talents. As for theater, you'll find several active local theater groups, thriving secular performance venues in some local churches, and, for those who prefer the role of spectator, the occasional national touring troupe.

In this chapter, we outline Savannah's major cultural organizations and venues for you. We provide plenty of telephone numbers and instructions on how to tap into specific schedules. You might also want to check out our Annual Events and Festivals chapter for further suggestions for an artsy afternoon or evening. Keeping abreast of the local cultural scene is fairly easy. The *Savannah Morning News* (see our Media chapter) offers its most comprehensive arts coverage in a Sunday *Accent* section. The *Morning News*'s Thursday *Diversions* section also contains event listings, but the coverage there tends to be more club and concert oriented.

CONNECT Savannah is a good resource on entertainment and the club scene, with the ads as informative as the articles and the listings among the city's most complete. Again, check our Media chapter for suggestions on where to find this publication, which is free and distributed at various restaurants and businesses.

VENUES

Lucas Theatre for the Arts
32 Abercorn Street
(912) 525-5040
www.lucastheatre.com
The restoration of the Lucas Theatre for the Arts seemed to take forever, but it has been worth the wait. The theater was built in 1921 and rode the popularity of the silver screen for decades. Alas, it fell into disrepair as the 1970s came on, and after some ill-fated attempts to keep it running (such as a short stint as a dinner theater and a period when the lobby was a restaurant), the magnificent building went into mothballs.

But the Italian Renaissance–style building with its ornate interior was just too fantastic to let go, and a lengthy fund-raising campaign was started to get this grand dame back on her feet. Restoration, however, is expensive, especially when you do things like bring in an Italian artisan to re-create the plaster moldings. Look for the 40-foot-wide ceiling dome, lots of gold leaf, and—a welcome sight to Savannah eyes—the bars upstairs and down. It took 13 years to pull it off, but the end result is beautiful. The marquee, with its chasing lights, adds an exciting touch to Savannah's nightlife, and the theater has helped spur redevelopment of nearby buildings.

The Savannah College of Art and Design

(SCAD) runs the theater, and while the college does use the facility for some activities, it remains open to the public for events. This venue serves as a major host for the Savannah Film Festival and the Savannah Music Festival, and is also the site for events sponsored by the Savannah Film Society and the Savannah Concert Association, along with privately promoted touring productions and events brought in by SCAD but open to the general public. The 2007–08 calendar takes guests from Argentina to Italy to Ireland, featuring performances by the Argentine group Tango Buenos Aires, Puccini's *Tosca* by Teatro Lirico, and the Celtic band The Boys of Lough, among many other performances.

Savannah Civic Center
Montgomery and Liberty Streets
(912) 651-6556
www.savannahcivic.com

This is a place, not an entity like a symphony or a drama group, but we list it here because it is the major performance venue in the city. The city of Savannah owns and operates this major facility, but groups, including private ventures and touring companies, stage the shows here.

The Savannah Civic Center has two main components, plus various meeting rooms and a ballroom. The arena, named for the late Dr. Martin Luther King Jr., can seat up to 9,000, depending on the event configuration. The theater, which seats about 2,500, is named in honor of Johnny Mercer, the famed Savannah-born lyricist ("Moon River," etc.). By and large, the more formal events, such as dramatic presentations or one-person shows, play in the theater, with the arena going for large-scale, pack-'em-in audiences for such events as rock or country music concerts, wrestling matches, and monster truck shows. But that isn't a hard-and-fast rule: When Mikhail Baryshnikov danced in Savannah with the touring experimental White Oak Dance Troupe, they filled the arena. The offerings at the Civic Center vary, depending on the tastes and daring of various promoters. The 2007–08 schedule included touring shows of

Cats and *Annie*, Disney on Ice, WWE Live RAW wrestling, and the Hermitage Russian Ballet. The concert scene has become more lively with the continued growth of the Savannah College of Art and Design and its built-in audience potential. To keep up with what might be available during your visit, check the media sources mentioned at the opening of this chapter, or simply check the large billboard on the Liberty Street side of the building. The number listed here is for the box office, and tickets generally are on sale well in advance of performances. We've always been pleased with our box office service, which is also helpful in arranging seating for the handicapped (there are some major virtues associated with dealing with a municipal facility).

The Civic Center consumes an entire block between Oglethorpe and Liberty Streets, with entrances on Montgomery Street and facing the parking lot. A word of warning about parking is in order: Popular events at the Civic Center put parking at a premium. A city-operated multilevel parking garage opened in 2005 across from the Civic Center, and it is open at night when there are performances. Because it is easier to get out of a street-side parking space, many patrons prefer to park along the surrounding streets. You don't have to feed the meters at night, but be sure not to block the crosswalks leading to the squares or make up any imaginative parking spaces—lots of parking tickets get handed out on the evenings of big performances. Also, avoid the temptation to whip into the vacant parking lots of obviously closed businesses: Many businesses choose to defend those spaces at night and will have after-hours parkers towed.

Savannah College of Art and Design
Various addresses and numbers
www.scad.edu

You may wonder what an art college is doing under the "Venues" heading. Actually, SCAD (as it is referred to locally; see our Education and Child Care chapter for additional information) is a major player in the local arts and culture scene, not just for its own students, but for the general public. Check out the SCAD art galleries listed later in this chapter, but first, two of the newest (including the most attractive and unique) theater entries are from SCAD. Trustees Theater, 206 East Broughton Street (912-239-1447), is a circa-1946 movie theater that has been refurbished and reopened as a 1,100-seat performance venue capable of handling both stage productions and movie screenings. Its basic purpose is to house performances and classes for SCAD's performing-arts majors, but it also offers performances to the public. Performers have included Tony Bennett, the Neville Brothers, and India.Arie. This is also a home venue of SCAD's annual film festival. The Lucas Theatre for the Arts, discussed elsewhere, is managed by SCAD.

THEATER

You have to be pretty agile to keep up with drama groups in Savannah. They come and go, and always appear to be operating on a shoestring. The amazing thing, though, is not their occasionally temporary nature—it's their resiliency. One particular group may wither away, but there's always another in the wings. Right now, we know of three independent groups, not to mention the productions put on by the City of Savannah's Leisure Services. Several churches maintain highly successful theater programs featuring secular works such as Gilbert and Sullivan offerings, and there are also collegiate theatrical groups. Armstrong Atlantic State University's Masquers produce reliably entertaining work. Check the event pages of the newspapers cited earlier for schedules and further information.

Asbury Memorial United Methodist Church
1008 East Henry Street
(912) 233-4351
This venerable church was dying out as its congregation aged and the neighborhood

i Scan the local paper for listings of performances by the Savannah Arts Academy. This public high school puts on some surprisingly professional performances, often in the spring. Its Skylite Jazz Band is particularly good.

changed, but it got a shot in the arm when a performance-minded pastor and the congregation opened their arms to the arts community. The church social hall serves as a performance arena. Don't mistake these productions for Sunday-school projects. They're at least on a par with the other local offerings (actually, all the local theater efforts involve different arrangements of essentially the same theater performers).

Although the offerings often have a religious theme (*Godspell* and *Jesus Christ Superstar*), this group has also tackled Gilbert and Sullivan. Ticket prices vary, usually around $15. Other local churches occasionally dip into secular drama, mainly to keep their youth groups involved, but this one definitely strives for and achieves a higher level.

Little Theatre of Savannah
P.O. Box 15775
Savannah 31416
(912) 631-3773
www.littletheatreofsavannah.org
The fortunes of this community theater group rise and fall, but it's still here. At one time, it owned its own theater, the Savannah Theatre, but the rigors of maintaining historic property proved to be too much for a small volunteer organization. That property is now used by a professional performing troop for a standing show, and the Little Theatre of Savannah has moved on. For a while, it performed on the stage at the Jewish Educational Alliance, and its current home is called the Savannah Actor's Theatre, 703D Louisville Road. (Even locals would have trouble with that address—it's what Liberty Street becomes after it crosses Martin Luther King Jr. Boulevard. The building is an historic [well, old, anyway]

Classical Music in Savannah

If classical music in Savannah were a patient on one of those prime-time Dr. McDreamy soap operas on network television these days, here's what the plot line would be: A generally healthy patient who has had a few periodic health problems suddenly drops dead; initial resuscitation efforts are lackluster and unproductive; desperate measures by unheralded medical heroes revive the patient; the patient now shows signs of life but it is unclear whether it will die, survive in a diminished state, or recover. Meanwhile, the patient's friends and family (read: fans of classical music) are hanging around the waiting room, exhausted from attending one possibly premature funeral and now uncertain about whether to hold another wake or host a get-well celebration.

Okay, so we strained a metaphor there, but you get the point. The Savannah Symphony Orchestra was a proud fixture in the city for over half a century, but it closed down amid managerial disputes and financial woes in the midst of its 2002–03 season. The symphony had been in and out of financial hot water for decades but always managed to survive. There were even a handful of well-publicized musicians' strikes. With the exception of the docks, Savannah isn't known as an organized-labor stronghold, so striking violinists were a newsworthy novelty—instead of walking picket lines, they set up free ensemble concerts in downtown squares at lunchtime. And there was always this sense that the show would go on—after all, the two free outdoor concerts sponsored annually by local government were major events, the visiting artists included the cream of the touring music world, and the symphony itself was very good.

So when the symphony closed its doors in early 2003, Savannah calmly waited for a corporate white knight or private patron to ride to the rescue. Said knight/patron never showed up.

For several years, all that Savannah had of classical music was a portion of the varied schedule of the Savannah Music Festival for three weeks in the spring, a few touring performances, and an effort to keep the fall Picnic in the Park program going with a pick-up orchestra of local remnants supplemented by regional imports.

Fast forward to 2007–08, and things are looking up. By the time you read this, they may have improved even more or failed miserably—but we've included Web sites so you can track the drama if this kind of music is important to you.

Basically, the revival efforts have gone in two different directions—one local, one tour-based. The Savannah Sinfonietta is a small professional orchestra with a local board that performed its first concerts in 2006–07. The Savannah Concert Association brings in touring classical artists for solo and ensemble performances.

Unlike its larger predecessor, which performed in the Savannah Civic

Center's Johnny Mercer Theater, the Savannah Sinfonietta performs each concert in two venues—donated church sanctuaries downtown in the Historic District and on Skidaway Island near The Landings, a wealthy residential community whose residents made up part of the original symphony's season audience. Audiences were skeptical at first, but the determined group was winning them over by the second season, giving reason to be optimistic about its future.

Savannahian William Keith is the director. The 2007–08 Masterworks series includes six concerts, plus a Handel's *Messiah* sing-along in December. As of this writing, only the first of that series has been performed, but it was critically well received. Don't scoff at the idea of using churches as music venues—the acoustics at Wesley Monumental United Methodist Church in the Historic District (site of the downtown concerts) and the handful of Skidaway churches among which The Landings sites circulate are surprisingly good.

Individual tickets are $30 to $35 for adults, with discounts for seniors and serious discounts for students. You can buy tickets at the door or on the Web site, www.savannahorchestra.org. You may have to be just a little patient when buying tickets at the door; volunteers are providing the manpower, and they're still working out organizational details. Here's an insider's tip for you: The costlier tickets are usually for the first three or four pews of seats, but based on our experience at last year's performances and the launch of the 2007–08 season, the sound is better farther back.

The Savannah Concert Association (www.savannahconcert association.com) schedule includes eight concerts for 2007–08. That season may well be over with by the time you read this, but the list of performers will give you an idea of the caliber of performance involved. The musicians included pianist Charles Wadsworth (appearing several times), pianist Hong Xu, pianist Dmitri Levkovich, violinist Chee Yun, and cellist Edward Aaron.

These concerts alternate between the Lucas Theatre and Trustees Theatre downtown, both operated by Savannah College of Art and Design (SCAD). Not only are both of these attractive venues, but they also come with an invaluable extra—professional box office service. SCAD's box office is at 216 East Broughton Street and is open during business hours during the week. Or you may call (912) 525-5050 and charge by phone. Ticket prices range from $12.50 to $35.00, with a special $2.00 rate for music teachers and students (which you must apply for in advance).

One encouraging sign we have noted: the two groups—Savannah Sinfonietta and Savannah Concert Association—are collaborating on a concert at the end of the current season featuring the Sinfonietta and the winner of the Hilton Head Island International Piano Competition. Maybe the first and hardest steps of the road back to a full-time professional orchestra have been taken.

freight station sort of behind and beyond the Savannah Visitors Center). This sounds confusing but there's a map on the Web site.

The 2007–08 season—the theater's 57th—included *The Nerd*, *Inspecting Carol*, the Agatha Christie classic *The Mousetrap*, *The Boyfriend*, and the Pulitzer Prize–winning *Crimes of the Heart*. Tickets are $20, $15 for seniors, $10 for those 12 and under, and cheaper all around if you buy season tickets. They may be purchased via the Web site.

Savannah Children's Theatre
2160 East Victory Drive
(912) 238-9015
www.savannahchildrenstheatre.org

Some performances at the Savannah Children's Theatre feature only children; others have adults in some roles. Some performances are culminating events in the classes the theater teaches; roles in others are open to aspiring young actors, child and adult, free of charge. The constant is the desire to expose children to the joys of live theater, both on stage, backstage, and in the audience. We've been impressed by what we've seen of this operation, which draws heavily on parent volunteers but which has a paid core staff. It is housed in space carved out of a long-vacant department store in a small strip mall (although experience has taught us that theater groups in Savannah are mobile, so check the Web site). Past productions have included *Beauty and the Beast* and a kids' version of *Guys and Dolls*. Actually, the list of past and planned performances is long: The theater is in almost constant production mode, and plays follow on one another's heels. Ticket prices vary, and they're $10 at the moment. You can buy them at the door, but it might be just your luck that's when the young star's entire extended family attends and the theater only seats about 150. You can also buy online. Limited concessions are available at most performances.

Savannah Theatre
220 Bull Street
(912) 233-7764
www.savannahtheatre.com

This professional troupe came to town in 2002, with a show titled *Lost in the '50s,* which was originally developed in Branson, Missouri. Since then, the bill has changed periodically, but stayed within the same framework. The group puts on an oldies-based review, changing the name and some of the program each year or so. In late November and until Christmas, it presents a holiday-themed musical. Then, it goes dark for a break of a couple of weeks and reopens with a new show. Particularly popular (and the best of its offerings) is *Broadway on Bull Street*. This show samples Broadway's greatest hits.

The Savannah Theatre is billed as the country's oldest live-performance theater (stretching it a bit, since the only remnant of the original building would be the foundations of the original building, destroyed by fire long ago).

The show became a successful local feature, attended by locals entertaining out-of-town guests, tourists, and—especially—tour groups, including the Girl Scout groups that flock to Savannah to visit the organization's founder's preserved mansion and other attractions.

The show changes, but some things remain the same. It still features a professional troupe that includes a couple of talented locals, there's still a little silly audience participation that fits in well with the atmosphere, and it's still lively and upbeat. Souvenirs and concessions are sold.

Tickets are $33 for adults, $16 for those ages 12 to 17, and $10 for those ages 5 to 11, with younger children free. Watch the Thursday entertainment section of the *Savannah Morning News* for discount coupons. Major credit cards are accepted and tickets may be purchased at the number above. Performances are at 8:00 p.m. Wednesday through Saturday and matinees are at 3:00 p.m. Saturday and Sunday.

The Puppet People
3119 Furber Avenue
Thunderbolt
(912) 355-3366

Puppets can be children's toys, but puppets can also be theater for grown-ups. Angela Beasley's Puppet People play to audiences of all ages. These are life-size creations that sing, dance, and vamp at everything from children's birthday parties to corporate bashes and retail openings. Beasley's been at it for 30 years, and her repertoire includes the characters around the Forsyth Park fountain, some very original Three Little Pigs, fish galore, and a Willie Nelson look-alike. These elaborate productions have been covered in the pages of *Southern Living* magazine and on cable network programming. The troupe does not perform on a regular schedule, but it is often featured at public events and festivals.

ART MUSEUMS AND COLLEGE GALLERIES

Savannah College of Art and Design
345 Bull Street
(912) 525-5527
www.scad.edu

This growing art college's campus is scattered throughout Savannah's Historic Downtown and Victorian District. Among its holdings are multiple on-campus galleries featuring rotating displays in a variety of media. Some feature the work of students, both graduate and undergraduate, or the college's faculty. Frequently, however, these galleries host works of internationally known artists such as Jasper Johns, Robert Rauschenberg, and Dale Chihuly.

The flagship galleries, most likely to feature professional work, are shopSCAD and the Red Gallery. These exhibits are free and open to the public. Times vary, particularly in keeping with the academic year, so call one of the listed numbers for hours and information on what is currently on exhibit. Also, check out the media outlets discussed earlier in this chapter for exhibit details. Following is a rundown of SCAD's galleries. Consider this list

fluid. As the college grows, the roles of its various galleries are subject to change—not to mention that it keeps acquiring new real estate.

shopSCAD
340 Bull Street
(912) 525-5180

This gallery, housed in an old armory building in the center of the Historic Downtown was among the first of the college's now-significant real-estate holdings. This gallery concentrates on visiting national and international exhibits and is among the easiest of the SCAD galleries for a visitor to find. If you are only doing one SCAD gallery, and the details on current exhibits don't give you a reason to pick one over another, do this one. A look at the Rococo building is worth the trip by itself.

Red Gallery
201 East Broughton Street
(912) 525-4950

This retail gallery, inside SCAD's library, features a variety of artists including SCAD alumni.

i Looking for one of the Savannah College of Art and Design's galleries? Locals, for the most part, try to be helpful when visitors ask for directions on the street, but most of us simply don't know the names SCAD gives its buildings. We don't call it Poetter Hall, it's the old Armory to us; the Jen Library is known to old locals as the old Levy Department Store and to younger locals as the Maas Brothers Department Store; Habersham Hall is the old jail. Take the online SCAD tour at www.scad.edu to learn more. And while we're on the topic of what locals don't know, don't expect us to know the individual names of the squares. We've been here for decades and except for a few prominent exceptions (Johnson Square comes to mind), we have to look the names up.

Statues stand in front of the Telfair Museum of Art. BETTY DARBY

Pinnacle Gallery
320 East Liberty Street
(912) 525-5063
This beautiful gallery space is primarily for exhibits.

Orleans Hall Gallery
201 Barnard Street
(912) 525-5063
You'll find student work for sale at this gallery, which doubles as a reception facility.

Other SCAD exhibit galleries include:

Alexander Hall Gallery
668 Indian Street

Hamilton Hall Gallery
522 Indian Street

La Galerie Bleue
3515 Montgomery Street

May Poetter Gallery
342 Bull Street

Pei Ling Chan Gallery and Garden
322–324 Martin Luther King Jr. Boulevard
(Exhibiting sculpture)

Telfair Museum of Art
Three addresses (see below)
www.telfair.org
The Telfair Museum of Art is actually three separate and distinct facilities operated by the same organization. The Telfair Academy of Arts and Sciences is a traditional art museum housed in an impressive historic mansion. The Jepson Center for the Arts, which merits a separate entry, focuses on modern art and has its own flashy modern building catty-cornered to the original Telfair. The Telfair also operates the Owens-Thomas House, a house museum covered in our Attractions chapter. We're covering both art museums here, under the heading of their parent organization.

Note that you can get better admission rates with a combination ticket for all three sites at $15 (family rate $30).

Buildings aren't all that has changed for these facilities. The new management has retooled the hours to better suit its audience—on Thursday the art museums are open after traditional business hours.

Jepson Center for the Arts
207 West York Street
(912) 790-8800
The Jepson Center for the Arts adds 64,000 square feet to Telfair's assets. In addition to large galleries for traveling exhibitions, it has space for regional and community work, outdoor sculpture terraces, classrooms, a 200-seat auditorium, a café, and a store.

In 2006 a city that made its reputation by preserving and restoring its historic architecture also offered something significant from the modern side of the architecture spectrum. The freestanding ultramodern Jepson Center for the Arts opened on the same historic square as its parent organization, the Telfair Museum of Art. The work of international modern architect Moshe Safdie has already sparked one of the blood feuds that Savannah's arts community so loves. After a long and showy fight before the city's Historic Review Board, the Telfair got the go-ahead for the construction of the new building, which features a three-story glass wall that gives outsiders a clear view of the multilevel atrium.

In a city where blending in has been the architectural watchword for decades, Safdie's design is guaranteed to make residents and visitors alike sit up and take notice. Safdie is Israeli born and educated in Canada. For several years, he was associated with Harvard University, and his design portfolio includes public and private projects from the United States to Singapore to Israel and back again.

Equally as different is the work on display within the new walls. There are 64,000 square feet of exhibition space, and it is here the Telfair concentrates its 20th- and 21st-century collections, both owned works and traveling exhibitions. That permanent collection was bolstered on opening with the gift of more than 20 works on paper by major contemporary artists honoring the late Kirk Varnedoe, a

Close-up

Savannah: Style Central for Architecture Buffs

Stroll along the streets of Savannah's Historic Downtown, and you'll be looking at a blend of buildings reflecting architectural styles prevalent in America during the late 18th and 19th centuries. Among these types were Federal, which was in vogue from 1790 to 1838; English Regency, 1811 to 1830; Greek Revival, 1820 to 1875; Gothic Revival, 1830 to 1885; Italianate, 1830 to 1900; Romanesque Revival, 1850 to 1890; and Victorian, 1860 to 1915.

Probably the city's most outstanding example of the Federal style is the Isaiah Davenport House, with its central hallway and arched fanlight doorway. This brick and brownstone house at 324 East State Street "reflects the balance and symmetry" of the Federal style, says Roulhac Toledano in *The National Trust Guide to Savannah,* and its double-entry stairway "must have set the standard for future graceful curving entry staircases leading to high stoops that dot the city in houses of all styles." The Davenport House, one of Savannah's many museum houses, was built in 1820; a successful effort to save it from demolition in the mid-1950s brought about the creation of the Historic Savannah Foundation preservation group. (Read more about the house in the walking-tour section of our Attractions chapter.)

The Regency style is best typified by the work of English architect William Jay and two of his designs, the Owens-Thomas House at 124 Abercorn Street and the Scarbrough House at 41 Martin Luther King Jr. Boulevard, open to the public. The porches and columns of these buildings are prime examples of the Regency style. A commission to build the house for cotton merchant Richard Richardson is what brought Jay to Georgia, and he "went on to create a series of buildings that qualify as the state's first architectural masterpieces," says Tom Spector in his book, *The Guide to the Architecture of Georgia.* These two houses "rank among the best works produced in America" during the early 1800s. The Owens-Thomas House, which Toledano deems "probably the finest example of English Regency architecture in America," was constructed in 1819, and the Scarbrough House was completed in the same year.

former Museum of Modern Art curator and native Savannahian. Included in that impressive gift were works by Jasper Johns, Roy Lichtenstein, Robert Rauschenberg, and Richard Avedon, among many others. On the traveling exhibit side, an Ansel Adams exhibit closed out 2007.

The Telfair Academy of Arts and Sciences
121 Barnard Street
(912) 232-1177
Savannah boasts many museums, but most are either theme museums (such as the Ralph Mark Gilbert Civil Rights Museum) or house museums—interesting homes whose main attraction is the historical significance of the building itself, backed up by the re-creation of

Greek Revival–style buildings are reminiscent of the temples of Greece with their long front porches supported by towering columns. To see two fine models of this style, take a look at the Aaron Champion House at 230 Barnard Street and the Sorrel-Weed House at 6 West Harris Street. Both houses were designed by Charles Cluskey, the Champion House in 1844 and the Sorrel-Weed House in 1841. Cluskey was Georgia's premier architect during the 1830s and 1840s.

Walk over to Madison Square for a look at what Toledano calls Savannah's "foremost Gothic-style house." The Green-Meldrim House at 1 West Macon Street, which can be toured by visitors, was designed by John S. Norris and built in 1853. Exterior features are the crenelated parapet, oriel windows, and the heavily detailed iron porch. (See our Attractions chapter for more on the Green-Meldrim House.)

The Mercer House at 429 Bull Street is another Norris design, but it is an example of the Italianate style, which has the look of an Italian villa—low-pitched roof, wide eaves, long porch, and cast-iron balconies. The house was designed before the outbreak of the Civil War but was completed in 1871 by two assistants of Norris. (For more on the Mercer House, see our Attractions and Savannah Celebrity chapters.) Another Italianate-style residence (and another of the city's house museums) is the Andrew Low House at 329 Abercorn Street (see our Attractions chapter).

The Romanesque Revival style is embodied by two Savannah landmarks, the Cotton Exchange at 100 East Bay Street and the Chatham County Courthouse at 124 Bull Street. Both were designed by William G. Preston. The Cotton Exchange, with its brick and terra-cotta facade and turned wooden posts, was constructed in 1886. Preston came to Savannah to build the courthouse three years later.

An interesting example of the gingerbread style of the Victorian period is the King-Tisdell Cottage at 514 East Huntingdon Street, which now serves as a black cultural museum. It dates from 1896.

a bygone lifestyle through period furnishing. (You can find out more details about these places in our Attractions chapter.)

The Telfair, however, is a true art museum, although the house museum description certainly applies to a portion of the Telfair mansion. Housed in the Neoclassical Regency mansion designed by English architect William Jay for the prominent Telfair family (a Georgia governor was among the family members), this is the oldest art museum in the South. Think of it as having three elements: It's part house museum, part permanent collection, part gallery for visiting exhibitions and programs.

The permanent collection includes paintings, sculpture, prints, and decorative arts. The collection includes examples of American impressionism, Ash Can Realism, and classical sculpture casts. Included are works by Childe Hassam, Gari Melchers, Robert Henri, George Bellows, and George Luks.

The museum also holds the largest existing collection of the works of Lebanese mystical poet and artist Kahlil Gibran, best known for *The Prophet*. His patroness, Mary Haskell, made her home in her later years on Gaston Street in Savannah. Because of the fragile nature of the artwork (it was done predominantly in pencil), it is only on display occasionally. On a more contemporary note, the Telfair is the new home for the *Bird Girl* sculpture featured on the cover of John Berendt's *Midnight in the Garden of Good and Evil*. Fans of the book hounded it out of its original setting in a family plot at Bonaventure.

The museum is branching out. It has taken up putting together its own traveling shows, bolstered by the success of 2001's "Frederick Carl Frieseke: Evolution of an American Impressionist." Its visiting exhibits have included Andrew Wyeth and Maxfield Parrish.

Admission to the Telfair is $10 for adults, $8 for seniors, $5 for college students, $4 for children ages 5 to 12, and free for children under 5. Chatham County residents are admitted free on Sunday, but, citing budget cuts, the museum has discontinued the practice of blanket free admission on Sunday. Hours are 10:00 a.m. to 5:00 p.m. Monday, Wednesday, Friday, and Saturday; closed Tuesday; noon to 5:00 p.m. Sunday; and 10:00 a.m. to 8:00 p.m. Thursday.

INDEPENDENT GALLERIES

Savannah has a large stock of art galleries. We listed those with collegiate connections separately. The following list consists of independent galleries. This is only a very small sample to get you started. The Sunday arts section of the *Savannah Morning News* usually offers a current listing of shows. And you'll stumble on others by accident: Lately half the coffee shops and little restaurants in town have turned their walls into impromptu galleries. For examples of this trend, check out Soho South (in our

Restaurants chapter) and the Gallery Espresso on Bull Street at Chippewa Square.

A. T. Hun
302 West St. Julian Street (City Market)
(912) 233-2060
Chuck Hamilton and Grant Nelson are partners in this gallery, which also shows other artists. It's all contemporary and includes many larger pieces. The nudes that sparked the birth of the gallery aren't shocking, just a good reflection of how conservative Savannah can be. Potters, jewelers, and photographers are represented as well, and there is an affiliation with an English gallery so there is a regular exchange of international work.

Don't look here for soft watercolors or memento landscapes of Savannah. It's young, funky, and even sells T-shirts sporting a Latin phrase that translates (roughly) as "We don't do snobby." Don't be misled, however; there's good stuff here.

Alvida Gallery
7303 Abercorn Street
(912) 355-5656
www.alvidaart.com
Who says you have to be downtown to be a serious art gallery? This one is perched on the major traffic artery in the midst of suburban commercial sprawl, but it's worth checking out. A framing operation and some gift items help pay the bills, but there's serious art on the walls. Included are the works of co-owners Anne El-Habre and Judith Metzger, but they have a rotating schedule of regulars from the region as well. We try to make it a point to attend this gallery's periodic show openings—good food, occasionally some folk music, all minus the usual gallery opening pseudo-haute attitude.

Chroma Gallery
31 Barnard Street
(912) 232-2787
www.chromaartgallery.com
This gallery, strategically located on a corner near City Market, represents many artists, but the works share some characteristics—large,

bold, colorful canvases. Although there is some regional work here, locals are well represented. We're particularly fond of the electric-bright renderings of marsh scenes. The gallery also displays art glass.

Gallery 209
209 East River Street
(912) 236-4583

This River Street gallery is the place to start your search for local artwork. Stuff here varies in quality, from some wannabe artists to the real thing. We especially like the enamel jewelry, such as a jewel tone seahorse. In addition to paintings that run the gamut from very good to not very, you'll find fiber art and interesting and affordable ceramics. This stuff will appeal more to consumers than art museums, but what's wrong with that?

LIBRARY RESOURCES

Live Oak Public Library
2002 Bull Street
(912) 652-3600
www.liveoakpl.com

The recent opening of an $8.3 million expansion and addition to the circa-1916 main branch on Bull Street has revitalized the entire library system. The building's addition is clad in marble and features park views from massive clerestory windows. The collection had drifted off into inadequacy and obsolescence until the renovation project gave it a shot in the arm—and a $3 million injection of public and private monies to stock the new shelves. (One anonymous couple chipped in $1 million.) While you may not think of libraries as places to visit while vacationing, there are resources here of interest to the traveler. Foremost among them is the local history and genealogy collection. Those in search of the dirt on their ancestors have been known to make the trip just to get into those records. Visitors can use the resources of the library without charge and can even check items out if they pay the $25 nonrefundable temporary card fee for out-of-towners. (It's $2 if you live here.)

PARKS AND RECREATION

Mother Nature gave our area a head start when it came to outdoor recreation facilities. Chatham County has more water than you can shake a shillelagh at, so opportunities for boating, sailing, and fishing abound. We're blessed with parks and parklike areas of every description and in every jurisdiction— national, state, regional, county, and city— and these provide settings for picnics and play and trails for hiking, biking, and jogging. Golfers and tennis players will find numerous venues that are open to the public.

Those who like their recreation organized can participate in a variety of team sports offered for adults and youngsters by the county, city, YMCA, and the recreation departments of the smaller municipalities; athletes age 18 and younger can keep busy playing practically year-round, and many do. Much of this organized activity takes place at facilities at Bacon Regional Park, a 500-acre complex in Southside/Midtown. This is the site of Memorial Stadium, where many of the area's high-school football games are played; Lake Mayer Community Park; and public facilities for golf (Bacon Park Golf Course), tennis (Bacon Park Tennis Complex), youth baseball and softball (Ambuc Park, William W. Scarborough Sports Complex, and Guy Minick Youth Complex), adult softball (Allen E. Paulson Softball Complex), soccer (Chatham County Soccer Complex), swimming (Chatham County Aquatic Center), and weightlifting (Paul Anderson-Howard Cohen Weightlifting Center).

On the following pages, you'll also find

i Although most city parks such as Forsyth and Daffin don't have gates that can be shut to keep people out at night, there is an ordinance stating that parks close at 9:00 p.m.

information concerning the parks and activities we've mentioned. While you're reading, keep in mind that a big part of the beauty of the area's recreational offerings is that, because of Savannah's mild climate, they're available to you just about every day of the year.

PARKS AND NATURE TRAILS
Historic Downtown

Forsyth Park
Drayton and Gaston Streets
(912) 351-3841

This downtown park on the southern boundary of the Historic District has sort of a split personality, but it's a delightful one. The northern portion consists of 11 acres filled with trees and shrubs and has an ornate fountain as its focal point. Splashing waters and shady sidewalks make this part of the park, which was laid out in 1851, a wonderful spot for strolling, relaxing on benches, and just plain goofing off.

The southern portion has a more active persona. Here you'll find a large playground, basketball and tennis courts, and wide-open spaces often used by folks engaged in softball, team Frisbee, and other athletic pursuits. The southern portion, a drill field for local military units before it was made part of the park in 1867, is also the site of monuments commemorating the Confederacy and honoring Georgians who served in the Spanish-American War.

Two dummy forts, structures built in 1909 and used for military exercises before World War I, straddle the line dividing the two areas. The fort on the western side of the park was renovated in 1963 as the Fragrant Garden for the Blind; the eastern fort will be converted into a restaurant.

The park was laid out on the site of a pine forest that was at the southern reaches of the city, a wood that made "sad and sea-like music, when stirred by the breeze," according to a historian of the late 1800s. Over time the pines were removed, died out, or were uprooted by storms. Of the park's numerous existing trees—44 per acre in the northern portion—a few are pines, but you'll see many more oaks, sycamores, and magnolias when you visit. Particularly impressive are the live oaks that line the central walkway stretching from the park's northern end at Gaston Street to its southern end at Park Avenue.

The monuments are on this wide promenade, as is the much-photographed fountain, which features a female figure surrounded by water-spouting swans and tritons (men with the lower bodies of fish). The fountain, said to be the largest in the United States when it was unveiled in 1858, is modeled after one in the Place de la Concorde of Paris. A lighted sidewalk that's much favored by walkers and joggers who live or work downtown borders Forsyth. According to the city, the distance around the park is 1.5 miles. The park is also the site of major annual events, including the Sidewalk Arts Festival and the Savannah Shakespeare Festival (see our Annual Events and Festivals chapter).

Islands

Old Savannah-Tybee Railroad Historic and Scenic Trail
U.S. Highway 80 East
(912) 652-6780
www.chathamcounty.org

When you walk, jog, or bicycle on this 6.5-mile trail, you're traversing the roadbed of a railroad that took passengers from eastern Savannah to Tybee Island for nearly 50 years starting in the late 1800s. Chatham County maintains the palm-lined, limestone trail on McQueen's Island and created it beginning in 1991 as part of the Rails Into Trails program, an effort to transform abandoned railroad rights-of-way into recreational areas. A trip along the entire length of the trail takes you past 18 fitness stations, past 30 wooden picnic tables, and across 10 wooden footbridges. Besides what it offers in the way of exercise, the trail presents visitors with vistas of marshland and the south channel of the Savannah River, opportunities for fishing and crabbing, and glimpses of wildlife indigenous to the marsh. Keep your eyes peeled for creatures such as the Eastern box turtle, the diamondback terrapin, the American alligator, the red-tailed hawk, the brown pelican, and the great blue heron, and don't be surprised if you walk up on a rattlesnake or two. We haven't seen any on our trips there, but we understand they enjoy sunning themselves on the trail.

The railroad was built over 17.7 miles of salt marsh, rivers, and tidal creeks by a group of investors led by Savannahian D. G. Purse, who in 1885 owned a good portion of Tybee Island and was trying to find a way to transport people there that was faster than the two-hour ride by steamboat. His solution was to build a railroad, and the idea was considered a harebrained scheme by local folks; they were convinced it was an engineering feat that couldn't be accomplished. But Purse persisted, and his Savannah and Tybee Railway began making regularly scheduled runs in July 1887.

A few years later, the line became part of the Central of Georgia Railway system and was operated from then on as the Savannah and Atlantic Railroad. The last passenger excursion was in July 1933; by then, the advent of the automobile and the construction of a road to Tybee (now US 80) had made the railway obsolete. But in its heyday, the little railroad carried thousands of Savannahians and out-of-towners to Tybee for days of sunning and swimming at the beach and nights of dancing at the Tybrisa Pavilion. The entrance to the trail places you at its midpoint and is on US 80 just east of the Bull River Bridge. The highway is well traveled, and there is not much space at the trail entrance, so be careful when you pull off the road to park. The trail is off-limits after darkness falls. Plans are to extend the trail all the way to Tybee Island itself, but that's in the future. (For much more on Tybee's interesting past and present, see our Tybee Island chapter.)

Skidaway Island State Park
52 Diamond Causeway
(912) 598-2300
www.gastateparks.org

Get back to nature on the Big Ferry or Sandpiper Trails at Skidaway State Park. Walking either will give you a good look at a maritime forest and the salt marsh, their plants, and possibly some of their animals, including fiddler crabs, egrets, deer, and alligators. The trails also take you to earthwork fortifications built as Confederate defenses during the Civil War and the remains of a moonshine still. Big Ferry can be hiked in either a 2- or 3-mile loop, with the latter taking about 90 minutes to walk. Sandpiper is a mile long, takes about 20 minutes, and can be traversed by people using wheelchairs (with a little help) and parents pushing baby strollers. A path connects the trails, enabling hikers to get in as much as a 5.5-mile walk.

The 533-acre park, created during the early 1970s and opened in 1975, is in the western portion of Skidaway Island and borders a stretch of the Intracoastal Waterway called the Skidaway Narrows. Other features of the park are a pool, a museum featuring the skeleton of a giant sloth, picnic sites, interpretive nature programs, and campsites (see the Camping section of this chapter). The 75-by-40-foot pool is open from Memorial Day to Labor Day, and the entry fee is $3. In addition to the picnic sites, there are five covered shelters available on a first-come, first-served basis. If you don't want to take a chance, you can reserve one at $50 a day; a group shelter accommodates 150 people and rents for $200 per day.

The park is open from 7:00 a.m. to 10:00 p.m. seven days a week. There's a $3 parking fee (more for multi-passenger vehicles) on all days except Wednesday, when admission is free. If you're planning to come here often or visit other state parks and historic sites in

i If you need information about where to find fish and how to catch 'em, drop by the Tybee Island Bait and Tackle shop and chat for a while with co-owner Ray Golden. He makes it part of his business to impart the lowdown on prime fishing spots, and he stocks a full supply of the equipment you'll need to have an enjoyable day on the water. You'll find his shop on Tybee's main drag, Butler Avenue, between 15th and Tybrisa Streets.

Georgia, you might consider purchasing an annual Georgia Park Pass for $30 ($15 for those age 62 and older). That will get you unlimited admission to all state parks.

Southside/Midtown

Daffin Park
1301 East Victory Drive
(912) 351-3841

When Savannah's Park and Tree Commission members conceived plans for Daffin Park in 1908, the recreational area was on the outskirts of the city. Now, Daffin is in the middle of Midtown, and it's a drawing card for residents of that area. The park, which is maintained by the city of Savannah's Leisure Services Bureau, covers 77 acres bounded by Victory Drive, Waters Avenue, Washington Avenue, and Bee Road.

Opportunities for enjoying the outdoors in a residential setting abound at Daffin, which has a large playground; grassy fields that accommodate softball, baseball, football, soccer, rugby, and, on occasion, cricket; basketball courts; nine tennis courts; a pool; a four-acre lake where you can fish for bass, bream, and catfish; and a pavilion on the lake that can be reserved for $75 per day for a variety of gatherings. Call (912) 351-3837 for reservations.

The eastern portion of the park is the site of Grayson Stadium, home of the city's minor-league baseball team (see our Spectator Sports chapter), and a picnic area shaded by towering pine trees. The playing fields on the southern side of the park—once the site of polo matches and a landing strip for airplanes before the city built its first airport in 1929—are also fine for flying kites, driving golf balls, and exercising Rover, when the fields are not otherwise occupied. If you're into walking or jogging, you'll find room to roam on the 8-foot-wide, 1.5-mile-long sidewalk surrounding the park. For a shorter jaunt, try the lighted sidewalk around Daffin Lake, which is a third of a mile long.

Lake Mayer Community Park
Montgomery Crossroad and Sallie Mood Drive
(912) 652-6780
www.chathamcounty.org

As the name implies, the centerpiece of this 75-acre park on the Southside is the lake, but there's more here than recreational offerings involving water. Lake Mayer is surrounded by a 1.5-mile walking and jogging track dotted with 18 fitness stations. The park grounds provide space for eight lighted tennis courts, two lighted basketball courts, an unlighted ball diamond, a conditioning course and a basketball court for people using wheelchairs, a playground, a remote-control auto race-track, and an outdoor skating rink designed to accommodate in-line hockey games. Picnic tables are sprinkled throughout the park, and two covered areas accommodate large groups: a pavilion with space for as many as 500 people and a shelter with room for 80 to 100. These can be reserved at fees of $175 and $150 respectively for five hours of usage; otherwise, they are available on a first-come, first-served basis.

Getting back to the 35-acre lake: Swimming is prohibited, but you can fish for bass, bream, catfish, and crappie if you have a freshwater license. The possibilities for boating abound; the lake is the site of the Savannah Sailing Center (see this chapter's Sailing section), which offers instruction to young people and adults, and of Red Cross classes in kayaking and canoeing. Windsurfing is per-

mitted on the lake, which is also where remote-control boat-racing enthusiasts come to compete.

Staff members at Lake Mayer present special events throughout the year, including egg hunts and kite-making and -flying contests on the weekend before Easter; fishing rodeos in April, May, and June; Senior Citizens Day in May; Family Nature Day in September; and Christmas Camp in December.

Lest we forget, numerous ducks and geese call the park home, and they are more than happy to take stale bread off (and out of) your hands. The park—created in 1972 and operated by Chatham County's Public Works and Park Services Department—is on Montgomery Crossroad near the intersection of Sallie Mood Drive. It's open from 8:00 a.m. to 11:00 p.m. in the spring and summer and 8:00 a.m. to 10:00 p.m. in fall and winter.

Southside Community Park
Science Drive
(912) 351-3841

Developed by the city of Savannah in cooperation with Armstrong Atlantic State University (see our Education and Child Care chapter), this 28-acre wooded area on Scenic Drive across from the ASSU field house features a nature walk that's two-thirds of a mile long. A playground and picnic tables round out the facility. The park opens at dawn and closes at dusk.

William E. Honey Waterfront Memorial Park
Mechanics Avenue
Thunderbolt
(912) 447-1900

The drawing card of this park in the east Chatham town of Thunderbolt is the T-shaped fishing pier, a facility that gives anglers and crabbers access to the Wilmington River and its aquatic bounty. The pier extends 82 feet from high ground out over the water, and the crossbar of the T paralleling the riverbank is 96 feet long and 16 feet wide. If you're here to picnic and not to fish, you'll find tables and a covered pavilion where you can enjoy a meal alongside the river. The park, opened on Labor Day 1997, is named for a Thunderbolt resident who donated funds for its creation. It's at the eastern end of Mechanics Avenue, which runs off US 80. The park and pier open at sunrise and close at sunset, and there's no charge for using them.

West Chatham

L. Scott Stell Community Park
195 Scott Stell Road
(912) 652-6780
www.chathamcounty.org
Helicopter pilots once prepared for war on the site of this 108-acre park southwest of Savannah. Now Chatham Countians come here to play ball on the four lighted diamonds of the Jim Golden Sports Complex, shoot hoops on the four lighted basketball courts, jog and walk on the 1-mile fitness trail, and picnic under the pines. There are also a BMX bicycle track, a tree farm, and a dog exercise area. During the early 1970s, the park site was Cu Chi Stage Field, a training area for South Vietnamese helicopter pilots stationed at nearby Hunter Army Airfield. Later in the decade, the county planted the seeds, literally, for the park by making garden plots at the site available to local residents free of charge.

You can still farm one of these 30-by-60-foot plots (there's no cost involved; you simply sign an agreement stating you will be responsible for your plot) in addition to taking advantage of the other recreational opportunities offered here since the park's completion in 1984. The fun includes fishing for bream, catfish, bass, and crappie in the pond. The park is open all year, from 8:00 a.m. to 10:00 p.m. during fall and winter and from 8:00 a.m. to 11:00 p.m. during spring and summer. Special events include garden workshops, fishing contests, Easter festivities, and a Halloween haunted house.

Savannah National Wildlife Refuge
South Carolina Highway 170
(912) 652-4415
www.savannah.fws.gov
By traveling the Laurel Hill Wildlife Drive, you can see some of the refuge's 29,174 acres of freshwater marshes and hardwood islands, which are known locally as "hammocks." This 4-mile gravel road is open to hikers, bicyclists, and motorists, and it takes you along dikes built during the late 18th and early 19th centuries by rice planters. The U.S. Fish and Wildlife Service, which manages the refuge, maintains 3,000 acres of freshwater pools created by the dikes, areas that serve as feeding grounds for wading birds and waterfowl. Unless posted as closed, all the dikes are open to foot travel, as is the Cistern Trail, a winding path that runs off the Wildlife Drive; however, if you're planning on leaving the drive to hike or bike, call ahead to ascertain the condition of the dike system.

The Wildlife Drive is open from sunrise to sunset throughout the year, except for two days during the fall, usually in October, when it's closed to the general public to allow a deer hunt by people using wheelchairs; you should check to see if this event falls at a time when you intend to visit the refuge. The drive and the dikes are great places from which to observe wildlife, in particular birds and alligators. A marvelous time for bird-watching is late December and early January, when the refuge is visited by 13 different types of ducks in concentrations of up to 30,000 birds. The best times for viewing gators are in March, April, and October, when the big reptiles crawl onto the banks of the refuge's canals to bask in the sun.

Laurel Hill Wildlife Drive and about half of the refuge are in South Carolina but right across the Savannah River from Chatham County; the entrance to the drive is only a couple of miles from the West Chatham town of Port Wentworth on South Carolina Highway 170, which is Georgia Highway 25 south of the river. The drive is not far from downtown

Savannah. To get to it from downtown, about a 15-minute trip, take U.S. Highway 17 north across the river to its intersection with South Carolina Highway 170, then turn south on South Carolina Highway 170.

You can fish from the banks of the Wildlife Drive and in the Kingfisher Pond year-round and in the remainder of the refuge's freshwater pools from March 1 to November 30, but the angling at these spots isn't anything to write home about, and you'll need a South Carolina license. You'll get better results fishing in the Savannah River along the refuge's boundaries, and a Georgia license will suffice if you stay in the main channels. The refuge manages hunts for deer, feral hogs, squirrels, waterfowl, and turkeys during the fall and winter. Permits to hunt there are required and can be obtained by mailing requests or applications to Savannah Coastal Refuge Hunts, Parkway Business Center, 1000 Business Center Drive, Suite 10, Savannah, GA 31405.

Savannah-Ogeechee Canal Museum and Nature Center
681 Fort Argyle Road
(912) 748-8068
www.savannahogeecheecanal.com
The 184-acre nature center and its several trails will give you a look at three environments: pine woods, hardwood tidal river swamp, and sand hills. Two of the trails start in the pines at the museum and follow the southern portion of the canal, which dates from 1830, faded from usage near the end of the 19th century, and has recently been cleared of brush and other growth. These trails—the Tow Path and the Heel Path—are each 0.4 mile long and lead you past Locks 5 and 6 of the canal to the Ogeechee River. The only bridge across the canal is at Lock 5 near the start of the paths, so don't expect to walk to the end of one and back on the other. However, a trail recently created as an Eagle Scout project allows you to walk from the end of the Tow Path (on the eastern side of the canal) to the 0.5-mile-long Jenkes Road Trail.

Jenkes Road, once a thoroughfare for wagon traffic, will also take you from the museum to the river. The road and the paths take you through the swamp; you can see the sand hills by walking the 1-mile Holly Trail. The nature center is open from 9:00 a.m. to 5:00 p.m. daily. Admission is $2 for adults and $1 for senior citizens and children older than age five. (For more on this site and the history of the canal, see our Attractions chapter.)

Tom Triplett Community Park
US 80 West
(912) 652-6780
www.chathamcounty.org
The first phase of this 193-acre park along US 80 just west of Dean Forest Road was opened to the public in October 1998. Visitors will find two pavilions and a 19-acre lake that's stocked with fish and circled by a paved path intended for walking, running, and bicycling. Plans call for the eventual construction of a boathouse and docks and the creation of campsites, hiking trails, picnic areas, and a playground. When it's completed, this county-owned park will be the largest in Chatham. The park is open from 8:00 a.m. until dark.

RECREATION
Recreation Programs

What follows are listings for three entities that help organize a wide variety of sports activities for youth and adults in Savannah and Chatham County. Note also that most of the smaller municipalities in the county have recreation departments, some of which are extremely active. To register to play on teams sponsored by these agencies, or to find out about their programs, call their representatives in Bloomingdale at (912) 748-0970, in Garden City at (912) 966-7788, in Pooler at (912) 748-5776, in Port Wentworth at (912) 966-7428, in Thunderbolt at (912) 447-1900, and on Tybee Island at (912) 786-9622.

Chatham County Public Works and Park Services Department
7235 Sallie Mood Drive
(912) 652-6780
www.chathamcounty.org

Operating out of offices on Sallie Mood Drive, the department's Sports Division provides league play for youngsters in a variety of sports. These include basketball (January through March for boys and girls ages 8 through 14), soccer (March through May for boys and girls ages 6 through 19), baseball (March through July for boys ages 6 through 14), fast-pitch softball (March through July for girls ages 6 through 18), and football (September through November for boys ages 5 through 12). The division also sponsors swimming and weightlifting complexes near Lake Mayer and holds a cheerleading competition for youngsters at Memorial Stadium in December and fast-pitch softball clinics in the fall. Entry fees are $75 per team for participation in basketball and $150 per team for participation in soccer, baseball, softball, and football.

City of Savannah Department of Recreation Services
7171 Skidaway Road
(912) 351-3852
www.ci.savannah.ga.us

The city provides team athletic competition for youngsters and adults throughout the year. Youth sports include basketball (January through March for kids ages 8 to 17), baseball (April through July for ages 6 to 17), football and cheerleading (September through November for kids ages 6 to 12), and soccer (September through November for girls and boys ages 6 to 19). For adults, there are leagues in softball in the fall and in spring/summer, basketball from January through March, baseball from April through July, and soccer from September through November. Entry fees for youth sports are $100 per team, with no fees charged for youth basketball. Fees for adult teams can run anywhere from $390 to $490, depending on how many games are played in the sport involved and the expenses incurred by the city in providing the program.

YMCA of Coastal Georgia
6400 Habersham Street
(912) 354-5480
www.ymcaofcoastalga.org

Besides the programs you'd expect to find at the Y (such as those involving swimming and other types of physical fitness for individuals), the YMCA of Coastal Georgia, through its five branches in Chatham County, offers youngsters opportunities to participate in youth basketball, baseball, softball, and soccer. Participants are registered and teams are formed at the branches, while leagues are set up and scheduled through each branch office. For the most part, games are played at facilities owned or leased by the Y.

Programs are open to nonmembers at fees slightly higher than those charged to members, and scholarships are available. Basic fees for individuals participating in under-six-year-old divisions in all sports are $30 for members of the Y and $45 for nonmembers. For all other age divisions, fees are $45 for members and $68 for nonmembers. To enroll your child in a program, contact the Y branch nearest you. The facilities are the Habersham Branch in Southside/Midtown at 6400 Habersham Street (912-354-6223), the Southside Branch at 11702 Mercy Boulevard (912-961-9622), the Tybee Island Branch at 204 Fifth Street (912-786-9622), and branches on the eastside islands (912-897-1192) and in West Chatham in Pooler (912-748-9622).

The last two branches are the latest, with the new West Chatham Branch opening in the spring of 2001 in a 32,000-square-foot facility that's more than two and a half times as large as its predecessor. The new branch features an outdoor pool, a day-camp facility, a Sprayground—a fully equipped playground that incorporates the use of water and two large gymnasiums. The new Islands Branch on Johnny Mercer Boulevard on Whitemarsh Island is built on 50 acres and has much more room for parking than the old Islands Y, where finding a space was often a problem. The new Islands Branch, which opened in January 2002, has new additions such as racquetball courts and a Sprayground. Both branches also are sites of a St. Joseph's/Candler Health Systems Children's Place to Be Fit, where children of elementary-school age are offered activities while their parents work out. In the summer of 2005, a new pool complex was completed at the Habersham Branch that includes a Sprayground, a kiddie pool, a 25-yard-long lap and instructional pool, and a 90-foot slide into a plunge pool. Later in the year, ground was broken on a new branch in Effingham County and on expanded youth facilities at Habersham.

All the Y branches provide health-screening services free to members via the Health Connection, which is staffed by St. Joseph's/Candler personnel.

Basketball

The county offers basketball for boys and girls ages 8 through 14 at a variety of sites between January and March. The city runs basketball programs for adults age 18 and older and for youngsters ages 8 to 17 during January, February, and March. Teams play at gyms in community centers and public schools, and the youth program puts 80 to 90 squads on the floor.

The YMCA hoops program attracts about 1,600 youngsters, making it bigger than both the county's and city's. Teams of boys and girls play in leagues starting at younger than age 6 and progressing to younger than age 18, and they do their dribbling and shooting at gyms at the Y's branches, previously listed.

Baseball/Girls' Softball

In April, the fancy of many a youngster in the Savannah area apparently turns to . . . baseball and softball. The city's youth baseball program involves about 120 teams in 6-and-under, 8-and-under, 10-and-under, 12-and-under, 14-and-under, and 17-and-under leagues. The county hosts about 65 teams in 6-and-under, 8-and-under, 10-and-under, 12-and-under, and 14-and-under competition, and the YMCA's program accounts for 75 teams in those age groups, plus an under-6 category. Some city and county teams play into July, while the Y program ends in May. City teams play at numerous locations including the Guy Minick Youth Complex and the William W. Scarborough Sports Complex, both in Bacon Park, and on diamonds in parks and at public schools. The city also conducts an adult baseball program, with games being played from April through July at fields in Daffin Park, at Savannah State University, and at Jenkins and Windsor Forest High Schools. Fees are $480 per team.

Diamonds are also best friends to many local young women: The county's softball program for girls ages 6 to 18 will field close to 65 teams between March and July, and the Y has leagues for under-10 and under-12 teams during April and May. The county schedules its baseball and girls' softball games at the Charles C. Brooks Sports Complex on the Islands, Ambuc Park in Southside/Midtown, Runaway Point Park in east Savannah, and the Jim Golden Sports Complex in West Chatham, all of which have restrooms and offer sales of snacks and beverages. Y teams play at the Y branches.

Ambuc Park
Sallie Mood Drive
(912) 351-6754
This 25-acre sports complex in Southside/Midtown has four lighted diamonds for baseball and girls' softball. Maintained by Chatham County, it's also the site of youth football games and soccer matches.

Charles C. Brooks Sports Complex
Johnny Mercer Boulevard
If you hear locals talk about this 20-acre county facility on Wilmington Island, they'll probably refer to it as "the landfill" because that's what it's built on. The complex, refurbished in 2006, has four lighted fields for baseball and softball, two multipurpose fields,

i If you're staying downtown and want to pedal around the Historic District, you can rent a bicycle from the Bicycle Link at 408 Martin Luther King Jr. Boulevard. Shop owner John Skiljon is a good source of information on where to ride, as is Mike Maynor, owner of Quality Bikes on the Southside.

a soccer field, and a football field that can be used for soccer matches. The road leading to the complex is on Johnny Mercer near that street's intersection with Quarterman Drive.

Guy Minick Youth Complex
Eisenhower Drive and Sallie Mood Drive
(912) 351-3858

This Savannah-owned facility is the site of many of the baseball games played by teams in city leagues. Four lighted fields are also used for soccer games played by teams in the younger age groups in the city's fall program.

Jim Golden Sports Complex
195 Scott Stell Road
(912) 652-6780

The 25-acre Golden complex has four lighted fields for baseball and girls' softball and an unlighted T-ball field. It's part of L. Scott Stell Community Park in West Chatham.

Bicycling

We mention in several places in this book that the Historic Downtown, with its quaint streets and squares and its laid-back attitude, is an ideal place for walking. It follows that this area is also a wonderful place to see from the seat of a bicycle. But if you opt to ride a bike rather than stroll around the downtown, be aware that you'll be competing with traffic that seems to become increasingly heavier as Savannah grows in popularity as a tourist destination. To avoid the worst of the traffic, consider taking your ride on a weekend morning before the sightseeing starts in earnest. Also, be sure to observe the same traffic laws as you would when driving your car, and give

serious thought to wearing a helmet. Georgia law requires kids younger than age 16 to use protective headgear; if you're older than the age limit, you can set a good example by wearing a helmet, and you might even save yourself a bump on the noggin. Keep in mind that adults are prohibited from riding bikes through Historic District squares.

Dedicated cyclists who delight in long rides will find that the city and county haven't done a great deal to accommodate them; however, there is a governmental committee on bikeways and greenways that's working to come up with facilities that will make bike riding more enjoyable. Until the committee devises some plans and officials implement them, however, bike riders will have to make do with the existing designated bike paths and bike trails at their disposal.

The city has two bike paths, each of which uses streets that are often heavily traveled by motorists:

The West to East Corridor runs along 52nd Street to Ward Street to LaRoche Avenue to the entrance to Savannah State University.

The North to South Corridor follows Habersham Street to Stephenson Avenue to Hodgson Memorial Drive to Edgewater Drive to Hillyer Drive to Dyches Drive to Lorwood Drive to Tibet Avenue to Largo Drive to Windsor Road to Science Drive at Armstrong State University.

The county offers a couple of trails for bicyclists:

The McCorkle Bike Trail ambles for 4 miles over 10 acres on Wilmington Island. The eastern end of this trail is at Walthour Road near Concord Road, and the western end is on Cromwell Road just past its intersection with Wilmington Island Road.

The McQueens Island Trail runs between Bull River and Fort Pulaski and is part of the Old Savannah-Tybee Railroad Historic and Scenic Trail (see entry in the Parks section of this chapter). This crushed-stone trail is best suited to mountain bikes.

Coastal Bicycle Touring Club

www.cbtc.org

This group of biking enthusiasts holds organized rides just about every weekend and special rides throughout the year. The club has about 150 members who meet monthly and receive a monthly newsletter. Annual membership fees are $20 for individuals and $25 for families. Members meet on the first Monday of the month at 6:30 p.m. at Tubby's TankHouse restaurant in Thunderbolt.

Bird-watching

Its location on the air route of migratory birds known as the Atlantic flyway makes Savannah a splendid place for watching birds. The premier spot for this activity is the Savannah National Wildlife Refuge (see entry in the Parks section of this chapter), a haven for thousands of mallards, pintails, teal, and as many as 10 other species of ducks that migrate here during the winter months. Transient songbirds and shorebirds stop by briefly during the spring and fall. The peak time for viewing ducks at the refuge occurs in late December and in January. According to Pat Metz of the U.S. Fish and Wildlife Service, you might also do some worthwhile bird-watching on the beach on the north end of Tybee Island during the spring, fall, and winter and on Skidaway Island during the spring and fall. Tybee's north beach is a good place for spotting gannets and purple sandpipers during the winter, and you might find migratory shorebirds and neotropical songbirds at Skidaway Island State Park and along the 4-mile trail on the northern end of the island running from the Georgia Marine Extension Service aquarium to Priest's Landing. Wild Birds Unlimited, the locally owned franchise of the national birding supply store, has an expert staff who are willing to answer questions—see our Shopping chapter.

Boating

Chatham County has about 86,700 acres of tidal marshlands laced by approximately 420 miles of navigable tidal waters. In other words, the area is a paradise for boaters.

Three of the most accessible scenic waterways are the Wilmington, Bull, and Skidaway Rivers, and they'll lead you to Wassaw Sound and the beaches of Wassaw, Williamson, and Beach Hammock Islands, where you can picnic, swim, sunbathe, and look for shells. The 7 miles of beach at Wassaw, a barrier island that's part of a national wildlife refuge and accessible only by water, are most inviting, particularly the "boneyard" on the northeast end where the bleached remains of toppled trees present opportunities for taking intriguing photographs. The southernmost and northernmost ends and the ocean beachfront of Williamson Island are open to boaters, but the middle of the island is a Critical Wildlife Area closed to humans; this area is reserved for birds such as the American oystercatcher. The basically pristine beaches of these islands are about a 25-minute trip from the marinas in Thunderbolt.

When you make a landing, you shouldn't have to worry about rocks, but be aware of what the tide is doing—if it's running out, you could get stranded for several hours if you're not careful. Also, be sure you're wearing shoes when you jump out of your boat into the water so oyster shells, broken glass, or the occasional stingray won't injure you.

The county maintains boat ramps at several locations that will provide you with access to local waterways. In the Islands area, there are two double ramps at Skidaway Narrows on the Diamond Causeway, and double ramps at Lazaretto Creek on US 80 East at Tybee Island and at Frank W. Spencer Park on the Islands Expressway just east of the bridge over the Wilmington River. In West Chatham, there are two double ramps at the Houlihan Bridge on Highway 25 at the Savannah River and at Kings Ferry on US 17 South at the Ogeechee River; and there is a single ramp at Salt Creek on US 17 South. All of the ramp facilities have restrooms and wooden docks. You'll find picnic areas at all the ramps (with the exception of Lazaretto Creek), and Kings Ferry has a swimming area and a playground.

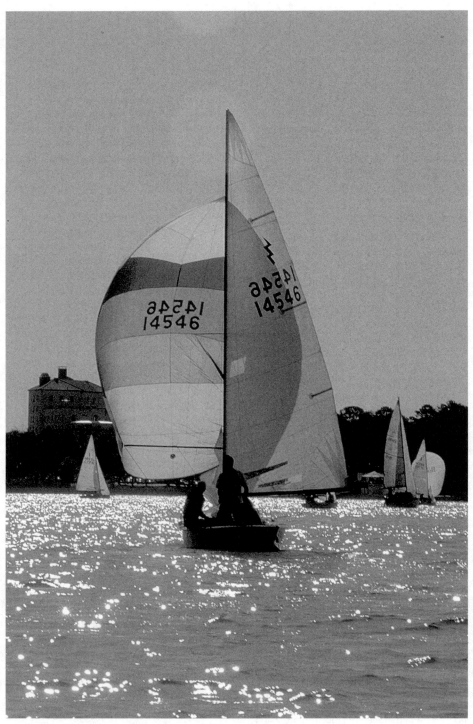

Chatham County is a boater's paradise. KYLE CASON

Downtown Via Boat

You can reach River Street and its shops, restaurants, and other attractions by boat via the Savannah River, but make sure to stay well clear of the commercial vessels using the shipping channel. These are huge ships, and they throw huge wakes. You can tie up alongside River Street at a 300-foot floating dock alongside Rousakis Riverfront Plaza.

The rate for using this city-owned facility is $1 per foot. If you plan to stay more than three hours, you must register with the city's Revenue Department, which can be contacted by calling (912) 651-6451. If you're tying up for less than a couple hours, there's no docking fee. You'll also find a dock at the Hyatt Regency hotel that's 414 feet long and available for boats 25 feet or longer. The fee for using the hotel dock overnight is $3 per foot, and electricity, water, and cable television hookups are provided, as is use of the hotel's indoor pool and fitness center.

Marinas

If you're traveling to Savannah by boat and are looking for a place to dock during your visit, or if you need somewhere to store your boat, you can choose from several marinas.

Bahia Bleu Marina
2812 River Drive
Thunderbolt
(912) 354-2283
www.bahiableumarina.com
Tie up at Bahia Bleu Marina and you're within walking distance of the restaurants and stores on the bluff at Thunderbolt. This facility, on the Wilmington River near Intracoastal Waterway mile marker 583, offers more than 3,000 feet of concrete dock and 240 enclosed racks, plus an extensive ship's store, restrooms, and showers. The marina, which reopened under new ownership in May 2002, has served local boaters since 1980.

Bull River Marina
8005 Old Tybee Road
(912) 897-7300
www.bullrivermarina.com
This marina sits on the Bull River some 4 miles from the mouth of Wassaw Sound, which borders the Atlantic Ocean. The location makes the marina about halfway between Savannah and Tybee Island. The marina provides boaters with 80 deepwater slips, a ship's store, restrooms, showers, live and frozen bait, gas, and diesel fuel. It offers private charters, boat rentals, inshore and offshore fishing charters, beach and island shuttles, and dolphin, sightseeing, and nature tours. The marina is just off US 80 at the western end of the bridge over the Bull River.

Hogan's Marina
36 Wilmington Island Road
(912) 897-FISH
www.hogansmarina.com
Situated on Turner Creek about 0.75 mile from the Wilmington River—the Intracoastal Waterway—Hogan's has more than 1,100 linear feet of dock space, a 16,000-pound boat hoist, and 272 dry-rack spaces. Name it and they've got it at this marina on Wilmington Island, which opened in the spring of 1991. You'll find a store with nautical gear and fishing tackle, gasoline, restrooms and showers, live and frozen bait, a fish-cleaning facility, and ice and beverages. Hogan's also repairs engines.

Isle of Hope Marina
50 Bluff Drive
(912) 354-8187
www.isleofhopemarina.com
On a picturesque bend of the Skidaway River sits the Isle of Hope Marina, which was established here in 1926 and installed concrete docks in 2003. The marina was the first dealer of Cris Craft boats in the nation and was the site of the dock scenes in the original production of the movie *Cape Fear,* the first in a long line of films made in the Savannah area. There are 100 wet slips and a ship's store. Gas and

Reworking the Concept of the Ideal Vacation: The Caretta Project

If your concept of the ideal vacation involves lazing on a sandy beach with accommodations that include air-conditioning and a hot tub, then you probably won't want to spend a week during the summer serving as a volunteer for the Savannah Science Museum's Caretta Research Project.

On the other hand, if you don't mind paying at least $650 for seven days and nights of no A/C, no hot water, no privacy, and lots of bugs, then working with the environmentalists who run this sea turtle monitoring program might be right up your alley.

About now you're probably wondering why anyone would want to fork out all that money to endure what sounds like the original Vacation from Hell. Well, it's simple. For your hard-earned dough, your time, and your sweat, you get the satisfaction of helping save a threatened species—the loggerhead sea turtle. Depending on when you devote a week of your life to the Caretta Project, you have the opportunity to either see loggerheads crawl up the beaches at Wassaw Island and lay their eggs, or watch hatchlings scramble down the beaches to take up residence in the Atlantic Ocean. It's a mystical experience that a 1998 volunteer from Albuquerque, New Mexico, described as "like a door opening on another world."

"People say the project changes their lives," said biologist Kris Williams, who serves as director of the undertaking. After their weeks on Wassaw, "many students have changed their majors to biology to work with sea turtles," she said.

The Caretta Project—*Caretta caretta* is the scientific name of the loggerhead—was in its 33rd year in 2005, and more than 2,520 volunteers from nearly every state and about a half-dozen foreign countries have participated since its onset. It's one of the oldest sea turtle monitoring programs anywhere and the only one in the United States whose volunteer sessions last an entire week and are thoroughly hands-on. Hands-on means that you'd better be ready to work if you volunteer. "We don't want people wanting to spend a vacation," said Williams.

Volunteers who participate in the sessions running from mid-May through early August spend their nights—we're talking from dusk to dawn—patrolling 7 miles of Wassaw's practically pristine beaches looking for turtles intent on digging a nest and laying eggs. Once a turtle is found, she is checked for an identification tag; tagged, if necessary; and measured. The turtle-monitoring team—which consists of six volunteers, a member of the Caretta Project staff, and an assistant—then either marks the nest and covers it with a screen to protect it from marauding raccoons or digs up the eggs and relocates them to a spot farther from the water's edge. Relocating the eggs is often necessary because erosion has caused a shelf to form along much of the beach at Wassaw; unable to climb up the shelf, the turtles sometimes dig their nests where the tide can wash their eggs out to sea.

"The eggs probably wouldn't hatch if we didn't move them," said Williams, noting that a major aim of the project is to maximize the survival of hatchlings. Seeing the hatchlings dash for the ocean is the lure for the volunteers who take part in sessions running from late July through mid-September. "We watch the nests and try to make sure we're there to ensure the hatchlings make it to the water," said Williams, explaining how volunteers ward off predators such as coons and ghost crabs. "We usually stay up until midnight, then get up at dawn to make sure no hatchlings are stuck."

While on Wassaw, a sea island southeast of Savannah that's accessible only by boat, volunteers sleep in a one-room, rustic cabin that's not air-conditioned; there's no hot water, and the shower is outside. Team members share housekeeping duties, including the preparation and cleanup of supper, the only organized meal of the day. "We eat well," said Williams, noting that suppers revolve around hearty dishes such as beef Stroganoff, pizza, spaghetti, and vegetable lasagna.

The registration fee covers a volunteer's food, lodging, and transportation by boat from Skidaway Island to Wassaw and back.

Volunteers should be 18 years old or older, but Williams said the program will accept those age 16 or even younger, provided they are highly motivated and independent types. "This is not a summer camp," said Williams. "This is a working vacation—it's not fun and games."

There's no maximum age limit, but participants in the program must be in good health and have reasonably good night vision and the ability to handle a moderate amount of walking. "Perhaps most important is your mental attitude," states the program's informational literature. "The project requires upbeat, adaptable folks who can cheerfully endure close quarters, insects, rainstorms, and the heat and humidity of a week in the subtropics without air-conditioning."

If you fit that bill and you're interested in participating, you can start the process of volunteering by calling (912) 447-8655 or writing to Caretta Research Project, P.O. Box 9841, Savannah, GA 31412. Project staffers start accepting applications in January, and it's a good idea to get yours in early.

"It's a very rewarding experience," Williams said of the volunteer program. "We've had people coming back for their 10th and 11th years."

Even with no A/C, no hot water, no privacy, and lots of bugs.

diesel fuel are available, as are showers, and there's an overwater pavilion available for rental. It's at Intracoastal Waterway mile marker 590.

Sail Harbor Marina & Boatyard
606 Wilmington Island Road
(912) 897-2896
www.sailharbormarina.com
As the name implies, Sail Harbor caters mainly to owners of sailboats, but this marina on Turner Creek near the Wilmington River will also accommodate powerboats. (For more on this facility, see this chapter's Sailing section.)

Savannah Bend Marina
Old Tybee Road
Thunderbolt
(912) 897-DOCK
This marina on the Wilmington River at Intracoastal Waterway mile marker 582 has transient dockage at 35 wet slips and a dry-storage building containing 262 racks for boats up to 29 feet long. The ship's store carries nautical apparel. You can relax and get a fine view of the river from one of the rocking chairs lining the porch of the store. Savannah Bend offers fuel service and has showers, laundry facilities, and restrooms. The marina is in Thunderbolt near the eastern end of the bridge over the Wilmington River.

Thunderbolt Marina
3124 River Drive
Thunderbolt
(912) 356-3875
www.thunderboltmarina.com
Yacht owners who dock at this marina, next to the boat works in Thunderbolt, get dough-

nuts delivered to them in the morning. The marina has more than 1,100 feet of dock space available for transient boaters. The marina offers a ship's store selling marine supplies, has gas and diesel fuel, will perform maintenance service, and provides a laundry and showers. Thunderbolt Marina is on the Wilmington River at Intracoastal Waterway mile marker 583.

Bowling

If you've got a yen to knock down some pins, you can go bowling at a couple of places in Savannah.

AMF Savannah Lanes
115 Tibet Avenue
(912) 925-0320
www.amf.com
Bowlers will find 50 lanes, a pro shop, a snack bar, and a full-service sports lounge at Savannah Lanes. This establishment in the Southside is the home of about 50 bowling leagues and two special promotions: Moonlight Bowling from 10:00 to 11:30 p.m. on Saturday and Extreme Bowling, which starts at midnight on Friday and Saturday and runs until 3:00 a.m. and from 9:30 p.m. to midnight on Sunday. Prizes are awarded during Moonlight Bowling; when it's time for Extreme Bowling, the regular lighting is turned off, disco lights are turned on, and a DJ plays Top 40 dance music. Daytime rates are $4.05 per game. After 6:00 p.m. all age groups bowl for $4.25 a game. Savannah Lanes is open year-round.

AMF Victory Lanes
2055 East Victory Drive
(912) 354-5710
www.amf.com
A well-received promotion at this establishment—which has 40 lanes, a pro shop, a full-service snack bar, and a lounge that opens at noon—is Friday Night Extreme Bowling, which features disco lighting effects from 11:00 p.m. to 2:00 a.m. Rates are $4.00 per game before 5:00 p.m. and $4.50 a game afterward. Victory Lanes is the home of sev-

---

i On July 1, 1998, the state of Georgia began enforcing minimum age limits for operators of boats and personal watercraft. Under these requirements, children younger than age 12 are not allowed to operate personal watercraft or boats longer than 16 feet.

eral leagues, plays host to bowlers seven days a week, and is closed only on Christmas Eve.

Camping

Skidaway Island State Park
52 Diamond Causeway
(912) 598-2300
www.gastateparks.org
The park has 88 pull-through campsites set amid the serenity of a maritime forest on Skidaway Island. Each has water, electrical hookups, cable television, hookups, and elevated tent pads; grills and tables are provided. You can build campfires in the fire rings found at each campsite, but please don't build them on the tent pads. The park is a popular spot because of its natural beauty and also because it's only about 35 minutes from the Historic Downtown (see the state park's listing in the Parks and Nature Trails section of this chapter). Many campers use the park as a "bedroom" while they visit the city, so the sites tend to fill up on major holidays and the weekend closest to St. Patrick's Day. If you're planning to stay at the park during those times, make a reservation by calling (800) 864-7275. Fees per night for campsites are $24.

Fishing

If you like to fish, you've come to the right place. Year-round, there's somewhere in Chatham County or offshore in the Atlantic Ocean where you can wet a line and catch something. Basically, we're talking about three types of fishing: inshore and offshore, which involve fish that live in saltwater, and freshwater.

The inshore area stretches from the beachfronts into the tidal rivers and creeks and includes Wassaw Sound. This is where you'll find spotted trout, red drum (also known as spot-tail bass), flounder, sheepshead, tarpon, croaker, and spots in the summer and whiting in the spring and summer. If you're visiting or new to the area and want to do some inshore fishing, hire a guide to show you some good fishing holes, which

local folks call "drops." There are countless drops in Chatham's inshore waters, and it pays to know where they are; if you don't, you might find yourself sitting in a boat doing nothing while anglers in a vessel less than 50 feet away are hauling them in.

It's also a good idea to consult the local tide charts before you go fishing inshore; Chatham County has a high tidal range, and when the tides are "springing" (i.e., rising to 8 to 10 feet), the fishing isn't good because the bottom is churned up and the water is muddy. Go fishing when the tides are in the 6- to 7-foot range and the water is clear. You can find tide charts on the weather pages of the *Savannah Morning News*.

When you fish offshore, you'll either be bottom-fishing or trolling for sport fish. Bottom-fishing will net you black sea bass, grouper, and a variety of snapper. The sportfishing is seasonal, starting in spring with bluefish, followed by cobia, king mackerel, bonito, wahoo, marlin, sailfish, amberjack, tuna, and Spanish mackerel. The sportfishing is good into November, and some veteran anglers say the optimum time to venture out is after Labor Day. Offshore angling is best in the Gulf Stream and at a particularly fishy live bottom called the Snapper Banks. The Snapper Banks are about 40 miles out, and a trip there from Wilmington Island will take about 2 hours; the Gulf Stream, the warm ocean current that flows from the Gulf of Mexico along the U.S. coast to New England, is about an hour farther.

If you're after freshwater fish in Chatham County, head for the Ogeechee River above Kings Ferry and the Savannah River above Port Wentworth. You'll encounter largemouth bass, shad, bluegill bream, redbreast bream, shellcracker bream, and crappie.

Make sure you have a Georgia fishing license, which will cover both salt- and freshwater angling; you'll be fined if you get caught without one. Licenses can be purchased just about anywhere you can buy fishing tackle, including discount department stores and online at www.georgiawildlife.dnr.state.ga.us.

i Crabbing is a favorite pastime of many Savannahians. It's a recreational pursuit that's relatively inexpensive, and you don't need a boat to do it. All you do need is a basket net, some bait (chicken parts, such as the necks, will do fine), and a tidal creek in which to crab. If you don't want to buy the basket net, you can affix your bait to a line with a lead weight attached, but you'll probably need a dip net for getting the crabs you catch out of the water. You can buy the items you'll need at bait shops or most hardware stores.

A one-day license costs $3.50. Licenses that are good throughout the year are $9.00 for residents and $24.00 for nonresidents. Seven-day licenses for nonresidents run $7.00.

Okay, now gather up your gear and bait and go fishing. To help you get started, we've listed a few charter services and marinas that cater to anglers. Also, the marinas included in our section on Boating can hook you up with charter boat captains and fishing guides.

Amick's Deep Sea Fishing
1 US 80
Tybee Island
(912) 897-6759
www.amicksdeepseafishing.com
Amick's offers mostly offshore fishing trips and can accommodate 23 passengers on its 41-foot, custom-built Morgan, the *Scat II.* Full- and half-day trips are available for private parties or individuals, and the company also has a 31-foot Morgan, the *Scamp,* for offshore fishing. Amick's is based on Tybee Island, just off US 80 at Lazaretto Creek. Open-boat trips to the Snapper Banks (approximately 10 hours) aboard the *Scat II* are $100 per person. Private weekend charters on the *Scamp* (also 10 hours) are $780 for six passengers.

Coffee Bluff Marina
14915 White Bluff Road
(912) 925-9030
Even if you didn't take advantage of the serv-

ices offered by Coffee Bluff Marina, the ride out to the end of White Bluff Road would be worth making just to get the panoramic view of the Forest River and the wide expanse of adjacent marsh. Anglers who make the trip will also find the marina's large convenience store with a supply of fishing tackle and equipment, a boat hoist, gas, oil, bait, and ice. The marina also offers boat storage in the water and in sheds, but there are no rentals. This facility is closed on Tuesday and Wednesday.

Miss Judy Charters
124 Palmetto Drive
(912) 897-4921
www.missjudycharters.com
Go fishing and have fun doing it with Miss Judy Charters. Why is it fun? Owner Judy Helmey, who started skippering boats in the mid-1960s at the age of 14, says it's because her company caters to customers by making them aware of their surroundings during trips, answering their questions, showing them rod and reel operations, and swapping a fish story or two. "They get to do everything that's fun and we take care of the hard stuff," she says. The Wilmington Island–based company— started in 1947 by Judy's father, the late Sherman I. Helmey—provides inshore and offshore fishing via the *Miss Judy Too,* a customized 33-foot Sportfisher, and from a variety of other boats. Trips leave from the company's dock on Turner Creek; the entrance to the road leading to the dock is on Wilmington Island Road about a mile south of Johnny Mercer Boulevard. Weekday rates for offshore fishing parties of up to six people are $500 for a four-hour trip, $600 for a six-hour trip, and $800 for an eight-hour trip; on weekends and Friday, rates are $500 for four hours, $700 for six hours, and $900 for eight hours.

Football

The county provides facilities and support for 8-and-younger, 10-and-younger, and 12-and-younger football teams that play games September through November at Ambuc Park, the Jim Golden complex, the Charles C.

Brooks Sports Complex (see previous listings for these venues), and Memorial Stadium. The city's youth football program is for 6-and-younger, 8-and-younger, 10-and-younger, and 12-and-younger teams. From 40 to 50 squads participate, playing games at Daffin Park (see previous listing) starting in mid-September and finishing just before Thanksgiving.

Golf

If golf is your game, you have several public and semiprivate courses in Chatham County from which to choose—one downtown, one on the islands, four in Southside/ Midtown, and three in West Chatham. We've also included write-ups on a couple of courses in nearby Bryan and Effingham Counties for those golfers who don't mind taking about a 30-minute ride to the links. The following listings will give you an idea of what's available; greens fees include cart rentals, and yardage is from men's tees.

Historic Downtown

The Club at Savannah Harbor
2 Resort Drive
(912) 201-2240
www.theclubatsavannahharbor.com
As you might expect of a course that hosts Savannah's premier golfing event—the Liberty Mutual Legends of Golf—this layout on Hutchinson Island has an impressive pedigree. This semiprivate course, which opened in 1999, was designed by golfing legends Robert Cupp and Sam Snead and is operated by Troon Golf. Set on 250 acres in the middle of the Savannah River, The Club takes golfers through a marshland environment and affords them spectacular views of Savannah's riverfront. The 6,627-yard, par-72 course features wide fairways and large, flat greens, and each hole bears an intriguing name. No. 8, for instance, is "The Briar Patch," a 132-yard par 3 with lots of marsh and a long green. Snead is celebrated at No. 10, nicknamed "Slammin' Sammy." The hole has a kidney-shaped green fronted by a large bunker; it's a par 3 that covers 363 yards.

The Club has a pro shop, chipping and putting green, and a driving range, and there's a grill that serves breakfast and lunch daily and dinner on Friday. Expect to pay $135 for a round of golf at The Club before 3:00 p.m. and $60 afterward. Walking is permitted at all times.

Islands

Wilmington Island Club
612 Wilmington Island Road
(912) 897-1615
Set amid the oaks, pines, and palms of southwestern Wilmington Island, this par-71 course rambles over 6,715 yards. Raised, undulating greens are planted in Tifton and Bermuda grass, and there's water on 10 holes, including No. 15 and No. 6, two of the course's four well-bunkered par 3s. The signature hole is 6, a 155-yard par 3 with a pond in front of the green and bunkers on the right.

Donald Ross designed the course, which opened in 1927 as part of a resort, the centerpiece of which was the eight-story General Oglethorpe Hotel on the Wilmington River. In the mid-1960s, the hotel was refurbished and renamed the Savannah Inn and Country Club, and the golf course was rebuilt and improved by Willard Byrd. The resort was later purchased by the Sheraton corporation, which gave the property a new name. The hotel closed in 1994, but the semiprivate golf club remained open under the name of the Sheraton Savannah Resort & Country Club. In May 1998, a family-run development company based in Macon bought the hotel and golf course and changed the name of the golfing facility to the Wilmington Island Club.

The developers built a $1.5 million clubhouse—a two-story, 25,000-square-foot building featuring gym and locker rooms, a card room, a lounge-grill area, a full-service kitchen, and a banquet room capable of seating 300 people. The course was upgraded with new cart paths and a new irrigation system, and a pro shop, lighted driving range, and practice green are also part of the layout.

Only club members are allowed to walk

the course. Greens fees are $56, and the course is open only to members on Saturday and Sunday mornings.

Southside/Midtown

Bacon Park Golf Course
Shorty Cooper Drive
(912) 354-2625

Bacon Park's 27-hole layout presents golfers with three 9-hole courses—Cypress, Live Oak, and Magnolia—featuring narrow, tree-lined Bermuda grass fairways and elevated greens. Cypress and Live Oak carry pars of 36, while Magnolia is a 37, and the combined length of any pair of the courses is more than 6,000 yards. Donald Ross designed the original layout, which is in the midst of suburban Savannah; it's owned by the city and operated by EDR Management Inc. The clubhouse contains a pro shop and full-service snack bar, and a driving range and practice green are available. You can walk the course on weekdays and after 1:00 p.m. on Saturday and Sunday. Playing 18 holes runs from $30 to $32, depending on the time of the week.

Cypress Course
The shortest of Bacon Park's three courses at 3,001 yards, Cypress has water on seven holes, including No. 3, the signature hole. This 185-yard par 3 has a large expanse of water on the approach to the green.

Live Oak Course
The first hole is long and narrow, a 384-yard par 4 with a green that's well bunkered. The ninth hole is the longest at Bacon Park, a 522-yard par 5 with a fairway that is crossed by a canal past midpoint; there's plenty more water along the remainder of the fairway and in front of the green. The course runs 3,163 yards.

Magnolia Course
This course starts with a long hole, a 466-yard par 5 whose green has lots of water on the right. Another interesting hole is No. 8, which is crossed near midpoint by a canal that runs down the left-hand side of the latter half of the fairway. Total length of Magnolia is 3,035 yards.

Henderson Golf Club
1 Al Henderson Drive
(912) 920-4653
www.hendersongolfclub.com

Henderson, opened in March 1995 and owned by Chatham County, offers a good mix of lengths among its 18 holes, ranging from just 127 yards on the 15th to 522 yards on the first hole. The course was built on farmland in southwest Chatham that contained 240 acres of wetlands, so there's plenty of water to look at. In most cases, however, the water is an intimidation factor rather than a sheer hazard.

In laying out the 6,273-yard, par-71 course, designer Mike Young took advantage of the wetlands and an abundant number of native trees by weaving them in with fairways and greens. Some of the holes eventually will be overlooked by homes; the area is being developed as a golf community where about 350 residences in the $150,000 to $400,000 range have been and are being built.

Rapidly gaining a reputation as Henderson's signature hole is the 18th, a par 4 that's 416 yards long. Accuracy is paramount here because there's water on the entire left-hand side of the hole and to the right of the green. The 6th hole also presents a worthy challenge; it's a long (437 yards) par 4 that plays more like a par 5 because of the usual prevailing winds from the southwest. This is the hole where the ability to hit long counts most. Henderson has a pro shop, driving range, practice green, and a grill serving hot food and sandwiches. It's the home of the Savannah Golf School, which offers a variety of lesson packages and hosts golf camps for youngsters.

Walking at Henderson is permitted anytime Monday through Thursday and after 1:00 p.m. on Friday, weekends, and holidays. Fees are $39 on weekdays and $48 on weekends and holidays. The course is off Highway 204 just east of the Interstate 95/Highway 204 interchange.

West Chatham

Crosswinds Golf Club
232 James B. Blackburn Drive
(912) 966-1909
www.crosswindsgolfclub.com
This semiprivate club boasts the area's only par-3 course, a 1,126-yard layout that's illuminated for nighttime play. The par 3 is suitable for families, people new to golf, and the occasional player, but it's challenging enough to allow veteran golfers to sharpen up their iron play. Water comes into play on five holes, and the par 3 has undulating greens similar to the club's 18-hole course.

The larger course at Crosswinds, which derives its name from its location—less than 2 miles from Savannah/Hilton Head International Airport—covers 6,032 yards and is different from most layouts in that it has four par 5s and five par 3s and is devoid of residential development. The front nine features tree-lined fairways, while the last nine holes offer a wide-open, Scottish links feel. Water is in play on 8 of the 18 holes, and No. 3, a par-4, 514-yarder, might give you fits because of a small green with lots of slope that provides the potential for putting balls in the drink.

Crosswinds, which opened for play in October 2000, has a spacious clubhouse featuring a full-service restaurant that's open for lunch seven days a week and a banquet room that seats 126 people. Also on the premises are a pro shop, an illuminated driving range, and putting and chipping greens. Walking is permitted on both courses. Greens fees for the 18-hole course are $49.50 Monday through Thursday and $59.50 Friday through Sunday. Discount packages are available. Fees for the par 3, which is open seven days a week, are $35 for cart and $41 to walk. Hours affect rates.

The club is just off Airways Avenue near that boulevard's exit (104) from I-95.

Mary Calder Golf Club
West Lathrop Avenue
(912) 238-7100
Owned by International Paper Company and located on the grounds of the company's kraft paper-manufacturing plant just east of Garden City, this par-35, nine-hole course exists mainly for the enjoyment of employees but is open to the public. Play 18 holes, and you'll cover 5,964 yards on a course that's not difficult but does present some challenges because of its tight, elevated greens.

The course, opened in 1937 on the site of Hermitage Plantation, has a pro shop, snack bar, and two putting greens. You can walk the course anytime. Fees for 18 holes are $25 on weekdays and $27 on weekends. You reach Mary Calder from downtown Savannah by driving west on Bay Street, turning north onto West Lathrop Avenue, and entering the manufacturing complex at Blue Gate 1.

Southbridge Golf Club
415 Southbridge Boulevard
(912) 651-5455
www.southbridgegc.com
Rees Jones designed this 6,450-yard, par-72 course, blending in the tall pines, graceful oaks, and wetlands of the West Chatham woodlands. Water comes into play on 11 holes on the course, opened in 1988 as part of the Southbridge residential community. The signature hole is No. 13, a par-3, 179-yarder involving a shot over water to an elevated green cut into three sections. The fourth hole is also challenging; it's a long par 5 typical of holes on the back nine. This hole was carved out of a thick forest. Water on the left side is involved in every shot on this 490-yarder, and bunkers guard the right side.

Southbridge is off Dean Forest Road at Interstate 16, making it about five minutes from downtown Savannah. An antebellum-style clubhouse adorns the semiprivate course, and the building houses a pro shop and Vickery's at Southbridge, a full-service dining room. The course rents clubs and has a driving range and putting green. Greens fees at Southbridge, which has cohosted the Georgia Open several times, are $39 on weekdays and $49 on weekends, with twilight discounts. Walking is allowed daily.

Outlying Courses

Black Creek Golf Club
Bill Futch Road
Black Creek
(912) 858-4653

Playing the 18-hole layout at Black Creek is a bit like competing on two different courses. The front nine has an open-links feel with its rolling hills and greens; the back nine, with its extensive wetlands, will remind you that you're not far from the coast (you're about 26 miles from downtown Savannah). Water comes into play on 11 holes on the 5,701-yard, par-72 course, which was designed by Jim Bivins of Atlanta and opened in September 1994. The signature hole, No. 15, was cut right out of a swamp and features an island-type green with a large pond in front of it and wetlands on the right and left. You want to make sure you use enough club on this par-3 140-yarder, because anything short of the green is in the water. All four of Black Creek's par 3s will test you, as will the green at No. 7, a par-4, 354-yard hole that presents a dogleg to the right.

The green is well bunkered and two tiered, with the right and left sides sloping away from you, so your shot to the pin has to hit in just the right spot. Semiprivate Black Creek—which is part of a golf community featuring homes priced from $210,000 to $350,000—features a Lowcountry-style clubhouse accommodating a spacious pro shop, a grill, and full-service bar. There's also a driving range and practice green. Walking is allowed late in the morning and in the afternoon. Fees are $32 on weekday mornings and $27 after 1:00 p.m.; on weekends, $39 before 1:00 p.m. and $33 in the afternoon.

To get to Black Creek, take I-16 to exit 143 and head west on U.S. Highway 280 toward the Bryan County town of Pembroke. Drive about 2 miles from the interstate to Wilma Edwards Road and turn right; the entrance to the club is less than a half mile on your right.

Lost Plantation Golf Club
1 Clubhouse Drive
Rincon
(912) 826-2092
www.lostplantationgolf.com

This semiprivate course near the Effingham County town of Rincon is a long one—7.5 miles from first tee to 18th green, so spread out that you'll never see another hole from the one you're playing. Narrow, tree-lined fairways set on rolling hills offer an abundance of hazards. There are ponds, lakes, or wetlands on 14 holes, and the Bermuda grass greens are big and protected by large bunkers. The signature hole of the 6,445-yard, par-72 course is No. 18, a 390-yard par 4 featuring a dogleg to the left and a lake that shields 70 percent of the green—on the front, left-hand side, and back.

Lost Plantation's rustic-looking clubhouse provides golfers with a well-stocked pro shop, a grill, and a card room. The course, which was built in 1988 and designed by Joe Lee, has a driving range and practice green. You can walk the course after 1:00 p.m.; fees are $32 on weekdays and $37 on weekends, with discounts for seniors and afternoon times.

Lost Plantation is 21 miles from downtown Savannah. You can get there from the city by taking Bay Street and Highway 21 to Fort Howard Road in Rincon and turning right. The road leading to the golf course is about a mile down Fort Howard Road on the right.

Ice Skating

Savannah Civic Center
Liberty and Montgomery Streets
(912) 651-6550

Believe it or not, you can enjoy this winter sport in Savannah, even at a time when it's liable to be downright warm. During December, the arena of the Civic Center is transformed into an ice rink where intrepid Southerners try their luck—and ankles—at skating. The rink fee of $6 (which is prone to change over the interval of a year that separates sessions) entitles you to the use of a pair of skates. Skating times vary, so call ahead for information on when the rink is available.

Running

You'll see lots of people running and jogging in Savannah, particularly during the more temperate months of autumn, winter, and spring. Good spots for running—places where you won't have to worry about colliding with motorists—are the sidewalks around Daffin Park and Forsyth Park and the jogging track at Lake Mayer Community Park (see listings in the beginning of this chapter). Each of these facilities covers 1.5 miles, so you can get a good workout by making a circuit or two. Some of the more experienced local runners drive out to the north end of Skidaway Island, park at the marine science center, and take to the roads there. These thoroughfares are fine for running because they are in good condition and sparsely traveled by drivers.

Savannah is the site of several major races, principally the Savannah River Bridge Run, a 5K and 10K race held in December (see our Annual Events and Festivals chapter), and the Tybee Marathon in February. If you're a competitive runner, you can probably find a race most weekends (except during the hot and humid summer months) within a two-hour radius of Savannah.

Savannah Striders
(912) 921-IRUN
www.savystrider.com

The Striders meet monthly, and many members get together for runs during the week. The club, whose membership numbers about 180, sponsors the Tybee Marathon, Half-Marathon, and 5K in February and the Women's Wellness Walk/Run 5K in September. Annual dues are $15 for individuals and $20 for families, and membership forms can be picked up at the Habersham Branch YMCA on Habersham Street. The listed telephone number is the Striders' information line, and calling it will provide you with data on club meetings and upcoming races. Members meet on the first Thursday of each month at 7:00 p.m. at The Exchange restaurant at 6710 Waters Avenue.

Sailing

Sailing is smooth in Savannah, as you might expect from the venue for the yachting events of the 1996 Summer Olympics. The best sailing is in Wassaw Sound, which is where the Olympic competition was staged. The sound has lots of deep water and few hazards, and you can bank on getting a tradewind breeze in the afternoon. Another good place for sailing is the Wilmington River, which is the site of several local regattas. The following are great places to get started.

Geechee Sailing Club
(912) 897-5597
www.geecheesailingclub.org

The club sponsors two major sailboat races, the St. Patrick's Day Regatta on the weekend after the holiday and the Oktoberfest Regatta in early October, and organizes about seven extensive cruises for members each year.

Members meet at Tubby's TankHouse restaurant in Thunderbolt on the second Monday of each month at 6:30 p.m. About 70 people actively participate in club functions. Membership fees are $125 a year.

Sail Harbor Marina & Boatyard
606 Wilmington Island Road
(912) 897-2896
www.sailharbormarina.com

Sail Harbor is on Turner Creek, right around the corner from the Wilmington River and about 7 miles from Wassaw Sound. This marina, whose office is closed Sunday and Monday, has 100 wet slips, 5 of them for transients; a ship's store offering a variety of sailing merchandise; and a laundry, showers, and restrooms.

Sail Harbor was the 1996 Olympic yachting marina, meaning it served as a shore base for officials coordinating the sailing events. The actual sailing was done from a floating marina in Wassaw Sound that was dismantled after the Olympics. Bare-boat charter fees are

$150 for the first day and $120 thereafter.

In May 2002, Sail Harbor acquired a full-service boatyard that has a 30-ton lift.

Savannah Sailing Center
Lake Mayer
Montgomery Crossroad at Sallie Mood Drive
(912) 231-9996
www.savannahsailingcenter.org
Youngsters and adults can learn to sail and sharpen their skills by participating in the programs offered by this community-based, non-profit organization. The center began operations in 1993 and trained all of the volunteers who served on the water for Olympic yachting in Savannah in 1996. Courses are taught at the boathouse at Lake Mayer. The center will accept children as young as age eight if they know how to swim. The center offers instruction on Saturday during the summer and every other Saturday during the spring and fall. Individual lessons start at $40 a session, but the pricing structure includes multi-session programs that work out to be much cheaper, including one for juniors that is $100. Scholarships are available, as are discounts for multiple sessions and multiple family members.

Soccer

Youth soccer is huge here, so big that there are spring and fall seasons. The county handles the spring program from March through May and typically has 60 teams in leagues for youngsters ages 6 to 19. The city coordinates

---

i Besides being fun and good exercise, kayaking is an excellent way to get a close look at the marshland environment. Kayaking continues to grow in popularity in coastal Georgia, and you can rent boats and paddle around the marshes by paying a visit to North Island Surf & Kayak (912-786-4000) or Sea Kayak Georgia (912-786-8732), both of which are on US 80 on Tybee Island.

---

play for a total of about 100 teams in those age groups during September, October, and November.

Most matches are played at the county's soccer fields on Sallie Mood Drive, but the city also stages matches at Guy Minick Sports Complex on Sallie Mood at Eisenhower Drive and in Daffin Park. In 1998 the city started an autumn adult soccer program, with fees set at $420 per team.

Teams participating in city and county youth leagues are members of the Coastal Georgia Soccer Association, which can be reached by calling (912) 691-2472. The YMCA of Coastal Georgia runs its own fall soccer program, fielding about 70 teams in the under-6, under-8, under-10, under-12, and under-14 age groups. Matches are played at the Y branches in the county between September and November.

Chatham County Soccer Complex
7221 Sallie Mood Drive
(912) 356-2503
Local youngsters get their kicks on eight lighted fields at this 50-acre complex on Sallie Mood Drive near Eisenhower Drive. There are three fields that are 64 by 110 yards, three that are 60 by 105 yards, and two that are 75 by 115 yards. On occasion, the larger fields are divided into smaller fields to accommodate matches being played by the youngest participants.

Adult Softball

Allen E. Paulson Softball Complex
7171 Skidaway Road
(912) 351-3852
Winter is the only time you won't find softballs flying at the city's Allen E. Paulson Complex, one of the finest facilities of its kind in the Southeast. Other times, the place is jumping with slow-pitch activity. About 90 teams compete in Savannah's open, church, and coed leagues during the spring and summer season, which ends around Labor Day. In September the fall leagues crank up, and about 60 teams hit the five lighted, 300-foot fields;

play ends around Thanksgiving. Paulson hosted two national tournaments in 1999, and there are tourneys of some description scheduled on most weekends during softball-playing months. Fees for teams playing in spring leagues are $490; teams that play in the fall leagues pay fees of $390.

Swimming

Chatham County Aquatic Center
7240 Sallie Mood Drive
(912) 652-6793
www.chathamcounty.org
Chatham County opened this state-of-the-art, $4.3 million facility in February 1998. A dome supported by air covers a 40,000-square-foot area containing an eight-lane, 50-meter pool and a six-lane, 25-yard recreational and instructional pool, both of which are accessible to the disabled. In addition to accommodating lap swimming, the large pool is used for district, regional, state, and national swim meets; there's seating for 976 spectators. The building also has men's and women's changing rooms, a pro shop, a snack vending area, and several offices.

The 50-meter pool keeps things calm with a water-motion stabilizer that minimizes swimmers' wakes, and a ventilation duct running around the inside of the center keeps the air temperature at 88 to 90 degrees and the humidity at comfortable levels. Swimmers enter the pool area through a revolving door that maintains the air pressure inside at the level needed to support the dome. The center offers a variety of programs for swimmers of all ages, those who want to develop their strokes and train for competition, and those interested in aquatic fitness. Swimming lessons are $50 for eight sessions; fees for aquatic fitness and coached swimming programs range from $40 to $85 per month. Recreational and lap swim times during the fall, winter, and spring and lap swim times during the summer run from 6:00 a.m. to 8:00 p.m. Monday through Friday, and from 11:00 a.m. to 6:00 p.m. on Saturday. Daily admission passes for Chatham County residents cost $5

for adults and $3 for children ages 10 and younger and $4 for senior citizens, college students, and active-duty military personnel, with kids age 2 and younger admitted free. Rates for noncounty residents are $1 more. The facility closed for renovation in the spring of 2007 and is scheduled to reopen in late 2007, when a restructuring of its rate schedule might be in the offing.

Tennis

About 1,500 tennis players participate in the United States Tennis Association league program here, making it the second-largest program in the state next to Atlanta's. A total of 150 of the teams in the program, more than a third of those involved, play at public courts. That number has grown from 50 teams in 1987. There are courts at city and county parks throughout the area, but the biggest public tennis complexes are at Bacon and Daffin Parks.

Bacon Park Tennis Complex
6262 Skidaway Road
(912) 351-3850
Tucked into a wooded area on Skidaway Road, this complex has 16 lighted hard courts open from 9:00 a.m. to 9:00 p.m. Monday through Thursday and from 9:00 a.m. to 5:00 p.m. on Friday, Saturday, and Sunday. A pro shop sells tennis merchandise and beverages. Fees are $3 per hour.

Daffin Park Tennis Courts
1001 East Victory Drive
(912) 351-3851
Daffin's six clay courts and three hard courts sit near the park's lake, so you can occasionally catch a breeze off the water. You can play for free on the lighted hard courts (available from 7:30 a.m. to 10:00 p.m.); there's a fee of $3 an hour for using the soft courts, which don't have lights and are open from 8:30 a.m. until 5:00 p.m. seven days a week.

Savannah Area Tennis Association
(912) 961-9862

The Savannah Area Tennis Association organizes and oversees the operation of the majority of United States Tennis Association leagues here. The board of directors of SATA meets at 6:00 p.m. on the third Monday of each month at the Exchange restaurant on Waters Avenue, and the meetings are open to the public. The association has about 1,500 active members. To join, contact the pros at public or private tennis facilities in the area. You'll pay a $40 USTA membership fee and a league fee of $11.

Weightlifting

Paul Anderson–Howard Cohen Weightlifting Center
7232 Varnedoe Drive
(912) 351-3500
www.co.chatham.ga.us

This facility is adjacent to Memorial Stadium in the Southside and is part of Chatham County's recreational setup. The 15,000-square-foot center is geared toward Olympic-style weightlifting and strength training for local sports teams, but it's open to the public from 9:00 a.m. to 8:00 p.m. Monday through Friday and from noon to 5:00 p.m. on Saturday. At the center, you can lift free weights or train on weight machines. Coaches are on hand to answer questions, and there are separate showers and saunas for men and women. The facility opened in February 1995 and is home to Team Savannah, the largest Olympic-style weightlifting team of its kind in the United States. Monthly fees are $10 for individuals and $20 for families, with daily visits pegged at $5.

Team Savannah
Paul Anderson–Howard Cohen Weightlifting Center
7232 Varnedoe Drive
(912) 351-3500

There are bigger regional weightlifting organizations in the nation, but Team Savannah is the largest one representing a specific locality. Team Savannah has 150 registered weightlifters and 12 coaches, including head coach Henry Meyers III. The team was founded by Michael Cohen, a former Olympian who started the organization in 1987 while serving as the strength coach for the Jenkins High School football team. Since then, Cohen's pupils have set numerous records and claimed a passel of championships. In 2004 two members of Team Savannah were part of the U.S. weightlifting squad that participated in the Summer Olympics in Athens, Greece, and Cohen served as the women's coach. Membership is $10 monthly and open to members of USA Weightlifting, according to weightlifting center director Meyers.

SPECTATOR SPORTS

Because there are so many opportunities to participate in recreational activities throughout the year in Savannah, most spectator sports tend to take a backseat. Even so, fan interest in minor-league baseball, professional golf, and automobile racing remains strong.

Minor-league baseball has been a part of the Savannah sports scene since the turn of the century (the 20th century, that is), with the most recent in the city's long line of diamond organizations being the Savannah Sand Gnats of the Class A South Atlantic League. The Sand Gnats are affiliated with the New York Mets, and they play their games in Grayson Stadium, the city's gem of an old-time ballpark.

Like baseball, automobile racing in Savannah has a long history, and operations in stock car racing and drag racing have been around quite a while.

In 1997 another type of racing exploded onto the scene, albeit briefly. The staging of the first Savannah Grand Prix that year marked the return of road-course auto racing to the city after an 86-year hiatus. Back in 1908, 1910, and 1911, famed drivers such as Ralph DePalma and Louis Chevrolet zoomed over the roads of Chatham County at speeds of up to 85 mph as Savannah stepped to the fore of the racing world with its Grand Prize and Vanderbilt Cup competitions. In 1997 Helio Castro Neves, Clint Mears, and other up-and-coming drivers hit 165 mph as they gunned their open-wheel racers around a newly built track on Hutchinson Island.

Unfortunately, the road-racing return has been sidetracked, at least for the time being. The Hutchinson Island circuit remains in place; only time will tell if big-time racing will ultimately get the green light in Savannah.

However, Hutchinson Island made a comeback as a spectator sports venue in April 2003 when the Liberty Mutual Legends of Golf seniors tournament made its extremely successful Savannah debut there. The tourney promises to be a fixture on the local scene.

If you're hankering for some big-league sporting action, you can find it within reasonable driving distance of Savannah. Atlanta, with its Falcons of the National Football League, Braves of Major League Baseball, Thrashers of the National Hockey League, and Hawks of the National Basketball Association, is five hours to the northwest. The NFL's Jaguars of Jacksonville, Florida, are even closer—about two and a half hours south on Interstate 95. Nearer still is Hilton Head Island, the site of a major sporting event in the spring: the Verizon Heritage PGA golf tournament (for more on this event, see our Hilton Head chapter).

If you're into intercollegiate sports, you'll find a lot to choose from close to home at the city schools, or you can hit the road for Georgia Southern University in Statesboro (about an hour away), the University of Georgia in Athens (four and a half hours), or Georgia Tech in Atlanta.

i Savannah's most heralded minor-league baseball player is pitcher Lew Brissie, who was wounded in action in World War II but led the Savannah Indians to the South Atlantic League championship in 1947. Brissie won 23 games that year while achieving an earned run average of 1.91, and he went on to appear in seven major league seasons with the Philadelphia Athletics and the Cleveland Indians.

AUTO RACING

Oglethorpe Speedway Park
Jesup Road off U.S. Highway 80
(912) 964-RACE
www.ospracing.net

This speedway gives the green flag to stock car drivers competing in the NASCAR Weekly Racing Series every Friday night from March through September. Special racing events are held on Saturday nights.

You'll see more than 115 entries competing each week on the half-mile dirt track in Weekly Series ministock, street stock, pure stock, 440, and late-model division events. The speedway also hosts other motor sports events, concerts, and festivals on weekends throughout the year.

The racing is handled by NASCAR officials, who keep things moving at a brisk pace. Oglethorpe Speedway is on Jesup Road off US 80 in West Chatham County. The 5,000-seat aluminum grandstand was built in 1995 and is wheelchair accessible. Tickets for Weekly Racing Series events are sold at the gate and are $10 for adults and teens and $8 for senior citizens and persons in the military. Children ages 6 to 12 are $3, and those younger than age 6 are admitted free. Parking is also free, there's a park for recreational vehicles, and primitive camping is available at no charge. The gates open at 5:30 p.m., and racing starts at 8:00 p.m.

BASEBALL

Savannah Sand Gnats
Grayson Stadium
1401 East Victory Drive
(912) 351-9150
www.sandgnats.com

If you believe there's nothing as American as spending an evening or Sunday afternoon at the old ballpark, a visit to Grayson Stadium to watch the Savannah Sand Gnats is for you. The city's Class A minor-league baseball team, an affiliate of the New York Mets, plays 70 regular season games at Grayson, where the brick grandstand was built in 1941. Located at

The Sand Gnats' mascot, Gnate the Gnat. COURTESY OF SAVANNAH SAND GNATS

the eastern end of Daffin Park, the stadium stands amid tall pines and oaks dripping with Spanish moss, and it's a great place to sit back, relax, and enjoy the national pastime while sipping a cold beer and devouring some peanuts—the boiled variety being the most popular in this part of the world.

Savannah began fielding a professional baseball team in 1904 and is a charter member of the South Atlantic League. Following lengthy affiliations with the Atlanta Braves and St. Louis Cardinals, the local club became part of the Los Angeles Dodgers organization in 1996, adopting the name Sand Gnats (see the Close-up on these pesky critters in our Area Overview chapter) and the unique team colors of burgundy, forest green, and tan. In November 1997, the team again changed its big-league organizational affiliation, becoming a part of the American League's Texas Rangers, and in 2003 linked up with the Montreal Expos of the National League, later the

Washington Nationals. In 2007 the affiliation became the New York Mets. The local team has in recent years developed a winning tradition: Savannah clubs captured Class A Sally League championships in 1993, 1994, and 1996. The 2007 season, however, was one of those "wait'll next year" seasons. A big part of the fun of following the Sand Gnats, regardless of their affiliation, is knowing that you might very well be watching a future big-league star.

Grayson's covered grandstand seats 5,000 people, and there's room for 2,500 in the bleachers. Most of the viewing area is screened from foul balls. If you can't resist eating while watching the old ball game, you can find plenty to munch on—in addition to the usual ballpark fare, Grayson in past years has offered Philly cheesesteaks, chicken fingers, and beef kabobs.

The Sand Gnats organization schedules numerous special events and promotions and giveaways of baseball caps, T-shirts, replica jerseys, bobbleheads, beer steins, backpacks, and baseball-card team sets. After-game fireworks are held several times each summer, and it's usually the best display available locally. Games start at 7:05 p.m. on weekdays and 2:05 p.m. on Sunday. General admission is $7 for adults and $4 for ages 4 to 14, senior citizens, and military personnel; kids younger than age 3 get in free.

Reserved seats are $8, and box seats run $10, if you can get them. There are usually a couple of free games a year, with admission sponsored by a company or organization. You can reserve tickets by calling the number listed, or you can order them online. Parking is free.

BIG-LEAGUE SPORTS

For years sports fans in Savannah have been making pilgrimages to Atlanta to watch the Braves, Falcons, and Hawks in action and enjoy the big-league surroundings. However, Savannahians no longer have to drive five hours to Georgia's capital to witness sports at

i If you attend a football game at the University of Georgia in Athens, you'll get a chance to see UGA VI (that's "UGH-uh Six"), one of the premier mascots in the nation. This white English bulldog, who lives at the home of Savannah attorney Sonny Seiler, is the offspring of the late UGA V, the mascot whom *Sports Illustrated* magazine called the best in the country. UGA V, who portrayed his sire, UGA IV, in the movie *Midnight in the Garden of Good and Evil*, appeared on the SI cover for April 28, 1997, promoting a feature story titled "America's Top 50 Jock Schools."

a top level—at least not during football season. Florida's Jacksonville Jaguars, in existence since 1996, play eight home games in a recently refurbished stadium that's half the traveling time of the Savannah-to-Atlanta junket. To order tickets to Braves, Thrashers, Falcons, and Hawks games, call Ticketmaster in Atlanta at (800) 326-4000. You can obtain Jaguars' tickets by calling (877) 452-4784.

GOLF

Liberty Mutual Legends of Golf
The Club at Savannah Harbor
1 Resort Drive
(912) 236-1333
www.libertymutuallegends.pgatour.com
Held during the third week in April, the Legends of Golf brings many of the sport's all-time greats to Savannah and the par 72 Club at Savannah Harbor course—players such as Arnold Palmer, Lee Trevino, and Chi Chi Rodriguez. Moved from north Florida to Savannah in 2003, the Legends is the second-oldest tournament on the Senior PGA tour—the event debuted in 1978—and boasted a total purse of $3 million in its first year here. Although legendary players are the main attraction of the tourney, the course is also a crowd-pleaser. Situated as it is on Hutchinson Island across the Savannah River from the

Close-up

Shoeless Joe Gets His Due in Savannah

Savannah did in 2003 what baseball has refused to do for decades—admit Shoeless Joe Jackson into a Hall of Fame.

Jackson, an all-time great outfielder who was banished from baseball following a gambling scandal involving the 1919 World Series, has been excluded from baseball's Hall of Fame in Cooperstown, New York, much to the dismay of fans who have sought his induction. His supporters point out that Jackson was never found guilty of charges of throwing the series.

But Shoeless Joe—a featured character in the films *Field of Dreams* and *Eight Men Out*—has found a place of honor in the Greater Savannah Athletic Hall of Fame (GSAHF). Although not particularly prominently displayed, his plaque and likeness adorn a wall on the second floor of the Savannah Civic Center, along with other members of the Hall's Class of 2003.

"There is only one athlete in any sport that interest is still being shown 80 years after he finished playing," states the inscription on his plaque. Also noted is that "his ties to Savannah began when he was sent here in 1909. . . . He loved Savannah and made it his home for years during and after his playing days."

Jackson, a native of South Carolina who died in 1951 at the age of 62, "owned and operated two businesses in downtown," his tribute states.

Shoeless Joe is among more than 200 athletes, coaches, mentors, administrators, executives, sportswriters, and organizations who have been inducted into the GSAHF since its founding by a group of 16 sports-minded residents in 1965.

The athletes participated in a wide array of sports—baseball, football, basketball, track, golf, swimming, diving, softball, automobile racing, weightlifting, and even lacrosse, kayaking, and racquetball. Those inducted range from media-mogul Ted Turner, famed as a yachtsman and as the owner of professional sports teams, to a quartet of the University of Georgia's bulldog mascots—UGA I, UGA II, UGA III, and UGA IV.

You can find out more about Savannah's sports history and the folks who have contributed to it the most by visiting the GSAHF, which is free and open to the public during Civic Center operating hours.

city's Historic District, The Club at Savannah Harbor offers spectacular views of the town. The 18 holes, designed by Sam Snead and Robert Cupp and bearing names such as The Briar Patch and Battery Point, also have a charm of their own derived from their marshy and woodsy environment.

The event features golfers competing in three divisions—the Demaret Division for players age 70 and older, the Raphael Division for those ages 50 to 69, and the Legends, which is the main competition and which will return to a team format in 2008. Golfers in the Demerat play on Monday and Tuesday of the event, those in the Raphael compete on Friday and Saturday, and the Legends takes place on Friday through Sunday. A pro-am fills out the week's action on Wednesday and Thursday. Tickets for all seven days of the event run $75, with senior citizens admitted for $65. Daily tickets are $25. Parking is free in lots at the nearby Savannah International Trade and Convention Center.

INTERCOLLEGIATE SPORTS

You can witness competition on various intercollegiate levels in football, baseball, men's and women's basketball, and women's volleyball and stay in town while doing so. Armstrong Atlantic State University, Savannah State University, and the Savannah College of Art and Design all compete in basketball; Savannah State plays football; and Armstrong, Savannah State, and SCAD field baseball and volleyball teams.

You'll have to do some driving to see the big-time college athletes compete. Georgia Southern University in Statesboro (a one-hour drive west) plays Division I-AA football and has won six national championships since 1985, the last in 2000. The GSU men's basketball team has been to the NCAA Division I playoffs twice since 1987, and the women's team has gone two times since 1993.

But the really big shows are in Athens at the University of Georgia, where the Bulldogs and Lady Bulldogs compete in the Southeastern Conference, and in Atlanta, where Georgia Tech's Rambling Wreck participates in Atlantic Coast Conference play.

DAY TRIPS

You obviously will find plenty to occupy your time in Savannah, but if you want to go roaming a bit, you'll discover lots to see and do in the rest of coastal Georgia. To get you started on your explorations of the territory to the south of Savannah, we've mapped out trips to Richmond Hill–Liberty County and to Jekyll Island.

The spotlighted sites in the Richmond Hill–Liberty County area are within an hour's drive of Savannah. It will take a little longer to reach Jekyll, which is about a 90-minute jaunt from Savannah. For those inclined to head north into the South Carolina Lowcountry, we've included a trip to Beaufort, a charming, history-filled town located 50 miles from downtown Savannah. Happy wandering!

RICHMOND HILL–LIBERTY COUNTY

Lovers of history and nature will enjoy a tour of Richmond Hill and Liberty County, an area of extensive marshlands, lush forests, and meandering rivers, where the past is rich in significant people and events. To adequately visit all the spots we'll be sending you to, you'll probably need more than a day. That said, you might want to split this tour into a couple of day trips or pick a few places that sound the most appealing and spend a day visiting those.

Begin your tour of the area by driving to the Bryan County municipality of Richmond Hill, a fast-growing town that's become a bedroom community of Savannah during the past 20-plus years. This one-time stomping ground of industrialist Henry Ford is 19 miles southwest of downtown Savannah and can be reached by heading west on Interstate 16 to Interstate 516. Then head south on I-516 to

the Southwest Bypass (Veterans Parkway), south on the Southwest Bypass to Highway 204, west on Highway 204 to U.S. Highway 17, and south on US 17 to the highway's intersection with Highway 144. Turn left from US 17 onto Highway 144 and head east through the heart of Richmond Hill; it's 1 mile to your first stop, the Richmond Hill Historical Society and Museum. The museum building, which once housed a kindergarten that was a project of Ford and his wife, is on the right on the corner of Highway 144 and Timber Trail Road.

Richmond Hill Historical Society and Museum
Highway 144
Richmond Hill
(912) 756-3697
www.richmondhillhistory.org
You'll learn the fascinating story of Richmond Hill's Henry Ford era (1925–1951) when you visit this museum. The billionaire Ford purchased 85,000 acres in Bryan County in the mid-1920s, in effect buying the town of Richmond Hill, which was then known as Ways Station. Ford spent his winters there, living on a plantation that accommodated a laboratory where chemists attempted to transform agricultural products into goods that could be used by the automobile industry.

Ford revitalized an area where moonshining was one of the major occupations; he put people to work on his plantation and at a sawmill that he refurbished, and he built medical clinics, houses, chapels, and the town's Community House. Ford also improved existing schools and built a trade school for boys and a grammar and high school for African-American youths. A museum staffer will tell you about Ford's accomplishments and their impact on the community while you look at photographs and artifacts from the period. You'll also learn about sites from the Ford era that you can visit, such as the Community House, which is now a funeral home, and one of the chapels, now a Catholic church.

Other sections of the museum depict the area's plantation era and offer displays of photos and some of the furniture used in the county's one-room schoolhouses and in a typical parlor of a Bryan County home in the early 1900s. One room is devoted to the re-creation of a country store whose shelves are filled with authentic tins and boxes that held products popular during the early 1900s, and if you're interested in the really distant past, be sure to check out the time line mural depicting the history of the area from prehistoric times to the present. An admission fee is not charged, but donations are accepted. The museum is open from 10:00 a.m. to 4:00 p.m. Monday through Friday.

After you've looked at the displays at the Richmond Hill Museum, hop in your vehicle and head east on Highway 144 to Fort McAllister State Historic Park. To reach the park, you'll drive 4 miles into the countryside on Highway 144 to Highway Spur 144, then turn left onto Highway Spur 144; the entrance to the park is 4 miles ahead, and the drive to it will take you past upscale Lowcountry-style and ranch-style homes, some of them with backyard boat docks on the beautiful and fast-flowing Great Ogeechee River, which can be seen on your left.

Fort McAllister State Historic Park
3894 Fort McAllister Road
Richmond Hill
(912) 727-2339
www.gastateparks.org
This 1,700-acre park between the Ogeechee River and Red Bird Creek has two alluring identities: It's a recreational area featuring amenities for campers and picnickers, and it's also the site of an earthen fort where much of the Savannah area's most significant Civil War action took place.

Prior to 1980 these two attractions

i Some of the attractions on our Richmond Hill–Liberty County day trip are in somewhat remote areas that aren't near restaurants, so you might consider packing a lunch for the day. You can dine in relative comfort at picnic areas at several stops on this tour, including Fort McAllister State Historic Park, Fort Morris State Historic Site, the Midway Museum, and the Fort Stewart Museum. Each of these picnic areas has tables and pleasant surroundings.

existed as Richmond Hill State Park and Fort McAllister Historic Site. That year, they were combined to form Fort McAllister State Historic Park, which today is operated by the Georgia Department of Natural Resources. There's a $3 parking fee to enter the park, which is open daily from 8:30 a.m. to 5:00 p.m. (campers arriving later can register at their campsites); admittance is free on Wednesday. To keep things as simple as possible, we'll discuss the recreational area and the historic site separately.

The Recreational Area
For day-trippers, the main attraction here is the tree-filled picnic ground running along a high bluff overlooking the Ogeechee River. Tall pines and hardwoods make this a shady, serene spot for walking or sitting in a glider-type swing and watching the river flow by. You'll find 50 sites with picnic tables and grills, a fishing pier that extends out over the river, and plenty of rustic-looking playground equipment for the kids in this area, which borders the main road leading to the fort. Across the road from this area is the start of a 3.5-mile nature trail complete with a primitive campsite that can be rented for $3 a night per person.

If you plan on making your visit to Richmond Hill–Liberty County last longer than a day and you like roughing it, consider staying at the park's Savage Island Campground, which has 66 campsites—54 for recreational vehicles and 12 with tent pads, and all with water and electrical hookups, grills, and tables. Two comfort stations provide campers with toilets, heated showers, and washer/dryers, and the campground also has a playground, nature trail, and dock and boat ramp on Red Bird Creek. The RV sites rent for $20 a night, and the tent pads are $18 a night, with reduced rates for senior citizens.

The Historic Site

Fort McAllister is one of the best-preserved earthwork fortifications built by the Confederacy during the Civil War. The southernmost of the defenses ringing Savannah, the fort withstood several attacks by Union warships before being overpowered by Federal forces on December 13, 1864, at the end of Gen. William T. Sherman's March to the Sea. The site was once owned by Henry Ford, who began an extensive restoration in the late 1930s, and the fort eventually fell into the hands of the state of Georgia, which restored it to its 1863–1864 appearance.

You can wander around the walls and through the interior of the fort and look inside its central bombproof, but be careful not to climb on these earthen structures, which are extremely susceptible to erosion from foot traffic. Take the self-guided tour of the fort and check out a 32-pounder smoothbore gun that fired red-hot cannonballs and the furnace where these projectiles were heated; the reconstructed service magazine, which held shells, powder, and fuses for the rebels' 32-

pounder rifled gun; and the fort's northwest angle, where the attackers placed the first U.S. flag planted on the parapets.

The fort site has a museum that's part of a visitor center that opened on September 1, 2001. The museum contains Civil War shells and weapons; implements such as those used in the construction of the fort; artifacts from the Confederate blockade runner *Nashville*, which was sunk in the Ogeechee by the Union ironclad *Montauk;* a diorama of the assault on the fort; a display depicting life at the fort as experienced by its 230 defenders; and exhibits involving the Guale Indians, who once inhabited the area, and Henry Ford's efforts to preserve the site. The fort is open from 9:00 a.m. to 5:00 p.m. Admission rates are $4.00 for adults, $3.50 for seniors, and $2.50 for youths; children younger than age 5 are admitted free.

After visiting Fort McAllister State Historic Park, head back to Richmond Hill on Highway 144 and then south to Liberty County and the Historic Liberty Trail. The first attraction on this tour of the trail is Fort Morris State Historic Site, and you can get there from Richmond Hill by turning left onto US 17 from Highway 144 and driving 2 miles to Interstate 95, heading south on I-95 for 11 miles, and leaving the interstate at exit 76. Next, turn left onto U.S. Highway 84/Highway 38 (Fort Morris Road) and stay on it for 7 miles until you come to the entrance to the site.

Fort Morris State Historic Site
2559 Fort Morris Road
Richmond Hill
(912) 884-5999
www.gastateparks.org
This peaceful little spot on a low bluff on the Medway River was the scene of one of the classic rejoinders in American history. During the Revolutionary War, the British besieged the American earthworks of Fort Morris and the nearby town of Sunbury, and the Redcoat commander demanded a surrender. The fort's commander, Col. John McIntosh, answered the demand in this defiant manner: "We, sir,

i Fort McAllister State Historic Park and Fort Morris State Historic Site are among the 18 bird-watching venues on the Colonial Coast Birding Trail, which stretches along Georgia's coast from Tybee Island in the north to Cumberland Island National Seashore and the Okefenokee National Wildlife Refuge in the south. You can see songbirds, wading birds, and waterfowl at Fort McAllister and Fort Morris, depending on what time of year you visit.

are fighting the battles of America, and therefore disdain to remain neutral till its fate is determined. As to surrendering the fort, receive this laconic reply, 'Come and take it!'" Lacking some expected support from another British force and the exact knowledge of the strength of the troops at Fort Morris, the Redcoats did not follow McIntosh's suggestion; instead, they retreated. Fort Morris, however, eventually fell to the British and was dismantled.

A smaller earthen fort, called Defiance in honor of McIntosh's reply, was built during the War of 1812 from the remains of Fort Morris, and you can explore it by visiting this site. Strolling around the walls of the fort under the majestic oaks towering over it, you have a wonderful view of the Medway and its marshes, and you might even get a glimpse of a shrimp boat trawling in the river. The interpretive center/museum at the site tells the saga of the fort and of Sunbury, the town it was built to protect, and there's also a 1-mile nature trail through marsh and scrub oak forest.

The Georgia Department of Natural Resources, which maintains the 70-acre site, offers several special events during the year, including the Independence Day Colonial Faire in July and the "Come and Take It!" reenactment in November. Admission to the site is $2.50 for adults, $2.00 for seniors, and $1.50 for youths ages 6 to 18; entry for children younger than age 6 is free. Fort Morris is open from 9:00 a.m. to 5:00 p.m. Tuesday through Saturday and from 2:00 to 5:30 p.m. on Sunday. It's closed on Monday, with the exception of federal holidays.

While you're at the interpretive center at Fort Morris State Historic Site, be sure to view the award-winning, 12-minute video, "Sunbury Sleeps: The Forgotten Town of Sunbury, Ga." This hauntingly beautiful tribute to one of Georgia's "lost towns" serves as the perfect introduction to the next stop on our day trip, the Sunbury Cemetery. The cemetery is a little more than a mile from the entrance to Fort Morris. After leaving the fort, turn right onto Fort Morris Road and keep to your left until you reach Sunbury Road. Turn left onto this dirt road and drive to Dutchmans Cove Road, then take a right and follow this unpaved lane a short distance to the cemetery.

Sunbury Cemetery
Dutchmans Cove Road
Richmond Hill

This small cemetery is all that remains of the once bustling town of Sunbury, which in 1764 had 80 dwellings, 3 stores, several wharves, and a trio of town squares. By 1773, Sunbury was a seaport beginning to rival Savannah as a place of commerce. That year the town saw 56 vessels clear port as compared with Savannah's 160. Sunbury also had another claim to fame: All three of Georgia's signers of the Declaration of Independence had a connection to the town—Lyman Hall lived there, Button Gwinnett resided on nearby St. Catherines Island, and George Walton was confined there when Sunbury was made a military prison after its capture by the British during the Revolutionary War.

By the end of the war, most of Sunbury had been destroyed, and the town never recovered. There were fewer than eight families living there by 1855, and all evidence of the town eventually disappeared—everything but the cemetery and the 34 grave markers that remain standing. When we visited Fort Morris, we knew when we left that there wouldn't be a great deal to see at the cemetery. But after viewing the Department of Natural Resources video about Sunbury, we felt compelled to take a look and pay our respects, so to speak. Maybe you will, too.

Now it's time to get back on the Historic Liberty Trail and head to the town of Midway. We recommend, though, that while you're on the way, you visit Seabrook Village, which you can find by turning right off Fort Morris Road onto Trade Hill Road.

Seabrook Village
660 Trade Hill Road
Richmond Hill
(912) 884-7008
www.seabrookvillage.org

This 104-acre site portrays the history and culture of African Americans living in coastal Georgia during 1865 to 1930. Using authentic buildings and displays of artifacts, Seabrook brings that period to life. Among stops on guided and self-guided tours of the village are Bowen's Farm, with its rice fields and a barn containing tools used in farming, gathering oysters, and making turpentine; the Ripley Corn Crib, where corn is ground into grits and meal; the Seabrook School, with its original wooden blackboard and desks made by former student John Stevens; the Gibbons-Woodward House, in which you can see a rural kitchen, a feather bed, and a replica of the original clay chimney; a mill and boiler house where stalks of sugarcane are ground by horsepower and cooked into syrup; the Delegal-Williams House, with its family photographs and local furnishings; and a train depot that was moved to the site from nearby Riceboro.

While you're visiting Seabrook, be sure to see the unusual artwork of Cyrus Bowen, with which he adorned local gravesites. Seabrook is open from 10:00 a.m. to 4:00 p.m. Tuesday through Saturday. Group tours lasting three hours and conducted by costumed guides are available, as are one-hour guided tours in the afternoon. Fees for group tours are $8 for adults, $7 for youths ages 10 to 18 years old, and $6 for children ages 5 to 10; fees for the one-hour tours are $5.

i If you're in the Richmond Hill area during mid-March to mid-April and you're interested in fish, consider paying a visit to the Richmond Hill Hatchery, a facility of Georgia's Wildlife Resources Division. This time period is when operations involving the spawning of striped bass are at their peak at the hatchery, and you can arrange a tour by calling (912) 756-3691. The hatchery, located about a mile west of the Richmond Hill business district on Highway 144, is open from 8:00 a.m. until 4:30 p.m. Monday through Friday.

The next stop on our tour is Midway, which was established in 1754 by a group of Congregationalists from Dorchester, South Carolina. Their Midway Society produced governors, cabinet members, U.S. senators and congressmen, numerous ministers, and foreign missionaries. The parish they settled, St. John's, was a hotbed of patriotic fervor during the years leading up to the American Revolution, and two of its residents, Lyman Hall and Button Gwinnett, were among Georgia's three signers of the Declaration of Independence. To get to Midway, head west on US 84 back to I-95 and stay on US 84 until you reach US 17. Turn right onto US 17. Clustered just up the road are the Midway Museum, Midway Congregational Church, and the Midway Cemetery.

Midway Museum
US 17
Richmond Hill
(912) 884-5837

This museum gives visitors an idea of what life was like for landowners in coastal Georgia during the late 18th century and early 19th century. The museum building is an elegant, raised cottage-style house erected in 1957 and based on a sketch made in 1828 of a home in nearby Riceboro. The rooms of the house are filled with original 18th-century furnishings; among the unique items are a walking cane-gun that fired a .45 caliber slug and a set of musical glasses that are played by rubbing vinegar around the rims. A museum staff member will tell you about many of the items in the three first-floor rooms of the house and will play a tune on the glasses; you're free to look at the upper-floor bedrooms and displays in the ground-floor rooms on your own.

This attraction, which is operated by the Midway Museum Board of Governors, is open from 10:00 a.m. to 4:00 p.m. Tuesday through Saturday and from 2:00 to 4:00 p.m. on Sunday; it's closed on Monday. Admission, which includes access to nearby Midway Congregational Church, is $5 for adults, $4 for seniors, and $2 for youngsters ages 6 through 17; children younger than age 6 are admitted free.

Midway Congregational Church
US 17
Richmond Hill

Built in 1792, this stately church reflects a style reminiscent of Colonial New England (some of the founders of Midway were descendants of Puritans from Massachusetts who had settled in South Carolina). The existing building replaced a church that was burned by the British in 1778. The church is a short walk from the Midway Museum, and you can obtain a key from a museum staff member and take a look inside. The church has no heating system or artificial lights, but services are conducted there each April by the Midway Society.

Midway Cemetery
US 17
Richmond Hill

Researchers believe Midway Cemetery was laid out in the late 1750s and that it contains about 1,200 graves. Among those buried there are James Screven, a brigadier general in the American army who was killed in November 1778 in a skirmish with the British about a mile south of his resting place, and Daniel Stewart, who attained the rank of brigadier after fighting in the Revolutionary and Indian Wars and was the great-grandfather of President Theodore Roosevelt; Fort Stewart, the U.S. Army's military reservation at nearby Hinesville, is named after him. The cemetery is open to the public, and a brochure featuring a map and self-guided tour of the site is available at the Midway Museum for 25 cents.

Midway Cemetery is also the burial site of Louis LeConte, who owned a rice plantation south of Midway where he created a botanical garden of great renown. You can reach the plantation by driving south on US 17 for 3 miles to the Barrington Ferry Road. Turn right onto Barrington Ferry and follow it for 5.5 miles to the entrance to the plantation site.

LeConte-Woodmanston Rice Plantation and Botanical Gardens
Barrington Ferry Road
Midway
(912) 884-6500
www.libertytrail.com

In its heyday during the early 1800s, Woodmanston Plantation covered more than 3,300 acres and was the largest inland rice plantation in Georgia. Louis LeConte came into possession of Woodmanston in 1810, and the garden he planted there gained fame throughout the United States and Europe.

The plantation was abandoned in 1869, but a restoration of a 63.8-acre site was begun in the late 1970s as a project of The Garden Club of Georgia. The project, being carried on now by the LeConte-Woodmanston Foundation, is a work in progress that so far has resulted in the creation of a 1.5-acre botanical garden featuring plants that LeConte might have grown and a 1-mile nature trail along a network of rice dams. The garden contains more than 100 different plants, including beds of older varieties of camellias and roses. Several structures that were part of the plantation—a chicken coop, a garden shed, a smokehouse, and a slave cabin—have been re-created on the site. Visitors can also stroll along a path through a three-acre bog containing flowering plants native to the area and observe rice being grown on two acres of wetlands.

The plantation is open to the public from 10:00 a.m. to 3:00 p.m. Tuesday, Wednesday, and Friday, and at other times by prior arrangement, and admission is $2 per person. Because LeConte-Woodmanston is in a somewhat remote spot, you might want to call ahead to the listed number before you visit, and you definitely should call to make arrangements for group tours. Also, be aware that the last 1.6 miles of the drive to the plantation is on dirt roads.

The last attraction on this tour is the Fort Stewart Museum, a military museum just inside the main entrance to Fort Stewart, the huge U.S. Army post at Hinesville. From

LeConte-Woodmanston, drive back to the intersection of US 17 and US 84 and head west on US 84 about 7 miles to Hinesville. Turn right onto General Stewart Way, which will take you to the entrance to Fort Stewart. The museum is on the post at the corner of Wilson Boulevard and Frank Cochran Drive.

Fort Stewart Museum
2022 Frank Cochran Drive
Hinesville
(912) 767-7885
www.stewart.army.mil

Displays at the museum focus on the history of Fort Stewart and its current occupant, the Third Infantry Division (Mechanized). Fort Stewart, now the largest army installation east of the Mississippi River, was established in the summer of 1940 as Camp Stewart and served as an antiaircraft artillery training center during World War II and the Korean War. During the early 1960s, the post was the site of a variety of tests and training by military units, and in the latter half of the decade it served as a training area for Army helicopter pilots.

In the mid-1970s, the Twenty-fourth Infantry Division (Mechanized) was activated at Fort Stewart, and the unit was based there until April 1996, when the post became the home of the Third Infantry. The story of the Third's service in the two world wars and Korea is related at the museum, portions of which are also devoted to the Twenty-fourth Infantry and the military history of coastal Georgia. Uniforms, weapons, and other items used by the Third Infantry and their opponents are on display in the museum, as is a T-72M-1 tank abandoned by Iraqi Republican Guard crewmen in an engagement with the Twenty-fourth Infantry during the earlier war in the Persian Gulf. There are also exhibits featuring Operation Iraqi Freedom and Audie Murphy, a Third Infantry hero in World War II whose exploits won him the title of "America's Most Decorated Soldier." Outside the museum, you'll find static displays of equipment used in warfare, including an M4A3

Sherman tank, a UH-1 Huey helicopter gunship, and numerous Iraqi artillery pieces and vehicles captured by U.S. forces during the Gulf War. Entry to Fort Stewart is open to civilians, and admission to the museum is free. Hours of operation are from 10:00 a.m. to 4:00 p.m. Tuesday through Saturday. Museum-goers should enter the post via the visitors' center at Gate 1 on General Screven Way.

JEKYLL ISLAND

Georgia's coastline is a fascinating and varied one. Savannah, which snugs up to South Carolina, marks its northernmost point. At the southern extremity, up against the Florida line, you'll find St. Mary's, with its access to Cumberland Island National Seashore. And in between you'll find the Golden Isles.

Four islands make up this cluster, accessible from Brunswick, a port and industrial city that retains a small historic district. It is the jumping-off point for the Golden Isles, reachable by causeway with one exception. St. Simons Island is the biggest and most developed of the Isles, with beaches, motels, restaurants, and historic sites. Little St. Simons is accessible only by boat and is open to a limited number of guests (by arrangement). Consisting of largely undeveloped beaches and marshlands, this island is a real treat for environment-minded tourists. Sea Island, largely residential and from a geographical point of view virtually part of St. Simons, is home to the extremely tony resort known as The Cloisters.

Jekyll Island is the southernmost of the four Golden Isles. We think it is likely to appeal to the same type of traveler who is attracted to Savannah. You'll find places to eat and sleep there, but development has not run wild. In fact, the state of Georgia owns the place, and the business and residential ventures there are really long-term leases. However, that policy is changing—in 2007 the state opened part of the island to high-dollar development. Enjoy the beaches (which are

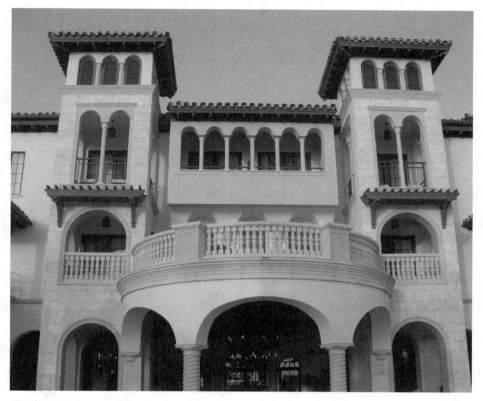

The Cloisters, a luxury resort on Sea Island. BETTY DARBY

all public, at least at the moment) and consider a trip along the extensive network of bike paths a must-do (bike rental places abound; check the lobby of larger motels). Jekyll, like the rest of the Golden Isles, is also covered with golf courses, most of which are accessible to the public at large.

The Jekyll Island Welcome Center, P.O. Box 13186, Jekyll Island, GA 31527 (912-635-3636, 877-453-5955), and the Brunswick & The Golden Isles Visitors Bureau, 4 Glynn Avenue, Brunswick (912-265-0366, 800-809-1790), are two general sources that can provide additional information, including lodging details and how to get onto the golf courses. Expect to pay a $3 "parking fee" as you drive onto Jekyll. There's also a Web site: www.jekyll island.com.

To get there, head south on I-95. It takes about 90 minutes. While it's not that long a trip (we know people who commute there from Savannah for work daily, in fact), it can be harrowing. This is the corridor that runs between the Northeast population centers and Florida, and it is always heavily traveled by time-conscious vacationers. Exits are clearly marked.

Jekyll and St. Simons Islands are not accessible from one another—you have to make the trip back to the mainland on the causeway and then take the other causeway to the next island. It's a pleasant drive through the marshes, watching herons and marsh rabbits, but it does take a little time.

St. Simons is a more developed beach community than Jekyll Island, but it has still retained its charm and individual character. There's a large year-round population, and they clearly cherish the winter months when the tourists aren't as prevalent. That doesn't mean visitors aren't welcome; it does mean a quieter pace of life in the winter. There's even a "downtown," a short strip of shops leading to the water and including the usual tourist stuff, an interesting toy store, a bookshop, etc. St. Simons has large, legible signs posted at key intersections, and the names of specific destinations are clearly listed. We get lost a lot elsewhere, but we get around just fine on St. Simons. The King and Prince Hotel is a good lodging choice (the selection is rather limited). It's by no means as tony as the Cloisters, the region's upscale resort, but they've got the amenities you'd expect in a beachside resort. The island offers multiple restaurant options, predictably leaning toward seafood. Since we've mentioned the Cloisters, we should expound a bit. This exclusive resort was built just before the bottom fell out of Wall Street and launched the Great Depression. It has long been a traditional destination of the if-you-have-to-ask-you-can't-afford-it crowd. Not that there aren't bargains to be had: Honeymooners are extended the right to rent rooms on their anniversary at the rate that prevailed at the time of the wedding—so if you meet someone celebrating their 50th, they're in high cotton. The owners tore the whole thing down a couple years ago and rebuilt it, using salvaged materials when possible. The result is a new-that-looks-old resort with stunningly landscaped grounds.

Jekyll Island Historic District Museum Visitors Center
Stable Road
Jekyll Island
(912) 635-4036
Georgia was originally founded as a refuge for debtors, but the richest and most powerful men in America originally developed Jekyll Island. They bought the island in 1886 and made it into a private resort where you need not apply unless your annual income included at least seven figures, all to the left of the decimal point at a time when that was really a fortune. Names that are synonymous with American fortunes were among the Jekyll Island Club's members: Rockefeller, Gould, Morgan. And they didn't stay in rented quarters, although the club was (and now is again) a fine hotel. Instead, they built "cottages"— mansions that took advantage of beautiful views, cooling breezes, and balmy weather. This was, indeed, the playground of the rich and famous.

Types of tours vary by season. The version that does not involve entry into any of the buildings costs $10 for adults and $5 for children and runs throughout the day. A more elaborate version that allows entry into two of the cottages that have been restored with period furniture runs at 11:00 a.m. and 2:00 p.m. daily (more often in some months). Cost is $15 for individuals. The stops usually include the mansion known as Indian Mounds, where once the Rockefellers roamed. There's bad news for independent-minded travelers: Only the guided tours get inside the choice restored buildings outfitted with period furniture. Several restored buildings, however, are in use as shops or galleries and, of course, are open to the public at no charge.

BEAUFORT, SOUTH CAROLINA

Beaufort is situated between Savannah and Charleston, South Carolina, and it exudes much of the charm of those two cities, but on a smaller scale. This town of about 9,500 residents has a historic district filled with elegant homes built in the 1700s and 1800s and a quaint but bustling waterfront shopping district that's brimming with intriguing stores and unique eating places.

The Beaufort area is rich in history. The Spaniards unsuccessfully attempted to found the colony of Santa Elena here in 1559, and French Protestants, led by explorer Jean Ribaut in 1562, tried to start a settlement called Charlesfort on what is now Parris Island. It failed, and the Spanish returned to the area in

1566, building a fort, San Phillipe, and the Mission of Santa Elena at Port Royal. According to the Historic Beaufort Foundation, this settlement was, by 1580, one of the largest Spanish towns north of Mexico. It was abandoned in 1586 following attacks on Spanish Florida by the English privateer, Sir Francis Drake.

The English laid claim to the area in the 1600s and by the turn of the next century had established a foothold at Port Royal. Beaufort was founded in 1711, and in the years leading up to the American Revolution, local planters turned profits by growing rice and indigo. During the Revolutionary War, residents of the area were sharply divided over the issue of independence from Britain and allegiance to the crown. British forces occupied Beaufort in July 1779 but evacuated later in the year. Cotton planting was introduced to the area after the Revolution. Subsequent crops made rich men and women of many of Beaufort's citizens in the years leading up to the Civil War. Early in the conflict, in November 1861, South Carolina's Sea Islands were invaded by Union forces, and Beaufort and the Port Royal area fell into Federal hands. Beaufort became the main base of Union squadrons blockading the South Atlantic. During the Union occupation, the first school for black freedmen, which eventually became Penn School, was established east of Beaufort on St. Helena Island.

Beaufort is about 55 minutes from downtown Savannah by car. To get there, take Oglethorpe Avenue west and drive across the Eugene Talmadge Memorial Bridge on US 17 into South Carolina. It's 5 miles from the bridge to the intersection of US 17 and Alternate South Carolina Highway 170; turn right onto Alternate South Carolina Highway 170 and stay on it for 6 miles, where it becomes South Carolina Highway 170 (also South Carolina Highway 46). Continue 3 miles to where South Carolina Highway 170 leaves South Carolina Highway 46. Turn left onto South Carolina Highway 170 and enjoy the scenery—a narrow, two-lane road shrouded by the moss-covered branches of gnarled oaks. Take a good look, because this area might not be heavily forested for much longer; civilization and the developers of subdivisions and shopping centers appear to be taking over.

You'll be on South Carolina Highway 170 for about 20 miles, which will take you into the outskirts of Beaufort. While on South Carolina Highway 170, you'll pass country roads with fascinating-sounding names such as Bulltomb, Bufflehead, Heffalump, Old Bailey's, Crippled Oak, Bellinger Bluff, and Mudbar, and you'll catch glimpses of marshland and open water. You'll cross the picturesque Chechessee River, drive through relatively pristine Lemon Island, and then find yourself marveling at the majestic expanse of the aptly named Broad River, which is spanned by a bridge that's 1.4 miles long.

South Carolina Highway 170 will lead you to U.S. Highway 21 South (also known in these parts as Boundary Street); turn right onto US 21 and stay on it for a mile until you reach the traffic light at Ribaut Road. Turn right onto Ribaut Road and drive to the third stoplight, then turn left onto Bay Street, which will take you about a mile past stately homes and a bay dotted with sailboats and into Beaufort's waterfront district.

The focal points of this area are Bay Street, which is lined on either side with shops

i While visiting Beaufort, consider taking a side trip to nearby Penn Center, a 50-acre National Historic Landmark District on St. Helena Island. Penn Center is the site of Penn School, one of the most significant African-American institutions in the United States and an active community center. The mission of the center is to preserve the history, culture, and environment of the Sea Islands. You can get there by taking US 21 east from Beaufort to St. Helena Island and turning right onto Martin Luther King Jr. Drive.

and restaurants, and Henry C. Chambers Waterfront Park, a pleasant, tree-filled swath of greenery lying south of Bay Street between the street and the bay formed by the Beaufort River. The park, with its wide walkways, swinging benches, and elaborate children's playground, is a wonderful place for strolling or sitting and catching a breeze off the nearby water. Several of the restaurants that dot the south side of Bay Street open onto patios and porches that offer outdoor dining on the fringes of the park. Among these eating places are Saltus River Grill at 802 Bay Street, which specializes in seafood; Plum's Cafe at 904½ Bay Street, which is known for its gourmet soups, salads, sandwiches, and homemade ice cream; and Panini's Cafe at 926 Bay Street, which features pasta, pizza, hoagies, and, of course, panini-style sandwiches.

The stores along Bay Street and on the narrow lanes running to the north off Bay provide a plethora of shopping opportunities. There are several galleries; a unique one is the Rhett Gallery at 901 Bay Street. In addition to selling prints and paintings, this gallery offers antique maps and nautical charts and Civil War art and artifacts, including pages from *Harper's Weekly* and *Frank Leslie's Illustrated Newspaper*—bits of history that make interesting artwork when matted and framed. Specialty shops you might want to visit include The Craftseller, at 818 Bay Street, which deals in local and regional arts and crafts; The Cat's Meow Shoppe, a gift shop on Bay Street that caters to collectors of all things feline; and Bellavista Antiques and Interiors at 206 Carteret Street. If you're looking for books, stop in at The Book Shop at 808 Bay Street, McIntosh Book Shoppe in the recently refurbished Old Bay Market Place at 917 Bay Street, or Firehouse Books & Expresso Bar at 706 Craven Street. Each has a good inventory that features books related to the region, and McIntosh has a large selection of rare, out-of-print editions.

Those in search of history will find it throughout town in general and in two locations in particular:

Beaufort Museum
713 Craven Street
Beaufort, SC
(843) 525-7077
Housed in an arsenal that was completed in 1798, the museum tells the story of Beaufort's history through its exhibits and displays of artifacts. Among the exhibits are those involving the Native Americans who lived in the area, the European colonization of the region, the development of the town in the era prior to the Civil War, the Union occupation during that conflict, and early-20th-century industries.

The museum has been situated in the arsenal since 1939 as the result of a WPA project to add a wing for a museum and relic room. The building was the site of National Guard musters until 1966, and it was acquired by the city of Beaufort in 1990 for the continued purpose of preserving the town's heritage and that of the surrounding Sea Islands. The museum is closed on Sunday and city holidays but is open the rest of the time from 11:00 a.m. until 4:00 p.m. Admission for adults is $3, and children age six and younger are admitted free.

John Mark Verdier House Museum
801 Bay Street
Beaufort, SC
(843) 524-6334
Beaufort can boast of many historic and beautiful residences, but the John Mark Verdier House is the only one that's open to the public on a regular basis. Revolutionary War hero the Marquis de Lafayette was entertained at the house during a visit to Beaufort in 1825, and the Union Army used it as a headquarters during the Civil War. Built in the late 1790s by one of the town's leading merchants, the two-story frame house rests on a tabby foundation and is an example of the Federal style of architecture. Interior features are the paneled reception parlor, first-floor dining room, graceful staircase, and spacious second-floor drawing room. The decor and furnishings reflect those of the period from 1790 until Lafayette's visit in 1825.

The house was condemned in 1942, but public-spirited citizens spearheaded a drive to save the structure, and a restoration effort was begun in the fall of 1975. It was completed a year later. The house is open to viewing Monday through Friday with the first tour at 10:30 a.m. and the final tour at 3:30 p.m. Admission is $6 for adults and $4 for students.

You can see more of Beaufort's elegant old houses—their exteriors, at least—by visiting an area called The Point, which is east of Bay Street. This oak-filled section of town is not large and doesn't take long to drive through, but it's abundantly graced with what the local historic foundation calls "Beaufort-style" homes. According to the Historic Beaufort Foundation, these homes were "designed for airiness and coolness" and "incorporated elements of Georgian and Colonial architecture as well as those of Greek Revival and semitropical Spanish." The foundation's guidebook states that the Beaufort-style home "differs from the more urban designs of Charleston and Savannah in that the Beaufort house is freestanding on a large lot, frequently with a formal garden, and is oriented to take full advantage of the prevailing southwesterly breezes. It more nearly resembles the plantation house, brought to town, as some indeed were, and adapted to the summer heat and the dampness of the Lowcountry." Many of these homes have fascinating histories, and some bear enchanting names, such as The Castle, Tidewater, Marshlands, The Oaks, Tidalholm, Riverview, and The Little Taj.

A wonderful way to view these homes and the rest of Beaufort's Historic District is on foot on your own; you can pick up free maps of the area at many of the downtown shops and at the visitor center, which is at the intersection of Congress and Carteret Streets. If you're looking for something that's a little more structured, there are numerous tours available, including those provided by appointment by The Point Tours at 1002-B Bay Street (843-522-3576) and by Carolina Buggy Tours (843-525-1300), whose carriages leave from the marina area of the waterfront; and by The Spirit of Old Beaufort, which conducts walking tours from its gift shop at 103 West Street Extension (843-525-0459). John Sharp (843-575-5775) provides a spookier look at Beaufort, with a lantern-lit narrative conducted in the graveyard of St. Helena's church.

RELOCATION/REAL ESTATE

Savannah is a popular relocation destination. Retirees come here, drawn by the weather, the availability of military benefits resources, the golf. Military discharges often opt to stay. Vacationers get hooked on what they see and come back year after year, finally pulling up stakes elsewhere and putting down roots here. And, in a phenomenon we probably couldn't document but which we would vouch for after 20-plus years of anecdotal observation, people who are reared here return to live here, despite the appeals of better-paved career paths, larger cities, and lower humidity. See a Savannah girl marry a beau from college in the Northeast and then strike out for California? Sure. Give her a few years—she and that husband will be back here to raise their kids.

If you are looking to relocate yourself, you want an area that has shown up on relocation radar. It's not that you are looking to follow the rest of the migrating herd—it's just that when you look at an area with a tradition of welcoming in new populations, you find a relocation industry already in place. The banks are all going to have packets welcoming you to the community; everyone from the voter registration folks to the library is going to be versed in helping newcomers; and chances are your kid won't be the only new face to turn up in class this year.

When you are starting out on a relocation quest, the first thing you want is information—lots of it. That's what this chapter is all about, and we'll refer you to the other chapters of this book that have details of particular information to newcomers (Education, Worship, etc.), but for some other sources, consider these.

Savannah Area Chamber of Commerce
101 East Bay Street
(912) 644-6400
www.savannahchamber.com
The chamber can provide you with its standard relocation packet via mail and free of charge. No one ever accused a chamber of being excessively unbiased, but this is still a good starting point. Materials and references will largely be restricted to chamber members, but with a few exceptions that doesn't lead to major omissions. Be sure to stress, when making your request by telephone, that you are looking for relocation info, not just tourist material, since the chamber's Convention and Visitors Bureau handles tourism materials, too.

Savannah Morning News
1375 Chatham Parkway
(912) 236-9511
www.savannahnow.com
We wouldn't even think of relocating to a town (assuming we had a choice) without reading the daily newspaper for a period of time. You could take out a mail subscription by calling the above number. The Web site offers essentially the full local news content of each day's paper, and it's free and available with no sign-up hassles. But with just the Web version, you miss the community flavor that goes with all the "other" stuff—wedding announcements, the neighborhood-oriented Closeup sections, and above all, the ads. (After all, if you are going to live here, don't you want a feel for where you'll be shopping? Of course, we take care of part of that for you in our Shopping chapter, but it doesn't cover such things as grocery stores.) Whichever form you choose, we recommend this information source as a reality check, since you

can usually assume a daily newspaper wasn't put together with any thought of luring in visitors or new residents.

THE BASICS

Consider this section a quick community review. You can read more in our chapters covering the area overview, history, education, and health care.

When you are talking Savannah, you are essentially talking three counties and multiple municipalities. Chatham County (population 232,064 in 2001, spread out over 451 square miles) is the biggest one in the area, and the sixth most populous in the state of Georgia. Savannah is the county seat, but you'll also find incorporated communities to the east and west—Thunderbolt, Tybee Island, Vernonburg, Pooler, Bloomingdale, Garden City.

Effingham and Bryan Counties make up the rest of what statisticians call the Savannah SMSA, or Standard Metropolitan Statistical Area. Both were established rural counties in their own right before becoming bedroom communities for Savannah as well. Effingham's county seat is Springfield, but the SUVs that commute into and out of Savannah are likely coming from Guyton and Rincon, for the most part. Bryan County's county seat is Pembroke, but the smaller municipality of Richmond Hill—south of Savannah's Southside—is the town you'll hear of most often.

Other counties—hey, Georgia boasts 159 of 'em—play a role in the local scene, too. Most prominent is Liberty County (county seat: Hinesville), which is home of Fort Stewart, to which Savannah's Hunter Army Airfield is attached in all but geography.

On the South Carolina side, essentially two counties play in the regional mix—Beaufort County, with its county seat of Beaufort and townships of Hilton Head Island and Bluffton; and Jasper County, home of Ridgeland and Hardeeville.

Hilton Head Island pioneered the concept of planned communities designed for relocating early retirees. As the island has increas-

ingly built up, you'll find similar upscale buildings spilling onto the mainland side, where the address is Bluffton. Next in line for the advent of gated communities will be Jasper County, which currently isn't heavily developed.

A geography review seems in order for those who are relocating from other parts of the country. Not for nothing is this section of South Carolina called the Lowcountry, and the land doesn't get any higher when you cross the Savannah River and hit Georgia. Invest in flood insurance wherever in this region you buy, and carefully evaluate the flood risks of any property you are considering buying. Remember that Savannah and environs all fall within hurricane impact zones. True, the last hurricane to really strike Savannah was David in 1979, and that was sort of a glancing blow. But Hurricane Hugo and Hurricane Floyd prompted evacuations before striking elsewhere, and the potential is there every fall.

In fact, put drainage at the top of your list of questions when looking at property. It doesn't take a particularly heavy rainfall to cause localized flooding, if it comes during a high tide when all the drainage ditches (we call them canals) are filled up with tidal water. Paving and development have increased the flood risk and drainage problems in some areas. Investigate thoroughly.

---

i Shopping for a home? Try the grocery store. A wide range of free real-estate publications, complete with photos and often in color, is distributed in Chatham County. Grocery stores are popular distribution points. There are at least five competing publications. Also, check the real-estate section of Sunday's *Morning News*. It includes, by zip code, listings of recent sale prices of properties. It's a good idea to check what stuff is really selling for, not just what is being asked for it.

INFRASTRUCTURE BASICS

Next up for review are infrastructure issues.

Electricity in this section of Georgia is provided by Georgia Power, a division of Southern Company. Natural gas is a deregulated industry in Georgia, as of several years ago. The result was a glut of marketers, confusing pricing, and billing fiascoes. Things have shaken out a bit now, but as a new resident you'll find yourself choosing among providers.

By the way, when investigating a new home, review your energy system seriously. The hot, humid summers make good air-conditioning a serious quality-of-life issue. And despite the fact that there may be a palm tree growing outside a house, winters can include some serious cold snaps—and many older homes lack good insulation.

The city of Savannah sells water, sewer, and garbage service to its citizens, and also sells water and sewer services under contract to various developments outside its city limits. In fact, you'll find these services provided by most municipalities. If you wind up in the unincorporated areas of the county—such as the popular Islands area—you may find yourself in an area served by a private water system, septic tanks, and private garbage contractors. Outside the city of Savannah, you may also encounter areas served by volunteer or combined pro and volunteer fire departments.

Chatham County and Savannah recently consolidated their police forces. The smaller municipalities still maintain their own. All you really need to know is that 911 works countywide.

Over the years, most of the "dead spots" for cell-phone coverage in this general vicinity have gone away, thanks to some aggressive tower building. You'll find most (but not all) of the area has access to broadband Internet service. Unless you pick a really remote area in Chatham County, you can expect to find it has cable television access, and most (but, again, not all) of those served also have access to cable modem service for high-speed Internet.

Does your new home involve construction or remodeling? Unless you are from some very isolated portion of the country, you're familiar with the idea and basic process of getting building permits. If your tastes have led you to the Historic District, be aware that the renovation permitting process can be extremely exacting—yes, you may find yourself (or your architect) having to defend the style of door handles you choose.

SAVANNAH NEIGHBORHOODS

We've been amazed at what real-estate prices have done in the last few years here. The beach was once a bargain (unbelievable but true); not anymore. Owning a home in the Historic District takes serious money and has for years. And a curse of trendiness sometimes descends on a neighborhood, sending prices skyrocketing all out of reason, as has happened in Ardsley Park, where circa-1930s and -40s bungalows command a quarter of a million dollars. Still, you can find livable selections. A well-maintained 1960s ranch home with three bedrooms and two baths can be had on the Southside for less than $120,000, and new construction of smaller homes on freshly opened-up sections of the southwest portion of the county are marketed for $138,000. According to the Savannah Area Chamber of Commerce, a home that would sell for $221,650 in Savannah would go for $271,250 in Atlanta and $598,333 in Stamford, Connecticut.

Historic District

The Historic District is a miniature city within a city. Inside the 2.5-square-mile area you will find restaurants, churches, antiques shops, museums, banks, government buildings, art galleries, and even some wildlife—that is, if you count the hundreds of squirrels who call the many squares and parks home.

Of course, there are also the houses. Hundreds of homes painstakingly restored to their original 19th-century splendor fill the area.

Available houses in the Historic Downtown area are becoming increasingly difficult to find. KYLE CASON

Within a few steps in the Historic District, you are apt to encounter wrought-iron balconies, brick courtyards, and other architectural delights such as historic downspouts shaped like dolphins that empty water into the street.

In addition to being a neighborhood, this is also a tourist attraction. Be aware that this is, or could become, a drawback of sorts: slow-moving and loud tour buses that the city does not regulate heavily; onstreet parking problems; walking tours that currently are at daggers-drawn with some irate residents; and so on. The charms outweigh the drawbacks, though (although we do admit to being taken aback, when we lived downtown, to people who would walk up to our windows and peek in as if the living room were an attraction).

The Historic District is also an area of great diversity. Some of Savannah's wealthiest and oldest families live a door or two away from art students who came to town from California or Ohio or Asia. In the Beach Institute area on the eastern edge of the district,

many long-standing African-American families raise their children in homes that have been in the family for generations.

The stock of run-down homes in need of renovation has fallen in the main district, although there are still fixer-uppers in the Victorian District and other historic areas outside the traditional "landmark" Historic District. Don't expect to find anything renovated for less than $250,000, although you may find some bargains in new condos, townhomes, or downtown lofts. The same housing market

i Residents of the Historic Downtown can apply for inexpensive parking stickers, which allow them to park their vehicles at meters near their homes without getting tickets. Everyone, residents and guests alike, however, needs to watch out for the posted weekly sweeping zone times, when parking is prohibited so the city street sweepers can do their job.

i There are dozens of neighborhood associations in Savannah. To find out information about a neighborhood group you are interested in, call the city of Savannah's Community Services Department at (912) 651-6520.

slowdown that has hit elsewhere in the country began affecting this area, too. Look for prices to correct to more realistic levels.

A good dose of "buyer beware" is called for when buying a historic home. Antique mantels are adorable; antique plumbing and wiring are not. If you are not familiar with the mixed blessing that comes with being the keeper of historic architecture, make sure you seek out expert advice about things like lead paint, fire escapes, and the like. And if you plan renovations of your own, any changes visible from the street will be under the watchful eye of the Historic Review Board.

The Victorian District

Just south of the Historic District lies the Victorian District, roughly bounded by Victory Drive, Gwinnett Street, Martin Luther King Jr. Boulevard, and East Broad Street. Here you will find the Victorian ladies of architecture—two- and three-story wooden houses with porches and gothic touches.

There's still renovation work to be done here, and gentrification is an active struggle here as well. Homeowners also confront the climate—Savannah's heat and humidity are a challenge to any paint job ever painted. The result is spotty: gorgeous homes next to boarded-up hulks, blocks that look homeless next to blocks that look pristine.

Some of these homes have as neighbors parts of the campus of Savannah College of Art and Design, which has spread beyond its Historic District roots to the Victorian District and even to surrounding industrial neighborhoods.

Starland

Once called "a cozy artists' neighborhood," this southernmost section of the Victorian

District had not seen much in the way of restoration until a handful of visionaries began rebuilding the blighted area into a diverse and friendly mix of residence and business. The name comes from an old dairy plant in the area.

Today you'll find the area still fairly early in the regeneration stages, with much of the work done by energetic sweat-investors rather than banks. There's a coffee shop, a dog park, art galleries (including a vet's office that sells art), and an eclectic feel of community.

If you are looking to buy here, come ready to do your own work—the stock of redone housing isn't large yet. But we suspect that to most Starland residents, that's sort of the point.

Southside/Midtown

Ardsley Park

Ardsley Park is Savannah's original suburb. Laid out in 1911, the development is south of the Historic District and the Victorian District in what Savannahians call Midtown. Although it was designed as a single residential subdivision, throughout the years it has grown to include a large area loosely bounded by Victory Drive on the north, Columbus Drive on the south, Bull Street on the west, and Waters Avenue on the east. Ardsley Park offers wide, tree-filled streets with many sizes and styles of older homes. Drive around and you will see large four- or five-bedroom mansions with elegant entrances, sunporches, and several fireplaces selling for $500,000 and higher. In other blocks, couples with young children live in very nice Craftsman-style bungalows with big yards. Because the area appeals to such a wide section of the community—from professionals to young families—it is a popular place to buy. In fact, as mentioned before, it is in the midst of the temporary curse of being trendy.

Looking in this neighborhood? Watch for flood-prone areas. Also, massive drainage improvement projects, ongoing for at least two years, have raised concerns about foundation damage near drilling sites. Also, don't invest without checking the after-work parking situation. Many of the bungalows either lack garages or carports, or else had them converted to living space—which means competition for street parking in some blocks is downright cutthroat. Columbus, Washington, and 52nd Streets have become fairly heavily traveled east-west routes.

An additional note: Across Waters Avenue and for several blocks behind the city's major Daffin Park is a neighborhood called Parkside, where you'll find much the same types of homes at, at least for the moment, slightly lower prices.

Gordonston

Gordonston is a small neighborhood nestled into Savannah's eastside. It is a popular spot for many local professionals including professors and others working in education.

Bordered by Skidaway Road, Gwinnett Street, and Pennsylvania Avenue, it was developed in the 1920s by the brother of Juliette Gordon Low, the founder of the Girl Scouts, on property that was once part of the family farm. In some ways, it is like a miniature Ardsley Park. Similar to its bigger cousin, throughout the development you will find tree-lined streets filled with a variety of older homes on large properties with front yards and backyards. Home styles include bungalows, cottages, and large mansions, and they tend to be less expensive than those in Ardsley Park. First-time home buyers might be able to find a two- or three-bedroom bungalow for around $200,000, while someone needing more space could find a large three- or four-bedroom home for $50,000 more.

Windsor Forest

When the city began suburban sprawl in earnest during the 1960s, south was the direction and Windsor Forest was the place. Windsor Forest is now a sprawl of neighborhoods between Savannah's malls. Here are classic American suburbs—ranch-style homes, split-levels, two-car garages, backyard barbecues, and so on. You can find virtually

i If you are choosing your home based largely along school-attendance lines, be aware that these can be—and often are—changed.

any price range here, even tony marshfront property, but it's a decidedly middle-class enclave. Here, you'll find your biggest, most elaborate grocery stores, your movie theaters, and on the nearby commercial arteries, the car dealerships and the fast-food franchises.

Georgetown

Although Georgetown debuted in 1974 on open land most Savannahians consider south of the Southside, you will still find homes going up there. More than 1,600 homes have been built throughout the development, located off the far southern reaches of Abercorn Street on King George Boulevard. There are nine subdivisions in total in the community offering a variety of home styles and prices. First-time home buyers should be able to find a two-bedroom home in Georgetown for around $140,000. Others wanting to move up to a larger house with many amenities like gourmet kitchens, Corian countertops, and hardwood floors will be able to find what they are looking for in Georgetown for $250,000 and up. There's also a pool and amenities center. Don't buy here without checking out the afternoon commute from Savannah, as this is an infamously congested route. Depending on where you're from, that traffic will either strike you as no big deal or a disaster.

Islands

The Islands area covers a lot of ground. Places such as Dutch Island and Skidaway Island, home of The Landings, are high end and exclusive (we mean that literally: They have gates). Islands such as Wilmington, Whitemarsh, and Talahi are more standard suburbia, and people who don't live there can't tell where one island ends and another begins. Tybee Island, the only one of the islands that actually feels like an island, covers a wide range of incomes and is sort of a world unto itself. (In fact, it has its own chapter in this book.)

Dutch Island

Dutch Island, an exclusive, gated enclave 20 minutes from downtown Savannah, is a popular choice for young professionals or those looking to move up to a larger home. The first neighborhoods on the island opened up in the early 1980s. Today, it is home to about 300 families and is expected to reach its maximum capacity of 500 homes within the next few years. Spacious homes with pristine lawns and traditional architecture can be found throughout Dutch Island. Home sizes range from 2,400 square feet up to 12,000 square feet, while prices go from $600,000 to "the sky's the limit."

Providence Plantation is the island's newest neighborhood. Half-acre lots start at $39,000, and homes begin at $225,000. Gourmet kitchens, hardwood floors, screened porches, and fireplaces are just some of the many amenities available. There is also a pool, playground, and lagoons stocked with fish for anglers. There are no recreation fees charged to use these facilities.

Isle of Hope

This peninsula in southeast Chatham County was an early summer resort for tourists. Situated with the Herb River on the west and the Skidaway River on the east, the community is one of Savannah's most picturesque. Beautiful old cottages with white picket fences and massive oak trees in the front yards overlook the waterways, while newer, typically suburban, homes scatter throughout other neighborhoods. The very old and very new mix together nicely.

There is a small-town feel even though large developments and the hustle of Savannah are just 20 minutes away. Longtime residents live on Isle of Hope as well as young families and professionals. Home prices vary

from modest, older two-bedroom bungalows around $200,000 to new three- and four-bedroom homes with all the amenities for $350,000 or more. The beautiful waterfront mansions on Bluff Drive are the stuff dreams are made of, and when one goes on the market, expect a multimillion-dollar price tag.

Long Point

More than 130 new homes have been built since 1992 at this popular Whitemarsh Island development. Conveniently located on Johnny Mercer Boulevard, it comfortably puts homeowners a short, 20-minute drive away from downtown or the Southside. Home prices start around $300,000 and climb to great heights for waterfront property and include many amenities like hardwood floors, cathedral ceilings, gourmet kitchens, and more. Styles differ throughout the development from sprawling single-story brick homes with circular drives to two-story stuccos with large front porches. Wide streets circulate through the community, and there is a guard gate that is typically occupied during the evening hours. According to local real-estate agents, when the most recent section of interior and lagoon lots opened at Long Point, 25 were sold within the first 60 days.

The Landings on Skidaway Island

Spend any time in Savannah and no doubt you will hear someone refer to "The Landings." This massive gated community takes up approximately 4,450 acres on Skidaway Island and is considered among Savannah's most prestigious developments. Started in 1972, The Landings is currently home to 6,500 residents from 45 states and 15 foreign countries. Since debuting more than 30 years ago, four phases have been built at The Landings, providing a diversity of architectural styles in a variety of prices ranging from $200,000 to $900,000. In Midpoint, one area of the development, you will find Colonial, Federal, and Southern Lowcountry homes, while traditional, ranch-style wooden homes can be found elsewhere. Granite countertops, custom cabinets, hardwood floors, cathedral ceilings, terraces, and bay windows are just some of the many amenities available in homes at The Landings.

All the homes are on nicely landscaped lots that are often filled with trees, giving the feeling that you're living in the country, not a development with thousands of homes. The Landings' other main selling points include 6 golf courses, designed by such golfing luminaries as Arnold Palmer and Tom Fazio; 34 tennis courts; 2 marinas; and a yacht club. At the Oakridge Fitness Center there is a pool, plus fitness and exercise rooms. At the Franklin Creek Activity Center, there is a pro shop, clubhouse, 25-meter pool with hydrospa, and a snack bar. Membership fees are required to use the various facilities.

Although all the original lots have been sold, there are usually about 100 listings, including resale homes and homesites, available at any one time, according to The Landings. Many interested people purchase a lot a few years before retirement in anticipation of eventually building a home. A more recent trend for a community made up so heavily of out-of-state retirees is the interest of affluent families already living in the area. All development at The Landings is closely monitored and must be approved by the Architectural Review Board. A number of restrictive covenants apply.

West Chatham

Southbridge

Southbridge is a 1,100-acre planned community 8 miles west of the Historic Downtown. Developed by Hall Development of Myrtle Beach, South Carolina, it is the first community of its size to open in West Chatham.

More than 350 families, including a mix of retired residents, young families, and professionals, have moved to Southbridge since its opening in 1987. As its literature explains, Southbridge is "a residential golf community

blending Southern tradition with the amenities of a country club." Traditional Southern architecture is the development's hallmark. Drive around the neatly landscaped neighborhoods and you will see classic Georgian- and Federal-style wooden, brick, and stucco homes nestled among trees or along fairways on the golf course. Inside are many extras including modern kitchens, high ceilings, parquet floors, formal dining rooms, fireplaces, and breakfast nooks.

Two-, three-, or four-bedroom home options are available from roughly 1,600 to 2,400 square feet; prices range from $200,000 to $500,000. One of the newest additions to the development is Steeple Run, offering three-bedroom town houses of roughly 2,000 square feet. These run from $165,000 to $185,000 and include such features as vaulted ceilings, hardwood floors, and skylights. If you prefer, you can purchase a lot for $30,000 to $100,000 and have a home built to your specifications. You pick the home style, wallpaper, where you want it on the lot, and the builders do the rest. The developers added golf course condos and large duplexes they call "villas" in 1999.

Golf architect Rees Jones designed Southbridge's 18-hole course, which is rated one of Georgia's 25 best courses by *Golfweek Magazine*. The semiprivate Southbridge Golf Club includes a 6,000-square-foot clubhouse with a pro shop, dining room, and lounge. Besides golf, there is the Southbridge Racquet and Swim Club, featuring 12 clay tennis courts, 2 hard courts, a swimming pool, and spa. Membership dues are required to use these facilities.

Godley Station

In the spring of 1999, construction began on the first homes in this planned unit, mixed-use development. It turned into an almost "instant community," with a growing population and adjacent "big box" retail all well established by 2001. Today it's an example of geometric growth. Remember the old adage about "retail follows rooftops"? This massive tract is near the Savannah International Airport and just off Interstate 95. As predicted, this has been the major new direction for suburban expansion in Chatham County. The neighborhoods here are heavily pitched to families and have a strong sense of traditional community. The residential section, which lies partly in Savannah and partly in the West Chatham municipality of Pooler, has protective covenants, sidewalks, and community amenities such as a pool and clubhouse.

Westbrook

This new gated community in western Chatham County began home construction in mid-2001. It is part of a larger development known as Savannah Quarters, where price points start at $140,000. Westbrook, however, is clearly the upscale part of the new development, with starting prices closer to $500,000.

This community may be unique because it tore up one designer golf course and put in another. A Robert Cupp course went in first. Then, Medallist Developments assumed full ownership of the development. Golfer Greg Norman is behind Medallist, and it was decided to replace the existing two-year-old course with one of Norman's design.

Other Westside

New residential development is booming around the West Chatham municipalities of Pooler and Bloomingdale. These tend to be smaller subdivisions, not the massive planned developments like those outlined earlier— solid, middle-class homes for folks who are willing to drive a bit to get out of the city. Many of these include starter homes in the $140,000 range. It is here you'll find national homebuilders like Centex and D.R. Horton competing in what was previously pretty much a local-builders environment.

But don't get the idea that these municipalities began with these neighborhoods. These fiercely independent little communities have been around for years, housing the blue-collar workforce for the industries of Chatham County (which are clustered toward the west)

and the remnants of the county's agricultural population. If you are looking to buy acreage, this is about your only remaining option in Chatham County, and you're probably too late.

Outside the County

Savannah has developed its own commuter culture as well, with people driving into Savannah from bedroom communities in adjacent Richmond Hill (Bryan County) to the south, and Rincon, Guyton, and Springfield to the west in neighboring Effingham County. Here, you'll find typical suburbia, with its typical advantages and disadvantages. A word of caution: Don't trust anyone's estimate of commuting time. Drive it yourself during peak morning and afternoon traffic times. We never thought we'd see it, but these routes are starting to develop rush-hour traffic problems.

Although Savannah doesn't approach the metropolitan gridlock of larger cities during commuting hours, it still takes time to cover distance. We've heard radio ads cheerfully tout these out-of-county addresses as "20 minutes from Savannah." Remember, Savannah is a big place, and perhaps whoever timed that trip was in a helicopter. Still, many families find the open spaces, near rural quiet, and a lightning-bug population that hasn't succumbed to mosquito spraying to be well worth a daily drive.

It's hard to leave this topic without at least mentioning the Ford Plantation in Bryan County. This literally was the Fords' plantation, as in Henry Ford. The land is being developed into ultraluxury homes designed as second or third homes for the jet set. There's a club, spa, marina, shooting, and other outdoor sports—you name it. Prices are predictably stratospheric.

REAL-ESTATE COMPANIES

Regardless of the area or price range you are considering, there are hundreds of local Realtors ready to help you with your real-estate needs. What follows is a rundown of some of the best in the area, but remember that this is a small sample. Companies are listed in alphabetical order.

You might also want to touch base with the Savannah Area Board of Realtors. They won't recommend one member over another, of course, but they can provide information about a member's credentials. Their number is (912) 354-1513.

Barroll and Barroll Realty Company
101 West Liberty Street
(912) 235-5665
Since returning to Savannah from Philadelphia in 1981, Margery and Larry Barroll have formed a family real-estate business that includes their two sons. Together the husband-and-wife team have been in the real-estate business since 1975. Although the Barrolls live in Ardsley Park and, in fact, have purchased many homes there themselves, they don't limit their business to that area—but it is one of their areas of expertise. Their listings are throughout Savannah and include Tybee.

David Byck Realty Company
13 East York Street
(912) 233-1276
Commercial and residential sales and property management are what this 25-plus-year-old company concentrates on. Although its commercial and residential departments often specialize in the Historic Downtown, its rental apartments and homes are located throughout the city, including the Southside. The company's commercial department is affiliated with a national network specializing in commercial and industrial leasing. They also work with a national relocation group with more than 900 agents throughout the country. According to owner David Byck, who has been selling real estate for 40-plus years, the company's agents strive to meet all the needs of someone relocating to Savannah, whether the person requires rental property or wants to buy a home.

Celia Dunn Realty Company
9–13 West Charlton Street
(912) 234-3323
Celia Dunn has been selling real estate in the Historic Downtown for more than 20 years. In fact, her offices take up the bottom floor of a beautifully restored three-story home overlooking Madison Square. Besides specializing in the historic area, she and her agents sell in several other areas of Savannah, including Ardsley Park, Habersham Woods, Tybee, and Thunderbolt, and recently branched out into neighboring areas of South Carolina. The firm is associated with Sotheby's International Realty.

Coldwell Banker Platinum Partners
6349 Abercorn Street
(912) 352-1222
This high-volume real estate firm is owned by Connie Farmer Ray. It handles property of all types in the Coastal Empire and neighboring South Carolina. The firm has six offices (that's the main address listed here) and more than 150 agents. It's hard to point to a neighborhood or price point specialty—these folks are everywhere in the residential market.

Konter Realty
22 Commerce Place
(912) 354-9314
Konter Realty is one of Savannah's largest real-estate companies, with 30 to 50 agents selling throughout the city and surrounding counties. It is also one of the oldest. Husband-and-wife team Lawrence and Harriet Konter founded the company 36 years ago in a small, two-room office in the Historic Downtown.

There are six individual divisions under the corporate umbrella of Konter Realty, including real estate, construction, and property management. The company also manages more than 500 residential units, along with 600,000 square feet of commercial/office space. Konter builds between 50 and 60 homes each year and is also involved in light commercial development including apartments, offices, and retail buildings.

i As a new homeowner in the region, one of the first services you are going to need is pest control. Mild winters, wet weather, and lots of green spaces all add up to bugs. Most locals make their peace with them outdoors, and wage chemical warfare inside their homes.

The Landings Company
1 Landings Way
(912) 598-0500, (800) 841-7011
This real-estate company is part of The Landings on Skidaway Island—Savannah's largest development and one of its most exclusive. Up to 20 agents are in the office, which, of course, specializes in selling homes, lots, and condos at The Landings. But you'll find their listings all over town, too.

Mopper-Stapen Realtors
31 West Congress Street
(912) 238-0874
Mopper-Stapen has been in downtown Savannah for almost 20 years. During this time, the company has been involved with many properties requiring renovation—sometimes entire neighborhoods with dozens of vacant houses. Besides specializing in historic properties, the company also concentrates on commercial real estate and property management.

Judy Nease Realty
924 Wilmington Island Road
(912) 354-9966
Judy Nease's specialty is her own backyard: She has called Savannah's eastern islands home for more than 30 years. This is also where she sells the majority of her real estate. Nease has been in the business since 1978 and started her own company around the beginning of 1996. There are seven agents in the office, all of whom have been selling real estate for many years and have built up their own areas of expertise. The company also offers relocation services for people moving to the area.

The Prudential Southeast Coastal Properties
1 Diamond Causeway
(912) 355-4171
There are 28 agents in this office, which is the only Prudential affiliate in Savannah. Reva and Bob Laramy started the company in 1982 and offer many services, including relocation, property management, short- and long-term rentals, and commercial sales. The company sells real estate throughout the city from West Chatham to the Southside. However, one of their main areas of expertise is The Landings on Skidaway Island.

RE/MAX Professionals
6813 Johnny Mercer Boulevard
(912) 897-1955
RE/MAX Professionals has 10 agents specializing in Wilmington, Tybee, and other islands. Owner Lynda Werntz has been in real estate since 1978. The office is one of three RE/MAX offices in Savannah, each with its own area of expertise and services.

Shore, Bell and Seyles Realty
401 Mall Boulevard, Suite 102B
(912) 356-1653
Relocation is the specialty of Shore, Bell and Seyles Realty. As part of their relocation efforts, owners Carey Shore, Nick Bell, and Charles Seyles, who each have more than 25 years of real-estate experience, will send you a relocation packet, give you a tour of Savannah, and even pick you up at the airport if you need a lift. They handle individual and corporate moves involving several employees. The company's main areas of concentration are Dutch Island and Long Point, two high-end island developments with properties ranging in price from $200,000 to $750,000.

Cora Bett Thomas Realty
24 East Oglethorpe Avenue
(912) 233-6000
Cora Bett Thomas Realty is a deluxe, high-powered real estate firm. This office specializes in prestige and historic properties, and

the clientele includes discreetly unconfirmed celebrities. Thomas is affiliated with the real-estate arm of Christies Great Estates, of British fame, for the marketing of unusual and high-end properties. The firm specializes in upscale properties, including new condo developments in the Historic District and on the waterfront. It has also expanded into planned developments in neighboring South Carolina.

APARTMENTS

Many apartment complexes complete with pools, recreation rooms, and clubhouses are available in Savannah. Most have been built within the last 10 to 15 years, if not more recently, and will be found on the Islands and Southside/Midtown. They are clustered in the Islands area because of the local reputation of the schools there, and on the Southside, in large part, because that is where off-base housing for Hunter Army Airfield tends to concentrate, close to base. The complexes are listed in several free publications offered in racks at area grocery stores.

The Historic Downtown also has a healthy market. Many residents have converted part of their private homes into apartments, and there are also a few apartment buildings to choose from. With the influx of students want-ing to live downtown, finding an apartment in this area has become more of a challenge. Prices have been on the rise. Until recently, you could find a one-bedroom apartment starting around $700 a month, and a two-bedroom for around $800. However, those prices have gone up and, depending on the apartment's size, quality, and amenities, monthly rents can go for $1,200 and up in some cases.

One of the best ways to find apartments in the Historic Downtown is to check in the *Savannah Morning News*. However, many owners don't bother advertising and simply post a FOR RENT sign on their apartment—a walk or drive around town is a good way to get leads.

You will also find houses for rent in several areas of Savannah, including Southside, Midtown, and the Islands. As the real-estate slowdown has made it harder for relocating homeowners to sell their properties, they are putting them into use as rentals. The homes vary from area to area and can include everything from older bungalows to new homes in gated developments. Like apartment rentals, many of the owners simply post a FOR RENT sign or advertise in a local newspaper. Some list their homes with local Realtors. Prices range anywhere from $500 (not many of those to be had) to $2,000 a month.

EDUCATION AND CHILD CARE

EDUCATION

Savannah and Chatham County offer a wide spectrum of educational opportunities. In addition to the forward-looking public school system, there are a variety of private high schools, a technical school, two state universities, and the largest art school in the United States. This chapter presents overviews of all these plus a broad look at what's available in the area of child care.

Public Schools

Savannah-Chatham County Public Schools
208 Bull Street
(912) 201-5600
www.savannah.chatham.k12.ga.us

The Savannah-Chatham school system serves some 34,000 students in prekindergarten (4-year-olds) through 12th grade. They are enrolled at 48 schools and participate in several alternative programs. Students in the system attend 30 elementary schools, 11 middle schools, and 7 high schools.

Twelve of the schools were added to the system between the mid-1990s and 2003 as part of an aggressive $221 million construction program. Among the new facilities is Savannah High School, built on the east side of town as a replacement for its namesake in Midtown on Washington Avenue. The old Savannah High, which was erected in 1937, was renovated and now houses the Savannah Arts Academy, which is dedicated to the visual and performing arts.

In another development involving a new school, a charter public middle school—Oglethorpe Academy—opened in August 1999 in west Savannah on the site of a one-time elementary school. The academy's charter is based on providing students with a

rigorous curriculum and an environment—that is, a student body—that's smaller than those of other schools. Another feature calls for parents or guardians of students being asked to sign contracts obligating them to accept responsibility for their children's behavior and compelling them to participate in the educational process.

Among the school system's alternative programs are two Corporate Academies, which promote the academic and social development of at-risk students by means of nontraditional programs, and the Adult Education Center, which offers basic skills and secondary education for persons seeking to pass the General Educational Development Test or enhance their personal growth through education. The system also operates the Coastal Georgia Comprehensive Academy for students with severe emotional and/or behavioral disorders and autism.

The system has an extensive academy program that enables students to concentrate on special talents and interests. Included in the program are the Montessori Academy at Ellis Elementary School; Advanced Learning academies at Bartow and Heard Elementary Schools; Fine and Performing Arts academies at Bloomingdale and Gadsden Elementary Schools, Shuman Middle School, and Savannah Arts Academy; the Traditional/Latin Academy at J.G. Smith Elementary School; the Renzulli Enrichment Academy at Mercer Middle School; and Honors academies at DeRenne Middle School and Jenkins High School. Two exciting innovations are the Children's Engineering Academy at Spencer Elementary School and the Marine Science Academy at Thunderbolt Academy.

The average class size at schools in the system is 25 students. There is an emphasis

Students perform in the square in front of Massie School on May Day.
KYLE CASON

on computer technology, and the system has more than 7,500 computers in its classrooms and access to the Internet at each school. The system has 278 partnerships with the business community through which businesspeople voluntarily assist individual schools in areas such as mentoring, accomplishing building projects, cleaning up campuses, and raising funds.

Two unique features of the local system are the Massie Heritage Interpretation Center and the Oatland Island Education Center (see our Attractions chapter). Massie, which is at 207 East Gordon Street, is the oldest standing school in Georgia (see the Close-up in this chapter). The school does not hold regular classes, but programs on the history of Georgia are offered. Teachers arrange for their classes to attend programs at Massie. Oatland, at 711 Sandtown Road, covers 75 acres, and its 1.75-mile Discovery Trail takes visitors through woodlands, past marshes, and to specially constructed habitats of endangered

and protected animals of the state—wolves, bison, panthers, and birds of prey among them. There's a re-creation of a Colonial settlement and a barnyard where youngsters can get a feel for life on the farm, past and present. The Oatland staff holds several special events throughout the year, including a festival featuring sheepshearing in March and a cane grinding festival in November (see our Annual Events and Festivals chapter).

Private Schools

Savannah's private high schools provide teenagers and their parents with alternatives to what's offered by the public school system. Most of the private schools are church-related, and all are focused on preparing their students for college. These schools are predominantly coed, but there is a school for girls and one that admits only male students. There's at least one private high school in each section of the city, with the majority being centrally located in the Midtown area.

Benedictine Military School
6502 Seawright Drive
(912) 644-7000
www.bcsav.net

This Catholic high school for boys dates back to 1902, when it was founded on Bull and 32nd Streets as Benedictine College. Having sons become "BC boys" is a tradition in many Savannah families, a circumstance that has led this military school for 9th through 12th graders to have an extremely faithful and active group of alumni. Sixty percent of those who attend the school are Catholic, but the remainder of the student body is as diverse as the faculty, which is composed of Benedictine priests and monks, laymen and laywomen, and military retirees. Enrollment is about 400.

Benedictine is a college-prep school, and 95 percent of graduates attend college. The school is housed in large, contemporary-style buildings on 100 acres in the Southside. It was moved there in the early 1960s; until that time, students received military training during all four years of school. Since then, however, Junior ROTC classes have been mandatory only for freshmen and sophomores and optional for juniors and seniors. More than 90 percent of upperclassmen continue to participate in JROTC, training that can give them an advantage should they elect to attend a military college or enter the armed forces out of high school.

The school's mission calls on its faculty to "value all individuals as children of God with emphasis on the Benedictine principles of prayer, work, and hospitality." The school offers opportunities for students to compete in a full range of sports and extracurricular activities. There are also rifle and drill teams. Extracurricular activities at Benedictine start an hour after the end of school so that participants can avail themselves of the after-school tutoring program. Benedictine partners with Edline, a program that allows students and parents to review grades, test scores, schedules, teachers' notes, and more on a daily basis by accessing the Internet.

Bible Baptist School
4700 Skidaway Road
(912) 352-3067
www.bbsav.org

The administration and faculty of Bible Baptist seek to educate the whole child while emphasizing the spiritual side of students' development. Bible is taught in every class of this traditional Christian school, which has an enrollment of 380 students in prekindergarten through high school. The coed, college-prep school is a mission of Bible Baptist Church, and it's located on a 19-acre church-school complex that includes a football stadium, a lighted baseball field, and a gymnasium with two full basketball courts. Although the school is open to students of all faiths, the teaching of Christian values is stressed.

Spacious classrooms give teachers plenty of room for learning centers and computer corners, and the average class size is 16 to 20 students. Ninety percent of graduates attend college. Among school traditions are the ceremony at which juniors are presented their senior-class rings by parents or friends and attend a social gathering afterward, with parents, grandparents, and siblings invited to join in. Bible Baptist, whose founders say it was formed in reaction to the ban on prayer in public schools and what was seen as a lack of

i Chatham Academy, a private school for students in grades 1 through 12, offers a full-day program of instruction for children with specific learning disabilities and attention deficit disorders. The school, located at Royce Learning Center at 4 Oglethorpe Professional Boulevard just east of Oglethorpe Mall, serves children of at least average intelligence who have been unable to function successfully in a traditional classroom. Chatham Academy provides a low student-teacher ratio and addresses the academic, social, and emotional needs of its students in classes grouped according to age and academic functioning level. You can contact the school by calling (912) 354-4047.

Benedictine Military School, a parochial high school for boys, stages a Pearl Harbor commemoration.
KYLE CASON

discipline there, has a full program of varsity athletics. The school is a member of the Georgia Christian Athletic Association and Georgia Association of Christian Schools.

Calvary Day School
4625 Waters Avenue
(912) 351-2299
www.calvarydayschool.com
This coed school in Savannah's Midtown is a ministry of Calvary in Savannah and is open to students of all faiths and creeds. The school and church occupy 22 acres at Waters Avenue and 63rd Street. The school started downtown with a kindergarten class in 1961 under the leadership of the Rev. John T. Tippitt Jr., and a grade was added each year. Calvary, which moved south to Midtown in 1964, now provides Christian-based education to more than 900 students in prekindergarten through 12th grade.

According to school officials, academics are blended with a strong program of athletics and other activities to help students evolve into well-rounded citizens. The student-teacher ratio is 18 to 1. The curriculum is designed to prepare students for college, and 98 percent of Calvary's graduates attend institutions of higher learning. Among the tools used in accomplishing the goal of readying students for life after high school are five computer labs, a high-school medical profession program, a middle-school technology lab, and two libraries. A new high school building opened in 2007.

The school offers a full program of athletics and has its own football stadium and track, a complex named M. C. Anderson Field. Cavalry offers before- and after-school programs for students prekindergarten through sixth grades.

Close-up

Massie School

Supporters of Massie School, the oldest operating public school in Georgia, celebrated the facility's 150th birthday in 2006. A public school from 1856 to 1974, Massie continues to serve as a focal point of education in its role as the Massie Heritage Center, a museum for teaching Savannah's history to students and adults. Housed in three Greek Revival–style buildings on Calhoun Square, Massie offers visitors a look at a 19th-century classroom and exhibits involving the history of the school, Savannah's city plan, the preservation of the city, its architectural treasures, American Indians in coastal Georgia, and the legacy of Savannahian W. W. Law, who was a civil rights leader, historian, and preservationist.

Massie began its long life as Massie Common School House in a single building designed by architect John S. Norris, who drew the plans for many of Savannah's important structures. A western annex was added in 1872, and the eastern annex was built 14 years later. The school was listed on the National Register of Historic Places in 1977, the year it began serving as an education and resource center under the aegis of the Savannah-Chatham County Public Schools.

From its location at 207 East Gordon Street, the center purports to offer local residents and visitors alike "the best orientation to Savannah's built environment." A highlight of this experience is a visit to the City Plan Room, which holds the only three-dimensional model of the city's Historic District. It's a huge layout that affords a bird's-eye view of the downtown. The room also contains maps and photographs describing the development and preservation of the city plan set forth in the 1700s by Savannah's founder, James Edward Oglethorpe. There's more to be learned about Savannah's buildings and efforts to preserve them via exhibits involving the city's classical architecture and the beginnings of the preservation movement—displays that make use of photos and artifacts.

Massie is open from 9:00 a.m. until 4:00 p.m. Monday through Friday. Self-guided tours are $3 per person, and docent-led visits run $5.

Memorial Day School
6500 Habersham Street
(912) 352-4535
www.memorialdayschool.org
Established in 1971 by the membership of Memorial Baptist Church, this college preparatory school in the northern part of the Southside focuses on equipping each of its students for the diverse challenges and opportunities of higher education and for responsible citizenship. With a fully degreed faculty and a schoolwide pupil-teacher ratio of 12 to 1, Memorial provides its 280 students with wireless laptop computer technology, software, and a variety of current media resources. Before- and after-school programs include remedial and enrichment activities for students through the age of 10, and there's a

fully licensed day-care program for children 6 weeks to 4 years old. The school offers extracurricular activities that encourage participation in academic competitive events in debate, public speaking, drama, music, and the literary arts, and in athletic programs involving football, basketball, baseball, softball, track, golf, and cheerleading.

St. Andrew's School
601 Penn Waller Road
(912) 897-4941
www.saintschool.com

The secondary division of St. Andrew's is the only high school on the eastside islands. St. Andrew's includes classes for prekindergarten and up. About 480 students are enrolled at the coed, nonsectarian, college-prep school, which is on 28 tree-filled acres on Wilmington Island.

The guiding principles of the school are high standards, a personalized approach to education, multiple opportunities for discovering talents and interests, small class size, and a strong sense of community. The student-teacher ratio is nine to one, and all graduates attend college. A series of seminars, multiple counseling sessions, and school-arranged tours of various colleges assist students in making their post-secondary decisions. Limited need-based financial aid is available for qualifying families. St. Andrew's offers a broad range of extracurricular activities, including participation in athletics, with St. Andrew's competing on the varsity level in the South Carolina Independent School Association because of its proximity to similar-size schools in the Palmetto State. The school's fine-arts programs are extensive.

St. Andrew's has its roots in a day school that was begun downtown in 1947 by Independent Presbyterian Church. During the 1970s, the church formulated plans for a larger institution, and the result was St. Andrew's, which was founded on Wilmington Island in late 1978. Although the school is no longer affiliated with Independent Presbyterian, St. Andrew's retains aspects of its Scottish heritage, including assigning students to six Scottish clans and hosting a field day in the fall when the school holds its own Scottish games.

The purchase of the former Islands YMCA adjacent to the school and the conversion of the facility into the St. Andrew's Early Education Childhood Center, which houses prekindergarten through third grade students, offers a nurturing environment with developmentally appropriate activities.

St. Vincent's Academy
207 East Liberty Street
(912) 236-5508

St. Vincent's—a Catholic, college preparatory school for girls—has been owned by the Sisters of Mercy since 1845 and is the only private high school in the Historic District. The three main buildings of the school cover a city block on the south side of Liberty Street between Abercorn and Lincoln Streets, and St. Vincent's also includes the Walsh Hall gymnasium on Harris Street and the Peg F. Dressel Library at Liberty and Lincoln. Although the Sisters of Mercy still operate the school, the majority of the faculty consists of professional lay teachers.

St. Vincent's teaches grades 9 through 12. About two-thirds of the school's 350 students are Catholic, but St. Vincent's is open to all young women regardless of creed, race, or socioeconomic status. Classes average about 20 students, with 95 to 100 percent of graduates attending college. The school administration believes the downtown location is an asset because it enables students to experience an urban environment and brings them into direct contact with Savannah's history and culture. St. Vincent's places an emphasis on Christian values and "the acceptance of individuals as God's gift to the world," says the principal, Sister Helen Marie Buttimer. This philosophy has led to a long tradition of graduates sending their daughters and granddaughters to their alma mater, up to the fourth and fifth generations. At the same time, St. Vincent's cherishes the diversity of

Thinking about homeschooling your child? You must first register with your local school board. You can find support for your homeschooling efforts in Savannah by meeting with members of Family Education for Christ, which can be reached by calling (912) 355-2722. This group schedules special activities for homeschooled students. Another organization, the Kingdom Builders Co-op, offers small classes for homeschoolers in a variety of subjects. For registration information involving the co-op, send email to dcwygant@cs.com.

its student body and makes its services available to all of Savannah's young women.

St. Vincent's offers an extensive program in visual arts, and the school's chorus is known throughout Savannah. St. Vincent's competes in eight varsity sports: volleyball, softball, basketball, tennis, track, soccer, riflery, and swimming.

Savannah Christian Preparatory School
1599 Chatham Parkway
(912) 234-1653

Savannah Christian is an independent, nondenominational Christian school for students in prekindergarten through 12th grade. The school's college prep curriculum produces above-average SAT scores and a college placement rate of 100 percent, and school spokespeople say Savannah Christian also seeks "to glorify God by partnering with families, churches, and the local community in educating future generations through Christ-centered training, application, and example."

Founded as the Evangelical Bible Institute with eight boarding students in 1951 by the Rev. George and Mrs. Harold Deane Akins, the school has contributed to the education of more than 5,000 students at some point during their academic journeys.

Savannah Christian maintains two campuses. The 254-acre Chatham Parkway campus hosts nearly 1,000 lower- and upper-school students and 160 day-care/preschool students. Facilities include 13 buildings with classrooms, labs, media centers, a gym, and a cafeteria; an outdoor pool; a track; five athletic fields; three playgrounds; and E.D.E.N. (Ecological Diversity for Educational Networking), a 125-acre outdoor learning center. A 14-acre campus on eastern DeRenne Avenue is home to more than 500 lower- and middle-school students, and facilities there include four buildings with classrooms, labs, media centers, a cafeteria, and two gyms.

Savannah Country Day School
824 Stillwood Drive
(912) 925-8800
www.savcds.org

Country Day strives to fulfill its motto—"Fostering excellence through knowledge, character, and service"—through a college prep program that emphasizes topflight performance in academics, the arts, and athletics.

The student-teacher ratio is 10 to 1, with class sizes averaging 21 students in the lower school, 16 in the middle school, and 15 in the upper school. The average SAT scores of students at Country Day are among the highest in Georgia, and the 67 graduates of the Class of 2005 were accepted to 117 different colleges. The coed school offers 19 Advanced Placement courses.

Country Day has 987 students. A broad range of athletics and extracurricular activities is offered, with the middle and upper schools fielding more than 40 sports teams. The school has 2 libraries with more than 25,000 volumes and 85 online services, 4 computer labs with 350 networked computers, 4 music and art studios, a fine-arts center, 3 gymnasiums, and a football stadium.

The Country Day campus is on 65 wooded acres tucked away in the Windsor Forest subdivision on the Southside. The school moved there in 1957 from a building on Forsyth Park that had been the home of the Pape School for Girls from 1905 until 1955, the year Country Day was chartered.

Since then, it has added several buildings. In 2007 it began construction of a new lower school building.

Technical Schools

Savannah Technical College
5717 White Bluff Road
(912) 443-5700
www.savannahtech.edu
Savannah Tech seeks to provide the local business and industrial community with highly trained workers—a service it has rendered since its founding by the Savannah Chamber of Commerce as the Opportunity School in 1929. Back then the school turned out mainly stenographers and clerks; these days, the emphasis is on providing students with the opportunity to acquire quality technical education and training that will allow them to be productive members of a global workforce.

From the mid-1940s until the summer of 1997, the school was governed mainly by the Savannah-Chatham County Board of Education. Savannah Tech is now governed solely by the Georgia Department of Technical and Adult Education and is part of a statewide network of 33 postsecondary schools. The school offers credit, noncredit, and specialized industry services and training. Credit offerings include technical certificates of credit, diploma programs, and associate's degree programs in allied health, business, and industrial technology. The school has more than 50 different credit programs, ranging from one-quarter programs in areas such as automotive technology and surgical technology to marketing and computer information systems. Some 4,000 students attend Savannah Tech.

The school serves four counties—Chatham, Bryan, Effingham, and Liberty. A state-of-the-art service center for students, new laboratory spaces, an expanded learning enrichment center, and a multipurpose learning center at the main Savannah campus on White Bluff Road opened in 2006. A $20 million Center for Allied Health Sciences and Learning Success is planned to support contin-ued enrollment growth. With the opening of the Army Education Center on Fort Stewart, the College has a presence on-post to serve military families with the necessary skills and education. The Liberty Campus continues to serve the educational needs of the community with programs in nursing, early childhood education, computers, and technology. The Crossroads Technology Campus in West Chatham, a key element in the development of a high-tech corridor along Interstate 95, is a catalyst for regional business development.

The college also partners with area employers to deliver programs off-site in area hospitals, specially equipped community education centers, and the public high schools. Provided are community-based studies in fields such as health care, masonry, early childhood care and education, and computer information systems. It also offers customized workforce training programs for new or expanding local industries as an economic development incentive.

Colleges and Universities

Armstrong Atlantic State University
11935 Abercorn Street
(912) 927-5277, (800) 633-2349
www.armstrong.edu
Armstrong Atlantic provides more than 75 academic programs through its College of Arts and Sciences, College of Education, College of Health Professions, School of Computing, and School of Graduate Studies. The university's teacher education program has gained state and national recognition, and its economics, computer science, and chemistry programs are also particularly strong. The College of Health Professions is the regional health professions education center for southeast Georgia. Among master's degrees are those offered in history, criminal justice, liberal and professional studies, nursing, education, public health, sports medicine, and physical therapy. Armstrong has an abundance of evening and weekend classes.

More than 7,000 students, including 810 graduate students, attend the school. They are taught by almost 500 professors. The great majority of students are commuters. The school is situated in the Southside on 268 acres in an arboretum setting.

The Lane Library has been newly renovated, and there's a new student recreational center. Since 2002, three student residential communities have been added to the campus, and they house 762 students in two- and four-bedroom apartments. Accommodations for an additional 96 opened in 2006.

Armstrong moved to the Southside in 1966 from Bull and Gaston Streets in the Historic Downtown, where it was founded in 1935 as Armstrong Junior College, which was then a city-supported school. It became a part of the University System of Georgia in 1959, gained college status in 1964, and achieved university status in 1996, when its name was changed from Armstrong State College to Armstrong Atlantic State University. The school fields NCAA Division II teams in men's basketball, baseball, tennis, and golf and in women's basketball, fast-pitch softball, volleyball, soccer, golf, and tennis (the 2005 team won the national championship). Armstrong hosts more than 200 cultural events each year, including a faculty lecture series, concerts, and dramatic presentations, all of them open to the public and most of them free.

Savannah College of Art and Design (SCAD)
342 Bull Street
(912) 525-5100, (800) 869-7223
www.scad.edu

The Savannah College of Art and Design has grown tremendously since its founding in 1979 with one building and 71 students. Today, SCAD is the largest art school in the country with its enrollment of more than 7,000 students. The college has almost 60 buildings (and seemingly constantly buying more) spread throughout the Historic and Victorian Districts, many of them of historic significance and beautifully renovated by the school. The college's restoration efforts have been so striking that the National Trust for Historic Preservation awarded SCAD the

National Honor Award for Historic Preservation in 1994.

The college offers bachelor's degrees in fine arts and master's degrees in arts, urban design, fine arts, and architecture. Among its 30 fields of study are historic preservation, interior design, painting, photography, furniture design, and production design. Programs involving computer art and graphic design attract scads of students, if you'll pardon the expression. The student-teacher ratio is 18 to 1.

The median age of students is 22, and they come from throughout the United States and from more than 80 foreign countries. Thirty-six percent live in the school's residence halls, several of which are former hotels, inns, or apartment buildings. SCAD has more than 50 student organizations and an intercollegiate athletic program fielding teams in basketball, golf, tennis, volleyball, swimming, rowing, cross-country, lacrosse, horseback riding, baseball, softball, and soccer.

Although founded and headquartered in Savannah, SCAD also has campus facilities in Atlanta and France.

Savannah State University
B. J. James Drive
Thunderbolt
(912) 356-2186
www.savstate.edu

Savannah State University has three colleges—Sciences and Technology, Business Administration, and Liberal Arts and Social Sciences—offering a total of 22 undergraduate degrees and 4 master's degree programs (social work, urban studies, marine sciences, and public administration). The campus, located adjacent to the town of Thunderbolt, covers 173 acres, many of them shaded by large oak trees festooned with Spanish moss. The eastern portion of the campus is bordered by salt marsh and the Wilmington River; that and the school's proximity to the Atlantic Ocean (about 8 air miles) led to its sobriquet of "College by the Sea," which it was called for many years before its upgrade to univer-

Savannah College of Art and Design has renovated old railroad buildings along Martin Luther King Jr. Boulevard. BETTY DARBY

sity status by the Georgia Board of Regents in 1996. Now it's known, not surprisingly, as the "University by the Sea." The school's location also lends a uniqueness to the university's marine sciences program; the program is the only one of its kind in the state situated in a natural setting. Among features of the program is the *Sea Otter*, a 35-foot cabin cruiser that's used for exposing students to marine science research.

The school was founded in 1890 as Georgia State Industrial College for Colored Youth and retained that name until 1950, when the regents dubbed it Savannah State College. It is the oldest public, historically black college in Georgia, and Savannah State has a student body that is 90 percent African-American, but university officials say the student population and faculty become more diverse each year. There are approximately 2,900 students and

145 instructors, about 70 percent of whom hold doctorates.

Savannah State has a full-scale athletic program and competes intercollegiately in football, baseball, men's and women's track and field, men's and women's basketball, and women's tennis, volleyball, and cross-country. The school achieved Division I status in 2002. There are 75 student organizations, including honor societies for high-ranking students in every major field of study, a theater group, concert choir, gospel choir, and marching band. Savannah State's Naval ROTC program sends more graduates to naval postgraduate school than all other small colleges in the country, according to university officials. The school also has its own FM radio station, WHCJ (90.3 FM), which broadcasts 16 hours a day.

i There's Hope for Georgia residents entering their first year at the state's colleges and universities. The Hope Scholarship pays tuition, some fees, and up to $100 per quarter for books to students attending a state school who have earned a B average in high school. B students attending eligible private colleges in Georgia can receive Hope in the amount of $3,000 per academic year for tuition. Students can renew these scholarships in their sophomore, junior, and senior years by maintaining a 3.0 grade-point average. Hope is funded by the Georgia Lottery for Education. For more information on the Hope program, call (800) 546-HOPE.

South University
709 Mall Boulevard
(912) 691-6000
www.southuniversity.edu

One of Savannah's oldest colleges, South University has grown from its humble beginnings as a two-year business college into a four-year institution offering degrees ranging from associate and bachelor's to master's and doctorates. Through its School of Business, School of Health Professions, School of Pharmacy, and a diverse offering of online programs, students can now pursue a wide variety of majors in the classroom, online, or through a combination of both.

i Looking for some non-credit educational opportunities? The Skidaway Community Institute was formed in 2005 to offer enrichment courses, primarily but not exclusively to residents of Skidaway Island's Landings Community. It has ambitious plans to build a community center to house its programs, but at present the classes are housed at Armstrong Atlantic State University and elsewhere. Learn more at www.skidawayci.org.

Within the School of Business, the university offers a bachelor of business administration and bachelor of science degrees in legal studies and information technology in addition to associate of science degrees in accounting, business administration, paralegal studies, and information technology. The School of Health Professions offers a bachelor of science in physician's assistant and healthcare management, master's degrees in physician's assistant, anesthesiologist assistant, and professional counseling in addition to its associate of science degrees in medical assisting and physical therapist assisting. South University was the first college or university in Savannah to award a doctorate degree through its School of Pharmacy. As of late 2005, the School of Pharmacy was one of only three such schools in the state of Georgia and, unlike other similar schools, it features a three-year, full-time accelerated program resulting in a doctor of pharmacy degree.

With more than 1,000 full-time students and hundreds of online students attending classes at South University, the average class size is 15 students per teacher, resulting in personalized attention from faculty who have been hired from some of the top universities in the country.

The school dates from 1899, when it was founded as a practical business college. The university was formerly located in downtown Savannah but moved to its current location on Mall Boulevard to accommodate the significant growth in students. Today, the campus covers more than 10 acres and features complete wireless computer access, student lounges, state-of-the-art classrooms and labs, and a 47-foot-high clock and bell tower that marks the center of campus.

The college was purchased by the South family in 1975, renamed Draughons Junior College two years later, and became South College in 1986 and South University in 2001. There is no athletic program, but the college does have a student government organization and several field-specific clubs.

CHILD CARE

The state of Georgia regulates the businesses of people who provide care for more than two children at a time. To comply with state law, a person who provides care for up to six children in his or her home—officially called a family day-care home—must be registered with Bright From the Start: Georgia Department of Early Care and Learning.

Persons operating businesses caring for more than six children must obtain licenses. Such businesses fall within two categories: group day-care homes, which provide supervision and care for 7 to 18 children either in a home or another location, and day-care centers, which provide care and supervision for 19 or more children. To be certified or licensed, the operator of a child-care business must be at least 21 years old, have a high-school or general-equivalency diploma, and pass criminal background and fingerprinting checks. They must have completed training in first aid and in infant and child cardiopulmonary resuscitation, and they must annually undergo 10 hours of continuing education in health and safety and child development.

When you're shopping for child care, make sure the provider you're dealing with is registered with or licensed by the state. Take a good look at the facility you're visiting: Ascertain that the inspection data on the fire extinguisher is current, that the smoke alarm and telephone operate properly, and that rooms are in good repair, well lit, and spacious. Check to see if instructions involving fire drills and other emergency procedures are posted. Ask about the program offered—it should provide age-appropriate toys and activities that encourage children to use their five senses.

As of October 2005, there were 415 family day-care homes and a total of 132 group day-care homes and day-care centers operating in Chatham County. They offer a wide variety of care—everything from the legal minimum to operations featuring state-funded and private prekindergarten programs, field trips, and other extracurricular activities, plus food programs that serve balanced meals.

Child Care Resource and Referral Agency of Coastal Georgia
7395 Hodgson Memorial Drive
(912) 925-7575, (877) 935-7575
www.cc4children.net
A great way to start your quest for the child care that meets your needs is by calling the Child Care Resource and Referral Agency of the Coastal Coalition for Children. This agency serves a nine-county area in coastal Georgia and assists parents searching for child care by presenting them with lists of referrals of licensed and registered child-care providers. Parents are also provided with information on how to choose quality child care, and these services are provided at no cost to families.

Parenting counseling is also available from Lutheran Ministries, which administers the A+ Parents program. This program provides support for people striving to be good parents and is a collaborative effort of Lutheran Ministries and the University of Georgia Extension Service in Chatham County. Lutheran Ministries is located at 6555 Abercorn Street and can be reached by calling (912) 355-0771.

Babysitting Services

Vacationers in need of babysitting or drop-in child-care services should speak to the concierge or desk clerk at their hotel, motel, or inn. Most establishments have lists of child-care providers who offer short-term services.

HEALTH CARE **H**

Savannah has experienced the good fortune of being a magnet for medical care almost since its founding in 1733. According to historians Preston Russell and Barbara Hines, the city's "first civic hero" was a physician, Dr. Samuel Nunes Ribeiro, who was among a boatload of Portuguese Jews who came to the town about five months after Savannah was settled. Georgia's founder, James Oglethorpe, credited Nunez, as he became known, with saving the colonists from the fevers that had killed several of them, including the only other doctor, William Cox.

The city was the site of Georgia's first hospital, a facility incorporated in 1808, and since the mid-1950s Savannah has been served by three large hospitals, two of which merged into a single health-care system in the spring of 1997. The other hospital, Memorial Health University Medical Center, is the regional tertiary medical center, a circumstance that draws many medical specialists to the area. It's also going into the doctor-production business: Memorial announced in 2007 that it is expanding its residency program with Mercer University School of Medicine in Macon to a full four-year medical school—a satellite of Mercer's existing one—by the 2008–09 academic year.

The latest available statistics involving health care indicate that Chatham County is the home of 635 physicians, giving the area a ratio of 1 medical doctor for every 365 residents. Georgia's first public health agencies were established in Savannah more than 100 years ago to combat yellow fever and improve the health of poor children. Since then, public health services have been expanded to offer preventive health services to all residents of the area and to provide primary care to those who do not have private physicians.

About the only medical services not available locally are transplant surgery and the long-term treatment of serious burns.

HOSPITALS

Memorial University Medical Center
4700 Waters Avenue
(912) 350-8000
www.memorialhealth.com
This 530-bed hospital in Savannah's Midtown offers tertiary care to residents of 35 counties in southeast Georgia and southern South Carolina. In this role, Memorial provides the region with several one-of-a-kind facilities and services, including the area's only pediatric intensive care unit (part of The Backus Children's Hospital), the only perinatal testing center, the only emergency helicopter service (LifeStarOne), the only ambulance specially equipped for sick newborns (Angel 3), and the only Level 1 trauma center, meaning the medical center offers extensive, immediate, round-the-clock services for emergency, life-threatening needs.

Memorial's Women's Health Institute is one of only six perinatal centers in Georgia, and the Neonatal Intensive Care Nursery is among only six in the state. The hospital's Curtis and Elizabeth Anderson Cancer Institute is southeast Georgia's referral source for cancer treatment, and its Heart and Vascular Institute is the regional coordinator of comprehensive cardiovascular services. Memorial's 50-acre campus is also the site of the Georgia Eye Institute, the Georgia Ear Institute, and The Rehabilitation Institute, which provides a comprehensive regimen of services for people recovering from illnesses and injuries.

Memorial opened in 1955 as a 300-bed general hospital. As a regional referral center, it now ranks in size among the top 5 percent i Free blood pressure checks are available daily at the city of Savannah's 14 fire stations and at the Southside Fire Department's stations.

of hospitals in the United States and employs more than 4,000 people, with about 1,000 of those working for CareOne, Memorial's home-care organization. CareOne brings home care to patients in 37 counties throughout southeastern Georgia and southern South Carolina, with its nurses providing services ranging from giving simple medications to highly technical care. Memorial is also a teaching hospital, and its name was changed in 1999 from Memorial Medical Center to reflect a closer connection with Mercer University School of Medicine in Macon, Georgia. Another feature of the medical center is its physician network of 35 practices for family doctors, internists, and other specialists.

St. Joseph's/Candler Health System

This health-care system was created in April 1997 as the result of the merger of Savannah's two oldest hospitals, 305-bed St. Joseph's on the Southside and 331-bed Candler in Midtown. The system offers general services and a wide range of specialized care, with St. Joseph's specializing in cardiovascular, oncology, and neurological services and orthopedics, and Candler specializing in oncology, pulmonology, outpatient surgery, the treatment of digestive diseases, and women's and children's services. Candler's Telfair Hospital is the area's only hospital dedicated to women. (By the way, there are only three general hospitals in Savannah: the Telfair Hospital at Candler, like the Backus Children's Hospital at Memorial, is merely a part of the larger hospital.)

In 1998 St. Joseph's/Candler opened The Children's Place on the campus of Candler Hospital. This pediatric acute-care program serves the special needs of sick children and their concerned parents. The Children's Place

utilizes a "kid-friendly" decorative theme in which each unit is adorned in primary colors from floor to ceiling. The hospital also offers "Bearly Sick," open to employees' children and to some extent to a larger public, child care services for mildly ill children who are too sick to go to school or day care. Also in 1998, the health system introduced its Care Call Center, which enables you to obtain a physician referral and information about treating minor health problems by dialing (912) 819-3360. A major addition to the system is the Nancy and J. C. Lewis Cancer and Research Pavilion, a $24 million, freestanding facility that opened in January 2005. The pavilion, located on Reynolds Street across from Candler, provides subspecialty cancer care and specialized research.

Beyond these hospital services, the system maintains a presence in almost every community in southeast Georgia via its network of primary-care physicians.

St. Joseph's Hospital
11705 Mercy Boulevard
(912) 819-4100
www.stjosephs-candler.org
This general acute-care hospital dates from 1875 when the Sisters of Mercy of the Roman Catholic Church took over operation of the Forest City Marine Hospital, a facility in downtown Savannah that specialized in the treatment of sick seamen. A year later the operation was moved to more spacious facilities at Taylor and Habersham Streets and was renamed St. Joseph's Infirmary. It was named St. Joseph's Hospital in 1901 and expanded several times before a new facility was built on the Southside in 1970.

In the years between the move south and the merger with Candler, St. Joseph's accomplished a $7 million expansion of its Emergency and Outpatient Building and opened its Sports Medicine Center, Multiple Sclerosis Clinic, and Diabetes Management Center. The hospital is situated on 28 acres and is affiliated with the Mayo Clinic Jacksonville and Nemours Children's Hospital in north Florida.

Close-up

Emergency Services

If you have an emergency or need general information about community resources, here are agencies you can contact. For emergencies requiring ambulance, police, or fire departments, call 911.

Alcoholics Anonymous	(912) 398-2977
Crime Stoppers	(912) 234-2020
First Call for Help	(912) 651-7730
Georgia Medical Society	(912) 355-6607
Helpline Georgia (crisis line)	(800) 338-6745
Poison Hotline Center	(800) 282-5846
Rape Crisis Center	(912) 233-7273
Safe Shelter	(912) 234-9999
Savannah Runaway Home	(912) 234-4048

Candler Hospital
5353 Reynolds Street
(912) 692-6000
www.stjosephs-candler.org
One of the longest continually operating hospitals in the United States and the first in Georgia, Candler was founded in 1805 and chartered in 1808 as the Savannah Poor House and Hospital. A new facility of the same name was built on Gaston Street in 1819, used as a Confederate hospital during the Civil War, and renamed Savannah Hospital in 1872. The first school of nursing in Savannah was established there in 1902, and 28 years later the Methodist Episcopal Church purchased the hospital from the city and renamed it Warren A. Candler Hospital in honor of one of its bishops.

During the 1960s, the hospital was renamed Candler General Hospital and expanded through the purchase of the Telfair Hospital (which became its obstetrical unit) and the Central of Georgia Railway Hospital. Construction of a new hospital at DeRenne Avenue and Reynolds Street began in fall 1978, and it was opened in late 1980. Its name was changed to Candler Hospital in 1992, with the word General being dropped to reflect the hospital's growth in specialized health-care services. Candler is affiliated with the Emory University System of Health Care.

PHYSICIAN REFERRAL SERVICES

Savannah has two services you can contact for help in finding doctors and obtaining free information about hospital services and your health. They are the Care Call Center at (912) 819-3360 and NurseOne at (912) 350-9355.

WALK-IN CLINICS

If you find yourself in need of medical care during your visit to Savannah, there are clinics where you can obtain treatment without having an appointment. These facilities are in addition to the emergency rooms at the three local hospitals.

Immediate Med
10410 Abercorn Street
(912) 927-6832
Immediate Med handles minor emergencies and comprehensive family medical care at its clinic in the Southside on Abercorn Street. The clinic is open from 9:00 a.m. to 9:00 p.m. every day except Sunday, when the hours are from 1:00 to 9:00 p.m. (Note that hours change from time to time; call ahead.) Major credit cards are honored, but Medicare and Medicaid are not accepted.

UrgentOne – Savannah Mall
14089 Abercorn Street
(912) 350-2121

UrgentOne – Godley Station
110 Medical Park Drive
(912) 748-1515
Memorial University Medical Center is the hospital behind these organizations. They offer physicians to handle urgent medical problems—the non-life-threatening kind. Hours are 9:00 a.m. to 9:00 p.m. daily, although we recommend calling to make sure nothing has changed. Note that the Savannah Mall location, in an outparcel location beside the mall, is on Savannah's far Southside, while the Godley Station location is in Pooler, one of the municipalities in the western part of the county.

HOSPICE CARE

Several organizations in Savannah offer specialized care for the terminally ill and assistance to members of their families, such as respite care and bereavement counseling. Hospice Savannah, which introduced this type of care to the area in 1980, provides living quarters for patients who cannot be cared for at home, as do Spanish Oaks Retreat and Heritage Park of Savannah. The three local

i The Georgia Infirmary, a day health center for disabled adults and the elderly, has played a unique role in the nation's health-care history. The center at 1900 Abercorn Street was the United States' first hospital for African Americans and the country's first training center for African-American nurses.

options for hospice care provide essentially the same services. They are Hospice Savannah Inc., 1352 Eisenhower Drive (912-355-2289), Spanish Oaks Retreat, 8510 Whitefield Avenue (912-356-0234), and Heritage Park of Savannah, 12825 White Bluff Road (912-927-9416).

COMPLEMENTARY MEDICINE

Although it's nowhere near a hotbed of complementary medicine, Savannah shows signs of beginning to catch on to this style of healing. More than two decades ago, at least one physician in town was practicing nutritional medicine, but an awareness of and growth in complementary medicine took shape in the 1990s. Now, there are a handful of full-fledged acupuncturists available and several medical doctors learning acupuncture techniques. You can avail yourself of the services of a slew of chiropractors, and there are also practitioners of osteopathy, herbal medicine, massage therapy, aromatherapy, and shiatsu (Japanese pressure-point massage).

If you're looking for practitioners of complementary medicine, a good place to start is the Brighter Day natural foods and organic produce store at Bull and Park Streets. Owners Peter and Janie Brodhead don't make recommendations pertaining to practitioners, but they do maintain a "community bulletin board" that might steer you in the right direction.

MEDIA

Need to know something? Well, you're in luck. Savannah is well equipped in the media department. We've got a TV affiliate for each of the major networks, cable access everywhere except a few remaining spots in the boondocks, radio stations in formats from country to classical, a daily newspaper, and several weeklies, monthlies, and specialty publications, even a city magazine.

To go along with this, Savannah has a solid journalism tradition. In the early 1980s, a now-defunct weekly won the Pulitzer Prize in editorial writing. In the days when such things were economically possible, there were competing daily newspapers in Savannah, and desktop publishing and niche markets periodically keep some variety moving in the print world.

As for TV, when you add all the morning, midday, evening, and night local newscasts up, they total at least 10 hours each weekday (and it keeps growing). Savannah has joined national media trends with absentee corporate ownership. The last locally owned television station was sold in 1998, meaning that all the major daily print and television media outlets now are owned by companies headquartered elsewhere. Radio has joined the trend. With a handful of exceptions—one independent holdout, two college stations, a public radio affiliate, some AM residue—three national corporations own all local FM radio stations.

NEWSPAPERS
Dailies

In addition to the *Savannah Morning News*, you can also get daily delivery of the *Wall Street Journal* and the *New York Times* (depending on which neighborhood you live

in). Ironically, however, you can't get home delivery of the *Atlanta Journal-Constitution*, the major paper from the state capital, in most neighborhoods, but you can buy it at convenience stores, newsstands, and vending boxes. (Check our Shopping chapter for info on where to get really out-of-town newspapers.)

Savannah Morning News
1375 Chatham Parkway
(912) 236-9511
www.savannahnow.com

Savannah's daily newspaper is the *Savannah Morning News.* It's part of Morris Communications, which owns several other Georgia papers (in Athens and Augusta, where the company is headquartered) as well as Jacksonville's *Florida Times-Union* and a host of other newspapers and publications.

Don't be confused if you hear the paper called the *News-Press.* Until 1996, the same company put out the *Savannah Evening Press,* and the combined weekend editions were known as the *News-Press.* The *Press* may be several years dead, but habit dies hard in Savannah and we still use the name from time to time.

Recent years have seen an emphasis on modern design and less focus on breaking hard news. Regular readers know where to find the regular features—the automotive section on Saturday, food coverage on Wednesday, a pullout entertainment tabloid called *Diversions* on Thursday, and lots of special sections on Sunday. Cost is 50 cents for single copies daily ($1.25 Sundays) and $14.00 monthly for home delivery.

The editorial pages feature a mix of local and nationally syndicated columns, but the real star of these pages is editorial cartoonist

Mark Streeter, who takes on local, national, and international topics with razor-sharp points, humor, and humanity.

A popular feature is "Vox Populi," consisting of a selection of anonymous phoned-in comments that are alternately rants and raves, reasoned commentary, whimsical observations, or frightening evidence of social disintegration.

Diversions, a tabloid that runs every Thursday, includes listings on everything from what movies are playing in local theaters to concerts, gallery exhibits, and more. A favorable review of a restaurant in *Diversions* will pack the place for a while.

Monday's edition usually includes a map showing locations of local reported crimes from a couple weeks previously.

The *Morning News* puts a lot of effort into its Web site, www.savannahnow.com, as well. Included here is a feature portion where people can post their own photos from events.

The Closeups are a selection of weekly neighborhood newspapers published as sections in the regular paper (*The Islands Closeup, The Intown Closeup,* etc.) for subscribers in those areas.

The *Morning News* moved to plush new quarters on the city's developing western suburb in late 2004. Facilities include a large lecture hall where the paper occasionally hosts public forums and lectures.

Ethnic Newspapers

Savannah has two weekly newspapers devoted to covering the African-American community. These papers had their roots in the days of segregation, when mainstream papers did not cover the black community. As that has changed, these papers have evolved. Although they still have news content—often of social events, church activities, achievement, or coverage of the historically black Savannah State University—they also devote a large portion of their pages to political commentary and opinion columns. Of the two papers, the *Herald* is the dominant.

i Looking for work? The serious job ads are in Sunday's *Morning News*—the weekday stuff is pretty run-of-the-mill. You might also want to track down one of the city's two African-American newspapers. Companies that are meeting corporate affirmative action commitments often make a special effort to advertise in those publications.

Savannah Herald
1803 Barnard Street
(912) 232-4505
This weekly newspaper was founded in 1945. The *Herald*'s motto is "Publishing Positive News for and about Savannah's African-American Community." Inside you will find local news stories, church news, sports, and editorials.

In "Around Town," columnist Jettie Adams fills people in on a variety of subjects, like who is having a birthday and the accomplishments of local children. The *Savannah Herald* is published on Wednesday, when 8,500 copies are distributed. Subscriptions are by mail, and the paper sells in vending boxes throughout town. Copies are also distributed at the larger African-American churches.

The Savannah Tribune
916 Montgomery Street
(912) 233-6128
The *Tribune*, as it is known, is Savannah's other weekly newspaper devoted to the black community. Publisher and Editor Shirley B. James includes local, state, and sometimes national items pertaining to African Americans. The *Tribune* is published on Wednesday. Subscriptions are predominantly by mail but it does have boxes as well.

Other Newspapers
The Business Report and Journal
340 Eisenhower Drive, Suite 240
(912) 351-9122
www.savdailynews.com
This weekly business niche newspaper was

launched in May 1998 and publishes every Monday in tabloid format.

Subscriptions are $44 a year. Single copies are $1 and are available at the newspaper office, a scattering of vending boxes, and restaurants and newsstands in the business district.

The publication is regional, covering 11 coastal Georgia counties and Hilton Head Island and Beaufort in South Carolina. It is written by a mixture of staff and freelance writers. Local nonprofits are covered as well as business news.

In 2007 this paper expanded its Web site and renamed it www.savdailynews.com—a site updated daily and expanded beyond the print version's business-only content. The publisher refers to this "virtual" newspaper, which does not appear in print format, as a daily "news(paper)."

Coastal Antiques and Art
1375 Chatham Parkway
(912) 236-9511

This monthly tabloid, distributed free throughout town, was purchased by the *Savannah Morning News*'s parent company in 1999. The ads are more useful than the editorial content if you are antiquing in Savannah.

Coastal Family
340 Eisenhower Drive, Suite 240
(912) 351-9122

In 1998 the same folks who put out the *Business Report* acquired this monthly devoted to such family-friendly content as parenting advice, coverage of schools, lessons and programs for children, and the like. It has evolved from essentially a press-release bulletin board to a monthly niche publication that's distributed free at area restaurants, various schools, physicians' offices, and stores that handle lots of kids' merchandise. It's also mailed to targeted households.

Coastal Senior
1375 Chatham Parkway
(912) 236-9511

This monthly publication, distributed free at racks throughout town, subtitles itself "Lifestyles of the 50+." Like its sister publication, *Coastal Antiques and Arts,* it was acquired by the *Morning News*'s parent company in 1999. Content is all geared toward older readers and includes advice columns from local physicians, schedules of senior-oriented events, and the like.

CONNECT Savannah
1800 East Victory Drive
(912) 238-2040
www.connectsavannah.com

This weekly newspaper is an alternative news voice, but its major focus is the entertainment and cultural scene. Expect some longer feature stories and a more outspoken editorial voice. Coverage here better serves younger, edgier readers. The format is tabloid, but it has a magazine-style cover to introduce its lead story. This publication conducts a very thorough, and apparently valid, readers'-favorite contest each year: If you are going to pay attention to posted brags like "Voted Best Sushi Restaurant," you're safer if you stick with this publication's version. *CONNECT Savannah* is available free at newspaper boxes, restaurants, and nightclubs. The Web site is particularly useful if you are looking for a quick rundown of what's happening on the entertainment front that particular evening.

La Voz Latina
5960 Ogeechee Road
(912) 925-7308
www.lavozlatinaonline.com

This monthly tabloid serves the growing Hispanic population of Savannah and surrounding region. The articles appear in both Spanish and English, although the ads are only in Spanish. (We loved the ones for Chinese restaurants.) Recent articles covered a string of robberies targeting Hispanics, gardening features, travel pieces, and coverage of local Hispanic organizations. *La Voz Latina* can be picked up free at a variety of locations—we find it at restaurants, both Mexican and otherwise.

i Want to read the latest without buying all these publications? Read the periodicals at any branch of the Live Oak Public Library. (You'll find more information on the library in our Arts and Culture chapter.)

MAGAZINES

Savannah Magazine
1375 Chatham Parkway
(912) 652-0291
Savannah Magazine is owned by Morris Communications, which also owns the city's daily paper, but it has its own staff. This slick, good-looking city magazine, which targets upper-middle-class and professional residents, is published eight times a year (every two months starting with January plus two other editions focusing exclusively on local interior design). The magazine was launched in the early 1990s, which means it has been around long enough to get all those tiresome stories about the 10 most eligible bachelors out of its system. Content is all local and ranges from pithy pieces such as the best lawyers in town (can't you imagine what those who were left out had to say?) to soft decorating features. It also covers the city's charity festivals and other annual events—sort of like the old-time society pages with better production values—and carries a regular listing of city events of all types.

Skirt!
1375 Chatham Parkway
(912) 525-0741
www.skirtmag.com
A Savannah/Beaufort/Bluffton/Hilton Head edition of this magazine showed up on the local scene a couple of years ago, one of the several different publications from the same people who bring you the *Savannah Morning News*. It's aimed at women—intelligent, well-heeled women who like to shop. At first glance, this publication appears extremely lightweight, but there is espresso beneath that froth. The articles are hyper-short, the

photos are big, and the essays tend to meditative pieces on self-discovery, all put together with a more liberal flavor than is typical in Savannah. But the ads share the stage in this publication (and you know how painful it must be for a writer to acknowledge that!). Those ads cover Savannah's retail scene with surprising thoroughness, provided you are looking for trendy stuff and are not on a budget. The monthly mag, produced in a supertab format on heavy newsprint, is available free at a wide range of shops.

The South Magazine
116A Bull Street
www.thesouthmag.com
Publisher Michael Brooks launched this bimonthly magazine in 2006. It's a glossier, edgier city magazine than the established city magazine against which it is competing. The target audience here is just as monied as that of *Savannah Magazine*, but also younger. The magazine draws heavily on Savannah College of Art and Design graduates, and the result is a dramatic showcase for photographic work. We admit we don't always get the fashion spreads, but perhaps that is the point since we are neither young nor rich. Stories range from personality profiles to meditative pieces on Confederate history and its modern-day devotees. The writing is good, but it is often upstaged by the design and photography, which are clearly in the driver's seat. Expensive real estate predominates in the advertisements, at least in 2007. Subscriptions are $19.00 a year, but you can pick up single copies at a wide range of local outlets for $3.95 an issue. Like its older competition, this publication comes out every two months—but its management cleverly picked to publish on the competition's off months. In other words, there's a February/March issue, instead of a January/February, etc. The Web version is a pretty complete reflection of the print product.

i The Savannah *Pennysaver* is a "shopper"— an ad-oriented publication with little or no editorial content. It gets tossed on just about every lawn in town Wednesday night and is especially valued for its garage-sale ads and lists of miscellaneous merchandise for sale: exercise machines, collector's dolls, used appliances, whatever. We aren't making this up: We really did once spot an ad in there offering to sell a parrot or trade it for a boat motor.

Rodale's Scuba Diving
6600 Abercorn Street
(912) 351-0855
www.scubadiving.com
This national magazine doesn't have any particular connection to Savannah (although we do have a dive community, of course), but we wanted to show that the city has a national presence on the publishing scene! The editorial and advertising departments are based here. This monthly covers anything and everything about scuba diving—adventure travel, diving techniques, health and fitness, etc.

TELEVISION

Remember those 10 daily hours of television news programming we mentioned earlier? They can lead to some strange newscasts, since many days, well, there isn't that much happening. As a result, sometimes the evening news looks like a televised version of a weekly newspaper, complete with stories about unusually large vegetables and congratulations to couples celebrating their golden wedding anniversaries. But let's not sell local efforts short—they also have mobile vans for live broadcasts off-site, generally good production values, and a willingness to cut into regular programming when real news breaks.

Weather coverage is particularly strong here—and a good thing, too, since the local National Weather Service (NWS) office fell victim to federal budget cuts several years ago,

and the nearest NWS location is now in Charleston. Stations give their meteorologists good equipment and ample air time. After all, outdoor lifestyles are the norm here, and we do live in a region of "active" weather. Want to see a news team drool with excitement? Just pick a station—any station—and tune in when the area is under a hurricane watch.

The newscast personalities are local celebrities, and they are generous with their time, visiting schools, taping public service announcements, and the like. The area is also served by small channels carrying such networks as the WB, UPN, etc., but since they do not maintain local news or other local programming operations, they are not discussed individually.

Notice that in the following listings the channel numbers are broadcast channels. If you are on a cable system—and most people here are—the channel numbers are different, but we've included the broadcast numbers so you'll know what people mean when they say "22 was at our wreck today" or "Was 11 there?" Comcast is the area cable provider (912-354-7531), having recently acquired a couple of smaller, neighborhood-specific systems.

WJCL—ABC (Channel 22)
WTGS—Fox (Channel 28)
10001 Abercorn Street
(912) 925-0022
These stations are jointly managed but separately owned. Traditionally the weakest player in local news broadcasts, the stations have been devoting more effort to news in the last few years. The network affiliations are a clue to what you'll find in handling of local direction. The Fox affiliate, for example, airs its late news at 10:00 p.m. instead of the more traditional 11:00 p.m.

WSAV—NBC (Channel 3)
1430 East Victory Drive
(912) 651-0300
WSAV is the city's major runner-up in the news race and has spent quite a bit of time

and money tinkering with its program. The newscast tends to be younger, and the content played more dramatically. The early morning newscast is a particularly good example of folksy without being overly cutesy.

WTOC–CBS (Channel 11)
11 The News Place
(912) 234-1111

This station has been the news ratings leader so long, it calls its 6:00 p.m. broadcast—both arrogantly and accurately—"THE News." While the demographics may be aging slightly, the station still holds a ratings lead. This station also runs a solid 90 minutes of local evening news that serves to remind that one of the virtues of news is that it is selective, not exhaustive. Much of the vast news hole winds up being filled with the likes of a syndicated cooking feature, canned consumer features on comparison shopping for this and that, and perky "brights" about the teen-of-the-week and the "Hometown Hero," along with occasional editorials so vehemently conservative they border on self-parody. Still, it has the biggest news staff among the local TV stations and can generally be counted on to get local breaking news quickly.

WVAN–PBS (Channel 9)
260 14th Street NW
Atlanta
(800) 222-6006

While airing the more familiar offerings, such as Sesame Street and NOVA, this PBS station also runs some very interesting local programming (on Georgia history, B&Bs, and such) in cooperation with its Georgia affiliate, Peach State Public Television.

RADIO

Radio isn't a serious player in the news game in Savannah. Where once the local media pack included radio reporters, they are all now either rip-'n'-reads out of the daily paper or making use of clearly promotional guest appearances from one of the television news teams. The only exception is the local public radio, WSVH at 91.1 FM.

The Savannah radio scene is experiencing some interesting developments, thanks to technology. Curiously enough, those developments are coming from its least commercial sectors. Consider HDRadio, the proprietary format where technology allows an FM station to parse its signal into up to three distinct stations, which can be received only by those who have specially equipped radios. That technology has made inroads mainly in major metropolitan areas and on a fairly limited scale. In Savannah, so far the only investor is a noncommercial religious station, HIS Radio at 91.9 FM.

The other interesting development is in Savannah College of Art and Design's (SCAD) Internet radio. One of the best things about working on a book like this is that it forces us to try things we ordinarily wouldn't bother with. We confess to a little age-related bigotry here—we assumed a SCAD Internet station would be both hard to hear and hard to listen to. We found out we were wrong when we were forced to actually check it out before writing about it. We went to www.scadradio.org and, despite the fact that we are not particularly technology-literate, managed to get hooked up with the station. And whaddaya know, where we were expecting something culturally unrecognizable to us as music, we found bluegrass! The station covers a wide range of music, not in some indigestible mixture, but in hour-or-more genre clumps. We like some, we don't like others, but it's great to hear live DJs. Turns out they're all students and all working for free. There's no commercials, just campus public service announcements put together by a creative student staff. We actually keep it on our computer and listen in occasionally while working. For one thing, it's a way to keep some awareness of what's going on at SCAD—a major part of life in Savannah, but also a separate universe that doesn't intersect all that often with those of us who live here full time.

If you are looking for entertainment, not news, the radio dial here can meet your ℹ️ Jerry Rogers operates the only locally owned FM radio station in town, WRHQ, where he regularly works a shift as DJ on the classic-rock-format station.

needs. The formatting is conventional, and at the moment is dominated by various versions of "oldies." One exception would be Savannah State University, which offers the only local broadcast college radio station (90.3 FM) and provides an interesting mix of jazz, hip-hop, alternative, and more eclectic stuff if you get tired of the tried-and-tested radio out there. Note that it is a low-power station and can be hard to tune in, so be patient. Another exception is Jerry Rogers' WRHQ, the only remaining locally owned FM station. Its playlist is sort of light rock/occasional oldies/a light touch of local groups/some new stuff—all perhaps best characterized by the format "stuff Jerry likes."

Adult Contemporary/Soft Rock
WAEV 97.3 FM
WYKZ 98.7 FM
WRHQ 105.3 FM

Various Oldies Formats
WGCO 98.3
WLOW 107.9 College Radio
WHCJ 90.3 FM
(Savannah State University)

Country
WJCL 96.5 FM
WGZR 106.9 FM

Gospel
WSOK 1230 AM
WJLG 900 AM
WHGM 1400 AM

Talk/News/Sports
WTKS 1290 AM
WBMQ 630 AM
WFXH 1130 AM

Top 40
WZAT 102.1 FM

Public Radio
WSVH 91.1 FM

Rock
WFXH 106.1 FM
WIXV 95.5 FM

Urban Contemporary/R&B
WQBT 94.1 FM
WLVH 101.1 FM (soft/oldies)
WEAS 93.1 FM
WWVV 104.9 FM (Blues, beach music, and jazz)
WTYB 103.9 FM

RETIREMENT

Savannah's moderate climate, recreational resources, and the other charms that make the city attractive to visitors are particularly important to retirees. Savannah is home to a large population of senior citizens—some with families that have been here for generations, others who have chosen this area specifically as their retirement getaway.

Recreational opportunities for the active retiree abound, from the opportunity to play golf virtually year-round on a variety of courses to sailing opportunities that are attractive, plentiful, and challenging enough to have landed the city Olympic venue status. Social opportunities are plentiful also, with a variety of organizations tailoring their offerings strictly to older members. Those who are eager to explore new educational horizons have the resources of area universities and their related programs.

Services for the changing needs of an elderly population are in place in Savannah, and they are growing in scope as the demand increases. If you have family members who are likely to need assistance with household chores or daily supervision because of Alzheimer's disease, programs are available to help both them and you. Expanded transportation, meal, and utility programs have been established to serve the elderly who need additional help.

SENIOR HOUSING OPTIONS

Savannah, like almost any other American city, has its full complement of nursing homes. As baby boomers and their parents age, however, the trend across the country includes residential options that provide a degree of support while stopping well short of the custodial/medical role of the classic nursing home. Some may be apartment complexes catering to older residents, while others offer a full "continuum of care" program where residents live independently in a complex's houses or apartments and, as their needs increase, move on to the complex's assisted-living quarters or on-site nursing home (usually marketed under more attractive terms, such as "skilled-nursing facility"). The personal-care home, which closely approaches the nursing home, is another in this new breed of senior housing options.

The broader spectrum of options began cropping up in Savannah about 20 years ago. This has been a real growth industry in the past few years here, but only recently did the upper end of the range—a full-scale continuing-care retirement community (CCRC) complete with capital investment requirements—launch here.

These types of housing options tend to fall at the extremes of the income range, with provisions for the lowest-income seniors in public-housing high-rises on one end and luxurious private quarters with amenities and prices to match on the other, with not much middle ground.

For the purposes of this book, we selected three of the options for further discussion: one because it is the newest and plushest of the lot, reflecting a concept familiar to people relocating here from larger population centers; another because it pioneered such options here and has proven to be a popular choice for middle-class and higher incomes; and one because it provides more affordable options while maintaining lots of amenities and resident choices.

ℹ️ Savannah's movie theaters offer discount ticket prices to senior citizens.

The Marshes of Skidaway
50 Diamond Causeway
(912) 598-5030, (800) 889-6238
www.marshesofskidaway.com

This CCRC shares a socioeconomic rung with The Landings, Chatham County's first gated, golf course–oriented community, although there is no formal connection beyond the fact that the two developments are neighbors on Skidaway Island. For initial investments that range from $221,000 to $579,000 (depending on size/format of housing), residents buy a residential agreement in various designs of freestanding homes, duplexes, or apartments. When residents die or relocate, the bulk of the investment (given certain conditions) is returned to the resident or estate. The facility offers assisted-living options and a nursing home.

A set monthly fee buys residents a broad array of amenities, including dining privileges in one of four dining rooms, maintenance, utilities, spa and pool access, scheduled activities, etc.

Construction began in 2003, and the first residents moved in in 2005.

Savannah Square Retirement Community
One Savannah Square Drive
(912) 927-7550
www.savannahsquare.net

This facility began offering independent-living, assisted-living, and skilled-nursing housing options in 1990. Financial arrangements call for a $500 deposit and month-to-month leases for apartments and cottages at rates ranging from $2,067 to $3,560. Amenities include communal dining, transportation, security, a library, a variety of community spaces, and other services. The facility covers a total of 15 acres and, between its apartments and cottages, incorporates 200 housing units.

Magnolia Manor on the Coast
141 Timber Trail
Richmond Hill
(912) 756-4300
www.magnoliamanor.com

This apartment complex for seniors emphasizes independence. There are 120 apartments in the three-story complex, which opened in 1990. Rents range from $1,520 for the one-bedroom, 600-square-foot units and go up to $1,920 for the 900-square-foot, two-bedroom units. Housekeeping and all utilities except telephone service are included. The dining room provides a midday meal that is designed to be the major meal of the day. Amenities include a full schedule of classes and activities, and the property includes a lakeside walking trail and other fitness options. A limited number of assisted-living units are available. It is affiliated with the Methodist church and offers a chapel and variety of spiritual activities, but is nondenominational and sets no religious requirements for eligibility. (Richmond Hill is a bedroom community just outside Savannah's Chatham County.)

SENIOR CITIZENS INC.

Think of this nonprofit organization, located at 3025 Bull Street (912-236-0363; www.senior citizens-inc.org) as a clearinghouse for senior services. Social and educational opportunities, as well as discounts provided by various merchants, are the primary benefits available to the younger segment of members. The range of services (some on a fee basis, others free or on sliding scales) runs all the way to home-delivered meals and utility assistance—whatever it takes to keep even frail and very low-income seniors independent as long as possible.

Senior Citizens derives much of its funding from federal grants, foundation donations, and personal bequests. It is also a participating member in the United Way of the Coastal Empire.

The next several listings provide information on Senior Citizens' offerings for active members of the retirement community. We follow those up with Senior Citizens' options that address social service needs.

Club 55
3025 Bull Street
(912) 236-0363

This separate suite within the Senior Citizens complex is designed as a social and educational center for all Senior Citizens' members. It includes meeting facilities, rooms for scheduled bridge games and other recreation, exercise facilities that include treadmills and other machines, computers for classes and Internet access, and a gathering place for health screenings, courses, and seminars on topics of interest to seniors. Dues are $12 annually. Current courses range from keyboarding to tap dancing to oil painting.

Merchants' Discounts

More than 170 participating merchants and service providers offer discounts to Senior Citizens' members (and many give price reductions to any senior citizen, member or not). Maintaining a current inventory of the very fluid list of participants and the terms of their discount offers has proven to be a pretty overwhelming challenge for the Senior Citizens' staff. Participating merchants are asked to display the Senior Citizens' logo where customers are likely to see it. If a freshly updated list isn't available when you join, and if you don't see a logo displayed by a merchant, the organization encourages you to show your membership card and ask if they participate in the program. After all, even if you don't have fixed-income problems, it's nice to pay less if you have the opportunity.

Ruth F. Byck Social Center
64 Jasper Street
(912) 234-6666

The Social Center's adult day-care program provides an option for families facing the hardships of caring for a loved one with Alzheimer's disease or similar chronic disor-

ders. Residents receive social interaction, exercise, and meals while family members are freed to go to work or take a break from constant care. The center is located at the rear of the Senior Citizens' complex.

Other Senior Citizens Inc. Services

Other services available to senior citizens in need include Meals on Wheels, which delivers hot lunches on weekdays; a transportation program; a Senior Companion program that offers a stipend to low-income seniors for assisting frail elderly persons they are paired with; social work assessment and advocacy; and the loan of fans and medical equipment. Senior Citizens Inc. programs make heavy use of volunteer labor, and active retirees are well represented among that corps of volunteers. To inquire about services or volunteer opportunities, call (912) 236-0363.

OTHER SENIOR SERVICES

Elderhostel
75 Federal Street
Boston, MA 02110
(617) 426-8056

Armstrong Atlantic State University
11935 Abercorn Street
(912) 921-5439

Savannah State University
P.O. Box 20523
Savannah, 31404
(912) 356-2253

Congregation Mickve Israel
20 East Gordon Street
(912) 233-1547

Elderhostel is a resource everyone age 55 or older who travels should become familiar with. It offers noncredit educational opportunities on a wide range of topics (and we do mean wide, from phonics to history to literature). Tuition is moderate, and arrangements are made for you to stay near the class site, usually in area motels. The program is generally arranged to allot time for classes, socializing, and taking in the various sights around the host location.

Elderhostel is a particularly thriving program in Savannah, where Armstrong Atlantic State University, Savannah State University, and Temple Mickve Israel/Jewish Educational Alliance all have course offerings that take particular advantage of the Savannah area setting. Other nearby units of Georgia's university system, such as Coastal Georgia Community College in Brunswick and Georgia Southern University in Statesboro, also participate.

Costs are moderate when you consider prices include motels, meals, and, in most cases, local transportation. The offerings we scanned ranged from $705 to over $1,000, with options that can add to the price. Preregistration is absolutely essential. Local residents can get discounts because they won't need the meals and lodging. They can register through the local addresses, but we really recommend you get the catalog and handle registration through the Massachusetts office.

Armstrong Atlantic's courses are based in two locations: at the university's Southside Savannah campus and on Tybee Island, Chatham County's beach municipality. Offerings are varied but tend to have musical themes. At Armstrong, the program has expanded into a Lifelong Learning Institute geared toward local membership. Courses are based at the Armstrong Center for Professional & Continuing Education, 11935 Abercorn Street.

Savannah State University has equally diverse offerings. The university's marshfront setting comes into play in a course on marine life of the Southeast, and other recent courses include Savannah history, phonics, and Gullah culture, which examines the language and African culture retained by a community of Lowcountry slave descendants. Among Savannah State's most popular Elderhostel offerings are its various jazz courses, taught by members of Savannah's thriving community of jazz musicians and scholars.

The courses sponsored by Mickve Israel tend to focus heavily on Jewish culture and history. The Mickve Israel congregation itself, as the oldest Jewish congregation in the South, is the focus of one course. Not all courses are centered on local topics, however. For example, check out "The Jewish Heritage of the American Musical."

Schedules change each quarter. Your best bet is to go to the www.elderhostel.org Web site and run a search on Savannah. Note that some courses involve Savannah teamed with other cities.

Retirement Services Office
Third Infantry Division (Mech.),
368 Hase Road
Ft. Stewart
(912) 767-3326
We've found that military retirees are well versed on the benefits they carry into retirement. They probably don't need a reminder that they retain shopping privileges at post exchanges and commissaries, and that there are active posts in Savannah for all the various military organizations. But those moving into or passing through the area might be pleased to know the extent of services available in the region, thanks to the major military presence here.

Hunter Army Air Field in Savannah is a subinstallation of Fort Stewart, which is about 40 miles southeast of the city. Some 4,300 soldiers are assigned to Hunter, and 16,000 are based at 279,000-acre Fort Stewart, the largest military installation east of the Mississippi. With that many personnel, you've got recreation facilities, and retirees have access to the Morale, Welfare, and Recreation programs at these installations. Although it is unlikely that many retirees are interested in the concerts staged for young

i The Live Oak Public Library offers records and cassettes of print items to those with vision problems and can also arrange to deliver items to homebound patrons. Call (912) 652-3600 for more information.

soldiers, they may well want to know about the golf courses, skeet shooting, movie theaters, and other activities and facilities at the two military reservations. Because it is far larger, many of these will be found at Fort Stewart in Hinesville, which is an accessible commute.

On the more serious side of things, Tuttle Army Health Clinic serves Hunter for primary and ambulatory care, and the larger, full-service Wynn Army Community Hospital is at Fort Stewart. The office listed at the head of this entry is largely concerned with such major tasks as straightening out retirement check problems or arranging veteran burials at sea, but personnel there can also provide information on other retiree services.

Hunter's main gate in Savannah is at White Bluff Road and Stephenson Avenue.

Hospital-Sponsored Clubs

Both of Savannah's two hospital systems offer special clubs to senior citizens, focusing not only on health care and wellness activities but also on education and social opportunities.

GenerationOne
7137 Hodgson Memorial Drive, Suite 12-B
(912) 350-7587
This club, sponsored by Memorial Health University Medical Center, offers health fairs and screenings, a member discount program, and visits to members hospitalized at Memorial. Classes in such areas as arts and crafts, line dancing, and bridge are scheduled, along with Senior Net computer classes and Internet access. Seminars are offered on health and retirement issues, healthy aging, and driver's safety. This group also has an active ongoing arrangement with a group-tour company. Eligibility begins at age 55. Membership is $12 per year.

SmartSenior
No. 8 Medical Arts Center
(912) 352-4405
This program of St. Joseph's/Candler Health System provides health seminars, educational

i State and local regulations give older property owners special exemptions on property taxes. Most, but not all, of the exemptions are keyed to income. If you are interested in purchasing a retirement home in Chatham County, learn more about your property tax status by calling the Tax Assessor's Office at (912) 652-7271.

programs, medical screenings, and visits to members hospitalized at either St. Joseph's Hospital or Candler Hospital. That may sound a bit stodgy, but it isn't—much of this group's activity is geared toward active retirees. There's a travel club that has gone from the Bahamas to Canada and points in between, ranging from two-week excursions to overnighters to catch an Atlanta Braves game. The holiday party is an enormous dine-and-dance bash. Activities scheduled throughout the year include tours of local industry, arts and crafts classes, and line dance lessons, for example. One of the unexpected annoyances that accompanies retirement is the loss of access to such office conveniences as a copier, and SmartSenior addresses that by providing free faxing, photocopying, notary services, and Internet access. In addition, the group provides member discounts at participating merchants. Annual dues are $12. Eligibility begins at age 55.

GOLDEN AGE AND OTHER SENIOR CENTERS

Golden Age Centers and Community Centers are daily gathering places that provide active senior citizens with an opportunity to participate in classes and other events. Lunches are served. The centers operated by the city of Savannah are known as Golden Age Centers. Senior Citizens Inc. operates three additional centers in arrangements with the municipalities of Garden City, Port Wentworth, and Thunderbolt. Pooler has its own center. All offer very similar programs.

The following is an alphabetical listing of The Golden Age Centers (all of them are area code 912): Cunningham Center, 121 East 36th Street (651-6779); Cuyler Center, 812 West 36th Street (651-6780); Frazier Center, 805 May Street (233-4796); Grant Center, 1310 Richard Street (651-6785); Savannah Gardens Center, 2500 Elgin Street (651-6775); Stillwell Towers Center, 5100 Waters Avenue (351-3855); Stubbs Towers Center, 1301 Bee Road (651-6776); Wimberly Center, 121 West 37th Street (651-6778); and Windsor Forest Center, 303 Briarcliff Circle (921-2104).

The three nearby community centers operated by Senior Citizens Inc. include the Garden City Center, 100 Main Street, Garden City (966-7791); the Port Wentworth Center, 100 Aberfeldy Street, Port Wentworth (964-5411); and the Thunderbolt Center, 3236 Russell Street, Thunderbolt (352-4846). The Pooler Center is at 100 West Collins Street, Pooler (964-5411).

WORSHIP

You won't have to look very far in Savannah for evidence that you are at least on the fringe of the Bible Belt—simply turn on a radio or television Sunday morning or stroll downtown, where you'll find normally stringently enforced parking regulations abandoned as suburbanites return to the downtown churches.

But don't let the label delude you into thinking you've wandered into a world of one-size-fits-all religion. Savannah is a city of great religious diversity, with more than 260 houses of worship that range from the splendor of a historic cathedral to the simple outreach of humble storefronts. You'll find the major denominations represented, along with other faiths that reflect the growing international community that comes to Savannah via the ports, local colleges, or seasonal agricultural needs for the nearby Vidalia onion harvest. You'll find out that religion in Savannah assumes a highly visible position in local life. Elsewhere, it might be unusual for a public meeting to begin with a brief prayer, but the practice still surfaces here from time to time and draws little, if any, public comment when it does.

Churches and synagogues are also active players in private education in Savannah. Not only is there a kindergarten through grade 12 Catholic school system—certainly not uncommon in any city with a significant Catholic population—but Baptist, Jewish, and Pentecostal congregations also sponsor private schools, along with other nondenominational Christian groups. (For information on many of these schools, see our Education and Child Care chapter.)

According to statistics compiled in the University of Georgia's *Georgia County Guide,* a third of Chatham County's population identifies itself with the Baptist faith. That identity covers a lot of ground, however, ranging from churches affiliated with the conservative Southern Baptist Convention to independent Baptist churches to those affiliated with historically African-American branches of the faith. The same survey shows roughly equal numbers of Catholics and United Methodists, each accounting for just more than 8 percent of the population. Smaller percentages are identified as belonging to other denominations or faiths, but the list contains no startling omissions. Local houses of worship include three synagogues (one each for Reform, Conservative, and Orthodox Jews) and a mosque.

Unlike several other of the original British colonies, Georgia cannot claim a religious motive for its founding. Instead, economic and social conditions were the driving force behind the settling of this, the thirteenth of the storied thirteen original colonies. Still, religion was a major part of Colonial life from the day Oglethorpe and his original settlers arrived (see our History chapter). The group was largely Anglican in its faith (no surprise there), but its charter provided for religious freedom—for the most part. Catholics were prohibited from settling in the colony in its early days, reflective of Georgia's early role as a military buffer between other English settlements to the north and the Catholic Spanish settlements in Florida.

That proviso about religious freedom got its first major test five months after the colony began. A shipload of mainly Spanish and Portuguese Jews, fleeing religious persecution in

> **i** John Wesley, a founding figure in the history of Methodism, is honored with a statue in Reynolds Square.

Spain, arrived in 1733. Whether the promised religious tolerance in the Georgia colony would have held up under normal circumstances is unclear, but this ship was made welcome—probably due, in no small part, to its showing up in the midst of a deadly fever epidemic with a doctor onboard. Thus, a Jewish community has roots that date back practically to the founding days of the colony. Temple Mickve Israel became the oldest congregation in the state of Georgia and is believed to be the third oldest in the nation (see our Attractions chapter for more on the temple).

Methodism, too, has deep historical roots in Savannah. John Wesley preached here in his Anglican days; he went on to become a founding father of the Methodist denomination.

The churches along the downtown Savannah squares house some of the oldest congregations in the country. Some members trace their membership back for generations; others have just moved to town. The buildings themselves are often historic, quite apart from their religious significance, but for the most part the congregations predate the current buildings. The earliest churches were destroyed by the fires that were a constant threat to the city in its earliest centuries.

Savannah's strongest claim to historical religious fame is in African-American history. Savannah is the founding point of the oldest black congregations in the country, and the two churches that sprang from slave roots—First Bryan Baptist Church and First African Baptist Church—are still active and influential participants in the city's spiritual and social life.

i The most elaborate of Savannah's many houses of worship is the Cathedral of St. John the Baptist, which you will find under those double steeples that command the skyline. A $5.3 million interior and exterior restoration project is complete, and this impressive structure is back in service, better than ever.

WHERE TO WORSHIP

Finding a spiritual match in an unfamiliar city is an important task that can be time consuming when you are relocating. If you are vacationing or staying for a short time, however, chances are you are more interested in simply continuing your usual religious observance while away from home. So, how does a spiritually observant traveler go about choosing a congregation to visit? Print media outlets provide several options in Savannah. The Savannah Morning News publishes a religion section every Saturday, and you'll find there a collection of religious news items, schedules of special events, and advertisements by various churches. The Herald, a weekly newspaper, provides detailed coverage of religious news in Savannah's African-American community. The Morning News (see our Media chapter) can be found in vending boxes all over town, especially around hotels and motels. You may have to look harder to find the Herald. It's in vending boxes in the downtown area, hospital lobbies, and major shopping centers, and you can call (912) 232-4505 to find out other locations. The Savannah Jewish News is a monthly publication serving Savannah's approximately 1,700 Jewish households. It is normally available by subscription only, but there's a good chance you can pick up a current copy at the Jewish Educational Alliance, 5111 Abercorn Street (912-355-8111).

New Age interests and other less-conventional spiritual paths are harder to track. You might check out the event columns of the Savannah edition of CONNECT Savannah, available free at a wide range of locations but especially copious at downtown restaurants and nightclubs.

Other good sources of info are the windows and bulletin boards of shops in the downtown area that sell New Age and nontraditional spiritual products (see our Shopping chapter), or stores that cater to a college-age population. This might seem a little hit or miss to you, but we've discovered that organizers

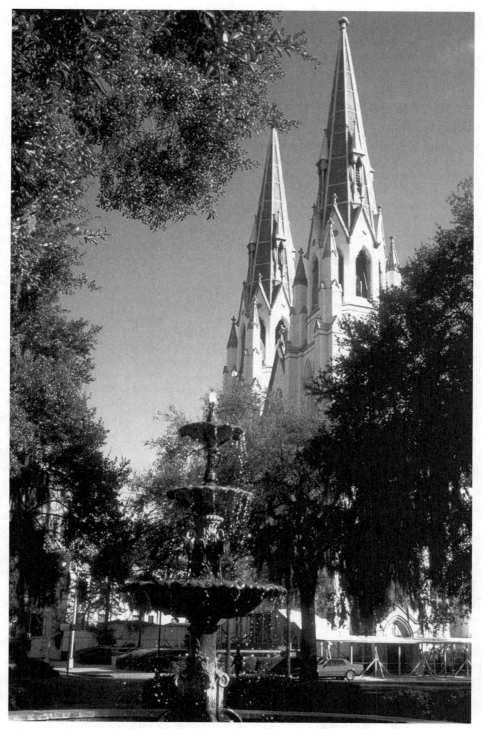

The twin steeples of the Cathedral of St. John the Baptist mark Savannah's skyline. KYLE CASON of such less-than-mainstream events are usually extremely diligent about getting flyers posted and word of events circulated.

SAMPLING SOMETHING DIFFERENT

If you are visiting Savannah, chances are good that you are staying in the downtown area. With that in mind, we scouted out some religious services in the Historic District that will enable you to carry on your worship habits while traveling, and still offer the chance to try something a bit different.

One of the newest developments in Savannah worship services is also one of the oldest. In 2005 historic Christ Church on Johnson Square instituted a candlelight Compline Service on Sunday night beginning at 9:00 p.m. It features a Compline choir assembled from within the church and from the community at large. In the dimly lighted sanctuary, a congregation gathers to hear organ selections and meditative chants, along with a brief sermon. Although the service is short, it draws heavily on introspection and silence, meaning it is probably not a good choice if you have young children in your group. An older audience would be more inclined to appreciate this special form of worship, which has its roots in ancient monasticism and which the church refers to as "saying good night to God."

Another new development in Savannah's religious life has been the growth of "contemporary" or "praise" services that are only loosely linked, if at all, to traditional denominations. These churches share many features: a willingness to embrace technology, emotional services that often call for active partici-

pation by the congregation, and lots of contemporary religious music, often using ensembles with percussion and brass. These congregations tend to be very large and, hence, located outside the downtown area for space considerations.

However, if you want to sample this type of service during your visit, try Savannah Christian Church's Late Church. Savannah Christian is well into the residential suburbs, but this Sunday-night service is staged downtown in the old Savannah Theatre, 222 Bull Street, in the heart of the Historic District. The church rents the space for its Late Church at 7:01 p.m. (yes, 7:01) and in fall of 2007 added a second service there at 11:01 a.m., saying that the evening service was at capacity. The target group is young adults and college students, but all are welcome. You can find out more at www.savannahchristian.com.

The two Sunday night services highlighted here show some of the contrasts you can find in Savannah's religious community, ranging from ultra-traditional to cutting-edge contemporary. If you are looking for daytime worship options, however, we suggest you follow your ears.

We asked our musical friends which churches they felt offered the most outstanding and uplifting sacred music. We had them focus on the geographic areas where visitors are likely to be staying and able to find their way around; that's why you'll note the predominance of downtown churches here. The list that follows is by no means comprehensive. Almost every church has music of some kind, and many play host to visiting singing groups. No doubt we've left some outstanding example off, but this brief list should give you a starting point.

A full carillon of bells can be heard beginning around 10:00 a.m. each Sunday morning, pealing out hymns from atop St. John's Episcopal Church, 1 West Macon Street, just off Bull Street. The church also has a good organ and choir. The Lutheran Church of the Ascension, 120 Bull Street, has what may be the largest organ in town, along with a fine choir.

i Savannah's churches are increasingly likely to offer services in languages other than English. Examples are a Korean Presbyterian Church, Catholic services in Vietnamese, and Baptist services in Spanish.

Wesley Monumental United Methodist Church, 429 Abercorn Street, boasts outstanding organ, choral, and even occasional handbell performances.

First Baptist Church at 223 Bull Street is known for its organ and choir. Bull Street Baptist Church, at the corner of Bull and Anderson Streets, has a wonderful pipe organ and choir. Farther south, another notable choir (accompanied by an electronic organ) sings at the White Bluff United Methodist Church at 11911 White Bluff Road.

If you are interested in religious architecture, you will want to check out at least three places: the Cathedral of St. John the Baptist (222 East Harris Street, corner of Harris and Abercorn Streets, www.savannahcathedral .com), Independent Presbyterian Church (207 Bull Street), and Congregation Mickve Israel (20 East Gordon Street, www.mickveisrael.org).

HILTON HEAD, SOUTH CAROLINA

INTRODUCTION/HISTORY

Something that strikes us when we're on Hilton Head Island—aside from the natural beauty of the place—is the relative newness of what has been built there. This becomes even more evident when the island is compared with the Historic Downtown of Savannah some 35 miles to the southwest, an area where much of what you see dates from the 1800s and early 1900s.

In contrast, most of the structures on Hilton Head are less than 60 years old, the result of two momentous events in the island's history that occurred in the mid-1950s. One was the opening of a set of two bridges connecting the 42-square-mile sea island with the South Carolina mainland. The other was the start of the Sea Pines residential/resort community by a southeast Georgian named Charles Fraser.

"The opening of the bridge had a major impact on development," states Porter M. Thompson in the book *Hilton Head Island Images*. "Suddenly building materials, equipment and people were able to come and go freely—Hilton Head had lost its isolation and a new era had begun."

Sea Pines, in its basic form a residential area built around a golf course, set the tone for the other planned communities that would be created on Hilton Head and spurred the development of the island as a mecca for retirees and vacationers. Back in the early 1950s, Hilton Head was home to about 100 families, "little more than a quiet community of farmers and shrimpers," as author Richard Rutt put it in *Hilton Head Island: A Perspective*. Now the island—with its natural assets of marshes, wide creeks, hardwood forests, and 12 miles of beach— is the site of 11 planned communities harboring a multitude

of stylish homes and upscale condominiums known locally as villas. Hilton Head boasts 25 beautifully manicured golf courses, almost 400 tennis courts, 10 marinas, 4 large hotels, a bevy of villa-style resorts and midsize hotels and motels, more than 250 restaurants, and 36 shopping areas with more than 200 shops. Permanent residents now number approximately 33,000, many of them engaged in satisfying the needs of visitors, of whom there are 2.5 million annually, according to the island's chamber of commerce.

All this growth has occurred in a manner that places an emphasis on preserving Hilton Head's natural surroundings: live oaks, magnolias, pines, palmettos, and other flora. Following ideas originally credited to Fraser, most islanders continue to adhere to the concept that buildings must blend in with the environment and that development be as unobtrusive as possible.

Although Hilton Head's modern era begins in the 1950s, the island's recorded history goes back considerably further—to the 1500s, when Spaniards and Frenchmen visited while exploring the area bordering Port Royal Sound, the large bay on Hilton Head's north shore that's one of the world's finest natural harbors. The Spanish and French fought over the sound for almost 50 years, with the Spaniards triumphing but never settling the area. That was left to the British, who in 1717 were responsible for the island's first English-speaking settler, John Barnwell.

Englishmen had been in the area well before that, however. In 1663 sea captain William Hilton sailed into the sound and came upon the island. He spotted a headland on the northeastern end and named it after himself. As time went on, the entire island came to be called by the name of this promontory, Hilton Head.

The settlers who came to Hilton Head in the 1700s eventually planted the land in cotton, indigo, sugarcane, rice, and other crops. They purchased slaves brought to America from Africa and used them to create large plantations. According to Richard Rutt, there were 24 plantations on the island by 1860, most of them producing cotton. Also by that time, South Carolina was on the verge of seceding from the Union and leading the South into the Civil War, a conflict in which Hilton Head would play an interesting part.

The island was invaded by Union troops on November 7, 1861, seven months after the war began, in an effort to control Port Royal Sound and establish a portion of the blockade of the Confederacy's Atlantic coast. In the Battle of Port Royal, a Union fleet of 15 warships and 31 transports and supply ships exchanged shots with 4 Confederate gunboats and 2 forts, one of them on Hilton Head. The Confederate guns were silenced, the forts were evacuated, and Union forces took possession of the island and held it until the end of the war.

The area near the fort on Hilton Head—called Fort Walker by the Southerners and renamed Fort Welles by its Federal conquerors—became a town during the Union occupation, when the population of Hilton Head mushroomed to 40,000. "Enlisted personnel—both soldiers and sailors—constituted the bulk of that population, or, 23–30,000 men," Rutt stated in his book. "The balance of Hilton Head's wartime population consisted primarily of freedmen who sought refuge on the island, civilian dependents, and Yankee tradesmen. The latter opened and operated a variety of business establishments, ranging from hotels, blacksmith shops, and theatres to photography studios, tattoo parlors, and bordellos."

The main street of the town, which was located in what is now Port Royal Plantation, was named Sutler's Row after the merchants who lined it. The military men who paid exorbitant prices for the sutlers' goods called it

i The town of Hilton Head's *Green Guide* asks that visitors help safeguard the island's flora and fauna by, among other things, staying off sand dunes and refraining from picking dune plants, feeding dolphins, or tampering with turtles' nests.

Robber's Row, the name now borne by one of the plantation's golf courses. Another settlement sprang up in what is now Hilton Head Plantation. It was called Mitchelville and consisted mostly of tents and barracks housing freed slaves who had fled to the island. When the war ended, the military and the sutlers left and, said Rutt, "the shops and houses of Robber's Row and Mitchelville rapidly disappeared from the island, no doubt torn down by freedmen seeking to build homes of their own."

From the end of the Civil War until the middle of the 20th century, Hilton Head was a sleepy sea island largely bypassed and forgotten by the rest of the world. All that began to change in 1950, when Fred Hack, C. C. Stebbins, and Lt. Gen. Joseph B. Fraser bought 8,000 acres of pine forest and formed the Hilton Head Company for the purpose of selectively cutting the pines. In 1956 the company's holdings were divided, with Fraser acquiring 4,000 acres on the southern end of the island. A year later Fraser's son Charles, a University of Georgia and Yale Law School graduate in his 20s, bought his family's holdings and another 1,200 acres and started planning and developing Sea Pines.

Meanwhile, Hack and O. T. McIntosh, who had purchased 12,000 acres on the northern end of the island in the early 1950s, began work on their own developments: Spanish Wells Plantation and Port Royal Plantation. (Sea Pines also used the term plantation in its name in its early years, as have many of the planned communities on the island; it refers to the antebellum plantations once located on the sites of the communities.)

"These few men," wrote Porter Thompson in referring to Fraser, Hack, McIntosh, and other developers, "began with the idea that large holdings of land could be subdivided into lots and sold for residential purposes. There was a twist to this. Hilton Head is ideally suited by climate and location for resort activity, so the communities developed would have to accommodate both resort and residential activities. It is Charles Fraser who is largely credited with first developing the concept that a resort/residential community could be successful, if a few considerations were made. He embodied two excellent and highly compatible interests: the understanding of development and a love of nature and of the natural beauty of the island."

Among the concepts advocated and practiced by Fraser were blending development with the environment, creating green spaces, keeping the density of housing as low as possible, cutting as few trees as necessary, and restricting the height of buildings so they were no taller than the tallest surrounding trees.

Under Fraser's direction, Sea Pines became, in the words of the Associated Press, "a big-time leisure landmark, a model for resort playgrounds and planned communities from Virginia to the Philippines." Other developers followed his lead, creating their own planned communities and, in the process, transforming Hilton Head into the world-renowned resort that it is today. Note that the island is virtually "built out" today. Just about the only vacant land is that set aside for green spaces, so new construction generally requires demolition of something that's already there. This has led to upscale development spilling off the island and onto the mainland, in the form of gated "plantation" housing, golf courses, and shopping centers. Although this Hilton Head "sprawl" is well outside the actual Bluffton, this area is called Bluffton.

GETTING THERE

Some people arrive at Hilton Head Island by boat or fly directly onto the island, but if you're like most visitors, you'll be coming by car, either from home in your own vehicle or from the Savannah International Airport in a rental. Whatever the case, here's how to get to the island.

By Car

Getting to Hilton Head by car is fairly simple because there's only one road onto the island, U.S. Highway 278, a four-lane that runs west to east through the South Carolina Lowcountry. Finding US 278 is no big deal, particularly if you're arriving at Savannah International Airport and renting a car for the 40-minute drive to the island (you can find information on flights to Savannah and car rentals in our main Getting Here, Getting Around chapter). US 278 is also easy to get to if you're coming from the south or north on Interstate 95, or if you're arriving from the west via Interstate 16 and I-95.

US 278 intersects I-95 just north of Hardeeville, South Carolina, so once you're on the interstate, all you have to do is watch for the exit for US 278 (exit 8). Take that exit and head east; it's an 18-mile straight shot to Hilton Head. You'll be on the island in 20 minutes and at the middle of it in about a half hour. To get to I-95 from Savannah International Airport, take Airways Avenue west for a little more than a mile to the interstate. Get on I-95 and head north into South Carolina. The US 278 exit is 16.5 miles up the interstate from where you left Airways Avenue.

If you're not renting a car, you can get to Hilton Head from the airport via the Gray Line Low Country Adventures Ltd. shuttle service. Low Country Adventures meets all incoming flights with private-ride or shared-ride shuttles; reservations are strongly recommended. Shared-ride fares from the airport to the island are $38 per person one-way and $66 round-trip, with multiple-passenger discounts available. You can reach Low Country Adventures at (843) 681-8212 or (800) 845-5582 or www.lowcountryadventures.com.

If you're visiting Savannah and want to pop over to Hilton Head for the day or spend a night on the island, you can drive there by following the I-95/US 278 route just discussed, or you can go the "back way." If you take the I-95/US 278 route, you'll be on multilane highways, and it will take about an hour and five minutes for you to get from Savannah City Hall to the Hilton Head Island Chamber of Commerce building at the middle of the island. (To get to I-95 from city hall, drive west on Bay Street through three traffic lights to Martin Luther King Jr. Boulevard, turn left onto MLK, and head south three traffic lights to the entrance ramp to I-16, then take I-16 west for 8.5 miles to I-95.)

The back way is shorter (about 55 minutes from city hall to the middle of Hilton Head), more scenic, and a little more complicated. It involves traveling on two-lane roads. If you want to try it, take Oglethorpe Avenue west to the Eugene Talmadge Memorial Bridge and drive north across the Savannah River into South Carolina. You'll be on U.S. Highway 17 for 5 miles from the South Carolina side of the bridge to the intersection of US 17 and Alternate South Carolina Highway 170. Turn right onto Alternate South Carolina Highway 170 and stay on it for 6 miles, where it merges with South Carolina Highway 46. Continue east on South Carolina Highway 46 for 12 miles to US 278. Turn right onto US 278 and head east—you'll be on the island in about five minutes. Along your way on South Carolina Highway 46 to US 278, you'll pass through piney woods, hardwood swamps, and the laid-back, offbeat little town of Bluffton with its Squat & Gobble restaurant and 30 mph speed limit (be sure to observe it). While in Bluffton, you'll come to a four-way stop; turn left to stay on South Carolina Highway 46. This route is an area of active, almost exponential, development, so you will be sharing the road with cement mixers and lumber trucks. Be careful and on your first trip, it's a good idea to plan to travel in daylight.

By Boat

If you're going to Hilton Head by boat, you can get there via the Intracoastal Waterway,

which runs along the west side of the island. There are several public marinas and harbors where you can tie up and enjoy your stay while aboard your vessel. These include Harbour Town Yacht Basin at Sea Pines (843-671-2704), Outdoor Resorts Yacht Basin at Intracoastal Waterway Marker 20 (843-681-3256), Palmetto Bay Marina at 86 Helmsman Way (843-785-3910, 800-448-3875), Shelter Cove Marina at Shelter Cove (843-842-7001), Skull Creek Marina at Hilton Head Plantation (843-681-8436), and Windmill Harbour (843-681-9235). The maximum length of the slips at these marinas ranges from 30 to 200 feet and the cost per night for docking runs from $1.00 per foot to $2.50 per foot, depending, in some cases, on the size of the vessel involved. Call ahead for specific details.

By Airplane

Hilton Head has its own airport on the north end of the island. The Hilton Head Airport is on Beach City Road, which runs north off US 278, the island's main drag. Beach City Road is at mile marker 4 on US 278, and the entrance to the airport is about a mile from US 278. There is a fixed-base operator across the runway from the airport terminal that can accommodate private planes. The FBO is on Gateway Circle off Dillon Road less than a mile north of US 278.

Hilton Head Airport
120 Beach City Road
(843) 689-5400
www.hiltonheadairport.com
Hilton Head's airport has an up-to-date, spacious terminal that is served by two commercial carriers, as of fall 2007 (remember, air travel is a volatile business and things change a lot). The longest established there is U.S. Airways Express (800-428-4322). U.S. Airways Express offers 8 to 14 flights each day to and from Charlotte, North Carolina, and direct flights to and from Washington, DC on weekends. Delta Connection (843-342-5380) offers three departures daily.

Six rental-car agencies maintain desks at

the airport: Avis Rent A Car (843-681-4216, 888-897-8448), Budget Rent A Car (843-689-3737, 800-527-7000), Enterprise (843-689-9910), Hertz Rent A Car (843-681-7604, 800-654-3131), National Car Rental (843-681-7368, 800-CAR-RENT), and Thrifty Car Rental (843-689-9990, 800-847-4389). There are nine taxicab and shuttle services operating from the airport. Rates from the airport are set by the cab companies and monitored by Beaufort County: Standard rates are $10 to the Hampton Inn; $17 to Hilton Head Plantation; $18 to the Marriott/Palmetto Dunes; $20 to Shipyard; $20 to the Holiday Inn Oceanfront; $23 to Sea Pines; $40 to Del Webb Sun City near Bluffton, South Carolina; and $70 to Savannah.

The airport has short- and long-term parking lots: Short-term rates are 50 cents for the first 15 to 30 minutes and 50 cents for each additional half hour, with a maximum charge of $6.50 for each 24-hour period; long-term rates are 75 cents for the first hour and 50 cents for each additional half hour, with a maximum charge of $5.00 for each 24-hour period and a weekly charge of $30.00. The first 15 minutes in the short-term lot are free.

Carolina Air Center Inc.
52 Gateway Circle
(843) 689-3200

In addition to the usual services you'd expect from a fixed-base operator, Carolina Air Center offers a shower, a nine-hole putting green, and courtesy crew cars on request. The ramp charge for single-engine aircraft is $10 per night, and 100 LL and Jet A fuel service is available 24 hours a day if you call ahead after normal business hours, which run from 6:00 a.m. to 10:00 p.m.

GETTING AROUND

The best way to get around on Hilton Head is by car. Walking isn't much of an option because things are pretty spread out. Bike riding is popular, but if you take to the splendid network of bike trails, be prepared to do some pedaling to far-flung destinations. If you haven't driven your own car or rented one, there are numerous taxi companies and limousine services to help you arrange transportation.

Driving on the Island

Finding your way around Hilton Head is fairly easy, but actually finding the places you're looking for can be a challenge. At first glance that statement might not make much sense, but consider this: Most of what a visitor would be looking for can be found on or very near three main roads (US 278, Pope Avenue, and South Forest Beach Drive), but spotting a specific restaurant, shop, or motel can be difficult because of town regulations limiting signage and promoting natural beauty. Businesses are not allowed to have signs off the premises, and the signs they do have must conform to strict rules involving size and lighting. These regulations, combined with the emphasis on preserving trees and foliage and having buildings blend in, can make it easy for you to drive right past your intended destination. This is particularly true when it comes to the island's main thoroughfare, US 278, a busy four-lane divided highway also known as the William Hilton Parkway. Most everything is set back off the road on tree-lined side streets that often resemble driveways.

William Hilton Parkway

Once you cross the Karl S. Bowers and J. Wilton Graves Bridges to Hilton Head on US 278, you're on William Hilton Parkway, which runs east for 5 miles to the northern end of the island, then bends south and continues 6 miles to Sea Pines Circle. This 11-mile stretch passes restaurants, motels, shopping centers, other businesses, and the entrances to resort communities such as Hilton Head Plantation, Port Royal, Palmetto Dunes, and Shipyard.

To aid motorists, the town has placed mile markers along the parkway, with the lower-numbered markers closer to the bridges and the higher-numbered ones closer to the traffic circle. In some write-ups on businesses on the parkway, we've included a mention of the mile marker nearest the business being discussed.

Sea Pines Circle

When you enter this traffic circle from William Hilton Parkway, you'll encounter exits to the Cross Island Parkway one-quarter of the way around, Greenwood Drive halfway around, and Pope Avenue three-quarters of the way around. Greenwood Drive is the main road leading into The Sea Pines Resort community. The stretch of the Cross Island Parkway directly west of the circle, also known as Palmetto Bay Road, was widened into a four-lane highway in 1997.

Pope Avenue

Pope Avenue runs east a tad more than a mile from Sea Pines Circle to Coligny Circle. On Pope, you'll find a variety of restaurants, stores, shopping plazas, another entrance to Shipyard, and the entrance to the public parking lot at Forest Beach.

Coligny Circle

The Coligny traffic circle is practically on Forest Beach, and it routes motorists from Pope Avenue to South Forest Beach Drive (one-quarter of the way around the circle) and North Forest Beach Drive (three-quarters of the way around). North Forest Beach Drive is residential and leads to many of the older vacation homes and permanent residences on the island; short side streets run east to the beach, but access is private and public parking is a no-no.

South Forest Beach Drive

There are several resorts and restaurants along South Forest Beach Drive, which leads to another entrance to Sea Pines. Access to the beach via the side streets is private unless marked otherwise.

Cross Island Parkway

The Cross Island Parkway, a four-lane toll road that bypasses the southern portion of William

Hilton Parkway and alleviates traffic congestion on that heavily traveled thoroughfare, was opened in January 1998. The 6-mile, limited-access highway stretches from near the intersection of William Hilton Parkway and Spanish Wells Road, at mile marker 2 in the northwestern portion of the island, to Sea Pines Circle. Part of the Cross Island Parkway is a 65-foot-high bridge that crosses Broad Creek at Palmetto Bay. The toll for riding the length of the parkway (one way) in a car has been set at $1.00; it's $1.75 for three-axle trucks and $3.25 for five-axle trucks. Planners say the new road saves motorists anywhere from 8 to 10 minutes in travel time.

Biking on the Island

Hilton Head has some 50 miles of paved public bicycle paths, and there are many more miles of paths within the island's resort communities. Among the public paths are those that run along William Hilton Parkway from Gumtree Road (just past mile marker 2) to Sea Pines Circle for 9 miles, along both sides of Pope Avenue from Sea Pines Circle to Coligny Circle for a total of 2 miles, along North Forest Beach Drive from Coligny Circle to the end of North Forest for 1.3 miles, along South Forest Beach Drive from Coligny Circle to Sea Pines' Ocean Gate for 1.4 miles, along the Cordillo Parkway from South Forest Beach Drive to Pope Avenue for 1.1 miles, and to the Folly Field Beach Park (see the Public Beach Access and Parking section in this chapter) from William Hilton Parkway for 0.8 mile. A 3.5-mile path along Gumtree and Squire Pope Roads in the northwestern part of the island was completed in 1998, as were a 1-mile stretch on Point Comfort Road and 1.1 miles of pathway on Arrow Road in the southern portion of the island. Also open for riding are a 2.2-mile path along Beach City Road and the wider paths along North and South Beach Drives.

You can make arrangements to rent a bike through the resort where you're staying or by calling one of the more than 20 bike rental outlets that can be found in the Yellow Pages of the local telephone directory. In season, expect to pay $25.00 to rent a bike for a week and $9.50 to $12.00 for a day.

Taxis and Limousines

In addition to the taxicab and limousine companies that serve the Hilton Head Airport, there are several other limo operators on the island, including Camelot Limousine & Tours (843-842-7777).

Taxi rates are not regulated by the city of Hilton Head and vary from company to company and point to point. To find out how much a trip will cost, tell the dispatcher where you are and where you're going and ask what the fee will be. Rates for limousines run from $65 to $75 per hour with a two-hour minimum.

Bus Service

The island is served by the buses of Beaufort County's Lowcountry Regional Transportation Authority (LRTA), but this public transportation service is mainly a means of getting working people from towns on the mainland on and off Hilton Head. These buses serve Hilton Head in the early morning and in the late afternoon, meaning the LRTA is not a means of conveniently getting around the island throughout the day. However, there is a limited-demand response system through which riders can schedule transportation by calling (843) 757-5782 (a round-trip to Bluffton using this system is $6).

Public Beach Access and Parking

The only public parking lots and metered parking spaces on the island are at Hilton Head's public beach access points. As far as parking on the rest of the island goes, there is an abundance of free spaces in the lots of restaurants, shopping centers, motels, and other commercial establishments, much of it shaded by trees, which can be a blessing in the summer months.

Alder Lane Beach Access

This access point is on South Forest Beach Drive. Metered parking for the access is on Woodward Avenue, which is across South Forest Beach Drive from Alder Lane. The meter fee is 25 cents for 15 minutes.

Burke's Beach Access

This access is at the end of Burke's Beach Road, which runs off of William Hilton Parkway between mile markers 6 and 7. There are 13 metered spaces here, with fees set at 25 cents for 15 minutes, and there are 200 free spaces at nearby Chaplin Community Park.

Coligny Beach Park

The access at Coligny Circle offers about 30 metered spaces and a parking lot with about 350 spaces. The meters allow you to park 15 minutes for a quarter. Rates when the lot is manned by an attendant—usually on Friday, weekends, and holidays—are $4 per day.

Driessen Beach Park

Located at the end of Bradley Beach Road, which intersects William Hilton Parkway just past mile marker 6, this access has a lot with 212 spaces where parking is 25 cents per half hour. The lot is about a half mile from the parkway.

Folly Field Beach Park

This access is on Starfish Drive, which runs off Folly Field Road. Parking at the 52 spaces here is metered, and the rate is 25 cents for 15 minutes. Folly Field Road also runs into William Hilton Parkway at mile marker 6; it's a little more than a half mile from the parkway to the access.

Islanders Beach Park

This facility is on Folly Field Road about a mile from William Hilton Parkway. The 150 spaces here are reserved for persons having annual beach passes (there are also 30 such spaces at Driessen Beach and 30 at Coligny). Passes are available only to Hilton Head residents or property owners; they cost $15 a year and can be obtained at the town's governmental offices near the entrance to Wexford Plantation.

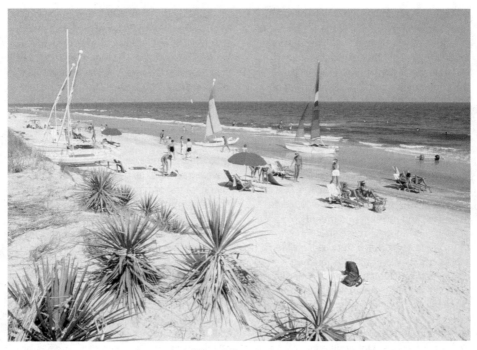

Visitors to Hilton Head will enjoy 12 miles of beautiful beaches. COURTESY OF HILTON HEAD ISLAND—BLUFFTON CHAMBER OF COMMERCE

SOURCES OF INFORMATION

Hilton Head Island–Bluffton Chamber of
Commerce Welcome Center
100 William Hilton Parkway
(843) 785-3673
www.hiltonheadisland.org
The chamber of commerce staffs a welcome
center at this site just past mile marker 1 on
William Hilton Parkway. Stop here and you'll
find displays and brochures involving shopping, dining, lodging, long- and short-term
rentals, golf, tennis, fishing, real estate, tours,
and events. There's a video display that will
introduce you to the island in several different
languages (you make the choice) and a large-
scale map of the island, plus smaller maps of
Hilton Head and the surrounding areas that
you can take with you. The center is open
from 9:00 a.m. to 5:30 p.m. daily.

The welcome center shares a building
with the Coastal Discovery Museum, which

offers exhibits involving the area's history,
native crafts, and wildlife. Admission is $2.
There's also an art gallery exhibit room.
Museum hours are from 9:00 a.m. to 5:00
p.m. Monday through Saturday and 10:00
a.m. to 2:00 p.m. Sunday, and there's a
museum shop featuring books on the Civil
War and topics of local interest.

PLANNED RESIDENTIAL COM-
MUNITIES

Hilton Head's 11 planned residential communities cover 65 percent of the island. All of the
island's golf courses (see subsequent listings)
are located within or associated with the communities, as are the four largest hotels and
many of Hilton Head's homes, vacation villas,
tennis courts, and marinas.

These communities are, for the most
part, private, meaning they have gates staffed

by security personnel who check the identities of arriving motorists. Some are more private than others: A few admit only residents and their guests; others are accessible to vacationers staying at hotels and villas within the communities and to golfers playing on courses that allow public participation. Sea Pines, which is the site of several restaurants and two shopping areas, allows the public to visit at a charge of $5 per car.

As we've mentioned before, the buildings in these communities are, in most cases, designed to melt into the landscape; stucco and wood are used extensively as building materials, and painting is in muted colors. The grounds surrounding these structures are often left in as natural a state as possible. In most communities, buildings must be approved by architectural review boards. This section comprises sketches of the island's 11 planned communities, listed in alphabetical order. For each we've provided, when possible, an address, telephone number, and/or Web site of a source for additional information: either a sales office, an administrative office, or the office of the property owners' association.

Hilton Head Plantation

Hilton Head Plantation is the second-largest planned community on the island, covering 4,000 acres on the northern tip of Hilton Head between Port Royal Sound and Skull Creek, which is part of the Intracoastal Waterway. Within the plantation's borders are 4,400 residential lots, four 18-hole golf courses, a beach fronting on the sound, the Whooping Crane Pond and Cypress Nature Conservancies, the Seabrook Farm garden plots, and tennis courts and swimming pools.

On the Skull Creek side of the plantation are Skull Creek Marina, a deepwater facility with 180 boat slips, the Old Fort Pub restaurant, and Fort Mitchel, a historic site that was a Union gun battery during the Civil War. Two of the golf courses within the plantation (the Country Club of Hilton Head and Oyster Reef) can be played by the public.

Outside the plantation's main gate, which is off William Hilton Parkway near mile marker 3, is Main Street, a development of shops and professional offices. The Hilton Head Plantation Property Owners Association is within the plantation at 7 Surrey Lane, and the telephone number there is (843) 681-8800. The Web site is www.hiltonheadplantation.com.

Indigo Run

Most of the homesites at this 1,775-acre development on the northern portion of Hilton Head border one of two 18-hole golf courses: The Golf Club at Indigo Run, a members-only layout designed by Jack Nicklaus and his son, Jack Nicklaus II, and opened in 1996; and the Golden Bear Golf Club, which was designed by Nicklaus's company and can be played by the public (see listing in this chapter's Golf section). All property owners at Indigo Run are entitled to join Golden Bear, and membership includes access to Sunningdale Park, which has six tennis courts, an Olympic-size pool, a kiddie pool, and a large playground for children. Membership in The Golf Club is open to owners of homesites and homes in Indigo Run.

As of March 2005, there were 680 homes on the 1,517 acres comprising Indigo Run's private residential community and another 60 in the building or design stages. These residences represent a wide range of styles and construction materials and are valued at $400,000 and up. Fifty of Indigo Run's homesites are in the River Club section along the banks of Broad Creek, and many owners of homes there have backyard boat docks. There are no villas at Indigo Run, and the only rentals allowed are long-term arrangements of a year or more.

Indigo Run is also the site of Indigo Park, a 258-acre retail and commercial center bordering William Hilton Parkway. Started in the mid-1980s by the Hilton Head Company, Indigo Run was acquired in 1991 by the Melrose Company and completed in 2001. The Indigo Run sales office is at 224 Pembroke Drive, just outside the main gate, which is off the parkway near mile marker 3. You can reach the sales office by calling (843) 681-3300 or (800) 487-2645.

Long Cove Club

The centerpiece of this community is a 6,548-yard golf course designed by Pete Dye that's been ranked best in South Carolina and as high as 19th in the nation. Property owners automatically become members of Long Cove Club, entitling them to use the golf course, the elegant 17,000-square-foot clubhouse, the pool, 10 tennis courts, and docks on Broad Creek that have slips for 100 boats. According to John McKenzie, president of Long Cove Club Realty, some club members live on other parts of Hilton Head but have bought lots at Long Cove just so they can play on the private golf course.

Development of Long Cove began in 1980, and all 570 homesites in the 600-acre community were sold by 1987. Ninety-seven percent of the sites have a view of a lagoon, marsh, or the golf course, and, as of fall 2005, about 415 homes had been built, all of them single-family residences. The median price tag for these homes—one- and two-story structures of stucco and cypress—is around $900,000. Privacy is prized here, and there are no short-term rentals. There's a sales office within the community at 44 Long Cove Drive, where the phone number is (843) 842-2442. The entrance to Long Cove is off William Hilton Parkway near mile marker 10.

Palmetto Dunes

Spread over 2,000 acres on the eastern side of the island, Palmetto Dunes offers 3 miles of beach bordering the Atlantic Ocean; 5,000 homes and villas, more than 500 of which can be rented by vacationers; three 18-hole golf courses; a world-class tennis facility; an 11-mile lagoon system; and two of the island's "big four" hotels—the 512-room Marriott Beach and Golf Resort and the 324-room Hilton Oceanfront Resort (see listings under this chapter's Accommodations section). All three of the golf courses—named for design-

ers Arthur Hills, George Fazio, and Robert Trent Jones—are accessible to the public (see listings in this chapter under Golf), as are the 23 clay and 2 hard courts of the Palmetto Dunes Tennis Center. Homes in Palmetto Dunes range from $500,000 to over $5 million.

Palmetto Dunes was started in the late 1960s and acquired in 1979 by the Greenwood Development Corporation, which since then has created the Shelter Cove Harbour yacht basin and retail complex and the Leamington community. Shelter Cove—a marina surrounded by shops, restaurants, and villas built in the style of a Mediterranean village—opened in 1982 and is directly across William Hilton Parkway from Palmetto Dunes. Leamington, covering 400 acres within Palmetto Dunes, is a private community with security gates that's centered on the Arthur Hills golf course. Development of this area was begun in 1986. You'll find the Palmetto Dunes sales office at the entrance to the community, which is off William Hilton Parkway near mile marker 8. The phone number is (843) 842-1111.

Palmetto Hall Plantation

Palmetto Hall is a golf-oriented community covering 775 acres in the northern portion of the island. Most of the 500 homesites border the fairways of the plantation's two 18-hole golf courses—the Arthur Hills and Robert Cupp Courses—both of which are open to the public (see listings in this chapter under Golf). Started by Greenwood Development Corporation in 1991, Palmetto Hall offers its residents a 16,000-square-foot clubhouse and an activities center with pools, tennis courts, and a children's playground.

The homes here, all of them single-family residences, reflect the style of the Lowcountry with their verandas, dormers, and colorful shutters. Residences range up to $900,000. Palmetto Hall is also the site of more than 100 acres of nature preserves. For information on home sales, call (843) 689-3333. Palmetto Hall's main gate is on Beach City Road about a half mile from the road's intersection with William Hilton Parkway at mile marker 4.

Port Royal Plantation

Living on the beach (or having easy access to it) is the main drawing card of this 1,000-acre community in the northeastern corner of the island. There are 2.5 miles of beach stretching along the plantation on the east and south-east—1.5 miles on the Atlantic Ocean and the rest on Port Royal Sound. The eastern side is the site of the actual Hilton Head, the bluff where English sea captain William Hilton looked out on the sound while exploring the region; it's the spot for which the entire island was eventually named.

Port Royal was one of the island's first planned communities, and the 920 homes within its gates reflect a wide variety of sizes and styles. They range in value from $500,000 to $5 million; most are in the $750,000 to $1.5 million range, and those on the oceanfront average about $3.5 million.

Another big attraction at Port Royal is golf. There are three 18-hole courses: Planter's Row, Barony, and Robber's Row, which are open to the public on a rotating basis (see listings in this chapter's Golf section). Residents of the plantation can be members at all three courses. Also outside the plantation but considered part of the Port Royal resort complex are the Port Royal Racquet Club, which has grass, composition, and hard-surface tennis courts; the 412-room Westin Resort Hilton Head hotel (see listing in this chapter's Accommodations section); and the villas at Island Links, Ocean Palms, Port Royal Village, Royal Dunes, The Links and The Lyons, Crown Reef, and the Barony Beach Club. The property owners' association office is at 10 Coggins Point Road just before the main gate, which is off William Hilton Parkway near mile marker 5. The phone number is (843) 681-5114.

The Sea Pines Resort

A Hilton Head architect once called Sea Pines the "daddy rabbit" of planned residential/resort communities. It's an apt description of the largest and oldest of the island's major developments—the first community of its kind in the nation.

The Sea Pines Resort covers 5,200 acres on the south end of Hilton Head and was started in 1957. It's the site of the island's first golf course, the Ocean Course, one of three courses in the community, all of which can be played by the public (see the Golf section in this chapter). The most popular of these courses is the Harbour Town Golf Links, which is the site of the island's biggest annual event, the Verizon Heritage, a PGA tour event that brings many of the world's best golfers to Hilton Head for four days during April. (See this chapter's Annual Events section for more on the Heritage.) The racquet club has 23 courts and offers comprehensive programs of tennis instruction under the direction of former Wimbledon champion and U.S. Olympic men's coach Stan Smith.

The Sea Pines Resort is the site of Hilton Head's best-known landmark, the red-and-white striped lighthouse at the Harbour Town Yacht Basin. Villas, shops, and restaurants ring the basin at Harbour Town; it's one of two marinas in Sea Pines, the other being at South Beach, where you'll find a New England–style village with shops, restaurants, and all sorts of watersports. Both marinas provide access to Calibogue Sound. More shops and eating places are available at Sea Pines Center.

Within the borders of Sea Pines are a 605-acre nature preserve, 5 miles of beach, the ruins of the Stoney-Baynard Plantation, two swimming pools, the Lawton Stables equestrian center, and a beach club that has an open-air grill, an oceanfront bar, a gift shop, live entertainment and dinner nightly in season, and picnic tables. The Sea Pines Resort offers 10,000 square feet of meeting space at the Plantation Club Conference Center, the Harbour Town Clubhouse, and the new Harbour Town Conference Center.

Sea Pines has nearly 3,500 single-family homes. A total of 530 villas and homes are available for rent by vacationers, and the new Inn at Harbour Town provides luxurious accommodations for those seeking a hotel-type setting. To learn more about The Sea Pines Resort, visit the welcome center at 32 Greenwood Drive or the Web site at www.seapines.com, or call (843) 785-3333 or (888) 807-6873. The welcome center is right outside the community's main gate, which is on Greenwood Drive just south of the Sea Pines traffic circle.

Shipyard Plantation

Shipyard has a mixture of single-family residences, condominiums, time-share units, and commercial developments within its 834 acres. There are about 265 residences ranging from patio homes starting at $400,000 to larger houses on golf courses that start at $500,000. The plantation, in the southeastern part of the island, is the site of more than 1,400 villas grouped in 22 different villa regimes.

The Shipyard Golf Club consists of 27 holes on 3 courses open to the public: Brigantine, Clipper, and Galleon (see this chapter's Golf section). Residents and guests have other forms of recreation available, particularly tennis and the beach. The Van der Meer Shipyard Racquet Club boasts 20 championship courts, and the eastern side of the plantation is on the Atlantic Ocean. Shipyard's ocean side is the site of the 340-room Crowne Plaza Resort Hotel (see this chapter's Accommodations section) and a beach club community house for residents. The plantation is also the home of the Hilton Head Health Institute, a resort for folks seeking to change their lifestyles by learning how to control their weight, reduce stress, and become more physically fit.

Ironically, Shipyard has no marina; its name is derived from the cotton plantation that once occupied the site. Administrative offices are at 10 Shipyard Drive, and the phone number is (843) 785-3310. They're just outside the main gate, which is off William Hilton Parkway near mile marker 10. There's a Web site at www.spoa.com.

Spanish Wells

There are some 200 single-family lots at this 350-acre community on the western portion of the island; the houses at Spanish Wells are on lots of at least 1 acre.

Spanish Wells is the most secluded of the island's communities; it's at the end of Spanish Wells Road, nearly 3 miles from William Hilton Parkway. The private golf club has a nine-hole course, two tennis courts, and a swimming pool. Many of the homes at Spanish Wells are on Calibogue Sound or Broad Creek, and those on Brahms Point, a narrow finger of land at the southwestern reaches of the community, have views of both bodies of water. The community derives its name from the wells from which Spanish explorers drew fresh water while visiting Hilton Head. Also of historical note is the fact that Spanish Wells is the site of Battery Holbrook, a Civil War gun emplacement. To learn more about Spanish Wells, call the property owners' association at (843) 842-4138.

Wexford Plantation

The emphasis is on privacy at Wexford, where rentals are prohibited and admittance is open only to residents, their guests, and prospective home buyers. This golf and yachting community covers 525 acres near the middle of the island. All of the 459 lots at Wexford are sold, and about 340 homes had been built as of summer 2005, most of them two-story, British Colonial–style houses valued from $750,000 to $5 million.

About a third of the homes are on the plantation's 35.5-acre harbor, which winds through the center of the community and is lock controlled to keep the water calm and at a minimum of 8 feet deep. The harbor, with slips accommodating yachts up to 66 feet long, provides access to Broad Creek. Most of the other homes are on Wexford's 18-hole golf course, a layout by Willard Byrd that's reserved solely for members and their guests and was recently restored to its original design. Other amenities take the form of a

i The Harbour Town Lighthouse, Hilton Head's most enduring symbol, stands 93 feet tall and is visited by a quarter-million people a year. The observation deck perches 66 feet above the base floor of the lighthouse on Calibogue Sound, and you reach it by climbing 110 steps. Completed in 1970, the lighthouse was the first one built on the Atlantic coast in more than 150 years. Flashing a white light every 2.5 seconds, it's a navigational aid for the sound and the Intracoastal Waterway, even though it's not operated by the U.S. government. (It's run by the company that owns Harbour Town.) The structure is open daily from 8:00 a.m. to dusk, and there's a $1 fee to tour it.

harborside clubhouse graced with pink Georgian marble and Tiffany glass skylights; a pool with a patio that overlooks the water; six tennis courts, four of them lighted; and a croquet lawn. Sales offices are at 2 Town Center Court and can be reached by calling (843) 686-8800 or (800) 345-2392. Wexford's main entrance is off William Hilton Parkway near mile marker 10, and you can reach the executive office at (843) 686-8810 or www.wexfordplantation.com.

Windmill Harbour

Designed for boaters and other folks who love being around the water, Windmill Harbour covers 172 acres in the northwestern portion of Hilton Head. Unlike the island's other planned communities, Windmill Harbour has no golf course, but it does have a 15.5-acre yacht basin with 260 boat slips. The harbor, the site of the South Carolina Yacht Club, has a lock system that keeps tides and currents to a minimum; the lack of movement of water also inhibits the growth of barnacles on the bottom of boats, allowing their owners to save on maintenance costs. The harbor lies on Calibogue Sound, which is part of the Intracoastal Waterway.

Eighty percent of the homesites at Windmill Harbour have views of the water. Among the residences at Windmill Harbour are estates on lots of an acre or more, villas, patio homes, and condominiums, all of them reflecting architectural styles seen in the historic district of Charleston and the South Carolina Lowcountry. Prices for condos start at $280,000; homes run from $500,000 to $2.5 million.

Residents seeking recreation other than boating can find it at the community's sports center, which provides an Olympic-size lap pool, seven clay tennis courts, and extensive workout facilities. The elegant building that serves as headquarters for the yacht club overlooks the harbor and offers a meeting place where members of the club can dine and attend cookouts, oyster roasts, and parties. Although Windmill Harbour is mainly a private community, the yacht basin is open to the boating public, and residents can rent out their dwellings for periods of 60 days or more. Shorter-term rentals are prohibited. The sales office is at 2 Harbour Passage Patio inside the main gate, which is off William Hilton Parkway just after you cross the bridges to the island. You can reach these offices by calling (843) 681-5600 or (877) 681-5600. You can also see more about Windmill Harbour at www.richardsongroupllc.com.

ACCOMMODATIONS

When you vacation at Hilton Head, you have the option of staying at hotels, motels, villas, or private homes that are being rented out by their owners. The hotels and motels range from modern, well-maintained establishments on the island's main thoroughfares to full-blown resorts situated in or adjacent to Hilton Head's luxurious golf communities. The villas are fully furnished condominiums set in apartment buildings and town houses, many of them with pools and locations close to beaches, golf clubs, and tennis courts.

There's plenty to choose from—Hilton Head has more than 3,000 hotel and motel rooms, 6,000 villa units, 1,000 time-share units, and an array of rental homes ranging from oceanfront mansions to laid-back cottages. We've provided a rundown of hotels and motels—places that offer nightly accommodations; for information on villas, timeshares, and private homes, which usually rent for longer-term stays (anywhere from three nights to two weeks), we suggest calling one of the island's numerous central reservations services. Among these are the Hilton Head Condo Hotline (843-785-2939, 800-258-5852), Hilton Head Accommodations and Golf Hotline (843-686-6662, 800-444-4772; www .hiltonheadusa.com), and Hilton Head Vacation Rentals (843-689-3010, 800-476-4485).

In general, rates for accommodations are higher from the end of April through September, although some places raise their prices starting in February, and others lower them after Labor Day. Call ahead to see what's available (well ahead if you're planning on staying during the summer, especially on weekends) and ask about special deals—many of the larger establishments have a variety of vacation packages from which to choose. Be aware that some motels and hotels will give you a lower rate if you stay with them early in the week when they might be struggling to fill up their rooms.

Most of the hotels and motels we surveyed don't allow pets and have nonsmoking and wheelchair-accessible rooms; we've noted the exceptions.

Price-Code Key

We have included a dollar-sign code with each entry denoting a price range for the average one-night stay, in season, for two adults. These prices do not include tax, gratuities, and add-on amenities such as room service.

$	100 or less
$$	$101 to $120
$$$	$121 to $175
$$$$	$176 to $225
$$$$$	$226 or more

Unless we've indicated otherwise, you'll have to pay to play golf or tennis at the resort where you're staying. Most places have packages or special deals involving these sports, and you should inquire about these if you intend to play. The following properties are listed alphabetically.

Adventure Inn Beach Resort and Rentals $$$
41 South Forest Beach Drive
(843) 785-5151, (800) 845-9500
www.advinn.com

Relax poolside under the graceful branches of the spreading live oak tree, take an early morning, guided walking tour of the beach, or play tennis for free at the Adventure Inn. This oceanfront establishment—which has been creating pleasant dreams for vacationers since 1963—offers a full slate of activities geared to youngsters from 9:00 a.m. to 5:00 p.m. Monday through Friday during the summer months. Some of the programs (such as scavenger hunts) are free, and there are fees for others (such as poolside bingo and beach-bag designing).

Tennis is complimentary on two courts across South Forest Beach Drive from the inn, health-club privileges for all guests older than age 14 are provided, and discounted golf packages for 21 courses on and off the island are offered. Although there is a five-night minimum stay in the majority of the units during summer, daily rentals are available. Some oceanfront efficiency rooms are well suited to families—each has a queen-size bed, a queen-size sleeper sofa, and a kitchenette.

Fitzgerald's, a restaurant serving dinner seven days a week, is on the premises. Because the units here are individually owned time-shares, there are no nonsmoking or wheelchair-accessible accommodations.

Comfort Inn & Suites $$
2 Tanglewood Drive
(843) 842-6662, (800) 522-3224
www.comfortinnhiltonhead.com

You can walk to the beach in five minutes from the five-story Comfort Inn, but if you'd rather not hoof it, you can hitch a ride on the hotel's beach buggy, which runs continuously from 10:00 a.m. to 4:00 p.m. from Memorial Day to Labor Day. If freshwater activities are more your style, take a dip in the hotel pool, where the surroundings have a Hawaiian flair, or zip down the waterslides at the adjacent Water Fun Park, where hotel guests are given a discount.

The 153-room Comfort Inn, situated on six acres graced by three lagoons, sits well back from South Forest Beach Drive, a block from the Coligny traffic circle. The hotel was refurbished in late 2005 and early 2006. Guests can partake of deluxe continental breakfasts from 7:00 to 10:00 a.m. in the registration building, which also houses 900 square feet of meeting space. Some of the rooms have refrigerators and microwave ovens, and there's a store nearby where you can purchase groceries. Golf packages are available. The hotel accepts pets for a cleaning fee of $25 plus $10 per night.

Crowne Plaza Resort $$$$$
130 Shipyard Drive
(843) 842-2400, (800) 334-1881
www.cphiltonhead.com

Built in a U-shape on the ocean in Shipyard, the Crowne Plaza opens onto a courtyard filled with subtropical gardens, extensive green spaces, and lagoons crossed by graceful wooden bridges. One bridge is a favorite spot for couples saying their wedding vows, and if you plan to get hitched there, you might consider enlisting the services of Crowne Plaza's notary public. The large courtyard is also the location of a pool, outdoor hot tub, toddler's pool, and Dockers, which serves light fare and drinks.

Amble down to the beach, and you'll pass by the beach snack bar, which specializes in snow cones and hot dogs. Nearby is the hotel's 7,000-square-foot outdoor pavilion, which is popular for meetings, dinners, and those weddings we referred to. The Crowne Plaza has 340 rooms, including 9 suites, with views of either the island, the courtyard, or the ocean. Portz restaurant offers fine dining

in the evening, and you can get breakfast and lunch indoors or outdoors at Brellas.

The hotel's leisure activities department operates Camp Castaway, a structured and supervised program for children ages 3 to 12. Among the many activities provided are shell hunts and turtle feedings for the youngest kids, games on the beach and in the pool for those ages 6 to 12, as well as bike tours. Fees for a full day of fun are $75 per child; children ages 3 to 5 are restricted to morning sessions, which are $47 per child. Afternoon sessions are $57. Adults seeking opportunities to exercise can find them at the Crowne Plaza's fully equipped fitness center and adjacent indoor pool and at Shipyard's golf courses and tennis courts.

Days Inn $
9 Marina Side Drive
(843) 842-4800

Each of the 14 suites at the Days Inn has a nice touch—French doors separating the bedroom from the large sitting room. The other 105 rooms at the three-story motel off US 278 just past mile marker 9 have king-size and double beds, and there is a pool. Guests in quest of another form of recreation might opt to play the adjacent Pirates Island miniature golf course. The motel's complimentary continental breakfast awaits guests in a dining room off the lobby from 6:30 to 10:00 a.m. The Days Inn is centrally located and near a slew of restaurants and shops.

Hampton Inn $$
1 Dillon Road
(843) 681-7900, (800) HAMPTON
www.hamptoninn.com

If you're not particularly interested in going to the beach, the Hampton Inn might be for you. This two-story, 125-room motel just off US 278 at mile marker 5 caters to business travelers and people visiting the island for the golf of it. And, heck, if you do desire to take a dip in the ocean, the Atlantic is only a little more than a mile away at the Folly Field Beach access. There's an outdoor pool for those who want to stay close by to do their swimming, an indoor putting green, and a well-equipped exercise room for the fitness-minded. The Hampton—which was renovated in 2004—offers deluxe, complimentary continental breakfasts from 6:00 to 10:00 a.m. and free copies of USA Today. Some of the rooms have kitchenettes with microwave ovens and small refrigerators, and some have whirlpool baths. A special feature of the Hampton is the "afternoon snack" of fresh-baked cookies.

Hilton Head Marriott Beach & Golf Resort $$$$$
1 Hotel Circle
(843) 686-8400, (800) 228-9290
www.marriotthiltonhead.com

With its 512 rooms and 46,000 square feet of meeting space, this Marriott is billed as the largest luxury oceanfront resort between Atlantic City, New Jersey, and Palm Beach, Florida. This 10-story hotel at Palmetto Dunes has the comfortable feel of a place where guests are kicking back and going on vacation. It's not unusual to see youngsters padding through the spacious lobby in their flip-flops on their way to a day at the pool or to take part in the activities provided by the Adventure Club, which is for kids ages 6 to 12. The camp provides fun (including nature walks and sand sculpting) via half-day and full-day programs available from Memorial Day to Labor Day. Rates are $35 for morning sessions; $55 for afternoon sessions, which usually include an off-site activity such as kayaking; and $85 for the entire day.

The pool is large, and there's also a 1-foot-deep pool for toddlers. Poolside, guests will find Quinn's II restaurant, which serves sandwiches, and the Point Comfort bar, specializing in frozen drinks. For indoor dining, there's The Cafe for breakfast, lunch, and dinner, and Conroy's for dinner and Sunday brunch. Conroy's Lounge overlooks the ocean and offers nightly entertainment. If you're in need of snacks, try The Grocery, an offbeat little convenience store on the hotel's lower level. Other shopping opportunities are found at the Coastal Coffee Boutique. If you crave exercise, you can work out in the Marriott's well-equipped fitness center, play a round of golf at one of five courses within walking or shuttle distance, or hit the courts at the Palmetto Dunes Tennis Center.

Hilton Oceanfront Resort $$$$$
23 Ocean Lane
(843) 842-8000, (800) 845-8001
www.hiltonheadhilton.com

Open hallways catching ocean breezes and lagoons winding their way through lush foliage give this beachfront Hilton Hotel at Palmetto Dunes a semitropical aura. The extra-large rooms have equally spacious balconies, each with at least a partial view of the beach and sea. All 324 rooms have kitchenettes and amenities such as ceiling fans in dining areas and separate vanities in bathrooms. The five-story hotel is built in a horseshoe shape that opens onto the beach, and the nooks and crannies of the spacious garden within the horseshoe feature small courtyards and rambling wooden decks.

The ground floor houses three eating places—the Palmetto Cafe, the Deli, and Mostly Seafood—and the Regatta Lounge, which serves as a sports bar in the afternoons and early evenings and a nightclub after dark Tuesday through Sunday. Guests can also eat lunch at the Buoy Bar and Grill at the main pool. There's also an adults-only pool for those seeking a quieter atmosphere. For more relaxation, try one of the two oceanfront whirlpool baths or the variety of services at the Ocean Tides Spa and Fitness Center.

The hotel offers special rates for golf and tennis at the courses and courts at Palmetto Dunes and special activities for children via Seaside Adventures Club. This day and evening camp program from Memorial Day to Labor Day is for kids ages 4 through 12 and is priced at $45 per child for a full-day session, $35 per child for a half-day session, and $30 per child for an evening session. The Hilton has 15,000 square feet of meeting space and the shorehouse open-air pavilion, and there's a shuttle from the hotel to all the activities Palmetto Dunes and nearby Shelter Cove Harbour have to offer.

Holiday Inn Express $$
40 Waterside Drive
(843) 842-8888, (888) 843-4136
www.hiltonheadexpress.com

Although the Holiday Inn Express sits only a block off busy Pope Avenue, the three-story hotel affords its guests peace and quiet because of the wooded areas surrounding it. Rooms on the rear side of the inn overlook a large lagoon.

Another drawing card for the 91-room hotel is its proximity to Forest Beach, which is a five-minute walk; for those wishing to take a dip and stay closer to home, there's an inviting pool at the inn. The hotel also provides guests with free continental breakfasts each morning from 6:30 to 9:30 a.m. Rooms at this inn, whose stuccoed exterior gives it a Spanish look, offer two different arrangements: a king-size bed or two queen-size beds. Some of the rooms with king-size beds have recliners.

Holiday Inn Oceanfront $$$
1 South Forest Beach Drive
(843) 785-5126, (800) 423-9897
www.hihiltonhead.com

Life's just beachy at the Holiday Inn Oceanfront, where the meandering, free-form pool is only steps away from the white sand of the Hilton Head strand. The contemporary decor of the inn's 201 rooms (all of which have refrigerators and open onto interior hallways) carry out the beach motif, as do the five-story motel's eating and drinking places—Grouper's restaurant, which has plenty of windows and great views of the ocean; the Island Eatery, which stands on a concrete peninsula jutting into the pool and serves lunch fare and ice cream; and the poolside Tiki Hut beach bar, which offers live entertainment. Large-scale renovations were completed in 2002, and additions include an oceanview banquet room that caters to receptions and meetings of up to 400 guests.

The inn offers numerous recreational activities, some of them free and many intended for the younger set. A children's program that runs from Memorial Day to Labor Day provides kids with activities such as relays on the beach, sand-dollar painting, and underwater treasure hunts. The inn also has a children's pool, kids' playground, and Dolly the Dolphin, a mascot who greets guests and interacts with youngsters.

Inn at Harbour Town $$$$
7 Lighthouse Lane
(843) 363-8100, (800) 732-7463
www.seapines.com

You won't find any soft-drink machines at this luxurious 60-room hotel in The Sea Pines Resort; butlers do the vending instead. This inn has private butlers who'll perform a multitude of tasks for guests, from bringing drinks and sandwiches to seeing that business papers are typed, shoes are shined, and pants are pressed. The butlers, some of them wearing Scottish attire in keeping with Harbour Town's Highlands heritage, are a big part of the concept of patterning the Inn at Harbour Town after small, fine European hotels. That concept extends to the rich furnishings of the common areas and guest rooms and the trappings of the bathrooms, which feature soaking tubs, walk-in showers, and lots of marble.

The inn, which opened in late November 2000, also has much to offer in the way of recreation. The hotel overlooks the first tee of the famed Harbour Town Golf Links, and the Sea Pines Racquet Club is a short stroll from the front door. Guests have access to the pool next to the Racquet Club and can take advantage of a complimentary shuttle service that will take them anywhere in Sea Pines at any time of day.

The inn serves a continental breakfast from 7:00 to 11:00 each morning at a cost of $9 per person, and there are lots of restaurants nearby, including the Harbour Town Grill and the eateries at the Harbour Town yacht basin.

Main Street Inn $$$$
2200 Main Street
(843) 681-3001, (800) 471-3001
www.mainstreet.com

A couple seeking a spot for a romantic get-away will find it at the elegant Main Street Inn off US 278 between mile markers 3 and 4. The 33 rooms are luxuriously appointed with classic furnishings: wooden armoires handmade on Hilton Head, beds adorned with Italian linens and goose-down pillows and comforters, and baths featuring pedestal sinks and Italian marble floors and shower walls. The Deluxe Queen rooms have fireplaces and balconies large enough for a wrought-iron table that's a perfect spot for breakfast.

The inn's crowning glories are the four Courtyard King rooms with their whirlpool tubs, glassed-in showers, and pine floors fashioned from the 150-year-old beams of a Lowcountry mill. In some Kings, French doors in the bathroom open onto an intimate courtyard abounding with fig vines, fruit trees, and jasmine. Guests staying in rooms on the upper two floors can step outside onto wide verandas complete with rocking chairs. From there, you'll see the Charleston-style gardens of the courtyard and a pool designed for swimming laps; the view beyond is of the lush 15th green and 16th fairway of Hilton Head Plantation's Bear Creek Golf Course and of the forested wetlands of a nature preserve.

Your stay includes buffet breakfasts served in the dining room/library, the dining room/lounge, or the courtyard. If all this isn't relaxing enough, try a massage, which is available on-site.

The Quality Inn & Suites $$
200 Museum Street
(843) 681-3655, (800) 995-3928
www.hhqualityinn.com

Located on the rapidly developing north end of the island, The Quality Inn boasts many of the features you might expect to find at a full-service hotel. Among them are an outdoor pool, a putting green, 2,000 square feet of meeting space, and same-day valet, laundry,

and dry-cleaning service. There's an Applebee's restaurant on the property, and the motel serves a complimentary continental breakfast daily from 6:30 to 9:30 a.m. The 127-room motel, which is on US 278 at mile marker 3, was completely renovated in 1999–2000.

Red Roof Inn Hilton Head $
5 Regency Parkway
(843) 686-6808, (800) RED-ROOF

This 111-room motel just off US 278 at mile marker 9 was thoroughly renovated in 2005. The two-story inn offers rooms with king-size beds and business kings (with dataports, speaker phones, and minifridges), along with four spacious suites complete with mini refrigerators and wet bars. According to the management, the emphasis here is on making guests "feel good and giving them value for their dollar." The inn is adjacent to Stack's Pancakes, which serves breakfast and lunch. The motel provides complimentary continental breakfasts from Memorial Day to Labor Day in a room off the lobby. A heated pool in an enclosed shaded area provides a spot where guests can relax or get some exercise.

Residence Inn by Marriott $$$
12 Park Lane
(843) 686-5700, (800) 331-3131
www.residenceinnhhi.com

The only all-suite hotel on the island rambles over a quiet wooded area in the Central Park office complex just off US 278 between mile markers 9 and 10. The centrally located Residence Inn provides full-scale hot breakfasts in the lobby daily. Each of the 156 suites has a balcony and fully equipped kitchen including a full-size refrigerator, and the King and bilevel loft suites have wood-burning fireplaces.

Loft suites are designed for entertaining, family gatherings, and romantic getaways—each has an enlarged dining area, a sleeper sofa, and a loft-type bedroom with its own bathroom. Complimentary social hours are offered starting at 5:00 p.m. Monday through Thursday. Golf packages are available, and there's a putting green near the pool. Guests can play tennis for free (using the hotel's rackets and balls, if needed) on two lighted courts on the backside of the property, which is also the site of a tree-shaded playground and picnic area. Pets are accepted with a $75 nonrefundable deposit.

South Beach Marina Inn $$$
232 South Sea Pines Drive
(843) 671-6498, (800) 367-3909
www.southbeachvillage.com

Were it not for the distinctly Southern foliage and marshlands within view, you might think you're in New England when you stay at the South Beach Marina Inn. This charming, 17-room hotel is part of a small complex of shops and restaurants patterned after a fishing village on Nantucket Island, Massachusetts. The rooms of the inn, a nightly rental property at Sea Pines, reflect the Yankee atmosphere via the highly polished heart-of-pine floors, brass beds, and colorful rag rugs.

All of the one- and two-bedroom accommodations have kitchenettes, and most have separate, cozy living rooms that will make you feel as if you've found a second home. Although the inn is deep within Sea Pines, the village and marina offer just about everything a vacationer would need. You could park your car and not leave, except to play a round of golf on the nearest course, which is a five-minute drive. At your front door is the marina on Braddock's Cove, which offers various recreational opportunities for hire—boat rentals, charter fishing, parasailing, kayaking, and windsurfing. Also, just outside your doorstep, you will find a pool, a dozen tennis courts, and 15 miles of paved trails for hiking, bicycling, jogging, and in-line skating. You can walk to the beach in three to four minutes, and there are six eating places within the village. All rooms are on the second floor; and there are no wheelchair-accessible accommodations.

Westin Resort Hilton Head $$$$$
2 Grasslawn Avenue
(843) 681-4000, (800) WESTIN1
www.westinhiltonhead.com

The architecture of the Westin radiates the charm of a classic, turn-of-the-century seaside hotel and is designed to complement the historic cities of Savannah and Charleston. A feeling of Southern hospitality carries throughout the five-story oceanfront hotel at Port Royal Plantation. The lobby features polished woods, palms, elaborate chandeliers, and Asian porcelains, and a mix of comfortable seating offers an ambience characteristic of the homes of the Old South. The Gazebo Lounge looks out on the hotel's spacious courtyard, where swans swim in a pond set amid lush foliage. In the cooler months, the lounge and its comfy drawing-room furniture and wood-burning fireplace beckon to guests. When the weather's warm, the courtyard is the place to be. You'll find two pools (a round pool and a lap pool) and extensive wooden decks where you can sunbathe, have a bite to eat at Turtles Beach Bar & Grill, and relax in rocking chairs and enjoy the scenery. A band often provides entertainment by the pool during summer afternoons, and you can get a massage at the water's edge if you're so inclined. There is also an indoor pool with a hydraulic lift for the physically impaired. Take advantage of the Westin Workout, powered by Reebok Gym.

Those seeking outdoor recreation can find it at the nearby Port Royal Golf Club, which has three championship courses (see the Golf section of this chapter), or at the Port Royal Racquet Club, which offers grass, clay, and hard-surface courts. A shuttle service is provided from the hotel to both sites. For youngsters ages 4 to 12, the Westin Kid's Club operates from Memorial Day weekend through Labor Day weekend.

There's fine dining during the evening at Westin's Barony Grill; casual dining and cocktails in the late afternoon and evening at Turtles, which overlooks the ocean; and family dining throughout the day at the Carolina

Cafe, which features a nightly seafood buffet, an 18-foot-long dessert table, and Sunday brunch. Completed in the spring of 2005, a $10.5 million renovation refurbished all of the hotel's 412 guest rooms and added an ocean-front outdoor pavilion and a 5,800-square-foot, open-air deck for group functions. The pavilion offers more than 2,800 square feet of covered space and accommodates about 200 people.

RESTAURANTS

The Yellow Pages of the Hilton Head telephone book contain more than 30 pages of listings and advertisements for restaurants. Make no mistake, there's a lot to choose from here in terms of eateries and cuisine. In this section, we look at some of the island's more popular restaurants in an attempt to provide you with selections offering a variety of foods in a variety of atmospheres at a variety of prices.

All the restaurants discussed here serve alcoholic beverages, and most have areas where smoking is allowed; we've noted the exceptions. Many of these eating places either recommend or require that you make reservations, and we've pointed out the ones that do. All take most major credit cards. Listings are in alphabetical order.

Price-Code Key

You can expect restaurants to be more expensive on Hilton Head Island than in Savannah. For our price code, we specify inexpensive, moderate, or expensive. Count on inexpensive entrees costing less than $15, moderate entrees costing up to $25, and expensive entrees costing more than $25.

Alexander's   Moderate–Expensive
76 Queens Folly Road
(843) 785-4999
www.alexandersrestaurant.com
Located on a lagoon at Palmetto Dunes, Alexander's provides casual but dressy dining in three settings: an enclosed porch, a wine

bar adorned with a fireplace, and a cozy dining room. Established in 1977, the restaurant serves dinner daily and specializes in seafood, including salmon Oscar and Neptune's seafood platter—a combination of fried shrimp, tilapia, scallops, and oysters. If you enjoy wine, you have your choice of 100 different bottles. Reservations are suggested.

The Barony Grill   Expensive
2 Grasslawn Avenue
(843) 681-4000
With its cozy hunt-club atmosphere, The Barony Grill provides an ideal setting in which to celebrate a special occasion. High ceilings, brick archways, comfortable chairs, and elegant table settings create an ambience that's refined yet relaxed.

A special feature is the wine-tasting room, where diners can find assistance in selecting the wines that will best complement their meals. The room—with its sand-colored stucco walls, polished wood floors, and wrought-iron wine racks—is also a spot where patrons can simply enjoy the experience of tasting various wines.

The Barony specializes in chops and seafood, and among the favorite dishes of diners are the pan-seared grouper and smoked prime rib. For starters, there are appetizers such as lobster bisque, roasted Carolina quail, and the onion soup, which features a three-cheese melt. Desserts, including the crème brûlée, are hard to miss—they're

> **i** A good source of information concerning the island's eating places is *Hilton Head Island Restaurants* magazine, which you should be able to find at rental villas, hotels and motels, shops, grocery stores, and other locations, including the chamber of commerce welcome center on William Hilton Parkway near mile marker 1. This free booklet of some 176 pages has listings for more than 100 restaurants and reprints of menus. The centerfold of this guide is a map that will help you locate these eateries.

displayed on a large marble and iron table situated at the entrance.

The Barony—located on the first floor of the Westin Resort Hilton Head at Port Royal Plantation—serves dinner Wednesday through Sunday and is closed during December, January, and February. This restaurant is completely nonsmoking.

The Big Bamboo Cafe   Inexpensive
Coligny Plaza
(843) 686-3443

According to the legend of The Big Bamboo, which appears on the front of the cafe's menu, this restaurant on the ocean side of Coligny Plaza shopping center has been constructed as closely as possible to the configurations of the original Big Bamboo, a bar and grill opened on the Pacific island of Tarawa in 1944 by ex–fighter pilot Jimmy Phipps. From the bamboo of the bar to the thatched palm fronds and camouflage netting of the ceiling to the World War II regalia tacked on the walls, Hilton Head's version of The Big Bamboo reflects the feel of the real thing—if there had been a real thing, that is. You see, The Big Bamboo of the Pacific is a figment of the imagination of a former owner, albeit one that has been brought vividly to life on Hilton Head.

What is real about this 85-seat dining room and bar is the atmosphere of fun that has been created—that and the interesting mix of dishes available, ranging from the roasted turkey sandwiches to the barbecue ribs, Greek pasta, and seafood fettuccine. Harder to believe is an item called the "war dog"—a hot dog stuffed with cheddar cheese, wrapped with bacon, dipped in beer batter and fried, then tucked in a toasted roll and smothered with chili, cheddar cheese, and onions. Wow! Or as Jimmy Phipps would have put it, "Whew!" The Big Bamboo—where you can gaze on a mix of authentic memorabilia and reproductions from the 1940s while listening to the Big Band music of that era—puts out the welcome mat daily for fighter jocks and other customers seeking dinner.

The Brick Oven Cafe   Inexpensive
25 Park Plaza
Office Park Road
(843) 686-2233

Gourmet pizzas from the brick oven and "Things to be Shared" give this restaurant in Park Plaza on Office Park Road an identity all its own. Among the pizzas on the menu are scampi, five-cheese, and mesquite-grilled chicken varieties, but you can also create your own. Dining parties are encouraged to share two or three dishes designed for that experience, including sesame-crusted tuna, calamari, and tempura chicken fingers. The wine list is extensive and offers numerous good values.

Cafe at Wexford   Moderate
Village at Wexford
1000 William Hilton Parkway
(843) 785-6300

The food and atmosphere of a cafe in the French countryside await you at this restaurant in the Village at Wexford near mile marker 10 on William Hilton Parkway. Wood floors and lots of brickwork give the 60-seat cafe an intimate aura. The menu offers a wide selection of country French cuisine; among the most popular entrees are the veal sweetbreads, which are sautéed in cream sauce with mushrooms and strips of ham; the cherry-glazed roast duckling; and the potato-onion-crusted fillet of grouper. For an appetizer, try the pâté de foie gras. The cafe serves lunch Monday through Friday, dinner Monday through Saturday, and brunch on Saturday and Sunday. Reservations for dinner are required.

Cafe Europa   Moderate–
160 Lighthouse Road   Expensive
(843) 671-3399

Excellent views of Calibogue Sound are available from just about all of the 140 seats at this restaurant. It's at the boaters' entrance to the Harbour Town Yacht Basin at Sea Pines, meaning the Cafe Europa is a wonderful place to watch a sunset. Linen-covered tables adorned with candles, the awning-covered ceiling, and large picture windows give the restaurant an ambience that's airy and upscale. The cuisine is continental with an emphasis on seafood. Customer favorites are the baked shrimp Daufuskie; the salmon Southern style, which comes with stone-ground grits and simmered greens; the Cuban fire-roasted tenderloin of pork, which features a mango barbecue sauce and smashed sweet potatoes; and the strip sirloin, which is accompanied by Lulu's smashed potatoes. Cafe Europa also has outdoor dining in an area at the base of the Harbour Town Lighthouse and overlooking the marina.

The cafe serves breakfast, lunch, and dinner seven days a week but is closed from November through mid-February. It's completely nonsmoking, and reservations are recommended.

Charley's Crab   Moderate–Expensive
2 Hudson Road
(843) 342-9066

Open-air decks and screened porches make this restaurant overlooking Skull Creek a splendid venue for waterfront dining. The location—just off Squire Pope Road about 1.5 miles from William Hilton Parkway—and the name clue you into the fact that Charley's specializes in seafood dishes such as caramelized catfish, crab cakes, and shrimp and grits. Steak, chicken, and pasta entrees also hit the mark. The fried green tomatoes—served with rock shrimp and crawfish salsa—constitute a can't-miss starter. Charley's, which has three dining rooms and a bar in a rustic setting, serves dinner nightly, lunch Monday through Friday, and brunch on Sunday.

Charlie's L'Etoile Verte   Moderate–
8 New Orleans Road   Expensive
(843) 785-9277
www.charliesofhiltonhead.com

Ask an islander where to eat on Hilton Head, and the first word out of his or her mouth is liable to be "Charlie's." This busy bistro near Sea Pines Circle serves lunch Tuesday through Saturday and dinner Monday through Saturday, specializing in more than a dozen types of fish cooked in many ways.

Charlie's is billed as a "French kitchen" (*L'Etoile Verte* means "green star" in French), but this eclectic-looking cafe serves, as its affable owner Charlie Golson puts it, "whatever we feel like cooking," "we" being Golson, his entree chef, and his dessert and appetizer chef. The three of them put their heads together and brainstorm during the day, a process that creates a menu that's different each night, written in longhand, and copied for distribution to diners.

Among the most popular selections are the chicken salad, Cobb salad, rack of lamb, pompano with mango sauce, and triggerfish in Parmesan crust.

Golson grew up in Savannah, apprenticed himself to a French chef for a year in 1970, and eventually moved to Hilton Head to serve as the chef at the now-defunct Hilton Head Inn. He opened Charlie's in 1984 in another location and has been enthralling islanders with his culinary artistry ever since.

CQ's Restaurant   Expensive
140 Lighthouse Road
(843) 671-2779
www.cqsrestaurant.com

Housed in the first structure built at Harbour Town in Sea Pines, this restaurant is filled with memorabilia reflecting the history of the South Carolina Lowcountry, Hilton Head, and Sea Pines, in particular. Modeled after a Lowcountry rice barn, the two-story building was originally an artist's studio, and many of its features are authentic—the flooring was part of a church in nearby Jasper County, roof beams were taken from an old Savannah warehouse, and the spindles on the staircase reportedly once graced the interior of a house of ill repute in Savannah.

Seeing as how the restaurant exudes all this local history, it's appropriate that the food served here tends to be regional in nature. Many of the dishes are American Southern, and among the featured entrees are the venison, lobster pasta, and crab cakes. The mouthwatering appetizers include seafood bisque and baked brie. There's also an extensive wine menu. CQ's has outdoor seating on a deck. Reservations are highly recommended at this well-known establishment, which serves dinner seven days a week.

The Crazy Crab   Moderate
104 William Hilton Parkway
(843) 681-5021

Lighthouse Road
(843) 363-2722

The island's two Crazy Crab restaurants serve fresh seafood and steaks in rustic wharfside surroundings offering splendid views of the water. At the Crazy Crab on the William Hilton Parkway near mile marker 1, the view is of picturesque Jarvis Creek and its marsh. The other Crazy Crab is among the shops alongside the Harbour Town Yacht Basin in Sea Pines. The menus at both restaurants are the same, with the mainstays being the fried shrimp and the steamed seafood pot, which consists of half a Maine lobster, crab legs, shrimp, and oysters. They are open for lunch and dinner seven days a week.

Hilton Head Brewing
Company   Inexpensive
7-C Greenwood Drive
(843) 785-2739

Billed as South Carolina's first brewpub since Prohibition and the only one on the island, this establishment in Hilton Head Plaza just off the Sea Pines traffic circle always has five

---

i If you need a bite to eat while traveling the "back way" to or from Hilton Head Island, consider stopping at the Pink Pig restaurant (843-784-3635) on Alternate South Carolina Highway 170 at a crossroads identified as Levy. This shockingly pink cinder-block eatery specializes in barbecue and is open for lunch and dinner Wednesday through Saturday. Locals swear by this place.

---

handcrafted beers ready for drinking: South Atlantic Pale Ale, Calibogue Amber, Old Duck Dark, Raspberry Wheat, and a seasonal brew. Although the pub takes on the atmosphere of a bar late at night, the restaurant offers casual dining for families at lunch and during the evening. Watching the turtles, ducks, and geese in the pond outside the pub's enclosed porch will keep the kids entertained. The menu yields a large variety of choices, including hand-tossed pizzas, burgers, steaks, and huge sandwiches. And then there are the chicken wings, named the best at the island's WingFest event in 2000, 2001, and 2002.

The pub, which opened in December 1994, has room for about 155 customers, including seats for 60 on the porch. On Wednesday evenings the staff removes the tables and chairs from the area around the large bar and a DJ presides over Disco Night.

Hofbrauhaus   Inexpensive–Moderate
Pope Avenue,
Executive Park
(843) 785-3663

This cozy, Bavarian-style restaurant off Pope Avenue offers old standbys of German cuisine such as sauerbraten and Wiener schnitzel, plus a variety of seafood, steaks, and fowl, including baked salmon, prime strip sirloin, and roast duckling. The Hofbrauhaus, in business since 1973 and featuring an accordion player squeezing out Bavarian music most evenings, serves dinner daily but is closed after Thanksgiving and during the first part of December. Reservations are suggested at the restaurant, which pours up to a dozen different German beers.

Hudson's on the Docks
1 Hudson Road   Inexpensive–
(843) 681-2772   Moderate
www.hudsonsonthedocks.com

The emphasis at Hudson's—a fixture on the Hilton Head restaurant scene since 1967—is on fresh seafood, much of it caught locally, including shrimp hauled in on the boats you might see tied at the docks just outside. The vessels and Skull Creek can be viewed from the main dining room, one of three at the 335-seat restaurant, which also has an oyster bar. Forty percent of Hudson's business involves shrimp—fried, steamed, or boiled—but the steamed oysters, scallops, and crab cakes (made with 100 percent lump backfin meat) are also big sellers. As you might expect, the dining rooms at Hudson's have a nautical look, and the tables and the oyster bar are made from shrimp-boat doors, the wooden pieces of equipment used in trawling.

The Oyster Factory Dining Room occupies the site of an oyster processing plant built in 1912 and bought by J. B. Hudson in the 1920s. The Hudson family added shrimp to the processing operation in the mid-1950s and opened the restaurant with 95 seats in the latter half of the 1960s. Brian and Gloria Carmines purchased Hudson's in 1975 and have expanded it since then.

Hudson's serves lunch and dinner daily. The restaurant is off Squire Pope Road about 1.5 miles from Squire Pope's intersection with the William Hilton Parkway between mile markers 1 and 2.

Juleps Restaurant   Moderate
14 Greenwood Drive
(843) 842-5857

The name is Southern and so are the surroundings at Juleps, which has the look of the fine old homes of Charleston. The food is continental, says owner/host Sam Cochran, but prepared with Southern ingredients by his chef and wife, Melissa. This combination produces entrees such as Kentucky bourbon rib-eye steak, roasted stuffed quail, jumbo shrimp stuffed with lump crabmeat, sautéed trout N'awlins with shrimp and crawfish, and Dixie cornmeal flounder. Among the appetizers are coconut pecan shrimp, which comes with a spicy citrus dipping sauce, and corn, crab, and sweet potato fritters. Specialty drinks can be ordered from the bar, including—what else?—mint juleps.

This restaurant in the Gallery of Shops near the Sea Pines traffic circle serves dinner

seven days a week. Reservations are recommended, and the owners request that diners wear shirts with collars.

Kenny B's
French Quarter Café   Inexpensive
70-A Circle BiLo Center
(843) 785-3315

Kenny B's brings a touch of The Quarter to Hilton Head at its eatery in the BiLo shopping plaza at the intersection of Pope Avenue and Cordillo Parkway. The cuisine is Creole with some Lowcounty tweaking, and murals, ceiling fans, and lampposts create a Big Easy atmosphere. Entrees lend to the aura—there's crawfish parade; voodoo pasta, which features seafood over penne; and Taste of the Bayou, a medley of N'awlins favorites (gumbo, jambalaya, red beans and rice, and shrimp étouffée). Drop by Kenny B's daily for breakfast, lunch, or dinner.

Marley's Island Grille   Inexpensive
35 Office Park Road
(843) 686-5800

Watch the chefs at Marley's prepare your dinner in the restaurant's open kitchen, where the focal points are a wood-fired grill and kettles for steaming shellfish—shrimp, mussels, clams, or a combination of all three. You choose how you want your selection cooked: with traditional tomato sauce, with an island curry, with the house ale and Old Bay, or in a garlic butter and sherry broth. Or try one of these other intriguing-sounding seafood dishes: tortilla-crusted tilapia, sesame-seared yellowfin tuna, or voodoo-spiced swordfish. From the wood grill, there are the red chili–rubbed flank steak, Havana cabana chicken, and Australian rock lobster. Marley's is open each evening; it's located in the Park Plaza shopping complex just southeast of Sea Pines Circle.

Old Fort Pub   Expensive
65 Skull Creek Drive
(843) 681-2386
www.oldfortpub.com

If you're looking for a romantic setting for a

meal, end your search at the Old Fort Pub. Set on a bluff along Skull Creek amid a tangle of live oaks, this restaurant offers evening-time diners candlelight, classical music, a rustic Lowcountry atmosphere, and spectacular sunsets over a creek and its marsh. There are great views of the water from the first-floor dining room, bar, and outdoor deck that get even better as you ascend to the second-floor Sunset Room and the rooftop widow's walk, a wooden deck reached via a cast-iron spiral staircase. Up there in the treetops, you'll find an ideal place for small cocktail parties, marriage proposals, and wedding ceremonies.

Old Fort Pub serves Lowcountry cuisine for dinner seven days a week and offers brunch on Sunday; reservations are a must in the evenings and should be made three to four days in advance. The dinner menu includes dishes such as Atlantic salmon, crab cakes, and herb-crusted rack of lamb.

While you're at Old Fort Pub, which was built in 1974 in a style inspired by the architecture of the Lowcountry, take time to stroll around the remains of Fort Mitchel, a Civil War gun battery on the site adjacent to the restaurant. Pathways wind through what were once the bunkers and moats of a fortification constructed by the Union Army after it captured the island in November 1861.

The restaurant is in Hilton Head Plantation on the northwestern part of the island (see the Planned Residential Communities section of this chapter). To get there, take William Hilton Parkway to Squire Pope Road, which is between mile markers 1 and 2. Turn north on Squire Pope and stay on it until you reach the Hilton Head Plantation gate; the guard there will give you a pass and directions to the restaurant.

The Old Oyster Factory   **Moderate**
101 Marshland Road
(843) 681-6040
www.oldoysterfactory.com

With its floor-to-ceiling windows, this multi-level restaurant offers splendid views of beautiful Broad Creek and the adjacent marsh from its 270 seats. Built of pegged timbers on the site of one of Hilton Head's oyster canneries and opened in 1989, the restaurant serves steaks and seafood, including oysters from surrounding waters prepared several different ways. The shrimp offered by The Old Oyster Factory comes from nearby Calibogue Sound, provided by Capt. Woody Collins and brought to the restaurant's dock aboard his boat. Shrimp is part of one of the restaurant's big sellers—the seafood medley, which also consists of scallops, oysters, and choice fish fillets. Another popular dish is the salmon en croute (in pastry), but you'll have to ask your server about it—it's not on the menu. The Old Oyster Factory is open for dinner daily and provides live entertainment on the dock from May through September.

Reilley's   **Inexpensive**
7-D Greenwood Drive
(843) 842-4414

Port Royal Plaza
Mathews Drive
(843) 681-4153

The easygoing atmosphere of the Reilley's in Hilton Head Plaza on Greenwood Drive is what you'd expect from a restaurant that has a deck once called the "Barmuda Triangle." Reilley's menu, adorned with shamrocks and leprechauns, lists a wide variety of offerings including several variations of Blarney Burgers and Super Sandwiches. If you're in the mood for a dinner, flip to the Longtime Favorites section, where you'll find steaks and a couple of dishes suited to Gaelic tastes—the corned beef and cabbage and the cottage pie, which is ground chuck seasoned with mushrooms and onions and topped with peas, homemade mashed potatoes, and cheddar cheese.

Reilley's takes credit for organizing the island's first St. Patrick's Day parade, a celebration started in 1983, the year after the restaurant opened in the Gallery of Shops. In 1995 the restaurant moved to its existing location in Hilton Head Plaza just south of the Sea Pines traffic circle. Reilley's serves lunch and dinner daily and offers a champagne-and-eggs brunch on Saturday and Sunday. The menu and atmosphere are much the same at the Reilley's at Port Royal Plaza on Mathews Drive, but there's no deck.

Sage Room   Expensive
13 Heritage Plaza
(843) 785-5352

Although the Sage Room nestles in one of the least-conspicuous locations of any restaurant on the island, that hasn't kept locals from flocking there. And if you make the effort to find it, you'll see why. The chefs work in an open kitchen, turning out a variety of dishes featuring seafood, fowl, and steak, plus Colorado rack of lamb and roasted pork tenderloin. Appetizers include some you won't encounter often—butternut squash soup, horseradish-crusted mozzarella, and the snow-pea martini. The Sage Room serves lunch Monday through Friday and dinner Monday through Saturday. As for that location, it's in the northwestern corner of Heritage Plaza, which is on the north side of Pope Avenue close to Coligny Circle.

Santa Fe Cafe   Moderate-Expensive
700 Plantation Center
(843) 785-3838
www.santafecafeofhiltonhead.com

Owner and chef Jim Buckingham spent his younger days in the Southwest, and he brings his appreciation for that region to his cooking. The upscale Southwestern cuisine of his Santa Fe Cafe is spicy food based on many types of chiles, resulting in dishes such as grilled pork tenderloin with smoked habañero barbecue sauce, black beans, and sweet potato fries; herb-roasted free-range chicken with jalapeño corn-bread stuffing and roasted garlic mashed potatoes; and grouper with chipotle (smoked chile) Parmesan au gratin. After several years of operating a limited chain of Mexican restaurants, Buckingham decided to concentrate his efforts on one establishment and in 1993 opened this cafe off William Hilton Parkway near mile marker 8. The stylishly Southwestern Santa Fe serves

i If you suffer a sweet-tooth attack while on the island, glide on over to Signe's Heaven Bound Bakery & Cafe at 93 Arrow Road. The main attractions are the truly angelic pastries and other goodies, such as the banana nut bread and the Key lime pound cake, but Signe's also serves breakfasts, salads, and hot and cold sandwiches. There's seating inside or on the outdoor deck.

dinner seven nights a week and lunch on Monday through Friday, and reservations are accepted.

Steamers Seafood Company   Moderate
28 Coligny Plaza
(843) 785-2070

Steamers specializes in fresh fish, shrimp, lobster tails, and certified Angus beef. For shellfish lovers, there's a platter consisting of steamed oysters, clams, shrimp, crawfish, mussels, and snow crab. At Steamers, you can eat outside on the decks beside the Coligny Plaza shopping center lagoon or inside in the fish-camp atmosphere of the dining room or raw bar. Barn and dock wood and corrugated tin on the walls and bars complete the pier-side look.

Steamers, which serves lunch and dinner daily, offers unique appetizers and more than 100 beers from around the world. This fun-loving restaurant has served seafood lovers on Hilton Head since 1991.

Stellini Italian Restaurant   Moderate
15 Pope Avenue, Executive Park
(843) 785-7006

This "little star" of an Italian restaurant shines forth from a wooded nook off Pope Avenue. Owner Joe Pesce and his partners have created the comfortable look of the Little Italy section of New York City at Stellini, which serves dinner Monday through Saturday. Especially inviting is the 40-seat Carolina Room, a porch with views of the surrounding forest. The restaurant also has a main dining room for 50. The menu provides an extensive selection of northern Italian fare, including chicken pancetta, a chicken breast sautéed in a light cream sauce with pancetta bacon and broccoli over angel-hair pasta; veal sorrento, medallions of veal sautéed in white wine topped with eggplant and melted mozzarella cheese in marinara sauce over angel hair; and zuppa di pesce, clams, shrimp, scallops, mussels, calamari, and grouper in marinara over linguine. One item you won't find on the menu is a special that's offered often: the veal chop stuffed with prosciutto and mozzarella. Pesce suggests making reservations to dine at Stellini, which opened in 1988. The restaurant is closed on Sunday and for a brief period during the winter.

Stripes: An American Grill　　Expensive
114 Office Park Road
(843) 686-4747

Co-owner and chef Steve Hancotte describes the food served at his restaurant near the Sea Pines traffic circle as "American regional." By that, Hancotte means that in creating his dishes he takes advantage of all the United States has to offer in the way of cuisine. Some examples of his red, white, and blue artistry: jumbo lump crab with garlic-dusted fries; char-grilled prime beef filet served with mushroom sauce and a gorgonzola custard; and Louisiana catfish fillet, pan-fried in Cajun spices and served with Smithfield ham on a black pepper cream.

Stripes, which opened in 1991, has seating for 72 in a casual atmosphere featuring caned chairs. The full bar offers a long wine list that's constantly changing and growing. The menu at Stripes is also revised on a seasonal basis. The restaurant is open for dinner seven days a week and is closed during the first three weeks of December. Reservations are recommended.

The Tapas Restaurant　　Moderate
11 Northridge Plaza
(843) 681-8590

Ever wanted to try something a companion is eating but felt self-conscious taking it from him or her? When you dine at The Tapas, such behavior is not only acceptable, it's expected. Tapas is Spanish for "little bits," and the small dishes served at this cozy, elegant bistro in Northridge Plaza off William Hilton Parkway between mile markers 4 and 5 are perfect for sharing. Say you're dining with three other people and each of you orders three different selections from the restaurant's menu of more than 50 items; that means you get a taste of twelve different dishes. Each item is served on an individual plate, and diners are provided with sharing plates.

Among the dishes you might try are the veal Anthony (tenderloin of veal sautéed in garlic butter, with cream sherry and mushrooms), escargot spinnochi (snails sautéed with garlic, spinach, and bacon cream sauce, topped with Parmesan cheese, and baked), and shrimp Parthenon (shrimp sautéed with feta cheese, oregano, and tomato bisque and served in a phylo shell). While you're at The Tapas, be sure to look up at the ceiling with its multitude of hanging wicker baskets. The 56-seat restaurant is open for lunch Tuesday through Friday, and for dinner nightly; reservations are suggested. Smoking is prohibited.

Truffles Cafe　　Inexpensive
71 Lighthouse Road
(843) 671-6136
www.truffles.com

Islander Price Beall has owned and operated this casually elegant restaurant in Sea Pines Center since its opening in 1983. With seating for 150, Truffles is larger than the typical cafe but retains the atmosphere of a bistro. The food is American in style, with specialties like chicken potpie made with white wine sauce and pasta New Orleans—a chicken breast served over pasta, tossed in a spicy cream sauce. Other favorites of regular customers are the ribs, grilled fish, pasta dishes, and Caesar and Monterey salads, both of which feature grilled chicken. Lunch and dinner are served daily.

NIGHTLIFE

Hilton Head is a resort that caters to families who are on the go throughout the day and to golfers with early-morning tee times, so it's not exactly a hotbed of nightlife activity. There are, however, nightspots at several hotels and motels, including the Regatta Lounge at the Hilton, Signals at the Crowne Plaza, the Playful Pelican at the Westin, and Conroy's Lounge at the Marriott. Some of Hilton Head's restaurants also have lounges where you can hang out and catch live entertainment.

There are three movie theaters on the island: Coligny Theatre in Coligny Plaza, Northridge Cinemas at 435 William Hilton Parkway at mile marker 5, and Park Plaza Cinemas in the Park Plaza Shopping Center off Greenwood Drive. Coligny Theatre has 1 screen, Northridge has 10, and Park Plaza has 5.

If you've spent your day knocking a tennis ball around, pedaling a few miles on bicycle paths, and frolicking in the surf, and you still haven't pooped out, you might consider these other nighttime entertainment options:

The Jazz Corner
The Village at Wexford
(843) 842-8620
www.thejazzcorner.com

This nightspot—appropriately tucked in a corner of the Village at Wexford shopping complex—offers live music and fine dining each evening of the week. The focus is on the smooth jazz of the 1950s and 1960s, but swing-era music and dancing and Dixieland is also featured. The Jazz Corner makes the most of an abundance of local talent while also presenting well-known performers such as pianist-singer Mose Allison and vocalist Tierney Sutton. Dinner is available, with entrees averaging $20 and including dishes such as crispy flounder, seafood-stuffed salmon, Oysters Gillespie (named for trumpeter Dizzy, no doubt), and veal piccata.

The Lodge
Hilton Head Plaza
(843) 842-8966
www.thelodgebar.com

The island's only cigar bar has an interior resembling a hunting lodge. You can satisfy your competitive instincts at four billiards tables and the shuffleboard table, or you can relax in front of one of the two fireplaces with a drink from the full bar or a cigar from The Lodge's large stock of smokes. In addition to wine by the glass, single malts, ales, cognacs, and bourbons, the bar serves a specialty drink, the chocolate martini. This establishment in Hilton Head Plaza, off Greenwood Drive near the Sea Pines traffic circle, opens at 5:00 p.m. daily.

SHOPPING

The shopping is plentiful on Hilton Head, which has stores of every description located in large shopping centers, in strip malls, and along the island's out-of-the-way streets and byways. To get you started, we've provided rundowns on a few of the bigger shopping areas and pointed out some of the stores you can find there. Knock yourself out.

Shopping Centers

Coligny Plaza
124 North Forest Beach Drive
(843) 842-6050
www.colignyplaza.com

Coligny Plaza, the island's oldest and largest shopping center, rambles over nearly nine acres at the Coligny traffic circle on the south end of the island. Sixty retail stores and restaurants—some of them tucked into nooks and crannies along the center's covered walkways—offer a wide range of goods and dining experiences.

The Plaza mixes specialty shops with conventional businesses such as a hardware store and a Piggly Wiggly supermarket. Among the specialty stores are Black Market Minerals, a rock and mineral shop; Jamaican Me Crazy, a clothing store that's Caribbean in

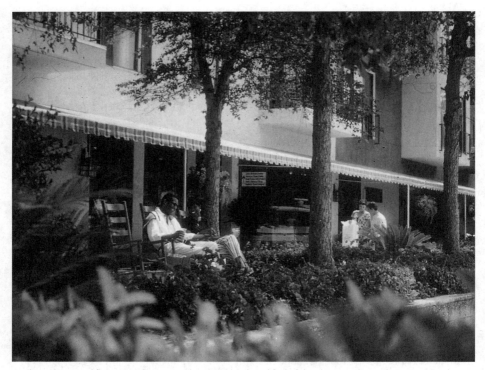

Rocking chairs and flowering plants contribute to the relaxed feel of the shops at the Harbour Town Yacht Basin in The Sea Pines Resort. COURTESY OF THE HILTON HEAD ISLAND VISITOR AND CONVENTION BUREAU

character; the Shell Shop; the Island Fudge Shop, where sweets are made before your eyes; the Coligny Kite and Flag Company; and The Magic Puppet & Toys Too. There are also a plethora of clothing stores, with the emphasis on beach and sportswear.

More than a dozen eating places offer everything from Italian cuisine at the Just Pasta Café to seafood at Steamers Seafood Company (see listing in the Restaurants section of this chapter) to sandwiches at the Art Cafe, Coligny Deli, and The Earle of Sandwich.

The shopping center was called Circle Square when it was started by J. Norris Richardson and his wife, Lois, in 1956. Consisting in its earliest form of the Forest Beach Market grocery store, a Laundromat, a real-estate office, and a beauty shop, the center has been expanded four times since the mid-1950s and was given its existing name in

1965. Members of the Richardson clan continue to operate the center, which is composed mostly of family-owned businesses.

On summer evenings, Coligny Plaza stages puppet shows and other family-oriented entertainment in the piazza off North Forest Beach Drive. The shopping center also hosts special events during the year, including an Irish festival held in conjunction with the island's St. Patrick's Day parade; a Halloween festival, during which shop owners dress in costume and open their doors to trick-or-treaters; and appearances by the Easter Bunny and Santa Claus, with the latter arriving at the shopping center via fire truck.

Harbour Town
Harbour Town Yacht Basin
(843) 363-5655
www.harbourtown.com

More than 20 shops and eating places grace the north side of beautiful Harbour Town Yacht Basin. When you're not busy wandering in and out of shops such as Camp Hilton Head, Currents women's apparel store, the Cinnamon Bear County Store, the Planet Hilton Head nature store, and Harbour Town Crafts; or dining at restaurants such as The Crazy Crab or Cafe Europa, you can relax outside by plopping down in one of the many rocking chairs and watching the activity in the boat-filled marina. The Harbour Town shopping complex is in The Sea Pines Resort. If you're not staying at the resort, be prepared to pay a $5 entry fee.

The Mall at Shelter Cove
24 Shelter Cove Lane
(843) 686-3090
www.mallatsheltercove.com
Hilton Head's only enclosed shopping mall accommodates more than 50 stores in a tropical setting featuring potted palm trees and other plants. Anchoring the northern end of the mall is a department store you might not expect to find on a Southern sea island—an Off 5th/Saks Fifth Avenue Outlet. At the southern end of the shopping center is the other anchor, Belk (for women and juniors); scattered in between are Belk for men, children, and home goods; and several stores offering high-quality wearing apparel including Ann Taylor, Banana Republic, Talbots, Express, Jos. A. Bank, The White House/Black Market, Chico's, Swim 'n Sport, and Victoria's Secret.

Shoppers seeking to pamper themselves should find products to their liking at Bath & Body Works and Crabtree & Evelyn, and there's a Waldenbooks store for those in search of reading material. Among specialty shops are The Blut Parrot gift shop, Bombay, and Williams-Sonoma cookware store. The mall has spacious corridors and a large center court that's the site of special events, arts and crafts shows, and prolonged visits by Santa Claus and the Easter Bunny. On the fringes of the center area is a food court with lots of seating and two vendors, Manchu Wok, and

Ice Creams & Coffee Beans. The mall, which opened in 1988, is off William Hilton Parkway near mile marker 9.

Pineland Station
430 William Hilton Parkway
(843) 681-8907
www.pinelandstation.com
This upscale shopping center, which dates back to 1979, was completely renovated in 1997. It wends its way over 10 acres on the north end of the island. Covered walkways lush with foliage and potted plants connect the four retail buildings, and there's a special events staging area set among gardens, a fountain, a waterwheel, and the center's well-known duck pond.

Shoppers will find stores offering apparel, including Children's Clothing Company, Tradewinds, and Tanner; several dealing in home accents and gifts, including Idyllic Endeavors, Baskets by Jean, the Bright Morning Star, An Added Touch, and Marco Polo Imports; a Stein Mart; a Starbucks Coffee Shop; Vic's Tavern; and five restaurants—Le Bistro, Philly's Cafe and Deli, Juniper Cafe, Il Carpaccio Ristorante & Pizzeria, and The French Bakery and Cafe. Pineland Station, which has more than 100,000 square feet of retail space, is between mile markers 4 and 5 on the parkway.

Village at Wexford
1000 William Hilton Parkway
(843) 842-2240
If you're looking for variety, you'll find it at the Village at Wexford, where the majority of the 30 stores and eateries are locally owned. This quaint-looking stucco retail and office complex sits on nine wooded acres off the parkway near mile marker 10, and houses La Cookery kitchen accessories, an Audubon Nature Store, Mum's the Word florist and gift shop, Pretty Paper stationery store, and Smith Galleries, which deals in artwork and jewelry. Several stores offer women's apparel, including Patricia's, The Honey Vine, and The Porcupine. Island Child specializes in clothing

Close-up

Hilton Head's Gone Gator

If you get near a body of fresh or brackish water on Hilton Head, which is hard not to do given the preponderance of the island's lakes and lagoons, there's a good chance you will see a creature that looks as though it has crawled right out of *Jurassic Park*. This is the American alligator, the largest reptile on the North American continent and one of the oldest surviving vertebrates on the planet.

Alligators abound on Hilton Head, where developers have provided readymade homes for them by creating the waterways that decorate the island's communities and golf courses. "If there's a mud puddle in the Low-country, there's an alligator in it," says Dean Harrigal, who coordinates the alligator nuisance program in the area. There have been no formal surveys of the alligator population on Hilton Head, but there are probably from 2,000 to 4,000 gators living on the island, says Walt Rhodes, the alligator project supervisor for the South Carolina Department of Natural Resources.

Alligators, which are protected by state and federal law, can grow to a length of 12 feet, but most of the gators removed from Hilton Head under the nuisance program are from 6 to 8 feet long, according to Harrigal. Even so, if left alone, alligators pose little threat to humans, say Rhodes and Harrigal. "Gators are naturally shy of people," says Rhodes. According to the two alligator experts, humans are more of a threat to gators than vice versa.

If the state receives a complaint about a gator on Hilton Head, and the animal is deemed a nuisance because of its behavior or location, the reptile will be removed. Removed, in this case, means destroyed, not relocated. Relocating a gator doesn't work because of the animal's strong homing instinct: Gators have been known to travel as much as 30 miles to return to their nesting areas, Rhodes and Harrigal say. About 50 gators are removed from Hilton Head each year because of complaints against them, but the two say that wouldn't be the case if people were more tolerant of the animals, who were here first (present-day gators are direct descendants of a

and shoes for youngsters. The restaurants at the Village at Wexford range from those offering fast food to those devoted to casual and fine dining; at one end of the spectrum are Wendy's and Subway, with the Iron Wolf Chop House, the British Open Pub, Antonio's, and the Cafe at Wexford (see this chapter's Restaurants section) at the other. The center is also the site of the Jazz Corner.

Bookstores

Barnes & Noble
20 Hatton Place
(843) 342-6690
This branch of the nation's largest bookseller opened in July 1998 and offers islanders and visitors more than 175,000 titles, a mind-boggling selection of magazines, and a cafe where you can sit, read, and drink juice, tea, or coffee

creature that lived in what is now Florida during the Miocene epoch, which occurred 25 million years ago). People don't like gators for a number of reasons. For one thing, the alligator's appearance is not in its favor. The gator looks like a big lizard, only uglier, and it seems to have a malevolent smile permanently plastered on its bumpy face. "It's not Bambi," says Rhodes. "It's not warm and fuzzy, it's cold and scaly." For another, most people don't know much about alligators and their relatively placid temperament. Folks confuse gators with the crocodiles found on other continents, in particular the 14-foot crocs seen devouring water buffaloes in sensationalized nature flicks. Gators, says Rhodes, "will let you alone if you let them alone, and they'll see you first."

Humans have a tendency to bring out the aggressiveness in gators by feeding them. If a person feeds a gator enough times, the beast's golf ball–size brain begins to associate the human with food. This is, if you'll pardon the phrase, a recipe for disaster that can be harmful to the human involved and fatal to the gator. It's also against the law: If you're caught feeding an alligator, you can be fined $200 or sentenced to 30 days in jail. There are cases of humans provoking gators into attacking them. Rhodes tells of a golfer who hit his ball near a gator that was sunning itself on a Hilton Head fairway, then smacked the animal with his golf club in the process of recovering the ball. The gator bit the golfer. "The gator did what you would do if someone hit you with a golf club," says Rhodes. There have been reports of people being pursued by gators, but Rhodes says he's handled in excess of 3,000 of the animals and has never been chased.

Rhodes's rules for coexisting with gators: Don't feed them; they find plenty to eat in the form of insects, crustaceans, fish, and snakes. Don't tease them. For goodness sake, don't try to pet them. Look at them all you want but do so from afar. "Give the animal the respect it deserves," says Rhodes. "It has as much right to be here as the deer, squirrels, and people."

and munch on gourmet cookies. Special features of the 20,250-square-foot store are the storytime sessions for children on Wednesday and Saturday at 10:00 a.m. The store's Special Order Express service will order any book from more than 1.2 million in print, and deliveries usually take place within seven days. This spacious store is just off William Hilton Parkway between mile markers 3 and 4.

The Island Bookseller
71 Lighthouse Road
(843) 671-3773
Although Joni and Jon Minier's bookstore at Sea Pines Center covers only 1,400 square feet, it offers a full range of fiction and nonfiction categories and includes a comprehensive collection of children's books. Another section of the store is devoted to volumes featur-

ing the Lowcountry, and the Miniers do their utmost to promote local authors.

During the summer months, The Island Bookseller keeps on hand a hefty stock of what Jon Minier calls "beach reads"—paperbacks for the side of the pool or the sand near the ocean's edge. This store, which has been in business in Sea Pines since 1983, does a lot of special ordering of books and also carries greeting cards, journals, calendars, puzzles, and games.

Port Royal Bookstore
Village at Wexford
(843) 842-6996

Owner John Stern refers to his small but well-stocked bookstore at the Village at Wexford shopping center as being old-fashioned—one where you can sit in a comfortable chair and read a book or have the staff special-order a hard-to-find volume. Stern constantly peruses catalogs in an effort to maintain an extensive inventory of books covering a wide range of topics including "The War of Northern Aggression," which is what some Southerners still call the Civil War.

The store rents best sellers by the day or week, a service designed with vacationers in mind. While you're at the store, take a gander at Stern's collection of miniature lead soldiers, which is displayed near the front of the shop.

GOLF

Hilton Head is heaven on earth for golfers. There are 25 courses on the island, many of them world-class and all of them dripping with Lowcountry charm. Seventeen are open to the public, and information on these follows.

The courses we've described have amenities such as pro shops, practice greens, and driving ranges. Many of these courses do not allow walking, but we've pointed out which ones do and to what extent. The greens fees listed include carts, and they reflect rates during the most popular playing times (generally spring and fall).

The rates included are for players not staying at the resorts associated with the courses. You can make arrangements to play these courses by calling directly, through the resort where you're staying, or via central golf reservation services such as Last Minute Tee Times (843-689-2262, 800-767-5423), Golf Island Call Center (888-465-3475), and Hilton Head Accommodations & Golf Hotline (843-686-6662, 800-444-4772).

That said, let's tee it up and take a swing at golfing on Hilton Head Island at . . .

Country Club of Hilton Head
70 Skull Creek Drive
(843) 681-2582
www.hiltonheadclub.com

Many of the greens on this par-72, 6,543-yard course at Hilton Head Plantation run near the Intracoastal Waterway, and the 12th is right on it. Designed by Rees Jones and built in 1985, the course has two holes longer than 540 yards, including the uphill, par 4, 556-yard 18th. Greens and fairways are Bermuda grass. Greens fees are $99.

Golden Bear Golf Club
72 Golden Bear Way
(843) 689-2200
www.goldenbear-indigorun.com

What a great name for a golf course! Interestingly enough, the chief architect of this Jack Nicklaus design was not the Golden Bear himself but the late Bruce Borland. Players of this 6,643-yard layout at Indigo Run will find a real challenge in the 11th hole—it runs 430 yards and features a long dogleg to the left and water on the left side of the green. This par-72 course has fairways and greens of Bermuda grass set among lagoons and stands of pine and hardwoods. Among the amenities are a bar and grill. You'll spend $87 in the morning, $60 after noon, and $50 after 2:00 p.m. to play this course.

Oyster Reef Golf Club
155 High Bluff Road
(843) 681-1745
www.hiltonheadgolf.net
The sixth hole at Oyster Reef—a par 3, 160-yarder—overlooks Port Royal Sound, giving golfers a fine view of that majestic body of water on the northern side of Hilton Head. The par-72 layout, which is the work of Rees Jones, covers 6,440 yards at Hilton Head Plantation. The greens were converted to Tif Eagle Bermuda grass in 2000. There are 9 ponds and 66 bunkers for players to contend with. At the end of a round, players can relax at the club's bar and restaurant. Greens fees run $95.

Palmetto Dunes Golf Courses
1 Trent Jones Lane
(843) 785-1136, (800) 827-3006
www.palmettodunes.com
Palmetto Dunes offers golfers three 18-hole courses from which to choose, each of them named for their heavy-hitting designers: Arthur Hills, George Fazio, and Robert Trent Jones. You can cover them on foot if you want to. Unrestricted walking is allowed at all times of the day. Rates on the Fazio and Jones Courses run $95, while the Hills Course is $148.

Arthur Hills Course
This heavily wooded par 72 was reconditioned during the mid-1990s, with all the greens being rebuilt. One of the most interesting holes is the 12th, a par 4 that's bordered by water along one side. The course measures 6,122 yards.

George Fazio Course
The Fazio Course covers 6,239 yards and is characterized by rolling fairways and lots of long par 4s—there are only two par 5s and three par 3s. You'll have to shoot 70 to make par on this layout, which ends with a hole where two bunkers provide a significant challenge.

Robert Trent Jones Course
If you like playing by the water, you'll enjoy this 6,570-yard course, which provides a winding lagoon system tied into 11 holes and a great view of the ocean from No. 10. Other hallmarks of this par 72 are open fairways and large greens.

Palmetto Hall Plantation
108 Fort Howell Drive
(843) 689-4100, (800) 827-3006
www.palmettodunes.com
Palmetto Hall offers golfers the opportunity to enjoy a Lowcountry-style clubhouse and 18-hole courses designed by Arthur Hills and Robert Cupp. The 16,000-square-foot clubhouse is a repository of historic artifacts (both Lowcountry- and golfing-related), antiques, and paintings and features a grill room with the aura of a club. Greens fees for the par-72 courses are $95.

Arthur Hills Course
The signature hole here is No. 18, a 434-yarder with water running up the left side of the fairway. It's a challenging par 4. Another hole featuring plenty of water is the 5th, but the water on this beauty is on the right side. The hole runs 490 yards and is a par 5. This 6,257-yard course was opened in 1991. Walking is prohibited.

Robert Cupp Course
Unrestricted walking is allowed on this 6,042-yard course, which was unveiled two years after the Arthur Hills layout. Vistas of marshlands and forests of oak and pine are features of this par-72 course, along with its straight lines and sharp angles.

Port Royal Golf Club
10 Clubhouse Drive
(843) 689-1760
www.hiltonheadgolf.net
This golf club at the Port Royal resort community has three 18-hole courses—Barony, Planter's Row, and Robber's Row—plus a bar and restaurant. Greens fees run $90 in the morning, $60 after noon, and $45 after 2:00 p.m.

i If you should somehow run out of golf courses to play on Hilton Head, be advised that there are several fine off-island layouts nearby. Among them are four on US 278, the road to the island—Eagle's Point (843-815-3100), Hilton Head National Golf Club (843-842-5900), Island West (843-689-6660), and Old South Golf Links (843-785-5353).

Barony Course

The long drivers will take a backseat to the shot makers on this 6,223-yard course, which has many small greens. The Barony, which was designed by George Cobb, presents players with a test of skill at No. 12, a par-4, 411-yard hole with water on both sides of the fairway.

Planter's Row Course

Willard Byrd was the designer responsible for Planter's Row, where golfers finish on a par-5, 511-yard hole featuring woods and water. If that's not enough of a challenge, consider No. 12, a narrow, 419-yard hole where you've got to cross water to.get to the green. The course measures 6,284 yards, and par is 72.

Robber's Row Course

Robber's Row represents a team effort by designers George Cobb and Pete Dye. The course was built in 1967 and reconfigured in 1994 by Dye, who added several water hazards. This par-72 course runs 6,311 yards.

Sea Pines Resort
www.seapines.com

Sea Pines is the home of three of the island's most popular golf courses, including the Harbour Town Golf Links, which is the site of Hilton Head's number one sporting event, the Verizon Heritage. Walking is allowed on all three courses.

Harbour Town Golf Links
11 Lighthouse Lane
(843) 363-8385, (800) 955-8337

The signature hole at Harbour Town is the one you've seen countless times on television—the windswept 18th, a par 4 on Calibogue Sound where shots to the green often end up among the fiddler crabs in the adjacent marsh. Consistently ranked among the world's top courses, this one was designed by Pete Dye and Jack Nicklaus and has some outstanding par 3s. The yardage at this par-71 course totals 6,040. Greens fees run $250.

Ocean Course
100 North Sea Pines Drive
(843) 842-8484, (800) 955-8337

The 15th hole on this oldest and newest of island courses offers a terrific view of the ocean. It's the oldest course because it was designed by George Cobb in 1962 and the newest because it was remodeled by Mark McCumber in 1995. Greens fees for this par-72, 6,172-yard layout run $114.

Heron Point Course
100 North Sea Pines Drive
(843) 842-8484, (800) 955-8337

You'll encounter wide fairways and lots of lagoons, trees, and marshes when you play this par-72 course, which was redesigned by Pete Dye and reopened after a year of work in September 2007. The previous name was Sea Marsh.

Shipyard Golf Club
45 Shipyard Drive
(843) 689-GOLF, (800) 2-FIND-18
www.hiltonheadgolf.net

Shipyard offers three interconnecting 9-hole courses appropriately named for three types of sailing vessels: Brigantine, Clipper, and Galleon. There is water involved on 25 of the 27 holes, which have Bermuda grass fairways and greens. There's a bar and restaurant on the premises. Greens fees are $90 in the morning, $60 after noon, and $45 after 2:00 p.m.

Brigantine Course

The work of designer Willard Byrd, the Brigantine is a 3,054-yard, par 36 surrounded by private homes and rental condominiums that blend in with the natural environment. You'll be challenged by No. 6, a long par 4; and No. 9, which is a par 5 that runs 494 yards and has water on one side of the fairway.

Clipper Course
The 3,302-yard Clipper has a tough 9th hole with lots of bunkers. Water comes into play on all the holes except No. 6, which is a par 4, 415-yarder. George Cobb also designed this course, which carries a par 36.

Galleon Course
This George Cobb–designed, par-36 course is best known for No. 2, a par 5 with an elevated green fronted by water and with bunkers all around. Total yardage for the course is 3,146.

TENNIS

If you'd rather be hitting a fuzzy yellow ball instead of a dimpled white ball, you'll find plenty of opportunities to do so at the numerous tennis facilities on the island. Among those open to the public for play are the following:

Palmetto Dunes Tennis Center
6 Trent Jones Lane
(843) 785-1152, (800) 972-0257
www.palmettodunes.com
An array of instructional programs and daily round-robin tournaments are featured at the tennis center at Palmetto Dunes. The tournaments are billed as "lively afternoon social competition with the emphasis on fun." There are 23 clay and 2 hard courts, 8 of which are lighted.

Reserved rates are $20 for guests and $25 for players not staying at the resort. Walk-on rates are $15 from noon to 4:00 p.m.

Port Royal Racquet Club
15 Wimbledon Court
(843) 686-8803
The Port Royal Racquet Club is the only tennis facility on Hilton Head—and in all of South Carolina, for that matter—offering all three

Grand Slam–type playing surfaces. There are 10 clay courts, 4 cushioned hard courts, and 2 grass courts. The club offers a variety of instructional programs and will custom design clinics for individuals and teams.

Located at Port Royal Plantation, the club has a well-stocked pro shop that provides a varied selection of men's and women's tennis wear and the latest in equipment. Reserved rates for clay and hard courts are $18 per hour, with walk-ons accepted at a fee of $12 per hour. You'll need reservations for the grass courts, and you'll pay $25 an hour to play on them.

Sea Pines Racquet Club
5 Lighthouse Lane
(843) 363-4495, (800) 732-7463
www.seapines.com
Programs and instruction take center court at the Sea Pines Racquet Club, which *Tennis Magazine* has ranked number two in the country. The flagship program is the Smith Stearns Tennis Academy, named in part after Stan Smith, the former U.S. Open and Wimbledon champion who serves as the club's touring pro and tennis consultant.

There are various programs for every age group, and 23 courts are available for play. The club has 11 instructors led by the genial Job de Boer, who specializes in teaching groups.

The club dates from the early 1970s. The pro shop offers players the latest in tennis fashions, equipment, and footwear. Court fees are $23 per hour.

Van Der Meer Shipyard Tennis Resort
116 Shipyard Drive
(843) 686-8804, (800) 845-6138
www.vandermeertennis.com
Twenty courts set amid the lush surroundings of Shipyard Plantation await the tennis buff at this racquet club, which the United States Tennis Association presented with its Outstanding Tennis Facility of the Year Award for 1997. There are 13 clay courts and 4 hard-surface courts outdoors and 3 DecoTurf courts

indoors (a total of 5 courts have lights). The club also offers a variety of tennis getaway weeks and weekends, stroke of the day sessions, daily drills, and intensive drills available year-round. The intensive drills are geared for players with 4.0-plus ratings and are designed to take skills to the next level.

The club, owned by premier tennis teacher Dennis Van der Meer, holds exhibitions by tennis professionals on Monday from March through October, with admission and refreshments free. The Shipyard Racquet Club has a large pro shop displaying an extensive variety of items, and it's also the site of the United States Professional Tennis Registry's International Tennis Symposium and $25,000 Championships, which are held annually during the middle of February.

Reserved rates for the club's clay courts are $25 per hour, with walk-ons paying $18 per hour from noon to 4:00 p.m. Fees for hard courts are $20 per hour reserved, $15 walk-on. Covered courts must be reserved, and fees are $40 per hour.

Van Der Meer Tennis Center
19 DeAllyon Road
(843) 785-8388, (800) 845-6138
This tennis center operated by well-known instructor Dennis Van der Meer provides a multitude of programs for adults and junior players in all stages of development, from beginners to aspiring professionals. There are

i Travelers intent on hiking, bicycling, and observing wildlife will find a pleasing venue in the form of the Pinckney Island National Wildlife Refuge, located off US 278 a mile west of Hilton Head Island. The refuge offers more than 14 miles of trails and accommodates large concentrations of wading birds and an active bald eagle nest. Pinckney Island, the largest land mass in the refuge and the only one open to the public, covers 1,200 acres. Admission is free.

17 hard-surface courts, of which 4 are covered and lighted, with fees for an hour of play set at $15. The center has a pro shop and is the headquarters of the Van der Meer Tennis University, which offers training programs for tennis teachers. The center is on DeAllyon Road, which runs off Cordillo Parkway on the south end of the island.

ANNUAL EVENTS

The island's most significant annual events occur during the spring. The biggest one—the Verizon Heritage—shouldn't be missed if you're a golf fan.

Verizon Heritage
Harbour Town Golf Links
11 Lighthouse Lane
(843) 671-2448, (800) 234-1107
www.verizonheritage.com
The Verizon Heritage brings 132 invited players and 125,000 spectators to famed Harbour Town Golf Links in The Sea Pines Resort during four days in April. In 2008 players will compete for $5.5 million in prize money ($990,000 to the winner) and the right to wear the Tartan plaid jacket awarded to the winner of this prestigious tournament. Boo Weekly was the 2007 winner, and Ernie Els finished second. Weekly is on a list of champions that includes Jack Nicklaus, Greg Norman, Nick Price, Hale Irwin, Tom Watson, and Arnold Palmer, who won the tournament in its inaugural year of 1969 when it was known as the Heritage Classic.

Attending the Heritage involves more than watching a golf tournament. The event is usually held during the second week in April, when the weather is generally lovely and nature is putting on a springtime show. It's a terrific time to get outdoors, amble around the verdant Harbour Town course, visit the shops and restaurants at the Harbour Town Yacht Basin near the first tee and 18th green, gawk at the high-priced boats docked in the marina, and observe the hordes of spectators doing all of these things. Sometime during their day at the course, those attending are invariably drawn to the 18th hole, which overlooks Calibogue Sound and has the Harbour Town Lighthouse as part of its backdrop, to see how the players finish up and deal with the wind blowing off the water.

During the three days leading up to the tournament, which starts on Thursday and ends on Sunday, there are two pro-am events and a pro-am fishing tournament. On the Monday afternoon before Thursday's first round of play, the Heritage presents opening ceremonies focusing on golf's Scottish origins and the game's long history in South Carolina (the South Carolina Golf Club of Charleston was founded in 1786 and is reputed to be the oldest membership golf club in America). The defending champion, tournament board members clad in plaid, and bagpipers from The Citadel military college parade along the yacht basin to the 18th green, where the defending champ gets the tourney under way by smacking a ball into Calibogue Sound as a Civil War–era cannon is fired. A practice-round badge—which entitles the wearer to admission to all Monday–Wednesday events, including the opening ceremonies and pro-am contests—was $35 in 2007.

A grounds badge, which is good for admission to the tournament grounds for the entire week of Heritage events, costs $115. A clubhouse badge, which gives you access for the entire week to the grounds, the clubhouse, and the Heritage Pavilion, a hospitality tent, costs $145. As stated earlier, practice round badges enable you to attend all the events leading up to the four-day tournament. Also, there are patron plans available for large groups of spectators; for details on these, contact the Heritage staff at the phone numbers listed for this entry. Parking for the Heritage is in lots within Sea Pines, and spectators are shuttled by bus to Harbour Town. The parking and the bus service are complimentary.

St. Patrick's Day Parade
Pope Avenue
(843) 842-4319
What started as a march by a few residents of Irish descent in 1983 has matured into the largest free spectator event held on the island. Some 20,000 onlookers gather to watch the two-hour parade, which is held on the Sunday before St. Patrick's Day or on the day itself when the holiday falls on Sunday. If you go, expect to see marching bands, in the neighborhood of 30 floats, dance groups, a bagpipe band or two, local dignitaries, and maybe even Budweiser's Clydesdale horses. The parade starts at 2:00 p.m. at Coligny Circle and proceeds west on Pope Avenue to Office Park Road and into Park Plaza. Tom Reilley started the celebration in 1983 when he and a few friends decided to march in honor of St. Patrick. Because they didn't have a parade permit, Reilley and his pals ran into some legal troubles with local officials, but they managed to straighten things out and resumed marching in 1985. Since then the parade has grown into the family-oriented event that it is today.

SpringFest
Various locations
(843) 686-4944, (800) 424-3387
www.hiltonheadhospitalityassociation.com
The Hilton Head Hospitality Association produces this celebration of the coming of spring, which takes place throughout March and features the St. Patrick's Day Parade (see preceding entry), WineFest, and cooking classes.

WineFest—billed as the largest outdoor tented wine tasting on the East Coast—is presented at Shelter Cove Community Park on the second or third Saturday of the month. More than 1,500 wines are available for tasting from 1:00 to 4:00 p.m. The $30 admission fee buys you a souvenir wine glass that's your ticket to the tasting; needless to say, WineFest is for persons age 21 or older.

ARTS AND CULTURE

Hilton Head has for years radiated a vibrant cultural presence. Some 20 community groups—ranging from the Hilton Head Art League to the Hilton Head Orchestra—foster and promote an appreciation of the visual and performing arts. Recently, the community created a new artistic resource, the Arts Center of Coastal Carolina, which has become the cultural hub of the island.

Arts Center of Coastal Carolina
14 Shelter Cove Lane
(843) 686-3945, (843) 842-ARTS
www.artscenter-hhi.org

A big-city facility on a resort island, this $10 million visual- and performing-arts center offers theatrical productions, performances by musicians and dancers, art shows, education programs, and community-service programs.

The center opened in March 1996 on 4.4 acres at Shelter Cove donated by the James C. Self family of Greenwood, South Carolina, owners of the Greenwood Development Corporation of Hilton Head. The result of the Self family gift and a fund-raising effort involving numerous corporations and the community, the center grew out of an idea hatched in 1985 by a group of local arts organizations. The group was incorporated as the Cultural Council of Hilton Head Island and was joined in its efforts by The Hilton Head Playhouse, which has produced more than 200 dramas, comedies, and musicals since its first performance in 1977.

Each year the center's 350-seat Elizabeth Wallace Theatre hosts up to six productions. Among the presentations for the 2007-2008 season were *The Full Monty, Camelot,* Agatha Christie's *Black Coffee,* and Mel Brooks's *The Producers.* The theater complex has dressing and costume rooms and a green room. A rehearsal hall has seating for 150.·

The center brings islanders a series featuring local talent and regional and national touring companies. Six to eight art shows are exhibited annually in the center's 2,300-square-foot Walter Greer Gallery, which has 12-foot-high ceilings and flexible lighting for showcasing art. Through its education program, the center cosponsors residencies by professional artists in area schools and brings children on field trips to the center for performances. The center also offers services and assistance to artists and art groups from throughout the island, providing technical support and space for a variety of organizations.

The center further serves the island by presenting free events such as the Community Christmas Tree Lighting, Family Fiesta Latina, Youth ArtsFest, and Gullah-Fest.

Hilton Head Art League
430 William Hilton Parkway
(843) 681-5060

As part of its mission to provide artists with opportunities to hone their skills and exhibit their works, the Hilton Head Art League presents "minishows" every four weeks at its gallery in the Pineland Station shopping complex. Each of these exhibits features the work of a league member, and each opens with an evening reception. The league sponsors two major art shows annually at the Walter Greer Gallery of the Arts Center of Coastal Carolina. One of the shows is juried, and the event attracts more than 700 entries from throughout the Southeast. The league also presents workshops that attract nationally known artists from throughout the United States (call 800-995-4068 for information). The Hilton Head Art League was started in 1972 by a handful of local artists. There are more than 950 members, 250 of whom are artists.

Hilton Head Orchestra
32 Office Park Road
(843) 842-2055
www.hhorchestra.org

The 65-piece Hilton Head Orchestra presents a 10-concert Monday Master Series, a 5-concert Sunday Series, and several special events, and sponsors a youth orchestra and international piano competition. About 40 percent of the musicians are from the local area, with the others traveling from Southern cities such as Savannah, Charleston, South Carolina, and Jacksonville, Florida, to participate in performances. Concerts are held at the First Presbyterian Church at 540 William Hilton Parkway. Mary Woodmansee Green serves as the orchestra's music director/conductor, having assumed that role in July 1998. Prior to coming to Hilton Head, she was the music director and conductor of the Kennett Symphony and Philadelphia Festival Orchestras, the Delaware Valley Chorale, and The Mary Green Singers. The orchestra was founded in the winter of 1982 by a handful of local musicians who incorporated the organization as the Hilton Head Chamber Orchestra later in the year. The name was changed to Hilton Head Community Orchestra in 1983; six years later, it became the Hilton Head Orchestra. The Hilton Head Youth Orchestra was organized in 1996. The Hilton Head Island International Piano Competition was also started in 1996. The competition is held early in March at the First Presbyterian Church. About 150 pianists apply, with 24 selected as quarter-finalists.

TYBEE ISLAND

HISTORY/OVERVIEW

While other beach communities succumb to high-rises, slick resorts, and gated communities with lawns pristine enough to putt on, Tybee stubbornly resists. Look around downtown during summer and you will see a hot-dog stand and souvenir shops hawking seashells and bargain T-shirts for less than $10. Meanwhile over at City Hall, council members busily guard ordinances restricting the height of buildings and giving older residents tax breaks so they don't get pushed out by outsiders with fatter wallets. The destruction of one of the island's oldest hotels (equipped with one of the island's oldest bars) in 1998 to clear the way for condo construction has sparked a drive for historic preservation.

Tybee is a place where folksy eccentricity is celebrated and many things have been practiced. Things like gambling, which took place in back rooms throughout Tybee until being exposed and cleared out in the early 1960s. A decade or so later, nearly every bar in town was shut down for staying open too late on Saturday night. Seems people were having too good a time to remember that selling beer on Sunday was illegal. That's the thing about Tybee islanders—they just sorta do their own thing.

"Once you cross Lazaretto Creek Bridge into Tybee you get a laid-back attitude. Not a don't care attitude, but a laid-back one," said Walter Parker, who served as Tybee's mayor four times and has lived there most of his life. "When you leave Tybee, you can't wait to get back."

Bluntly put, the place is a little scruffy looking, but if you'll get your nose out of the air, you might appreciate the quirky appeal. You'll find million-dollar beachfront construc-

tion next door to cinder-block shacks (and don't necessarily assume the owners of the fancy home are the richer: Tybee knew shabby before it was chic). This is a locals' beach at which tourists are welcome. They're glad to see you come and, good naturedly, glad to see you go when the season is over and they get their oddball little island back to themselves. The Beach Bums Parade, wherein locals on makeshift floats armed with large-scale water guns do battle with spectators spraying garden hoses, marks the beginning of the tourist season—a fun, messy launch to the crowds of summer. Later, mid-September ushers back in "Tybee time," when the residents have the place to themselves and the particular pleasures of a warm winter beach.

There are flashier, better-groomed places to vacation, places with more activities and scheduled events. However, we spent one of the best vacations of our lives in a rented cottage near the foot of the lighthouse, with a nor'easter howling outside as we squinted in inadequate light to work a jigsaw puzzle that probably didn't have all the pieces. If you are at peace with the fact that everything doesn't have to be plastic, maybe Tybee is for you. Bring your own 499-piece jigsaw puzzle and find out.

Tybee's past is as colorful as its present. It served a role in several wars and has been home to Lt. Col. George C. Marshall (creator of the Marshall Plan) and to a quarantine station for people with infectious ailments. In the early 1800s, scientists believed the marshes in and around the island held harmful vapors or miasma that rose from the marsh vegetation and were carried by the wind into Savannah. However, it was also widely theorized that the vapors were counteracted by the healing properties of sea air. That was a notion that eventually played a role in Tybee's foray into tourism in the late 1880s.

Native Americans were the first Tybee islanders. They settled this small island (2.5 miles long and about 0.6 mile wide) and also are generally credited with giving the island its name, which means salt, though there are other competing theories. Next came the Spanish in the 1500s, followed 200 years later by Georgia's founder, Gen. James Edward Oglethorpe.

Because of its location at the mouth of the Savannah River, Tybee was important strategically. Soon after his arrival, Oglethorpe ordered the construction of a lighthouse, which was completed in 1736. During the War of 1812, the lighthouse (see Things to Do in this chapter) was used to warn Savannah of possible attack by the British, but this attack never materialized. A fortress known as a Martello Tower, designed with round walls that supposedly would deflect cannonballs, was built on Tybee Island in 1815 to help guard the Savannah River from attack. It was one of only a few such structures in North America.

On the western end of the island, a quarantine station was set up to house sick passengers coming in off ships. This is how Lazaretto Creek got its name. *Lazaretto* is an Italian word for an institution or hospital for those with contagious diseases. "They kept them in quarantine there for four months," said James Mack Adams, local Tybee historian. "If they got sick and died, they buried them right there."

In 1829 construction began on Fort Pulaski (see the Things to Do section in this chapter). The fort, now a national park, stands off U.S. Highway 80 as you approach Tybee. It was constructed of 25 million bricks and has walls 7.5 feet thick. Robert E. Lee was one of the engineers who planned and supervised construction. During the Civil War, Union forces attacked the fort using a new weapon called "rifled cannon." It took only 30 hours of bombardment for the fort to fall into Union hands. The attack had such devastating effects on the brick fort that after the surrender, all forts like Pulaski were considered obsolete.

Following the war, Tybee turned its attention toward tourism. In its early years, Tybee was reached by boat, a voyage that could take two hours from Savannah. That changed in 1887 with the construction of a rail line through the marsh and over various creeks and rivers between the island and the mainland. That same year Tybee was officially incorporated as Ocean City. A year later it was changed to Tybee, only to be changed in 1929 to Savannah Beach. It wasn't until many decades later, in the early 1970s, that it became Tybee again. A reference today to Savannah Beach is likely to raise the locals' dander.

Day-trippers, as they were known, would come on the train, rent bathing suits from a local hotel, and spend the day at the beach. Some would arrive later in the day to dance to Big Band music supplied by outfits playing at one of the island's biggest attractions: the Tybrisa Pier. When the Tybee Road opened in 1923, the stream of people coming to the island continued to grow. In a column that ran in the local newspaper in 1931, E. B. Izlar reflected about the "good old days" on Tybee. "The decline of mosquitoes, of picnickers, of bars and of yardage in women's bathing suits constitute the most radical changes in reviewing the past thirty years on Tybee Island," the column stated. "Today, Mr. Izlar declares that mosquitoes, except in the dense wooded places, are rare, and he bears out his statement by remarking that he has only seen three this season."

Reminiscing on the bathing suits of the early years, Mr. Izlar lamented the time when

i Tybee hasn't had a major hit from a hurricane in more than 100 years. The most damaging hurricane occurred August 27, 1881. It landed with a massive storm surge that covered the island and destroyed nearly every structure in its path.

suits were sold for $2.50 to $4.00 a dozen (except, of course, when special suits for women were as high as $12.00 a dozen) in the days when women "wrapped up" to cover everything. As for bars, Mr. Izlar said that though they abounded in bygone days, there was little disorder—only friendly fights. "There was not even need for a jail in those days."

While the islanders focused on tourism, the U.S. War Department began construction of Fort Screven on the north end of the island. The fort was made up of seven gun batteries that ended up being fired only for practice, not for war. During World War I, part of the Eighth Infantry Regiment was assigned to Fort Screven. One of its commanders was Lt. Col. George C. Marshall, who after leaving Tybee became a five-star general and served as secretary of state, secretary of defense, and author of the Marshall Plan for rebuilding western Europe after World War II.

In the meantime, Savannahians were beginning to build houses at the beach for the summer months. The ocean breezes would give them relief from the city's sweltering summer heat. Many of these magnificent old beach homes can still be found on the island today. Current resident Walter Parker recalls how empty the island was in those days. "I can remember in the winter you could go for several blocks before you saw a light on," said Parker. "No one lived here year-round."

Eventually, that began to change and Tybee's year-round population slowly grew. However, several factors—beach erosion, pollution, the closing of Fort Screven—resulted in several years of decline on the island beginning in the 1940s. Residents cultivated an outlaw attitude during this era by engaging in back-room gambling and illegal drinking, which got the attention of the news media. It

also helped fuel the island's reputation in some circles as Georgia's unruly stepchild. Eventually, local and state law enforcement agencies cracked down to curb Tybee's wanton ways. The pollution, gambling, and other sins were eventually cleaned up, and Tybee once again became a popular tourist spot.

Since 1980 or so, the island's year-round population has been on the rise to its current level of around 4,000. Today, locals who have called Tybee home for generations live amongst a thriving community of artists and writers, most of whom migrated during the 1980s. There are also many retirees whose hometowns are places far away from Tybee. Every socioeconomic group is represented, from the poor to the very wealthy.

"I think Tybee is an easy place to live," said Parker. "I think it has more than its share of characters. . . . But it has a small community feeling and most want it to stay that way."

GETTING THERE, GETTING AROUND

Tybee is about 18 miles east of Savannah. There is only one road to get you there: US 80. You can reach it from the Historic Downtown by heading east on Bay Street. In less than a mile, it will run into President Street, then President Street Extension. After about 3 miles, it merges with US 80 East. From Midtown, hop on Victory Drive and head east— you are also on US 80 East.

After entering Tybee, US 80 turns into Butler Avenue, the community's main drag, which will take you past hotels, beach houses, and the small downtown area. You will know US 80 has become Butler Avenue after going around a fairly sharp curve. You can't miss it. Follow Butler a mile or so farther into downtown, and you will be deposited in a city parking lot next to the pier.

Most places you need to visit on Tybee should be accessible from this main strip. Near the beginning of Butler Avenue, streets running east and west are numbered, starting with 1st Street at the northern end of the city

i Geologically speaking, Tybee is very young—only about 1,000 years old. Savannah's other islands, including Wilmington and Skidaway, are more than 40,000 years old.

and ending with 19th Street at the southern end. These are crossed by north- and-south-running streets that are named and numbered, starting with Butler Avenue closest to the beach and ending with 6th Avenue.

If you are going to spend the day at the beach on Tybee, you will have to pay for parking. The streets closest to the beach are metered at $1 an hour, and all meters require quarters. The city operates three parking lots, all accessible from Butler Avenue: at the end of Tybrisa (which used to be 16th Street), 14th Street, and at North Beach. The parking lots, and the streetside spaces near them, are equipped with modern pay-and-display meters that print a receipt to display on your dashboard. The modern meters can take credit cards for a $2 minimum. Officially, parking is patrolled every day year-round from 8:00 a.m. until 8:00 p.m. In reality, and in typical Tybee fashion, it's a more practical system: starting up about 8-ish or 9-ish and depending on the weather or crowds. If it's raining or the crowds are light, the parking enforcers may knock off early, but be aware that you are gambling if you assume they have. Like the Savannah authorities, the parking enforcers are very generous when doling out tickets and are fairly vigilant. So if you don't want an expensive ticket, don't leave your meter expired. It usually isn't too much trouble finding parking on Tybee, except for a few very busy weekends. Planning a longer stay? Parking stickers that allow you to park in all lots and at all meters without further payment are available. Property owners get them free; other frequent visitors buy them from Tybee City Hall at $75 a year. Tybee's parking services can be reached at (912) 786-4573, ext. 121, with office hours beginning at 9:00 a.m.

ACCOMMODATIONS

Affordable hotel rooms, sprawling beach houses, and oceanview condos are some of the choices you will find when searching for accommodations on Tybee Island. Tybee is known as a family beach, so a lot of what is available is geared toward those lugging not only beach chairs but high chairs as well. Regardless of where you land, more likely than not you will be within comfortable walking distance of the beach.

Tybee's season runs typically from the middle of April through the middle of September. After that, the streets become less crowded and rates go down. Stay during the peak season, especially on weekends, and the rates are going to be higher. A few weekends, including July 4, are especially busy. Weekend hotel rates are considerably higher than weekday rates.

Tybee's accommodations scene is very atypical. There's a healthy scattering of hotels, but few in the way of major national chains and none that you would consider truly upscale. (In fact, lots of them are rather shabby, although you'd never guess it from their rates.) Nor is development moving in that direction. When a developer breaks ground on Tybee these days, chances are that developer is building condos. These run the gamut from strictly investment properties to purely private residences, but it's safe to say the tourist housing market on the island is skewing increasingly to condo rentals. At least one motel has converted to condos, in fact.

While we list some Realtors who can help land you in a beach house and condo, some owners handle property rental on their own. Most simply post a FOR RENT sign in the front yard—when you're in town, pick one of these places that you like and jot down the number for future reference. Some private owners also put listings in the *Savannah Morning News* (see our Media chapter for more information), so check there as well. Our listings begin with hotels and motels, we throw in a couple of bed-and-breakfasts, then move on to rentals. Note that Tybee's rental market for houses and condos, just like its real-estate market, is booming—so rates are volatile and could well climb between this writing and your reading.

Price-Code Key

Our price code is designed to make it easier for you to gauge the cost of staying at one of Tybee's hotels, motels, or bed-and-breakfasts. The dollar sign indicates the average cost for a one-night stay for two adults during peak season, typically mid-April through mid-September. Weekends cost more.

$	$50 or less
$$	$51 to $100
$$$	$101 to $150
$$$$	$151 or more

Hotels and Motels

There are only a handful of hotels and motels to choose from on the island. Most are smaller chains with names you will recognize and offer standard, sometimes modest accommodations. The ones we list have non-smoking and wheelchair-accessible rooms and come with free parking. Although Tybee is outside Savannah, it shares area code 912.

Beachside Colony $$$–$$$$
404 Butler Avenue
(912) 786-4535, (800) 786-0770
www.beachsidecolony.com

This started life as a motel, but thanks to an ongoing demolition/rebuilding/renovation project, it is now a condo-only facility. Aside from the fact that you are renting a larger, pricier place, you won't note much difference, since most of the units are investor owned and rented out steadily. Two- and three-bedroom units are available, and rates range from $150 to $350 per night. The complex is on the ocean and boasts a pool, sundeck, and cabana. There's a workout club and a casual but elegant restaurant (see the Restaurants section later in this chapter). The grounds are particularly well maintained, which cannot really be taken for granted on Tybee. Parking is also rigorously defended at this complex. (God help tenants if it weren't.) These folks handle several properties.

Best Western Dunes Inn $$–$$$$
1409 Butler Avenue
(912) 786-4591, (800) 528-1234

The Best Western Dunes Inn is across the street from the beach and a block or so away from Tybee's small shopping district, where you can find everything from a new swimsuit to suntan lotion. This motel offers spacious rooms comfortably furnished with two double beds or one king-size bed. Some have balconies overlooking the pool, and a few kitchenettes are also available. Complimentary coffee is served every morning.

DeSoto Beach Hotel $$$–$$$$
212 Butler Avenue
(912) 786-4542
www.desotobeachhotel.com

The only thing old about this place is the name, which once served one of Tybee's oldest hotels. That place is long gone, but on this narrow sliver of land between condo developments, careful design has led to 37 rooms, most of which are technically oceanview and a few of which have a magnificent view. The hotel is on the ocean side of Butler, and it is one of the first motels or hotels you will encounter when driving onto the island. There's an oceanfront pool and a game room that's partially open to the elements. The room decor is fresh and crisp-looking, and you'll find such amenities as hair dryers and coffeemakers. Rates in season range from $130 to $210.

Howard Johnson Admiral's Inn $$$–$$$$
1501 Butler Avenue
(912) 786-0700, (800) 446-4656

A nice, two-story hotel, Admiral's Inn has 41 spacious rooms, a swimming pool, and is across the street from the ocean. The standard room comes with two queen-size beds, but if you need a little more space, deluxe king rooms with sitting areas are available. For those coming to Tybee after tying the knot, there is also a bridal suite. The hotel's meeting room holds up to 75 people.

Computer, phone/fax, and copy service

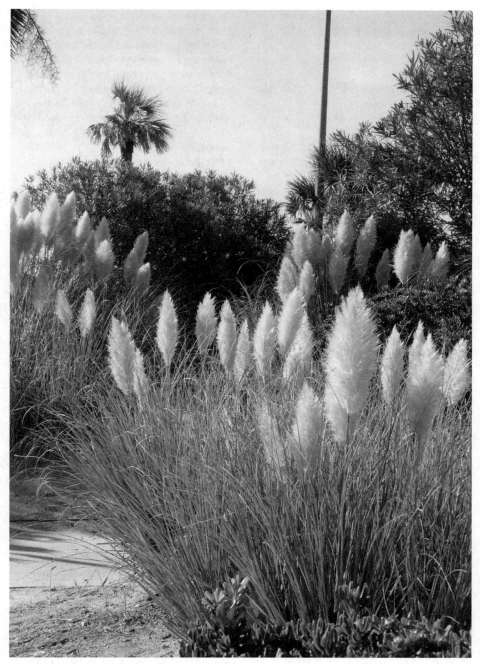

Tybee Island vegetation. BETTY DARBY

are available for those unfortunate souls who have to work while at the beach. The hotel is within comfortable walking distance to "downtown Tybee."

Ocean Plaza Beach Resort $$–$$$$
15th Street and Ocean Front
(912) 786-7664, (800) 215-6370
www.oceanplaza.com

This is Tybee's largest hotel, with 240 rooms and suites and two swimming pools. It is also one of the few properties that offer direct room views of the ocean. Head out your door, walk through a parking lot, and within a few steps you are on the sand. Located on the southern end of the island, there are actually three buildings at Ocean Plaza, including two four-story structures facing the ocean. The rooms are spacious and decorated in bright pastel colors. All oceanfront rooms have balconies overlooking the Atlantic.

Many room options are available, including a single room with a king-size bed, one-room suites with queen-size beds, and two-room suites with one king-size and one double bed. Kitchenettes are also available. Regardless of the room type, all come with a choice of poolside or oceanview location. Rollaway beds can be rented for $10, and cribs cost $5. The Ocean Plaza offers free HBO and a conference center. The Dolphin Reef Restaurant, bridging two of the motel buildings, serves breakfast, lunch, and dinner seven days a week.

River's End Campground and R.V. Park
915 Polk Street
(912) 786-5518, (800) 786-1016
www.cityoftybee.org/campground.aspx

This little campground and RV park used to be an out-of-the-way facility, but then skyrocketing real estate prices suddenly meant it wasn't so out-of-the-way anymore. The City of Tybee Island bought the park in 2006 to preserve its use as a campground, fearful of impending condo development. Aside from the unusual ownership arrangement, this is a standard campground. There are close to 100

RV sites with water and electric and 18 primitive campgrounds. Among the amenities are a swimming pool, air-conditioned bath houses, cable, wi-fi, a laundry, and similar touches. Rates start at $30 a night for the primitive campsites, and go up to $45 for the most utility-rich RV sites. Rates are cheaper by the week, and even cheaper by the month.

Sand Castle Inn $$–$$$
1402 Butler Avenue
(912) 786-4576

The Sand Castle Inn is within walking distance to Tybee's "downtown." It is on the beach side of Butler Avenue—Tybee's main thoroughfare. The motel offers a pool and free continental breakfast each morning. The rooms are fresh, with bright colored bedspreads and white walls. Although just a short stroll to the beach, none of the rooms have ocean views.

Bed-and-Breakfasts

Hunter House $$–$$$
1701 Butler Avenue
(912) 786-7515
www.hunterhouseinn.com

When John Hunter purchased a beach house on the southern end of Butler Avenue with hopes of converting it into a bed-and-breakfast, he had his work cut out for him. It was 1988, and the 14-unit apartment house he bought was nicknamed "Animal House." Since then, Hunter has successfully converted the three-story, 1910 beach house into a four-room bed-and-breakfast, and one of Tybee's finer restaurants is also on the premises (see this chapter's Restaurants section).

All rooms are modern in design and include queen-size beds and private baths with separate entrances and range in size from a single to a large, four-room suite complete with living room and small kitchenette. In one smaller room, you will find bright pink walls and a white wicker settee and matching headboard, while another includes a four-poster queen-size bed with a massive fireplace in the living area. There is a wonderful wraparound porch perfect for relaxing and taking in the ocean breezes. It's a good place to enjoy your continental breakfast, which includes coffee, cereal, and other goodies. Hunter describes his establishment as having "Southern Charm with a Beach Atmosphere."

The Lighthouse Inn $$$$
16 Meddin Drive
(912) 786-0901, (866) 786-0901
www.tybeebb.com
Susie Morris and her husband, Stuart Liles, opened this charming B&B in the fall of 2000 in a circa-1910 home they have restored. It features three fully decorated guest rooms and baths, as well as a front porch for relaxing. The couple lives on the ground floor. The location is close to the north beach (a less-developed segment of Tybee's beaches) and the lighthouse (as the name no doubt cued you). The North Beach Grill is also close by.

Rentals

Tybee Beach Vacation Rentals, Inc.
Solomon Properties
211 Butler Avenue
(912) 786-0100, (800) 967-4433
www.renttybee.com
Solomon Properties is a local company of Realtors with several private condos and homes for rent. Their offices are on the right after you round the bend (US 80/Butler Avenue) heading toward downtown Tybee. Like all the rental agencies listed here, inside the offices are lists of properties, pictures, rates, and other valuable information. The rental rates seem outrageous compared with what they were a few years ago—$1,700 a week for a two-bedroom house that is near but not on the beach was a landlord's dream in, say, 1997. It's a reality today.

Tybee Island Realty
1016 First Street
(912) 786-7070, (800) 379-2298
www.tybeeislandrealty.com
John and Judy O'Neill, a husband-and-wife team, own this real-estate company, which also deals with several private rentals. You can stop in at the offices, located on your right a mile or so after crossing Lazaretto Creek Bridge into town, and pick up one of their rental brochures. Again, these give all the information you need: pictures of available properties, price ranges, and lists of amenities. When we stopped by, they had many listings—everything from oceanfront condos for $1,175 per week to beachfront homes that sleep 14 for $2,500-plus a week. Many rentals were also available nightly.

Tybee Island Rentals, Inc.
US 80 and Second Avenue
Savannah
(912) 786-4034, (800) 476-0807
www.tybeeislandrentals.com
Beach homes, condos, and cottages of all shapes and sizes can be rented from Tybee Island Rentals. Check out the varied selection at their offices, located about 2 miles past the bridge onto Tybee. Whether you are looking for a romantic getaway for two or a place to bring the whole family for a week at the beach, you should be able to find something that suits your needs. Choices include everything from a five-bedroom, six-bath home overlooking the ocean for $2,200 a week to a one-bedroom efficiency for $375. Remember that rates are seasonal.

TYBEE REAL ESTATE

Like the Historic Downtown in Savannah, Tybee has been one of the most popular places to buy real estate in the last few years. Prices have been on the rise and in many cases have jumped significantly—up more than 100 percent in some cases. The small-town atmosphere, along with its proximity to Savannah, has made this island community attractive as a year-round residence for many. However, the real estate downturn of 2007 seems to have slowed things down a lot here.

This interest has led to much development and a few growing pains. After a large hotel went up on the beach, a movement was started to restrict the height of all develop-i Wonder why the new homes here (and some of the older ones) are built so high off the ground? It leaves ample room for an open parking area under the house, but the real reason is the building codes that require lifting the finished floor out of the reach of floods.

ment on Tybee to avoid a resort full of high-rises. Many residents want to keep the beach community what it is—a small town by the sea.

It is hard to identify distinct neighborhoods on Tybee. In some neighborhoods, you might find older beach houses next door to modest, one-story homes. A few doors down there could be two or three new homes or a set of two or three new town houses. Near Fort Screven or North Beach, you will find a few new housing developments that can offer large two- and sometimes three-story homes with ocean views and wraparound porches on fairly large lots. A few streets away there could be a modest home needing quite a lot of work. It's worth noting that streets often don't follow a particular pattern on Tybee; many are dirt roads that zigzag, and in some cases just stop.

Tybee's older beach homes are usually found along Butler Avenue, the city's main thoroughfare, which goes to the southern end of the island. Here the streets follow a grid pattern with the numbered streets increasing the closer you get to downtown. Again, in many blocks, there is a smattering of new homes followed by several older ones. During the last few years, many older homes have been torn down to make room for condos, townhomes, and the like. Single-family homes on the island range from around $200,000 for older, modest homes to $500,000 for new construction to the-sky's-the-limit on oceanfront. All new homes must be built several feet off the ground to prevent flooding. The realty companies listed earlier are ready to assist you with inquiries concerning the Tybee Island real-estate scene. Call for more details.

RESTAURANTS

Tybee's restaurant scene is evolving. Locals don't have to be that old to remember when most eateries were burger and ice-cream joints where you could come in your bathing suit, and where you were likely to find the door locked shortly after Labor Day. Those places are still there, but they have been joined by a sprinkling of reasonable family restaurants. Latest on the scene: upscale dining that draws a dinner crowd of Savannahians willing to make a moonlight drive through the marshes for dishes with Caribbean flair or seafood with a sophisticated sauce. It personifies Tybee, in a way—white linen tablecloths and a lengthy wine list in a restaurant next to a trailer park, and no one thinking anything strange about it. One thing you won't find (and another personification of Tybee's individuality) is much in the way of fast-food franchises—with the exception of an Arby's. A burger joint on Tybee would be named something like Earl's instead of McDonald's.

We've labeled restaurants as "inexpensive," "moderate" or "expensive." Of course, prices vary to either extreme on most menus and you can tip the bill over into the next category. But just so you'll know what to expect, count on inexpensive entrees costing less than $15, moderate entrees costing up to $25, and expensive entrees costing more than $25.

The Breakfast Club   Inexpensive
1500 Butler Avenue
(912) 786-5984

If you want to get a table at The Breakfast Club without waiting in line, you may have to get up a little early, especially during the summer months. Lines start forming outside this very popular eatery about 7:00 a.m. on weekends. During the week, sleep in much past 8:30 a.m., and you will most likely find yourself waiting outside with a handful of other people. Regardless, it is worth the wait. As the line (which moves fast) attests, this diner on the southern end of the island near downtown is one of Tybee's best. For more than 20 years, members of the Farrow family have been serving up breakfast specialties like chorizo con huevos (flour tortillas, sausage, sharp cheese, salsa, and sour cream) and pecan waffles. For $8.95 you can get the surf and turf omelette, complete with fresh ribeye and local shrimp with garlic butter. While omelettes are a menu favorite, you will also find many other choices, from grits to burgers. Chef Jodee Sadowsky, who purchased the diner from his mother, Helen Farrow, was named one of North America's 101 best cooks in *Cooking Across America*. After the season, when the locals reclaim the island, you'll find them sitting here, sharing the gossip. Warning: This place doesn't look like much but don't let that mislead you.

The Crab Shack — Moderate
40 Estill Hammock Road
(912) 786-9857

Going to The Crab Shack is as much about atmosphere as it is about seafood. Located in Chimney Creek, a hamlet off US 80 just past the Lazaretto Creek Bridge (you can't miss the signs), The Crab Shack's motto is, "Where the Elite Eat in Their Bare Feet." What started as a small, rustic restaurant on the marsh has grown into a tourist favorite. Now they've even added a licensed live alligator habitat. While munching on giant servings of seafood delicacies such as Georgia blue crab, snow crab, golden crab, Alaskan king crab, shrimp, and oysters, you can sit out on the huge porch overlooking the marsh. Oak trees decorated with white lights give The Crab Shack a casual, relaxed, fun flair. If you want to try a local specialty, try the Lowcountry boil, which includes boiled shrimp, corn, potatoes, and sausage. As for drinks, the frozen margarita is a good choice along with the piña coladas and daiquiris. Dress is casual. The restaurant can handle parties of up to 150 people and boasts a separate gift shop, dubbed (what else?) The Gift Shack. Some scenes from the movie *The General's Daughter*, starring John Travolta, were shot here in the summer of

1998, which is appropriate—the place has a movie set feel anyway.

Fannie's on the Beach — Moderate
1613 Strand
(912) 786-6109

This restaurant and bar, which commands an ocean view across a parking lot, added an upstairs outdoor deck for dining and a band on the weekend. It's open lunch, dinner, and late night. Specialties include a shrimp burger—a concoction made of ground shrimp, sautéed onions, and celery. Quesadillas are meals, not appetizers, and include shrimp and scallop varieties. They also offer sandwiches, salads, and burgers, but the staff considers the pizzas to be the signature dish. You can get everything from the standard version to one sporting smoked salmon, capers, cream cheese, scallion, black olives, and sun-dried tomatoes. After dark, the club atmosphere comes to the fore and the band cranks up in summer, playing for a crowd of diverse couples.

Georges' on Tybee — Expensive
1105 US 80 East
(912) 786-9730

This is one of Tybee's priciest restaurants, but it's worth that price. The proprietors of the North Beach Grill, George Spriggs and George Jackson, staked out a spot a couple of rungs up the socioeconomic ladder for their second restaurant, where a talented team of chefs produces what they dub American fusion cuisine. Look here for such creations as sautéed black grouper over multiple grains with tomato relish and a sweet corn/Vidalia onion puree. Or there's grilled beef tenderloin with oven-roasted purple potatoes, sautéed cauliflower, grilled asparagus, local lump crab, and mustard-cream sauce. The menu is intentionally small—say, eight entrees covering seafood, beef, chicken, and even a vegetarian offering—but widened by a large selection of generous appetizers. There is an extensive wine list and a full bar, along with a dessert menu that most diners would find a challenge

Close-up

Hitting the Beach with "Crawfish" Crawford

There is good news for swimmers diving into the ocean off Tybee, according to John "Crawfish" Crawford, a University of Georgia educator and expert on Tybee and its marine life. The 30 to 40 species of sharks lurking in the waters offshore probably aren't that hungry. "We have well-fed sharks here," said Crawford. "The water is full of plenty of food which they would rather eat instead of fooling with something the size of a human being."

Words to live by. Although shark attacks are so rare they are nearly unheard of on Tybee, Crawford says to reduce your risk even further by avoiding swimming during twilight hours when sharks typically feed. Also, don't use a flutter kick—to a shark it could sound like a wounded fish.

Besides sharks, beachgoers might encounter an abundance of other marine life on Tybee, according to Crawford. Some of the more common things you might come across during your day at the beach include:

Sandpipers—These tiny, fleet-footed birds seen running up and down the beach are born and nest in the Arctic tundra. They fly all the way to Tybee just to engage in a little 50-yard beach dash for food.

Ghost Crabs—Look near the dune line, and you might see whitish-colored crabs scurrying—then disappearing—into a hole. Besides spending their time digging their hole homes, these crabs serve as beach garbage collectors, picking up parts of dead fish and others things cluttering their front yards.

Jellyfish—Several different species of jellyfish live in our waters. The cannonball variety has a brown rim around the edge, and you can't be stung by

after the large portions. This is definitely an upscale restaurant, and not a place to wear your beach duds, but because it is in a beach community, the dress code is a little more relaxed than the menu and atmosphere would otherwise imply. (Translation: Guys can get by without a jacket and tie, but they won't feel odd with one, either.) The restaurant launched in the summer of 1998 and is going strong. Reservations are strongly recommended.

Hunter House   Expensive
1701 Butler Avenue
(912) 786-7515
Hunter House was the first of Tybee's current crop of formal restaurants. Housed in a 1910

bed-and-breakfast at the southern tip of the city's main thoroughfare, it features three intimate dining rooms that seat only a few people at a time. Wooden walls line the entryway, and each room is decorated in simple and sophisticated decor. Owner John Hunter says he likes the small size of his restaurant and would rather concentrate on serving 40 quality meals instead of 60 or more mediocre ones. Offerings include seafood Patrick, which is jumbo shrimp broiled in olive oil, wine, and garlic and served with buttered pasta, fresh basil, tomato bits, and Asiago cheese. Among new entries is "fillet of scarlet snapper," which involves a macadamia nut crust, papaya, lime salsa, black beans, saffron rice . . . you get the them. The sea nettle, which comes out typically in the late summer and has long wispy tentacles, is responsible for the most stings off Tybee. If you get stung, putting meat tenderizer on the sting helps ease the pain, according to Crawford.

Ghost Shrimp—If you run across tiny holes just above the low-tide line, you most likely have encountered a ghost shrimp. These tiny shrimp live in a network of burrows that twist and turn in the sand and are only three-fourths of an inch in diameter. Those little brown things you see near the entrance of the hole are their droppings.

Sand Dollars—These small disks are actually live animals. Many people mistakenly take them home while they are still alive, Crawford said. If you find a sand dollar on the beach and it is a greenish color on top and reddish on the bottom, it is still alive, so leave it on the beach. A white color indicates that the sand dollar has died.

Sting Rays—If you happen to see a sting ray while swimming in the surf, don't panic—they aren't aggressive and won't bother you a bit. If you happen to be unfortunate enough to step on a sting ray, however, they do consider this an attack and will sting. To avoid such a confrontation, shuffle your feet back and forth while walking in the surf. This gives them enough time to realize you are coming and head in a different direction.

Sea Turtle Nests—Sea turtles regularly nest on Tybee Island. The city's public works department patrols the beaches for the nests to mark them with wire so people don't run over them. If you do come across a nest, don't disturb it.

picture. There's also chicken, steaks, and a wide range of appetizers. Because of the restaurant's small size and popularity, reservations are recommended.

The North Beach Grill   Moderate
41-A Meddin Drive
(912) 786-9003
The North Beach Grill is a place you have to go looking for but are glad once you find it (it's sorta beside the Tybee Museum, across the parking lot from the lighthouse). Located steps from the sand on Tybee's North Beach, it specializes in lunches and long, relaxing dinners with a Caribbean flair. If you are in a hurry, you might want to try someplace else. Sit out on the patio or inside the small, invit-

ing dining room to enjoy the many menu choices—there is a constantly evolving set of entrees and appetizers. You will find things like plantain, jerk chicken, jerk salmon, crab cakes, flounder, and much more from which to pick.

The restaurant is one of those entrepreneur dream stories where two friends were tired of working for others in the restaurant business and launched their own effort in what was little more than a shack at the time. (They've since launched Georges', described in a previous listing.) It has become a place Savannahians have added to their repertoire for entertaining visiting guests.

Sundae Café	Inexpensive lunch,
304 First Street	Moderate dinner

(Highway 80 and Jones)
(912) 786-7694
www.sundaecafeattybee.com

When on Tybee, it is important to remember that appearances can be deceiving. This little restaurant is in a small strip shopping center at a major intersection, next door to a convenience store. So what? The good food and unusual menu have given this restaurant a buzz, however modest its exterior. Consider, for example, a dinner entrée of grilled mahimahi served over blackened green tomatoes with boursin potato cakes, crab buerre blanc, and a shrimp succotash. There are other equally elaborate dishes, along with simple fried grouper, shrimp, scallops, and oysters. Lunch runs to soup, salad, and sandwiches. The restaurant includes a full bar. Lunch and dinner every day but Sunday. Reservations are recommended for dinner.

THINGS TO DO

The Beach. Okay, if you came to Tybee, it stands to reason you wanted to go to the beach. Actually, you have two options: South Beach, where the most development (restaurants, shops, entertainment, etc.) and largest crowds are, and North Beach, which is more residential in nature, although hardly what you'd call deserted. Go south for people watching, north for shelling. You're at South Beach when you park in Tybee's downtown, main-drag Strand area. North Beach parking is across from the lighthouse and behind the museum. At low tide, you can walk from one to the other, but if you miscalculate the incoming tide, it can be a long walk around.

During the season, Tybee's beaches have lifeguards. Hours and days depend on the weather and crowds. The lifeguard stands are clustered near the public parking. Early on, they're only staffed on weekends. Don't take it for granted that there's a lifeguard on duty, and even if there is, they call it a day when the crowd starts to thin. Be careful! Ocean swimming can be tricky, even for the strong swimmer. Tybee is prone to riptides.

Beach regulations prohibit glass containers or cans. Dogs aren't allowed on the beach, either, and you'll get a ticket if you bring one. The beach is patrolled by officers in shorts and T-shirts, either walking or on all-terrain vehicles.

Vendors on the beach rent canvas rafts, umbrellas, boogie boards, and the like.

Fort Pulaski National Monument
US 80 East
(912) 786-5787

Explore a 19th-century fort from top to bottom at Fort Pulaski. Located about 15 miles outside Savannah on the way to Tybee, the fort is remarkably preserved and gives a fascinating glimpse into coastal warfare. The fort was completed in 1847 and considered the ultimate defense system of its day. Audio stations provide information on the fort's pivotal role in the Civil War and how it changed defense strategy worldwide after an attack by Union forces. The 5,600-acre monument also provides picnic areas, a boat ramp, and nature trails, along with panoramic views of the Atlantic Ocean and scenic salt marshes. Bring your camera—this is one of the area's most photogenic spots. The fort is open from 9:00 a.m. to 7:00 p.m. but closes two hours earlier in the off season (September–May). Cost is $3. Children age 16 and younger enter free.

Lazaretto Creek Marina
US 80 East, just across Lazaretto Creek Bridge
(912) 786-5848, (800) 242-0166
www.tybeedolphins.com

Dolphin tours, fishing, diving, and sunset cruises are offered at Lazaretto Creek Marina. Dolphin tours are $15; offshore fishing ranges from $250 to $850, depending on the length of the trip.

The Tybee Arts Association
P.O. Box 2344
Tybee Island 31328
(912) 786-5920
www.tybeearts.org

This nonprofit group is dedicated to developing and promoting arts throughout the area. Besides operating the Lighthouse Gallery near Tybee Lighthouse, the organization holds exhibits and gives art classes for adults and children. Adult classes can include pottery, stained-glass making, and painting, while children's classes include wearable art, make-your-own puppet, sand and beach art, and painting and drawing, among others. Weekly classes are $60; times vary.

Tybee Island Branch
Live Oak Public Library
405 Butler Avenue
(912) 786-7733

Chances are there aren't too many public libraries around with an ocean view. Granted, you have to have pretty good eyes to see it, but the view is there, along with an impressive entryway sculpture by ironwork artist Ivan Bailey. (Look up!)

Local library regulations are very kind to guests. Here, as elsewhere in Chatham County, nonresidents can buy a temporary library card with full privileges for $25, valid for nine weeks. Some paperbacks and children's books can be borrowed without a card. (Library cards are free to residents.)

The collection includes books, magazines, audiobooks, and videotapes. The branch is not large, but it has access to the library system's full collection, if you can wait for delivery.

Tybee Island Lighthouse
30 Meddin Drive
(912) 786-5801
www.tybeelighthouse.org

Throughout history there have actually been four Tybee Island Lighthouses. The original was completed in 1736, but it sat too close to the shore and was washed away during a storm. Hurricanes, fires, and even an attack

i Like to collect seashells? According to expert seashell hunters, Tybee's North Beach provides the best bounty.

by Union forces during the Civil War led to partial or complete destruction of two other stations. In 1866 the fourth Tybee Lighthouse was authorized and was a combination of old and new. It used the lower 65 feet of the 1773 Tybee Light as the base, then 94 more feet were stacked on top. The light, a first-order Fresnel lens, was displayed for the first time on October 1, 1867, and it has been there ever since. It is 1 of only 2 of the 15 original light stations built in Georgia that is still functioning.

Learn about the history of the lighthouse and take a 154-foot climb to the top for a wonderful view of the area. Hours are 9:00 a.m. to 5:30 p.m. daily (last ticket sold at 4:30) except Tuesday, when it is closed. Closed for major holidays. Cost is $6 for adults, $5 for seniors, military, and children ages 6 to 14; children younger than age 6 get in free. The price includes admission to the Tybee Museum (see listing). A major restoration project spruced things up in 1998 and 1999, and again in 2006. By the way, we're famous! The Tybee Lighthouse was one of five southeastern lighthouses featured on a set of U.S. postage stamps in June 2003.

Tybee Island Marine Science Center
14th Street parking lot
(912) 786-5917
www.tybeemsc.org

Learn about Tybee's marine life at the Tybee Island Marine Science Center. Located just steps from the sand in the 14th Street parking lot, the center has aquariums with species indigenous to the area, such as starfish and jellyfish. There is a small library, a touch tank, and displays featuring such things as sharks and shells—always favorites with the kids. Don't expect anything polished or Sea World-ish, but it is informative. Beach walks are one of the most popular programs offered. Folks are invited to stroll the beach to learn about the things that inhabit it. The center staff also

Stroll out to the Tybee Pavilion. BETTY DARBY

throws a seine net into the ocean to see what they might catch. The center is open from 9:00 a.m. to 5:00 p.m. daily, closing at noon Tuesday. Adults $4, children $3.

Tybee Museum
30 Meddin Drive
(912) 786-5801
www.tybeeisland.com

Besides learning about Tybee's history, visitors to the Tybee Museum get to walk around one of the few remaining structures at the former Fort Screven. Inside Battery Garland, one of the original seven-gun batteries built at the fort, you can learn about hundreds of years of Tybee lore—from the arrival of Native Americans to Tybee's role in the Civil War to the beginning of tourism on the island. Open from 9:00 a.m. to 5:30 p.m. daily, but closed Tuesday and major holidays (note that St. Patrick's Day is a major holiday in these parts). Admission is $6 for adults, $5 for seniors, military,

and children ages 6 to 14; children ages 5 and younger get in free. The fee includes admission to the Tybee Island Lighthouse just across the street (see listing).

Tybee Pier and Pavilion
16th Street

The $2.5-million wooden pier was unveiled in time for the 1996 Summer Olympics, when the yachting events were held in the area. It was built in almost the exact location of the Tybrisa, Tybee's former pier and pavilion that was known for its Big Band concerts before it burned down. Wander out to the end of the pier, and you will witness anglers casting into the ocean to see what they might catch. You can rent fishing poles and bait on the pier, and you can pick up a snack, too. The pier's pavilion, a large wooden platform you cross before heading out over the ocean, is also a popular spot for concerts. Concerts are often free (and even when they aren't, you can sit on the beach and listen in). It's also a good place for a romantic evening stroll without getting your feet wet.

SHOPPING

Tybee isn't exactly a shopper's paradise, but you can buy what you need. Beach essentials and tacky souvenirs are easy to come by in a variety of stores clustered around the action. Some places merit more attention, however, and we mention a few of them here.

T. S. Chu Co.
6 Tybrisa Street
(912) 786-4561
T. S. Chu emigrated from China early last century and slept in the dunes until he got things going financially. And get them going he did. His early enterprise has grown to a prosperous local retail empire. For the most part, it's

convenience stores and gas stations. But the original store remains on Tybee, a sprawling, dimly lit, and unconventional place that sells tourist junk and beach supplies near the door and lightbulbs, hammers, dishpans, and other housewares and hardware farther inside.

Tybee Market
1111 Butler Avenue
(912) 786-4601
The mark of a dedicated Tybee Islander is a refusal to leave the island unless he or she absolutely has to. That makes Tybee's only grocery store (aside from numerous convenience stores) a godsend for some. It's small and the selection is limited, but it serves the purpose. If you are whipping up a complex recipe in your vacation digs, you might have better luck in the conventional supermarkets you drove past on the suburban islands on your way out to Tybee.

INDEX

ABOUT THE AUTHORS

RICH WITTISH

When Rich Wittish took a job with the daily newspaper in Savannah in 1974, he intended to stay for a short while, then move on to a larger media market. The charm and leisurely lifestyle of the region won him over, and 30 years later, he continues to enjoy the city and its surrounding areas. He and his wife, Linda, often spend parts of their weekends rediscovering the pleasures of meandering through the squares of Savannah's Historic Downtown or strolling on the beach at nearby Tybee Island.

Rich feels that one of Savannah's most attractive qualities is its size—it's large enough to be interesting and small enough to make you feel at home. That atmosphere reminds him of the city where he grew up, Jacksonville, Florida, and the way it was in the late 1950s and '60s before it boomed and became the "Bold New City of the South."

Although Rich was born in New Jersey, he considers himself a Southerner. He spent his boyhood in north Florida, attended college at Auburn University in Alabama, was stationed in rural North Carolina during much of his military service, and is married to a lady who's a Georgia country girl at heart. Rich came to Savannah after serving almost five years in the U.S. Air Force, a stint he began immediately after graduating from Auburn with a degree in journalism. He was a navigator and attained the rank of captain while employed by Uncle Sam.

After fulfilling his military obligation, Rich left the Air Force to see if he could put into practice what he had learned in college. He got plenty of opportunities at the *Savannah Morning News* while covering a variety of beats as a reporter—including police, politics, and business—and serving as an editor on the city desk and in the state news depart-ment. During his last seven years at the *Morning News,* Rich headed up the company's community newspapers department.

After working at the paper for 22 years, Rich decided in May 1996 to go in a somewhat different direction and try his hand at freelance writing. Since then, he's coauthored a book on the aviation history of Savannah, done some public relations work, and written numerous articles for *Savannah Magazine* and *The Savannah Business Report and Journal,* a newspaper that focuses on the local business community. He also writes a weekly column in the daily newspaper.

Rich and Linda are parents of a daughter, Erica Wittish Parker, who works as a teacher and coach. In addition to staying in touch with what Erica, her husband, Josh, and their daughter, Jaylen, are doing, the Wittishes keep busy with activities at their church, First Presbyterian, where they are involved with the congregation's community outreach ministries.

BETTY DARBY

Betty Darby is a journalist who has made Savannah her home since 1980. She is a 1977 graduate of the University of Georgia, where she majored in journalism and minored in political science. She even studied Russian, with some vague idea of covering the 1980 Olympics in the Soviet Union. The subsequent American decision not to participate in those games was a bit of a relief, since she hadn't mastered much of the language.

Betty got her first newspaper assignment in the summer following her freshman year at college, working for the Rome (Ga.) *News-Tribune* in her hometown. She returned to the paper for summer and holiday breaks throughout her college years, then joined the reporting staff full time. She later took a reporting position with the *Savannah Morning News*, where she covered various hard-news beats along with writing movie reviews and serving a stint as a copy editor. Over the course of her newspaper years, Betty covered politics, crime, and education; wrote features; and interviewed subjects ranging from John Wayne on his final movie promotion junket to George Bush in his vice presidential years.

After nine years with the Savannah newspapers, she moved into public relations and marketing work with public schools for several years. Later, she wrote and edited a quarterly magazine for a Savannah hospital. She spent several years as the managing editor of *The Savannah Business Report and Journal,* a niche publication covering business news along the entire Georgia Coast and in Hilton Head Island, South Carolina. She teaches creative writing courses in local continuing education programs. She continues to write for magazines and other outlets and occasionally dusts off a half-finished novel manuscript she's working on.

While in Savannah, Betty has ranged wide over the city's residential real estate. She has lived on some of the grandest squares in the Historic Downtown (albeit in some of the humbler apartments) and in the suburban enclaves of the Islands area. She spent 12 years in the city's Midtown section in a circa-1930s bungalow and has now moved to the Southside's suburbs.